ROUTLEDGE HANDBOOK OF FOOTBALL MARKETING

Edited by Nicolas Chanavat, Michel Desbordes and Nicolas Lorgnier

LONDON AND NEW YORK

First published 2017
by Routledge
2 Park Square, Milton Park, Abingdon, Oxon OX14 4RN

and by Routledge
711 Third Avenue, New York, NY 10017

Routledge is an imprint of the Taylor & Francis Group, an informa business

British Library Cataloguing-in-Publication Data
A catalogue record for this book is available from the British Library

Library of Congress Cataloging-in-Publication Data
A catalog record for this book has been requested

ISBN: 978-1-138-28932-1 (hbk)
ISBN: 978-1-315-26720-3 (ebk)

Typeset in Bembo
by Apex CoVantage, LLC

Printed and bound by CPI Group (UK) Ltd, Croydon, CR0 4YY

ROUTLEDGE HANDBOOK OF FOOTBALL MARKETING

Football is big business. The top teams and leagues in world football generate billions of dollars in revenue and serve an audience of billions of fans. This book focuses on the marketing of football as the apex of the contemporary football industry. Drawing upon key theories and concepts in sport marketing, it highlights the critical strategic and operational elements that underpin effective marketing in football clubs around the world.

From the English Premier League to Major League Soccer, this handbook addresses the most important developments in sponsorship, marketing communications, digital marketing strategies, customer relationship management and social media. Written by a team of leading football marketing experts, it presents the latest cutting-edge research in case studies from countries including the UK, USA, France, Spain, Germany, Italy, China and Japan.

The only up-to-date book on football marketing written from a truly international perspective, the *Routledge Handbook of Football Marketing* is an invaluable resource for any researcher or advanced student with an interest in football marketing, as well as all marketers working in the professional football business.

Nicolas Chanavat is Director of the first year of the sport management Master's degree program at the University of Paris-Saclay, France, and Director of Research Grants for the French Centre for Olympic Studies. He is a specialist in football marketing and mega sporting events and has published several books and academic articles in these areas. Mr Chanavat has worked for professional sport clubs such as AS Saint-Étienne and organised several mega sporting events (FIFA, IOC, UEFA). In addition, he works as a consultant for the French Soccer Federation and the "Grand Stade" of the Olympique Lyonnais.

Michel Desbordes is a sports marketing professor at the University of Paris-Saclay, France, and the academic director of INSEEC Sport business school. He is also an associate professor at the University of Ottawa, Canada, and the Shanghai University of Sports, China. Mr Desbordes has published 25 reference books in the field of sports marketing, as well as numerous academic articles. As a media consultant, he is regularly consulted by BFM, France Télévisions, Europe 1, *Le Monde* and *L'Équipe* to discuss matters of sports business. Since 2009, he has also been the chief editor of the *International Journal of Sports Marketing and Sponsorship*.

Nicolas Lorgnier is an associate professor at Canisius College, USA. He has over 10 years of teaching experience in sport management and has worked with universities in Europe, North America and Asia. Mr Lorgnier has written over 30 publications, including articles in leading sport management and service management journals such as *European Sport Management Quarterly* and *Service Business*. He also serves as a reviewer for various academic journals, such as the *Journal of Sport Management*, the *International Journal of Sports Marketing and Sponsorship* and the *Journal of Strategic Marketing*.

CONTENTS

ILLUSTRATIONS

Figures

Tables

CONTRIBUTORS

Wladimir Andreff is professor emeritus at the University of Paris 1 Panthéon-Sorbonne, honorary president of the International Association of Sports Economists and the European Sports Economics Association, and president of the Scientific Council of the Observatory of the sports economy (Secretariat of the State of Sports), and he has taught at 16 universities abroad. Mr Andreff is an editorial board member of 15 scientific journals and has authored more than 420 scientific publications in economics, as well as 29 books, including *La mondialisation économique du sport. Manuel de référence en économie du sport* (De Boeck, 2012).

Verónica Baena is the marketing chair at the European University of Madrid, Spain. Her research focuses on strategic branding. She has written six books, nine book chapters, more than 40 articles and more than 40 conference papers. In 2010, her work was selected as the best study on brand management at the XXII National Congress of Marketing (Spain). The award was presented by the Foro de Marcas Españolas Renombradas and the Spanish office of patents and trademarks. In 2011, Ms Baena received the award for best researcher at the European University of Madrid, and most recently, she was one of two finalists for the European Award of Excellence in Teaching in the social sciences. She also received the Literati Award for Excellence in 2013.

Emmanuel Bayle holds a PhD in management science and is a professor of sport management at the Institute of Sports Science, the University of Lausanne (ISSUL), Switzerland. He has published several books and articles in the fields of sports governance and sport management (the great sport leaders, the governance of sports organizations, CSR and sports, etc.) and the management of nonprofit organizations. He currently manages a project on the professionalization of international sports federations.

Yoshifumi Bizen holds a PhD and is an associate professor at the Department of Health and Physical Education at Kokugakuin University, Japan. He received his doctoral degree in sport science from Waseda University, Japan. His research interests include sport consumer behavior, company sport, sport policy and athlete endorsement. His research articles have appeared in academic journals such as *Japanese Journal of Sport Management* and *Japan Journal of Lifelong Sport*. Mr Bizen has also served on multiple committees for local governments and nonprofit sport organizations.

Jens Blumrodt is an assistant professor at the ESC Rennes School of Business, France, and the director of the MSc program in Sports, Leisure and Tourism Management. He teaches and conducts research in sport management and tourism. Recent activities within the Research Center for Responsible Business are related to strategic brand management and the questions dealing with a company's social responsibility. He acts as a consultant to sports and tourist companies and organizations.

Guillaume Bodet is a professor at the University of Claude Bernard Lyon-1 (University of Lyon), France, in the Management of Sport Organizations Department, the College of Sports Sciences, where he teaches marketing and sport management and co-directs the Master's program "Sport Management". He is a member of the Centre for Research and Innovation in Sports (CRIS) and the Laboratory for Vulnerability and Innovation in Sports (L-Vis) and is a visiting fellow at the University of Loughborough, UK. His research topics are mainly focused on the marketing and consumption of sports services, products and brands. He has been asked to share his expertise with many organizations such as the British Swimming Federation, UEFA, the ATP, the Korean Ministry of Sports and the Institute for the Industrial Development of Sports at the University of Shanghai.

Claude Boli holds PhDs in history (De Montfort University, Leicester, UK) and sociology (University of Nantes) and is a researcher associated with De Montfort University and a board member of the executive committee of the Sports Writers Association. His fields of research include contemporary England, the museography of sports and the history of black people in Europe. Since 2006, he has headed the department for the Research of the National Museum of Sports (Nice). He is the author of *Manchester United. L'invention d'un club* (La Martinière, 2006), *Football. Le triomphe du ballon* (the National Sports Museum, 2008) and Claude Boli, Patrick Clastres and Marianne Lassus (eds.): *Le Sport à l'épreuve du racisme, de l'antisémitisme et de la xénophobie au xxe siècle* (New World, 2015).

Eric Brownlee is an assistant professor of sport marketing at the Dahlkemper School of Business at Gannon University. He has industry experience in the marketing and sales of major collegiate sports in the US, and his primary research focuses are assessing the value of corporate partnerships in sports and the development of effective sports sales techniques in both major professional and collegiate sports in the US. Dr Brownlee has presented his research internationally and has been published in publications such as the *International Journal of Sport Management*, the *Journal of Brand Strategy* and *Sport Marketing Quarterly*.

André Bühler is a marketing professor at the University of Nuertingen-Geislingen, Germany. He also heads the German Institute of Sports Marketing. He specializes in sport management and marketing, with a particular interest in sponsorship, relationship marketing, social media and neuromarketing applied to sports.

Vincent Chaudel has been a consultant in the sports sector for 10 years. After conducting a professional thesis in Canada, he founded a consulting practice for sports marketing companies (Showteam) before joining Deloitte in 2001, Ineum in 2003 and then Kurt Salmon in 2011. He offered his broad expertise (strategy, organization, marketing, communication) for the media, sports organizations (federations, leagues, clubs) and public entities (governments, ministries, local authorities). In 2009, he was elected Vice President of Sports and Citizenship, the first European think tank centered around social issues linked to sports. Since 2012, he has run the blog for sports and business blog for *Figaro/Sport 24*, and he contributes to *France Football* as a columnist.

Aurélien François holds a PhD in management on the CSR practices of professional French sports clubs. Currently an associate researcher at the Sports Research Centre (RCSCS) at the University of Ottawa, Canada, he continues to publish on this theme through articles and book chapters. He has recently expanded his interests to other themes revolving around professional sports such as sports equipment and the question of the funding and the professionalization of women's football.

Christopher Hautbois is an associate professor at the University of Paris-Saclay, France, where he co-directs the Master's program "Management of Events and Sporting Activities" (MELS) and teaches economics and sports marketing. Able to conduct research, his works focus on the strategies of nonprofit organizations in sports, particularly national sports federations and local governments. He is the author of the economic editions of *Sport et marketing public* (2008) and *Marketing des fédérations sportives* (2014).

Boris Helleu is an associate professor at the University of Caen Normandy, France, where he directs the Master's program "Sport Management". His research is a part of the field for the marketing of sporting events, and it focuses on the use of social media in building the fan experience. He shares on his Twitter account (@bhelleu) a daily review of international marketing news and sports economics and maintains a blog dedicated to the same themes (Hell of a Sport).

Sarah Jürgens obtained a Bachelor's degree in international marketing as part of a Spanish–British joint program at the University of Wales, UK, and the Escoex International Business School, Spain. In August 2014, at the Munich Business School, Germany, she completed her dual Master's programs, "Corporate Strategy and Innovation" and "International Finance". She is currently employed at the sports marketing company 12 Unleash where she develops communication campaigns and conducts reports.

James Kenyon is an associate professor in sports management at Loughborough University, UK, and an early career researcher, having recently attained a PhD in sport management and marketing from the Centre for Olympic Studies & Research (COS&R) based at Loughborough University in 2013. His research interests include, among other themes, the marketing of major sporting events and football. An avid amateur footballer, James scored a hat trick in the 2010 Kensington Plate Final held at Goodison Park, Liverpool.

Dongfeng Liu is a professor of sport management and co-dean of the School of Economics and Management at Shanghai University of Sport, China. He is also international professor with INSEEC Business School, France, and guest professor with University College Dublin, Ireland, and Kufstein University, Austria. He is a member of China Sports Strategy Society, a think tank of China's Sports Ministry.

Gerd Nufer is a professor of management science with a specialization in marketing and sport management at the ESB Business School, the University of Reutlingen, Germany. He is also the director of the German Institute of Sports Marketing. Mr Nufer has a particular interest in event management, communication and international marketing. He has won several awards, both in teaching and in research.

Elena Radicchi holds a PhD in economics and business management and is an associate professor of sports marketing at the University of Florence, Italy. From 2004 to 2012, she taught classes for economics, sport management and event marketing for the Master's program "Sports Management" at the University of Florence. Currently, she teaches event and sport management for the Master's program "Design of Sustainable Tourism Systems". Since 2008, she has conducted research activities within the Sports Management Laboratory. Her publications concern, in particular, sports tourism, sporting event marketing, modern media and experiential marketing.

Shintaro Sato holds a PhD and is an assistant professor of marketing in Feliciano School of Business at Montclair State University, USA. He received his PhD degree (sport management) from the University of Florida, USA. Mr Sato has published his research in distinguished peer-reviewed academic journals such as *Journal of Sport Management* and *European Sport Management Quarterly*. His research interests include sport consumer behavior, advertising and crisis management in sport and tourism settings. Specifically, he is interested in how consumers process information and make certain judgments and behaviors.

Nicolas Scelles is an associate professor for sports economics at the University of Stirling in Scotland, UK. His thesis in 2009 dealt with the uncertainty of the outcome of professional sports leagues. He was awarded the Grand Prix UCPF (Union of Professional Football Clubs) in the category of "Research". Nicolas Scelles has published scientific articles in several international journals (*Applied Economics, Economics Bulletin, International Journal of Sport Finance, International Journal of Sport Management and Marketing, Journal of Sports Economics*). He intervened regularly as part of the Master's program "Executive in Sports Organisation Management" (MEMOS) proposed by the International Olympic Committee (IOC).

Patrizia Zagnoli is a professor of economics and management at the University of Florence, Italy. In 2002, she started the first Italian Master's program in "Sports Management" where she was also the chair of the Sports Marketing Department. Since 2008, she has created and directed the Sports Management Laboratory. Currently, she teaches the marketing of tourism and sports within the Master's program "Design of Sustainable Tourism Systems". Ms Zagnoli has been published in the field of sports marketing and modern media. Her scientific training on the industrial economy and the economics of innovation focused on the processes of local development and how the evolution of the technological paradigm, ICT, has provided crucial knowledge to build a framework for economic analysis on which to understand sports.

INTRODUCTION

Nicolas Chanavat, Michel Desbordes and Nicolas Lorgnier

It is undeniable that football is currently enjoying a special status in France, and generally throughout the world. Its exceptional power is illustrated by its impact on the economy, society and the media.

As such, marketing has become a key function, or even a state of mind, required for the expansion of football professional sector. Therefore, it is now essential for professional sports organizations to differentiate their brand and to innovate with their customer service and economic partners. That way, digital activities can be at the core of the stakeholder strategies in the ecosystem of a professional football that is constantly changing.

Towards a football marketing boom

In the context of the globalization of the football product, the financial stakes are incessantly growing due to the increase in broadcasting rights and investments of private partners. If the figures and marketing information devoted to football are everywhere, and if they are evocative of the stakes of professional sports entities, let's mention some most telling examples.

The amount of FIFA's revenue for the 2011–2014 budget cycle, which amounts to 5.7 billion US dollars (FIFA, 2015), is a business success record. Thus, cumulative audiences of the 2014 World Cup Final are estimated at 910 million viewers. One can then wonder how this public enthusiasm is beneficial for advertisers and the media.

Furthermore, the aggregate turnover of the 20 most powerful clubs in the world amounted to 6.2 billion euros for the 2013–2014 season, which represents a substantial increase of 14% compared to the previous business year (Deloitte, 2015). Given these substantial figures, it seems a worthy endeavor to define and study more closely the specifics of their business model.

On January 31, 2013, the arrival of David Beckham to PSG created an unprecedented craze never seen before for a football player in France. How well does this fit in the globalization strategy of French football and the globalization of the Paris-Saint-Germain (PSG) brand?

For its part, on December 20, 2013, the Association Sportive de Saint-Étienne (AS Saint-Étienne) inaugurated its museum dedicated to the club's history. Although this represented an undeniable source of additional revenue, it is above all a real lever for the development of a "green brand" suggesting a lasting, tangible and unique experience. To what extent does this marketing initiative make sense for clubs with a less powerful brand equity?

During the 2013–2014 season, the innovative partnership between Qatar Tourism Authority (QTA) and PSG resulted in an image contract and a sponsorship of 150 million euros for the first year and reaching 200 million in subsequent years. In the same vein, since the 2015–2016 season, Manchester United has been sponsored by the supplier Adidas with about 94 million euros per year (for 10 years), which is added to the partnership (begun during the season 2014–2015) with Chevrolet for a period of 7 years and an amount of 560 million euros (80 million euros per year). How is it that the amounts committed reach such sums? Furthermore, how do we measure the effectiveness of such operations?

Ever since 2005, the family of Allianz stadiums has been located in six countries and on three continents: Parque Allianz in Sao Paulo, Allianz Stadium in Sydney, Allianz Riviera in Nice, Allianz Park in London, Allianz Arena in Munich and Allianz Stadion in Vienna. Basically, more so than naming rights, what are the expected benefits via these platforms of global brands?

In 2014, Cristiano Ronaldo's fan community crossed the symbolic level of 100 million Facebook fans: a first. This Portuguese player gets on average a new fan every second. Here the importance of digital media makes sense and opens up many questions about the marketing potential of such a sports brand.

And it will be in the 2016–2019 period that the annual amount of TV rights to the Premier League will reach a record 6.92 billion US dollars. On average, operators will then spend 13.7 million euros to broadcast every match. Is this not without consequences for the other European leagues?

These particularly powerful data elicit debate and encourage further reflection on the marketing of football. They illustrate the need to analyze marketing strategies and the operationalization of French and European professional football sports entities. This book is written from this viewpoint.

For relief from financial supervision and increased club revenues?

As an object of considerable global growth, the economy of football has faced new challenges over the last decade. For European professional clubs, the advent of the financial fair play rule (FFP) proves to be the most important.

This system was unanimously approved in September 2009 by the Executive Committee of the UEFA, the aim being to improve the overall economic health of European clubs and to end what Michel Platini, the president, called the "victory on credit". This was fully supported by clubs and professional leagues, national federations and the EU institutions (European Parliament and European Commission). Therefore, beginning with the 2013–2014 sporting season, participation in the Champions League and the Europa League is conditioned by new rules. The revenues of the clubs should not exceed their spending by more than 5 million euros over the previous two seasons (and the previous three seasons since the 2015–2016 season). A maximum amount of 45 million euros is tolerated if the club's shareholders cover excess expenditures (30 million euros for the 2015–2016 season).

This helped to significantly reduce the losses of the European clubs: from 1.7 billion euros in 2011 to 400 million euros in 2014. Although this device undeniably allows a cleanup of the finances of European clubs, wouldn't it be appropriate to soften it in order to promote growth and competition and to stimulate the entrance of new investors?

Thus, couldn't the Financial Control Body for the clubs (ICFC), founded by UEFA, accept a temporary deficit for clubs guaranteeing the creditworthiness of investors and a multi-year plan with a forecast of rising income?

In any case, at a time when France has just lost its 5th rank in the UEFA's classification in favor of Portugal, French clubs are destined to grow and become more professional. Beyond certain exceptions, they are failing to compete as a sport on the European stage. The challenge is in their vital economic power to purchase players, or in the development of working infrastructures which promote the development of competitive clubs. In this environment, the organization of Euro 2016 is intended as a lever for the development of French football to be able to catch up with European competitors. Whatever concessions and changes are to be made to the financial framework of future clubs, this new context is not without consequence for strategic orientations, marketing and sales aspects in which clubs are constantly innovating.

An innovative book on marketing issues facing football

It was in the 1980s that the first specialized academic journals in sports marketing and management appeared (*Sports Business Daily* in 1979 and *Journal of Sport Management* in 1986). The seminal book of Mullin, Hardy and Sutton (1993) considered the precursor of a new sports marketing research field and is at the origin of multiple analyses on sponsorship, consumer behavior in a sports context, event management or strategic marketing applied to sport (Amis and Cornwell, 2005; Beech and Chadwick, 2007; Stotlar, 2009; Desbordes and Richelieu, 2012).

In France, the theoretical foundations of sports marketing were set forth by Desbordes, Ohl and Tribou (1999). Today, there are many reference books.

The proliferation of academic journals also reflect the maturity of the discipline: *Business and Management: An International Journal; European Sport Management Quarterly; International Journal of Sport Management and Marketing; International Journal of Sports Marketing and Sponsorship; Journal of Sport Management; Sport; Sport Management Review; Sport Marketing Quarterly*; etc.

Although football is the most popular sport in the world and generates huge revenues, so far too few publications have been dedicated to the marketing analysis of its professional clubs.

This book does not attempt to provide a set of "infallible recipes or models" guaranteeing the marketing performance of professional football clubs. However, this unique contribution brings together the insights of numerous experts in the marketing field applied to professional football. Thus, the objective is to address the various complex marketing issues related to the development of football clubs. In addition, strong with solid theoretical bases and practical examples, it provides an inventory, defines key concepts, identifies good practices, places them in relation to academic literature and offers unprecedented lines of inquiry in the matter.

In this context, we will successively address several topics, starting with the evolution of sports marketing and its specificities. It seems necessary to look at how clubs can differentiate themselves from one another and make themselves more attractive vis-à-vis their own fans, those of other clubs and non-fans as well as the media, sponsors or communities. Moreover, is there a predominant economic model for French clubs? What are the growth drivers on which they and their European neighbors can draw? What differences are there in terms of marketing development between the clubs in Major League Soccer (MLS) and European clubs? Can we imagine that European football is on the edge of a new "big bang"? Don't the growing disparities in budgets available to clubs give rise to particular marketing logistics? On the other hand, are marketing arrangements inherent to each club replicable? In addition, how did Euro 2016 fit into the marketing dynamics of French clubs? Also known is the importance of integrating the sports facilities within the club's development strategy, but does it necessarily determine their success? How can transfers of players give rise to a unique marketing strategy? What are the trends in sponsorship in professional football? What about connectivity of stadiums, ticketing and customer experiences? How can professional football be used in a strategy of territorial marketing and/or an overall development strategy? What role do digital business or corporate social responsibility play in the marketing development of professional sports entities? Basically, what is truly known about the marketing logic of professional football clubs?

This type of practice actually covers a large number of activities and entities with purposes, scopes of activities and means, which are all very diverse. They potentially lead to unique marketing strategies and variations that we ought to consider.

This book takes a strong managerial stand. It aims to be the result of a common approach in which professionals in the field and researchers collaborate to articulate concepts with marketing action. This book is for teachers – researchers working on the marketing of sports and particularly on football marketing. It is also intended for professional football players and all socio-economic actors in connection with this sector. With this book, students in sport science, economics, political science, commerce or communication would be able to better define the marketing orientations of football's professional sports entities. A new understanding is given to several French Ligue 1 clubs and to some clubs of the other four biggest European championships. The book is divided into three parts.

The first part aims to define the context and better understand the marketing of football from national, European and world perspectives. Chapter 1, written by Nicolas Chanavat and Michel Desbordes, allows a better understanding of the realities of football marketing. Recent models of income and costs of a football club in France are specifically discussed in Chapter 2 by Wladimir Andreff and Nicolas Scelles. In Chapter 3, Eric Brownlee and Nicolas Lorgnier analyze successful marketing activities in the MLS. Then an interview with Christophe Bouchet, a great witness of sport marketing for the last 15 years, addresses sports marketing agencies in Chapter 4. Finally, Chapter 5, written by Vincent Chaudel, discusses the economy of European football.

It is in the second part that strategies and marketing initiatives essential to the success of professional football sports organizations are discussed. Chapter 6, written by Nicolas Chanavat, Michel Desbordes and Nicolas Lorgnier, analyzes the fundamental elements for sports sponsorship. Chapter 7, from Boris Helleu, presents the current state of football 2.0. Chapter 8, written by Christopher Hautbois, examines the strategic aspects linked to the coexistence between regions and professional football clubs. Finally, it is in Chapter 9 that Aurélien François and Emmanuel Bayle offer a comparative study of societal practices in European professional football.

The third part illustrates the strategies and types of operations of European professional clubs through nine concrete cases, while the strategic development of Asian football leagues is addressed in the last two cases. They can be considered as the many implementations of marketing principles mentioned previously. Clubs that have been studied represent a wide range of possible configurations: German, English, Spanish, French and Italian clubs more or less important in terms of budget or number of fans, national, European or global standing, etc. Chapter 10, from Chanavat Nicolas and Michel Desbordes, studies the marketing aspects of the PSG and especially its globalization strategy since the arrival of Qatar Sports Investment (QSI) in the capital of the club. Along these lines, the Olympic Lyonnais (OL) development strategy is the subject of Chapter 11. Certain marketing aspects of the Parc Olympique Lyonnais' and the "Grand Stade" are the subject of special attention. Chapter 12 deals with marketing logic deployed by AS Saint-Étienne. It focuses on the issue of operationalization of marketing innovations that create value for the club. Written by Verónica Baena, Chapter 13 focuses on the role of sport as an agent of social change and of performance marketing through the case of Real Madrid. Analysis of the brand management strategy of Borussia Dortmund is the subject of Chapter 14, written by Gerd Nufer, André Bühler and Sarah Jürgens. Another German case studies the VfB Stuttgart branding image and examines the purchasing behavior of its fans. This takes place in Chapter 15 by Jens Blumrodt. The analysis of the marketing strategy of ACF Fiorentina, based on the power of the local identity of the city of Florence, is in Chapter 16, written by Patrizia Zagnoli and Elena Radicchi. Then James Kenyon and Guillaume Bodet address the issue of fan support via social media by examining the case of Liverpool FC. In Chapter 18, Claude Boli reveals, through the case of Manchester United, how the establishment of the history of a club can become one of the bases of its economic success. Then, the focus of the cases changes to discuss the development of emergent football leagues. In Chapter 19, Dongfeng Liu explains how the development of professional football is coming as a response to the social development of China. In the final chapter, Chapter 20, Yoshifumi Bizen and Shintaro Sato present the structure and strategies set forth by the J League (Japan).

Even if the marketing strategies presented are numerous and diverse, they are not intended to be an exhaustive list. This book is the result of collaborative work, enriched by the experience of professionals and observers of the professional football sector, who agreed to share their expertise and vision of this rapidly changing industry. We thank them, as well as those who have contributed in some way to the success of this project.

Bibliography

Amis J. et Cornwell T.B., *Global Sport Sponsorship*, Oxford, Berg, 2005.

Beech J. et Chadwick S., *The Marketing of Sport*, Upper Saddle River, NJ, Pearson Education, 2007.

Deloitte, *Commercial Breaks, Football Money League, Sport Business Group*, 2015, pp. 1–40.

Desbordes M., Ohl F. et Tribou G., *Marketing du sport*, Paris, Economica, 1999, 2004.

Desbordes M. et Richelieu A., *Global Sport Marketing: Contemporary Issued and Practice*, London and New York, Routledge, 2012.

Drut B., "Les règles de fair-play financier dans l'UEFA: quelles conséquences pour le football européen?", *International Review on Sport and Violence*, numéro 7, 2013, pp. 89–96.

FIFA, *Rapport financier 2014*, 2015.

Mullin B.J., Hardy S. et Sutton W.A., *Sport Marketing*, Champaign, IL, Human Kinetics, 1993, 2007.

Stotlar D., *Developing Successful Sport Sponsorship Plans*, Morgantown, WV, Fitness Information Technology, 2009.

PART I

Towards a professionalization of the marketing of professional football clubs

The first part aims to define the context and explain the marketing of football from national, European and world perspectives. Chapter 1, written by Nicolas Chanavat and Michel Desbordes, allows a better understanding of the realities of football marketing. Recent models of income and costs of a football club in France are specifically discussed in Chapter 2 by Nicolas Scelles and Wladimir Andreff. In Chapter 3, Eric Brownlee and Nicolas Lorgnier analyze successful marketing activities in the MLS. Then an interview with Christophe Bouchet, great witness of sport marketing for the last 15 years, addresses sports marketing agencies in Chapter 4. Finally, Chapter 5, written by Vincent Chaudel, discusses the economy of European football.

1
THE MARKETING OF FOOTBALL
History, definitions, singularities, strategies and forms of operationalization

Nicolas Chanavat and Michel Desbordes

Since the 1970s, professional football clubs have gradually integrated marketing as a key function necessary for their development and sustainability. In France, this change was spurred either by businessmen, such as Jean-Claude Darmon, or by some clubs, or rather by their presidents, visionaries and pioneers in this area, such as the AS Saint-Étienne (ASSE) of Roger Rocher, or the Olympic Lyonnais (OL) of Jean-Michel Aulas, to name a few.

Indeed, Roger Rocher and his team quickly grasped the importance of generating revenue independent from the team's undetermined sporting results: television rights, sponsorship rights, merchandising, etc. The launch of the hymn "Go green!" in 1976 illustrates the excitement around the European adventure of the AS Saint-Étienne. The commercial success that has followed highlights the growing media exposure of football, and particularly one of its consequences: the birth of economic issues related to licensed merchandise (Moneghetti, Tétart and Wille, 2007; Charroin and Chanavat, 2014). This phenomenon is not without repercussions for the economy and the marketing of clubs.

Currently, a professional sports club faces several challenges: promoting its brand and innovating its products and services to offer to the fans. It should then set in motion a strategy to attract, maintain and develop customer relationships. The other challenge consists of meeting the needs of businesses via sponsorship activities, public relations and all of the services and products needed by business partners. For example, the PSG marketing department innovated itself by adding the name of a partner to one of its buildings. Normally, a club advertises its brand within its stadium, but here PSG innovates by partnering with a mobile operator at its training center. Le Camp des Loges was then renamed the Ooredoo Training Centre in 2013. There is also talk of building and/or renovating its sporting arena to equip and prepare itself for the customer journey in the modern 2.0 football stadium. Finally, since consumers are increasingly connected, marketing and event related activities lead sports entities to turn to digital technology. The fan is looking for an emotional experience through watching football, but he also equally seeks convenience to experience his or her passion. In 2014, Manchester City became the first English club to offer free wireless broadband in its stadium, "Etihad Stadium". It is now possible for fans to download content and share the moments lived at the stadium through social networks. This is an important step in the digital strategy of the club.

This first chapter aims at explaining the context. The goal is to better understand the place of marketing within professional football by analyzing the evolution of sport business and its role.

We will then redefine and analyze the key concepts and characteristics of the discipline and then address the question of the economic value and marketing potential of clubs, players and coaches. It is then necessary to study French football's factors of growth and decline. In this context, the construction of the brand remains the key issue of every professional sport entity. The marketing strategy and the operationalizations are then chosen decisively. Supported with primary data collected from several professional sports organizations (clubs, leagues, federations, etc.) and personalities from sports business, the chapter discusses different football marketing, topics which are then further studied in the following thematic chapters and/or case studies of clubs.

Sport business and professional football: between genesis and globalization

For 15 years, the sport business enjoyed considerable development. But the use of the sport and its values conveyed through marketing and sales aren't something from this millennium. For over a century, companies have measured the power of sponsorship communication, whose emotional impact is based on both the uncertainty of the outcome and the commitment of its participants and the public. What is the role of football in this development? Beyond sponsoring activities, who has gradually developed other profit centers of sports organizations? What clubs, institutions and football personalities helped through the steps until the advent of Sportainment? To what extent is it necessary to understand the globalization of the football product? Who are the new investors in this sector? Our analysis relates to world football, but it also focuses particularly on French football.

From the appearance of professionalism to the concepts of "Sportainment" and "e-sports marketing"

The development of economic activities, marketing and sales in the sports sector (commonly known as sport business) can be divided into five distinct phases.

The global professionalization of football's business activities leads us to address in particular the advent of sponsorship, merchandising and television broadcasts. Analysis of the strategies deployed by the AS Saint-Étienne, the Matra Racing and the Olympique Lyonnais, which are all driving forces on trade and marketing issues, brings us to the year 2000. This period marks the advent of Sportainment. This notion, combining "sport" and "entertainment", symbolizes the marriage between sport, entertainment and money. This triptych led to the advent of sports-entertainment with the goal of optimizing the fan experience. If the sporting competition forms the DNA of the event, the fan is now at the center, which has consequences for aspects of interactivity, activation or animation. The 2010s has seen the strengthening of digital activities, or so called *e-sports marketing*. This discipline includes the marketing and sales practices which aim to educate consumers using new communication technologies.

The key periods of sport business development

The appearance of professionalism and the engagement of the first businesses and sponsors within the world of football in the 1930s correspond to the first period.[1]

The years between 1970 and 1980 represent the second phase. It is characterized by an increased presence of television in homes, the advent of licensed merchandise and the strengthening of partnership logics. Therefore, the newfound ability to broadcast football on television offers to clubs, which are considered to be true business enterprises, an increasing revenue. This transformation can be observed very early in England with Manchester United and eventually spread all over Europe (see Chapter 18 dedicated to Manchester United). In France, this period is illustrated in particular by the popular enthusiasm aroused by the AS Saint-Étienne (Charroin and Chanavat, 2014). The management of the club is among the first to grasp the extent of the phenomenon and to transform the business structure of the football spectacle (Boli, 2005). At this time, the emergence of large-scale financial stakes in sports is undeniable. The concept of "cash is king" then transforms the professional sport, thereby qualified as sports business, a denomination which emphasizes the commercial dimension attached to it. As a result, the sport has become a product, "like any other" service. The advent and characteristics of the phenomenon exacerbate competitive logic, the unequal nature of remunerations and the social hegemony of the sport. At this point in time, one sees the first sport marketing agencies thrive in the United States.

The 1990s were marked by a new and third phase. Worldwide, the marketing of sports entities was strengthened by the Dream Team basketball players during the 1992 Olympics in Barcelona. In France, the organization of the Winter Games in Albertville and the epic run of the Olympique de Marseille (OM) of Bernard Tapie during the 1993 European Championship seem to have played a role in this development. Sports federations, meanwhile, return to an evolutionary process that led to making marketing a core function of their organization (Hautbois, 2014). Strengthened by expertise and experience in organizing temporary international sporting events (the Winter Olympics in Albertville in 1992, European football Championship in 1984) or recurrent events (French Open "Roland Garros", the Tour de France), this discipline is not new in France. However, the year 1998, marked by the victory of the French football team sponsored by Adidas, is considered the end of sport business prehistory (in France) (Desbordes, 2011). This date is symbolic in several ways. First of all, sponsorship became an element of the marketing mix of brands and no longer a visibility or reputation operation. Brand activation devices developed accordingly. Second, the victory of "Les Bleus" convinced the elites of the importance of sport in society and therefore of its economic potential. More private in the French world, the activity then propelled itself to the rank of noble activity. From then on, there has been a great deal more money in sports, and marketing activities have become more professional. In Europe, the sport more and more takes on the dimension of a growing business, driving companies to invest heavily in this sector. Indeed, the profitability of the sport, especially in the case of a home team victory, is transformed into a "jackpot" for the company. This is why, following the most logical and classic investments of sports equipment manufacturers (Adidas, Nike, Puma, Le Coq Sportif, etc.), which were present in the market for a long time, one observes the very important arrival of, in theory, illegitimate sports companies (insurance companies, banks, consumer goods, airlines, etc.). Thus, we speak of "sports marketing" for equipment manufacturers, while we say that the sponsors (those who invest in sport without 'natural' or semantical link to it) are, in turn, "marketing through the sport" ("sport marketing").[2]

Then, in the 2000s, everything becomes more complex: marketers understand that the optimization of the investment was going through a successful "threesome or foursome" (at least), each representing a different brand. This corresponds to multiple, sport sponsorship events (Chanavat, 2009). Several brands, the club, the equipment manufacturer and the sponsors in this way come together as a whole on the same jersey. The club FC Barcelona is the perfect illustration. The blue and garnet jersey of the Catalans never had a sponsor's name (with the exception of the equipment manufacturer) since its founding in 1899. It was, in the image of Athletic Bilbao, an exception in European football. But since 2006, UNICEF has been visible, free of charge, on the jersey. This operation, described as "citizen sponsoring", allows the Catalan club to see its number of fans increase worldwide, in addition to allowing the club to increase its rates for sponsorship.

Since then, another partner, Qatar Airways, appears next to UNICEF on the jersey. Overall, one can legitimately wonder whether each brand of the FC Barcelona quartet with Nike, Qatar Airways and UNICEF, represents the same values and how this brand proliferation impacts the perception of the consumer. If one can observe an increase in the number of brands, then the number of stakeholders has also increased: agencies (Sportfive, Havas Sports, Sportlab, etc.), media (Canal +, France Televisions, BeIN Sports, Team 21, etc.), law firms and consulting specialists,[3] sports agents, equipment manufacturers, leagues, federations, confederations, clubs, athletes, etc. This was a time of globalization and Sportainment. Since 2005, Max Guazzini, then president of the Stade Français rugby club, has been recognized as a precursor for the screenwriting of sporting events material in France. He revolutionized the "rugby cassoulet" (traditional meal in the countryside in the southwestern part of France) by making it multicultural: he managed to bring in women and children to the stadium, and his event strategy and marketing strategy will inspire sports organizations in football. "This trend detector thus introduced into his stadium cheerleaders, colorful costumes, music, jingles, a small remote controlled cars, floats of scantily clad dancers; a brief spectacle" (Allaire, Gonguet and Villepreux, 2014, p. 163). Mathieu Renaud, sales and marketing director of LOU-Rugby products, added that

> this was a first in French rugby: to fill up the Stade de France with 80 000 people, seats previously reserved for the French football team, les bleus, or for track and field meets. He opened the era of marketing relocation and many clubs will follow suit: RC Toulon rugby at the Velodrome in Marseille, Lyon Olympique University rugby at Gerland in Lyon, Aviron Bayonnais rugby and Biarritz Olympique rugby at Anoeta de San-Sebastien, USAP Perpignan rugby at Montjuic in Barcelona and the Union Bordeaux-Bègles tugbyat Chaban-Delmas.[4]

The 2010s mark the advent of e-sports marketing. The development of new digital technologies characterizes the fifth and final stage of the development of sports business. The article from Chanavat and Desbordes (2014a) demonstrates the creativity of business in regards to ambush marketing and considers the 2012 London Olympic Games as the first truly mega social and digital event. Since then, sport marketers must take into account the fans' new habits of communication and consumption, and make them unique experiences. It is in this context that the 2.0 marketing made its appearance. In a digital world, social networks help meet the marketing logic of professional sports entities. In any event, marketing activities now play a central role in the development of the professional sport, and particularly in professional football.

The advent of professional football

Football is sometimes regarded as "more than a sport". It could even be considered as a total social phenomenon which draws appeal from the simplicity of its rules because it is able to combine, like no other sport, individual talents with collective effort. This sport which unleashes passions in every corner of the planet can be seen as a metaphor of the human condition, where there are more losers than winners, where all is not heroic or epic, where the most stubborn do not necessarily see their efforts rewarded, where there are setbacks, cheating and injustice, and where it is often required to go through difficult times. Because sports in general, and football in particular, appear to be an inexhaustible source of symbols and social representations, marketers do not hesitate to extensively use them in order to persuade consumption. One can then wonder how football has become more professional?

Since its birth in the particular context of Victorian Britain (the industrial revolution, urbanization, colonization), football has continued to add to its missions, at first educational, then political and economic, which makes it more than a sport, a social tool. In the beginning, one of soccer's priorities was the education of an elite capable of undertaking, governing and contributing to the British Empire's settlement policies. In the public schools, where British upper-class youth were welcomed, the practice of games which used balls (foot or hand) was developed. The Football Association, whose members played with their feet, was codified in 1863. The English federation, named The Football Association (FA) built itself throughout the whole country and began by creating the FA Cup in 1871. While the FA authorized the reimbursement of expenses for players who competed in the matches it organized in 1882, a professional team was not established until 1885. The Royal Arsenal of London, created in 1886, became the Woolwich Arsenal. In 1891, they obtained the first professional club status before changing its name in 1913 to become the Arsenal Football Club (Nys, 2010).

The spectacle of professional football matches attracts the masses: 110,000 spectators attended the FA Cup final in 1901, and there was a total of more than 8 million viewers for the 1913–1914 season following the FA League matches (Vamplew, 1988). The swift growth in professionalization, spectacularization and media coverage of British football makes it the reference model. The first clubs founded by the British in France are those of Le Havre Athletic Club (HAC) in 1872 by engineers and workers of a railway company, and the Taylors English Club in 1877 in Paris by fabric traders. Now a product of mass culture, football affirmed its position during the interwar period as the "king of sports" (Wahl, 1989) in the majority of European and Latin American countries. Founded in 1904, FIFA, which is based in Zurich, has long had the monopoly on the sport. After World War I, the spectacularization of football grew, as evidenced by the growing number of home crowds at Wembley Stadium, opened in London in 1923 (126,000 seats); at Colombes stadium in Paris, which was built for the 1924 Olympics (64,000 seats); at the Centenario Stadium in Montevideo for the first World Cup (60,000 seats); or at the Mussolini stadium in Turin for the 1934 World Cup (70,000 seats).

In addition, while one observes an increase in international football matches by the end of World War I, (Waquet and Vincent, 2011), the increases especially heightened with the success of the Olympic tournaments in Antwerp (1920), Paris (1924) and Amsterdam (1928). FIFA then becomes autonomous, separate from the Olympic movement, with the creation of the World Cup, which is first held in Uruguay in 1930 (Charroin and Waquet, 2008). In Central Europe, football is also experiencing increased professionalization: Austria in 1924, Czechoslovakia in 1925, Hungary in 1926 and France in 1932. There is also the establishment of professional leagues in South American countries: Brazil in 1933 and Argentina in 1934 (Dietschy, 2010). It should be noted that the development of professional teams took place primarily in urban areas. These areas have the support of powerful industrialists who use football, just as they used motorsports and cycling races for decades, as a promotional lever (FCSM for Peugeot, Fiat for the Juventus of Turin, etc.).

With its role as international sports-entertainment, football becomes acquainted with first political drifts. For instance, it is used for propaganda purposes, such as in Italy in 1934, where Mussolini utilized the World Cup and the Squadra Azzura victory for his own benefit.

After World War II, and then in the 1950s, it is from old Europe that comes the new impetus given to football. In a context of strong economic growth and development of new media coverage of football with the arrival of television, a wind of liberalism was in the air. This led club executives and media leaders, such as the newspaper *L'Équipe*, to impose their visions unto governing bodies: "UEFA was ahead in creating a more spectacular form of football and a greater economic profitability," explains Jacques Ferran (French journalist and former editor of *L'Equipe,* former director of France Football and creator of the European Cup of Champion Clubs).[5] It is in this context of revival that we witness the creation of the European Champion Clubs' Cup; the first final was won by Real Madrid, facing the Stade de Reims on June 13, 1956, at the Parc des Princes (Dietschy, 2010).

The advent of European football and "catholic football" (Dietschy, 2010) represents a breaking point in the history of football. Since the 1950s, the sport and the media have developed jointly by taking advantage of the convergence and complementarity of their interests: football provides programing and viewership for television, while television provides funds and a means of promotion for football. We will touch on this aspect later. So, we are speaking on the subject of professional sports' TV addiction (Andreff and Staudohar, 2000). In the 1970s, the landscape of televised sports broadcasts expands with cycling, football, boxing and rugby. Before the arrival of television advertising (1968), audiences and revenues were not concerns for professional sports organizations. However, they become increasingly important as television broadcasts the sports spectacle to the masses. In this context, Roger Rocher quickly grasps the potential benefits that may arise from television media coverage of a professional football club. In September 1975, he signed an agreement with Georges de Caunes, owner of TF1's sports service. In exchange for 400,000 francs, the channel received the rights to live broadcast four matches along with the rights to install advertising billboards behind the goals. Roger Rocher negotiated in the contract that TF1 is committed to promoting "Les Verts" through documentaries and promoting attendance at the Geoffroy-Guichard stadium, which holds over 40,000 seats. At that time, the precautionary principle requires that the announcements of the game can only be done during the evening news, and games must be broadcasted in the late evening. It is true that at this time, the income generated at the stadium constitutes the bulk of the club's budget (81% in the 1970–1971 season[6]). TV rights are only beginning to have an effect on income. With sponsorship, they only became the main source of revenue at the end of the 1990s. Now almost all football executives have legitimate concerns for their main sources of funding.

The AS Saint-Étienne under Roger Rocher: the first company of sport entertainment?

In England, since 1961, the outstanding economic success of Manchester has largely been linked to political loyalty from supporters. The year 1973 was marked by the creation of the Manchester United Commercial Department, an entity entirely dedicated to the commercial activities of the Mancunian club. A significant change appears in 1990 with the recruitment of marketing experts who contribute to the economic growth, the creation of a loyalty strategy and additional, profound changes. The entrance onto the stock exchange in 1991 and its effects on the club's organizational transformation resulted in turning fans into real consumers (Boli, 2005). Overall, starting from a loyalty policy of local supporters, clubs are expanding towards a global loyalty policy.

A pioneer in sports marketing in France, Jean-Claude Darmon, understood that football could tap into a significant financial windfall. This self-made man had a revolutionary idea: fill sports arenas with billboards. In 1969, he began marketing boards for FC Nantes. In this way, he convinced the entrepreneur Michel Axel (first sponsor of the club) to pay 15,000 francs a year to put his logo on the jerseys of FC Nantes. Six years later, the Hachette group paid 400,000 francs for the same benefit. Gradually, Jean-Claude Darmon was in charge of the advertising billboards in stadiums and research partners on behalf of several major French football clubs. He became a key figure in the areas of advertising football stadiums and television rights. He begins at FC Nantes where he also turns out to be the first to register a trademark for a football club, "FC Nantes Promotion", and to market licensed merchandise. Familiar to the world of football, friend to the then president of the French Football Federation (FFF), Fernand Sastre, he became the adviser of the FFF and the National Football League (LNF) in the mid-1970s. This earned him the nickname "The great financier of French football".[7]

Meanwhile, Roger Rocher, the emblematic president of the AS Saint- Étienne, understood, especially during the epic European saga of the 1970s, that the club had become an entertainment company which should generate non-sport resources in order to further develop itself. On the whole, the spectator and the television viewer are increasingly sought after by professional clubs. Viewers are convinced to become supporters and buy products. Roger Rocher and "AS Saint-Étienne Promotion" (the counterpart of Jean-Claude Darmon and "FC Nantes Promotion") prove to be pioneers in this area. Indeed, during the years from 1990–2000, this "prologue" in merchandising snaps with the saga of "Les Verts" (Moneghetti, Tétart and Wille, 2007). A pioneer in merchandising, sponsorship and sports marketing, competition innovation, training and institutional structuring of clubs, especially at the level of division of labor and delegation policies, the AS Saint-Étienne club will continue to significantly contribute to the professionalization of sports business in France (Charroin and Chanavat, 2014). Our analysis echoes the words of Jacques Ferran, who Roger Rocher describes as "by far the only major executive of a French club. I see no other coming close. He transformed the AS Saint-Étienne into an exemplary club in all areas related to organization, communication, and money."[8]

Box 1.1 The "green merchandising"

Being aware of the importance of fans in the development of the club, Roger Rocher wished to win the loyalty of a group of supporters. In 1969, the club appealed to interested persons through forming a single entity called "Associate Members". This followed discussion initiated by Lucien Dumas, a man close to Roger Rocher. A new association was established within the club's Board of Directors in which two seats are reserved for these "new" fans: the associates' office.

Stengthened by this new status, Roger Rocher began listening to "associates", initiators of "Green merchandising". Alex Mahinc, a charismatic member close to Roger Rocher, recounts:

> The Associate Members were in charge of the club mail. People asked for pictures of players, signings and things to sell. Just look at Charles Paret who does not believe in it, but who gave us 500 remaining pennants that he had on hand. They sold like hotcakes. Given the success, the 'accociates' proposed to Roger Rocher to diversify their sales through mail order or direct sales on game night. Against Kiev, it was madness, it was necessary to get on the table with a nightstick so as not to be overrun by fans. Thus, in 1974, the 'Associate Supporters' took initiative through the sale of licensed merchandise. Once again, Roger Rocher listened to the associates' advice. With his agreement, they manufactured various gadgets: T-shirts, flags, scarves, hats . . . that were sold either to the House of the Associates or by mail. This is a success and, by itself it inaugurated the 'birth' of sports merchandising in France.

"AS Saint-Étienne Promotion" is then created and operates the first "Boutique des Verts". In this dynamic, Roger Rocher proves himself to be innovative once again with the inauguration of the first store dedicated to "Les Verts", on the 14th of September 1977, the day of the match against Manchester United. The "Boutique" is built in the parking lot of Geoffroy-Guichard stadium. Covering an area of 400m^2, it offers a wide range of products with the club's brand. Success was awaiting. The additional revenue generated by this sports shop is necessary for the club's financial stability. The idea of the president is to generate profits with the goal of helping the sports side. The AS Saint-Étienne is the first French club to create and market products bearing its image. At the European level, Bayern Munich, AC Milan, Inter Milan, Real Madrid, FC Barcelona, Leeds United, and Liverpool FC proved themselves to be advanced on these issues, while Juventus was the first club to export products. In this context, "Roger Rocher was forced to study the operation of foreign clubs. . . . He knew how to climb up to the level of the big foreign clubs, he was the only one in France able to do it." Overall, France was one of the pioneering countries to implement an entrepreneurial model and logic with a football club.

Source: Charroin and Chanavat (2014, pp. 124–125).

The Matra Racing of Jean-Luc Lagardère: The "galactical" strategy for a search of profit

In 1982, Jean-Luc Lagardère (Chairman of Matra – big international company involved in communication, media and weapons) decided to invest in football and to build a great club in Paris. The French group Matra, specializing in electronic equipment and defense, was inspired by major international companies such as Fiat or Philips. In fact, Jean-Luc Lagardère wanted to have his own football team. Matra acquired Racing Club de Paris, a club with a glorious past, but floundering in the second division at the time. Racing Club de France was renamed to Matra Racing in 1987. Beginning in 1985, Jean-Luc Lagardère decided to build a "galactic" armada in order to immediately climb back up to Ligue 1. This was to be achieved with players such as Pierre Littbarski (star of the German team), Luis Fernandez (iconic PSG player), Maxime Bossis (star of the French team), Enzo Francescoli (star of the Uruguayan team) or Arthur Jorge (a few weeks after his success in the European Cup of Champions Clubs with FC Porto). The strategy of the club faced a double objective: to be profitable and to integrate the elite of European football within the decade. The club was well regarded as a genuine subsidiary of the group in search of profit. In the image of Florentino Perez, the president of Real Madrid (see Chapter 10 dedicated to PSG), the club was very ambitious and invested a lot of money into the recruitment and salaries of stars. However, this policy of stardom and soaring wages will last several seasons without ever truly bearing its fruits. Exasperated by the failures of the team, disappointed by a lack of popular support, and no longer wanting to see the name of his company tarnished by football critics, the Group withdrew (despite tens of millions of francs invested) due to a financial return deemed as insufficient. Ultimately, this avant-gardist project proved to be economically unviable (Bolle, 2005). When Jean-Luc Lagardère announced the withdrawal of his group from professional football, the stock saw an increase of 5% in the share price of Matra. Matra's financers then seemed relieved by the decision to give up that liability. It was about trying to take control of the group and bring it to the highest European level (like Agnelli with Juventus or Silvio Berlusconi with AC Milan; Bayer chemical group with its two clubs in the Bundesliga, Leverkusen and Uerdingen; or Philips, partner of PSV Eindhoven), but ultimately the Matra Racing campaign did not succeed.

Olympique Lyonnais, Jean-Michel Aulas: towards a new dynamic?

Starting in 1987, Jean-Michel Aulas (JMA), early in his presidency of the Olympique Lyonnais, contributed to the development and professionalization of French football (see Chapter 11 dedicated to the OL). The Gerland stadium was temporarily equipped with a giant screen and the first, end of season fireworks were launched. These were innovative steps in football in the late 1980s, which gradually led JMA to the operation of his own spectacle. Thus, the concept of the creation and operation of a private stadium made its way in the mind of JMA, and it symbolized the idea of "Sportainment" (François Bayle, 2014). The diversification of activities and incomes of the Olympique Lyonnais team (OL), an unprecedented structuring which took place in the 2000s of French football, has been largely dictated by the desire to gain access to public offerings. The club has now been publicly on the stock market since 2007.

There is clear evidence that companies believe that the elite of French football does not constitute a lucrative investment. This is why Colony Capital and US investment funds held PSG for several years before selling it (see Chapter 10 dedicated to the PSG). Sponsorship reasserts itself as a result of the arrival of Bernard Tapie in Marseille and the 1993 victory against AC Milan in the Champions League. Since this European victory, several groups, such as Canal + (PSG), M6 (Girondins de Bordeaux) and Socpresse (FC Nantes), or businessmen such as Olivier Sadran with Toulouse FC, Bernard Caiazzo and Roland Romeyer with the AS Saint-Étienne, Loïc Fery with the FC Lorient and Michel Seydoux with the LOSC of Lille, invest in French professional football.

To a globalization of the football product

The Bosman ruling of December 1995 has a considerable reach not only for football, but also for all professional disciplines. The Court of Justice of the European Communities considered that, if it was up to sporting federations to determine the rules of the game, the economic dimension should be subject to Community law. This case law has had several effects: a legal effect with the end of the sports exception; an economic effect because it opened the professional football contract market to international competition and accelerated the liberalization of professional football; and a sporting effect because the movement of players within Europe has led to a reorganization of clubs' staffing. The freedom of the movement of players (the legal component) has promoted the development of both the sport and the professional football industry (economic component), which consequently had an impact on the competitive balance of competitions (economic component). Thanks to the revolution of the Internet and social networks, the 2000s marked a media explosion, which opened the era of instant information and knowledge flow. For Andreff (2012), Sportainment refers to the advent of sports-entertainment in a context of globalization and globalization of the sports economy. In France, this phenomenon is illustrated in particular by the arrival of foreign investors investing in club capital and the passion to internationalize displayed by several entities.

The life cycle of the football spectacle

While the international dimension was quickly revealed, today's football is apprehended as a global product that is constantly developing. Lionel Messi's or Cristiano Ronaldo's recognition rate is higher than that of the Pope! Our analysis echoes the words of Philippe Diallo, Director General of UCPF,

> Football is only at the beginning of its economic expansion. I have no worries about the development of football, even in the territories that have not yet been conquered. The scope of the growth is very large. Europe remains a major point of this development, but its status may become challenged. A bit like in the rest of the economy, if US,

> Brazil, China are there, it means that players may want to move. The MLS, for example, is well organized.[9]

The environment which is evolving professional football remains peculiar. French football possesses undeniable assets in this ultra-competitive market. "In this context, France has several very positive factors: the stadiums, the human competence, the quality of training, a sound championship: no corruption, etc., an increase in the television contracts."

In the concept of the life cycle (representing sales of sporting goods over time), as presented above by Andreff (1989), it is considered that companies attempt to export their products during the decline phase, trying in this way to stem the decline through internationalization. The attempts to penetrate Asian and North American markets (promotional tours, sales of TV rights, development of shops, websites, social networks) seem to agree with this theoretical explanation. For 30 years, the process of "commodification" of professional sports has represented an undeniable reality and appears as a clear theme of the contemporary evolution of the sport. The most publicized and spectacularized sports clubs are in this way transforming into businesses that are approaching the characteristics of conventional companies (Chantelat, 2001). Thus, football is a particularly significant example used to illustrate this phenomenon. For example, professional clubs, like Real Madrid, Manchester United and PSG, develop their marketing and financial strategies in a global perspective.

The sport business has considerably advanced itself through mobilizing techniques conventionally used for products of mass consumption. Facing a partially saturated European football market, Asia appears to be a credible "way out" for clubs who are looking for new sources of funding and are eager to internationalize their brand (Desbordes, 2007). Some athletes transcend their sport, becoming full-fledged brands and global icons in their own right. They are presented as marketing tools who are facilitating trade within a specific market. It is then necessary for

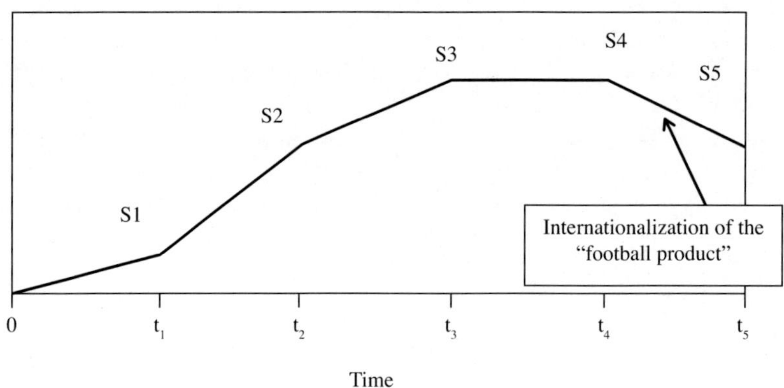

Legend:
S1: sales corresponding to the needs of high-level competitors
S2: sales covering all of the sport side
S3: sales covering the national market (including purchases of non-sports fans and the renewal applications)
S4: sales corresponding to the beginning of the decline phase

Figure 1.1 The life cycle of the sport product (sales over time)

Source: Andreff, 1989.

clubs to recruit international players based on their marketing profile increasing their potential in terms of merchandising and the interest they generate on the media. This strategy, symbolized by the arrival of David Beckham to PSG, was particularly used with Asian players such as Junichi Inamoto for Arsenal FC and Park Ji-Sung to Manchester United.

From an international perspective, the strategies deployed by the NBA and the Premier League are seen as prime examples.

In France, as part of the international development of the Ligue 1, the PSA signed in 2015 a unique agreement with FC Miami City. This is Miami's official football club, which operates in the "Premier Development League" bringing together 65 American teams. Through this academy, FC Miami City organizes trainings throughout the season for licensees and an after-school program with dozens of partner schools. With more than 600 players in the academy and hundreds of children trained in the schools, FC Miami City has become the football reference in Florida. This partnership aims to promote the Ligue 1 to young American audiences. American children are becoming increasingly passionate about the practice of "soccer", as evidenced by the number of graduates of the American Football Federation (over 4 million) and the development of the MLS. This agreement will thus enable FC Miami City to represent professional French football in the US by becoming an Official Ligue 1 *Soccer Academy* in Florida. This initiative is part of the Ligue 1 brand strategy of internationalization on the North American continent, which was implemented during the "Champions Trophy" in 2015 in Montreal. The logic is the same for clubs that multiply marketing initiatives. To set itself up as a global sports brand, the PSG's central strategy is based on a globalization process (see Chapter 10 dedicated to the PSG).

The arrival of new, foreign investors

If these club presidents sometimes happen to be millionaires, they do not owe it to football. For examples, Olivier Sadran, Chairman of Toulouse FC (Toulouse FC or TFC), owns a catering company, and Louis Nicollin, president of Montpellier HSC (MHSC), owns a waste treatment company. One observes that more and more foreign billionaires and multimillionaires invest in acquiring football clubs in Europe.

The globalization of football is also illustrated by the arrival of foreign investors in football clubs.

Since 2011, French football is characterized by the arrival of the sovereign Al Thani family of Qatar to Paris Saint-Germain (PSG), the Russian oligarch Dmitry Rybolovlev to the Association Sportive de Monaco (ASM), the businessman Hafiz Mammadov of Azerbaijani to the Racing Club de Lens or the Chinese group Ledus to Football Club Sochaux Montbéliard (FCSM). This last example is symbolic. It shows the end of 87 years of "cohabitation" between the Peugeot group, which was at the inception of French professional football, and the FCSM.

Since 2003, Roman Abramovich has invested several hundred million into the Chelsea club. Globally, the Mexican Carlos Slim is the richest football club owner, with a fortune estimated at 73 billion US dollars. He owns two professional sports organizations in Mexico (Club Pachuca, Club Leon) and one in Spain (Real Oviedo). In any case, billionaires do not become owners of a football club envisioning economic profitability. Indeed, it seems impossible to manage a football club as a solid and profitable business, since there will always be competing owners who do not care about profitability and who will spend whatever price it takes to win titles (Kuper and Szymanski, 2012).

Drut (2014) mentions several motives that lead them to invest. Veblen's theories of leisure and conspicuous consumption (1899) seem possible for some businessmen. If it is necessary to be rich or have the power to attract the esteem of men, it is essential to evidence these qualities.

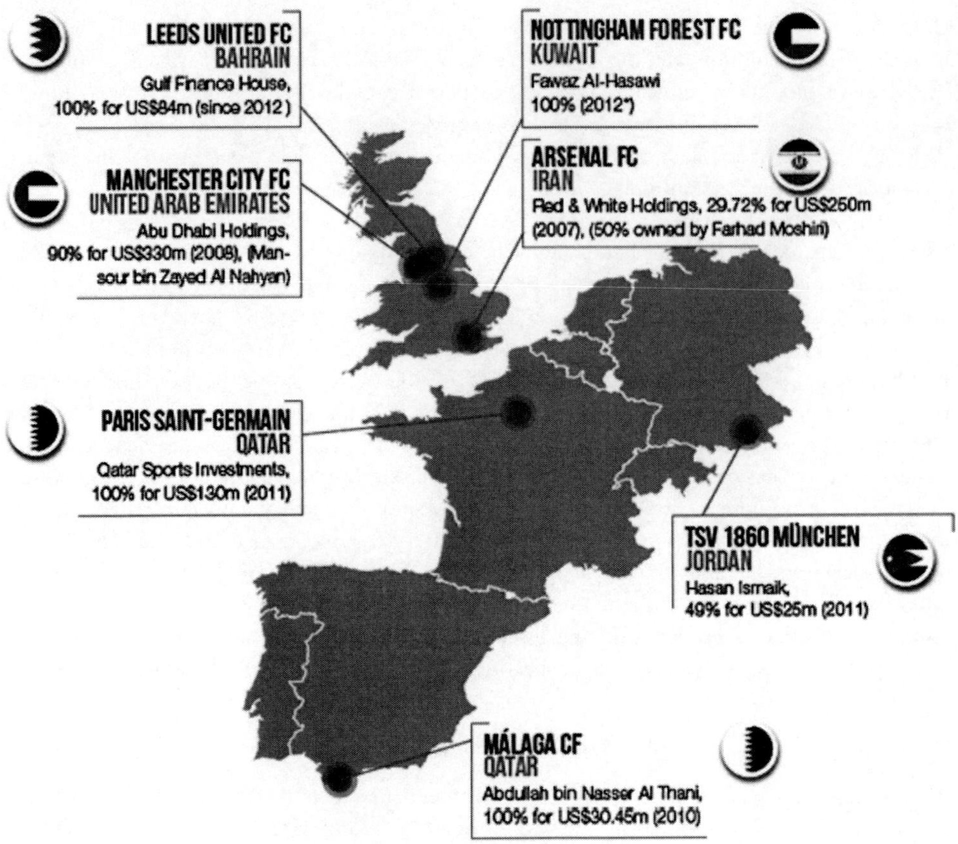

Figure 1.2 Middle Eastern owners of European football clubs

Source: Repucom, Emerging Giants, 2015, p. 7.

Football enjoys a unique status in Europe, given its exceptional media exposure. Thus, the gains, in terms of awareness, image and affect, appear to be a credible motivation for other billionaires. The acquisition of social and political acceptance (after a series of financial scandals) seems to explain the purchase of the Fulham club by Mohamed Al-Fayed. Note that while PSG is the only French club owned by Middle Eastern shareholders, six more clubs in Europe are as well, as shown in Figure 1.2.

Qatar and PSG

If French football is marked in recent years by the arrival of foreign investors, the purchase of PSG by QSI refers to a singular model. This investment is part of the overall strategy of the development of Qatar, a tiny Persian Gulf country, which makes sports a pillar of its growth strategy.

From 1995 to 2013, Qatar has been headed by the Emir Hamad bin Khalifa Al Thani, who provided the country with a new constitution and created the Al-Jazeera channel to increase awareness of the emirate. Qatar sees, within the strengthening of its international brand equity linked to sport, a way to consolidate its diplomatic influence and, therefore, to protect its independence.

Qatar has developed an influence strategy through sports based on the following, major activities: the acquisition of professional sports organizations; organizing recurring and one-off events; the acquisition of television rights; the creation of a brand for equipment manufacturing; contracting partnerships; head hunting by offering to pay a fortune to those with sports skills; and the choice of a Qatari at the top of a sporting body (Chanavat and Desbordes, 2014b) (see Chapter 6 dedicated to sponsorship). Regarding football, Qatar organized its first international competition in 1995 when it hosted the World Cup for players under 20. It should be noted that the event was organized in just 3 weeks in Nigeria and was rejected at the last moment by FIFA due to an Ebola outbreak.

Qatar's strategy appears to exceed the emirate itself as it influences the entire international perception of the Middle East. The development of the "Qatar Brand" can make of a tiny state a diplomatic and economic reference in a region with powerful countries like Saudi Arabia or the United Arab Emirates.

If it still seems difficult to measure the effectiveness of this new marketing strategy based on sports, the takeover of PSG by Qatar emerges as the centerpiece of the plan. PSG has developed several initiatives aiming to move strategically towards internationalization for the last 15 years, but the club's globalization process clearly coincides with the arrival of the QSI in the club's capital. Moreover, the club's central strategy is now based on this approach of internationalization that is the subject of a detailed analysis (see Chapter 10 dedicated to the PSG).

What are the characteristics of football marketing?

Marketing aims to be a "state of mind" useful to the development of football. But what makes it unique? It is important to specifically study its event-related components, its uniqueness as a sports service and the stakeholders who make up the ecosystem of professional football. The notion of a professional sports entity is reviewed and defined here. The analysis of the discipline's characteristics leads us to offer a definition of the concept of football marketing.

The sporting event, a sharing of emotions

"A sporting event represents a large social event, with a specific image and a generally uncertain outcome, promoting the sharing and the exchange of consumer perceptions and feelings against various entities that it brings together" (Chanavat, 2009, p. 117).

This definition of the sporting event leads us to clarify certain points. First, a social event consists of ways of acting, thinking and feeling that are external to the individual and which strongly influence people. The event provides the necessary energy to the system. As evidenced by its etymology, it is likely to have a strong impact on social groups – fans. Indeed, the word "event" comes from the Latin word *eventus* meaning "which has happened, and that affects a person or a human community." Therefore, the sporting event can be considered as such. Its impact is related to the fact that it represents a carrier of identity in what we can call "affectionate communities" (Maffesoli, 1988).

We can ask ourselves: what would be the impact of a sporting event without uncertainty in terms of results? We can legitimately think that sporting events lacking this component do not give rise to the same interest or the same enthusiasm for its attendees, viewers and hence companies. Thus, the attendees and the viewers tend to stay focused on a match with an indecisive score, since uncertainty as to the winner remains. In 2014, during the final of the FIFA World Cup between Germany and Argentina, the audience ratings peaked during the extra time.

On the other hand, a sporting event could lose its appeal if it is not broadcasted live and the result is therefore known. More so, when the result of an event is known, spectators begin to leave the sports arena to avoid traffic jams. A sporting event is objectively perceived as the possibility of a win. But when the result is predictable, interest and emotion disappear, leaving little room for the possibility of a win. Consequently, we can ask ourselves: what would be the attraction of the football product without the standard components of the event? The sporting event offers the best conditions for emotional communication to occur. This phenomenon operates directly for the spectators, but also through TV or social networks. Therefore, what would be the sporting event – a football match – without emotions? What would it look like without joy, anxiety, hope, anger, sadness or pride? Deprived of its emotional component, it certainly does not offer the same interest to consumers and therefore to advertisers. In other words, emotions are what make life worth living (Crocker et al., 2003). They color and influence all of our perceptions without us truly realizing it. Thus, a football match is appreciated to the extent that it is emotionally experienced by fans. This is why a growing number of advertisers have invested in sponsorship activities to engage in an emotional relationship with consumers of sports entertainment.

Stakeholders in professional football

Although the ecosystem of professional football brings a multitude of stakeholders, here we will focus especially on professional sports organizations

The ecosystem of the industry

The 2014 barometer of the economic and social impacts of professional football (EY-UCPF, 2014) presents the ecosystem of the French professional football industry. It breaks down into three levels: the clubs; local stakeholders (subcontractors, suppliers, partners, etc.); and the industrial and sectoral world (media, sports equipment, real estate, etc.).

Professional sports entities: at the heart of the system

From a marketing perspective, professional sports organizations are at the center of the professional football system and include:

- Sports organizations (professional sports structures, confederations, federations, leagues, national teams, events and organizers of sports events, etc.);
- Sports celebrities, active or retired (athletes, referees, coaches, club presidents, etc.);
- Sports facilities (stadiums).

Because of their media exposure, these entities have a marketing potential, an image of their own and the ability to impact the reactions of the general public as part of a sponsorship pairing. The various forms of professional sports entities helps us to grasp the marketing of football. They represent full-fledged brands and evolve more often within a competitive logic, where economic issues are significant. In this capacity, the Ligue 1 is in competition with the Serie A; Manchester United organizes tours in Asia in order to sell more jerseys than FC Barcelona; the PSG website is available in eight languages to promote the internationalization of the brand and to compete with Real Madrid, who has a website in seven languages. . . . This competition is so fierce that, in Europe and the United States, some brands seem to reach a plateau in these virtually saturated markets.

Towards a definition of football marketing

We will successively address the marketing concepts, highlight the characteristics of sport services, and distinguish between the concepts of sports marketing and the marketing of sports. This will lead us to offer a definition of football marketing.

Marketing

The sport marketer is first of all a marketer. It therefore becomes necessary to understand an outline of marketing logic. Overall, marketing aims to respond to consumer needs. A myriad of definitions have been proposed to define marketing. Thus, according to the American Marketing Association (AMA), "marketing is the activity, set of institutions, and processes for creating, communicating, delivering, and exchanging offerings that have value for customers, clients, partners, and society at large" (AMA, 2013). For Kotler et al. (2006, p. 5), "marketing is to identify human and social needs, and then respond to them." If these definitions are relevant, they do not fully cover all the areas occupied by marketing activities. Marketing remains above all a "state of mind" which consists of understanding the consumer's point of view to meet his or her needs. It follows the development of new technologies. One sees the appearance of newer, more interactive forms of marketing, such as viral marketing, street marketing, etc.

Marketing activities of an organization must be designed jointly and represent fully integrated marketing programs with the aim to create, communicate and deliver value to the consumer. Thus, a marketing program is a set of decisions on marketing actions to employ. The concept of the marketing mix suggests a classic way of presenting. It brings together the tools available to an organization it requires to achieve its goals in the eyes of the target market. These tools are grouped into four components of the marketing mix (called "the 4 *P*s"): product, price, place (or distribution) and promotion (or communication). Each component of the marketing mix is equipped with levers of action. Sponsorship represents one of the communication (or promotion) techniques available to organizations.

When it comes to studying a particular industry under the lens of marketing, the question of unique models used may arise. There is clear evidence that the ins and outs of marketing applied to the sports sector are a part of the same perspective as the "classical" marketing we just mentioned. However, the specific features of the sports sector lead to certain peculiarities. In France in particular, the properties of the discipline have in this way been questioned by Desbordes, Ohl and Tribou (1999) from the theoretical structuring of the field, and then by Desbordes and Richelieu (2012).

What are the characteristics of sport services?

Sport services are specific when compared to services known as traditional. We can therefore distinguish four dimensions:

- Sport services have an emotional dimension: the intangible nature of sport services adds to the highly emotional characteristic, which gives it density. This dimension is reinforced by the uncertainty of outcome that sets the sporting spectacle apart from other types of spectacles. A sporting spectacle without the passionate comments of a journalist or unaccompanied by public manifestations of emotions is at risk of losing its originality.

- Sport services have an environmental dimension: the sporting environment greatly influences the sensation of sports pleasure and the degree of satisfaction for the regular consumer. We can even say that the environment is an integral part of the service.
- Sport services presuppose the active participation of the consumer: the process of the cooperation of the regular consumer in the production of the service is also a feature of sport services. Hence the term, "consum'actor". The involvement of the consumer, and his or her efforts, give value to the service. The consumer plays a key role in the creation of valued service.
- Sport services have a symbolic dimension: while all consumptions, sporting or not, display a symbolic character linked to social representations, sports consumption presents even more of it. Sports take place in the public eye, which allows for the demonstration of a certain social position.

Sport marketing, marketing of sport: what are we talking about?

In this context, it is necessary to distinguish two concepts: *sport marketing* and the *marketing of sport*. These concepts may be ambiguous for both professionals and university scholars.

Thus, according to Mullin, Hardy and Sutton (2007, p. 11),

> Sport marketing consists of all activities designed to meet the needs and wants of sport consumers through exchange processes. Sport marketing has developed two majors thrusts: the marketing of sport products and services directly to consumers of sport, and the marketing of other consumer and industrial products or services through the use of sport promotions.

This definition which alludes to two distinct models is accepted by the international scientific community.

Sports marketing aims to promote sports products and services to sports consumers. In this way, it brings together the strategies, techniques and marketing operationalizations applied to sports entities (professional sports entities, suppliers, etc.). Teams and clubs of all sizes (not just professionals) are therefore able to practice sports marketing.

Marketing through sports or the marketing of sport consists of, on the other hand, using sports for purposes of promotion and communication for entities that have no intrinsic link with sports. It typically concerns businesses and refers to the notion of sponsorship (see Chapter 6 dedicated to sponsoring). The idea is for the sponsoring brand to "capture" the values or images conveyed by the sponsored sporting entity in a marketing perspective.

The marketing of football

Football marketing brings together all of the marketing strategies, techniques and marketing operationalizations applied to football entities. These marketing logics help to generate resources by diversifying the offers and services, in particular vis-à-vis consumers of sporting events and economic partners. The marketing of football seeks to streamline its activities in relation to the professionalization of the industry and to the better understanding of the needs of stakeholders who make up its ecosystem. It particularly concerns the professional clubs or federations which, as professional sports entities, have in their DNA a sporting essence, and it refers back to the model of sport marketing.

What are the economic values and marketing potentials for professional sport entities?

This section addresses the economic and marketing value of professional sport entities. Clubs, players and coaches are the subject of a particular study.

An economic approach

If we put aside the competitive aspects, and it is also in this light that it is the most often mentioned, there is no doubt today that football has an economic dimension. Clubs have to enhance their attractiveness through their marketing strategy by taking into consideration all the brands and stakeholders they bring together. The fan is more attracted to certain sporting bodies than others. Many studies aim to measure and estimate the marketing value or price of a professional sports entity. According to Christophe Bouchet, "The evaluation of a club is the exact amount that someone agrees to pay. A club is not a 'puppet' although the elements that give it its value are those that the buyer will use to serve its network and its image. They are very important but hard to quantify."[10] Measuring the value of a professional sporting entity proves to be a complex exercise. In this context, several institutions establish rankings based on the value of clubs, players or coaches. Let's review some of them: the Football Observatory, Deloitte, Forbes and Brand Finance.[11]

The Football Observatory of the International Center for Sports Studies (CIES)

The CIES Football Observatory, affiliated with the University of Neuchâtel in Switzerland, has issued an annual report between 2006 and 2014. This is a very rich document in which the market value of the players of the Big 5 is presented. A ranking is determined according to different parameters and various estimates. Among the criteria taken into consideration, the most notable are the player's age, the duration of his contract, the position held, individual performance through performance statistics by position indicators, the results of the club, results of the national team if he plays internationally, the player's history to analyze his consistency and make projections, etc.

In 2014, for its ninth edition (CIES, 2014), the report of the study placed Lionel Messi as the Big 5 player with the highest value on the transfer market. According to the econometric model developed by the Observatory of Football, the estimated value for the FC Barcelona player is almost two times higher than that of Cristiano Ronaldo: 216 million euros as opposed to 114 million euros. This difference can be explained given the young age of the Argentine. However, unlike the Portuguese player's market value, Messi's value decreased in the last year because of a decline in performance (-19 million euros).

Luis Suarez, the person behind an outstanding season with Liverpool, was among the Big 5. The price of his transfer is between 98.5 and 114.5 million euros. Eden Hazard is, however, as of 2013, outside of the Big 5. After his second year at Chelsea, his value varied between 75.9 and 88.3 million euros.

The first representative of the French Ligue 1, Edinson Cavani, 3rd in 2013, occupies the 9th position today. His rating dropped slightly (now between 48 and 55.8 million euros, from between 58.3 and 67.8 million euros in 2013). The former Monacan player, James Rodriguez (25th, between 34.2 and 39.8 million euros), and the Parisian, Lucas (37th, between 30.6 and 35.6 million euros), complete the top three of the French championship.

As for Paul Pogba, he is the first Frenchman. He holds the 6th place. Pogba's value is between 60.6 and 70.4 million euros. Olivier Giroud, striker for Arsenal and the France national team, is 48th (between 28.1 and 32.7 million euros).

Note that since January 2015, the Football Observatory publishes a monthly report which analyzes themes of professional football news: team composition, transfer values, career development, field performance, top talents, etc.[12]

Deloitte consulting group

Deloitte is one of the world's four major audit and consulting firms in which tens of thousands of dedicated professionals from independent firms work together in order to advise on topics of risk management, taxation, legal and finance for internationally renowned customers. These firms are members of Deloitte Touche Tohmatsu Limited, a UK private company. Each member firm provides services in geographical areas and is subject to professional laws and regulations of the country. The total revenues for the 2014 fiscal year were measured at 34.2 billion USD.

In France, Deloitte is seen as the leading auditing and consulting group, with a revenue of 984 million euros, up 10.5%. At the beginning of each year, the firm publishes a study entitled *Football Money League*. The ranking compares the financial power of the biggest football clubs worldwide. The study divides economic resources into three types of revenue. The "matchday" combines ticket sales and revenues from consumption on the day of the match. The study also takes into account the "broadcasting" of clubs, that is to say everything that concerns TV rights. Finally, it relies on the "commercial" aspects which correspond to the different partnerships as well as the sale of licensed merchandise.

The results of the 2015 study showed wide disparities between the incomes of big clubs. The financial resources of Real Madrid (549.5 million euros), ranked first, are twice as large as those of

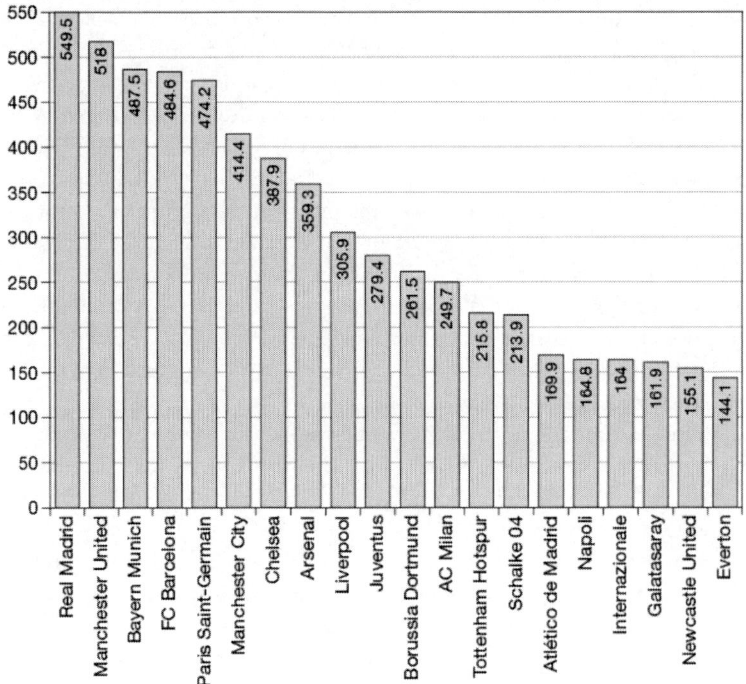

Figure 1.3 Revenues of big football clubs

Source: Deloitte (2015).

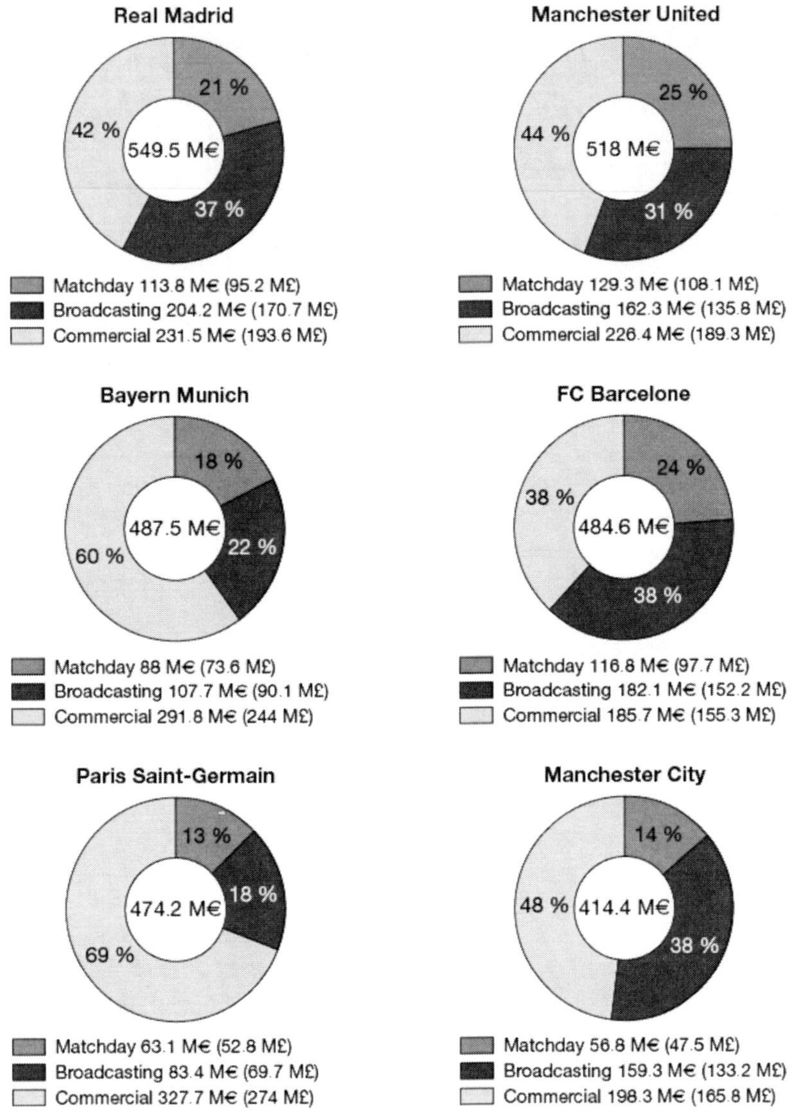

Figure 1.4 The economic model of the six most powerful professional football clubs in the world

Source: Deloitte (2015).

Juventus, ranked tenth, three times more than those of Atletico Madrid, ranked 15th, and almost four times more than Everton, ranked last. Almost all of the clubs that appear in this ranking participate in European tournaments and the notable Champions League, which guarantees significant revenue. Within its own league, La Liga, Real Madrid sometimes plays against clubs whose budget is 20 times lower than its own. In this context, the competitive balance, a pillar of the economic analysis of the sport and a guarantor of the uncertainty of the outcome, is seriously at risk.

Overall, a modern football club is financed by ticket sales (oftentimes ticket sales have become less important, even though historically it was the first resource of clubs), television rights and commercial resources (these include the sponsorship and sales within areas of public relations, VIP boxes and business seats). PSG and Bayern Munich are the exception. More than half of their revenues are commercial. This source of revenue amounts to 327.7 million euros for the French club. This amount is twice as large as all of Inter Milan's revenues, which are estimated at 164 million euros (ranked 17th). Among the six most powerful clubs, FC Barcelona and Manchester United have the most balanced business models.

Forbes *magazine*

Since 2004, *Forbes*, the New York-based business magazine (founded in 1917), publishes an annual ranking of the 20 or 25 most powerful football clubs in the world in terms of their financial value (most valuable soccer teams). This is an estimate of a club's value based on its ability to generate revenue. The Forbes measurement tool includes the value of club assets (players, stadium, ticket, etc.) and the marketing developed around the brand: merchandising, sponsorship or television rights. The top 20 clubs in the 2015 edition include eight English clubs, four Italian clubs, three German clubs, three Spanish clubs, one French club and one Turkish club. La Liga is valued higher than the Premier League as it contains the two highest rankings of the Big 5. Real Madrid is in first place with a value amounting to 3.26 billion USD (slightly lower compared to the results of 2014). It is directly one place ahead of the Catalan club whose market value is estimated at 3.16 billion US dollars. Manchester United enters the ranking with an estimated street value of 3.1 billion US dollars. The gap is closing between the Mancunian club and Spanish clubs. The value of Atlético Madrid, a finalist in the Champions League in 2014, is estimated at 436 million US dollars, more than seven times less than Real Madrid, winner of the event. PSG, the only Ligue 1 club, appears in 12th place. The Parisian club is valued up to 634 million US dollars.

Overall, these teams have a very strong brand equity, a high love rating, a prestigious history and an important base comprised of local and foreign fans.

The consulting group Brand Finance

Since 2010, the London firm Brand Finance, specializing in economics, also offers an annual ranking of football clubs based on the value of their brand. The concept of *royalty relief* is used as a method of calculation for each brand. It measures the price a third party would pay to acquire

Table 1.1 The ranking of football clubs in terms of their financial worth in millions of dollars

1	Real Madrid	3,260	**11**	Borussia Dortmund	700
2	FC Barcelona	3,160	**12**	PSG	634
3	Manchester United	3,100	**13**	Tottenham Hotspur	600
4	Bayern Munich	2,350	**14**	Schalke 04	572
5	Manchester City	1,380	**15**	Inter Milan	439
6	Chelsea	1,370	**16**	Atlético Madrid	436
7	Arsenal	1,310	**17**	Naples	353
8	Liverpool	982	**18**	Newcastle United	349
9	Juventus	837	**19**	West Ham	309
10	Milan AC	775	**20**	Galatasaray	294

Source: Forbes, 2015.

the right to use the brand commercially. This value is derived from the sum of the next 5 years of cash flow that a club is entitled to. This calculation takes into account the athletic performances, the economic environment of the club's country, the quality of infrastructure (stadium), the affects of the fans and the aura of the coach.

The 2014[13] edition of the top 50 ranking includes 16 English clubs, eight German clubs, six Italians clubs, five Spanish clubs, four Brazilian clubs, five French clubs, three Turkish clubs, two Dutch clubs, and one Portuguese club. Thus, thanks to the amount of its television rights, the Premier League positions the vast majority of its clubs in the ranking. Better yet, half the top 10 is made up of English clubs.

The Brazilian club the Corinthians, who increased 33% (80 million euros), rises to the top 20. This is the only South American club challenging the arch-domination of European clubs.

PSG is ranked tenth with an estimated value of 238 million euros, and it jumped 14 ranks to reach the top 10. This club has the highest value compared to the previous edition (62 million euros in 2013). Les Girondins de Bordeaux (41 million, 47th), the LOSC (62 million, 36th), the OM (67 million euros, 32nd) and the OL (81 million euros, 25th place) represent the other French brands in the world ranking. Bayern Munich remains the most valued brand-club in the world with 659 million euros. Real Madrid is second with 565 million euros. Estimated at 543 million euros, Manchester United is third. Barcelona remains in 4th place with 457 million euros. With a value of 375 million euros, Manchester City gains three places and occupies the 5th position.

A marketing approach

The marketing approach of professional sports entities is illustrated by the work of Repucom. Repucom is considered a world leader in sports marketing studies. In 2010, the company merged with the company SPORT + MARKT and, 2 years later, they acquired Sports and IFM Sports Marketing Surveys.

The ranking of players with the highest marketing potential, published by Repucom and based on the Celebrity DBI Index, measures and describes the perception that the

Table 1.2 The ranking of football clubs based on their brand

2014 RANK	2013 RANK	CLUB	BRAND VALUE 2014 (US$ Million)	(£ GBP)	(€ Euros)	LEAGUE	COUNTRY
1	1	FC Bayern München	896	534	659	Bundesliga	
2	3	Real Madrid CF	768	457	565	La Liga	
3	2	Manchester United FC	739	440	543	Premier League	
4	4	FC Barcelona	622	370	457	La Liga	
5	8	Manchester City FC	510	304	375	Premier League	
6	6	Arsenal FC	505	300	371	Premier League	
7	5	Chelsea FC	502	299	369	Premier League	
8	7	Liverpool FC	469	279	345	Premier League	
9	10	Borussia Dortmund	327	195	240	Bundesliga	
10	24	Paris Saint-Germain FC	324	193	238	Ligue 1	

Source: Brand finance (2014, p. 6).

general public has of celebrities. This study is developed in collaboration with *The Marketing Arm*, a company specializing in image management strategies and intellectual property rights of celebrities for multinational and local brands. This includes evaluation, negotiation, execution and management of the stars and the rights of third parties on behalf of brands across all activations.

If football is considered a sporting spectacle produced by the players, they are considered to be "artists" who capture much of the wealth of clubs. In this context, Cristiano Ronaldo possesses the best marketing potential of all football players. The captain of the Portuguese national team has a recognition rate of 83.9% and a fan base of a record 82 million fans on Facebook[14] and 26 million followers on Twitter. Lionel Messi is in 2nd place. The Argentinian is known by 76.1% of the people. He has 57 million fans on Facebook and 2 million followers on Twitter. The Spaniard Gerard Piqué finishes 3rd with a recognition rate of 58.1%, 12 million Facebook fans and 8 million Twitter followers. In total, four Spaniards who were world champions in 2010 are part of the Top 10. It should be noted that Thierry Henry is the only Frenchman in this ranking, with a recognition rate of 51.6%, 16 million Facebook fans and 0.3 million Twitter followers. The only player from the Ligue 1 present in this classification is Zlatan Ibrahimović. The only ranked athlete (9th place) who did not participate in the 2014 World Cup in Brazil, he has the 6th highest recognition rate (55.8%) (Repucom, 2014).[15]

The aforementioned definition of a professional sports entity includes coaches as well as clubs and players (which are often the subject of study). This is because they have a real impact on marketing.

Therefore, Repucom innovated in 2015 by conducting a study on Ligue 1 coaches for the first time. The results of the study show that Laurent Blanc is the coach with the highest marketing potential of the French elite. He also was awarded best Ligue 1 technical player in 2014–2015 and was awarded the UNFP trophy (see Chapter 10 dedicated to the PSG). What about Marcelo Bielsa? The Argentine technical player, a real sensation during the Ligue 1 season (2014–2015), mainly because of a clashing personality, seems to have convinced the experts but not the crowds. Ranked among the "freshmen" in the categories proposed by Repucom (with the "stars", "historic figures", "rising stars" and "discreet"), the Argentinian suffers from a lack of awareness, and he is known only by 34% of the sample (10th in the ranking).

Table 1.3 The ranking of football players according to their marketing potential

Rank	*Player*	*DBI Score*	*Global Reputation*	*Likes on Facebook (May 2014)*	*Followers on Twitter (May 2014)*
1	Cristiano Ronaldo	79.49	83.87%	82 million	26 million
2	Lionel Messi	75.87	76.07%	57 million	2 million (not active)
3	Gerard Piqué	62.90	58.08%	12 million	8 million
4	Fernando Torres	62.69	59.64%	3 million	2 million
5	Wayne Rooney	59.47	55.82%	20 million	9 million
6	Andrés Iniesta	59.47	55.82%	20 million	9 million
7	Neymar Jr	59.36	53.33%	22 million	11 million
8	Iker Casillas	59.09	49.43%	18 million	1 million
9	Zlatan Ibrahimović	59.07	55.81%	15 million	1 million
10	Thierry Henry	57.56	51.62%	16 million	0.3 million

Source: Repucom (2014).

Box 1.2 The marketing potential of Ligue 1 coaches

Paris, April 1st, 2015 – A few days before the end of the French Football Championship, Repucom analyzed the perceptions that French people have of Ligue 1 coaches. While the players are the headliners and are regularly used by clubs and brands to promote their image, it appears that some coaches also have substantial marketing potential. Based on the perception of French people, calculated with the Celebrity DBI index (index measuring marketing impact of celebrities), Laurent Blanc, coach for Paris Saint-Germain, appears as the star of this championship. He enjoys an outstanding reputation (96%) and a high level of sympathy (74%) among the general public. Transgenerational, he resonates with all age groups, with his past as a player that began in the 1980s (the French national team, prestigious clubs), and his success as a coach/team manager. He stands out especially thanks to the media exposure afforded by his current position with PSG.

Laurent Blanc is the most well known, and Willy Sagnol is the most likable.

At the top of the ranking of the most famous coaches, we find Laurent Blanc (96% of the population says they know him). Next are Claude Makelele, who was on the bench of SC Bastia until November 2014 (86%), and Rolland Courbis, coach for Montpellier Hérault SC (67%).

In terms of sympathy, three young coaches stand out. The first, Willy Sagnol, the new coach of Girondins de Bordeaux, is perceived as likeable by 76% of people who say that they know him. He is followed closely by Jocelyn Gourvennec (EA Guingamp; 75%) and Christophe Galtier (AS St-Étienne; 75%).

Pierre-Emmanuel Davin, director of Repucom France, analyzes that

> For a football club, and in general for a rights holder, it is essential to measure the marketing impact of its personalities, whether it is coaches, players or executives. Coaches represent and sometimes embody their club, in this way playing an important role among the general public, fans and sponsors. Thus, to understand their perceptions of different targets that would affect a club or a brand is an essential element in a communication and sponsoring strategy.

Source: http://repucom.net/fr/laurent-blanc-star-entraineurs-ligue-1/ – "Laurent Blanc, star des entraîneurs de ligue 1", article published on repucom.net, April 1, 2015. Last accessed on May 12, 2015.

We have just examined the economic value and the marketing potential of European professional sports entities. We will now analyze the growth areas of professional football.

What are the growth areas utilized for professional football?

"The question of what are the sources of funding for clubs is clearly the main problem for owners and decision makers" (Maltese and Danglande, 2014, p. 8). First, we will analyze the financial situation of French clubs and identify the limitations to their growth. Then we will study the principal sources of funding utilized by clubs.

The financial situation of French clubs

What about the growth of the professional football sector in France? How has the structure of club revenues evolved? What growth areas are developed? What are the limits? Our analysis raises the question of the deployment of new revenue necessary to the success of clubs.

An illusory growth of the professional football sector in France?

In 2014, the third barometer of professional football (EY-UCPF, 2014) demonstrates the power of the economic sector within French professional football. However, the study points out that it does not express its full potential. Its strong media and social impact faces a competitive environment that's now globalized and liberalized. The professional football sector experienced a growth of 19% in the 2012–2013 season since the last edition of the *Barometer* (2010–2011 season) and reached a total revenue of 6 billion euros. Employment is also increasing, with a current workforce of 26,000 people, an additional 1,000 jobs. This study also shows the indirect economy created as a result of professional football, particularly at stadium construction sites for Euro 2016 and in sports betting.

Three factors help to explain this increase: the increase in broadcasting rights during the period (+50 million euros, related to audiovisual rights for European competitions), the tripling of the amount of sports betting on football activity and construction (or renovation) of sports arenas in preparation for Euro 2016 (from 34 million euros for the 2008–2009 season to 249 million euros for the 2012–2013 season).

Doesn't this provide a "trompe l'oeil" growth? If this growth is very significant, it refers above all to the 2012–2013 season and the development of two clubs: PSG and to a lesser extent AS Monaco.

What is the economic balance for clubs?

The DNCG report published in 2015 (for the 2013–2014 season) focuses on the financial situation at the core of the industry: the French professional clubs. It shows a cumulative net loss of 93 million (and an operating loss of 231 million euros) for the 40 professional clubs. This is a strong increase compared to last season.

The report also highlights the difficulties of professional sports organizations: developing their operating revenues (estimated at 1,707 million euros), of which nearly half (43.4%) comes from the two clubs with distinctive characteristics mentioned above (PSG and AS Monaco).

Otherwise, one observes a rebalancing of the operating income structure compared to the 2012–2013 season: the television rights are down 7%, sponsorship and advertising see a 9% increase, and stagnation on the part of game day revenues and other products.

The rebalancing of product breakdown is explained by the decrease of audiovisual rights earned by clubs (713 million euros, –3%) under the contract signed by the LFP with broadcasters over the period from 2012 to 2016; this resulted in the growth of all other revenue items, especially sponsorship and "other products".

Game day revenue, traditionally considered the Achilles heel of the French clubs, continues to grow, even though it does it so moderately (165 million euros, +4%). The significant increase in attendance at Ligue 1 sporting arenas in 2013–2014 (+10%) is explained by the entry into service (total or partial) of some stadiums like the Geoffroy-Guichard or the Allianz Riviera stadium, as well as by the support of clubs by the LFP in optimizing the operation of stadiums.

The limits to the growth of clubs

French professional football suffers from a form of "structural un-competitiveness". The report published in 2014 by the Union of Professional Football Clubs (UCPF, 2014) on the reasons behind the large sporting and economic "drop" of French clubs highlights four major obstacles to their development: severe disavantages (social charges, a penalizing tax system, restrictions

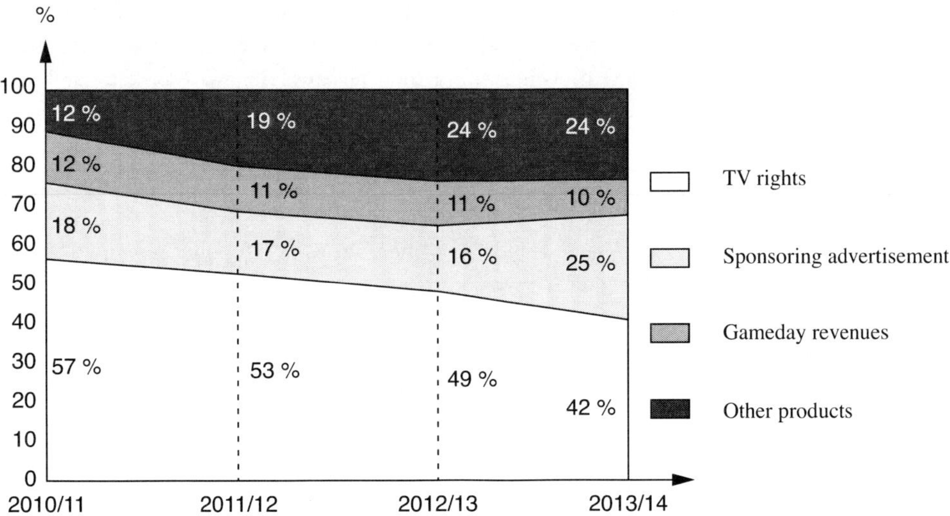

Figure 1.5 A breakdown of club revenue

Source: DNCG, 2015.

on sponsoring); sports erosion (the exodus of the best French players, etc.); a lack of economic competitiveness (television rights, sponsorship revenues on game day, low subscriptions, the difficulty of pronouncing stadiums, etc.); and fragile finances (under-capitalization, under-developed revenues, etc.).

Thus, social, business and estate taxes are greater and weigh a great deal heavier than those of France's European competitors. "Despite the significant efforts and positive results of some clubs, the competitiveness of the French professional football has deteriorated vis-à-vis its main European competitors, particularly as a result of the unfavorable tax and social environment," says Philippe Diallo. French clubs are not able to recruit star players, which is not conducive to their sporting success; it limits their revenue, grows their deficits and restricts their investment capacity. "In Europe, the clubs who sign big marketing contracts are those with super stars,"[16] explains Bruno Belgodère, CFO and marketing director at UCPF. On the same subject, Philippe Diallo adds that "if tomorrow Cristiano Ronaldo comes to OM, we will sell millions of jerseys and say that we are marketing geniuses. Our difficulty is to find out how to provide OM the means to pay Cristiano Ronaldo. In Paris, the problem was solved by the arrival of a shareholder."

In summary, a comparison of the five largest budgets of French clubs with those of other European clubs (from England, Germany, Spain and Italy) highlights three key elements:

- The analysis of operating expenses shows France's disproportionate business and federal taxes when compared to the other European nations mentioned above;
- Training in France is one of the best in Europe, which allows clubs to generate a high volume of revenue from transfers of trained players. However, they earn less revenue on transfers from non-trained players when compared to their main European competitors;
- The study of revenue shows that the French economic model struggles with developing its operating revenue when compared to its European competitors.

Therefore, French clubs have difficulty catching up with their European counterparts in terms of profitability and results. In this context, it seems inevitable for clubs to better control their expenditure, development and the diversification of their revenue. But what are the traditional sources of funding for clubs? We will now examine each of them in detail.

The "traditional" sources of funding for clubs

In their book published in 2014, Maltese and Danglande (2014, p. 10) point out that there are different configurations, depending on the type of organization putting on the sporting event. If we distinguish various growth engines, five commercial offers relate to the world of professional football: the sale and resale of players or coaches; ticketing; private and public contractual partnerships; media rights, essentially for television or mobile phones; and licensed products or services that might involve merchandising as well as on site restauration and consumption.

Although the multiplication of a growth engine is a necessity, income diversification is a prerequisite for the French clubs wishing to be listed on the exchange. OL must, for example (this is a must!), have at least 20% of its revenue derived from sources of income other than those directly related to sports results in order to ensure a certain stability results and therefore the share price. Beyond the commercial offers, it is important here to study the principal means of financing for clubs.[17]

Sale and resale of players or coaches

The trading of players consists of selling players at a higher price than what a club bought them for a few years ago, or by reselling players trained by the club. This also applies to coaches. At the end of the 2009–2010 season, the FFF had offered 1.5 million euros in compensation to the club Girondins de Bordeaux to hire Laurent Blanc.

Even if the strategic direction of the French clubs aiming to focus their training on quality has led to lower number of players in training programs, the French training method is recognized worldwide. OL, which makes training one of the pillars of its development, is one of the best European training clubs (see Chapter 11 dedicated to OL). To achieve this excellence, French professional clubs invest nearly 120 million per year (UCPF, 2014). The premature departure of promising young players, often the best players with the most potential, weakens training and contributes to the medium-term impoverishment of French sports clubs, to the benefit of

Table 1.4 The principal means of funding for a club

Means of Financing
Sale and resale of players or coaches
The debt waiver
Ticket sales and revenue from matches
Public funding
Contracts for private partnerships
Media rights, essentially television or mobile
Licensed products or services

Source: Adapted from Maltese and Danglande (2014, p. 10).

strengthening its neighbors. In this way, Paul Pogba left Le Havre very young to join Manchester United. The report of the UCPF (2014, p. 20) notes that

> these early departures are due in part to the legal framework of the first professional contract: in other European countries, the duration of the first professional contract (recommended by FIFA) is 5 years, while in France it is only 3 years, facilitating early departures abroad.

To reduce the level of their deficits, clubs utilize two classic levers: the trading of players (based mainly on training) and, when necessary, the support of their shareholders. With 179 million euros, the positive results of transfers have in this way helped to support their activity (DNCG, 2015).

What role(s) for shareholders?

Overall, shareholders provide the financial support necessary to guarantee the activities of their clubs. According to the report of the DNCG (2015), withdrawals from current accounts are at a historic level of 125 million euros for the 2013–2014. This record high is almost twice as much as the previous season and seems to confirm the upward trend that began in recent seasons. Without taking into account these withdrawals, the net loss of the 40 professional clubs would be 217 million euros.

Clubs appear to be dependent on either shareholders, large groups or even some states (Qatar, for example). Richard Olivier, President of DNCG, stresses that this phenomenon "does not promote the attractiveness of the sector and the arrival of new investors" (DNCG, 2015, p. 3). Although the DNCG is vigilant as to the creditworthiness of potential new shareholders of the club, clubs should ensure the implementation of internal controls regarding the origin and arrival of funds.

Towards a development of ticket sales and match revenues?

This activity has long been considered as the unwanted relative of marketing. However, it constitutes a means of development for sports organizations, including football clubs. The time when the spectator considered an absolute fan arrived the day of the match to buy his or her ticket is gone. The ticket is similar to a service that the marketing teams of clubs must develop to retain their customers and attract new ones. We talk about conquering loyalty.

The maturity of the discipline presents itself as the creation of businesses specialized in service and consulting (eForSports). Both are designed to support the event organizers in every sense, to develop and implement a ticketing strategy. The development of marketing ticket sales is based on the explosion of online sales. This has triggered the ticket dematerialization process (transition from the "thermal ticket" to the e-ticket), favoring the improvement of the customer experience and the proliferation of virtual outlets.

To ensure public support, the strategy of the Euro 2016 organizing committee has innovated. For the first time, a category 4 was created to sell 250,000 tickets: from 25 euros for the cheapest seats to 895 euros for the best locations in the final. Going from 16 to 24 teams, Euro 2016 has also increased the number of matches from 31 to 51, and therefore, the number of tickets on sale has never been higher. In total, there are about 2.5 million tickets, of which 1.8 million (almost 75%) are intended for the general public and fans of teams who qualify. These affordable rates are supposed to make the spectacle accessible to the "real" fans.

In any case, our analysis suggests that the economic model of clubs, based on TV rights, trading and withdrawal from shareholders, could include moving towards a rebalancing of growth engines, particularly in ticketing.

Public funding

Regardless of the sport or the team, the identity of professional sports clubs always passes through the attachment to a territory, especially in a city. This is often noted in the press by identifying clubs by their home city: "Paris" to describe the PSG team, "Lille" for the LOSC, "Liverpool" for the Liverpool FC. And when several clubs share the same city, names of neighborhoods or places identify the clubs (Arsenal, created not far from the old "Royal Arsenal", which employed all players; Chelsea, the name of a London neighborhood close by, etc.). It turns out that the link between local governments and professional clubs in France is thick and, for the latter, essential.

First of all, we observe the financial link which binds communities and their professional clubs. We know that the first frequently funds the latter, generally by allocating public subsidies, sometimes with the signing of purchase contracts benefits. Public grants to professional sports clubs have also often had bad press, quite wrongly. These well supervised devices are often very useful for communities, as explained by Guillaume Dufeutrelle, advisor of top level sports for the mayor of Paris:

> subsidies are not intended to enrich a club. Moreover, they are capped by the Buffet Act.[18] However, they allow to keep a close link between the community and the club, integrating social objectives or animation of local sporting communities. It is simply community support for a club that wants to put its image, its reputation and its expertise in service to the city. The club gains in image, but it is especially beneficial for people who can expect to see their team and club invest in local life off the field.[19]

However, the financial link between the community and its professional clubs is far from being the only one. We know that in France even the most important clubs are not the owners of their stadium.[20] This is for example the case for PSG, a simple tenant of the Parc des Princes which is owned by the city of Paris.[21] Discussions on topics such as the license-fee or the maintenance work make the city the club's main interlocutor. The license-fee required by the municipality depends largely on the profitability of the activity taking place within the stadium. It is well known that the economic model for many clubs, based in part on match revenues, is subject to the quality of relations with the city owning the stadium or arena.

In addition, professional clubs have needs in terms of sites for training, preparing or even housing players. While some clubs have dedicated training centers (the Ooredoo training center for PSG, the Commanderie for the Olympique Marseille, etc.), most are dependent on the time slots allocated in municipal facilities. "Some of our clubs are clearly dependent on communities in order to conduct their business," explains Guillaume Dufeutrelle. "Take the example of the Paris Football Club. It uses time slots in two facilities for its practices and games: the stadium Charléty in the 13th district and the Park of Choisy fields, owned by the City of Paris. Therefore, each year there are subtle negotiations between the city and the club in order to determine the use of these facilities and their rental cost. Concurrently, the association supporting the club operates in a third site, the Docteurs Déjerine stadium, in the 20th arrondissement, for the training of youth teams." The PFC also appeals to the local community to assist in the housing of its players, a concern that can quickly become complex and expensive in some major cities.

We are beginning to understand how the support of local authorities is key for many professional clubs. The economic survival of the club depends in large part on political will. What grants? What license to use the stadium? What housing facilities for players, offices, lodging? Add to that the fact that in order to fill the stadium, clubs need to communicate. This requires their website or the media, but even in the digital era, poster campaigns are still very effective. However, they often have an exorbitant cost. Communities often have spaces dedicated to them for their poster displays. Offering a club the opportunity to freely display posters for its next game becomes a form of additional support. As Guillaume Dufeutrelle concludes,

> As soon as you leave the Ligue 1, the top clubs are often very rich. For their survival and for them to preserve their recruitment budget, which determines their sporting success, the support of the city is essential. For many clubs, it is local authorities and their sports policy that decides their sporting and economic future.

Private partnership contracts

As we have seen previously, the revenue from sponsorship and advertising accounted for 25% (opposed to 16% the previous year) of revenues (total products excluding transfers) of Ligue 1 clubs (DNCG, 2015). This increase is mainly explained by the amount of partnerships formed by the PSG and QTA, or that of AS Monaco and the AIM society.

In addition, according to the report from Repucom (2014) and the Landscape Industry Sector Report 2013/2014, sponsorship in European football is worth over 2 billion euros. Overall, revenue generated from sponsorship throughout the world continues to grow. Sportswear companies remain the most prolific actors in terms of sponsorship on the football market, with 422 million euros invested across Europe. Nike appears to be the leader in this field, with a total investment of 166 million euros in 21 clubs from the top five European leagues. In 2014, revenue from sponsoring of the five major champion leagues and their 98 clubs reached about 2.1 billion euros. This report focuses on the sponsorship of European football, especially on sectoral origins of the firms involved in the sponsorship of the best leagues and clubs. The results of the study include, for the first time in the analysis, advertisers investing in billboards on the field and league sponsors. Premier League clubs have once again generated the highest revenue in Europe in terms of sponsorship. The Premier League is the most attractive league for global advertisers. Currently, 77% of the Premier League's total business sponsorship comes from companies outside the United Kingdom, with 16% coming from the Middle East. Middle Eastern companies play an increasingly important role in the European football industry and are now investing the largest amounts by partnership contract (10.6 million euros).

Sponsorship remains a growing revenue in European football, but there are wide disparities in the amount of jersey sponsorship deals. Sponsorship and marketing activities can be internalized or outsourced to specialist agencies. These sports marketing agencies market various professional sports organizations in the world of football. In France, there are several agencies, and Sportfive is the leader in the market. The strength of these specialized structures is having special relationships with leaders of sponsorship companies and access to their marketing and communication services. For the executives of football, the question arises of whether or not to use such services. "FIFA, UEFA, the clubs, have internalized and externalized sponsorship. There are no rules. Tomorrow if I was club president, objectively I would not know what strategy to follow," said Mathieu Ficot, Economic Development Manager for LFP. In any event, there is no one model that prevails over the others.

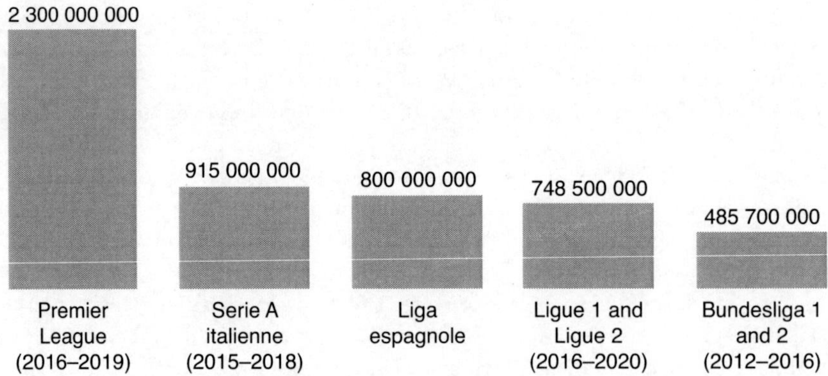

Figure 1.6 Comparison of the annual TV rights of the five major European leagues (in Euros)

Source: http://www.leparisien.fr/sports/football/angleterre-les-droits-tv-du-foot-atteignent-un-record-a-7-mds-eur-10-02-2015-4522199.php – "Angleterre: les droits TV du foot atteignent un record, à 7 Mds €!", article on the site leparisien.fr, February 10, 2015. Accessed on May 14, 2015.

The situation of agencies is different in different countries. In Germany, the business is very developed, contrary to Italy where it finds itself in dire straits (see Chapter 4 dedicated to agencies).

In any case, sponsorship is progressively moving from a sponsorship of power, centered solely on ground visibility, to a sponsorship of meaning where brand activation plays a key role. Fertility and liberalization of activities reveals several trends: regional sponsorship, citizen sponsorship, participatory sponsorship and state sponsorship (see Chapter 6 dedicated to sponsoring).

Revenues from television rights

Television media rights represent the primary source of revenue for French (+4% compared to the 2010–2011 season) (EY-UCPF, 2014) and European professional football. However, one can observe a decline in television rights in the breakdown of revenues of French clubs: 57% in 2010–2011; 53% in 2011–2012; 49% in 2012–2013; and 42% in 2013–2014. It should be noted that the early sale of the broadcasting rights for LFP Championships for the 2016–2020 period allows clubs to have a medium-term visibility. The increasing sums as a result of broadcasters (825 million euros per season on average, against 655 million currently) (DNCG, 2015) should allow clubs to calmly consider the development of their other growth engines.

Box 1.3 TV rights in other major European leagues

In France, the football rights have also reached a record high last year. However, the amount is more than two times lower than in England. The war between Canal + and BeIN Sports over the rights of French football for 2016–2020 had delivered its verdict in April 2014. The Professional Football League had allocated a record amount of 748.5 million euros a year in broadcasting rights for Ligue 1 and Ligue 2 for the 2016–2020 period.

In Spain, unlike other championship leagues, the teams of La Liga negotiate their own contracts with TV stations. Exact numbers are hard to obtain, but in total, they would reach the 800 million

Euro mark (600 euros for the domestic market, 200 euros for international) per season. Both Real Madrid and Barcelona receive 140 million euros per season.

In Germany, the 36 clubs of the first and second leagues have an exclusive 4-year contract, signed in 2012 by the German League (DFL) with Sky Germany. On average, Sky spends 485.7 million euros per season to broadcast 612 live games.

In Italy, the rights of Serie A amount to 915 million euros for 2015, renewable 1 year for the same sum until 2018. Sky and Mediaset share the package. Sky spends 572 million euros for all the games (380), Mediaset spends 343 million euros for the matches where big teams are involved.

This raises the question of the sale of TV rights for the Ligue 1 championship abroad.

How to be more efficient in the sale of television rights in the championship of France abroad? For Mathieu Ficot, "The presence of stars in a league and clubs in the Champions League are the two ingredients that allow for the development of international rights."

For the 2016–2019 period, the Premier League has a record amount of 6.92 billion euros (2.3 billion per year) with the renegotiation of rights in the UK. The incumbent Sky (126 meetings, 10 more than presently) and BT (42 games) thus share the rights of the championship league for this period. Starting in May 2017, the last ranking in the Premier League will receive 136 million euros from television rights. The champion will receive 210 million. In comparison, the LFP earns three times less, since the rights were 748.5 million euros per year.

Revenue related to licensed products and services: merchandising

Generally known under the name of merchandising, the concept refers to all the techniques intended to improve the presentation of products in a retail space in order to make people want to purchase them (Floch, 1989). In the sports business sector, the notion of merchandising refers to all licensed products and services, the trademarks of a sports entity. For a professional sports organization, brand extension aims to reduce financial uncertainty by subscribing to a unique and innovative marketing logic.

Generally, revenue from the sale of licensed merchandise accounts for a small percentage of the club's revenue. Instead, they promote the development of their brand. "The merchandising of football clubs is between 5% and 10% of the commercial activity. This is what merchandising represents for PSG. Its purpose is to develop in the same proportions. However, it must continue to support the development of the club from an economic point of view," said Frédéric Longuépée, Deputy General Manager in charge of business for PSG.[22]

While there still exists a risk of diluting the brand through spreading it in all directions, peripheral revenue generated by the licensing of the OL demonstrate that a professional football club can generate additional revenue through the power of its brand. The club allows a company to design, develop and market its brand in exchange for royalties. Professionalization and complexity of contracts is observed here. The club-brand and the respect for it are now highly protected today. The contracts between the two entities are becoming more precise. They are usually written by experts. Thus, OL, a club-brand par excellence, has developed activities that have led to the extension of the target customer (see Chapter 11 dedicated to OL). Others have done the same, with some products that may appear as unexpected, like the diapers bearing the image of Sevilla!

Overall, "myopic" marketing that still existed 10 years ago seems to have disappeared in France. The clubs carry out studies to measure the needs of their clients. While clubs have developed considerably, some do not have a marketing department as such. There is sometimes a communications director or business manager who serves as the director of marketing. Although the marketing structures of clubs are "poor", this does not explain the weakness of the French market. Some reasons seem to be specific to the consumer's demand in sporting spectacle: French fans do not support their team like British or Spanish fans who travel abroad and who buy jerseys bearing the image of the club. The gross import, without adapting the model of Manchester United, was a failure for clubs in France. It is necessary to adapt to the needs of the consumers of French sporting spectacles. There is clear evidence that a successful merchandising strategy is related to customer knowledge, quality of products sold, relevance of product distribution, sports results of the club and player behavior.

Even though the sale of licensed merchandise remains limited for French clubs, it is an important source of income for European clubs. These clubs are constantly developing new products around the club's brand. The two Spanish giants prove to be the most successful in the field. The Euromericos study (2015) shows that Real Madrid, as the market leader, would have sold 2.5 million copies of their official jersey during the 2014–2015 season. FC Barcelona ranks second with 2.4 million jerseys sold and Bayern Munich in third place with nearly 2 million jerseys sold. Known for their success in terms of internationalization, English clubs are not in the top 3 ranking. Manchester United ranks 4th with just under 2 million jerseys sold. Regarding the French clubs, PSG is in 6th place with 1.7 million garments sold. Finally, Juventus and AC Milan are respectively 9th and 10th in the standings with about 1 million jerseys sold for each of the two clubs.

In any case, merchandising requires strong congruence between the identity of the club brand (the DNA of a professional sports organization) and the choice of products. Also, the strategic brand management constitutes a fundamental element necessary for the development of clubs that should now be examined.

The strategic management of football brands

Now we will focus on one of the fundamental aspects for a professional sports entity: the strategic management of its brand. In a marketing perspective, there are several concerns, the first is to define and promote the brand.

The concept of the brand applied to professional sports entities

We study here the strategic importance of the brand and its application to professional sports entities.

The strategic importance of the brand

Politicians, artists or athletes may be considered as brands unto themselves. But they are not alone in this regard. In most areas, if an individual wants a successful career, they should ensure that their stakeholders (colleagues, superiors, etc.) know their talents, skills and their attitude or stance on positions (Keller, 2008). This approach is done to create one's own brand. The first reference to brands dates back to Roman times (Malaval, 2002). There existed no commercial purpose. However, it now seems impossible to address marketing, consumer behavior or the value of an entity without mentioning brand power (Lewi and Lacœuilhe, 2007). Indeed, the brand symbolizes our consumer society. It is a complex idea, of which it is possible to find hundreds of definitions depending on whether it is considered as a distinctive sign, a symbol or a source of added value. Today, it represents a product and provides benefits for both the consumer and the company. The key to management is to ensure that consumers perceive differences between the products of the same category. Thus, brands are changing the perception and experience that consumers have of a product and facilitating the process of deciding on what to purchase (Keller, 2008).

We can distinguish six different approaches of the brand: legal, marketing, financial, discursive, utilitarian and systems. Symbolized by the definitions of Kotler and Ries, the marketing approach allows the brand to offer products differentiated in a given competitive field. Thus, for the American Marketing Association's (AMA) definition: a brand is "a name, term, sign, symbol, design or combination thereof used to identify goods and services of one seller or group of sellers and to differentiate them from those of the competition." This definition is based on the notions of identification and differentiation related to distinctive signs. It is part of a commercial and competitive logic.

Therefore, it is necessary that the brand is unique and that it is a barrier to entry for competitors. The brand is now considered an essential tool for differentiation. It is with this logic that the big brands of the first half of the 20th century were developed and that professional sports organizations strive to develop.

Management and creation of sports brands

Ubiquitous in our society, the issue of brand administration (brand management and marketing or branding) concerns various industry sectors and a wide range of product categories. Gerke, Chanavat and Benson-Rea (2014) point out that, while studies and research in marketing have focused on the creation and the management of the brand, little else is known on the subject of sports brands.

However, the sport sector is not exempt from this phenomenon to the extent that many clubs, teams, leagues, events or competitions have become popular brands. And the management of the brand now constitutes the most important asset for a sports organization (Bauer, Sauer and Schmitt, 2005). Thus, the brand power of a sports organization often determines the degree to which consumers can become fans by purchasing items or clothing for themselves in order to identify with their club (Richelieu and Pons, 2006). This is even reinforced by the fact that the brand equity of a club can generate revenue independently of its club's sporting results (Gladden and Milne, 1999). Bauer, Sauer and Schmitt (2005) show that the strongest brands often represent the most successful teams. Thus, any sports organization has a brand, and it is in its interest to develop its brand equity through a marketing approach. Professional sports teams have the potential to build brand equity by leveraging shared emotional relationships with fans. Therefore, the objective of brand equity in the sports business sector is to establish a strong link between the consumer (fan) and the club. (Former) football players are also considered trademarks as such, like David Beckham, Cristiano Ronaldo or Lionel Messi. An analogy can be made between a brand and an athlete, a sports event or a sports team. Professional sports organizations are particularly concerned by this approach.

Strategic brand building in professional sports

On the basis of work in brand management (Kapferer, 2007), the strategic construction of the brand in professional sports, typically on behalf of the clubs, has been the subject of several publications (Mullin et al., 2007; Chanavat and Bodet, 2009; Chanavat Bodet, 2010; Richelieu, 2011).

Specifically, based on the work of Chanavat and Bodet (2009) and Richelieu (2011), we propose a four-step process to demonstrate the strategy of constructing a sports brand. This approach proves itself particularly suitable for a club:

- Defining the identity, the brand image
- Segmenting
- Positioning the sports entity on the market
- Developing operational marketing actions through the "4 *P*s" which will support the brand strategy.

The definition of the identity and of the desired brand image, segmentation and positioning are key strategic elements. The marketing actions which arise are merely extensions. These elements are in line with the ideas of François Vasseur, associate marketing director of the FFF: "In the clubs, it is about having this discussion around the brand at the beginning, in your building supply, this approach then allows you to develop a consistent marketing program that you sell to your partners."

These four steps are presently detailed and illustrated by some cases that are the subject of a specific chapter (see the third section on clubs). Other examples, like the ones of the Toulouse FC or the FFF, are also fueling the discussion.

Defining identity and brand image

How does a professional sports entity want to be perceived? What is its DNA? To which values does it wish to be attached? How does it foresee itself as characterized by its fans? What image does it aim to convey? The crucial first step related to the strategic construction of a professional sports entity is to define its identity and its values.

The definition of brand image proposed by Keller (1993) seems to be accepted by the scientific community. It represents, "the perceptions of a brand as reflected by the associations to a brand held in the consumer's memory" (Keller, 1993, p. 3).

Thus, the ambition is to build QSI PSG as an international sports brand. The slogan "Let us dream bigger/Dream Bigger" of PSG demonstrates the willingness of the club to move towards a global sports brand. The desire to affiliate itself with the city of Paris is also expressed through the creation of a new logo. "The values that we wish to convey to PSG are: elegance, aesthetics," explains Frédéric Longuépée. These include the characteristics of the city of Paris that led Qatari investors to buy PSG.

In its strategic development plan, AS Saint-Étienne stated its willingness to move from a "family" club, to a "regional/national" crowd, to a unifying club in European influence, relying on its historical foundation and rich and clean values. For the club, it is not about concealing its glorious past. The 2014–2015 strategic plan of the club shows that it is based on the color green; a history since 1933; a victory list; iconic players; combativeness, the warrior spirit; sharing, the family spirit; regional roots; popular fervor; and the Geoffroy-Guichard stadium[23] (see Chapter 12, dedicated to the AS Saint-Étienne).

The clubs OM or AS Saint-Étienne have two of the best track records in French football and a clearly known identity. Boris Lafargue, the man responsible for the marketing and media for Toulouse FC, states, "Despite dark sports years, the AS Saint-Étienne has never betrayed its identity. They are a good example." For the OL, "the women's section is part of the DNA of the Olympique Lyonnais club," emphasizes Thierry Sauvage, the CEO of OL. The club proves itself to be a forerunner in this field.

Overall, the clubs, as well as the national football teams, have a strong identity built over time through their history, their fans, the historical players, their titles, their culture, etc. (Chanavat and Bodet, 2009). These represent the starting point of a lasting brand strategy. The more a team is equipped with a strong history and is integrated into the socio-economic fabric of the community, the more it is able to capitalize on the emotional connection that binds it to its supporters, and the more its brand will be strong (Richelieu, 2011). "When you are a football club, you are a company and you need to develop a brand. This brand needs to have asperities to capture an audience," says Boris Lafargue on this subject.

It is essential to define the identity of the club, its project, what it aims toward. The definition of identity goes beyond the club's objectives. If it feeds on them, it also exceeds them. In the same way that the identity of an individual cannot be reduced solely to his or her identity card, that of a club is not just its economic or legal characteristics. The identity defines a means to achieve its goals, a vision. A strong brand identity can potentially increase the fans' emotions towards the club and build their confidence and loyalty. Thus, they will be more receptive to marketing initiatives implemented by clubs with the purpose of attracting and seducing fans (Richelieu and Pons, 2006). After having defined the identity and the brand image it wishes to convey, the club must never betray them. Fans can understand when their team loses games, however, they are not able to accept that their club's identity or image could be ridiculed. The identity is not negotiable, it is not for sale and it must be prioritized. But while it is necessary for a club to define a strong and distinct identity, it is essential that it is perceived as such. Dobni and Zinkhan (1990) stress the importance of the perception of reality at the expense of reality itself.

Segmented demand: the different categories of fans

Therefore, clubs should know who are their supporters, their fans. What are their profiles? Clubs must analyze the different types of consumers who are likely to become a part of their identity. Marketing Segmentation is the action of dividing a population (the supporters) into homogeneous subsets according to various criteria (demographics, etc.). The chosen segmentation criteria are aimed at obtaining population segments of sufficient size. This approach provides the possibility of creating differentiated marketing campaigns based on segments and to possibly propose a suitable, specific offer. These segments must be appropriate for the club.

The strategy deployed by the AS Saint-Étienne in this way illustrates how the clubs segment their offers and no longer address "traditional supporters" only. From a marketing perspective, the club aims to reach new audiences and does so regularly in order to evolve its offerings to meet consumer expectations. According to the 2014–2016 strategic plan of the club, the segmentation of the AS Saint-Étienne is done to satisfy the general public (fan groups, associations), individual season ticket holders, viewers (local and regional populations), friends of the club (geographically dispersed), families/teenagers and the business to business element (local business and national investors) (see Chapter 12 dedicated to the AS Saint-Étienne).

Several studies have led to an examination of a series of fan profiles (Bourgeon and Bouchet, 2001; Bourgeon-Renault and Bouchet, 2007; Richelieu, 2011; Chanavat and Bodet, 2014; Pimentel and Reynolds, 2004).

Thus, we can retain the following five categories:

- *Emotional fans*: these fans go to the stadium to cheer their team before anything else. They represent the core of the clubs, the most loyal fans. Their strong attachment, their devotion to the club, can present itself in several ways. According to Pimentel and Reynolds (2004), they are willing to attend all of their team's matches, even the away games;

organize their holidays according to the schedule of their team; collect products of the club. The concept of "love for the brand" is used to describe this type of "absolute fan". In marketing, studies reveal the appeal of this concept that seems to interfere with variables related to positive word-of-mouth, commitment and even the anguish of a possible separation from the brand (Albert, 2014). If a victory for the club is considered a personal victory for the fans, the defeat can be seen as a personal failure (Richelieu and Pons, 2005).

- *Aesthetes fans*: this type of fans is in love with the game, and above all they are in love with the beauty of the game. These fans are passionate about the sport. Richelieu (2011, p. 16) notes that "they see themselves as and try to be recognized as experts in the sport." Unlike emotional fans, a defeat of their favorite team will not truly impact them. This group of fans does not seem to approve of the dramatization of the sporting event and the advent of Sportainment. In other words, the entertainment before, during and after the event and the event marketing devices of a club are not very well received by them.
- *Relational fans*: Above all, they come to the stadium for its social dimension. Even if they could develop a particular affection for a club, they mainly see an opportunity to get together with friends, fans and family. Richelieu and Pons (2005) emphasize that these fans are supposed to be more open to entertaining than the aesthetes fans, to the extent that the getaway at the stadium is considered to be an experience in itself. The use of sports events may actually be based on research experience lived individually and/or collectively (Bourgeon-Renault and Bouchet, 2007; Chanavat and Bodet, 2014).
- *Opportunistic fans*: they measure the benefits they can personally gain from attending a sporting event. For Bourgeon-Renault and Bouchet (2007, p. 98), "the behavior results in a relative neutrality and sometimes by a demonstrative support required by a collective 'overarching' movement, in the hope of reaping the benefits of this commitment." They are not necessarily experts, but are typically present in a business perspective, to build a network, make contacts, etc.
- *Normative fans*: they go to the stadium to meet the social pressure of the group to which they belong (Pimentel and Reynolds, 2004). In the same vein, not to be at the margin, some consumers will follow their national team during an international competition like the FIFA World Cup or the European Championship of Nations.
- *The e-fans*: they have developed a fondness for critical thinking, especially with regard to the club brand, its external communication, content, technologies and innovations. The hyper-connected e-fans are more demanding of the clubs. They want a more humanized report, more direct and participatory.

Obviously, a fan can belong to multiple categories.

Positioning the sports team on the market

The crucial question concerning the positioning of a club consists of responding to the following question: "why would a spectator of sporting spectacle select to consume my club brand over another?" The identity and brand image are the elements on which the club can rely to differentiate itself. When an organization is able to highlight the uniqueness of its brand, it can more easily stand out from the competition.

For clubs, one of the means of differentiation is that of sporting results, that is their record of achievements. This is a key factor. However, it would be wrong to think that only sporting results can make a difference in the eyes of the targeted audiences. Localization, the catchment area in marketing, frequently plays a major role, although this aspect is more or less controlled by the organization. In other words, the lack of status is not prohibitive.

Toulouse FC has found an original positioning. For lack of being a viable contestant in terms of sports in the Ligue 1, the club clearly assumes the role of a media contestant in the championship. Basing itself on its dynamic side, spontaneous and quirky, the club is innovative on digital issues. Despite a tight budget, it has expressed a desire to exist beyond the sporting side. The words of Boris Lafargue explain the approach adopted by the club,

> We do not have a worthy record of achievements. However, there is a capacity to form professional football players. We have relied on it for 10 years. Once we said we were the South West club and it's quite nice to live in this region . . . the idea is to find what will enable us to stand out. And we found this vein: make people smile. It works great for two reasons: 1) no one does it, 2) it is consistent with the image that people can have of our region. We were quickly judged as being legitimate on this issue.

Although the Toulouse FC has stood out quickly, the club can legitimately ask itself, what have their fans thought of them? As Boris Lafrague explains,

> The approach has been well received, to our surprise. Now it is about not destroying it and trying to maintain it properly without falling into a caricature of what we do. We are on a thread, it disrupts our natural audience. We try to educate our population on what we actually are. We are not a football club in fact.

Personal and social factors significantly influence the perception of clubs, such as the perceived congruence between class values associated with the local team and those related to the foreign team (AS Saint-Étienne and Liverpool, for example) (Chanavat and Bodet, 2009). Peer influence, and in particular the one of friends with regard to which club to support, seems to highlight the social role of sports and opens perspectives in terms of tribal marketing (Bodet and Chanavat, 2010).

Business activities prioritize the perception surrounding the brand of the sports entity. The act of selling an object is not enough. It should give it meaning so that the fan can identify with it. The slogan "Mès que un club" ("More than a club") from FC Barcelona, the symbol of Catalonia, singles out the club.

The first three steps (identification, segmentation, positioning) necessary for strategic brand building lead us to the implementation of the marketing mix.

Articulate coherent marketing actions

A professional sports entity must define how it wants to be perceived. On the basis of a clear, defined identity, it must segment and position itself but never betray itself. Marketing operationalizations that arise should not in any way deviate from this strategic vision. Instead, they must feed the positioning of the club and promote differentiation. Moreover, the most difficult challenge for the club is to be self-sustainable.

This is why the clubs should ask themselves the following question: "How do you write down initiatives, and then implement them so that they are not perceived as commercial activities?" Having a defined direction and an established set of specifications helps many clubs to communicate and be more creative. This is the case of Toulouse FC and its offset strategy that aims to "make people smile," says Boris Lafargue. The actions put in place by the club give power to its image as championship agitator in the media.

Box 1.4 Toulouse FC and Zlatan Ibrahimović

Toulouse FC, master of hype in Ligue 1

After Rihanna, Cristiano Ronaldo or Cavani, there is Zlatan Ibrahimović, who has recently participated in a media stunt for Toulouse FC. Just look at the Parisian star's birthday present which was offered by TéFéCé and the media strategy of the club from Toulouse.

This is not really a surprise for the fans of Ligue 1, but the Toulouse FC has once again created excitement. For Zlatan Ibrahimović's 33rd birthday, "les Violets" sent a package to the Swede with two jerseys with the names "Vincent" and "Maximilian" (note: the names of the sons of Ibrahimović) and a copy of the video game Call of Duty, that the Swede loves. We do not know if his children will wear the jerseys, but the latter should undoubtedly use his favorite game console to "Zlatan" gamers! It is now Zlatan's turn to create the hype after the famous #HobbyCavani tweets that Toulouse launched on the sidelines of the TFC–PSG match. TFC's strategy is simple: getting the word out about the club by getting as much media (including Internet) exposure as possible. It's also a way to match the top names in Ligue 1 in terms of media coverage, while minor clubs are struggling to stand out, as a result of the rising stardom of OM or PSG. Toulouse FC is also one of the leaders on the Internet in France, as the club is 5th in terms of Twitter followers (behind Paris, Marseille, Lyon and Monaco), but more importantly, it has second highest number of views on their Dailymotion channel (more than 8 million views, nearly 180,000 of them for the video about the package delivered to Ibra)!

Source: http://lerdvsportif.fr/tfc-maitre-du-buzz-en-ligue-1/ – "Le TFC, maître du buzz en Ligue 1," article by Henry and Thomas appeared on lerdvsportif.fr. Last accessed on May 12, 2015.

We have just reviewed the steps necessary for the strategic construction of a sports brand. This analysis, fundamental for a professional sports entity, specifically concerns the clubs. Now we will study the possible developmental levers which can be utilized for the better performances of French clubs.

Toward new balances and new conditions for success?

It turns out that French Professional Football plays a social, territorial and economic role. It is then about making French football more attractive, competitive and efficient in a European perspective. A dual commitment of public authorities on one hand and football institutions on the other seems to be necessary to foster the development of clubs. We do not aim to make an inventory of all the new marketing logics deployed by the clubs, but rather we aim to highlight some of them which are used to improve competitiveness. In any case, strategies and marketing operationalizations should reinforce themselves to serve the best interests of the sport.

The role of public authorities

First of all, the competitiveness of the clubs can be supported by public institutions. Improvements in a club's fiscal, legal and social environments would allow them to better compete with their European rivals. For example, in France, the weight of taxes for players is the highest: it is five times more than in the UK, 12 times more than in Italy, five times more than in Germany and 66 times more than in Spain!

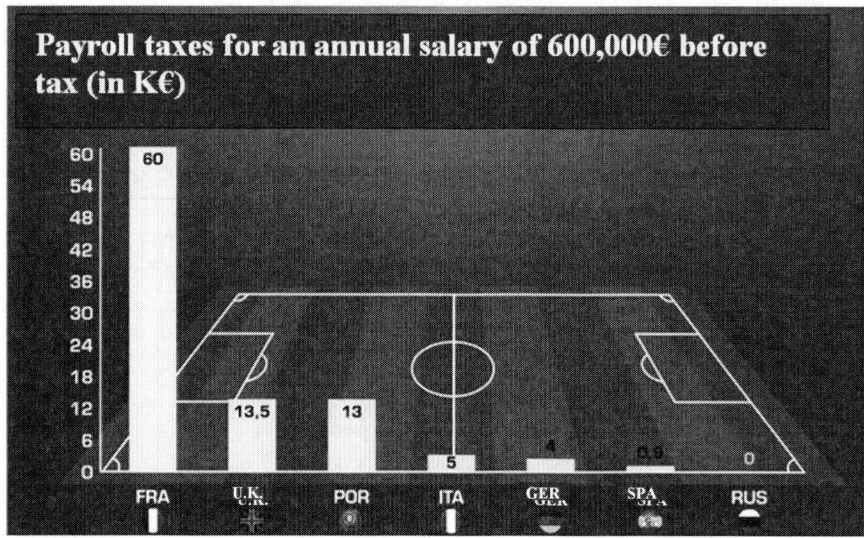

Figure 1.7 Comparison of European football players' payroll taxes

Source: UCPF, 2014, p. 6.

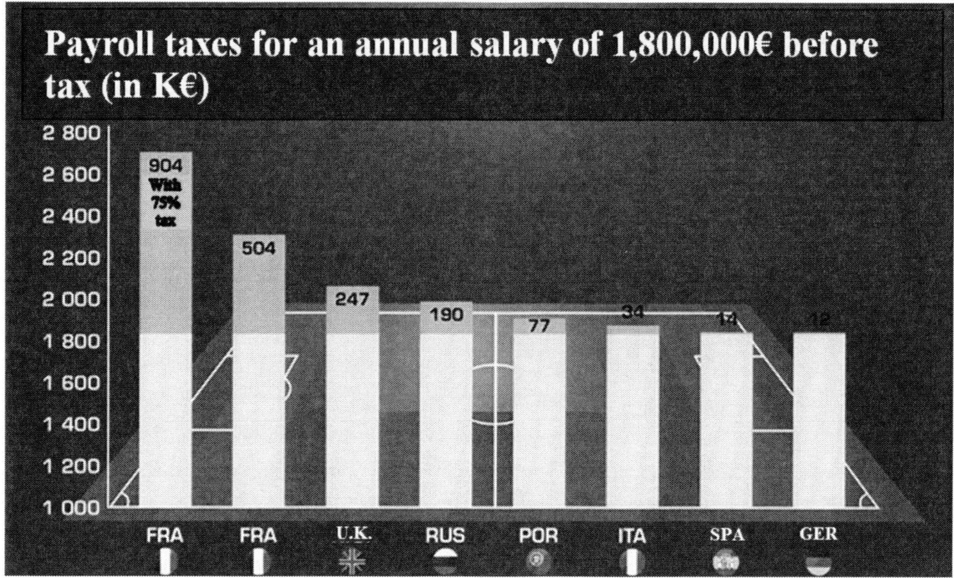

Figure 1.8 Comparison of European football nations in terms of employer contributions

Source: UCPF, 2014, p. 6.

The weight of payroll taxes in France is a real handicap in terms of competitiveness vis-à-vis other European nations studied, where the charges are either lower (Italy, Portugal, United Kingdom, Russia), or quickly capped (Germany, Spain). With a salary of 1.8 million euros per year, the gap is even widening with the impact of the "75% tax."

Since the Evin law in the 1990s, football clubs are forbidden to sell beer or allow advertising for alcohol brands, which complicates the marketing dimension. However, many of our European neighbors benefit from economic resources related to such partnerships. In Germany, in addition to sponsoring revenues, the sale of beer reported 40 million euros per year for the Bundesliga clubs.

In the same vein, the funding and operating model of sports venues must promote the development of clubs. This aims to make the stadium a developmental tool, a real growth engine. On this subject, Samuel Guillardeau, stadium manager and director of organization and security of OGC Nice, states that "the public-private partnership is clearly not for to the advantage of the clubs. It is preferable to be operating and investing in digital media."[24]

Although the fact that if a club owns its stadium it allows the stadium manager to have a certain degree of freedom in decision making, the PPP (public-private partnership) does not seem to be the most appropriate for them. In addition, the arrival of new investors and sponsors for clubs should be promoted through a new regulatory system.

Box 1.5 Advantages and disadvantages of the public-private partnership

One year after the opening of the Allianz Riviera, we can now assess the operating model chosen in Nice: the public-private partnership (PPP).

At the operating level: having to set up and disassemble for each event significantly increases the cost of a season when we could otherwise invest in security work for our audience and reduce the cost of our operations (dividing the stadium, setting up nets in the visitors' area, etc.). From a commercial point of view, the events that take place in the stadium outside of the OGC Nice activity are competing for the club's VIP club and general-public markets. The budgets for business' public relations are not expandable and what they consume for other events will not be used for the club's matches. The club thus undergoes an increase in operating expenses and a decrease in revenues. Arrangements are found for everything to function properly, but it nevertheless requires always being in a special agreement and valuing all valued assets to the private party in the agreement. For example, all our heavy equipment, our furniture showroom, our gates, our screens, . . . remain available for use by the private operator in its business events and other events. The problem of the model is that the club's representatives are more interested in serving the one-time organizers than to serve the OGC Nice, which creates tension in cohabitation. As other events generate inconvenience to club residents, it creates further tensions with the private operator. Fortunately, beyond the rigidity of the signed contracts, the men on the ground make an effort to get along with each other so that everyone can carry out their tasks.

The first advantage of PPP during its implementation, should normally benefit the community by avoiding additional debt. Although, this is no longer the case since January 2011, the year which began the construction of the Allianz Riviera.

The second advantage was intended for the clubs. Even if they had to pay a much higher rent than before, they remained reasonable and proportional to revenue. This advantage was threatened when auditors of the regional chamber of Alpes-Maritimes (Nice region) questioned the model imagined by asking the community not to finance depending on the sporting performance (thus determining higher fixed rents).

Now that these advantages have disappeared, I believe that public authorities should break these contracts. This would allow clubs to directly operate stadiums, without costing them more with regard to rising rents requested by the regional audit. In turn, public authorities should see a lowering of their debt since private rents paid back for the equipment are two to three times more expensive in the end. In addition, private companies borrow at higher rates than public bodies or authorities; now these rates are passed on to the overall cost and interest which are due in addition to state tax. Breaking these contracts may even eventually allow clubs to lower their rent.

Source: S. Guillardeau, "Stadium manager de club professionnel: quelle cohabitation avec un exploitant privé ?", *Jurisport* 147, November, 2014.

The role of the "football family"

Undeniably, the public sector can contribute to the development of the clubs. However, football authorities, and foremost the clubs, need to find new financial balances and set in motion new strategies themselves.

The reflection on the part of the football authorities, particularly on the reform of competitions (format, date, etc.), seems paramount. On May 21, 2015, the board of the LFP (National Professional Football League) voted in the principle of two promotions and two relegations between Ligue 1 and Ligue 2 (and two promotions and two relegations between Ligue 2 and the National League) instead of three, starting in the 2015–2016 season. This decision, intended to reassure investors who wish to have more security, is going in the right direction in regards to the modernization of the clubs. Others should follow. Furthermore, one may wonder if investors will not end up turning to other markets and abandon France. This is evidenced for example that the franchises in the United States are so highly regulated that investors know of what is happening.

In this context, it seems necessary to modernize the governance of clubs and professionalize their organization.

Overall, it should make the product more attractive and effective from a sporting and economic perspective. This refers to the question "When should we play?" For Arnaud Jaouen, things are very clear:

> When we play on Sunday at 2pm. Geoffroy-Guichard is practically sold-out. The fans are driving up to 2 hours to come to the stadium. People come in the morning, eat there, go to museums, to the store and leave in the evening. However, if the match takes place on Saturday at 8pm or on Sunday at 9pm, a lower consumption is observed.

Thus, there are time slots more conducive to the optimizing of clubs' marketing and business policies. Bundesliga matches are, for example, programed in the afternoon. This allows the stadiums to fill, to have a family audience, and to optimize clubs' marketing and sales revenues. According to Frédéric Longuépée, "The future may be in the allocation of centralized resources at the league level, funded by the league, with new revenue."

At the European level, the UEFA also seems to contribute to the growth of French clubs. As UEFA wishes to improve the finances of clubs, it could consider a fiscal homogenization mentioned above. At a time of the financial fair play rule, couldn't the UEFA imagine a system which takes into account the peculiarities of each country in a fair perspective? This question echoes the words of Bruno Belgodère for which "UEFA has ignored a labor cost that particularly disadvantages France. Won't the FPF be a barrier to sponsorship, and more generally to the development of football in Europe?"

In this context, we believe that there are no risks and that clubs have several advantages. To do this, executives must invest in the invisible. Of course, the sports side of a professional club remains essentially the growth engine. However, the marketing unit should not be forgotten. On the contrary, it must be strengthened and professionalized. On this subject, Philippe Diallo noted that "sports can sometimes, if not often, make the decision in relation to strengthening the structuring of marketing services." These words echo those of Frédéric Longuépée:

> Today, football clubs are primarily focused on the sports side. When a club has revenues, it often rushes to invest them in buying players to aim for the highest ranking, even if that requires to set budgets depending on sporting results. For me that is nonsense. Budgets should be based on what you control, not on what you cannot not control.

A number of marketing initiatives aim to develop the image and the emotions of the fan with regard to the club brand. These do not directly impact sales, but they favor above all the creation of value and revaluing of businesses products. For Philippe Diallo, three points can be highlighted from the perspective of the development of French clubs: "First, the idea is to clean up the clubs. Second, one can raise the question of stadiums. Third, social networks and the brand sponsors." These three points are related to clubs' marketing activities that that we will discuss below.

Toward new marketing approaches: between innovative strategies and operationalizations

Overall, clubs study innovations developed by competition. But the marketing initiatives of a professional sports structure must, as we have emphasized, observe a genuine long-term marketing logic. Indeed, they must be able to generate additional revenue, but also respect the identity and the image of the sports entity. This is why the development of a museum is a recent example of a new product enabling both increased profits and the development of the club brand. If the fact of attending a game has a strong emotional charge, the visit to such a museum is a marketing tool to relive the moments that fostered and developed the emotions of consumer originally felt vis-à-vis a sports entity. The tradition of the museum is very rooted in the great European clubs like Liverpool FC, Manchester United or Bayern Munich. The AS Saint-Étienne is the first French professional club to have founded a museum to capitalize on its history. There are other options for teams with less glorious pasts or with a changing profile. The museum concept has a position that will highlight aspects other than the more traditional nostalgia with, for instance, a general entertainment experience.

This section does not aim to provide an exhaustive list of mobilized levers and innovations proposed by the clubs. However, we study some of them to show the vitality of the clubs in the matter of sports arenas, the experiential customer, the concepts of CRM and FRM, the social responsibility and the digital activities of clubs. Other activities could be addressed. In addition, some elements covered here are detailed in Parts II and III of the book, particularly in the case studies of clubs.

Sports arenas: (to the service of) the customer experience?

Today, a viewer comes to the stadium to watch a sporting event, but even more for the experience: to take advantage of the atmosphere to which he or she contributes. Businesses, as for themselves, want to maximize their investments and measure the impact of their partnership initiatives. This is where marketing for clubs makes most sense. The objective consists of developing the club brand and sporting entity's revenues so that it can grow from a sporting standpoint. For all that, a football brand does not support itself like a typical brand. It depends on the news of professional sports entities that is comprised of players, coaches, the president, etc.

If television rights were the main source of development for spectator sports in the 1990s, sports arenas have once again become both a priority and a discriminating factor in the economic and athletic performance of professional clubs. This is due to a convergence of interest between stakeholders for which sports arenas represent a major challenge: the professional clubs, governments, commercial enterprises (construction, architects, etc.), sponsors, media, advertisers, and leagues or federations (Bolotny and Gouze, 2008).

Sports facilities are now at the heart of the economic model of the sports business. It constitutes an asset, a source of revenue through ticket sales, lodges, restaurants, licensed merchandise and the ecosystem in which it has inserted itself. It is a major challenge for the clubs. Our analysis is consistent with the words of Philippe Diallo, "The stadiums are added as a new pillar of growth for the first ten clubs of Ligue 1." France lags far behind in terms of modern sports facilities (stadiums or arenas) in tune with the requirements of professional sports. It turned out that France failed to take advantage of the 1998 (football) and 2007 (rugby) World Cups. This delay has been repeatedly emphasized, particularly by reports including Besson (2008), Seguin (2008), Augier (2009), Delpierre (2010), Douillet (2010) and Costantini (2010). Yet, modern sports arenas represent a necessary tool for the development and sustainability of professional sports structures whose modernization is an integral part of the competitiveness of clubs.

In this perspective, renovation or construction projects are developing. If hosting the Euro 2016 event is profitable for stadiums that will host matches during this competition, other outdoor sports facilities for the event have also emerged: "Park & Suites Arena" in Montpellier, "MMArena" in Mans, "KindArena" in Rouen or "Matmut Stadium" in Lyon. Obviously, the economic success of French professional clubs in the upcoming years seems closely related to the propensity of clubs to incorporate their sports facilities within their business model. While Premier League clubs have invested billions of euros during the last 15 years in the stadiums that they own, almost all French clubs are still the single tenants of often obsolete stadiums, which for most of the time only host an event twice a month. A sports arena should be seen as a profit center and a multifunctional space, thanks to the mobilization of technological advances helping to optimize revenue along with the comfort and safety of fans. In a sector marked by risks, diversification of spectacles and activities, it is absolutely essential to dilute the financial risk related to possible bad sporting performance.

Economic development enjoyed by German clubs thanks to the 2006 World Cup should be a reference for French football. Contrary to popular belief, the capacity of stadiums does not necessarily have to be scaled upwards, as evidenced by the examples of Juventus or Toulouse FC. In any case, the major French and European clubs want to renovate their stadium in a perspective of development. The commercial optimization of the stadium and the ability to fill it are major issues of professional clubs. Thus, they have measured the importance of marketing tickets ahead of time and expanded their targeted market. Likewise, another big trend is related to the service to the fan and the Internet connectivity in the stadiums, two crucial issues for the development of attendance and ticketing. The stadium, previously neglected by the football clubs and institutions, is now becoming the tool of preference (or coming back), the catalyst.

Although increased attendances remains an objective, the trend is to foster the quality of the facility by seeking to make of the live sports spectacle a "unique experience" for consumers. The average revenue per viewer remains a real Achilles' heel for the French sport. The quality of the service, the comfort of the stadium and the overall quality of the spectacle are all elements that could allow for a gradual increase in pricing.

The article by Chanavat and Bodet (2014) titled "Experiential marketing in sport spectatorship services: a customer perspective" addresses this theme. The results of the study show that experiential marketing influences a club's reputation and brand image. Today, possessing a strong brand in terms of stock market capitalization is not enough. The era of transactional marketing is gone and has been replaced with notions of relational proximity between the brand and its consumers. Continually improving contact between the brand and its customers is the priority for marketers. The needs of the fans are no longer confined to the sporting event, to the match itself, but they extend to the services and experiences that surround it. The quality of services and the experience offered to spectators must be a priority for clubs. It should be noted that the LFP assists clubs by conducting studies to improve "the experience of spectators in the stadium" in Ligue 1 and Ligue 2. Furthermore, in the future, it would be able to have the power to "establish a consulting structure which would conduct studies and would visit the clubs, spending 4 or 5 days to assist them in the ticket office", suggests Mathieu Ficot.

For a better understanding of the spectator: from the CRM to the FRM

A professional football club should be able to identify the needs of its consumers. It is even a prerequisite for winning the loyalty and hearts of new customers. This requires the development and qualification of a database comprised of customers and prospects. CRM (Customer Relationship Management) includes all the tools and techniques designed for capturing, processing and analyzing information on customers and prospects to win their loyalty by providing the best service. In the context of sport business, the concern is FRM (Fan Relationship Management) to the extent that the fan is at the center of the approach.

The establishment of a database of supporters through a membership card does not aim to collect information, even if it represents its basic function, but to process the information in-depth. For Arnaud Jaouen, "the main goal is to qualify customers." If the membership card reinforces the sense of belonging to the club, it also represents a stake in terms of partnership. The club has more leverage with its partners, thanks to the collected information on supporters that may interest them.

Along these lines, customer knowledge is a major marketing challenge for the FFF, as evidenced by the words of François Vasseur:

> One of the priorities for the FFF is to create electronic scoresheets. We will meet the needs of licensees using a CRM database with our partners. This is a technological revolution to the extent that we will be able to follow the path of all licensees and make available information concerning sponsors.

Would CRM be the cure for all ills? Frédéric Longuépée remains more reserved:

> CRM is not a panacea. First you have to put in place a strategy to fill a stadium. To generate other income, there needs to be a full stadium and a nice place to go before the start of the match. Some places grow consumption and some that don't. One must create welcoming conditions which allow the fan to convince his wife to come with the children.

Today only a minority of Ligue 1 clubs have systematized the establishment of such an approach, but it is expected to quickly grow.

The social responsibility of clubs

The activity of clubs is also reflected in regards to social responsibility. During the 2012–2013 season, professional football has undertaken 950 operations for the promotion of amateur football, affecting 3,500 clubs, whose 700 transactions involve professional players and/or technical staff: each of the 44 professional clubs is in direct relation with 90 amateur clubs on average each season. Clubs are involved in many causes: integration, supporting local associations, the fight against racism, etc. In 2012–2013, 860 operations have been carried out to support local charitable causes, domestic and international. Clubs have affirmed for a number of years their desire to be anchored in their territories and to participate actively in the life of the city, to enrich and energize, by conducting educational, social and sporting activities. Three French clubs that we contacted while writing this book have established a foundation to structure and finance their social activities: Toulouse FC, OL and PSG.[25]

Didier Kermarrec, director of development for OL,[26] points out that "it is not a craze (for Lyon). Therefore a structural investment has been done for years in terms of CSR within the club. For instance, the Sport initiative in the city has been put into place since 1999."

Overall, this social dimension allows clubs to involve economic partners in carrying out their work and missions of general interest, and enhance the image of the clubs. It should be noted that other professional sports organizations have integrated social activities in their overall development strategy: Le Havre AC, OGC Nice, FC Lorient, SM Caen and the AS Saint-Étienne. For example AS Saint-Étienne founded the association "ASSE-Cœur-Vert" (Green-Heart-AS Saint-Étienne). In addition, clubs are committed to Fondaction Football through the UCPF: "clubs exert individual social responsibility and participate in cooperative programs at the heart of their territory and in people's daily lives," explains Philippe Diallo (see Chapter 9 dedicated to CSR).

Digital activities: a professional football revolution?

From the point of view of expanding the audience beyond the live (90% of the broadcast), broadcasters are looking to upgrade the football spectacle through diversified content (per target, per time-period, per screen). Thus, more than 20 million Internet users visited at least one sports site in 2013 (EY-UCPF, 2014), to which there will be added social networks, video platforms and websites of clubs.

For over 10 years, the scale of social media has grown steadily with the creation in 2004 of the most globally known network: Facebook. The advent of Mark Zuckerberg's network was accompanied by the appearance of several other platforms such as Twitter, Instagram, LinkedIn, Ping, Pinterest, Vine and Snapchat. Each of the networks possesses its own specificities relative to its proposed functions. This, combined with the increased use of smartphones and computers, is not without consequences for professional sports entities.

Brand communities continue to grow via social networks and facilitate the gathering of "fans". These communication tools have become necessary for any brand wishing to have a presence on the sports business market. The fan becomes a media that speaks and generates, comments on, or consumes content related to his favorite team 24/7 (Helleu and Karoutchi, 2013) (see Chapter 7 dedicated to social media). The proliferation of new digital platforms for fans has led professional sports entities to innovate on digital issues. After only a few tries, PSG has significantly internationalized. It now has more foreign fans than French fans. This new global professional sports entity should in this way respond to the "virtual" needs of fans who will never move to Paris. Clubs (French), often managed as small businesses, should in this way develop expertise worthy of the largest multinationals whose digital tools (website, social media, etc.) are only the visible part. "Thinking digitally, you have a great interest in the 20-year-olds on your team when you start to think about Snapchat, Pinterest," said Boris Lafargue.

In clubs, innovations are observed, including the monitoring of players' physical and physiological data on live broadcast and continuously. At the intersection of the emotional and functional, digital media is supposed to promote the development of clubs. The upsurge in digital activities combines with the rejuvenation of traditional audiences and the renewed vitality of clubs.

In France, the Toulouse FC is considered as the ultimate "digital club". It has managed to grow, innovate and make an impression in the digital field without a huge budget. According to Boris Lafrague,

> The Toulouse FC was the first professional sports team to rely on an official website. The first club to have online ticket sales, an online channel on Daylimotion, and an 'active' account on Twitter. We find in the records that OM and PSG have been launched before, except when we launched it, it was active, which is not the case of the other two.

Overall, the club quickly measured the usefulness of social networks in a marketing perspective. It is well positioned on several media networks and gives meaning to each particular network according to their uses. The real trend in digital audience is measured in the growth of social communities. "What's interesting with digital campaigns is that it is possible to reach a certain percentage of our target with a limited budget. And most importantly it is possible to quantify this percentage," he adds.

One of the key factors for success seems to be the privileged access to the professional team: "The marketing cell has the ability to build an activation agenda for the Toulouse FC mark with 150 to 200 dates a year. When talking with marketers, we feel that we are envied. Even by great clubs," concludes Boris Lafargue on this subject.

Overall, today the digital world opens up a wealth of opportunities for sport business in general and professional football in particular. The development of digital technology has made its appearance in the sports industry and therefore influences the economy of football. Following the example of American sports venues, the modern French stadiums will be connected, such as the future "Grand Stade" of OL (see Chapter 11 dedicated to OL).

Obviously, digital innovation will be at the center of the strategies employed by professional sports entities. It should especially make it possible to improve the relationship with fans and to promote the marketing activities of sponsors.

Conclusion

This chapter has allowed us to lay the foundations of football marketing. Our first goal was to examine the development of sport business through five key phases. If the sport is built through business investment, football history shows us that professional clubs have long underused their marketing potential. In the 1960s, they paid equipment manufacturers for their outfits. Today, in a globalized environment where the football product gives way to Sportainment, e-sports marketing and the experiential customer, Nike pays around 30 million euros a year to claim the title of PSG's official supplier. Plus, the amount of English football TV rights rises to new heights.

In the second part, our analysis of football marketing characteristics promotes the understanding of its emotional impact, its specificities as a sports service, and the definition of the professional sports entity by combining the central stakeholders of its ecosystem.

We observe logically a wealth of tools, studies and businesses allowing us to measure the economic value and marketing potential of clubs, players and coaches, who are the subject of the third part of this chapter.

Since the Bosman ruling in 1995, and an opening of European borders made without harmonization or regulation, French professional clubs have suffered from both a sporting and economic stall. In the fourth part, we focused on the economy of the French clubs and their main means of financing. Four major obstacles allowed us to better understand a facade of growth in the sector of French Professional Football: severe disadvantages, sporting erosion, economic competitiveness at half-mast and fragile finances. To balance their books, the vast majority of clubs have been forced to sell some of their best talents each year. Also, AS Saint-Étienne's[27] new marketing strategy aims to generate more revenue (10 million euros) and to move towards a new economic model. "If I spend 10 to 20 million, the club does not sell more players. The idea is to help a sports cell become a more competitive team," explains Arnaud Jaouen, marketing director of the AS Saint-Étienne. Therefore, one cannot help but imagine for a moment that AS Saint-Étienne would be stronger if they still had Kurt Zouma (left to Chelsea for 15 million euros), Pierre-Emerick Aubameyang (left for Borussia Dortmund for 13 million euros), Dimitri Payet (left to Lille for 9 million euros) or Blaise Matuidi (left to PSG for 8 million euros), to name a few from one club.

Fifth, we focused on strategic construction of a brand based on four key steps: defining an identity and brand image, the segmentation, the positioning of the sports entity in the market, and the development of operational marketing actions.

Last but not least, we focused on the new balances and conditions needed for the success of French clubs. Our analysis points out that if the competitiveness of clubs requires support from public and government institutions, clubs must innovate without betraying their values. The deployment of marketing innovations, well in line with this identity, can create value to the club brand. Several issues were approached to demonstrate the creativity of clubs. Overall, it refers here to numerous themes: sports grounds, consumer behavior, licensed merchandise, partnerships, brand management, the digital world, television rights, corporate social responsibility, ticketing. . . . In addition, several marketing innovations continue to create new wealth and are detailed thereafter: the creation of a museum or a foundation, the development of sponsorship projects, the implementation of a customer relationship, the development of digital activities, the implementation of brand activation, etc.[28]

In this way, a thorough understanding of supporters should allow professionals to better adapt their marketing strategies to supply and respond to their needs. It is now necessary for clubs to "qualify" their customers, which requires a significant work on the parts of CRM/FRM.

In addition, couldn't clubs work more on building their brand? It is, of course, easier to sell jerseys with the name of Zlatan Ibrahimović on the back, but do clubs put every effort to think ahead about their strategy, their brand identity and the image that they want to convey? There is clear evidence that this approach facilitates the itemization of a coherent operational marketing program. Therefore, if a club wants to exist, to find its place in a multitude of other professional sports structures, it should be able to stand out in front of consumers. It is about becoming a clan, a tribe or a community at a time when some clubs want to make *socios* of their fans. To magnify the sense of community, can't the club give a real role to the fan? This is not about the consumption of sports services, but it is about convincing other target audiences, about becoming in some way the best ambassador for the club-brand.

At the time of the "all digital", shouldn't football marketers share their knowledge more? This question echoes the words of Boris Lafargue: "We must stop working in our own separate corner thinking that we can revolutionize things. For example, in terms of social media in Toulouse, we should pool our forces." More than a strategy or technique, marketing is above all a *state of mind* useful to the growth of professional football.

Considered today as a real show, professional sports must provide an emotional experience to their fans. A fan goes to the stadium to attend a sporting event, but even more for the experience, to enjoy the atmosphere to which he or she contributes to. Plus the social media, and editorial content at large, should promote the experience.

Finally, with Euro 2016 taking place in France still to come and a ticketing strategy tailored to different target audiences, it does not seem impossible that the event will favorably impact the development of professional football and bring "back" sports fans to the Ligue 1 stadiums. Therefore, one can legitimately think that this international event will help to create a momentum of popularity around football in general and help to develop interest from both several types of audiences (children, women, etc.) and important economic partners for future professional football. We believe that the strategies and their implementations studied in this book will contribute to a better understanding of football marketing.

Notes

1 An entire chapter is devoted to sports sponsorship in the world of professional football in this book.
2 A definition of the concept is offered in the chapter devoted to sport sponsorship.
3 Law firms take care of the various parts, especially the signature and contract compliance.
4 Interview done by Nicolas Chanavat on May 13th, 2015, at the LOU Rugby headquarters.
5 Interview by Nicolas Chanavat, Arnaud Waquet and Arnaud Richard, on November 22, 2013, under the Memos program (Memory for Sport) of the CEOF (French Olympic Study Centre) and the ANOF (French National Olympic Academy), at the interviewee's home. Jacques Ferran was at the initiative of the first draft of the Regulation of the European Clubs Cup, on the February 4, 1955.
6 For more information, see Chapter 2 on economic models.
7 Technically, the birth of Sportfive requires a takeover bid of Canal + on the Jean-Claude Darmon group, RTL already owns 28% of capital and 34% are still in the hands of its founder, the rest being public. Following the merger, and depending on the success of the tender offer, RTL Group and Canal + will hold equally between 39.5 % and 46.5% of the new group, considering that Jean-Claude Darmon must keep 5% of it. Primarily based on football, Sportfive will manage the sporting, marketing and television rights of hundreds of clubs around the world (see Chapter 4 dedicated to agencies).
8 Interview by Nicolas Chanavat, Arnaud Waquet and Arnaud Richard on November 22, 2013, as part of the Memos program (Memory for Sport of the CEOF – French Olympic Study Centre) and the ANOF (the French National Olympic Academy), at the interviewee's home.
9 Interview conducted by Nicolas Chanavat on October 10, 2014, at the headquarters of UCPF.
10 Interview conducted by Michel Desbordes and Nicolas Chanavat on April 1, 2015, at the Infront headquarters.
11 Other rankings as proposed by the German website transfermarket could have been discussed here.
12 See http://www.football-observatory.com/-Publications.
13 Brand Finance, *Brand Finance Football 50, The Annual Report on The World's Most Valuable Football Brands*, 2014.
14 Currently, the player has over 100 million fans (103 millions on May 14, 2015).
15 http://repucom.net/media/ronaldo-most-marketable-footballer – "Ronaldo crowned the most marketable footballer globally ", article published on repucom.net on May 28, 2014. Last accessed on May 12, 2015.
16 Interview conducted by Nicolas Chanavat on October 10, 2014, at the headquarters of the UCPF.
17 Some financing sources are illustrated by sporting events such as Euro 2016.
18 Law n° 99–223 of March 23, 1999, called Loi Buffet (Buffet Act). This law limits the amount of public subsidies for professional sports club to 2.3 million euros and forbids using the funds to pay the players.
19 Interview by Nicolas Chanavat on May 11, 2015, at the City Hall of Paris.
20 In France, AJ Auxerre (Abbé Deschamps stadium) and AC Ajaccio (Francois Coty stadium) are the only professional football clubs currently owning their stadiums. Olympique Lyonnais will join them in 2016, with the delivery of its "Grand Stade" (see chapter dedicated to OL).

21 PSG pays a fee of €1.06 million per year +3% to 7% of the revenue of the stadium to the City of Paris. Source: Directorate of Youth and Sports of Paris, 2015.
22 Interview conducted by Nicolas Chanavat and Michel Desbordes on January 22, 2015, at the headquarters of PSG.
23 Association Sportive de Saint-Étienne, confidential and unpublished documents, provided by Arnaud Jaouen, ASSE 2014–2016 Strategic Plan, 2014.
24 Interview conducted by Nicolas Chanavat on November 18, 2014, at the headquaters of OGC Nice.
25 Respectively, the Toulouse FC, the OM Attitude and the Montpellier Hérault SC.
26 Interview conducted by Nicolas Chanavat on November 18, 2014, at the headquaters of OL.
27 Interview conducted by Nicolas Chanavat on July 8, 2014, at the headquarters of the ASSE.
28 Some activities are the subject of a specific chapter and/or are thoroughly covered in the case studies of clubs.

Bibliography

Albert N., "Le sentiment d'amour pour une marque: déterminants et pertinence managériale", *Management et Avenir*, 72, 2014, pp. 71–89.

Allaire R., Gonguet J.-P. et Villepreux O., *L'histoire passionnée du rugby français et international*, Éditions Hugo et Compagnie, Paris, 2014.

American Marketing Association (November 24, 2016). Available at https://www.ama.org/AboutAMA/Pages/Definition-of-Marketing.aspx

Andreff W., *Économie du sport*, PUF, 1989.

Andreff W., *La mondialisation économique du sport*, Louvain-la-Neuve: Belgium, De Boeck, 2012.

Andreff W. et Staudohar P.D., "The evolving European model of professional sports finance", *Journal of Sports Economics*, 1, 3, 2000, pp. 257–273.

Association Sportive de Saint-Étienne, Documents confidentiels et non publiés, communiqués par Arnaud Jaouen, *Plan stratégique ASSE 2014–2016*, 2014.

Bauer H.H., Sauer N.E. et Schmitt P., "Customer-based brand equity in the team sport industry", *European Journal of Marketing*, 39, 5/6, 2005, pp. 496–513.

Bodet G. et Chanavat N., "Building global football brand equity: Lessons from the Chinese market", *Asia Pacific Journal of Marketing and Logistics*, 22, 1, 2010, pp. 55–66.

Boli C., "Convertir les supporters en fidèles consommateurs: une politique commerciale à Manchester United", *Communication et organisation*, 27, 2005, pp. 70–82.

Bolle G., "Les spécificités françaises dans le mode de gestion du football", in G. Bolle et M. Desbordes (ed.), *Marketing et Football: une perspective internationale*, Paris, Presses Universitaires du Sport, 2005, pp. 5–23.

Bolotny F. et Gouze G., "L'Exploitation des enceintes sportives, modèles économiques, optimisation commerciale et sécurité juridique", *Les Échos*, février 2008.

Bourgeon-Renault D. et Bouchet P., "Marketing expérientiel et analyse des logiques de consommation du spectacle sportif", *Revue Française du Marketing*, 212, 2/5, avril 2007, pp. 87–102.

Bourgeon D. et Bouchet P., "L'expérience de consommation du spectacle sportif", *Revue européenne de management du sport*, 6, 2001, pp. 1–47.

Bourg J.-F. et Gouguet J.-J., *Économie politique du sport professionnel – L'éthique à l'épreuve du marché*, Paris, Vuibert, 2007.

Brand Finance, Brand Finance Football 50 "The Annual Report On The World's Most Valuable Football Brands", 2014.

Chanavat N., *Étude de l'efficacité du parrainage sportif multiple événementiel: une application à trois entités sportives professionnelles et à un annonceur*, thèse de doctorat en sciences du sport, Lyon I, Université Claude Bernard, 2009.

Chanavat N. et Bodet G., "Experiential marketing in sport spectatorship services: A customer perspective", *European Sport Management Quarterly*, 14, 4, 2014, pp. 323–344.

Chanavat N. et Bodet G., "Sport branding strategy and internationalisation: A French perception of the 'Big Four' brands", *Qualitative Market Research: An International Journal*, 12, 4, 2009, pp. 460–481.

Chanavat N. et Desbordes M., "Towards the regulation and restriction of ambush marketing? The case of the first truly social and digital mega sport event: Olympic Games London 2012", *International Journal of Sport Marketing and Sponsorship*, 15, 3, 2014a, pp. 79–88.

Chanavat N. et Desbordes M., "Le parrainage sportif multiple événementiel: atouts, défis et conditions de succès", *Revue Gestion (HEC Montréal)*, 38, 4, 2014b, pp. 27–36.

Chantelat P., "Présentation", in P. Chantelat (éd.), *La professionnalisation des organisations sportives: nouveaux enjeux, nouveaux débats*, Paris, L'Harmattan, 2001, pp. 17–40.

Charroin P. et Chanavat N., "Roger Rocher, Président de l'Association Sportive de Saint-Etienne (ASSE) des années 1960–70: un visionnaire bâtisseur", in E. Bayle (dir.), *Les grands dirigeants du sport 23 portraits et stratégies de management*, Louvain-la-Neuve: Belgium, De Boeck, 2014, pp. 113–134.

Charroin P. et Waquet A., "L'universalisme professionnalisant du football contre l'amateurisme internationaliste olympique", in Th. Terret (dir.), *Les Paris des Jeux olympiques de 1924*, Biarritz, Atlantica, vol. 2: Le Paris sportif, 2008, pp. 445–490.

CIES, *L'Observatoire du football*, rapport annuel, 2014. Available at http://www.football-observatory.com/?lang=fr

Crocker P.R.E., Kowalski K.C., Hoar S.D. et McDonough M., "Emotion in sport across adulthood", in M.R. Weiss (éd.), *Developmental Sport and Exercise Psychology: A Lifespan Perspective*, Morgantown, WV, Fitness Information Technology Inc., 2003, pp. 333–355.

Deloitte, *Commercial Breaks, Football Money League, Sport Business Group*, 2015, pp. 1–40. Available at https://www2.deloitte.com/content/dam/Deloitte/uk/Documents/sports-business-group/deloitte-football-money-league-2015.PDF

Desbordes M., "Introduction", in M. Desbordes et A. Richelieu (éd.), *Néo-marketing du sport, regards croisés entre Europe et Amérique du Nord*, Louvain-la-Neuve: Belgium, De Boeck, 2011, pp. 1–8.

Desbordes M., "Introduction: New directions for marketing in football", in M. Desbordes (éd.), *Marketing and Football: An International Perspective*, Oxford, Butterworth-Heinemann, 2007, pp. 1–15.

Desbordes M., Ohl F. et Tribou G., *Marketing du sport*, Paris, Economica, 1999.

Desbordes M. et Richelieu A., *Global Sport Marketing: Contemporary Issued and Practice*, Londres et New York, Routledge, 2012.

Dietschy P., Chapitre 4, "Professionnalisme et premières Coupes du monde", in *Histoire du football*, Paris, Perrin, 2010, pp. 149–195.

DNCG, Rapport annuel, *situation du football professionnel saison 2013–2014*, 2015.

Dobni D. et Zinkhan G.M., "In search of brand image: A foundation analysis", *Advances in Consumer Research*, 17, 1990, pp. 110–119.

Drut B., *Économie du Football professionnel*, Paris, La Découverte, 2014.

EY-UCPF, "Baromètre 2014 des impacts économiques et sociaux du football professionnel", *Entre ombre et lumière*, 2014. Available at http://www.ey.com/fr/fr/newsroom/news-releases/communique-de-presse---3eme-barometre-foot-pro-ucpf---ey

Floch J.-M., "La contribution d'une sémiotique structurale à la conception d'un hypermarché", *Recherche et Applications en Marketing*, 4, juin, 1989, pp. 37–49.

François A. et Bayle E., "Jean-Michel Aulas: un précurseur pragmatique", in E. Bayle (dir.), *Les grands dirigeants du sport*, Louvain-la-Neuve: Belgium, De Boeck, 2014, pp. 359–376.

Gerke A., Chanavat N. et Benson-Rea M., "How can country of origin image be leveraged to create global sporting goods brands", *Sport Management Review*, 17, 2014, pp. 174–189.

Gladden J.M. et Milne G.R., "Examining the importance of brand equity in professional sport", *Sport Marketing Quarterly*, 8, 1, 1999, pp. 21–29.

Guillardeau S., "Stadium manager de club professionnel: quelle cohabitation avec un exploitant privé?", *Jurisport*, 147, novembre 2014.

Hautbois C., "Le marketing des fédérations sportives françaises: spécificités et pratiques", in C. Hautbois (dir.), *Le marketing des fédérations sportives*, Economica, 2014, pp. 47–102.

Helleu B. et Karoutchi M., "The internet, online social networks and the fan digital experience", in J. Beech et S. Chadwick (éds.), *The Business of Sport Management*, Harlow, Pearson, 2013, pp. 298–320.

Kapferer J.-N., *The New Strategic Brand Management: Creating and Sustaining Brand Equity Lon Term*, Londres, Kogan Page, 2007.

Keller K.L., "Conceptualizing, measuring, and managing customer-based brand equity", *Journal of Marketing*, 57, 1993, pp. 1–22.

Keller K.L., *Strategic Brand Management*, Englewood Cliffs, NJ, Prentice-Hall, 2008.

Kotler P., Keller K.L., Dubois B. et Manceau D., *Marketing Management*, 12e édition, Paris, Pearson Education, 2006.

Kuper S. et Szymanski S., *Soccernomics*, Glasgow: HarperSport, 2012.

Lewi G. et Lacœuilhe J., *Branding Management: la marque de l'idée à l'action*, Paris, Pearson Education, 2007.

Maffesoli M., *Le temps des tribus, le déclin de l'individualisme dans les sociétés postmodernes*, Paris, La Table Ronde, 1988.

Malaval P., "La promotion des ventes en marketing business to business", *Décisions Marketing*, 27, 2002, pp. 7–18.

Maltese L. et Danglande J.-P., *Marketing du Sport et événementiel sportif*, Paris, Dunod, 2014, p. 82.

Moneghetti M., Tétart Ph. et Wille F., "De la plume à l'écran. Sport et médias, 1945–2005", in Ph. Tétart (dir.), *Histoire du sport en France, tome 2: Le temps des masses, 1850–2005*, Paris, Vuibert, 2007.

Mullin B.J., Hardy S. et Sutton W.A., *Sport Marketing*, 3e edition, Champaign, IL, Human Kinetics, 2007.

Nys J.-F., "La surenchère des sponsors dans le football", *Géoéconomie*, 3, 54, 2010, pp. 63–77.

Pimentel R.W. et Reynolds K.E., "A model for consumer devotion: Affective commitment with proactive sustaining behaviours", *Academy of Marketing Science Review*, 5, 2004, pp. 1–45.

Repucom, *Industry Sector and Landscape Report 2013/2014*, 2014.

Richelieu A., "La construction stratégique de la marque dans le sport", in M. Desbordes et A. Richelieu (éds.), *Néo-marketing du sport, regards croisés entre Europe et Amérique du Nord*, Louvain-la-Neuve: Belgium, De Boeck, 2011, pp. 11–24.

Richelieu A. et Pons F., "Reconciling managers' strategic vision with fans' expectations", *International Journal of Sport Marketing and Sponsorship*, 6, 3, 2005, pp. 150–163.

Richelieu A. et Pons F., "Toronto mapple leafs vs football club barcelona: How two legendary sport teams built their brand equity", *International Journal of Sports Marketing & Sponsorship*, May, 7, 3, 2006, pp. 231–250.

UCPF, *Le décrochage*, novembre 2014.

Vamplew W., *Pay Up and Play the Game: Professional Sport in Britain*, Cambrigde, Cambridge University Press, 1988.

Veblen T., *The Theory of the Leisure Class*, New York, Macmillan, 1899, pp. 64–70.

Wahl A., *Les archives du football. Sport et société en France (1880–1980)*, Paris, Gallimard/Julliard, 1989, p. 34.

Waquet A. et Vincent J., "Wartime rugby and football: Sports elites, French military teams and international meets during the First World War", *International Journal of the History of Sport*, 28, 3–4, 2011, pp. 372–392.

Webography

http://lerdvsportif.fr/tfc-maitre-du-buzz-en-ligue-1/ – "Le TFC, maître du buzz en Ligue 1", article écrit par Thomas Henry et paru sur lerdvsportif.fr. Dernier accès le 12 mai 2015.

http://repucom.net/fr/laurent-blanc-star-entraineurs-ligue-1/ – "Laurent Blanc, star des entraîneurs de Ligue 1", article paru sur repucom.net le 1er avril 2015. Dernier accès le 12 mai 2015.

http://repucom.net/media/ronaldo-most-marketable-footballer – "Ronaldo crowned the most marketable footballer globally", article paru sur repucom.net le 28 mai 2014. Dernier accès le 12 mai 2015.

http://www.euromericas.com/que-club-vende-mas-camisetas/ – "¿Qué club vende más camisetas? ", article paru sur euromericas.com le 22 mai 2015. Dernier accès le 23 mai 2015.

http://www.forbes.com/pictures/mlm45fkkle/1-real-madrid/ – "Real Madrid Tops Ranking Of The World's Most Valuable Soccer Teams", article écrit par Mike Ozanian paru le 6 mai 2015. Dernier accès le 12 mai 2015.

http://www.leparisien.fr/sports/football/angleterre-les-droits-tv-du-foot-atteignent-un-record-a-7-mds-eur-10–02–2015–4522199.php – "Angleterre: les droits TV du foot atteignent un record, à 7 Mds € !", article paru sur le site leparisien.fr le 10 février 2015. Dernier accès le 14 mai 2015.

https://twitter.com/EURO2016 – Tweet du comité d'organisation de l'Euro 2016 après l'annonce des tarifs de la billetterie de l'Euro 2016 par Jacques Lambert le 12 mai 2015. Dernier accès le 14 mai 2015.

https://www.ama.org/AboutAMA/Pages/Definition-of-Markeaspx – "Définition du marketing selon l' Association Américaine de Marketing", publié en 2013. Dernier accès le 12 mai 2015.

2

ECONOMIC MODEL OF A PROFESSIONAL FOOTBALL CLUB IN FRANCE

Nicolas Scelles and Wladimir Andreff

The economic model of football clubs is a revenue model, but also a cost model in relation to their objective. It can be defined as the search for balance between revenues, costs and objective, and the latter can vary: profit maximization, sporting maximization under strict constraint ("hard" constraint) or "soft" budget constraint (Andreff, 2009). In France, the revenue model of football clubs has evolved with time. This mutation fits in the switch from an SSSL (Spectators-Subventions-Sponsors-Local) model to an MMMMG (Media-Magnats-Merchandising-Markets-Global) model at the European level (Andreff and Staudohar, 2000). Before 1914, sport financing came mainly from practitioners (Bourg and Gouguet, 2001, p. 19). Thereafter, with competitions being a spectacle, spectators have become the primary source of revenue, ahead of the subsidies granted by the local authorities and industry patrons. Advertising revenues have gradually become more and more important, and in the 1960s and 1970s, sponsorship increased significantly as firms were seeking a more direct identification in terms of audience, image, reputation and sales (Andreff and Staudohar, 2000, p. 259). In France, during the 1970s, operating revenues of first division football clubs came mainly from the spectators, supplemented by subsidies and sponsorship. The SSSL model was at its peak, with its "L" finding its justification in the fact that the revenues were generated from local or national residents.

The 1980s is the starting point of a continuous increase in the share of TV rights income for French clubs. The major event explaining this rise of TV rights is the emergence of a new television actor in 1984 following the abolition of the ORTF (Office de Radiodiffusion – Télévision Française, French Radio broadcasting – Television Office) public monopoly: Canal +. From the 1984–1985 season, the TV channel signed an exclusive contract for the football first division. It will then gradually increase its investment in French professional football in addition to having ownership of the Paris Saint-Germain from 1991 to 2006. The 1980s also mark the birth of commercial investments with the advent of merchandising, but also the appearance of the listing of football clubs on the stock exchange in Europe. Therefore, in England, in 1983, Tottenham introduced its title on the London Stock Exchange (also called the City). In the 1990s, the rise of the stock market listing and merchandising coincides with financial stakes. According to Bourg and Gouguet (2001, pp. 22–23), they "encourage more firms to take control of clubs by directing investment towards a discipline, football, and one team, often prestigious". After a first wave of takeovers of some clubs by business magnates (from Lagardère to Aulas) and media (M6/Bordeaux, Canal +/Paris Saint-Germain, PSG), a second wave of club acquisitions by institutional investors followed – Colony Capital then Qatar sovereign fund for PSG – and oligarchs (Dmitry Rybolovlev/AS Monaco, Waldemar Kita/FC Nantes, Hafiz Mammadov/RC Lens). These elements show the emergence of the MMMMG model for major European clubs (about 30), translating into professional sports the cumulative effects of deregulation, financialization and globalization of the economy (Bourg, 2004, p. 50).

In 1990–1991, the revenue model of the French first division football clubs corresponded mainly to the SSSL model, since only 15% of revenues excluding transfers came from TV rights and merchandising (7.5% each). In 2012–2013, the distribution of revenues for French clubs as a whole seems to indicate a reversal towards the MMMMG model, with 74% of revenues excluding transfers coming from TV rights (49%) and other products, mainly merchandising (25%). Nevertheless, it seems necessary to observe the reality of the different clubs before generalizing the existence of a single-revenue model. Besides, considering only revenues excluding transfers does not allow a complete overview of the revenue model idea, as transfer revenues should also be considered knowing that they are at least partly tied to the expenses excluding transfers and to the possible imbalance between the latter and the revenues excluding transfers. On the level of the expenses excluding transfers, player salaries represented 61% of the total in 1990–1991 (Dermit-Richard, 2003) against over 66% in 2012–2013 despite a drop in their weight compared to the previous season (70% in 2011–2012). For both seasons considered, revenues were sufficient so as to face expenses. However, these two seasons are far from representative of the 1990–2013 period during which expenses consistently exceeded revenues.

In this chapter, recent models of revenues and costs of a football club in France are considered first (1). These models lead to recurring deficits and debts despite management control of the clubs (2). The impacts of financial fair play implemented by UEFA and the organization of the Euro 2016 by France associated with the construction/renovation of stadiums are then discussed (3) before considering the place of marketing in recent and future economic models (4). The last section is the conclusion (5).

1. One or several models of revenues and costs?

The purpose of this section is to address the revenue model and the cost model of a football club in France, but would not it be preferable to speak about some models of revenues and costs of the clubs? Thus, several models will be differentiated, both for revenues excluding transfers (1.1) as well as costs excluding transfers (1.2).

1.1 Which models of revenues excluding transfer?

In Ligue 1, Paris is itself a case apart since 2011–2012, with only 21%–23% of the revenues excluding transfers from TV rights (around 60% on average for other clubs) and 56%–58% from other revenues (around 11% for other clubs). In 2012–2013, revenues excluding transfers of the French capital club were four times higher than those of the other three French clubs with the highest revenues excluding transfers, namely Marseille, Lyon and Lille (€400 million against €100 million). That year, Lille came closer to Marseille and Lyon in terms of the distribution of revenues excluding transfers, its new stadium allowing it to be less dependent on TV rights by generating more revenues from sponsorship and matchday (nevertheless, with less merchandising than Marseille and Lyon). However, it is difficult to differentiate the revenue model excluding transfers from these clubs compared to that of a number of French Ligue 1 clubs, as their ability to generate more revenues excluding transfers seems to be a consequence of their more favorable local market (and potentially their participation in the Champions

League). For Marseille, Lyon and Lille, as for most other clubs in Ligue 1, TV rights represent between half and two-thirds of the revenues excluding transfers. Variations may occur depending on sports results (e.g. Montpellier with 73% of TV rights in 2012–2013, when the club participated in the Champions League).

Some specific cases other than Paris can be noted in Ligue 1. For example, Nice has always been in the upper range of TV rights in the period 2010–2013 (from 69% to 71% of its revenues) even though it had a weak capacity to generate matchday revenues. Its new stadium, opened in 2013–2014, should have allowed a rebalancing of revenues in relation to the strong growth in average attendance (24,186 spectators in 2013–2014 against 10,246 in 2012–2013). The other particular cases in Ligue 1 over the period 2010–2013 have been Arles in 2010–2011 and Ajaccio in 2011–2012 and 2012–2013, with nearly 80% of revenues excluding transfers coming from TV rights, which questions their ability to generate other revenues excluding transfers and to belong sustainably to the elite (only one season for Arles, and three seasons for Ajaccio, when taking into account the 2013–2014 season, after which the club was put aside). If the analysis period is extended to the 2013–2014 season, for which the economic and financial data of the clubs were not available at the time of writing this chapter, it is very likely that Monaco has presented a breakdown of its revenues bringing it closer to Paris Saint-Germain than to other French clubs.

In Ligue 2, the distribution of revenues excluding transfers differs from Ligue 1 from the standpoint of TV rights (just over 50 % instead of 60%), sponsorship (over 20% instead of 16%–18%) and other products (15% to 20% instead of 11%), but not so much for matchday revenues (from 10% to 11%). In 2012–2013, Ligue 2 clubs generated almost 6.5 times less revenues than Ligue 1 (slightly over €200 million against nearly €1.3 billion). A club going down from Ligue 1 to Ligue 2 gets 40%–60% less revenues excluding transfers. So, as a result, the club has to adapt its expenses accordingly, as the transfers can hardly cover the shortfall in revenues.

1.2 Which models for expenses excluding transfers?

For Ligue 1 and Ligue 2, expenses excluding transfers break down roughly into 60% of payroll expenses and 40% of other expenses excluding transfers. However, in Ligue 1, among other expenses excluding transfers, the depreciation charges of transfer fees represent around 12% against only 3%–4 % in Ligue 2. Incorporating agent fees (2%–3% in Ligue 1; 2% in League 2), we can estimate that about 75% of the expenses excluding transfers of Ligue 1 clubs are linked to employees and their agents against a percentage more along the lines of 65% in Ligue 2.

Beyond the distribution of charges excluding transfers, it is important to consider what percentage of revenues excluding transfers they represent. Expenses other than payroll charges, depreciation charges of transfer fees and agent fees correspond to charges related to travels, organization of matches, external services, taxes, other depreciations and provisions and other charges. We assume that they are more or less fixed for a given club at a given level outside the rent increase caused by a new stadium, and therefore clubs may not actually decrease them. In Ligue 1, they represent around 30% of club revenues (32.5% in 2012–2013 when excluding Paris Saint-Germain) against 48% in Ligue 2 in 2011–2012 and 2012–2013 when excluding Monaco (44% in 2010–2011) which is characterized by greater heterogeneity between clubs (standard deviation of about 15% against 6% for Ligue 1). Clubs that have the highest percentages in Ligue 2 are former Ligue 1 members (Grenoble in 2010–2011, Metz in 2010–2011 and 2011–2012, Le Havre, Le Mans, Nantes and Sedan throughout the period 2010–2013, Lens in 2011–2012 and 2012–2013, Auxerre and Monaco in 2012–2013) including Le Havre, which played its first season in its new stadium in 2012–2013. By removing these clubs from the calculation, the percentages are

Table 2.1 Ratio between payroll expenses/revenues excluding transfers of Ligue 1 and Ligue 2 clubs during the 2010–2013 period

	2012–2013	*2011–2012*	*2010–2011*
Ligue 1	66.4%	73.6%	74.6%
Ligue 1 without Paris	71.4%	78.6%	75.2%
Ligue 2	99.3%	93.2%	77.2%
Ligue 2 without Monaco	83.5%	87.0%	77.2%

Source: LFP/DNCG.

between 37.5 and 40% for Ligue 2. We can therefore estimate that previous expenses for a Ligue 1 club represent one-third of its revenues and 40% for a Ligue 2 club. A club seeking to achieve balance for its profit and loss account excluding transfers should reduce its expenses in payroll, depreciation charges of transfer fees and agent fees by two-thirds of its revenues in Ligue 1 and by 60% in Ligue 2.

Among the latest expenses mentioned, the approach taken is to focus on payroll expenses and what they represent as a percentage of revenues excluding transfers. Table 2.1 reports percentages exceeding the target to reach for a club seeking balance excluding transfers (except in Ligue 1 when including Paris in 2012–2013) even though the depreciation charges of transfer fees and agent fees are not taken into account. This excess is even stronger in Ligue 2 than in Ligue 1, particularly in 2011–2012 and 2012–2013, and the same result holds even when removing Monaco. From then on, the majority of clubs base their revenues on player transfers to try to balance their books. Some rely on the contribution of shareholders to clear their deficits. However, deficits and recurring debts of French football clubs show that economic models could be improved.

2. Deficits and debt: "soft" budget constraint and management control

The French football clubs operate in a system of open league, with promotion of better ranked clubs to higher leagues (or to European competition) and relegation of lowest ranked clubs to a lower league. In such a system, the purpose of the clubs is necessarily to maximize their number of wins on the field in order to be promoted or to avoid relegation. As a consequence, beyond the different models of clubs identified above, they all seek to recruit as many talented players as possible within their budget and beyond. Therein lies the origin of their "soft" budget constraints (2.1), their difficulties to control the wage bill and the need for management control (2.2).

2.1 The "soft" budget constraint responsible for deficits

Apparently, football clubs spend without constraint in France and Europe, that is beyond what their income would allow, especially to recruit and pay player salaries, particularly superstars. A "soft" budget constraint characterizes any business, organization or football club which can spend more than its income, not occasionally but repeatedly, without becoming bankrupt (Kornai et al., 2003; Andreff, 2014). The immediate consequence is the current and persistent deficit of the club. Repeated deficits then drive the football club into a cycle of debt. This is the case when football clubs are not given the goal of maximizing their profit, but rather of maximizing their wins on the field and, to that end, of recruiting the best possible talents. In the system of open leagues, virtually no football club is ever made bankrupt because of recurring or sustainable deficits, either in France or in other European countries; the survival rate of football clubs is extremely high despite recurring deficits (Kuper and Szymanski, 2009), although 56% of European football clubs in first divisions had a deficit in 2009–2010, and 63% in 2010–2011 (UEFA, 2012). The "soft" budget constraint of football clubs is perfectly illustrated by the fact that many of them are on the verge of insolvency without ever being put into liquidation (Storm and Nielsen, 2012).

A football club spends lavishly, beyond its income, when it knows that it will benefit from the financial bailout of its deficit and debt by banks, as is the case in Spain (Ascari and Gagnepain, 2006); or by the state, as in Italy (i.e. the plan *salve calcio* of 2002, Baroncelli and Lago, 2006); or by *sugar daddies*, that is *sunk investors* who do not expect financial returns but rather an image, prestige, a reputation, as happens in the English Premier League with Russian oligarchs, with sheikhs from the Middle East or with rich Americans. For a football club, a more common modality to release budget constraint is to simply not pay its debts, knowing it will not be put into liquidation, and thus to accumulate debt in the form of outstanding payments; this is the modality of mismanagement adopted by several French football clubs, even though some clubs are also in the hands of oligarchs (Rybolovlev, Kita, Mammadov) or Qatari funds.

2.2 Growing debt and management control

A football club's outstanding payments may be due to suppliers, or other clubs. It may consist of unpaid back wages, and often of back taxes and unpaid social security contributions. Even though the French Professional Football League (LFP) considers itself to be the best managed in Europe, thanks to the National Direction of Management Control (DNCG), this has not prevented Ligue 1 from being in deficit before tax every year from 1999–2000 to 2012–2013, except for 4 years, in 1999–2000 and from 2005–2006 to 2007–2008 (Table 2.2). Table 2.2 also shows the extent of arrears in debt and in total liabilities of Ligue 1 clubs. Outstanding payments rose from €363 million in 1999–2000 to €725 million in 2012–2013 and represent usually 85% or more of the total debt of the clubs. This has increased from €427 to €830 million between 1999–2000 and 2012–2013, and its weight has gone from half of the Ligue 1 liabilities in 1999–2000 to three-quarters of them in 2012–2013. In other words, we can see a deterioration of the aggregated balance sheet of Ligue 1 clubs that has no reason to stop as long as the budget constraint will remain "soft", whereas the clubs can continue to accumulate debts without the threat of having to stop their business – meanwhile liquidation and termination of activity is the usual rule in all sectors of the economy except for sports leagues.

The fact that Ligue 1's debt is much lower than that of the English Premier League (over €2 billion) would not justify that some French football clubs revel in financial indiscipline, deterioration of their accounts and an increasing debt. It is especially the debt structure that is of concern, with outstanding payments that have climbed up to 91% of the debt in 2008 and still remained at 87% in 2013. In 2011, 10 Ligue 1 clubs (and 10 Ligue 2 clubs) were in deficit and as such in increasing debt: Bordeaux (deficit of €6.5 million), Caen (€1.6 million), Lens (€5.9 million), Lille (€8.7 million), Lyon (€35.1 million), Marseille (€14.7 million), Monaco (€0.3 million), Nice (€1.2 million), Paris Saint-Germain (€0.2 million after covering) and Valenciennes (€3.7 million). There were nine in 2012 (Auxerre, Bordeaux, Lyon, Marseille, Nancy, Nice, PSG, Toulouse, Valenciennes) and still seven in 2013, despite the prospect of a future implementation of the financial fair play rule by the UEFA: Ajaccio (deficit of €1.8 million), Bordeaux (€7.7 million), Brest (€2.2 million), Lille (€3.1 million), Lyon (€27.9 million), Nancy (€4.1 million) and PSG (€3.5 million). However, if five clubs had a deficit of over €5 million in 2011, the maximum amount that will be tolerated with the implementation of the financial fair play rule, they were

Table 2.2 Deficit and debt in Ligue 1, 1999–2013 (€ million)

	1999–00	*2000–01*	*2001–02*	*2002–03*	*2003–04*	*2004–05*	*2005–06*	*2006–07*	*2007–08*	*2008–09*	*2009–10*	*2010–11*	*2011–12*	*2012–13*
Result before tax	2.2	–53.6	–46.3	–151.2	–35.9	–32.5	27.7	42.7	25.0	–14.7	–114.1	–46.1	–82	–4
Total of liabilities including:	803.2	929.3	847.2	720.5	601.0	668.7	819.3	892.8	999.7	947.7	929.3	925.1	1007.8	1112.6
Equity	89.3	84.0	142.8	93.2	139.4	111.7	159.6	208.6	213.4	265.6	189.0	183.7	143.2	167.5
Shareholder accounts	163.5	223.1	141.7	119.9	60.1	53.1	75.2	51.2	61.8	56.6	104.9	100.9	214.6	83.5
Risk provisions	123.0	101.0	59.6	49.9	37.3	37.5	52.5	54.0	34.6	32.7	25.4	29.0	24.6	32.1
Financial debts	64.5	96.3	86.1	112.7	66.1	63.0	70.4	71.3	62.4	60.2	94.2	87.2	105.2	105.0
Other liabilities[1]= *(1)*	362.9	424.9	416.9	344.8	298.1	403.4	461.6	507.7	627.6	532.6	515.7	524.3	520.2	724.6
Total debt	427.4	521.2	503.0	457.5	364.2	466.4	532.0	579.0	690.0	592.8	609.9	611.5	625.4	829.6
(1) / *Total debt*	85%	82%	83%	75%	82%	86%	87%	88%	91%	90%	85%	86%	83%	87%
Total debt / Liabilities	53%	56%	59%	63%	61%	70%	65%	65%	69%	63%	66%	66%	62%	75%

[1]Outstanding payments, back taxes and social contributions and player transfer fees

Source: LFP/DNCG.

only two in 2013, namely Bordeaux and Lyon (but PSG's large deficit was covered by Qatari funds that the club attempted to identify as a sponsorship contract with Qatar Tourism Authority; see *infra* the penalty decided by UEFA).

The overall debt of the football league is not due to poor governance (and administration) of all clubs, of course, but some of them, usually with repeated deficit and accumulation of debts like Bordeaux, Lille, Lyon, Marseille and PSG. For the latter, the debt is the sure sign of poor administration linked to lax governance engendered by the "soft" budget constraint (Andreff, 2007). Judging from this situation, it appears that a football club management control is absolutely essential – this is the role of DNCG with LFP in France – just as it is important to harden the budget constraint by putting an end to the clubs' recurring deficits and their non-repayable bailout – which is the objective of the financial fair play rule. The DNCG action – management recommendations, expertise in payroll, temporary ban on recruitment, budget limitation, projected payroll limitation or club relegation to a lower league – did not cause the deficits and debts of financially undisciplined clubs to decline. It is appropriate to ask if, with the cumulative effect of the DNCG management control and the implementation of financial fair play starting in 2014, the French football clubs will finally all reach balanced management (expenditure = income) in compliance with budget constraints fixed by the rules of UEFA.

3. What are the impacts of the financial fair play rule and the Euro 2016?

Two major factors are likely to impact the economic models of French football clubs: on the one hand, UEFA has introduced a financial fair play device; on the other hand, France hosts the Euro 2016, an event constituting an opportunity for the stadium construction/renovation of several French clubs. This section discusses respectively the expected effects of financial fair play (3.1) and the Euro 2016 associated with the construction/renovation of stadiums (3.2).

3.1 What will be the impact of the financial fair play rule?

The financial fair play rule applies to clubs participating in European competitions. It authorizes a deficit not to exceed €5 million for a 3-year period. However, expenses related to training, investment in club infrastructure and spending on social welfare activities are excluded from the calculation (Scelles and Dermit-Richard, 2015). In addition, for the first period of application of this device, that is at the end of the 2013–2014 and 2014–2015 seasons, the clubs are allowed to present a cumulative deficit within the limit of €45 million, provided that it is financed by their shareholders. This threshold will be reduced to €30 million at the end of the three seasons for the period 2015–2018. Paris Saint-Germain has already been punished by UEFA at the end of the 2013–2014 season for non-compliance with the financial fair play rule, regarding the obligation of respecting a surplus of player purchases compared to sales of a maximum of €60 million and the stabilization of its payroll (Haddouche, May 16, 2014). The scope of this measure was reinforced a few days later by the news that the legality of the mechanism was going to be confirmed by the European Commission (Haddouche, May 21, 2014). However, this did not prevent the Paris Saint-Germain from buying David Luiz from Chelsea for an estimated amount of nearly €50 million, a transfer which is obviously associated with an increase in the club's payroll (L'Equipe, May 23, 2014).

In the context of French football, one may question the real impact of the UEFA financial fair play rule, since the DNCG has controlled the club accounts since 1990. The fundamental difference between the two mechanisms lies in the fact that the DNCG ensures club solvency, while the financial fair play aims to achieve financial balance between the revenues and the expenditure of each club. The DNCG authorizes recurring deficits if the clubs are able each time to ensure the funds required to meet their expenses; conversely, the financial fair play rule wants to reduce those deficits and eventually cancel them. The consequence which is to be expected in France is a limitation of the economic benefit of the richest clubs, who also often have the greatest deficit and debt. At the same time, financial fair play is at risk of freezing positions by not allowing clubs with lower potential to take advantage of the investment in players made by wealthy shareholders. Thus, Monaco is part of an urban area with a low number of inhabitants compared to other Ligue 1 clubs (around 70,000) and performs in front of limited crowds – 8,900 spectators on average in 2013–2014, which is the second-lowest average attendance despite its second place in the championship. The club therefore risks being thwarted in its ambition to play regularly in the Champions League, except if it can generate significant sponsorship revenues (whose amounts must nevertheless be justified in the light of market prices and not be overvalued as was the case for the contract between Qatar Tourism Authority and the Paris Saint-Germain; Haddouche, May 16, 2014) and/or internationalize itself.

Another potential consequence of the financial fair play rule is its impact on changing transfer revenues. By limiting the richest clubs' scope for spending on players, the financial fair play rule should reduce the transfer revenues of other clubs since part of the richest clubs' expenditure is made to less wealthy clubs. Thus, the economic model of a number of clubs, based on player sale in order to ensure financial balance, could be called into question. From that point on, two alternatives are available to these clubs: to develop new revenues and/or reduce their payroll. The second alternative is constrained by the fear of not being able to attract enough talented players to achieve the sporting objective, that is no promotion or relegation in the open league system. The first alternative requires particularly the optimization of the working tool: the stadium. In this context, the Euro 2016 can be an opportunity.

3.2 *What will be the impact of the Euro 2016 and the construction/renovation of stadiums?*

In 2016, France hosts the men Euro football championship, the European championship in men category for all nations playing this sport. Ten stadiums were selected: the Stade de France (Saint-Denis), the Stade Vélodrome (Marseille), the Stade des Lumières (Lyon), the Stade Pierre-Mauroy (Lille), the Parc-des-Princes (Paris), the Stade Bordeaux-Atlantique (Bordeaux), the Allianz Riviera (Nice), the Stadium (Toulouse), the Stade Geoffroy-Guichard (Saint-Étienne) and the Stade Bollaert-Delelis (Lens). The first eight belong to the first seven French urban areas (Saint-Denis is part of the Paris urban area) – the seven cities with more than 1 million people – while the last two are located in urban areas with more than 500,000 inhabitants and with a strong potential audience. Among the 10 stadiums, four are new (Lyon, Lille, Bordeaux and Nice) and five are renovated (Marseille, Paris, Toulouse, Saint-Étienne and Lens), while the Stade de France is the only one not to be changed. In addition to these 10 stadiums, since 2005, other stadiums were built (Stade Parsemain for Istres, Stade des Alpes in Grenoble, MMArena in Le Mans, Hainaut Stadium in Valenciennes, Stade Océane in Le Havre), while the Stade Auguste Delaune (Reims) was renovated, the Stade de la Mosson (Montpellier) was also renovated before suffering from flooding in 2014 and Niort has a new stadium project (Montpellier has also announced such a project in May 2016). These constructions or renovations are often presented as opportunities for clubs. Several following chapters will discuss in more detail these opportunities, which are supposed to help develop revenues excluding transfers other than TV rights, and thus limit

TV dependency and the need to sell one's best players in order to achieve financial balance. If the next section briefly considers the economic and marketing optimization of the opportunities offered by the construction/renovation of stadiums, the point of view chosen here tackles, on the contrary, the risks associated with a new oversized stadium.

A new stadium obviously has a cost and requires funding. A Public Private Partnership (PPP) has been the preferred scheme in a number of recent cases (Le Mans, Le Havre, Lille, Nice or Bordeaux), in which infrastructure construction was done with funding in whole or part by the private partner, which acquires the use of the facility for 30 years and an annual rent paid by the community and the club in return (Gayant, 2014). The major problem with this arrangement is that the dealer is interested in operating revenues from the infrastructure business, tending to oversize it with harmful consequences for the clubs (beyond undesirable effects for taxpayers): the payment of a rent which is higher than it should have been while the additional revenues generated by the new stadium do not exceed the level that would have been achieved with a properly sized stadium. Moreover, this notion of "properly sized stadium" is very relative in view of the promotion/relegation system in place in Europe: a stadium suitable for Ligue 1 for a given urban area is oversized if it becomes part of Ligue 2 (not to mention a relegation to an even lower level). Thus, Grenoble and Le Mans found themselves in great difficulties, from a financial but also from a sporting standpoint, after their relegation from Ligue 1, as they were unable to spend enough to keep their best players. The result is known: the double sporting and administrative relegation from Ligue 2 for both clubs. Valenciennes, relegated from Ligue 1 at the end of the 2013–2014 season, is also in serious financial trouble. As for Le Havre, the opening of its new stadium at the end of the 2012–2013 season resulted in expenses outside of the payroll expenses, depreciation charges of transfer fees and agent fees from 50% to 75% of revenues excluding transfers. However, it was quite predictable that the club would not be able to fill its 25,000-seat stadium in Ligue 2 (average of 8,500 spectators in 2012–2013, only 7,500 in 2013–2014 despite a better sporting performance).

The aforementioned elements show the need that clubs have an appropriately sized stadium. Niort seems to have understood the challenge of having a suitable stadium, that is to say, modern and with sufficient capacity to avoid "losing" attendees without being too big. Indeed, the club's project – inspired by the Matmut Stadium of Lyon Olympique Universitaire (rugby) – plans a new stadium with modular structures whose capacity could range from 9,400 seats for the Ligue 2 to 12,500 seats in case of promotion to Ligue 1 (Jounier, March 26, 2014). However, the relegation of the club to National (i.e. third league) would make oversized this otherwise "reasonable" project. This is the dilemma faced by the promotion/relegation system, both generator of sporting stakes, and therefore attractive to the public, but also challenging for the economic model of a club.

4. What is the role of marketing in the economic models of clubs?

Recent events (including the financial fair play rule and the organization of the Euro 2016) are not without consequences for the future of economic models of professional clubs in French football. The implementation of the financial fair play rule suggests the need to balance revenue and expenses in the long run. The organization of the Euro 2016 is a potential pillar to generate new revenues. This requires suitable marketing and thus consideration of the place to be given to marketing in future club business models (4.2). Beforehand, it is important to note the role of marketing in recent economic models (4.1). In other words, what are the revenues and expenses that are already impacted by marketing?

4.1 The role of marketing in recent economic models

First, it seems important to clarify that TV rights and ticketing revenues – related to attendance that impact sponsorship revenues and merchandising sales – partly depend on outcome uncertainty (Scelles, 2009, 2010). This is itself induced by the competition format and sporting stakes associated (Scelles et al., 2013a, 2013b). These elements defined by the LFP (under the condition of French clubs qualified in European competitions) can be seen as a marketing tool to optimize the attractiveness of the products offered (Scelles et al., 2011). TV rights and ticketing revenues also depend on the capacity of the LFP and clubs to sell their products through effective communication (Scelles et al., 2015). In a more general way, the audience at large – which explains (directly or indirectly via the expected benefits by sponsors) all revenues (Bolotny, 2004) – is related to product quality, relevant pricing, distribution via appropriate channels and adequate communication as many elements of the marketing mix. Therefore, marketing is necessary to optimize club revenues and therefore requires support from specialists in its thinking and implementation. All clubs today have marketing units, more or less developed according to their economic capacity. Payroll dedicated to this marketing unit remains limited in comparison to player expenditure and seems to have a significant impact on revenues, although further study would be required to verify this more precisely. Such a study should consider the recent and future developments which could impact marketing and future club business models.

4.2 The role of marketing in future economic models

The observation of recent trends should help to anticipate the role of marketing in future economic models. Among these trends, the development of social and digital networks (commonly called "social media" even if this naming is questionable; Stenger and Coutant, 2011) changed the communication of clubs which use Facebook and Twitter to interact with their fans. These networks seem to create financial value even if the exact process of value creation remains unclear (Scelles et al., 2014b). Scelles et al. (2013c) hypothesize that the numbers of Facebook fans and Twitter followers could be two indicators of club internationalization, which is sometimes difficult to comprehend on the basis of available economic data. The internationalization of French clubs and more generally LFP – favored by the arrival of institutional investors and foreign oligarchs – is a major component of future economic models including the growth of TV rights internationally and needs the development of a marketing strategy conceived within a globalization strategy. In addition to being a possible indicator of internationalization, social and digital networks are increasingly used on stadiums. In this context, the organization of the Euro 2016 encourages the construction/renovation of stadiums conceived to combine the use of socio-digital networks, marketing that could take advantage of it and generation of new revenues. This reflection on engaging clubs in modernity must be done with respect for their past and lend value to their historical sports performances, which constitute a major determinant of their financial value (Scelles et al., 2013d, 2014a). The example of the AS Saint-Étienne museum illustrates perfectly the benefits of a marketing strategy which links modernity and tradition. The capacity to bring together different elements which have been mentioned above constitutes a major challenge in future economic models of clubs which must seek to diminish the portion of revenues and expenses "undergone", that is to say, which depend upon the environment in broad terms (Dermit-Richard and Scelles, 2014).

Conclusion

At the end of this chapter, it seems important to summarize the issues discussed. Section 1 shows that it is more appropriate to speak about some models rather than one unique economic model for French football clubs. Indeed, all the clubs do not have the same structure of revenues and costs excluding transfers, and the need to sell players is not the same for everyone. Moreover, promotions and relegations are changing the economic model of a given club, which can result in significant financial difficulties for relegated clubs. However, the latter are not the only ones presenting deficits and debts, since Section 2 shows that a number of clubs do not comply with the financial discipline of not spending more than one's income.

Will the financial fair play rule of the UEFA, considered in Section 3, put an end to these recurring deficits and debts? In the long run, this should be the case for clubs participating in European competitions, as they are obliged to comply with the rules set by UEFA. Assuming that every club wants to get the opportunity to participate in European competitions, the financial fair play rule is supposed to annihilate the deficits and debts of all clubs. To do this, a new economic model must be implemented by clubs, striving to be less dependent on TV rights and transfer revenues. In this context, optimizing the stadium tool seems the best option. Nevertheless, optimization does not mean "megalomania". Some clubs have learned it the hard way since the beginning of the decade (Grenoble, Le Mans and Valenciennes). The organization of the Euro 2016 by France is an opportunity for several clubs to build a new stadium or upgrade the current one in order to optimize its use and the associated revenues. However, these constructions and renovations are a necessary but not sufficient condition, since along with this, clubs have to implement a suitable marketing strategy to take full advantage of the new tool.

More generally, Section 4 highlights the importance of marketing in recent and future economic models for clubs. These economic models are largely based on the optimization of TV rights and ticketing sales that depend in particular on sporting stakes and outcome uncertainty. In this regard, marketing plays a role on two levels: through the choice of the format of its competitions by the LFP (action on its products); and via the communication made on the importance of sporting stakes by the LFP, media and clubs. In the future – but the process is already in motion – social and digital networks should take a leading role in the marketing of the LFP and clubs. Considered in the framework of economic models, they can be seen as an inexpensive tool (mostly wages of professionals that are expert in digital communication strategy) that could enable new opportunities of interaction with fans and generate new sources of income. The chapters that follow study in detail the contributions of social and digital networks, and more generally of new forms of marketing.

Bibliography

Andreff, W., "French Football: A Financial Crisis Rooted in Weak Governance", *Journal of Sports Economics*, vol. 8, n° 6, December 2007, pp. 652–661.

Andreff, W., "Équilibre compétitif et contrainte budgétaire dans une ligue de sport professionnel", *Revue Economique*, vol. 60, n° 3, May 2009, pp. 591–634.

Andreff, W., "Building Blocks for a Disequilibrium Model of a European Team Sports League", *International Journal of Sport Finance*, vol. 9, n° 1, February 2014, pp. 20–38.

Andreff, W. & Staudohar, P.D., "The Evolving European Model of Professional Sports Finance", *Journal of Sports Economics*, vol. 1, n° 3, August 2000, pp. 257–276.

Ascari, G. & Gagnepain, P., "Spanish Football", *Journal of Sports Economics*, vol. 7, n° 1, February 2006, pp. 76–89.

Baroncelli, A. & Lago, U., "Italian Football", *Journal of Sports Economics*, vol. 7, n° 1, February 2006, pp. 13–28.

Bolotny, F., "C'est l'incertitude qui crée la valeur", *Cahiers du football*, January 26, 2004.

Bourg, J.-F., "Les sports collectifs professionnels en Europe: Quel modèle économique?", *in* J.-J. Gouguet (ed.), *Le sport professionnel après l'arrêt Bosman: Une analyse économique internationale*, Presses universitaires de Limoges, Limoges, 2004, pp. 43–60.

Bourg, J.-F. & Gouguet, J.-J., *Économie du sport*, La Découverte, Paris, 2001.

Dermit-Richard, N., "L'absence chronique de rentabilité financière des clubs de football professionnels: Une proposition d'explication", *Revue Européenne de Management du Sport*, n° 9, juillet 2003, pp. 1–34.

Dermit-Richard, N. & Scelles, N., "Rentabilité économique du football français: Le pressing de l'environnement, obstacle à l'action stratégique", *Revue Européenne de Management du Sport*, n° 41, April 2014, pp. 35–49.

Gayant, J.-P., "Valenciennes, relégué en Ligue 2, victime de la malédiction des nouveaux stades?", *Le Monde*, May 8, 2014. Retrieved from http://ecosport.blog.lemonde.fr/2014/05/08/valenciennes-relegue-en-ligue-2-victime-de-la-malediction-des-ppp/

Haddouche, C., "Fair-play financier: le PSG sanctionné par l'UEFA", *Le Figaro*, May 16, 2014. Retrieved from http://sport24.lefigaro.fr/football/ligue-des-champions/actualites/fair-play-financier-le-psg-sanctionne-par-l-uefa-694811

Haddouche, C., "L'Europe confirme la légalité du fair-play financier", *Le Figaro*, May 21, 2014. Retrieved from http://sport24.lefigaro.fr/football/ligue-des-champions/actualites/l-europe-confirme-la-legalite-du-fair-play-financier-695513

Jounier, P., "La vraie clé, c'est le stade", *La Nouvelle République*, March 26, 2014. Retrieved from http://www.lanouvellerepublique.fr/Deux-Sevres/Sport/Football/Ligue-2/n/Contenus/Articles/2014/03/26/La-vraie-cle-c-est-le-stade-1845418

Kornaï, J., Maskin, E. & Roland, G., "Understanding the Soft Budget Constraint", *Journal of Economic Literature*, vol. 61, December 2003, pp. 1095–1136.

Kuper, S. & Szymanski, S., *Why England Lose & Other Curious Football Phenomena Explained*, Harper Collins, London, 2009.

L'Équipe, "Accord confirmé avec Chelsea et David Luiz", May 23, 2014. Retrieved from http://www.lequipe.fr/Football/Actualites/Accord-confirme-avec-chelsea-et-david-luiz/467846

LFP / DNCG. *Comptes des clubs professionnels, saisons 2004/2005 à 2012/2013*, 2006–2013.

Scelles, N., "L'incertitude du résultat, facteur clé de succès du spectacle sportif professionnel: L'intensité compétitive des ligues: Entre impacts mesurés et effets perçus", thèse de doctorat en sciences et techniques des activités physiques et sportives, Université de Caen Basse-Normandie, Caen, France, 2009.

Scelles, N., *La glorieuse incertitude du sport. L'intensité compétitive des ligues professionnelles: Entre impacts mesurés et effets perçus,* Éditions universitaires européennes, Sarrebruck, Allemagne, 2010.

Scelles, N. & Dermit-Richard, N., "Maladie des coûts' et régulation financière du football professionnel français et européen", *in* B. Zoudji and D. Rey (eds.), *Le football dans tous ses états: Regards croisés sur les acteurs du ballon rond*, De Boeck, Louvain-La-Neuve, Belgique, 2015, pp. 169–179.

Scelles, N., Desbordes, M. & Durand, C., "Marketing in Sport Leagues: Optimising the Product Design. Intra-Championship Competitive Intensity in French Football Ligue 1 and Basketball Pro A", *International Journal of Sport Management and Marketing*, vol. 9, n° 1/2, 2011, pp. 13–28.

Scelles, N., Durand, C., Bonnal, L., Goyeau, D. & Andreff, W., "Competitive Balance versus Competitive Intensity before a Match: Is One of These Two Concepts More Relevant in Explaining Attendance? The Case of the French Football Ligue 1 Over the Period 2008–2011", *Applied Economics*, vol. 45, n° 29, 2013a, pp. 4184–4192.

Scelles, N., Durand, C., Bonnal, L., Goyeau, D. & Andreff, W., "My Team Is in Contention? Nice, I Go to the Stadium! Competitive Intensity in the French Football Ligue 1", *Economics Bulletin*, vol. 33, n° 3, 2013b, pp. 2365–2378.

Scelles, N., Durand, C. & Ferrand, A., "Identification et maîtrise des facteurs clés de succès par les dirigeants: Le cas des ligues sportives professionnelles (basket, football et rugby masculins en France)", *La Revue des Sciences de Gestion*, vol. 272, 2015, pp. 55–65.

Scelles, N., Helleu, B., Durand, C. & Bonnal, L., "Globalization, social media and professional sports clubs value", Proceedings – IBEC 2013: 12th Annual International Business & Economy Conference in Caen, College of Business, San Francisco State University, San Francisco, 2013c.

Scelles, N., Helleu, B., Durand, C. & Bonnal, L., "Determinants of Professional Sports Firm Values in the United States and Europe: A Comparison between Sports Over the Period 2004–2011" , *International Journal of Sport Finance*, vol. 8, n° 4, November 2013d, pp. 280–293.

Scelles, N., Helleu, B., Durand, C. & Bonnal, L., "Professional Sports Firm Values: Bringing New Determinants to the Foreground? A Study of European Soccer, 2005–2013", *Journal of Sports Economics*, 2014a, OnlineFirst, doi: 10.1177/1527002514538976.

Scelles, N., Helleu, B., Durand, C., Bonnal, L. & Morrow, S.H., "Social media and professional sports club values reconsidered", 22nd Conference of European Association for Sport Management, Coventry, UK, 9–12 September 2014b.

Stenger, T. & Coutant, A., "Introduction", *in* T. Stenger and A. Coutant (eds.), *Ces réseaux numériques dits sociaux*, Hermès, Paris, vol. 59, 2011, pp. 9–17.

Storm, R.K. & Nielsen, K., "Soft Budget Constraints in Professional Football", *European Sport Management Quarterly*, vol. 12, n° 2, April 2012, pp. 183–201.

UEFA, *The European Club Licensing Benchmarking Report. Financial Year 2011*, UEFA, 2012.

3

MARKETING OF PROFESSIONAL SOCCER IN THE UNITED STATES

A case study of Major League Soccer

Eric Brownlee and Nicolas Lorgnier

Introduction

Near the end of 1993, World Cup USA's CEO Alan I. Rothenberg fulfilled a long-term promise from USA Soccer to the Fédération Internationale de Football Association (FIFA) by announcing the formation of Major League Soccer (MLS) and unveiling the league logo (Abnos, 2015). In 1994, shortly after the World Cup in the U.S., ESPN and ABC announced the first television rights deal for a new professional soccer league in the U.S. that had no players, coaches, or even a single team in place. This league was named Major League Soccer (MLS), and the first seven teams were placed in Boston, Columbus, Los Angeles, New Jersey, New York (Long Island), San Jose, and Washington D.C. The first regular season game was played in 1996 between D.C. United and the San Jose Clash with a crowd of almost 32,000 fans, and the league has been expanding rapidly ever since. A pivotal point in the history of the league occurred in 1999 when the Columbus Crew opened up the first soccer specific stadium for professional soccer in the U.S. Another major milestone occurred in 2006 when the Red Bull company purchased an existing MLS team and renamed the team the Red Bulls, thus creating the first corporate named team in major American professional sports (Sports Business Journal, 2015).

As the league has continued to grow, several teams have been added as well as soccer specific stadiums, and player salaries have increased dramatically. This includes the 2007 contract signed by David Beckham for approximately 6.5 million US dollars per year that is still the largest contract in the history of the league and prompted the league to enact the Designated Player Rule, also nicknamed the "Beckham Rule" (Sports Business Journal, 2015). While the 2013 salary cap for the MLS was 2.95 million US dollars, several teams exceeded this figure due to factors such as the single entity structure of the league. More specifically, unlike many other major professional sports leagues throughout the world, the MLS player contracts and the ownership of all teams is controlled by the league. Team owners in the MLS only own the rights to operate the franchise, but do have some rights to negotiate with players in terms of salary distribution. This includes the Designated Player salary, which will be discussed in more detail later in the chapter and has perhaps the most profound impact on the salary distribution of teams (Coates, Frick, & Jewell, 2014). While the single entity structure only allows team owners minimal rights to negotiate player salaries, this structure allows for significant freedom when it comes to marketing, sales, and service. One of the biggest aspects that the owners can control is the facility their team plays in, and there is a current push for more soccer-friendly stadiums for MLS teams.

Since 1999, the MLS has built 12 soccer-specific stadiums with several more already in the planning phase, and this is a key aspect to the development of the league because the league is still heavily reliant on ticket sales revenue and fans are looking for a unique in game experience. For instance, a recent national survey indicated that 54% of American football fans preferred attending MLS games over National Football League (NFL) games. The respondents cited the in-venue atmosphere and that camaraderie among fans at MLS games was superior to NFL games (King, 2014). This is interesting because the NFL has long been viewed as the most successful major professional sports league in the U.S., and these survey results potentially indicate that the MLS is becoming one of the most popular U.S. professional sports leagues primarily due to the one of a kind match day experiences for fans. Similar to the NFL and other major professional sports leagues in the U.S., the MLS is going above and beyond by offering top-level soccer in new venues and is focusing on creating new rivalries among MLS teams and capitalizing on existing city rivalries. Not surprisingly, many of the recently added or potential MLS teams are in NFL cities like Atlanta, Los Angeles, Minneapolis-St. Paul, and Miami (Davis, 2016). This chapter will further explore the successful marketing practices of the MLS while examining some of the distinct structural features of the MLS such as the Designated Player Rule and salary cap. The chapter includes interviews of MLS marketing executives and provides recommendations of sales and marketing tactics for soccer professionals and sport marketing students.

Attendance

The MLS finished the 2015 season with a 12.7% net positive gain in attendance, bringing the average attendance for an MLS game past 21,000 for the first time in the history of the league. This major milestone represents the first time the MLS has been able to rival the attendance figures for other major sports leagues in the U.S. like the National Basketball Association (NBA) or the National Hockey Association (NHL). It is also important to mention that one MLS team, the Seattle Sounders, is averaging over 44,000 fans per game, and this figure is similar to English Premier League (EPL) teams like Manchester City. The future of the MLS looks bright, and some league professionals believe that within the next few years average attendance at MLS games will surpass 20,000 fans per game (MLS, 2015; Thomas, 2014a). Table 3.1 further illustrates the continued importance of ticket sales and revenue for the continued success of the MLS.

The MLS primarily depends on gate or ticket sales as the main source of revenue, and while this dependence is expected to decrease from 31% of total revenue in 2008 to 28% of total revenue in 2018, it appears that ticket sales will remain the main source of revenue for years to come (Broughton, 2014). With that being said, the major area of growth for the MLS is television broadcast rights, and this revenue stream has increased significantly, with 32% more viewers on ESPN platforms in 2016 (Stephenson, 2016). Understanding the factors that drive attendance to MLS games is important due to the heavy dependence on ticket sales revenue by the league and the success of the league in growing attendance and increasing ticket sales. While the MLS may not be the same caliber of play as major European soccer leagues, the attendance and television viewership growth has been dynamic. Additionally, the combination of new media rights and newly built soccer specific stadiums has increased the average value of an MLS team to 157 million US dollars in 2015 (Barrabi, 2016). Consequently, there may be several sales and marketing strategies employed by the MLS that can be helpful for all soccer professionals.

Table 3.1 2015 MLS Attendance

Team	*Average Per Game (Change from 2014)*
Chicago Fire	16,003 (–0.5%)
Colorado Rapids	15,657 (+3.8%)
Columbus Crew	16,985 (+0.6%)
D.C. United	16,244 (–4.6%)
FC Dallas	16,013 (–4.7%)
Houston Dynamo	20,658 (+2.7%)
LA Galaxy	23,451 (+10.3%)
Montreal Impact	17,750 (+1.9%)
New England Revolution	19,627 (+17.7%)
New York City FC	29,016 (N/A)
New York Red Bulls	19,657 (+1.2%)
Orlando City	32,847 (N/A)
Philadelphia Union	17,451 (–1.0%)
Portland Timbers	21,142 (+1.6%)
Real Salt Lake	20,160 (–0.9%)
San Jose Earthquake	20,979 (+40.3%)
Seattle Sounders	44,247 (+1.2%)
Sporting KC	19,687 (–1.6%)
Toronto FC	23,451 (+6.2%)
Vancouver Whitecaps FC	20,507 (+0.5%)
League	21,574 (+12.7%)

Source: (MLS, 2015; Thomas, 2014a).

MLS expansion and growth

The MLS started with 10 initial teams in 1996, and by 2016, the league had doubled in size. There are now 20 teams, with additional expansion scheduled in the near future. Furthermore, there will be 24 teams by 2020. This tremendous growth in the number of MLS teams has paralleled the growth in attendance, television ratings, and franchise value. The newest MLS teams are Atlanta United FC, Los Angeles FC, Minnesota United FC, and Miami (name yet to be determined), and these teams are expected to be added between now and 2020. Sacramento and St. Louis are currently mentioned as the top candidate cities for an MLS team in the near future, with several other cities showing interest in hosting a team (Davis, 2016). To say the growth of the MLS has been prolific would be an understatement, and the MLS has experienced tremendous growth during the first 20 years of its existence. As noted in Table 3.2, the MLS is now the 7th largest soccer league in the world in terms of average attendance per game, and if attendance keeps increasing at the current pace, the MLS could be one of the top five soccer leagues in terms of attendance within the next few years (MLS, 2015). The following sections outline the three major reasons for the initial growth of the MLS over the past 20 years.

Table 3.2 Highest average attendance (by league)

Team	*Average Per Game (2015 Season)*
Bundesliga (GER)	43,177
Premier League (ENG)	36,487
La Liga (ESP)	28,773
Liga MX Apertura (MEX)	24,625
Serie A (ITA)	23,893
Chinese Super League (CHN)	22,580
Major League Soccer	21,574
Primera A Division 2014–2015 (ARG)	21,374
Ligue 1 (FRA)	20,904
2.Bundesliga (GER2)	19,147
Eredivisie (NED)	18,398
Série A (BRA)	17,300
Championship (ENG2)	17,118
J-League (JPN)	16,891
A-League 2014–15 (AUS)	12,513
Premier Liga (RUS)	12,459
Primeira Liga (POR)	12,005
Allsvenskan (SWE)	9,845
Premier League (SCO)	9,904
Super Lig (TUR)	9,206

Source: (MLS, 2015).

Issue one: Beckham Effect

In 2007, it was announced that the MLS was signing one of the most well-known international soccer players, and during this time David Beckham was signed by the LA Galaxy. This was the start of a significant growth period in the MLS, and this momentum has continued years after Beckham retired. For example, attendance grew by over 3,000 fans per game during the Beckham era, and teams also started to build soccer specific stadiums during this time period. Researchers have also noted that David Beckham generated more than twice his annual salary in unique ticket sales for the LA Galaxy and their opponents during the Beckham era. Beckham had such a profound impact on the MLS that the league has continued to grow faster than any other major sports league in the U.S., and the number of teams in the MLS has increased from 12 in 2007 to 20 in 2015 (Lamport-Stokes, 2015; Lawson, Sheehan, & Stephenson, 2008).

This profound effect that Beckham had on the MLS and U.S. soccer has been termed the "Beckham Effect," and as Beckham is scheduled to start a new MLS team in Miami in the near future (as a majority owner), fans interest and support continues to grow. Before Beckham the MLS was growing, but it was more of a slow growth, and the league was focused more on survival than aggressive expansion. During the Beckham era, fans attended games that he played in at a 55% higher rate than when he did not play, and the MLS saw its first fully sold out games, with nearly 30,000 fans in attendance. This prolific increase in attendance as well as the talk show appearances and the American pop culture icon status of David Beckham forever changed fan perceptions of the value of the MLS product, and the current aggressive expansion and growth is due at least in part to the "Beckham Effect" (Davis, 2016; Lamport-Stokes, 2015; Lawson, Sheehan, & Stephenson, 2008).

Issue two: foreign partnerships

While David Beckham, who formerly played for Manchester United, Real Madrid, and the LA Galaxy, was possibly the first major successful international partnership or venture for the MLS, this is an area where the MLS has been focusing much of their resources recently. The Beckham signing set the groundwork for the MLS to partner with international leagues and teams, since his signing demonstrated the league was serious about signing the best talent possible and improving the quality of play in future seasons. The MLS recently announced a partnership from 2015–2018 with Fox Sports Africa to broadcast live MLS games in Sub-Saharan Africa. This deal is a direct result of the significant growth in the number of key African MLS players, such as Didier Drogba from the Ivory Coast, and shows the commitment of the MLS to create additional foreign partnerships and increase international viewership (Davis, 2016; Lamport-Stokes, 2015; Lawson, Sheehan, & Stephenson, 2008; MLS Soccer Staff, 2015). In addition to the recent African broadcast partnership, the MLS has announced additional long term media partnerships to broadcast their games in Latin and South America, Africa, Asia, Europe, and the Middle East. The eventual goal is for the MLS to be broadcast around the world, and the MLS hopes to move beyond television partnerships in the near future and establish specific relationships with international soccer franchises such as Bayern Munich (Thomas, 2015).

Issue three: soccer-specific stadiums

As the MLS has continued to grow both domestically and internationally, there has been a demand to improve the quality of the product by making sure games are played in soccer-specific stadiums and players are paid more and more each year until the pay is similar to high-level European professional soccer. New soccer specific stadiums have been a key aspect of the MLS securing international television deals and demonstrating that the league offers a quality product. Since the Premier League has been broadcast on NBC Sports Network in the U.S., viewership of the eight MLS games broadcast on NBC has increased by 60%. It is important that discerning fans who are comparing and contrasting major European professional soccer with the MLS view the MLS as a viable alternative and a competitive league with quality facilities. Populous Sports, which is a major sport architecture firm that has been responsible for the design of several new, soccer specific MLS stadiums, has designed many of the MLS stadiums in the same manner as famous European soccer facilities such as Parc Olympique Lyonnais (Miller, 2016).

The Columbus Crew were the first MLS team to build a soccer specific stadium in 1999, and this was kind of an anomaly until 2010 when several other teams such as Los Angeles, Dallas, Chicago, etc. decided to build soccer specific stadiums. This first wave of new, soccer specific stadiums were designed to limit costs, and they did not have many high-tech features. As the MLS continued to grow and sign major television broadcast deals, the stadiums become more and more important, and teams like Portland and Kansas City recently built soccer specific stadiums with many of the same features of major European professional soccer teams (Newcomb, 2015).

Research has shown that the newly created soccer specific stadiums can have a significant effect on initial attendance, and this is known as the "Novelty or Honeymoon Effect." In addition to this initial attendance increase, some of the features of these new stadiums are necessary and expected to improve the fan experience. For instance, fans used to attending major sports events in the U.S. expect high-quality scoreboards with high-definition display and high quality audio. Also, fans expect a variety of food and craft beer options when attending professional sports events in the U.S., as this has become the norm. The newest MLS teams such as Minnesota United continue to add features to their facilities. The MLS plans to offer all of their games in high-tech, soccer-specific stadiums in the near future (Love, Kavazis, Morse, & Mayer, 2013; Newcomb, 2015). Overall, the MLS has experienced significant growth in everything from attendance to viewership and even the addition of new teams/soccer-specific stadiums, and the MLS is an excellent case study for sport marketers interested in learning about how a fairly new league has been able to grow and become competitive within a short period of time. The next section of this chapter further outlines the unique structure of the MLS, and the final section of this chapter includes interviews of MLS sales and marketing professionals so that readers may gain insight into how the MLS has effectively grown the league.

MLS salary cap rules

Issue one: league structure

The MLS is currently the only major professional sports league in the U.S. to operate under a single entity structure. This means the league has primary ownership of all teams and controls all player contracts. MLS team owners own the rights to the business operations of the team. In other words, the MLS owners primarily focus on marketing and sales because these are the aspects of the organization that they can directly oversee (Coates, Frick, & Jewell, 2014). Consequently, it is important to understand the league structure of the MLS because this is not only very unique in the landscape of major American professional sports, but it is also very different than the private ownership structure of most of the major European professional soccer leagues like the Bundesliga or the Premier League. The MLS is a closed league structure and does not have a promotion or relegation system similar to European professional soccer. The single-entity structure of the MLS also has a direct and major influence on player salaries through the use of a league mandated and controlled salary cap (Parrish, 2013).

In the context of U.S. sport, the MLS is unusual, and the single entity structure is more similar to the initial setup of the National League (which gave birth to the MLB) than any of the current major professional sports leagues. Free agency does not currently exist in the MLS, and while salaries have increased in recent years, there is not an open labor market, and technically all MLS players are employed by the same employer under this system. This system was challenged in the *Fraser vs. MLS* antitrust lawsuit in 1996, but the MLS ultimately prevailed in this case in 2002 and remains a single entity. During this case, eight MLS players sued the league, arguing that the single entity structure created a monopoly, and they wanted a free agency system. The MLS successfully argued that a free agency system would destroy the profitability of the league, and while the league has investors, the team owners are more like operators than majority owners we would see in major U.S. professional sports. The success of the MLS in this legal battle has helped the league to maintain its original structure, and the salary cap system for the MLS is significantly different than any other major professional sport in the U.S., as outlined in the next subsection (Arangue Jr., 2015).

Issue two: salary cap

Similar to most other major professional sports leagues in the U.S., the MLS operates under a salary cap structure. The salary cap structure of the MLS is considered to be similar to a "soft" cap system, similar to the NBA but significantly different than the NHL or the NFL. This means that while there is a salary cap in place for MLS teams set by the league, there are certain exceptions to the salary cap and ways that teams can pay players above and beyond the cap. Both the NHL and the NFL have what are considered "hard" salary caps, or caps with less exceptions and methods of paying players beyond the cap (Coates, Frick, & Jewell, 2014).

The MLS salary cap system is very different than the Union of European Football Associations (UEFA) Financial Fair Play rules, which are much more similar to the Major League Baseball (MLB) luxury tax regulations. The UEFA Financial Fair Play rules essentially penalize soccer clubs for falling below a salary floor or spending too much money on player wages and losing specified amounts of revenue over the course of a season (Thompson, 2015). The MLB luxury tax system does not have a salary floor and "taxes" or penalizes teams financially that spend beyond a specific threshold. The collected "taxes" are redistributed to smaller market teams that in theory can use the money to become more competitive in the future. However, this is rarely the case, and there is typically a major disparity in performance of MLB teams based on team spending (Coates, Frick, & Jewell, 2014). The MLS "soft" cap system is a combination of a salary cap with major exceptions such as the Designated Player rule and small luxury tax similar to MLB. This luxury tax in MLS is outlined in Table 3.3 below, and the next section of this chapter will further explain the Designated Player rule in the MLS.

Table 3.3 History of the Designated Player rule

Year	*Salary Cap*	*Cost of First DP*	*Cost of Second DP*	*Cost of Third DP*
2005	US$1.9 mill	N/A	N/A	N/A
2006	US$2.0 mill	N/A	N/A	N/A
2007	US$2.1 mill	US$400,000	US$325,000	N/A
2008	US$2.3 mill	US$400,000	US$325,000	N/A
2009	US$2.3 mill	US$415,000	US$335,000	N/A
2010	US$2.6 mill	US$335,000	US$335,000	US$335,000 + $250,000 tax
2011	US$2.7 mill	US$335,000	US$335,000	US$335,000 + $250,000 tax
2012	US$2.8 mill	US$350,000	US$350,000	US$350,000 + $250,000 tax
2013	US$2.9 mill	US$368,750	US$368,750	US$368,750 + $250,000 tax
2014	US$3.1 mill	US$387,500	US$387,500	US$387,500 + $250,000 tax
2015	US$3.5 mill	US$436,250	US$436,250	US$436,250 + $250,000 tax

Note: DP = designated player; mill = million; NA = not available.

Sources: (Coates, Frick, & Jewell, 2014; Mayers, 2014; Tannenwald, 2015).

Issue three: Designated Player rule

In 2007, the MLS instituted the Designated Player (DP) rule that allowed teams to sign one highly marketable player without having that player's salary count against the salary cap. The DP rule was initially enacted to allow the Los Angeles Galaxy to sign David Beckham, and subsequently the DP rule has often been informally referred to as the "Beckham Rule." While the DP or "Beckham" rule was originally designed to allow teams to sign one superstar player without going over the salary cap, the rule has been amended several times over the years, and currently teams may have up to three designated players (Parrish, 2013). The financial information related to the DP rule is outlined in Table 3.3, and a few studies have outlined the effectiveness of increasing MLS attendance with designated players (Lawson, Sheehan, & Stephenson, 2008; Parrish, 2013).

Scholars and practitioners have noticed that the Designated Player rule tends to favor large market teams with more financial resources. The DP rule is similar to NBA salary cap exceptions like the "Larry Bird Exception" that allow NBA teams the ability to sign a star veteran player to a higher salary than competing teams before the player becomes an unrestricted free agent. The DP rule favors larger-market teams with more financial resources because this is the one major area of player salaries that can be controlled by team owners. In other words, teams with wealthy owners or higher revenues can purchase the maximum designated players, while other teams that are not as successful financially or located in a smaller market with a smaller stadium may not be able to afford all three designated players. The DP rule is unique in U.S. professional sports and is important to understand because it significantly influences the marketability and success of teams. For instance, while David Beckham played for the Los Angeles Galaxy, the team accounted for 20% of all league revenue (Coates, Frick, & Jewell, 2014).

MLS strategic plan

The unique structure and ambitious expansion plans have significantly impacted the MLS strategic plan, and the main aspects of this plan are discussed below. First, the MLS has a strong focus on marketing to millennials. Currently, 65% of the MLS audience is between the age of 18 and 34, and the MLS plans to not only increase viewership among millennials, but to also target multicultural millennials. To date the MLS has been very successful in gaining younger viewers, and the seven major corporate sponsors of the MLS have seen significant increases in sales during the MLS season among younger customers. The MLS plans to improve online streaming and increase social media presence in order to continue to reach millennial fans, and they currently have the youngest average fan base of any major professional sports league in the U.S. (Heitner, 2015).

Second, the MLS plans to expand the number of teams, soccer specific stadiums, and broadcast markets significantly in the next 4 years. The expansion into new U.S. markets will open up additional domestic television markets and hopefully increase viewership. Additionally, the MLS has been focusing on international viewership by expanding into specific broadcast markets based on the origin of the key players in the league. Overall, digital viewership in the MLS has increased by triple digits the past few years. The MLS is one of the first leagues to fully embrace online streaming as a viable broadcast method, and more games have been available live online every season (Heitner, 2015).

Finally, the MLS is extremely focused on data acquisition and fan engagement, and this is evident by their recent partnership with SAS. The recent partnership with SAS has started with the LA Galaxy, and the plan is for all MLS teams to be using SAS Visual Analytics and SAS Visual Statistics in the near future to mine the data they collect from fans during the purchase process and market to them effectively and improve their fan experience. For instance, this software can help teams like the LA Galaxy pick which promotion to offer a specific fan to achieve the best possible chance for purchase or satisfaction. The teams will also be able to predict potential revenues per game and for the season very accurately with this software (SAS, 2015). Overall, the MLS is very innovative in its approach to sales and marketing. This is further investigated in the next section with interviews of MLS sales and marketing professionals.

MLS marketing executive interviews

The following section presents information from interviews of key MLS marketing and sales executives. This section is written from the perspective that the MLS is a very innovative league with tremendous growth in a short period of time and unique and successful sales and marketing strategies. Consequently, the following interviews were conducted from the point of view that European professional soccer offers fans the best product in terms of quality of play, and the MLS is an excellent case study of how to market and sell an emerging soccer product. Some of these strategies may be applicable to all soccer marketing and sales professionals and sport marketing students.

Interview one: Mike Ernst, senior vice president of ticket sales, service, marketing, and club operations for the Chicago Fire

What is your background?

I completed a Bachelor of Arts degree in Marketing and Communication from St. Ambrose University. Shortly after graduating college, I worked for a phone company in the collections department, and this is when I realized very quickly that this was not what I wanted to do for the rest of my life. So, I enrolled in graduate school at the University of Iowa and completed a Master of Arts degree in Sport Management. At this point in my life, I had heard that the best way to break into the sports industry was through the sales department, and I applied for a sales position with the Seattle SuperSonics NBA team. I was hired in an entry level inside sales account executive position with the Seattle SuperSonics, and I worked for the team for approximately 2.5 years. After the team moved to Oklahoma City I accepted a position with the Chicago Fire, and during the past 6 years, I have worked my way from inside sales to Vice President of Ticket Sales.

What are the major marketing and sales tactics used by the Chicago Fire and the MLS? How do these practices compare and contrast with European Soccer Leagues?

The three key market segments we target at the Chicago Fire include "Soccer Moms," Millennials, and Hispanic fans. Soccer Moms are the families who live in the Chicago suburbs. The Millennials are the younger soccer fans who grew up playing the game and often live in the city. The Hispanic fans are an interesting segment for Chicago because in a city of a little over 10 million people, the Hispanic demographic accounts for more than 1 million of these people. Marketing to "Soccer Moms" and Hispanic fans usually includes targeted zip code television advertisement buys and billboards. For Millennials, we purchase mass transportation advertisements on trains and buses, as well as Internet and social media advertising. The biggest challenge with the Hispanic demographic is that they usually follow another team from their home country or one of the major European clubs, and it is challenging to transition these fans from being fans of their favorite team abroad to fans of an MLS team. Consequently, we have realized that it makes the most sense to let fans know that they can follow the Chicago Fire and their team abroad. Overall, the MLS has to be more aggressive than top level European clubs in terms of marketing and sales. The number one goal of the MLS is to fill the stadium. This may be similar to teams that have been relegated or those that are a notch below the upper tier of European Soccer Clubs.

What are the most effective marketing and sales strategies used by the MLS and the Chicago Fire and why?

This depends on the criteria, but social media engagement is the most effective strategy used by the Chicago Fire. We have found that we get the best Return on Investment (ROI) with social media engagement and advertising. We use many Facebook ads and we are more aggressive with social media due to the younger demographics. The MLS believes strongly in mobile video content and pushes this out through social media and the match day app. Unique and engaging content is best.

How do you think some of the major marketing and sales practices used in the MLS could be applied to European soccer? In other words, what could European soccer clubs learn from MLS clubs in terms of marketing and sales?

The MLS uses a more aggressive sales push than European clubs. This includes using outside agencies like the Aspire Group. The MLS uses a very mature approach to selling tickets that involves extensive training and research. The MLS National Sales Training Center is the only operation of its kind in the U.S. and possibly the world. Future ticket sales account executives attend the National Sales Training Center, and after extensive training and subject to performance the graduates are employed by one of the MLS teams. The MLS has perhaps the most developed and aggressive sales tactics of American professional sports.

How do the MLS Designated Player, Draft, and Salary Cap Rules compare and contrast with the UEFA Financial Fair Play Regulations? Also, how do these practices influence business and marketing in the MLS?

There is less debt for US franchises and less errant spending due to a salary cap and lower player salaries. The MLS is the only major professional sports league in the U.S. that is not the top league in the world in terms of competition. The MLS draft does not have a significant impact because of the homegrown rule, and teams are getting more players from overseas.

How could European soccer clubs benchmark MLS teams, and in your opinion, which MLS franchises are the most successful in terms of sales and marketing and why?

New teams are most successful, Toronto, Seattle, due to being in a smaller marketplace and having less competition with other sports. The future success of the MLS depends on success in the bigger markets. All of the teams are very successful and I would recommend benchmarking the league itself rather than specific teams.

What are the major opportunities in terms of marketing and sales for the MLS and the Chicago Fire in the next 5 years?

The MLS is a huge growth market because of the large number of younger Americans playing soccer. Also, soccer is currently the sport of choice for younger Americans. It is only a matter of time before these potential buyers will have purchasing power. The success of the U.S. Men's and Women's National Soccer teams is also key to the future success of the MLS.

What are the current challenges for the MLS and the Chicago Fire in terms of marketing and sales?

How do you market a second-rate product? This is a challenge we face because soccer fans in the U.S. are becoming more knowledgeable about all of the soccer leagues. It is the only league that is not the top in the world in terms of player competition that is based in the U.S.

Interview two: Jeff Beryhill, director MLS National Sales Training Center

What is your background?

I went to the University of Minnesota and completed a Bachelor of Arts degree in Sociology and thought about teaching. My senior year I took a basketball class for one credit and I met someone from the NBA team the Minnesota Timberwolves. This person offered me an internship in basketball operations that was part of group sales for selling tickets to teams who could play at the Target Center. After that, I worked for the Minnesota Lynx Women's National Basketball Association (WNBA) team, and eventually got a job in inside sales with the Minnesota Timberwolves. I led the team in revenue production and ticket sales and eventually became group sales manager for the Timberwolves and the NFL Jacksonville Jaguars. I also briefly worked in minor league hockey in Mississippi and worked as Group Sales Manager for the MLS Chicago Fire. I have been the director of the MLS National Sales Training Center for 3.5 years.

What are the major marketing and sales tactics used by the MLS? How do these practices compare and contrast with European soccer leagues?

Every team is different, but the fans are much younger and more engaged than other major professional sports leagues in the U.S. The in-game experience is very interactive with chants and drums, and the "Supporter" sections are very young. The league embraces people being different. The major European soccer leagues sometimes feel they don't have to do sales and marketing due to the demand. However, European soccer leagues are realizing the importance of sales and service and can look to the MLS for a well-developed model. The MLS = best sales and marketing and the European = best players. Several outside leagues have used the MLS sales center training to improve their sales and service performance. For instance, we have worked with a Japanese soccer league.

What are the most effective marketing and sales strategies used by the MLS and why?

Digital sales is the most effective because conversion rates are higher than other leagues like MLB, NFL, but less likes or followers. The MLS is much more efficient than some of the other leagues because of the digital engagement of fans.

How do you think some of the major marketing and sales practices used in the MLS could be applied to European soccer? In other words, what could European soccer clubs learn from MLS clubs in terms of marketing and sales?

The MLS uses more targeting, and the MLS National Sales Training Center could possibly be recreated or emulated in another country with a significant amount of planning and work with the current training center. Data-driven sales techniques could be employed to better tailor sales and marketing.

How do the MLS Designated Player, Draft, and Salary Cap Rules compare and contrast with the UEFA Financial Fair Play Regulations? Also, how do these practices influence business and marketing in the MLS?

The MLS is unique in that there is a pretty unfair advantage in leagues like the EPL, but the MLS has significant parity. The MLS is single entity so owners only operate the club, they do not own them. High profile designated players can increase season ticket sales immediately. Stars can draw more on the road also, and Clint Dempsey is currently a big draw for the entire league.

How could European soccer clubs benchmark MLS teams, and in your opinion, which MLS franchises are the most successful in terms of sales and marketing, and why?

There is success across the board and attendance has increased for the past 5 years. Portland, Kansas City, and Seattle are selling out all of the games, and they are selling 35,000 season tickets.

What are the major opportunities in terms of marketing and sales for the MLS and the in the next 5 years?

The big focus right now is growth, and there is a new TV deal, and the biggest area of growth is TV viewership.

What are the current challenges for the MLS and in terms of marketing and sales?

Building relevance and finally having a generation of fans who have grown up with soccer. Every MLS team continues to build its fan base, and soccer is for the new generation.

Interview three: Jamie Ponce, director of ticket sales and service, New York Red Bulls

What is your background?

I attended John F Kennedy High School in Paterson, New Jersey, and competed in wrestling, baseball, and cross country. After high school, I attended Centenary College in Hackettstown, New Jersey, and completed a Bachelor of Science degree in Business Administration with a specialization in Sport Management. While in college, I competed in National Collegiate Athletic Association (NCAA) Division III wrestling and baseball.

Shortly after college, I was hired by the New Jersey Nets of the NBA and worked there from 2005 to 2011. I started working in the Inside Sales program and was promoted less than a year later to Account Executive. During my time as account executive I was the top ticket seller once and the second highest seller during the following season. After a few years as an account executive, I was promoted to a Premium Seating Executive, focusing on the team move from New Jersey to New York City and to help drive season ticket interest in Brooklyn. In my 5th year with the Nets, I was promoted to Inside Sales Manager, which allowed me to help grow the next sales talent for the organization, and grew the department revenue by over 200% from the prior year. In my last position at the Nets, I was the Assistant Director of Ticket Sales and was one of the first team members located in Brooklyn when the team moved from New Jersey to New York City. During this experience, I was leading a small staff to drive season ticket sales for the newly constructed Barclays Center grand opening.

Currently, I am the Director of Ticket Sales and Service for the New York Red Bulls and have been overseeing our strategy from a sales and service perspective. I have also been involved in our ticket operations to help find new ways to enhance the customer experience with speed of entry and looking for new ways to help make all our systems work together and attain all the information we can to gather detailed data and truly enhance the fan experience.

What are the major marketing and sales tactics used by the New York Red Bulls and the MLS? How do these practices compare and contrast with European soccer leagues?

From a marketing perspective, many of our efforts revolve around digital campaigns and re-marketing in the digital space. We have a ton of grassroots events, such as viewing parties at local pubs and youth soccer festivals in key areas, to help grow our club. These events help to show our involvement in the community. From a sales perspective, we look to have synergy with our training academy as they are involved in many areas with people who have an interest in playing and watching soccer. This helps us provide a way to send an offer to an upcoming match as well potentially gain new season ticket holders.

What are the most effective marketing and sales strategies used by the MLS and the New York Red Bulls, and why?

Our digital campaigns for the club have been the most effective because it is the one way that we can actually track our spending and provide real-time feedback as to how the campaign is doing. With this type of feedback, we are able to tweak what is said on the banner, try different players or action shots and really see which is capturing the most attention and driving someone to go on our website and purchase a ticket.

How do you think some of the major marketing and sales practices used in the MLS could be applied to European soccer? In other words, what could European soccer clubs learn from MLS clubs in terms of marketing and sales?

In many of the European clubs, sales is not approached in the same way, where we are looking to fill the building and gain new fans, while European clubs are looking to grow their reach and gain more dollars from large corporate sponsors. In other words, most European clubs don't have many seats to sell and need to seek revenue from sources other than tickets. European clubs that do have available inventory handle the outbound sales approach differently and seem to focus less on service and retention than MLS clubs. Improving the customer experience and overall engagement of fans is currently very important in the MLS and is gaining importance in European soccer. A few of the leaders of European clubs are being hired from several major U.S. sports because of their experiences in fan retention and service.

How do the MLS Designated Player, Draft, and Salary Cap rules compare and contrast with the UEFA Financial Fair Play Regulations? Also, how do these practices influence business and marketing in the MLS?

I am not too involved in this portion of the business so I am not sure about the differences.

How could European soccer clubs benchmark MLS teams, and in your opinion, which MLS franchises are the most successful in terms of sales and marketing and why?

Of course I would have to say we would be a club that European teams should use as a benchmark. Despite the amount of sports options in the New York City marketplace, including a new MLS team (New York City FC), the Red Bulls have still been able to show growth in all categories including season tickets, sponsorships, and training academy revenues. Powered by a strong leadership team, we look to stay at the forefront of new technologies and software such as mobile ticketing, cashless/ticketless card systems, and RFID scanners to speed up entry.

What are the major opportunities in terms of marketing and sales for the MLS and the New York Red Bulls in the next 5 years?

One of the major opportunities from our club perspective is the advancement of mobile technology, such as having a team specific app and a source for fans to have a "one stop shop" to check in on the club, manage their seats, and interact with our rewards portal all in the same space.

What are the current challenges for the MLS and the New York Red Bulls in terms of marketing and sales?

The current challenges are with the New York City market, which has several sports and entertainment option. Our funds at times can be limited, and it is tough to break through the crowded space and spend at the same levels that a couple of the other MLS teams are able to accomplish. In a sense we have to do a significant amount with a little, so each event we put on has to be special and has to make an impact with our fans.

MLS unique marketing and sales strategies: National Sales Training Center

The MLS National Sales Training Center opened in Blaine, Minnesota, in 2010, and the first cohort had 175 applicants for approximately 20 available positions. The sales training center is the only league operated sales training facility in major professional U.S. sports. Since the inception of the center, potential sales executives have made over 1 million sales calls, and over 150 graduates of the sales training center programs have been placed with MLS teams. Two sales coaches are based at the sales training center, and students live on the campus during their training period and make sales calls for several MLS teams. Students learn about the sales process the MLS way, and there is a specific curriculum that is used to teach them. The call center helps drive sales for MLS clubs and provides the students with one of a kind sales training that can help prepare them for a future career in sales with an MLS team (Thomas, 2014b). The MLS National Sales Training Center is perhaps the most successful sales training program in professional sports, and it provides a potential model for other soccer leagues to use for training their sales staff.

Lessons for soccer marketing and sales professionals

This section outlines a few potential lessons for current or future European Soccer Professionals.

- Highly targeted marketing and sales can be very effective. MLS teams and the league seem to have excellent knowledge of their fans.
- While television broadcast rights are very important in terms of revenue, the in-game experience is also important, and this is very evident in the MLS.
- The unique single entity structure, DP rule, salary cap, and luxury tax in the MLS allow the teams in the league to remain more competitive than their European counterparts. It is also important to note that most of the MLS teams are profitable due to this unique structure.
- Sales and service training are very important, and the MLS invests significant resources in developing future sales employees. The MLS National Sales Training Center is a very effective sport sales education initiative, and perhaps this program could be adopted in Europe.
- Overall, the MLS is very focused on sales and service, and the importance of sales and service for European soccer leagues may continue to increase as fans become more discerning and are interested in more than just the quality of competition. In other words, the MLS is very good at providing an excellent in game experience, and this is something that could be examined and implemented by European professional soccer clubs.
- Engaging fans is very important in the MLS, and the MLS uses technology to engage fans and improve service. This includes creating team apps, mobile ticketing, and interactive mobile rewards and discounts.

Bibliography

Abnos, A. (2015). The birth of a league. *Sports Illustrated Online*. Retrieved from http://www.si.com/longform/2015/mls/

Arangue, Jr., J. (2015, March 3). 'It is simply a cartel': The story behind MLS winning the labor wars against players. *Vice Sports Online*. Retrieved from https://sports.vice.com/en_us/article/it-is-simply-a-cartel-the-story-behind-mls-winning-the-labor-wars-against-players

Barrabi, T. (2016, June 2). Is major league soccer scoring with fans? *Fox Business*. Retrieved from http://www.foxbusiness.com/features/2016/06/02/is-major-league-soccer-scoring-with-fans.html

Broughton, D. (2014, October 6). Forecast: Big growth ahead. *Sports Business Journal*, 1.

Coates, D., Frick, B., & Jewell, T. (2014). Superstar salaries and soccer success: The impact of designated players in Major League Soccer. *Journal of Sports Economics*, 1–20.

Davis, J. (2016). Rivalries are central to major league soccer's expansion plans. *ESPN FC*. Retrieved from http://www.espnfc.us/major-league-soccer/19/blog/post/2874585/rivalries-key-to-major-league-soccer-expansion-plans

Heitner, D. (2015, December 22). How major league soccer is closing the gap with the big four. *Forbes Sports Money*. Retrieved from http://www.forbes.com/sites/darrenheitner/2015/12/22/how-major-league-soccer-is-closing-the-gap-with-the-big-four/#214e906b7b39

King, B. (2014, June 2). Soccer's growing reach. *Sports Business Journal*, 1–8.

Lamport-Stokes, M. (2015, March 5). Beckham effect "pretty significant" on MLS. *Reuters*. Retrieved from http://www.reuters.com/article/us-soccer-mls-beckham-idUSKBN0M12KC20150305

Lawson, R. A., Sheehan, K., & Stephenson, E. F. (2008). Vend it like Beckham: David Beckham's effect on MLS ticket sales. *International Journal of Sport Finance*, 3(4), 189–195.

Love, A., Kavazis, A., Morse, A. L., & Mayer, K. C. (2013). Soccer-specific stadiums and attendance in major league soccer: Investigating the novelty effect. *Journal of Applied Sports Management*, 5(2), 32–46.

Mayers, J. (2014, March 7). Looking at changes to the MLS roster and competition rules for 2014. *Seattle Sounders FC Blog Seattle Times*. Retrieved from http://blogs.seattletimes.com/soundersfc/2014/03/07/looking-at-changes-to-the-mls-roster-and-competition-rules-for-2014/

Miller, B. (2016). The driving force behind MLS stadium design. *Populus*. Retrieved from http://populous.com/posts/driving-force-behind-mls-stadium-design/

MLS (2015). MLS sets new attendance records, Seattle hold highest average in league. Retrieved from http://www.mlssoccer.com/post/2015/10/26/mls-sets-new-attendance-records-seattle-hold-highest-average-league

MLS Soccer Staff (2015). MLS, FOX sports Africa announce partnership to broadcast MLS in Sub-Saharan Africa. Retrieved from http://www.mlssoccer.com/post/2015/11/18/mls-fox-sports-africa-announce-partnership-broadcast-mls-sub-saharan-africa

Newcomb, T. (2015, September 4). Defining characteristics for new wave of MLS soccer-specific stadiums. *Sports Illustrated Online*. Retrieved from http://www.si.com/planet-futbol/2015/11/05/soccer-specific-stadium-mls-orlando-dc-united-minnesota-miami

Parrish, C. (2013). Soccer specific stadiums and designated players: Exploring the Major League Soccer attendance assumption. *International Journal of Sport Management Recreation & Tourism*, 12, 57–70.

SAS (2015, March 9). NHL's LA Kings and MLS' LA Galaxy shoot to score with fans using SAS® Analytics. Retrieved from http://www.sas.com/en_za/news/press-releases/2016/march/customer-intelligence-sports.html

Sports Business Journal. (2015, March 2). Timeline: Two decades of MLS. Retrieved from http://www.sportsbusinessdaily.com/Journal/Issues/2015/03/02/In-Depth/Timeline.aspx

Stephenson, C. (2016, July 27). TV ratings for MLS are up from last year on all ESPN platforms. *MLS*. Retrieved from http://www.mlssoccer.com/post/2016/07/27/tv-ratings-mls-are-last-year-all-espn-platforms

Tannenwald, J. (2015, May 1). MLS announces 2015 roster rules, finally. *The Goalkeeper Blog Online Philadelphia Inquirer*. Retrieved from http://www.philly.com/philly/blogs/thegoalkeeper/MLS-announces-2015-roster-rules-finally.html

Thomas, I. (2014a, November 3). MLS average attendance pushes past 19,000. *Sports Business Journal*, 31–32.

Thomas, I. (2014b, November 24). Bryant Pfeiffer, MLS national sales center. *Sports Business Journal*, 3–4.

Thomas, I. (2015, March 30). MLS makes headway with international deals. *Sports Business Daily*, 4.

Thompson, E. (2015). Financial fair play explained. Retrieved from http://www.financialfairplay.co.uk/financial-fair-play-explained.php

4

FIFTEEN YEARS OF SPORT MARKETING REVISITED

Interview with the "great witness" Christophe Bouchet, former president of Olympic Marseille, former CEO of Sportfive and director of Infront in France

Interview conducted by Michel Desbordes and Nicolas Chanavat on April 1, 2015

Michel Desbordes and Nicolas Chanavat (MD & NC): Good Morning, Christophe Bouchet! We are pleased to meet you to talk about the evolution of the agencies and your view of 15 years of sports marketing.

Christophe Bouchet (CB): The mission that you assign me here is singular: to evoke the agencies' job. It is singular because when I was president of the OM, I concluded without much elegance, it must be said, our contract with the agency that was working for the club, considering its inadequate work. A few years later, while I was running Sportfive, I spent most of my time convincing the leaders of the benefits of a sports agency in managing their club or their institution. We can therefore speak of a sharp turnaround. Of a contradiction? We shall see.

MD & NC: What is an "agency" for you?

CB: Before we dig deeper into the subject, it is important to quickly throw around some definitions to understand properly. What are we talking about? In the business of football, we are sometimes talking about agency *or* marketing agency *when a third company markets products on behalf of a club, league or federation. To define the marketing agency, we should also define the term* sports marketing, *which is a little unsuitable. If you want to keep the anglicism* marketing, *first note that it is "marketing of sport". Like the sports journalists who are primarily sports journalists. And, believe me, they are rarely athletic. This marketing is the marketing of various entities participating in sports: athletes, events, championships, clubs, federations or confederations. Here we seek to promote these various actors through their reputation or values that they carry to the greatest number, the audience that you want to touch deep down, the passion for sports.*

MD & NC: We often say "go through an agency". What does this mean for you?

CB: The expression "going through an agency" means that we do not sell in-house, with its own teams, some products that can be very varied, panels at the stadium, location on the shirts, luxury boxes, hospitality areas, naming the stadium or room, etc. In sport, not only in football or rugby, but in all the ball sports in general, the marketing agency is not an advertising agency (although it operates in part on the same basis), and it does not work (or works little) in the merchandising field, or in ticket sales, two areas somewhat neglected in France.

However, some time ago, the agency *was marketing TV rights of clubs (the European Cups) for the league (international) and for the French Football Federation (FFF). Under the combined pressure of the Union of European Football Associations (UEFA) on the one hand and the broadcasters on the other, the intermediary business has almost disappeared in France and is no longer the majority in Europe. It remains more prevalent on other continents (Africa, Latin America or Asia). The clubs, leagues, federation or confederation (the "*beneficiaries*") claim to have "sold" or "outsourced" their rights, and the agency says "they have the rights".*

MD & NC: Is sports marketing special in football? Is there any hindrance from the fans?

CB: In the football industry, the most restive and the most paradoxical supporters can also designate this activity by the well-known term, although often controversial, of "football business". These are usually the same people who demand the best players, or massive injections of tens of millions of euros in the service of their logo, "pure" money that would fall from the sky, but not through the marketing of a team or A brand. The paradox in this field reached its peak when the Marseille fans, frustrated by the lack of results of their team, commanded to Robert Louis-Dreyfus from the highest courts: "Give some money back." Emphasizing also that if they are fussy about the over-commercialization of their club, they are less fussy about the origin of the funds invested by shareholders. The supporter that doubts commercialization often criticizes the remuneration of sports but condones the methods their generous patrons have used to amass fortunes before injecting a part in their passion. Although it is not the topic of this book, there would surely be a lot to write about on the origin of the funds invested. We also note that the same fans were formerly quite morally flexible on the display of means used to gain a victory.

MD & NC: What allows this marketing to generate money?

CB: Marketing is the optimal way to monetize the results of a club, its popularity or the values that it carries. Marketing therefore seeks to extract from its club values adapted to get the maximum revenue. Having been at the head of marketing of the three biggest clubs, OL, OM and PSG, I can say that everyone here, through an agency or not, has a very different strategy. We do not sell the OM like the OL. The Marseillais sell the irrational: a passion, a legend, a merger with its city, a popularity. The Lyonnais are based on a rational approach, a method, an efficiency and a training. The Parisians, finally, sell the result and a brand, Paris, which gives them the advantage of wider opportunities internationally. Professionals must therefore approach the brands adapted to their socio-style. We sell more OM and PSG to sponsors in search of reputation, we sell more OL for its association with efficiency. Beyond these generalities, sellers can obviously somewhat vary their arguments for different products (panels, business seats, lodge, jersey, etc.) and geographic segmentation. From this point of view, French clubs greatly lag behind their English and Spanish competitors that have mastered the art of selling the same product in different territories and thus are able to leverage brands and incomes depending on their location. With its new reputation, PSG now has territorial exclusivities.

MD & NC: But ultimately, what really is sports marketing in football?

CB: If you stay in football, there is a final component in "sports marketing" which is rarely discussed: the overall improvement of the product, its better image, its greater penetration. Milk industries know that improving the image of their product will make a splash in any industrial sector. French football executives have an historical problem to improve their fundamentals. The increase in income would however be much greater if they attempted to improve collectively rather than individually, with the exception of a massive influx of funds (PSG). The English and the Germans have perfectly applied this strategy through collective proactive policy, with an explosion of their income over the past decade as the result. The English chose to exorcise all their demons, and they created a common entity, the "Premier League"; the Germans learned from their sporting setbacks in the late 1990s.

MD & NC: It is conventional to speak fairly of "errors" in France, the famous "French bashing" . . . Do you think that this make senses in the marketing of football?

CB: I just want to give an illustration of the strategic mistakes made in France from this point of view. The example dates back to about 10 years ago, but in terms of sports marketing, we are in an activity of long, even very long cycles. In the early 2000s, the LFP decided, like every 3 or 4 years, to put into play the TV rights. To scrape up a few million euros, guided in its choice by the marketing committee (which I was on), the LFP chose to mess with the famous Téléfoot *broadcast, which was a staple of the Sunday programing on basic television station, in a time slot which was a real milestone for the sympathizers of the historic landmark. For a bargain price, the show went on France Télévision, who ultimately "killed" the show. The supporters, not necessarily those who are willing to watch a game in full or to go to the stadium, lost their only interaction. This issue, however, was decisive in the phenomenon of monopolization and the identification of brands. We can say here with certainty that the disappearance did not help paid television and that it left many people feeling abandoned.*

The Germans, in marketing their TV rights, have understood. They never touched the equivalent broadcasting on a basic television station which airs on Saturday afternoon. Certainly, they sold far cheaper TV rights, but by promoting their product, they dramatically developed the appetite of the Germans for their football. Revenues from "marketing" of German football clubs, for ticketing and marketing spaces (including naming stadiums), are now incomparable to that of the French clubs. However, this example alone does not fully explain the difference in income between the two countries, but it helps to understand it better.

The leaders of football, instead of bickering constantly, of fighting vain ego battles for their clubs, should, once and for all, lay down the foundation for a clear 10-year strategy, which would also be a good definition of the term sports marketing.

MD & NC: Can you go back to the genesis of the agency business in France? When did it start?

CB: In France, the agency business has long been embodied by one man: Jean-Claude Darmon, who was named "the great financier of French football" by Thierry Roland. The Marseillais had begun his career in Nantes by selling advertising banners, then extended his scope to other products, to other clubs in the football league, the FFF, the Confederation of African Football (CAF), to build an empire. Indeed, at the time, we did not speak of agency. We were "in Darmon" or not. Said Darmon, after various takeovers and consolidations in the industry, became Sportfive. The latter, now property of the Lagardère Group, remains the largest agency in France, although in serious decline. Cunning and hardworking, going to bed early and getting up at dawn, Jean-Claude Darmon inspired, without other alternatives, admiration, fear or repulsion. He fashioned this activity to its greatest advantage and then to that of certain shareholders of Sportfive. But he also applied a methodology largely explaining the decline of this business in France, which will never recover its enormous profitability. In this way, Jean-Claude Darmon was the origin of a true movement of rights outsourcing. A stream that was reversed with a wave of re-internalization of rights, powerful and durable. The sales marketing agency is also very far from the revenue it generated 10 years ago, and there is a safe bet that it will not return to its levels of revenue or profitability.

MD & NC: How had this dual antagonist movement been possible?

CB: In the midst of discovering the value of football in sponsoring and, later, the one of TV rights, Darmon accummulated good profit for his clients. He brought money to clubs that had low-income sources (far from current revenues) and that had never expected to generate income from advertising. He profited largely from taking important commissions. No one complained about this new resource and nobody reproached him about his margins. In this game, J.C. Darmon has collected a lot of money in a world that did not yet know the financial windfall of TV rights.

MD & NC: It is sometimes said that Darmon introduced "banking services" in the system.

CB: The club leaders then became his debtors. This balance of forces was of great use to him from when TV rights took off in the mid-1980s to the time when Canal + began to offer money to the league in exchange for the broadcasting of its meetings. Well placed in the bodies, a friend of Jean Sadoul, president of the LNF until his death in 1991, he was able to emerge as the essential intermediary. When the TV rights quickly exploded, the commissions collected amounted to significant sums. Especially as Darmon quickly realized that the life of the party would now be the owners of TV channels. He learned quickly to pamper Patrick Le Lay (TF1) and Pierre Lescure (Canal +), to whom he refused nothing.

Darmon quickly became a financial alternative for clubs (or even the FFF) down funding. He knew that to intervene was to help at the right moment. He never forgot his goals, negotiating counterparties with customers at bay. He also improved the profitability of its contracts in terms of percentage and duration. Clubs thus found themselves "locked" by contracts extending over decades, especially in the case of descent in Ligue 2.

MD & NC: Did the management style and management of JCD not reach its limits at some point?

CB: Jean-Claude Darmon excelled in sales. But at the heart of this never-ending whirlwind, he did not really care (or very little) for the image, sport, football, club or the real interest of sponsor. In his defense, the French leaders are not as busy as him. Thus, nobody in the agency really thought about the quality of the product or about its behavior in time, let alone a long-term strategy to improve the product.

MD & NC: Which excesses?

CB: The jerseys of French clubs have become [decorated like] Christmas trees, brands have succeeded each other without strategic vision. However, the necessary condition for the recognition of a sponsor is the long association between the brand and the team. The agency is not providing a strategic added value; the foundations of a decline were laid.

MD & NC: Why is the case of Sportfive emblematic of a growth that will eventually lead to an inevitable decline?

CB: The agency business is inseparable in France, and with the Sportfive case in Europe, the story of a breakup begins. Sportfive is an excellent "business case" for all business schools, strategy option or merger/acquisition. Around 2005, after choosing not to buy Canal +, Arnaud Lagardère had a strong idea: there is no point investing in the pipes; it must opt for the contents. To transform this sensible idea, Lagardère Group chooses to bring himself to the audiovisual production companies and then, later, to the shows. As for sports, the group created a fourth branch, Lagardère Sports (which became Lagardère Unlimited). One of the first decisions of this emerging entity is to acquire Sportfive, owned by the Advent fund. The company, which then released 65 million euros of EBITDA, is the object of a lively battle. Lagardère finally gets through and despite the lowest financial offer (865 million euros), the group purchases the company at the expense of the Russian Blavatnik (associated with Robert Louis-Dreyfus) who proposed 905 million euros. Even the lowest, the French offer is still considerable. Indeed, it represents more than 13 times the results, but mostly heavy clouds are accumulating on the horizon. Much of Sportfive profits take on two high-performance products: the marketing of TV rights of the clubs in the UEFA Cup and those of the national federations in the qualifying matches for the Euro and the World Cup. With regards to the clubs, the UEFA decided at the time – and has already announced – that it would internalize its rights. With regard to the federations, rumors also suggest that the UEFA is considering grouping to sell itself. Another great source of profit is the French Federation of football. The French branch released over 10 million euros EBITDA, much of which comes from a very favorable contract with the FFF. The latter, whose economic affairs are directed by Christmas Graët, is furious. Even before the takeover, Arnaud Lagardère got involved with Noel Graët to renegotiate the contract, for a lower price of course. In return, Christmas Graët will make a public statement suggesting that if Sportfive comes under a foreign flag, it could completely break its contract. Still in France, the contracts with the major clubs, OL and PSG, come to an end. Finally, Sportfive is not a unified society, the French branch (former Darmon) does not speak to the German branch (former UFA Sports) and each has its own services. Restructuring costs can prove to be expensive, especially as the Geneva office (which manages the rights of Euro 2008) has also taken a lot of independence.

In short, the price offered by Lagardère seems very high for the acquisition of Sportfive, and those who pushed the French group into this acquisition obviously had substantial interest (fees and other success fees or employees of the group who saw themselves properly direct the case).

Simultaneously, the management of Lagardère Sports, and thus the acquisition, is entrusted to a trio inexperienced in business life and unknown to the world of sports. To prepare for the future, we must reinvest heavily in the French and German clubs. Sportfive also invests heavily (75 million euros) in the naming of the future stadium Juventus of Turin or in a new motorsport (Transoriental). It offers very substantial minimum guarantees to the IOC without reaching the goals. S5 invests heavily, probably between 350 and 500 million euros.

MD & NC: What conclusions can we draw from this "business case" in 2015?

CB: Ten years later, the UEFA has dried up, as planned, the sources of the UEFA Cup and the qualifying matches of the federations. The UEFA decided to not renew the contract with S5 for the rights of the Euro and S5 has never gotten the naming rights for the Juventus either. It has not managed to find agreement with the FFF, which resumed its independence, and the waltz of the leaders proved very costly. Only the African branch, detached from France, continues to make good profits thanks to a contract signed with CAF and a marketing fee of around 35%. However, the balance sheet is very heavy: the Lagardère group consumed over a billion euros of cash for a company struggling for several years just to break even, and whose market value is now very low. In addition, another thing to remember, can a listed company hold such rights as an intermediation company? Indeed, a listed company is obliged to publish much of its results and contracts, while this agency business demands an absolute secrecy about the mechanics of contracts. Despite this disappointment, the Lagardère group has decided to continue its adventure in the sport, even if Arnaud Lagardère announced in March 2015 a change in strategy, moving rights to target the management of athletes.

MD: Sportfive yet seemed "untouchable" with no real competitor.

CB: Yes, the situation seemed good. Darmon had to face an opponent at some point in time. To compete, the agency Havas tried its luck in the mid-1990s with an interesting idea. Taking the subject from the other end: that of the sponsors. Since it mastered the advertising budget of brands, it was able to advise a possible investment in sport and in developing of new budgets. The advertising group therefore created "Havas Sports", which found there was also a good way to make commissions on both sides, the brand that it advised being on one side, the copyright on the other. A superb martingale. Havas Sports (HAS) then took exclusive mandates with some clubs. The promise was attractive, and the company could quickly move up the ranks, constituting itself a quality portfolio among French clubs (Saint-Étienne, Marseille, Toulouse) and even abroad (Roma).

MD & NC: How did Havas start to expand its customer base? With what speech?

CB: The selling point was easy to decline, "We are Havas, we will bring you what nobody else can bring you." HAS was able to evoke its different expertise and once again its global network. In short, it smelled of expertise and money.

MD & NC: With what results?

CB: HAS took for itself all the beautiful market share especially as some prestigious clubs tasted some of the practices of Darmon. Bernard Tapie, the most powerful leader of football between 1986 and 1993, held Darmon for a vulture and Damon felt the same about Tapie. In between the two, the atmosphere was electric, even a little more. . . . So that, for example, the Marseillais Darmon could never have the OM contract.

Havas Sports could get in the game so easily. Only its double hat was quickly fatal to the whole. The balancing act which was to advise brands on one side and the other clubs quickly found some limitations, especially as the two entities, the ad agency on the one hand, and the marketing agency on the other, had the same name of the removed Charles Havas, founder of a press agency.

MD & NC: That's interesting. Could you illustrate this with a few examples?

CB: Judge for yourself: it was difficult for Havas to advise Peugeot to associate its golf or rugby brand, while at the same time Havas was not able to find a car sponsor for its football clubs. Worse, the very name of Havas became inconvenient for certain steps: to reach Renault, it had to go by its main rival, Publicis. Another example: Havas advised Carrefour not to touch pro-football, but encouraged its client to contract with the FFF, which was managed by . . . Jean-Claude Darmon. Imagine the head of the club leaders under contract with the HAS. The model did not survive. Havas Sports retains its primary role of providing expertise in sports-related brands and developing itself worldwide.

MD & NC: What is the major underlying problem of these agencies?

CB: The most fundamental problem of Darmon (Sportfive) and Havas Sports was, for many years, not bringing a real marketing expertise. Again, to their credit, the owners of clubs and federations, more concerned with the little scratches on their center forward, never had a good vision on the matter asserted. Monopolized by their daily sports scores, concerned about the ticket sales because it is also acts as a political instrument, club presidents had little interest in this area and often did not look past the financial line. The agencies have not fulfilled their promise of expertise, centralization of knowledge, new product offerings, market knowledge. They have often been lacking imagination. But then, for this game, the leaders were tempted to pay the vendors themselves. They did it because the agencies have trained many of them, but also because many trainings have emerged, flooding the market with young people who are often intelligent, structured and delighted to get a place in the flashy world of football. How can one not mention Limoges that sent its students on a mission, which now occupy interesting positions? Many business schools followed, naturally offering a very large pool. The shareholders have thus preferred to re-internalize their rights. This movement has meant above all a saving of paid commission, therefore a tangible result from the first year, but rarely an improvement of trade policy. They asked their teams to immediately bring money, not to build long-term plans, for the simple reason that the club itself rarely has a strategic plan.

It is now unlikely that the motion be reversed again. At issue are the employees of clubs, often well paid, walking in the shadow of Darmon, dependence, etc.

MD & NC: Are there any other models more original or "hybrid" that have developed in recent years?

CB: The UEFA has played, over the past decade, a decisive and pervasive role in the market for marketing agencies. For many years, three European agencies (S5, Kentaro and Infront) have made significant profits with the national federations. They held the rights of these federations for qualifiers for the Euro and the World Cup. For their part, the UEFA and FIFA marketed the rights of their final phases, while sometimes helping agencies (Euro 2008/Sportfive). Under the leadership of Michel Platini, the UEFA decided to capture this market by offering the federations to buy their rights to form a package and resell those rights in blocks to European and world televisions. Behind this homogeneity, there was also the real intention of limiting the gain of the agencies whose income irritated the president of the institution of European football. Only friendly matches remained with the agencies, but the UEFA bought them too. To compensate for this loss of friendly matches, the UEFA decided to organize the European Championship every 4 years, alternating with the Euro. The market of intermediation of federation meetings has completely disappeared. But the amazing thing is that once the UEFA grouped all its rights, it launched a tender to agencies. All classic agencies were rejected in favor of a new competitor, CAA Eleven, a vehicle created for the occasion: an association between the American CAA and two former Lagardère Sports, which had lost the rights but with Lagardère recuperated them in the CAA Eleven. This structure thus has a market share with a rule that is a little bit restrictive: CAA Eleven must work exclusively with its beneficiary. The UEFA has based this model on the exclusive relationship maintained with Team Marketing. This agency is fully dedicated to the commercialization of the Champions League and the Europa League. Team Marketing and CAA Eleven are thus, in two different ways, models of a hybrid agency, admittedly agency, but only one copyright holder.

MD & NC: And how did Sportfive react to all this?

CB: During the recovery by Lagardère, to counter this rather abrupt movement, Sportfive has banked its offer. According to a model that IMG and Sportfive had experimented with in Germany, S5 promised to buy the rights of the clubs or of the federation on a long-term basis (10 years) by paying a signing fee almost equal to 5% of turnover, business projected over the period. This constituted a substantial check for 11 million euros to Lens for example, and up to 28 million euros for the OL. Always in search of cash because of their structural inability to borrow, some clubs have plunged. The strategy of S5 was clear: buy the rights of the seven or eight most popular clubs and mesh the territory to create a national football product having more value. This implementation failed because OM and S5 could not find an agreement, and the Qataris, though shareholders of Lagardère Group, broke ties with S5.

With the clubs taking up their rights, the LFP and FFF also, agencies have lost much of their income from football in France. They have not managed to conquer rugby, which nevertheless generates substantial marketing income. Rugby in its forced march professionalism benefited from the experience of football, and all major clubs have preferred to proceed internally. The agencies are now working with the leagues and federations of indoor sports, but revenues are in no way comparable.

MD & NC: Are there still more models in the market of sports marketing of football that are now at maturity?

CB: Infront, which opened an office in France 3 years ago, has chosen another model. Instead of negotiating exclusive contracts with the "beneficiaries", the company signed a series of non-exclusive mandates with numerous beneficiaries of the market, providing opportunities piece by piece. This method is much less capital consuming, but is also less profitable since the agency cannot pay all the cash flows. It has the advantage of pacifying the relations between the parties, since one feels prisoner of the other. Infront or S5 can also provide a range of paid services in marketing assistance and consulting. In addition to its exclusive governance model, Sportfive has followed the lead of its rival with a non-exclusive offer of the same nature. This is not without problems for S5 clubs. The agency first attempts to market what it does not have in store rather than to serve customers bound by a contract from which they cannot get out of. Sport and CO, founded by Eric Conrad (ex-Havas Sports), has contracts that are entirely based on the S5 model (Bastia, Nimes, Tours), paid by a commission, but it also has more hybrid forms of fees including marketing aid and commissions for activities made in different territories (Evian, Lorient, Nancy). However, total income of the agencies fell sharply.

MD & NC: Is Infront really a new player on the market?

CB: Not quite. During the past decade, very unfavorable to Sportfive, its Swiss competitor Infront followed a reverse path. The Zug company was built on the remains of the prestigious ISL founded by

Horst Dassler, who alone held the rights of FIFA and the IOC. But then, upon the premature death of Horst Dassler (son of the founder and CEO of Adidas), ISL erred in bad investments in the United States, South America and in tennis. In bankruptcy, the ISL was bought by the German magnate Kirch television that also made it bankrupt. Robert Louis-Dreyfus bought the company and renamed it, choosing a very stable management. The same team is in charge for 10 years under the leadership of Philippe Blatter. Some members of this team are even from the dead ISL and have solid experience and a large address book. Besides the football industry, very profitable (thanks to the Italian market), and the branch of audiovisual production (HBS), which historically produced images of FIFA, Infront has embarked in sports a priori less profitable. Thus, Infront holds much of the rights of winter sports federations. Following the death of Robert Louis-Dreyfus, the company was sold for around 500 million euros to the Anglo–US fund Bridgepoint, which has retained the company for 3 years. The fund delivered Infront on the market in 2014. Following a battle between professionals (including CAA) and various funds, it is ultimately the Wanda Group, which won the auction by placing more than 1 billion euros on the table, 12 times the operating income of the Swiss company. The Chinese group, mainly active in real estate, had already made some inroads in the sports world in China with the club Dalian, but also in Europe, where the group holds 20% of Atletico Madrid. Wang Jianlin, the founder and president of Wanda and one of the three richest Chinese (according to Forbes), has great ambitions for Infront, including significant extensions into Asia and Africa. This purchase marks a decisive foray of the Chinese into the universe of the global sport.

MD & NC: How can we compare the situation in the countries of the "Big 5"?

CB: The situation is not the same everywhere in the big five European football countries (England, Germany, Italy, France, Spain). First, because the sponsorship market is extremely variable from one country to another. Germany, where the sector is flourishing, Italy, completely devastated, each country has its peculiarities.

MD & NC: Your outlook interests us on this point. Could you illustrate your thoughts?

CB: Yes, of course. In order not to lose too much, take one example of the clubs.

In Germany, with the exception of the prestigious Bayern Munich, most clubs work with an agency, IMG, Sportfive, Infront or even UFA Sports. It is the king country of the agencies. The market is very strong on the one hand and relief (banking services) system each play an important role. In Italy, hit hard by the crisis, incomes are complicated to pick, and market for intermediaries clubs is virtually nonexistent. Concerning the big clubs, they rarely have an exclusivity strategy and yield products to opportunity agencies. Infront is the most present, which seems normal in a country where the Swiss company markets the entire Italian league in TV rights. A unique case in the Big 5, other professional leagues do not use an installed agency (which does not mean without intermediary – see the case of Mr. Wehrli, below).

MD & NC: And in other countries, what are the changes?

CB: In Spain, as in Italy, the difference in income is abysmal between the two giants (Real and Barça) and the others. The two Spanish clubs have their own sales force, but do not hesitate to sign contracts according to the territory of expression. S5 has signed with Barcelona for the African territory.

The other feature is the pervasive role of Mediapro, which is both a broadcaster of its own channels and those of the two rival clubs (Real, Barça), a producer of images and agency. The clubs also give way to centralized billboards (Umedia owns 80% of this market). This leads to a serious paradox: it is taken for granted that the exclusivity of a trademark is the most profitable or reverse, a company that pays a high price logically imposes exclusivity in its product category. But, in Spain, Barça is equipped by Nike, but Adidas and Puma can be displayed on the stadium panels installed at its enclosure.

In England as well, the offer is segmented by product. Generally, clubs have their own sales teams for high-value products (shirt, lodges, naming rights). However, they also use an agency for the billboards which are, as is the case in Spain, a lesser resource.

MD & NC: Are there any new jobs that have emerged in this changing landscape?

CB: In the French market agencies have completely melted. If the agencies suffer from their reputation, it is not the case of all intermediaries. Some even made a place in the sun and with strong revenue, while combining different caps to subsidize them. This is the case of Yves Werhli and his cabinet, Clifford Chance. The French lawyer has indeed convinced his partners to specialize in the field of sport and more particularly in the trading of rights. Hardworking, shrewd and inventive in the negotiations, Yves Wehrli has attracted most leaders. First of all, those of the organizing committee of the World Cup in 1998, Jacques Lambert and Michel Platini. Then he entered the LFP where everyone was happy to have such a prestigious firm. Suddenly, the club presidents, who complained about extravagant agency commissions, have never balked at paying hefty fees (fees and results bonus) to the law firm, which has become essential to the LFP, the FFF and in some other clubs (he directed the IPO of the OL, recapitalized RC Lens). Charming, always smiling, Mr. Wehrli knows how to be as compelling with a Graët as with a Thiriez or an Aulas. He even managed to become the council of Sportfive as he dried up the market further. With his friendships and undeniable people skills, it is he who made the repurchase of the company for the Lagardère Group, who also was both the S5 board and its legal adversary, the FFF. It remains council of the Lagardère group but also CAA Eleven that came to win all the rights of the UEFA under the nose of . . . S5. He set up with Jacques Lambert the file of France for the Euro 2016 of which the key decision maker was Michel Platini. All without taking into account its position to the UEFA in the investigation regarding financial fair play.

MD & NC: We feel that broadcasters have also been instrumental in changing the ecosystem.

CB: Yes, you're right. For 15 years, agencies lost market share after market share. In addition to the lack of marketing expertise of the agencies, the professional teams among beneficiaries or the centralization of others (UEFA), you have to add the intrusion of broadcasters. They buy the rights to certainly retransmit on their own network, but also for resale in other categories or in other territories. The textbook case is that of the international rights of the LFP. The League Championship owns the rights outside France. It historically gives commercialization. Darmon was inevitably the first agency to operate them. The League then gave its rights to IMG. In 2007, the LFP still put its rights on the market. An unpublished final agency opposed an agency to a broadcaster, Sportfive, to Canal +. A fight anyway for a losing battle since Méheut Bertrand and Frederic Thiriez had agreed previously. Canal + has become the owner of those rights for Africa, but also for the world. The LFP has renounced to develop its own product: a short-term policy. At the snap, the rights went to BeIN for a long time (until 2024). The Qatari bouquet of channels can feed its versions into the United States, North Africa and the Middle East. The remaining rights are sold, either directly or through other agencies; BeIN is working primarily with the powerful Spanish MediaPro and Italian MP Silva for these deals of resale.

The broadcasters seek to achieve their absolute dream: to remove any intermediary with the shareholders and become masters of the game. Thus, Canal + has gone twice a step further by creating its own agency. Without the expected success. This was first Sport +, initiated under the leadership of Jérôme Valcke (current secretary general of FIFA). Sport + was quickly merged with Darmon and UFA-Sports to become Sportfive. A few years later, Canal +, with Jean-Louis Dutaret, the former right hand of Jean-Claude Darmon, created "Canal + Events" to carry and resell the rights, but also to create events on the model of ASO, and to own the rights without having to pay them. His life was a little longer, but Canal + Events was also quickly sold to its employees.

This quest for the absolute, tempted by Canal +, sought by BeIN, is produced by MediaPro in Spain. The Spanish company founded 20 years ago by the Catalan producer Jaume Roures turns all the wheels. Agency (with major rights), producer (via MediaLuso) and broadcaster with two television channels, free "La Sexta" and pay "Gol TV", 100% football. MediaPro holds a lot of rights of Liga and broadcasts Real Madrid. It did have the rights of Barça stolen by Telefonica but remains an absolute model. This presents a danger for the world of sport, as it could someday face bankruptcy in a difficult landscape.

MD & N: How is this happening to FIFA or the IOC?

CB: This dissociation by product occurs also by territory. It is also very fashionable in large global organizations, FIFA or the IOC. These last two remain in their own sales territories, which have a double benefit: that of being the most profitable side and the one whose processes are controlled both for sale and for recovery. Especially since these organizations have hired known professionals. This does not prevent some worries. Broadcasters of the safest countries may also experience some problems. The latest example was the defeat of the Spanish market, hit hard by the economic crisis, which has preferred to forego certain purchases of rights called "premium". Besides, these direct sales – FIFA and the IOC do not hesitate to outsource TV rights of the most fragmented territories to specialist agencies – take longer to process and are more complicated to achieve. Large institutions and agencies allow markets to clear their risks and perils. The IOC outsources more than three-fourths of African countries to Infront; FIFA still outsources much of Asia to Infront. These organizations sometimes yield hybrid products by mixing high-potential countries and other countries that are harder to sell. Agencies have to provide guarantees and take risks.

MD & NC: What major professional leagues?

CB: The big professional leagues proceed in the same manner, retaining their domestic duties but marketing their international rights. The Italian MP Silva is thus oriented towards the sale of such rights. In France, a small flexible structure such as TVMS has specialized in the sale of rights in the countries of Africa that FIFA, UEFA and the IOC do not negotiate directly (usually the Maghreb countries and the area of influence of South Africa which pay satellite bouquets, Al Jazeera/BeIN and SuperSport dominate the market).

This mixed method (cutting by product and territories applied by the major beneficiaries) seems to have a bright future. To regain market share, the agencies will have to make serious but dangerous offers with a minimum guarantee or further improve their marketing expertise.

MD & NC: With your experience and hindsight, and after going on both sides of the fence, do you think we need an agency to optimize the marketing of a football club?

CB: This question often arises for the leaders of football. Take an agency or not? There is no easy answer. Let us study the French clubs. First, discussions arise differently depending on the size of agglomerations, the ownership structure of clubs and the personality of their leaders. Consider three clubs called "intermediaries" in Caen, Guingamp and Tours. In Caen and Guingamp, the chairs are perfectly integrated into the economic systems of their city and their region. Jean-François Fortin in Caen is a recognized industry sharing the ownership with some of its industrial peers. Who better than they can, in Normandy, maximize revenue by combining their networks and knowledge? Presumably nobody. Same as Guingamp, family Graët finally holds some shares, but the club has prepared a fine mesh for companies that contribute to the development of the region. This mesh is at the heart of economic policy and logic. It is difficult to do better than them to get a sum of income. Besides, the two clubs do not weigh enough to really interest national brands. Do they need an agency? Not likely.

In Tours, the ecosystem is very different. For over 10 years, there have been two sole successive shareholders, Frederic Sebag and Jean-Marc Ettori, that share common characteristics: they are not Touraine, do not live in Tours and only moderately appreciate Touraine life. The first led the club from Paris, which has not prevented him from raising the club to the CFA 2 League. The second led the club from Corsica. They have a fairly low knowledge of Tours, ignore the various economic and political networks, which constitutes a heavy handicap. The presence of an agency is probably desirable. The club also employs an agency, Sport and Co, which has built a portfolio among the clubs of equivalent size in Bastia, Nimes, Nancy, Lorient. According to the clubs, Sport and Co, founded by Eric Conrad (former Havas Sports) does not have the same type of contracts, but has created a specificity in supporting clubs.

MD & NC: What about the big clubs?

CB: In the most important clubs in terms of trade turnover, PSG broke its contract with S5 since the arrival of Qatar, and OM has not resumed agency since the break with Havas Sports despite repeated approaches of S5 and Infront. Bordeaux and Lille go forward without agency. Conversely, OL has a long-term contract with Sportfive, like Lens, Nice and Saint-Étienne. Who is right? The truth is probably in between. To sell internally certainly saves a commission. Nevertheless, direct sales, to be optimal, often face the same obstacle: sports hazard. It's part of the game, but the subject is not there. Internal marketing teams rarely resist the psychological pressure in the event of defeat, and their leaders have many other priorities when the wind is unfavorable. Furthermore, internal teams are renewed less, having less control over the market. One solution is to have an agency to prepare cases, to enhance them, and for internal teams to participate (with the agency?) in the pure sale.

MD & NC: Christophe Bouchet, we thank you for your expertise and enlightening comments, it's been instructive for our readers.

CB: Not a problem, it was a pleasure.

5

EUROPEAN FOOTBALL IS NEARING A NEW "BIG BANG"

Vincent Chaudel

The draw of the Champions League took place Thursday, August 28, 2014. Only 334 points separated France (6th) from Russia (7th) in the UEFA index. Beyond the sporting prestige, the entire economy of French football finds itself in the risk zone, and it may suffer permanently from a counter-performance from our clubs in the Champions League and Europa League 2014/2015. How to explain that the second strongest economic power in Europe could be at the brink of a sporting "relegation"?

The Bosman ruling, "big bang" of football business

Issued December 15, 1995, in a dispute between a Belgian player (Jean-Marc Bosman) and a Belgian football club (FC Liège), the decision of the European Court of Justice will fundamentally transform the organization of team sports competitions in Europe. In short, the judgment had deleted the notion of quotas of foreign players, European players initially and, by extension, all of those from countries that have concluded agreements with the European Union. Before that fateful date of December 1995, European competitions were an opposition of style between the Italian *catenaccio*, total Dutch football, the British kick-and-rush, the Spanish "mad", and the football of Nantes for us French. Twenty years later, we are seeing an opposition that is more economical than a sporting competition, where the weight of nationality and cultural tactics of coaches and/or players are more and more discreet.

On the economic front, there was also a business model competition between the great nations of European football before the famous "big bang" that was the Bosman ruling. In England, the Premier League has grown in favor of a disagreement within the federation about the TV rights of the lower leagues, allowing the league to negotiate directly with a company that will become more than a partner, one of the two pillars of its business model: B-Sky B. The other economic pillar of British football resides in its popularity in both stadiums (and a little too much in the streets at that time) and on the screen. The peculiarity of the Bundesliga lies in the wide wireless media exposure of German football (80 million potential viewers) that allowed the league to generously market itself to advertisers in the late 1980s. As for Spain, the organization of clubs as non-profits and their famous "*socios*" allowed clubs to benefit from additional sources of income: revenue from matches, commercial revenue, TV rights and contributions from *socios*. Already in the 1990s, the Calcio distinguished itself by its TV dependence. Under the leadership of Silvio

Berlusconi, the main transalpine clubs enjoyed a favorable environment (individual negotiation of TV rights) and a rivalry between two pay-TV operators. Not benefiting from a strong attendance, major TV rights or sponsorship deals, French clubs have fully recovered their main asset: training. Just as Spanish clubs have developed in part through the contributions of *socios*, player trading (buying/selling players) has long been the specialty of French clubs, the AJ Auxerre of Guy Roux being the best example.

As of the 1996/1997 season, one could observe a correlation between the economic power of clubs, their ability to recruit great talents (almost regardless of any barrier of nationality) and their sporting performance. "Tell me what is your budget, I will tell you what rank you'll end up." For the most romantic of us, if this correlation exists, it remains linked to the public factor. In his research on economic modeling of team sports, Professor Stefan Kesenne[1] establishes a direct link between the local potential (in terms of audience and sponsorship) and the economic power of a club. He demonstrates mathematically that the revenue of a club is linked to its local potential (public and economic) and its concentration of talent (as a result of proposed salaries). As for costs, they are mainly due to the amount of talent hired by the club and its remuneration. To be competitive from a sporting standpoint, a "post-Bosman" club must have a substantial financial base to attract top talents. To do this, it must have a large fan base. If the mathematical proof seems implacable, the consequence of this is to condemn, more or less long term, the "small city" clubs to give up their dreams of the European championship.

The uncontrolled runaway of the economy of European football

Nearly a decade after the Bosman ruling, one could observe an economic plan with a double trend in European professional football: the strengthening of the dominant position of a small number of very big clubs and a forced return to reality for clubs that have been living beyond their means. This period should have offered a unique opportunity for French clubs (and their more prudent management under influence of the DNCG) to position themselves as leading outsiders, behind some clubs still unaffordable in economic terms.

After a spectacular growth of inflows in the second half of the 1990s, the growth of French clubs has significantly slowed in the early 2000s (with a return to League 1 consisting of 20 clubs). Although attendances in 2003/2004 were up 1.7% from the previous year, the stagnation of revenues observed since 2000 is confirmed in 2002/2003 with an overall increase of 7% of revenue excluding transfers for League 1, but a 4% decrease in sales for medium clubs in League 1, which reflects the move to 20 clubs and the integration of two "small budget" clubs.

Meanwhile, wage inflation has been relatively contained in 2002/2003. The ratio of wages to sales was stable at 68%. This ratio nevertheless remained high, resulting in income, excluding trading players, of negative 68 million euros for all of Ligue 1.

Unfortunately for French football, the transfer market turnaround has been confirmed. Transfer fees received by the clubs in League 1 in 2002/2003 accounted for one-third of the amount of compensations received in 2000/2001. At the same time, the average number of professional contracts by the club went from 27.44 to 21.95. The balance of transfers for League 1 clubs, after having been at a large deficit during three seasons between 1998 and 2001, was close to equilibrium in 2002/2003. From this fact, the accounting result was strongly negative in 2002/2003, although the origins of these difficulties were mainly from management operations of players between 1998 and 2001.

Over the same period, the English league was the only major European league to record a percentage of double-digit growth in revenues in 2002/2003. Over the previous five seasons, the English, German and Spanish championships had recorded a significant increase in their average attendance per club (+14%, +13% and +29%). The average attendance per club of the French League 1 championship was stable (+1.5%), partly as a result of the transition to 20 clubs. The Italian championship itself was in decline with a fall of 17% of inflows over the period. If the German championship was already one that had the highest average attendance in Europe (with a stronger growth potential than the English league that filled its stadiums to almost 95%), Britain remained by far the championship generating the most ticket revenue, in addition to enjoying an average ticket price 50% higher than the Spanish and Italian championships, twice that of the German Bundesliga and three times that of the French Ligue 1.

Wage inflation was and remains to this day the Achilles heel of the business model of European football. For the first time in 2002/2003, the clubs of the Calcio have seen their wages decline. The Premier League still showed an increase of 7.7% as a result of the "Chelsea price" phenomenon, although the transfer market was finally in very sharp decline throughout Europe. Excluding players transactions, English and German championships showed positive results with an increase of 179 and 115 million euros, in contrast to Italy which recorded in 2002/2003 for the second consecutive season a result outside the operations of players that was very negative (–381 million euros). After trading in players, the net income before tax of English league paradoxically became very negative (–230 million euros), which corresponds mainly to the cumulative loss of six clubs (Leeds, Fulham, Sunderland, Middlesbrough and already Chelsea and Manchester City).

In each championship, clubs (FC Valencia, Borussia Dortmund, Leeds United, Glasgow Rangers) took financial risks to try to follow the furious pace of locomotives clubs (FC Barcelona, Manchester United, Bayern Munich), going so far as to omit or defer the payment of fees and/or taxes. The situation of Italian clubs already seemed to be the most disturbing.

Michel Platini and the return to fundamentals

On January 26, 2007, Michel Platini was elected for his first term as President of the UEFA. As in a "classic" election campaign, he built a real program that could be summed up in these few words: a football with more financial fairness and more uncertainty in sports. In sporting terms, Michel Platini wished to reaffirm the necessary investment of clubs in training with the rule of "locally trained players". Financially, failing to establish a European DNCG (to the chagrin of the president of the LFP, Frédéric Thiriez), his presidency will remain marked by the introduction of the UEFA license.

In the summer of 2008, the subprime crisis first hit the United States and then spread to Europe. Resulting from the investment potential of sponsors or from the purchasing power of the fans, the consequences of this crisis appeared quickly. In 2009, total revenue of the clubs in the first league was 11.7 billion euros. Unfortunately, the increase in these revenues was accompanied by a significant increase in costs (primarily related to transfers and wages of players), generating an overall net loss of 1.2 billion euros.

Many football clubs, including the most prestigious, have encountered serious financial difficulties that resulted in the doubling of overall losses of first league clubs within the year. In this context, the unanimous consensus that has formed in the football family around the recently approved financial fair play concept (FFP) will play a key role in order to meet the expected financial distress which other clubs will suffer in the future. Keeping control of costs and maintaining them at a sustainable level is and will remain the main challenge of the clubs. The sustainability of the football sector as a whole is at the heart of the philosophy of financial fair play, which aims to balance income and expenditures, and to prioritize investments in the long-term.

This was the stand of Michel Platini in the editorial of the benchmarking report on the licensing procedure to clubs in early 2010.

Expenditure control, importance of training, new stadiums for Euro 2016, the environment seemed so favorable for the hexagonal football that in 2012, Frédéric Thiriez loudly showed a newfound ambition: the return of the LFP on the stage of the European Championships. The arrival of new foreign investors (QSI for PSG, Dmitry Rybolovlev for Monaco or Hafiz Mammadov for Lens), a potential increase in TV rights and a number of competitors invited by the FFP should have allowed our championship to transform its economic dynamics into sports performance (and in UEFA points). Since then, French professional football clubs show an overall deficit of 39.5 million euros (June 30, 2013). The OM has finally (but at what cost) opened the new Velodrome stadium with 67,354 seats, and the OL-Land and the stadium of Bordeaux are (still) not completed. Moreover, if the eruption of BeIN sports in PAF (French broadcasting landscape) has had an upward impact on the rights of League 1, it is only for the period 2016/2020. Not to mention a collateral effect (perhaps under-estimated) of the Financial Fair Play rule on clubs that should have been the locomotives of our league: PSG and AS Monaco.

Despite these positive signs, the cumulative deficit of French professional clubs increased from 39 million euros in June 2013 to 200 million euros in 2014. Obviously, the leaders of French football explained these poor results by pointing out the (temporary) adverse effects of taxes (75% on high wages), the additional cost of wage costs, all generating a real distortion of competition. If these items are correct, the deficits in football result from what one might call a "scissor effect" between the expenditure which, in the last transfer window, exploded under the leadership of AS Monaco and PSG, and the erosion of revenues, with a ceiling of TV rights in the last two contracts, and sales of smaller players in the past, a result of the financial difficulties of "clients–buyers clubs". In fact, European football is not immune to global economic trends. We are witnessing a phenomenon of concentration of wealth in a few actors and a stagnation or even impoverishment of challengers. For an indication, with 259 million euros, Manchester United was, in 2004, the club that generated the largest revenue. Then, Olympique Lyonnais ranked 18th with a budget of 88 million euros. A decade later, Manchester United (518 million euros) is now second, behind Real Madrid and their 549.5 million euros of revenue. Despite its 120.5 million euros, Olympique Lyonnais fell out of the Top 20 economic ranking. Over the same period, the average budget of League 1 clubs has increased from about 50 to 65 million euros. This increase is mainly explained by the extraordinary budgetary development of PSG. France does not distinguish itself from its neighbors in this regard. Whether in Spain, Italy and to a lesser extent in Germany, there is a phenomenon of championships polarization, in which three or four clubs generate as much revenue as the 15 or 18 other clubs. The double level of competition (continental and national) and the preponderance of TV rights in the budgets of the clubs, regardless of the championship, are the stumbling blocks of the audiovisual honey pot of the ecosystem of modern football. In Italy, as in Spain, the individualization of the rights leads to significant imbalances, therefore leading "small clubs" to the brink of bankruptcy.

Because a domestic league cannot be reduced to the opposition of two, three or four clubs, Italy has agreed to review its method of marketing and rights redistribution. Twenty years after the Bosman ruling, the economic model of football seems to harmonize itself at the European level: major TV rights, modern stadiums (connected when possible) and well attended (attendance rate above 90%), in a favorable location (strong catchment area and many companies) and especially owners with a sufficiently broad financial base to assume the economic consequences of a sporting under-performance. Facing an incredible inflation of budgets of the "big teams" and an unprecedented growth of TV rights, the authorities have sought to structure their clubs to avoid excesses of all kinds. The response from France was the DNCG where the UEFA has set up the Financial Fair

Table 5.1 Rankings in the Money League

2013/14 Revenue (€m)

Position	Change	Positions changed	Club	Revenue (€m)
1	→←	0	Real Madrid	549.5
2	↑	2	Manchester United	518.0
3	→←	0	Bayern Munich	487.5
4	↓	(2)	FC Barcelona	484.6
5	→←	0	Paris Saint-Germain	474.2
6	→←	0	Manchester City	414.4
7	→←	0	Chelsea	387.9
8	→←	0	Arsenal	359.3
9	↑	3	Liverpool	305.9
10	↓	(1)	Juventus	279.4
11	→←	0	Borussia Dortmund	261.5
12	↓	(2)	AC Milan	249.7
13	↑	1	Tottenham Hotspur	215.8
14	↓	(1)	Schalke 04	213.9
15	↑	5	Atlético de Madrid	169.9
16	n/a	new	Napoli	164.8
17	↓	(2)	Internazionale	164.0
18	↓	(2)	Galatasaray	161.9
19	n/a	new	Newcastle United	155.1
20	n/a	new	Everton	144.1

2012/13 Revenue (€m)

Position	Change	Positions changed	Club	Revenue (€m)
1	→←	0	Real Madrid	518.9
2	→←	0	FC Barcelona	482.6
3	↑	1	Bayern Munich	431.2
4	↓	(1)	Manchester United	423.8
5	↑	5	Paris Saint-Germain	398.8
6	↑	1	Manchester City	316.2
7	↓	(2)	Chelsea	303.4
8	↓	(2)	Arsenal	284.3
9	↑	4	Juventus	272.4
10	↓	(2)	AC Milan	263.5
11	↑	1	Borussia Dortmund	256.2
12	↓	(3)	Liverpool	240.6
13	↑	2	Schalke 04	198.2
14	→←	0	Tottenham Hotspur	172.0
15	↓	(4)	Internazionale	164.5
16	↑	3	Galatasaray	157.0
17	↑	3	Hamburger SV	135.4
18	n/a	new	Fenerbahçe	126.4
19	n/a	new	AS Roma	124.4
20	n/a	new	Atlético de Madrid	120.0

■ Position in Football Money League
■ Change on previous year
■ Number of positions changed

Source: Deloitte Football Money League – 2015.

Play (FFP). In an open and non-harmonized (payroll, taxation) environment, the UEFA approach proves to be both a source of tension at the international level and a real opportunity for French football. With the organization of the Euro, and the comeback of our locomotive clubs (PSG, AS Monaco, OM, OL), it seems that France was able to move up the European hierarchy, except for endogenous stress (e.g. removal of image rights or the application of the 75% tax).

And tomorrow, what business model for European football?

With the financial Fair Play rule, the real challenge was to find a favorable outcome, a.k.a. acceptable sanctions for new stigmatized investors, whether they are Qatari, Emirati or Russian. The UEFA President Michel Platini gambled with his credibility and in effect his political future (to be one day at the head of FIFA) and could do without these penalties. Too heavy, they could have adverse consequences. First, because these investors are now important customers of the UEFA, directly or indirectly. Second, because in case of legal appeal from the penalized clubs, nothing says that the UEFA, although it has worked legally, even if its intentions are laudable, would be winning out. Because under EU law, there is always room for discussion. Finally, what could still prevent an entrepreneur from putting money in other subsidiaries? After all, all of these clubs pay for their expenses, which is not the case of some indebted clubs – such as Real and Atletico Madrid to name the finalists in the Champions League – who themselves are not worried by the financial fair play rule. Finally, the European body could go through to see the famous closed league project wielded by big clubs. Better not take any risk and therefore not antagonize PSG, Manchester City and AS Monaco (too much) in the future.

Sanctions have fallen. PSG will have to pay a fine of at least 20 million euros initially, which did not seem to particularly touch QSI. This is akin to a "luxury tax", a common mechanism in American sports. If you exceed the fixed ceiling, you pay a fee. The great baseball clubs such as the Mets or the Yankees do it regularly without protest and without real weakening. By investing fast and hard, PSG has certainly made a mistake with regard to financial fair play criteria, but it has also offered itself time and the opportunity to be at the point of being able to "skip their turn" during a transfer window . . . which was unfortunate for the League 1 clubs. For PSG, the essentials of the sports investment were made. The constraints on the recruitment and payroll imposed by the UEFA could even be an asset as they limit the club's temptation to disrupt the workforce and thus promote stability, which remains one of the best guarantees of athletic performance.

Whether in sports, in business, in politics or in football, there is too often a gap between willingness and flexibility that is needed to achieve the expected results. This is particularly true of the UEFA and its FFP vis-à-vis the PSG and Manchester City. Through their financial power and their activity during the transfer window, these clubs are allowing many other clubs to make a living, forcing the UEFA to have some leniency. And as in football too, we only lend to the rich, there are always small arrangements between friends, to better circumvent the rule. Didn't PSG get the TFC loan from Serge Aurier with an option automatically and unconditionally raised a year later? It's simply a purchase with a deferred payment which diverts duress. Even more subtle, Manchester City opens "subsidiaries" in the United States and Japan, which enables it to offer very soon – a practice already common in the US sports – a career plan for players like multinationals in offering yuppies. Meanwhile, this device has helped safely attract Franck Lampard in the eyes of the UEFA.

With a renegotiation of TV rights amounting to 6.92 billion euros for the 2016–2019 period, the Premier League club will give its clubs "legal" ways around the constraints of the financial fair play rule. With ownership of players by third parties, it is the influence of players' agents and speculation of new players with the UEFA seeking to contain the spread (see the referral with FIFPro of the European Commission to declare illegal this practice by investment funds). With the 2022 World Cup in the winter, it is the European leagues and their clubs that should suffer economically from the calendar change. These are all elements that suggest that European football is on the verge of a new big bang, with perhaps a takeover of the players (see ATP), broadcasters (see Murdoch in Southern Hemisphere rugby) or a confirmation of the UEFA's power at the head of European football.

Note

1 *The Economic Theory of Professional Team Sports – An Analytical Treatment,* by Stefan Késenne, University of Antwerp and Catholic University of Leuven, Belgium.

PART II

Topics related to the marketing of professional clubs

It is in the second part that strategies and marketing initiatives essential to the success of professional football sports organizations are discussed. Chapter 6, written by Nicolas Chanavat, Michel Desbordes and Nicolas Lorgnier, analyzes the fundamental elements of sports sponsorship. Chapter 7, from Boris Helleu, presents the current state of football 2.0. Chapter 8, written by Christopher Hautbois, examines the strategic aspects linked to the coexistence between regions and professional football clubs. Finally, it is in Chapter 9 that Aurélien François and Emmanuel Bayle offer a comparative study of societal practices in European professional football.

6

SPORTS SPONSORSHIP AND PROFESSIONAL FOOTBALL

Nicolas Chanavat, Michel Desbordes and Nicolas Lorgnier

In the media, the importance of sponsorship is often mentioned in quantitative terms. Moreover, certain published figures have a dramatic character. While in 1990 global investments were around 5.5 billion euros, the amount of invested expenses reached 57.5 billion US dollars in 2015 (IEG, 2015). Activities related to the sporting industry represent approximately 70% of the total sums.

And in the football sector, the income from FIFA coming only from sponsors for the 2014 World Cup amounted to 1.4 billion US dollars. Concerning the French Football Federation, we see that 40% of its 200 million in annual revenue came from sponsorship.

Regarding the professional football clubs, the results of the study from Repucom (2015)[1] show that revenue generated from "jersey" partnerships have continued to grow in Europe. There was a record 20% increase in revenue in this area: from 570 million euros in 2013–2014 to a total of 687 million euros in 2014–2015.

Since the 2015–2016 season, Manchester United has been sponsored by the equipment manufacturer Adidas for an amount of approximately 94 million euros per year over a period of 10 years. This contract comes after the partnership started in the 2014–2015 season by Chevrolet for a period of 7 years, amounting to 560 million euros (80 million euros per year). The total amount of these partnerships for the Mancunian jersey is the most expensive in the world of football. Despite grim sporting results, Manchester United has set the tone for over a decade for the price of jersey sponsorship for major European football brands.

In addition, partnerships (and sales of licensed merchandise) for PSG have generated 327.2 million euros, representing 69% of the club's revenue (Deloitte, 2015). This amount reflects a form of unprecedented partnership between PSG and QTA, which is considered *nation branding*. Beginning in the 2011–2012 season, the contract will allow PSG to pocket 150 million euros in the first year and up to 200 million in the subsequent years.

While these amounts may be considered "excessive" and partnerships seemed to be solely dedicated to a single sponsorship category, the reality is quite different. Currently, all companies (multinationals, SMEs, etc.) are involved in sponsorship and, contrary to popular belief, the admission ticket, even in a highly publicized environment such as professional football, remains "affordable".[2] In France, the liberalization of the activity can be explained by the LFP initiative that put a stop to the restriction of six sponsors and the prohibition of marketing certain locations.

Once considered a simple financial contribution, this communication technique is now an integral part of the marketing strategies of companies. It meets the same criteria for evaluating an advertising or promotional campaign and can have an effect on the consumer's reactions with regards to brands in terms of cognitive reactions (to be made known), affective reactions (to be well liked) and conative reactions (to act) (Chanavat, Martinent and Ferrand, 2009).

The concepts of "naming", "activation", "ambush marketing", "co-branding", "money can't buy", etc. are frequently associated with this topic. The fruitfulness of the technique brings out other trends that will be addressed in this chapter: regional sponsorship, state sponsorship, citizen sponsorship, multiple sports event sponsorship, participative sports sponsorship, etc. There has been clear evidence that sponsorship practices have evolved, which are expressed most often by football partnerships. Hence, this is why we stress the importance of better understanding of the ins and outs of this discipline.

This chapter aims to highlight the essentials in terms of sponsorship in the professional football sector. The objective is to define and illustrate key concepts, to compile an inventory, to examine the best practices and then examine them side by side through the academic literature. Sports sponsorship covers various fields of application, which we will examine before observing the objectives and targets that are discussed. Although it is difficult to precisely quantify the actual effect of the sponsorship, it is still necessary to address its impact from an economic point of view. We will analyze the managerial development of sponsorship that has gone originally from a focus on the enhancement of exposure to the activation of the brand to consumers of sports entertainment. In this way, rights holders and sponsors have expressed their will to provide sports consumers with unique experiences and offer them the "unobtainable". The analysis of new trends, in particular the place of the digital experience on the professionalization of the discipline, is the subject of special attention.

Several semi-structured interviews with the clubs (OL, AS Saint-Étienne, PSG, OGC Nice, Toulouse FC), federal authorities (LFP, FFF) and agencies (Sportlab, SponsorLive, Infront) and numerous examples of concrete cases enhance this analysis.

Sports sponsorship: definitions, characteristics and features in the world of professional football

Before understanding the developments and changes of sponsorship practices and before discussing new trends and innovations in professional football, it is necessary to understand the logic and the foundations behind the practice. This is why we address the genesis of the discipline. The analysis of the different terminologies and specific fields of application in the world of professional football will lead us to a proposed definition of sports sponsorship in football.

The genesis of sponsorship: the professionalization of football as a trigger?

Returning to the practice's beginnings is interesting as it is necessary in order to understand the development of sponsorship practices. The word "philanthropy" comes from *Gaius Cilnius Maecenas*,[3] Minister Counsellor for the Emperor Augustus. Thanks to an excellent education in Greece, the famous Roman knight developed a taste for the arts and literature and took under his protection great artists and writers such as Horace and Virgil. The term *Maecenas* (or patronage) remains affiliated with his actions. Therefore, the origin of sponsorship is identified with the time of ancient Greece (Burton, Quester and Farrelly, 1998). Also of Latin origin, the term sponsorship comes from *sponsor/sponsors*. It signifies the bond, the guarantor, but also the godfather of a neophyte. This term was developed especially in England, a country with strong sports culture, which may explain why its scope has often been restricted to sports.

In France, the origin of sponsorship dates back to 1891 with the Paris-Brest bicycle race, supported by Michelin, and then in 1903 with the Tour de France directed by Henri Desgrange, editor of the magazine *L'Auto*, considered as one of the first sponsors of the event (Bœuf and Leonard, 2003). In Europe, the beginning of sponsorship is illustrated in football by the support of FIAT to Juventus (1897), Bayer to Leverkusen (1904), Philips to Eindhoven (1913), Peugeot to Sochaux (1925) and Casino to Saint-Étienne (1933). Thus, in 1929, while Jean-Pierre Peugeot modernized his company through centralizing its plants on the Sochaux site, he created a professional team with the FC Sochaux. Its role was to represent the club's pennant (Peugeot cars) throughout France during the games where it competed against the best national teams, and to enhance the brand's image of the lion (Dietschy and Mourat, 2006). To make this form of communication as effective as possible, the club recruited top players for a fortune and organized charity matches in Europe against increasingly prestigious teams. Because FC Sochaux was restricted from official matches due to its status of not being a professional club, Jean-Pierre Peugeot created his own competition in 1930: the Peugeot Cup. This competition brought together the best French teams and in this way predicted the outcome of the French professional championship. Once FC Sochaux was recognized as a professional organization by the French Football Federation in 1932, the club had fully (and officially) acted as a representative of the Peugeot company throughout France. The use of professional football for advertising purposes is therefore claimed by the firm (Dietschy and Mourat, 2006). Consequently, the development of professionalizing football organizations in France corresponds to the origins of sponsorship (Chanavat, 2009).

In the 1930s, it was common for English professional football players (Dixie Dean, Stanley Matthews, etc.) to sing the praises of cigarette brands or cosmetic products for men. In the 1960s, with the arrival of television into households, football was widely utilized as an advertising platform. According to Nys (2010), the 1966 FIFA World Cup, hosted and won by England, marks the starting point of football's media coverage and the appeal it continues to generate among sponsors. After World War II, the professional football player gradually became an advertising platform. The authorization to advertise on jerseys dates back to 1968. This change is not to everyone's liking. In 1970, *Le Miroir des sport* (Mirror of Sports) castigates footballers by comparing them to "human billboards", who lose their dignity by wearing a shirt that promotes the benefits "of a diaper or a ready-to-wear clothing brand" (Wahl and Lanfranchi, 1995).

In any case, it seems that during the second half of the 19th century companies quickly realized the power of communication through sponsorship, whose emotional impact is based on both the uncertainty of the outcome and the commitment of its supporters, its participants and the public (Ferrand, 1993). Without going into the historical debate surrounding the genesis of sponsorship, it should be noted that, contrary to popular belief, it is not a recent idea and that professionalization of football played an important role in the development of this discipline.

Different terminologies related to sponsorship

Sponsoring, patronage, partnership, event communications or communication through the event are (many) words typically used to address the phenomenon of sponsorship. This has caused some problems for researchers and engendered semantic debates in schools. Previous researchers have already analyzed the evolution of different terminologies which have addressed the phenomenon (Derbaix, Gérard and Lardinoit, 1994; Fleck-Dousteyssier, 2006; Chanavat, 2009). Therefore, beyond a comprehensive review of all of the terms used to address sponsorship in the academic literature, we focus our attention on the qualitative evolution of the concepts of patronage, sponsoring and sponsorship as well as the event-related approaches of the phenomenon.

Patronage

Patronage, as highlighted by ADMICAL (the Association for the Development of Industrial and Commercial Sponsorship), represents,

> "a way for the company to assert its interest in its cultural and social environment and to be where the audience does not expect." The decision made on January 6th, 1989 defines philanthropy as "material support, provided with no direct counterpart from the part of the beneficiary to a work or to a person for the undertaking of activities of general interest".

In order to distinguish differences regarding the definitions of patronage, they agree on the concept of support for the performance of activities of general interest relative to the decision made on January 6, 1989, referred to above.[4]

Sponsoring

Since the early 1970s, we find that the notion of sponsorship has been defined at various times. Sponsorship was formerly defined as a single payment made for advertising. Today, the proposed definitions aim in particular to emphasize and clarify the nature of the stakeholders involved (sponsor and sponsored entity), their exchanges and the objectives pursued by the use of this communication technique. Nevertheless, it seems difficult to define sponsorship given the variety of situations that characterizes this type of operation. In this context, Ferrand, Torrigiani and Camps i Povill (2006) define sponsorship as a

> communication strategy integrated in the different strategies of the organization. It pursues business and/or institutional objectives through making use of the related rights, and the direct partnership between an organization, a brand, a product with another organization, an event or a personality. Finally, it involves a commercial transaction between the concerned parties.

Sponsorship

Since the early 1990s, several definitions have been proposed in French literature.[5] Walliser (2003, p. 67) notes that "there is generally no accepted definition of a sponsorship." However, the minimum consensus around the phenomenon could be characterized by an exchange between a sponsor and an entity, and the search for communication objectives through making use of a combination of both (Walliser, 2003). Fleck-Dousteyssier (2006) defines sponsorship as "a communication technique which involves, for any organization, brand or product, creating or directly supporting a sponsored entity, socio culturally independent from itself as well as partnering with the media in order to achieve marketing communication objectives." This definition is interesting as it is suitable for the two most common definitions used in the framework of French-language searches, which are Derbaix, Gérard and Lardinoit (1994) and Walliser (1994). It further illustrates the diversity of possible partnership between sponsor and the sponsee. Nevertheless, it has a limit: the nature of the sponsored entity is not restricted to an event, a discipline, a partnership, a foundation, a group of people, an individual or an audiovisual program.

Event-related approaches

Even if they do not characterize the plurality of sponsorship practices, different expressions have appeared in order to highlight the dynamic aspect of the phenomenon. In this way, Cegarra (1987) suggests the concept of promotion through action, while Giannelloni (1993) highlights the concepts of event communication or communication through the event, and Ferrand (1995) mentions the expression of communication through the athletic event. Desbordes, Ohl and Tribou (1999, p. 308) define event communication as, "a technique which consists of persuading an audience that there is a link between the company and the event that it supports, in order to reap the benefits in terms of image and reputation". However, this approach has not generated debate. The few definitions which have been observed can be explained by the existence of perspectives within the body of research concerning the pair of "marketing and the event". Also, we identify three approaches. The first approach concerns "marketing events" or "organizational marketing." It focuses on situations in which the central source of revenue is the event. Here, it is suitable to market through traditional marketing tools. The second approach, "marketing with events", refers to studies on the creation and staging of an event by the company itself. The third and final approach "marketing near or at the events" includes research on the use of an independent event in order to communicate a business's own advertising messages. Sponsorship therefore falls under the third category. The confusion connected to the use of the words communication or event has likely contributed to the use of other semantic referents by researchers.

What are the areas of application in the world of football?

The challenge here is to focus on the different areas of sponsorship and to consider the specifics of professional football in the matter. This work will allow us to propose a definition of football sponsorship.

The focus areas in sponsorship

The activity of sponsorship, which is in perpetual development, is based on different areas and many performance levels that are at the root of a variety of managerial practices. Sponsorship covers various fields of activities in our present society. Chanavat (2009) proposes a classification in six areas of sponsorship: sports, culture (music, art, etc.), education, social causes (charity, etc.), science (environment, health, etc.) and the media. Please note a preponderance of the sports sector, including football, with over 70% of its investments in sponsorship, which encompasses the vast majority of partnerships. However, studies suggest the growth of other business areas. In this sense, Walliser (2006) emphasizes that culture constitutes a privileged sector for sponsors, while the social, environmental and audiovisual aspects represent important development areas of sponsorship practices.

What are the specific features of sponsored entities within sports and within football?

The work of Fleck-Dousteyssier (2006) points out that sponsorship can operate at several levels in different areas. To examine the typology of possible sponsorship operations, three distinct areas are proposed: organization (club, federation, etc.), event (match, championship, tour) and individual (athlete). The appearance of the naming of stadiums and other places of life within a club requires us to split the "organization" category into two areas: "organization" and "place" in order to distinguish the practices. In addition, the development of the practice led us to specify and/or modify certain fields. Thus, in the sports sector, advertisers can individually support athletes who left their professional careers. Zidane retiring after the German World 2006 is a perfect example. Here we are talking about the brand associating themselves with former sportsmen for their values as men. The term athlete suggested by Fleck-Dousteyssier (2006) does not reflect the diverse nature of the entities, particularly as the brands are also encompassing the coaches (who have not necessarily once been of top athletes) or referees. Examples of Jose Mourinho, the current coach of Chelsea, and Pierluigi Collina, former Italian referee of international football, illustrate our point of view.

Moreover, at the convergence of the sports and media industries, we identify the clothing sponsorship among sports journalists. In this way, the sports services of Canal + and RMC are primarily related to the Serge Blanco brand. This form of partnership reflects the current professionalization and diversity of sponsorship operations. Despite the clarifications made to the type of sponsorship operations proposed by Fleck-Dousteyssier (2006), it will be necessary to refine our classification, which is only a contribution to the intellectualization of sponsorship activities that never stop developing.

Therefore, the classification of sponsorship operations that we have proposed highlights several categories which refer to the types of entities subject to sports sponsorship: organization (federation, league, club, team, etc.), individuals (athletes, coaches, referees, officials, journalists, etc., or person who held this function), event (contest, competition, show, game, round, etc.) and place (sports arena, stadium, training center, television, etc.), as shown in Figure 6.1. Here, we are talking about intra-domain sponsorship.

Although an advertiser can engage in different levels of performance within one type of entertainment, they can also intervene in several different areas of entertainment (sports, culture, etc.). This is called cross-domain sponsorship. Brands choose their most favored form of expression: choice of the activity, choice of the sponsored entity or choice of the form of activation, taking into consideration the goals to attain. The choice of an athlete is found to be the most difficult in the sense that its performance is varied, as it is a human subject to performance and underperformance as opposed to an event or a team. At the 2010 World Cup in South Africa, Quick announced the

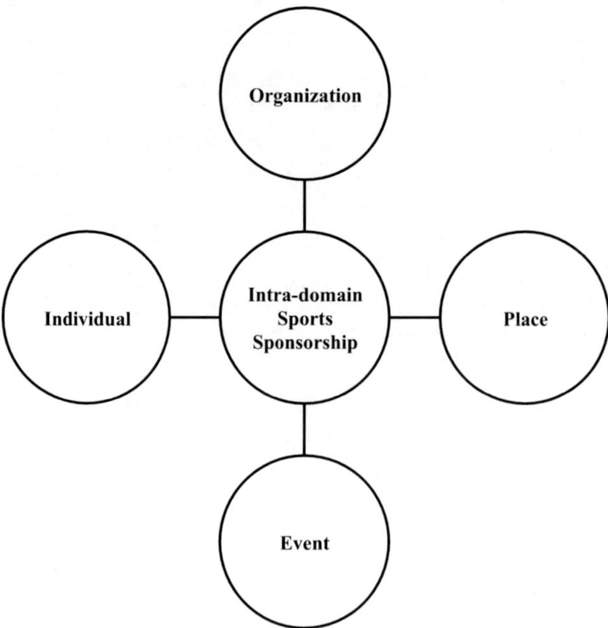

Figure 6.1 The different types of sponsored sports entities (or "sponsees")

suspension of its advertising campaign for Giant Max featuring the player Nicolas Anelka. The sponsor changed its strategy after a controversy over alleged insults the player lodged against Raymond Domenech. This large-scale communication reversal resulted in the decision to replace all the posters where the player appeared with another poster just featuring the burger only, 48 hours after the event. However, the television campaign had already been launched a few days before the scandal was stopped. At the time, Quick did not mention the financial impact of the operation to the extent that if poster replacements had been planned ahead of time, the company would have done better without this issue which happened in a one-time marketing operation with Nicolas Anelka.

Box 6.1 The sports sponsorship strategy of the company Emirates

For 20 years, Emirates has sponsored sports events both in the United Arab Emirates and elsewhere in the world, starting with the very first speedboat race, which took place in Dubai in 1987.

His Highness Sheikh Ahmed bin Saeed Al-Maktoum, Chairman and CEO of Emirates Airline & Group, believes that sponsorship is a vital part of the airline's marketing strategy. "We believe that sponsorship is one of the best ways to establish contact with our passengers. It allows us to share and support their interests and to establish a closer relationship with them," he explains.

Football

Football remains one of the main sports of the Emirates sponsorship portfolio, including partnerships with some of the greatest European football clubs.

Rugby

Enriched with long heritage in this sport, Emirates has benefited from a special opportunity to highlight its vast, first-class sponsorship portfolio during its first partnership with the 2011 Rugby World Cup.

Tennis

The growing presence of Emirates in the field of tennis was recently illustrated by the acquisition of the US Open Series, including the US Open, the fourth and final major tournament of the year.

Motor Sports

Emirates is proud to be the International partner of the Formula1, giving the airline a premier presence in the Grand Prix worldwide.

Horse racing

Thanks to its strong presence in the world of horse racing, Emirates has close relations with the horse shows, the authorities, the stables and high level races.

Golf

Emirates sponsors more than 15 golf events worldwide, ranking as one of the most prominent brands in this sport, particularly since its partnership with the 2010 Ryder Cup.

Cricket

Cricket continues to have a great importance for Emirates, and it is enhanced through relationships with the prominent ICC, the ICC elite referees and the Deccan Chargers.

Australian football rules

Emirates is proud to be the main sponsor of the Collingwood Football Club, one of the greatest sporting institutions in Australia.

Arts and Culture

In addition to its comprehensive portfolio of sports sponsorships, Emirates intends to promote the growth of arts and culture in the world as part of its sponsorships.

Source: http://www.emirates.com/fr/french/about/emirates-sponsorships/sponsorships.aspx – Parrainages Emirates, published on emirates.com. Last accessed on May 8, 2015.

A sports entity (person, place, event or organization) is usually sponsored by several advertisers simultaneously. Indeed, during the 2014–2015 season, 24 brands were contractually associated with PSG: top four sponsors (Emirates, Nike, Ooredoo and QNB); a major partner (Aspetar); five official partners (BeIN Sports, Orange, Citroën, PMU, Huawei); eight official suppliers (GDF Suez, Panasonic, Nivea Men, Coca-Cola, Man, Puressentiel, McDonald's, MoneyGram); and six official labels (Go Sport, Aurel BGC, Hublot, Viagogo, Hugo Boss, EA Sports).[6]

In the same vein, for a given event, a brand may be associated with multiple entities of different types. During the 2014 World Cup in Brazil, Adidas was, for example, simultaneously an official partner of FIFA and of the organizing committee. The equipment supplier was also associated with nine national teams and 254 players, including Lionel Messi.

In addition, as part of an event, various mediums are available to sponsors: the jersey, billboard, television broadcasting, new media, etc. In this context, the sponsor may be associated with entities of various types. The reality of the situation thus demonstrates the inherent plurality of sponsorship to the extent that (1) almost all of sponsorship operations does not imply one, but several sponsors; (2) many sponsors are also not associated with one but several entities within the framework of a given event (Chanavat, Martinent and Ferrand, 2010). Moreover, engaging in another area (social issues) can be beneficial to the initial areas's (sports) maximization of marketing oriented objectives.

The role of agencies

The concept of a sports marketing agency refers to different businesses that particularly support the development of marketing, sponsoring, commercial or communication activities in professional football. We observe a proliferation in the number of agencies involved in the professionalization of the sector. The SPORSORA Association (2014, p. 30) distinguishes four types of agencies in the panorama of sports marketing agencies:

- The consulting agencies in communications specializing in sports marketing, whose mission is to support brands in all or part of their communication cycle in sports. This is seen as an opportunity for creating value for brands through communication programs and building real content strategies.

- Agencies specializing in marketing rights: they negotiate the rights from sports institutions (federations, leagues, clubs and event organizers), develop marketing products and ensure the sale to advertisers.
- The agencies in charge of hospitality: they manage the design and provide public relations packages for businesses who wish to receive their customers and other professional relationships around a sporting event in a privileged and exclusive environment.
- The agencies that organize sports-themed events which are characterized by their heterogeneity (one-shot or recurring events in a sports arena or proximity, etc.), for their own account or on behalf of advertisers or institutions.

In France, the trade agency has long been personified by Jean-Claude Darmon. The development of marketing agencies in football is the object of particular attention.

Towards a definition of sports sponsorship in football

As we have seen previously, a number of terms are used to address the subject of partnership activities: patronage, sponsorship, event marketing or communication through the event, etc. The terms sponsoring and sponsorship appear as global and unifying concepts. It seems difficult to define the concept of sports sponsorship in football (or football sports sponsorship) because of the plurality of situations that characterizes this type of operation. However, this concept can be defined as the partnership between a sponsor and a sports entity (organization, person, place or event) to achieve management and marketing communication objectives as part of a football-related activity.

What are the goals and impacts of sports sponsorship practices?

This section aims to study the purposes of sponsorship. After studying the key factors necessary for a successful sport partnership, we will discuss the objectives and targets of the practices. The examples provide insight on the logic of exchange, the basis of the phenomenon. What follows is a study on the amounts which have been invested in the sector. Particular attention is paid to the economics of professional football club jerseys.

The key factors for success, the targets and objectives of a sponsorship

Now we will analyze the key factors for success and the targets and objectives of sponsorship.

The key factors for a successful sports sponsorship

A powerful sponsorship requires integrating the objectives of this plan in a proper marketing and brand communication strategy. It should not be a "heart stopper", but an ensemble that promotes good management and development of the company. This entails giving meaning to the sponsorship strategy and ensuring that it is in line with the values and projects of the brand. The SPORSORA Association (2014, p. 55) distinguishes four key factors for success in a sports partnership.

These elements are in line with the remarks of Christophe Bouchet, director of Infront, for whom, "In order for a sponsor to be recognized there must be a long-standing partnership between the brand and the sponsored entity." In addition, four elements make up a virtuous cycle in a sponsorship: the strategy, the acquisition of rights, activation and know-how.

Moreover, a sponsorship should set goals and aim to reach certain targets. Several objectives and impacts can be searched by an organization that leads a sponsorship initiative. Of course, these depend on the target audiences. Table 6.2 proposed by Meenaghan (2005), recaps the objectives and impacts related to the different audiences. We will examine some of them.

Table 6.1 Key factors for a successful sponsorship

Factors	*Definitions and Examples*
Coherence	The consistency of the partnership with the overall strategy of the company and the values it wants to highlight is essential. It also means making a thorough analysis of the brand's values and a careful identification of target audiences. Finally, the choice of sports and partners' rights holders is obviously a crucial element for a successful sponsorship
Objectives	The company's goals should be clear, identified and shared both within the organization and with its partners. A desire to achieve too many objectives at once can be counterproductive. It is better to favor the growth of a partnership in time that will meet all of the brand's objectives.
Duration	Duration remains a key element as it is needed in order to anchor the brand's image in the public's mind and preferred targets. Beyond efficacy, it also guarantees that sympathy is strengthened, and that the relationship will stand the test of time even when potential storms could challenge the company outside of its commitment to the sport.
Meaning or Content	The meaning or the content of the sponsorship program are fundamental today. A sponsorship strategy can no longer rely solely on visibility criteria. One must give meaning to the speech, by telling a story (storytelling), which will have the effect of strengthening the public support and accelerating the brand status, brand awareness and the process of brand preference.

Source: Adapted from Sporsora (2014, p. 55).

Table 6.2 The objectives, targets and the impacts of sponsorship

Targets	*Objectives*	*Effects*
General public	Moral and civil dimensions of the company	Valorization of the image of the company
	The social responsibility of the company	Creation of a feeling of kindness
People in the company	Organizational culture of the company	Increased feeling of pride and belonging to the company
	Image of the company	Creation of brand image
Politicians / Executives	Offering places for a show, breakfasts or receptions	Providing entertainment, building a relationship
	Creation of a feeling of kindness	Aids/platforms for lobbying
Media	Offering places for a show, breakfasts or receptions	Creation of a positive image for the company
Shareholders	Ubiquitous visibility	Reassuring feeling
Vendors	Relationship management	Enhanced business relationships
Negotiators	Relationship management	Enhanced business relationships
Targeted market	Brand advertising	Stimulation of brand recognition
	Sponsoring of the brand	Developing company's values
	Brand relationships	Provoke a change in attitude
	Sales	Provoke brand attractiveness
		Stimulate tests or sales of a product
Oneself/Peers	Choice of the president	Status reinforcement
	Personal enhancement	Personal fulfilment

Source: Adapted from Meenaghan (2005, p. 247).

The target audiences of sponsorship: the event as a focal point

> A sporting event is actually very social, has a specific image and a generally uncertain outcome, facilitating the consumer's sharing and exchange of perceptions and feelings with regard to various entities that gathers.
>
> (Chanavat, 2009, p. 117)

First of all, it is appropriate for the entity that wishes to invest in sports sponsorship to identify the targets it wants to reach. Sponsorship initiatives may aim towards external targets or internal members of an organization (Meenaghan, 2005). It is therefore appropriate here to underline the multiplicity of the potential audiences targeted for sponsorship. Anne (1992), distinguishes two audiences: the direct and indirect audience. Entities that are in direct contact with the event are constitutive of direct audiences: the spectator, rights holder, co-sponsor, etc. Therefore, they are the stakeholders present at the event venue while the event is taking place. This target, often narrow, does not always generate substantial investments by the advertiser (Fleck-Dousteyssier, 2006). The sponsor aims at the indirect audience which includes, in turn, entities indirectly associated with the event through the media. According to Anne (1992), this audience is made up of viewers, listeners and readers.

Moreover, the population targeted by the action can be considered as an internal or external target by the sponsoring organization. External audiences targeted by sponsorship action include customers, prospects, the general public, prescribers and experts, suppliers, distributors, financial actors, the media, governmental authorities, etc. Sponsorship also provides to the organization a platform to the public audience. These are mainly staff and shareholders. These audiences are an integral part of the sponsorship system. The combination of direct and indirect audiences at the event, as well as internal and external communications modes to locate stakeholders within a particular model, is shown in Figure 6.2.

Finally, the advertiser seeks to reach the part of the event audience corresponding to its own objectives of external communication. This is "useful" audience.

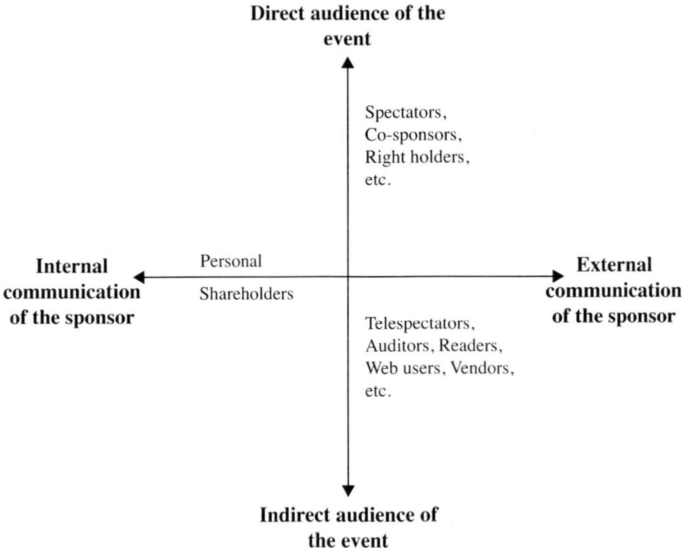

Figure 6.2 Combination of audiences and communication modes as part of a sponsored event

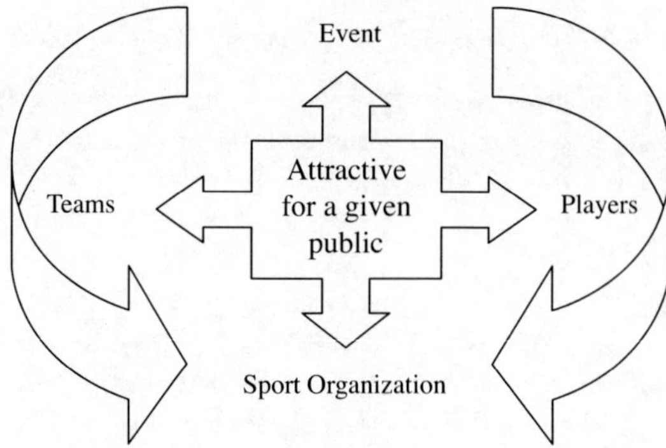

Figure 6.3 The event as the focal point of public attraction

Source: Adapted from Chanavat and Desbordes (2014a, p. 29).

Sports sponsorship represents a communication used to persuade sports consumers that there is a link between the sponsoring brand and the sporting event, which is represented by an organization, an individual, an event or a place. In this context, the event represents a focal point of attraction for the targeted audiences.

The objectives of the sponsorship

After identifying the target, the idea is for the company to define the objectives of the sponsorship. The sponsorship action does not necessarily replace advertising, to the extent that it does not always use the same communication medium, It is, however, a complement. The basis of success for a sponsorship strategy lies in the benefits it offers. Three main objectives are generally attributed to advertising: to gain attention, to persuade and to provoke a behavior (De Baynast and Lendrevie, 2014). The communication through the action also represents an effective means of influencing the cognitive, emotional and conative reactions of the consumer; an idea also highlighted by the model of Cornwell, Weeks and Roy (2005) in their overall approach linked to the consumer in a sponsorship action. In general, sponsorship seeks ultimately to increase the sales of an organization. However, the act of purchasing (or re-purchasing) depends on many variables relating to the consumer, the environment or marketing action. In addition, the sponsorship objectives sought by an organization are mainly the development and loyalty to the brand until it is publicly recognized and the change and the strengthening of the image. Sponsorship is primarily a hot media; advertising will advocate and present the benefits of products. However, the sponsorship will bring emotion, values, image. It also helps goals to be met. More specifically, the sponsorship may be used to increase the credibility and brand awareness, influence its image, generate a feeling of benevolence towards the sponsoring brand, contribute to human resource management, develop *business-to-business* relationships or boost sales. We will pay particular attention to some of these objectives through examples in football.

- *Providing credibility to the product*
  Sponsorship is an opportunity for a sponsor to provide evidence of technical performance, good quality and expertise in its products and/or services. Whether directly or indirectly associated with the sponsored entity, the objective is to enhance and legitimize the sponsor.

The product or service is therefore placed in a position of use to demonstrate its superiority over its competitors. This type of action relates primarily to companies involved in the technical and/or technological sectors (the Adidas sports shoe on the occasion of the FIFA World Cup).

- *Increasing awareness*
  Brand awareness measures the perception of a brand, its roots as a node in the memory of the consumer. Increasing brand awareness is one of the fundamental objectives sought by the sponsors. Of the organizations that are involved in a sponsorship campaign, 67 per cent pledge that purpose (IEG, 2014). Three indicators of brand awareness help us to understand the effectiveness of a sponsorship action: *top of mind* (measurement of superiority), unaided awareness (measuring the presence within the mind), aided awareness (a measure of recognition). A special meaning is given to each indicator, and two of them are related: unaided awareness and top of mind. Unaided awareness is the percentage of individuals able to spontaneously name a brand in the sector considered. This indicator is used to evaluate memory storage as it measures the level of brand recognition in the consumer's mind. The top of mind indicator or the first, spontaneous association, measures the brand which is most often cited. Finally, the aided awareness score takes into account the percentage of people recognizing the brand in a list on a given product category, taking into account that there are fictitious names and/or names that do not belong to the category studied in the list. This indicator measures more the recognition than the memorization of sponsors. It can also identify the phenomena of persistence or confusion. The calculated score is usually the highest of the three. Thus, the effectiveness of sponsorship has enabled Nissan to develop its reputation considerably. Through its sponsorship of UEFA, Nissan gives itself new media exposure through sports. Nissan is also a partner of Usain Bolt, as well as the 2016 Olympic Games in Rio. In addition, in France, the automaker is involved with the Paris marathon where it promotes its electric models.

Box 6.2 Nissan, the official sponsor of UEFA Champions League

In September 2014, the Japanese brand became the official sponsor of the famous UEFA Champions League for a period of 4 years. This partnership will make Nissan one of the biggest promoters of the sport worldwide.

After years of "affiliation" to a competitor, the UEFA Champions League changed its automotive partner. This sporting competition, which is highly followed in Europe, will offer a certain reputation to Nissan, which will strengthen the long-term sponsorship, signed until the 2017/2018 season. This has been the largest sponsorship deal ever made by the manufacturer.

> Innovating differently is what Nissan does and, as UEFA partners, we will seek to implement new ways to enrich the experience of the Champions League, said Roel de Vries, Corporate Vice President and Global Head of Marketing & Communications at Nissan. The most prestigious football competition in Europe will be an important global forum for Nissan. Our goal is to create enthusiasm for both football and our cars among fans throughout the world. Both are the work of great people who are passionate about what they do.

Commenting on the agreement, Guy-Laurent Epstein, Marketing Director of UEFA Events SA, said:

> We are delighted to have Nissan as the official partner of the Champions League next season. Nissan is a global company and one of the largest automotive groups. We believe that the partnership will result in a lot of innovation and enthusiasm across all global markets and we are confident that Nissan will be able to utilize the UEFA Champions League in order to strengthen its current success.

The partnership with the Champions League is another example of Nissan's commitment in global sports, already including multiple sponsorships: the 2016 Olympic and Paralympic Games in Rio, the Brazilian and Mexican Olympic teams, the British Olympic and Paralympic teams, the Africa Cup of Nations, the Canadian Football League (not forgetting that they are the sports ambassadors of the brand), the Olympic gold medalists Usain Bolt and Sir Chris Hoy, the institutional partner of the Trust/Heisman Trophy and the official global automotive partner of City Football Group.

As an official partner of the UEFA Champions League, Nissan will have extensive rights to the games, the pregame workouts, content, media, hospitality, events and the final. This should offer its customers a wide range of promotional activities!

Source: http://www.nissan-idm.com/actualites/nissan-sponsor-officiel-de-l-uefa-champions-league – "Nissan, sponsor officiel de l'UEFA Champion League", published on January 5, 2015. Last accessed on April 15, 2015.

However, the proliferation of brands engaged in sponsorship on behalf of a given event does not facilitate the recognition of sponsors. This results in an advertising overload likely to impact the effectiveness of the sponsorship operation. It is important to not confuse awareness and image. A known sponsor can enjoy a disastrous image. Conversely, there are lower profile brands that have a "good" image.

- *Creating, enhancing or modifying the image*
  The image corresponds to all the associations attached to an entity. The development and enhancement of brand image are major objectives for the sponsorship activity. As part of a sponsorship action, the sponsor seeks to take on the image of the sponsored entity. In this way, we are talking about image sponsorship. This may be the image of the company, its brands or its products. The goal may be to orient the image toward values such as innovation, dynamism or elitism. Indeed, more than half of the organizations aim to modify their image (IEG, 2014). This element is in line with the academic literature in sponsorship which emphasizes that the first goal of many sponsors is to develop, enhance or modify the semantic associations linked to a brand. This is why the study of the effectiveness of sponsorship on the image, as well as the study of related concepts expressing the cognitive dimensions related to brands, is frequently studied (Chanavat, 2009). The acquisition of image elements can be explained by a strengthening or a transfer of partnerships. Note that this concept of transfer (McCracken, 1989) is based on the theories of conditioning and of reinforcement. This objective in regards to the brand's image can be tied to external and internal targets. In this way, during the France–Brazil match on March 26th, 2015, a communication operation set up by Volkswagen, sponsor of the FFF, caused people to talk about the brand, activate the partnership and allowed for the development of the car brand's image.

Box 6.3 The communication operation of Volkswagen during the match between France and Brazil, on March 26, 2015

France-Brazil #VOLKSWAGEN

Perhaps you noticed the "small" error that has crept into our billboards during the match between France–Brazil on March 26. Indeed, in France, the brand is difficult to write, and often the victim of misspellings. Last night, we wanted to play a little game: the viewers and the audience in the stadium could read at the edge of the field "#Volkswagen supports the Blues". The error present throughout the 1st half was largely relayed by social media, with the belief of an error of the brand. Finally, all of this was a communication operation planned from the beginning to generate discussion around the name Volkswagen. At halftime, we responded on TF1, Twitter and of course on the same billboards around the field with the slogan, "Yet that's easy to get it right," the brand's signature in the 1980s.

Source: http://volkswagen-fff.fr/operation-volkswagen/ – Last accessed on May 8th, 2015.

François Vasseur, associate marketing director of the FFF, explains

It was their idea. This is a brand that often innovates in communication. A bit irreverent. They like to take the opposing view. This was not detrimental and did not pose a problem to the French team. But the FFF did not think that it would have much impact. This affirmed that the LED panels were being watched. It's good for the sponsors.

Figure 6.4 Display of the Volkswagen advertising campaign "Volkswagen supports the Blues"

- *Contributing to the management of human resources*
  As mentioned previously, sponsorship potentially concerns the external targets just as much as it concerns the internal staff of a structure. Nevertheless, the impact on the human resources of an organization is only rarely the sole purpose assigned to sponsorship. However, the sponsorship can promote the development of the corporate culture, the motivation to work and to seek a result, or to federate and to build up the internal cohesion of an organization. These factors contribute to the management of people which represent a necessary condition for achieving results for an organization. In the first place, the fact of being associated with an entity can arouse the interest of a company's sales force and can, for example, serve as a platform for a development operation with commercial results. This may therefore bring about an emulation sponsorship, inducing a form of competition between sellers with the goal of rewarding the best of them through inviting them to the event with a special status. As part of the partnership between the FFF and Credit Agricole, the coach of the France team unveiled on March 19, 2015, the list of players selected for the friendlies against Brazil and Denmark at the headquarters of Crédit Agricole. For François Vasseur, associate marketing director of the FFF, "This press conference with Didier Deschamps has enabled a mobilization of the bank employees. It is a beautiful example of an initiative that contributes to the management of the sponsor's human resources."[7] In general, it is appropriate to associate human resources directly with the sponsored entity. Furthermore, the objective is also to communicate internally in order to involve staff and obtain their membership to the global communication project.
- *Boosting business-to-business (B-to-B) relationships*
  Actions regarding hospitality, also called public relations operations, conducted as part of a sponsorship activity, represent a solution to develop trade relations between professionals. The sponsor must choose a sponsored entity that is suitable in this way to related activities from the perspective of fostering individualized and privileged relations. The proposed environment must combine social selectivity and a pleasant and unique experience. Thus, the sponsorship activity can contribute to the stimulation of a distribution network. This is about creating a direct or indirect association to the operation. This partnership can present itself under different forms: animation or special operations. Moreover, the relationship between the co-partners of a sponsored entity can be promoted.
- *Sales development*
  The act of buying is influenced by many variables, including those related to marketing action. As mentioned earlier, sales development is considered as the ultimate goal of the sponsorship. The objectives previously identified only represent the intermediate goals of the sponsors (Walliser, 2006). A study published by International Events Group shows that sales and other results produced by an activation of managerial processes are the most important factors in the decision to renew or abandon a sponsor (IEG, 2014). Overall, the sponsorship has to sell. Therefore, if the impact of this communication on the cognitive and affective dimensions of the consumer seems necessary, it must be recognized that the increase in sales remains inevitable. However, it remains difficult to isolate and quantify the direct impact of a sponsorship campaign on sales. Therefore, more studies are measuring purchase intent than sales or turnover. Combining a promotional sales event that delivers tangible benefits to consumers helps contribute to the evaluation of this action. Moreover, special circumstances appear to be essential for there to be an immediate effect on sales. Thus, "the stimulation of sales through sponsorship has the greatest chance to occur when products have a strong connection with the sponsored activity and, somehow, have proven themselves during the

action" (Walliser, 2006, p. 44). Many examples illustrate that sales development is an objective clearly assigned to the sponsorship action.

The logic of exchange in a sports sponsorship

We can therefore highlight that goals related to sponsorship impacting the cognitive, affective and conative dimensions of the consumer. In other words, the action aims to transfer part or all of the values of the sponsored sporting entity (and the elements of the culture associated with it) to the company as an institution and to its products or its brands. The idea is to make it more efficient on the market, that is to say, to better meet the needs of consumers. This gives rise to a financial support, material or intangible, done in order to make known the company, its products and brands, and to reap the rewarding benefits in terms of image.

Therefore, to properly choose the most effective sponsorship action, one should know precisely who is the direct and indirect audience of an event. From a quantitative and qualitative standpoint, this includes demographics, lifestyle and consumer universe. In this perspective, studies of media audiences have multiplied (KantarSport, Repucom, Institut français de démoscopie, Sport Lab, Sport Research International, Eurodata TV, BVA, etc.). As a form of communication with commercial purpose, sponsorship naturally seeks to increase sales. However, the act of purchase or re-purchase is influenced by many variables related to the buyer, the environment and the marketing action. More specifically, the sponsorship will be used to increase the credibility and brand awareness, to influence the image, to boost the distribution network and sales force, to develop business-to-business relationships, etc.

A comprehensive development of the amounts invested

We have laid out the theoretical foundations and have examined the characteristics and purposes of the phenomenon of sports sponsorship in football. It is now necessary to study the economic importance of this activity.

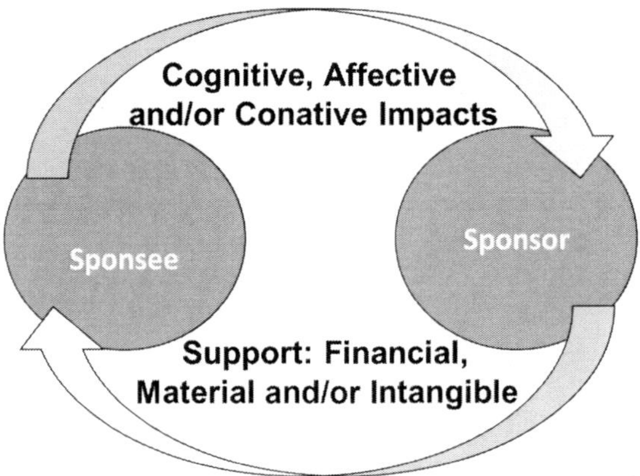

Figure 6.5 The logic behind the exchange in a sports sponsorship

Source: Chanavat and Desbordes (2014a, p. 30).

An overall increase in the sports sponsorship sector

In the early 1980s, the Union of Advertisers (UDA) estimated the worth of the sports sponsorship industry at 30 million US dollars. This period corresponds to the explosion of sponsorship spending. Chauveau (1992, p. 111) mentions that there has been a "very rapid increase in power since 1985". Thus, according to the IREP (Institute and advertising research), the expenditures of French sponsoring companies have more than doubled between 1985 and 1990. The investigation by the UDA in 1988 concluded that companies had gone from the discovery and exploration of sponsorship to its rational utilization. The pioneer era was therefore over. The early 1990s corresponds to the *users age*. While in 1990 global investment hovered around 5.5 billion euros, the amount of invested expenses reached 9 billion euros in 1996 (IEG, 1996) and represents no less than 57.5 billion US dollars in 2015 (IEG, 2015), nearly two decades later.

According to the latest report by the Institute for research and advertising studies (IREP – France Pub, 2014), expenses on advertising in France amounted to more than 29.6 billion euros in 2014. Sponsorship and patronage respectively accounted for 0.8% and 0.3% of the market share expenses on advertising.

These figures are probably underestimated to the extent that they do not take into consideration, for example, the additional expenses of activating the brand to optimize its spending. If this element is necessary for a sponsorship, then it is essential to understand it. For each euro invested in the partnership, one to three euros have to be invested in order to promote the association with the sponsee and to extract the maximum profit. However, this ratio is informative only because it situates the brand activation strategy in the general marketing strategy of the company. Everything depends on the definition of the agreed upon sponsorship. Some sports marketing operations, public relations or direct marketing are listed as expenditure items other than that of sponsorship.

In a turbulent environment, sport business and football seem to resist the crisis. The LFP–UCPF–IPSOS "barometer" (2015) on the image of professional football clubs confirms the strong link between Ligue 1 and Ligue 2 and the French people. They place these championships as leading sports entertainment. This survey establishes football as the favorite sport of the French (before tennis and rugby): 17 million of them are interested, and 14.5 million are following it regularly, 36% (+2 points versus last season) and 31% (+3 points) of the national population (LFP–UCPF–IPSOS, 2015).

Football sponsorship: entrance tickets

While figures, studies and amounts of sponsorship agreements in football are often mentioned, let's try to observe some of them in order to better understand the discipline.

In February 2008, the French Football Federation (FFF) announced that the firm Nike would provide uniforms for the French Football Team (EdFF), between 2011 and 2018 for a total budget of 320 million euros for seven and a half seasons (42.6 million per year). Nike's strategy has always been to associate its image with the best teams. The American equipment manufacturer has made EdFF the most expensive national football team in the world. For François Vasseur, "This is a partnership of eight years, which also concerns amateur clubs, regional teams, all youth teams, and all national competitions. The equipment manufacturer's partnership involves the most. We work hand in hand with Nike to optimize this partnership."[8]

For its part, as mentioned above, the English club Manchester United has been sponsored by Adidas since the 2015–2016 season for an amount of approximately 94 million euros per year for over 10 years. This contract is combined with the partnership started by Chevrolet in the

2014–2015 season for a period of 7 years amounting to 560 million euros (80 million euros per year). These amounts are an important part of professional clubs' budgets and are naturally increasing as the sporting results of the club improve. Thus, sports sponsorship represents almost 16% of the operating revenues for Ligue 1 and Ligue 2 clubs, while match revenues are only 11% (EY-UCPF, 2014). In other words, sponsorship is a major source of funding for professional clubs (Chanavat, 2009; Tribou, 2007).

Partnership contracts allow athletes to significantly increase their revenues. While the annual salary of Lionel Messi from the club is 36 million, the 17th edition of "the salaries of stars" from France Football (2015) places the Argentinian as the highest paid footballer in the world, with 28 million euros of revenue coming from the utilization of his image. In addition, a study by Badenhausen on behalf of *Forbes* magazine (2015) shows that the sponsored athlete David Beckham generated 75 million US dollars in 2014 during his first full year of retirement. With his numerous partnership contracts, the Englishman is ranked second among the best paid retired athletes behind Michael Jordan. Among active athletes, the Portuguese Cristiano Ronaldo, the number one football player, occupies second place in the Forbes ranking (2014) of the highest paid athletes. The amount of the player's salary is estimated at 52 million US dollars with 28 million US dollars coming from his sponsors: Emirates, Nike, Samsung Electronics, Toyota, etc. Thus, 35% of his revenues come from sponsorship activities. Sports sponsorship is therefore emerging as a preferred communication means for many advertisers. Beyond his performance on the field, Cristiano Ronaldo is also very present on social networks. He has the largest community among sports players with more than 100 million Facebook fans (see Chapter 7 dedicated to social networks).

As for sporting events, they also depend on sponsorship, and this promotional activity is a significant part of the corporate marketing budget (Grohs and Reisinger, 2005).

However, this share is still modest for the LFP (about 1/100), given the large amount of television rights in its business model. Yet the LFP hopes to develop *naming rights initiatives* starting in 2016. The Ligue 1 would like to get backed by a trademark as they were by Orange between 2008 and 2012. The goal is to collect at least 10 million euros per year from the 2016–2017 season on. This amount is lower than what is collected in England with Barclays (48 million euros per year), with BBVA in Spain (23 million euros) and in Italy with Telecom Italia Mobile (15 million euros), but slightly higher than the rate achieved by the Bundesliga thanks to Hermes (8 million euros). The cost of the association between a sponsor and a sponsored sports entity has continued to increase in recent years.

In 2014, Nissan became the official sponsor of the Champions League, the most prestigious European football cup, for 4 years. Note that the car firm is also title sponsor of several clubs including: New York City, Melbourne City and especially Manchester City. The Japanese automaker became the official sponsor of the City Football Group (CFG), which includes such entities. Thus, beyond the association with the values and performances of the clubs, the strategy of the sponsor brand is to sponsor a competition. Whatever the sporting results, this "multi-association" offers a strong media exposure.

As of the 2015–2016 season, Chelsea and Yokohama have signed a jersey partnership for an amount of 55 million euros per year for 5 years. Sometime later, Manchester City and Etihad concluded an agreement two times higher for 110 million euros per year. If Etihad is an airline of Abu Dhabi, the country of the club's owners, UEFA seems to consider that the agreement is in line with the rules of financial fair play.

Among the companies active in the field of sports sponsorship in France, the majority of brands communicate through football. Unsurprisingly, football remains king to the extent that it brings together, on the French market, more than half of the brands represented during sporting events. Thus, in order to partner with a leading French Ligue 1 club, the brand Eovi, a mutual fund for interprofessional, national health insurance, became the main partner of the AS Saint-Étienne (ASSE) from the 2015–2016 season on. Note that this was already the main sponsor of the women's team "Les Verts". Similarly, after the financially complicated years, Le Coq Sportif made a comeback in terms of football partnership, beginning in the 2015–2016 fiscal year. The French manufacturer is sponsoring the AS Saint-Étienne and Fiorentina (see Chapter 12 dedicated to the AS Saint-Étienne).

As for Hyundai, the 4th largest global automaker, they have partnered with FIFA for the World Cup since 2002, with the European Championship of Nations and UEFA for 14 years, and with the Ligue 1 for 2 years (as a partner of OL). It is a way for them to be present throughout football (see Chapter 11 dedicated to OL).

The status of football is the same internationally. The FIFA World Cup in Brazil 2014 was beneficial on a new level in terms of sponsorship. Income generated only from FIFA sponsors for the World Cup in 2014 amounted to 1.4 billion US dollars. It amounted to 750 million euros on the part of its six official partners at the German World Cup in 2006.

The particularity of sports sponsorship is that the market is not standardized. The figures are not very precise, even if more and more specialized research institutes are working on the subject. Sports sponsorship, constantly changing due to an extremely large selection, became an economic activity, and it makes sense to measure its effectiveness in a managerial perspective. Since the 1998 FIFA World Cup in France, sponsorship became considered as a separate activity in France, while the Anglo-Saxon countries had considered it as such for many years. At the time, the sports industry essentially brought together the sporting goods manufacturers such as Adidas and Nike and distributors. Today, telecommunications, the banking sector, and general public electronics companies as well as airlines are the sectors most represented. Here we have a growing market, consisting of many advertisers developing an extremely large offer with a wide range of investments. As a result, this variation produces significantly different "entrance tickets" in terms of the disciplines and types of sponsorship. This variation also exists in the football sector.

Moreover, the large amounts of some of the contracts can contradict new practices of market liberalization. Thus, as noted above, the entrance ticket for a jersey sponsorship for a Ligue 1 club has proved possible for less than 10,000 euros.

A focus on the jersey sponsorship of European football clubs

The jersey is considered the main marketing outlet in the football sector. The Repucom study (2015) shows that jersey sponsorship revenues continue to grow in Europe. The results of this study, based on an analysis of six major European leagues (Premier League, Bundesliga, La Liga, Ligue 1, Serie A and Eredivisie) show a 20% increase in revenue in this area: 570 million euros in 2013–2014 for a total of 687 million euros in 2014–2015. This is a record increase for the past 15 years. It suggests that the sponsoring brands wish more measures and a better understanding of the impact of sponsorship. In this context, the Premier League and La Liga have enjoyed a 30% increase in 1 year. Over the same period, the revenues for Ligue 1 have increased by 13%, Serie A by 21% and 9% for the Bundesliga. Only the Eredivisie, the Dutch league, is down with a 5% decrease. This increase is made possible especially by the massive investment of Middle East economic partners, which happen to be the main providers of income related to sponsorship. Companies in UAE and Qatar have invested nearly 160 million euros in European football sponsorship. Eighty-six percent of sponsorship revenue for La Liga are the result of foreign investment. FC Barcelona and Real Madrid were pioneers with contracts signed respectively with Fly Emirates and Qatar Airways. Other clubs followed, like Real Sociedad, who signed a jersey sponsorship deal with Obao, a Chinese company. The importance of the phenomenon is also reflected by 68% of sponsorship revenues for the Ligue 1 and 75% of revenues in the Premier League. Also, according to the Repucom study (2015), the UAE, *via* Emirates, represents the largest investor with its notable five "big" contracts with Real Madrid, PSG, AC Milan, Arsenal and Hamburg. Emirates has at least one team from each major European league, showing its large investment in the sector and in the business of football. Next is Qatar, which has developed unique partnerships with PSG (Ooredoo, QTA, QNB, etc.) (see Chapter 10 dedicated to PSG) or with Barcelona (Qatar Foundation and Qatar Airways).

We can also highlight the partnership between Etihad and Manchester City. The major clubs in this way share their jerseys with airline companies. Behind the Middle Eastern countries, German companies are the second largest suppliers of revenue with 112 million euros of income invested, followed by US companies (82 million). The Premier League is the league that collects the most revenue, 213 million euros, of this nature. They are also the league that recorded the highest growth in revenue between the 2013–2014 and 2014–2015 fiscal years (+36%). Partnerships signed by Manchester United discussed in the introduction of this chapter explain this significant increase. Indeed, each club's jersey partnership accounts for an average of 10.65 million euros. Next is the Bundesliga, with 139 million euros in revenue, which is ahead of La Liga that reached 113 million euros in revenue.

The German league has a strong internal market, as German companies have traditionally invested in the jersey partnership with clubs. However, this championship records a growth rate below the Liga (9% vs 30%). Ligue 1 ranked 4th in the standings with 96 million euros in revenues despite a smaller growth rate than Serie A (13% vs 21%). Note that Ligue 1 totals 68% of revenues from foreign companies against only 47% for the Serie A.

Finally, note that the amount of revenue from jersey partnerships for the MLS (45 million euros) is higher than the Dutch league (42 million euros). However, these results must be slightly modified to the extent that the MLS has more clubs than the Eredivisie (see Chapter 3 dedicated to the MLS). Also, the Dutch league catches up with the MLS in terms of average income per club. This decrease in revenue is illustrated by Ajax. While the club was receiving 12 million euros per season from its Aegon partner, the new contract with Ziggo amounts to 8 million euros.

Although these amounts are colossal, they are based on those of Manchester United, the club of reference in this matter. Since the partnership developed with Vodafone in 2000 for 12 million euros (then 16 million euros), the club has tripled the sponsorship fee on this outlet. Subsequently, in 2003, Real Madrid took this into account for its partnership with Siemens Mobile, and signed for 16 million euros annually. Season after season, Manchester United increased the amount of its jersey partnership: from 20 million, to 23 million, and finally to 25 million euros for its agreement with AON. This financial budget of 25 million euros is the same amount as the partnership between Emirates and PSG, between the Standard Chartered and Liverpool, between T-Mobile and Bayern Munich or between Bwin and Real Madrid. The emergence of the Asian market is reflected in turn by the contracts signed by Huawei with PSG, Olympique Lyonnais with Hyundai or Goldenway with Swansea.

The presence of Qatar Airways on the FC Barcelona jersey (for 30 to 35 million euros per year) in 2011 and the renewal of Emirates with Arsenal for an equivalent sum rekindled the race for jersey sponsorship. However, in July 2012, at the announcement of the sponsorship agreement forged between Manchester United and General Motors for its Chevrolet brand, a new step had been taken. The agreement provided for 2 years of "invisible" sponsoring until 2014 for 15 million euros and seven years of presence on the Manchester United jersey for 50 million euros (with an annual 2% increase), without premiums.

In 2015, the partnership between the Japanese brand Yokohama Rubber and Chelsea for a 5-year period, amounting to 275 million euros (including 25 million in performance bonuses) attests of the same. While Nike paid 13.1 million euros to be the official supplier of Juventus, Adidas is paying at least 29 million euros per season for 6 years (since 2015–2016) to be the new official supplier of the club.

If the amounts of contracts with partners were already consistent, they have been experiencing a record evolution. The "jersey sponsorship" is an important part of the income of professional sports structures to the extent that it represents about 10% of their budget.

Managerial development of sports sponsorship: evolution, mutation and new trends

Over the last 15 years, sponsorship has changed considerably; therefore, we intend to highlight three striking elements. The first concerns the activation of the sponsor's brand to optimize its partnerships. The second is related to relationship marketing. Finally, we can highlight the growing impact of new and digital technologies in the relationship between the sponsored sports organizations and the sponsoring brands. The concept of brand activation is the subject of special attention in this section. The concepts of naming, ambush marketing, regional sponsorship, state sponsorship, citizen sponsorship, sports sponsorship of multiple events and participatory sponsorship are successively examined and illustrated.

The advent of brand activation

We can observe an evolution of sponsorship over the past 30 years. Beyond the evidence presented so far, we identify three distinct periods. First, sponsorship was a technical communication that was integrated at best into the corporate communications strategy. Subsequently, companies have sought to utilize the synergies between their sponsorship strategy and the other variables in the marketing mix to ensure the best possible return on the investment. Today, the challenge is first to incorporate sponsorship from the various business strategies and, second, to enable the brand to sponsor different targets. Successful brand activation requires consistency in all the initiatives implemented by the sponsor for a long period of time, to supply, build and enhance a story. The goal is to have a clear story. Our analysis echoes the words of François Vasseur for who

> sponsorship takes time to settle in. You have to dig a furrow with a real story you tell, and all your activations come to feed this history of the partnership. That's the hard part: not to do isolated actions, a commercial hit, a successful event, etc. It takes consistency.

An alternative communications technique through sponsorship

The 1980s were marked by the rapid development of sports events supported by increasing media exposure. Many companies were involved in sponsorship operations, particularly in order to stand out from traditional modes of communication. It was done to develop a closer relationship with their targets and enhance their brand image and reputation. This period was marked by a significant growth of the sports sponsorship market. All sports organizations (federations, clubs, event organizers) then began to look for sponsors. Sponsorship appeared as a new source of funding. The structures which had the rights to the event were especially concerned about the availability of this new service and had not yet entered a marketing approach. Customers were not satisfied to the extent that their expectations had not yet been analyzed. Some organizations did not have the expertise and skills to approach and negotiate with sponsors. Moreover, they did not know how to design a sponsorship offer to satisfy the expectations of sponsors. Thus, after a period of enthusiasm, policymakers began questioning the selection and effectiveness of these operations. This was an "educational" period in which stakeholders were seeking to better understand this outlet and to streamline their strategy. Thus, the 1980s led to a better assimilation of sponsorship into the communication strategy. This demonstrates that sponsorship must contribute to the achievement of marketing objectives. It remains integrated into communication.

An interaction between sponsorship and the variables of the marketing mix

The 1990s witnessed the development of sponsorship interaction with other variables in the marketing mix. The communication to which the sponsorship is attached was also better integrated into marketing. Thus, the concept of Integrated Marketing Communication (IMC) was gradually used. This was reflected by a greater focus on results, which made evaluation and ROI one of the major issues of this decade. Finally, the players within the system organized to fight against pseudo-sponsorship strategies, mentioned above, that emerged in the mid-1980s. Of course, the evolution certainly respected the objectives of the sponsorship action but focused mainly on integration among the variables of the mix. During the 1990s, the design and use of sponsorship evolved. Operators learned to develop synergies between the sponsorship and the variables of the mix. The work of Dambron (1991), titled *Sponsoring and Marketing Policy*, reflected the will to rationalize the relationship between sponsorship and marketing management as well as focused in particular on its interconnectedness with the variables of the marketing mix: product, price, distribution and communication. It was based on a qualitative survey of large French companies, some of which are subsidiaries of American or Japanese firms. This analysis expresses the challenge of this decade for sponsors and sports organizations. This is an integrative approach in which the sponsorship is treated according to the above four macro variables (i.e. product, price, distribution and communication). Moreover, during this time, local authorities discovered sponsored events as a tool for developing the territory and as a way to improve the image of their brand (Ferrand and Chanavat, 2006).

Activation of the sponsor to generate the desired brand experience

The sponsors began investing more and more to promote their sponsorship actions. In the early 2000s, the concept of activation gradually replaced the one of enhancement. There began to be no "good sponsorship" without brand activation. This represents a strategic tool contributing to brand building. Its main role is to accelerate consumer contact and the actual purchase by rewarding and creating meaning, and increasing proximity to the consumer in everyday life. The brand brings a real benefit to the consumer. It must be an encounter (experience) in the emotional context of the event. Several definitions have been proposed in the academic literature. Maltese and Danglande (2014, p. 82) define activation as "operational modalities of sponsorship implementation during the event in order to connect fans (or direct audience) to the sponsors' brands". For Ferrand, Torrigiani and Camps i Povill (2006, p. 64), "Activation is a marketing strategy designed to provide the concerned persons with the desired brand experience during the sponsored event."

All stakeholders – right holders, agents, consumers, sponsors, etc. – want to make a profit from this activity in their own way. The challenge is to measure everyone's expectations in order to establish an ideal approach (Chanavat, Desbordes and Hautbois, 2014). It can be measured through contests: games *via* social networks, web games, games reserved for customers with the opportunity to win sporting goods, outings with some athletes or tickets to attend or discover an event. The initiatives of sponsors, including brand activations, are favorable to the development of professional sports organizations (Chanavat, Desbordes and Hautbois, 2014). For Samuel Guillardeau, stadium manager and director of organization and security at OGC Nice,[9] "The club relies on its partners to further its development. Most organized activities were made in collaboration with Allianz."

It is also desirable that the club quickly defines a specific activation budget with its partner. He adds,

> The club has the ambition to deploy other strategies with its partners in order to maximize its image and values. To facilitate this strategy, the club must change the way it works in terms of contract negotiations. The activation budget of the partnership should be defined immediately to facilitate their approach.

The logic of brand activation is also developed on behalf of the federations. As François Vasseur explains,

> We assisted the partners in terms of activation. It is structured so that the account managers are dedicated to partners. They are tasked with thinking about the making of the operation that often money cannot buy. This is a real concern for the FFF.

Although expectations from clubs and partners are changing in terms of sponsorship, it is now compulsory to stand out from the competition with these activation budgets. Several concrete examples of initiatives developed in the football sector are discussed in this chapter.

The "money can't buy" *events*

In football, rights holders want to provide their fans with the most unique experiences with the players and the club: kicking off the proceedings, getting on the players' bus, participating with the training, accompanying the players on the plane during an out-of-town game, etc. A "money can't buy" initiative consists of offering consumers the unattainable. Literally, there are events that money can't buy. While for the sponsor the idea is to promote and activate the partnership, this type of device also proves beneficial for many of the stakeholders in sports events:

- The rights holder (club, federation, etc.) that allows you to experience this unique fan experience and to create buzz;
- The sponsor who manages to activate its rights in an innovative way;
- The sports marketing agency that works to meet the needs of a rights holder and an advertiser;
- The customer who will live an extraordinary moment;
- The fan's community, who can identify with the winning fan.

AS Saint-Étienne's marketing agency Sportfive and Orange gave the opportunity for a fan of "Les Verts" to live an unforgettable moment. This demonstrates the will to innovate and the club's ability to create a marketing buzz. "Initially, the club suggests an innovative idea and asked Sportfive to work on the concept and offer brands," says Arnaud Jaouen.[10] Thus, an AS Saint-Étienne supporter could camp out overnight in the stadium of his favorite club, Geoffroy-Guichard, in Saint-Étienne (see Chapter 12 dedicated to the AS Saint-Étienne).

The mobile operator Orange is a brand very involved in sports. Indeed, for years, the brand has been present in football, rugby and sailing. Although investments in sports brands were numerous, sometimes without any real coherence, the vast majority of counterparties was not used for some advertisers. For Orange, it seems that things have changed. The brand has decided to value its investments by activating in a rather forceful manner, including through new media.

The objective of the Orange brand is twofold. First, it wants to create content around partnerships, to make them live on its supports. In other words, the aim is to activate the partnership. Second, the idea is to offer consumers an unattainable dream. Overall, in the context of football, the goal is to deliver fans unique experiences, which are closer to the players and the club. The idea is to move towards innovative brand activations. In this perspective, Orange has decided to digitize its activation sponsorship around two sites – the "12th man" (football partnerships) and "Together with the XV" (rugby partnerships) – and around social media (Twitter, Facebook, Dailymotion). For the implementation of this device, Orange aims to create buzz, publicize and optimize its partnerships. This digitalization tries to create brand preference to retain subscribers and attract new customers. To do so, the essential advertising promise within the message ("the claim") is as follows: if Orange can help you achieve your dream in sports, what would it be? In football, this is the fan who creates his or her own event via the "I Have a Dream" Facebook page.

To carry out this project, Orange has very strong partnerships with Ligue 1 clubs as well as various other teams. This allows them to organize special events, to mount communication campaigns such as Live L1 (following L1 matches on Twitter with bloggers). To complete this soccer device, the brand is based on the "Orange Team". The team consists of players who make themselves available to meet with the winners of contests and other operations. For this, they sign trade and image partnerships. Among them are Christophe Jallet, Guillaume Hoarau, Kévin Gameiro, Eric Abidal, Andre and Jordan Ayew, Matuidi Blaise, Bafétimbi Gomis, Jérémie Janot or Mevlüt Erdinç. The main interest of this Team Orange resides with the meeting with the fans; however, it is missing a connection to the rest of the program behind this activation. A lack of sense that the brand is expected to fill quickly. Among all the operations organized by the 12th man, one can observe the contests of higher quality: VIP seats, meetings with players (Eric Abidal, the Ayew brothers), exceptional events (visit of the Parc des Princes), but also the OFC. With this strategy, Orange shows the possibility of utilizing sports partnerships with the aid of a digital platform. It is good to create content and bring a community to life, and thus achieve business goals using social media. The brand is one of the first to have launched a new media, which was still not preempted by advertisers. It thus proves that by improving the means, social media can become a fully fledged tool for 360-degree marketing strategy.

In the same vein, in 2015, PMU, official sponsor of PSG, activated its partnership with the club by launching an unprecedented recruitment for a dream "job". Through the program "Paris Saint-Germain Insider", a fan was given the opportunity to go behind the scenes of PSG for a month. Accustomed to "Money can't buy" activations, PMU and PSG in this way allowed a supporter of the club to discover the daily life of the club's operations. The insider immortalized special moments and shared them with community of fans *via* social media. The fan was recruited by a jury composed of PSG and PMU employees to participate in different events: practice close to the staff at the Ooredoo training center; go one-on-one against a player, Blaise Matuidi; travel to a game at the Stade Velodrome for the OM match against PSG; experience PSG vs Lille as a VIP member on the sideline; and participate in a Paris Poker Live tournament. This is an innovative tool for activating the PMU sponsor. Indeed, after the defeat of PSG 3 goals to 1 against Barcelona in the quarter-final of the first leg of the 2014–2015 Champions League, the aforementioned insider tweeted: "3–0 at the Nou Camp, we believe in it!" #WebetwithPMU.

Box 6.4 Paris Saint-Germain Insider: David landed his dream job thanks to the PMU

After 3 weeks of recruitment, the face of the Paris Saint-Germain's Insider was unveiled Friday at the Parc des Princes, before the match against Lorient. David Boyer, known as @David24HD on Twitter, an unconditional fan of the club from the capital, has done well in the face of four other formidable competitors!

For 1 month, he will take the role of reporter for Paris Saint-Germain on behalf of PMU and share with all supporters of the club, on social networks, privileged anecdotes and moments alongside the players behind the scenes of the club.

David: Paris Saint-Germain's Insider

David, a 28-year-old administrative assistant at ESSEC, has been an unconditional supporter of the club for over 20 years! Also passionate on social networks, he never misses an opportunity to tweet. Whether it's general/sports news or games of his team, any event is used for an original and humorous analysis. This, according to him, allowed him to differentiate himself and thus gain access to the final phase: the interview with the jury composed of Paris Saint-Germain and PMU representatives.

> The interview for the final phase of recruitment took place last Friday, I was prepared for it but that did not stop me from waking up early and being relatively stressed. During this interview, I explained to the jury my vision of the perfect Insider, my desire to share and to discover football differently, to offer something new. I wished to emphasize the details that make the Paris Saint-Germain a great club and to relay to all the stories I'm going to experience – meetings with some of the best players in the world, Classico from the press box of the Velodrome (Marseille stadium), home games . . . gathering anecdotes and witnessing intimate moments between players. I think that they enjoyed all of that. I am very pleased to take on this role for a month. A big thank you to Paris Saint-Germain and PMU, who have allowed me to realize my dream!

From March 25 to April 25, David will spend a month in contact with the players, discovering the daily life and functioning of the club through various appointments: a poker tournament at Parc des Princes, a practice at the Ooredoo training center close to the staff, a face to face meeting with Blaise Matuidi, a trip to the Stade Velodrome for the match between Marseille and Paris Saint-Germain and a home game, against Lille. There was a great deal of feedback on the *Paris Saint-Germain Insider* by PMU. Launched on February 23, the digital operation of PMU, the *Paris Saint-Germain Insider,* was a great success: more than 20,000 applications were filed, generating more than 90,000 shares on social networks via #PSGINSIDER. Through this unprecedented operation, PMU set out in search of the assigned reporter from Paris Saint-Germain, offering him the chance to infiltrate behind the scenes of the club, to live closer to the players and share those special moments with fans *via* social networks. To follow the operation on social networks, go to: #PSGINSIDER.

@PMU_OnParie @PSG_Inside @David24HD

Source: http://sportmedia.pmu.fr/communique/15548/Paris-Saint-Germain-Insider-David-decroche-job-de-reve-grace-au-PMU – "Paris Saint-Germain Insider: David lands his dream job thanks PMU" published on March 25, 2015. Last accessed on April 20, 2015.

Although clubs are inventive about the use of their players, our analysis suggests that new initiatives will take place. For instance, the LFP could allow a fan to ask a question at a press conference, to be with photographers on the lawn at the game, etc.

A digital sponsorship activation

Digital activations undertaken by Hyundai and Ooredoo, respectively OL and PSG partners, demonstrate the vitality and fertility of sports sponsorship in professional football.

Hyundai aims to increase its visibility and build brand image in France. This is why the brand has been a major partner of the Olympique Lyonnais for three seasons. In a brand activation perspective, Hyundai wants to contribute to the improvement of the "fan experience" through emphasizing its communication on digital media. This digital activation approach led Hyundai: to develop, in collaboration with OL services, the *SociOL Room*, a VIP box uniquely connected to social networks in France. This is the first "Social Media Center" to be developed by a professional entity in Ligue 1. Thanks to this interactive experience, the brand also won the 2015 Sporsora trophy for the "SociOL Room by Hyundai" in the category of best activation, as well as the prize for the best digital sports activation at the 2014 *Sport Numericus*. Although there are benefits to the sponsor for commercial development, the goal is to develop OL's image and to support its community of fans.

Box 6.5 Hyundai, trophy winner of Sporsora 2015 for the "SociOL Room by Hyundai"

Hyundai, trophy winner of Sporsora 2015 for the "Sociol Room by Hyundai" in the category "Best activation around a sporting event"

Launched by the Olympique Lyonnais and Hyundai in December 2013, the "SociOL Room by Hyundai" aims to aggregate fan communities in four charity matches: AS Saint-Étienne, OM, ASM and PSG.

A little over a year later, the brand was awarded the Sporsora 2015 trophy for the best activation around a sporting event.

Hyundai has been the major partner of the Olympique Lyonnais since the 2012–2013 season. Through this partnership, Hyundai benefits from the power of the OL brand to continue its conquest of the French market. With 1.9 million fans on Facebook and nearly 560,000 followers on Twitter, the Olympique Lyonnais is among the top three in Ligue 1. In this way, Hyundai and Sportfive worked with the club, a leader on digital media, to create innovative digital content broadcasted on SociOL Room.

The SociOL Room by Hyundai was the first "Social Media Center" to be born in a Ligue 1 stadium. Making influencers, players, fans, and community managers participate, they average 120,000 fans per game who interact on SociOLRoom by Hyundai. This craze has naturally benefited the Hyundai brand which saw its number of Facebook fans increase from 100,000 to 264,000 in a year. Affecting a total of more than 2 million people to date the SociOL Room displays on the broadcast content a commitment rate of 15%.

For Lionel French-Keogh, director of Hyundai Motor France:

> Engaged in football, both at the global, European and national level with the Olympique Lyonnais, one of our goals is to share our passion and our emotion with the sports fans.

> The digital SociOL Room perfectly meets this desire. This activation is part of a larger 360 program which proposes to allow the fans to undergo a unique and memorable experience every time the opportunity is offered to us.

For Vincent Baptist Closon, marketing director of the Olympique Lyonnais:

> The club has always wanted to be a pioneer in the digital domain for the benefit of our partners, but also of all of our supporters; our digital expertise is recognized by all and we welcome this new award for the SociOLRoom by Hyundai. This story will be all the stronger and more beautiful in our future 2.0 stadium!

For Laurent Moretti , CEO of Sportfive France:

> This is the second award that Hyundai and OL has received for SociOL Room, and we are very proud to contribute to this success story. In view of the Olympique Lyonnais stadium, this is a project that has high resonance and a great future. Congratulations to the team for their dynamism and their involvement in the conduct of such an innovative project.

Source: http://www.hyundai.fr/actualites/116 – "Hyundai winner of the 2015 Sporsora Trophy for the SociOL Room by Hyundai" published on February 10, 2015. Last accessed on April 19, 2015.

Ooredoo is an international company (from Qatar) and a leader in telecommunications, providing mobile, fixed and broadband services tailored to the needs of individuals and businesses across the Middle Eastern, North African and Southeast Asian markets. Their activation of partnerships has proved to be highly effective. Ooredoo and PSG have enabled young people to get involved in football through mobile technology.

Box 6.6 Ooredoo launches its global campaign "Fans Do Wonders"

Ooredoo announced the launch of a new global communication campaign with Paris Saint-Germain today. The company wants to capitalize on the attractiveness of football to inspire young generations. This is the largest international advertising campaign ever by a partner of the Paris Saint-Germain, with the aim to raise global visibility for both brands.

In this innovative campaign called "Fans Do Wonders", five of the most famous players from Paris Saint-Germain – the center forward Zlatan Ibrahimović, defenders Thiago Silva and David Luiz, and midfielders Blaise Matuidi and Lucas Moura – communicate with young fans around the world from the Parc des Princes with Ooredoo high-speed mobile networks and an Internet connection.

Fans can participate in this interactive campaign by connecting to the www.fansdowonders.com microsite where they can send messages directly to players via the website or via Twitter with the hashtag #fansdowonders.

Fans that send messages will have the best chance to win a trip to Paris and to attend a Paris Saint-Germain match and a practice with the players. As a bonus, the best messages will also be displayed on the billboards of the Parc des Princes stadium for several matches. A 360-degree campaign, coupled with a strong presence on social media and social networks, will be unfolded to publicize "Fans Do Wonders" to a global audience.

Dr. Nasser Marafih, CEO of the Ooredoo group, said:

> This campaign represents one of our most important global initiatives to date, to the extent that we would reach young fans worldwide. Paris Saint-Germain is one of the best teams at the moment and working with this club offers Ooredoo the opportunity to share their message and enrich people's lives through technology. We want to support the digital lifestyles of our customers in all our activities and this campaign provides an excellent platform to showcase our mobile networks which are the best and the fastest.

Nasser Al-Khelaïfi, president of Paris Saint-Germain, said:

> The ambition and the quality of the campaign perfectly illustrate the goals shared by Paris Saint-Germain and Ooredoo and should find a strong echo throughout the world among our fans and the clients of our partner. On the eve of a very important match for us, this campaign expressing at the time the talent of our players, the enthusiasm of our fans and the proximity that exists between the two is a great signal, for which we are very proud of. This campaign is evidence of the strong commitment of our partner Ooredoo who has already been with us for nearly 2 years.

Throughout the campaign, Ooredoo will highlight its leadership and its networks, which are the best and fastest in the world. The company has indeed introduced 4G in five of its nine major markets. It is also the leader in data in Algeria, Iraq, Qatar, Tunisia and the Maldives.

Ooredoo wants to address the wants of football fans on its Middle Eastern, North and Southeast Asian, and African markets. Local versions of the campaign will highlight people from different countries in which Ooredoo is present.

"Fans Do Wonders" was designed in line with the unprecedented success of the campaign "Simply Do Wonders" of Ooredoo, which was the most watched commercial online video 2014in the Middle East and North Africa, with more than 11 million views.

Ooredoo began its collaboration with Paris Saint-Germain in September 2013 to inspire young people and support community development in countries where Ooredoo is present in the Middle East, North Africa and Southeast Asia. Both organizations have collaborated on the project "Paris Saint-Germain Academy brought to you by Ooredoo" who organized football camps for young people of Qatar, Tunisia, Oman, Kuwait and which will soon be in Algeria and in other countries where Ooredoo is present.

Source: http://www.psg.fr/fr/News/112002/Article-Cote-Club/70794/Ooredoo-lance-sa-campagne-globale-Fans-Do-Wonders – Ooredoo launches global campaign "Fans do Wonders", released Tuesday, April 14, 2015. Accessed on April 19, 2015.

Overall, it is important to promote packages and partnership activations. Therefore, brand activation is not just about billboard visibility in a sports arena. To truly "emerge" it is necessary to (1) activate through customer databases, (2) set up contests to create a unique customer experience and (3) utilize digital media. It is necessary to truly think about social media. Creating an international community is an indispensable, strategic approach.

What are forms of naming in football?

In 1926, William Wrigley, entrepreneur of the chewing gum brand Wrigley and owner of the Chicago Cubs, gave his name to the baseball team's stadium: "Wrigley Field". This is the first case of naming a sports infrastructure. On May 9th 2013, Levi Strauss & Co signed a naming rights contract for 220 million US dollars with Santa Clara Stadium and the NFL franchise the San Francisco 49ers for a period of 20 years. Levi's & Co enjoys maximum visibility inside and outside "Levi's Stadium". In France, the first initiative of stadium naming was taken in Le Mans with the new stadium called "MMArena", which was opened on January 29, 2011. This name refers to the insurance company from Le Mans: Mutuelles du Mans Assurances (MMA). They have agreed to pay 10 million US dollars over 10 years. In addition, they pledged an initial 3-million-euros contribution from the MMA company under the naming agreement. This allowed for the completion and the financing of the new stadium as well as alleviation of the financial burden generated by the project on taxpayers (Besson, 2008). The second football stadium which had a naming rights agreement is that of OGC Nice. Opened in September 2013, the Allianz Riviera benefited from an agreement of 9 years (for a total estimated at 16 million euros). They find themselves at the heart of the club's development project, explains Samuel Guillardeau, stadium manager and organization and security executive at OGC Nice.[11]

This practice is still struggling to gain a foothold in France because of the reluctance of local authorities to associate with a brand on public properties. Regarding the naming of its stadiums, Germany is at the forefront and illustrates the close links between German companies and football. However, the evolution of naming will be sensitive in France with the construction or renovation of infrastructure, particularly on the occasion of the 2016 UEFA European Championship.

Indeed, "naming consists of selling the name of a sports stadium to a sponsor's brand over a long period" (Chanavat, Desbordes and Renaud, 2014, p. 42). Note that this sponsorship technique comprises technical variants. They aim to give or lean against the name of the sponsor in a competition (e.g. the Liga BBVA in Spain) or a club (such as the football club the New York Red Bulls).

Started in the last 30 years in North America, the practice of naming stadiums developed especially in Germany, England and the Netherlands. In France, although the practice has existed for many years in sailing, motorsports and cycling, the development of naming stadiums is relatively recent. Since the "MMArena" at Le Mans, other projects have emerged, such as in Montpellier where the first new generation multipurpose arena was built. Called "Park & Suites Arena", this arena has welcomed concerts, and sporting events, as well conferences and exhibitions since May 2011. The Matmut Stadium of LOU Rugby was built in September 2011, and a few months later, the Sports Palace ice rink at Morzine-Avoriaz became the "Škoda Arena". The Morzine-Avoriaz Hockey Club became the first hockey club in France to practice naming. Meanwhile, the Rouen Sports Palace, named "KindArena", was opened in September 2012.

In any case, the optimization of this new form of sponsorship seems to be in favor of building new infrastructure. If it is possible to "rename" a preexisting installation, assuming it was deeply renovated, the amount of the agreement will generally be lower. The naming represents, for the sponsors, a communication technique to significantly impact cognitive (image and reputation), affective (brand loyalty) or conative (purchase) reactions of consumer in regards to the sporting spectacle. These effects are reinforced in view of the long-term partnership, which is one of the keys to a successful sponsorship.

The activity of naming is not in itself an innovation. However, the idea to attach for the first time the name of a business partner to one of the club's sports facilities is an innovation of PSG in the matter. Thus the famous "Camp des Loges" was renamed "Ooredoo Training Center", after the Qatari telephone operator, who sponsors the club until 2018 for 13 million euros per year. Since the Parc des Princes is the property of the City of Paris, and the club wants to develop new sources of revenue, other partnerships of this type should be created in the near future. For Frédéric Longuépée, deputy general manager in charge of PSG business operations, "New PSG facilities will be named, including important places for PSG at the Parc des Princes. The club has the desire to tell great stories and we are looking for assets to do so."

It is required that the sponsor brand adds value if there is to be a successful action of naming. The story with the *asset* must be beautiful to mention. There must be a form of congruence between the project and the brand of the partner. Therefore, other French clubs have innovated in terms of naming. By becoming the "official watch maker" of OM, Rodania is sponsoring the countdown time on the new giant screens and appears on different media throughout the Stade Velodrome. The brand also presents its watches in the new stadium's VIP hallways for Ligue 1 matches. The sponsor therefore already has visibility on training outfits, LED billboards during games, the Velodrome's scoreboard and signs used for players' substitutions by the referees. Moreover, in 2014–2015, Rodania launched a new assortment of watches with the OM colors for children and adults. The goal is to strengthen the Swiss brand, to activate its partnership with OM through an innovative naming: The Rodania Mobile of OM.

While some Ligue 1 clubs have decided to undergo the process of naming their stadium, some of them, such as LOSC, have not been able to find a partner. At the European level, other clubs like Juventus have experienced similar difficulties. However, some English clubs like Arsenal or Manchester City have agreements with Emirates and Etihad. Note that the practice of naming stadiums is widespread in the Bundesliga, to the extent that 15 of the 18 clubs have developed such a practice. In France, our analysis suggests that a new naming trend could quickly emerge. For example, one could imagine that the LFP creates a special naming for trophies: "Trophy for the best fans", "Trophy for the most beautiful pitch", "Trophy for best dribbler", "Trophy for best tackler", etc.

Box 6.7 Rodania and the Olympique de Marseille: The Rodania Mobile

The Rodania Mobile of OM

This concept, unique to the world, was designed by Marcelo Bielsa, its construction directed by Olympique Marseille, and funded by Rodania, the official watch maker of the club. This tool is primarily an educational resource, used to facilitate the development of professional players. It can also be used for training young footballers of the club. Olivier Guilbert, technical director of OMtv and designer of Rodania Mobiles, tells the story of these vehicles of a new kind, designed in just 3 months:

> It all started in early December when Marcelo Bielsa presented his idea to us. Therefore we started to work on the creation of the vehicle that fits all requirements. The coach and his players are delighted to have such a tool and want to quickly use it on the fields of the Robert Louis-Dreyfus center.

Rodania Mobile will:

- Promote the perception, attention and concentration of the players,
- Increase the effectiveness of training,
- And accelerate the pace of the performances.

The Rodania Mobile is a vehicle which contains the following technological resources:

- A high-tech screen that allows the coach to explain the exercises and analyze live sessions,
- A mechanism that allows the HD recording of live trainings,
- Real time slow motion to correct errors and clarify the instructions,
- A whiteboard to show the tactics,
- And a digital timer to have a perfect command of the time.

Rodania, official watch maker of the Olympique Marseille, facilitates the training for the club's teams through sponsorship of these technological vehicles.

Source: https://www.om.net/videos/172926/la-rodania-mobile-arrive-lom – "La Rodania Mobile arrive à l'OM", published on April 10, 2015. Last accessed on May 8, 2015.

However, the FFF does not seem able to implement naming activities as clubs have done. Although this device makes sense in the federal system, it is mainly expressed through competitions. "The Coupe Gambardella Crédit Agricole works fine. But the naming of infrastructures, for the FFF is not possible. Operations of naming yes, but not structural naming," explains François Vasseur.

Figure 6.6 Marcelo Bielsa and the Rodania Mobile of OM

The ambush marketing of sporting events

History and end goals

The term ambush is defined as the surprise attack of a moving foe. The concept of ambush marketing can be defined as "a marketing communication technique, which relies on the voluntary and unilateral association to a brand, product, institution, or event (or an item related to it)" (Fuchs, 2008, p. 5). The association between the pseudo-sponsor and the sponsee is voluntary and deliberate, and not, as might happen, the result of an error made in good faith by the consumer. The concept was introduced by Jerry Welsh in the 1980s. At the time serving as the marketing director of American Express, he conceived it as a legal and ethical competition tool that can be utilized in the strategy of a brand that does not officially sponsor an event. The phenomenon resulted in the distribution of an advertising campaign indirectly associating the Visa bank brand with the Lillehammer Olympics (1994).

Ambush marketing activities are distinguished by several categories according to the nature and practices of their reach. Overall, these measures have three objectives: (1) drawing attention to the pseudo-sponsor; (2) diluting the effectiveness of the official sponsor; and (3) altering the reactions of consumers in a favorable manner for the ambusher.

Ambush marketing, also called pseudo-sponsorship, pirate marketing, trap marketing, commercial ambush or parasite marketing, dates back to the 1976 Montreal Olympics. Later, as part of its marketing strategy for the 1984 Olympic Games in Los Angeles, Kodak sponsored broadcasted games on ABC, as well as the official film of the American team. Kodak aimed to dilute, in a thoughtful and planned way, the effects of the sponsorship obtained by Fuji, the official partner of the event. Contrary to popular belief, ambush marketing is not a recent phenomenon. During the 1988 Seoul Olympics, each sponsor had at least one competitor which was using an ambush marketing strategy. During the 1996 Atlanta Olympics, the British athlete Linford Christie wore lenses with the colors of his supplier, Puma, during a press conference even though Reebok held the commercial rights for the event (Chanavat, Desbordes and Ferrand, 2013).

The pseudo-sponsorship phenomenon has rapidly developed over the past 20 years, particularly because of its efficiency. Moreover, while the amounts of tickets increased, it appeared easier to associate with an event implicitly given the myriad of professional sports entities that it brings together (athlete, team, player, coach, referee, etc.). Football proved itself to be fertile ground for this type of initiative.

Overall, mega sporting events like the football World Cup or the Olympics are a "laboratory" for brand related marketing initiatives (Chanavat and Desbordes, 2014b). Ambush marketing is a source of diluting reputation. The idea is to get a gain in reputation without incurring the costs of a formal partnership.

The ambush goes digital

To cope with the increase in pseudo-sponsorship activities, sponsors and rights holder entities are multiplying initiatives. Thus, they (1) are pressuring the organizers to protect the event; (2) will link field sponsorship and broadcast sponsorship; (3) will anticipate the promotions of competitors; (4) must use secure sponsorship rights; and (5) can always resort to legal action in case deficiencies are found. However, this debate is not closed considering the multiplication of sponsorship contracts. In football, ambush marketing strategies are very common, as the players play in a club with a collective contract with a supplier, while at the same time they have individual contracts for their shoes, often provided by a rival supplier. The message is then blurred (Desbordes and Richelieu, 2012). For example, Cristiano Ronaldo, a player from Real Madrid, wears the Adidas brand on his jersey, as it is the official equipment provider of the club. However, the Portuguese player is bound to Nike by an individual contract. In this context, during the 2014 Football World Cup in Brazil, Pepsi used its partnership with 18 players, including Sergio Aguero, Lionel Messi and Robin van Persie, so they would take part in advertising campaigns before and during the competition. Although this initiative is not necessarily aggressive, it uses players to gain visibility, especially on social media. The tweet below illustrates how the brand refers to the World Cup, even though Coca-Cola is the official partner. In addition, Van Persie was seen again in advertisements after his magnificent goal scored against Spain on June 13, 2014.

In this context, which is more akin to parasite marketing, FIFA decided to reinforce the security of the rights of its partners. Following up on the ambush of previous initiatives (Bavaria, Beats, etc.) the international federation launched a major international campaign for awareness and precaution against ambush marketing for the benefit of trading partners, notably *via* their digital tools. We must recognize that the Organizing Committee of the 2014 FIFA World Cup has been the most restrictive FIFA Organising Committee to date, to prevent *ambush marketing*. The marketing of the event is managed under the exclusive authority of FIFA and its organizing

Figure 6.7 Pepsi advertising campaign with Robin van Persie, with a tweet quoting "when training allows you to reach perfection #futbolnow"

committee. Without their permission, it is prohibited to refer to the World Cup through logos, designations or other marketing products and services. That's why FIFA requires countries which are candidates for the games to adopt a specific "World Cup" legislation. For the 2014 World Cup, for instance, there were bans on advertising in any form whatsoever within two kilometers of the stadium. This space was named "trade restriction zone".

In this context, François Vasseur analyzes that "with the explosion of digital content, it's very easy for brands to find news about the French team. We saw that during the 2014 World Cup. They have a core of activity linked with the sporting side. You can easily talk about players, put a negative spin on the stories, it's annoying."

Rights holders fight against ambush marketing when pseudo-sponsors benefit by obtaining profit without a contractual agreement. However, the over-reaction often involves extensive media coverage. Therefore, ambush marketing activities are proving to be increasingly visible on interactive media such as YouTube, Twitter, Facebook, etc. Furthermore, sponsors are faced with the creativity of messages from pseudo-sponsors that can cause confusion in the minds of consumers, a poor attribution and/or understanding.

Regional sponsorship, a new stage for clubs?

Definition and stakes

Regional sponsorship can be defined as a partnership expected to sell locally the image rights for a professional sports entity within a specific territory by segmenting the market. This new trend of sponsoring presents a twofold challenge. First, it allows a club to generate additional economic resources. It also promotes the globalization of club brand in given areas.

The leader: Manchester United

Overall, English football is proving to be the precursor of this form of sponsorship. Manchester United developed in 2008 a partnership with the brand Smirnoff Vodka, their drink partner responsible for Asia and Pacific. The report published by Repucom, *European Football Clubs Income Stream Report* (2014), dedicated to the periods of growth for European football clubs shows that Manchester United remains the leader in regional partnerships. This report examines the 20 most powerful European clubs, accounting for about 5 billion euros in revenue. For the 2013–2014 season, the study identifies 84 regional sponsorship deals for the 20 European clubs studied, which corresponds to an additional income of 54 million euros. Over 59% of this total was generated by Manchester United, or about 32 million for 38 partnerships. With this specific strategy, the club generates 350% more income than the runner up, FC Barcelona. In terms of the number of partnerships, Chelsea FC and FC Barcelona are the first clubs to have followed this trend. Asia represents the most appropriate market for this new kind of sponsorship with 47 contracts in total. Next comes Europe (15), Africa (10), and South and Central America (4). Thailand is the country's largest contributor with 17 partnerships. Also, with 20 contracts, finance is the sector that invests the most in this type of contract, followed by telecommunication (16) and food (11) industries.

A strategy for new European clubs

Although Manchester United currently dominates the regional sponsorship market, other European clubs have the ambition to integrate this form of sponsorship in their partnership strategy. Liverpool FC has formalized the signing of a new regional sponsorship contract for the 2015–2016 season. For the first time, the club has signed a partnership with the Asian firm Cobra Energy Drink. This agreement relates exclusively to the market of Burma. There plans to be an advertising campaign nationally circulated in Burma through promoting energy drinks and featuring several players from the club. Cobra Energy Drink plans a brand activation by organizing many contests throughout the year, enabling its clients to win the club's products. Thus, a drink bearing the image of Liverpool was produced and sold in 2015 for a limited edition in the Burmese market.

For its part, PSG formalized in 2015 its first regional partnership in Indonesia with the Indonesian food group GarudaFood. The new beverage of the group, SuperO2 Sportivo, becomes the official water of the club in Indonesia, where PSG has over 2 million fans on Facebook (PSG has developed a version in Bahasa Indonesia of the official site for its local fans). Frédéric Longuépée who was himself present for the formalization of the partnership explains:

> In November 2013, the website of the club was available in Indonesian, with the idea of opening a market which has extraordinary potential for football fans. Today, there are as many Indonesian fans as French fans on Facebook. When we saw that, we decided to invest time and to reach out to brands. After 6 months, we landed a partnership. This is the example of Jakarta and GarudaFood.

PSG has measured the opportunity to position themselves in interesting territories in terms of number of subscribers on Facebook (62 million in Indonesia) and where matches are broadcasted (especially by BeIN Sports and Channel B). This example illustrates the international expansion strategy developed by PSG. The club takes another step in its international expansion by signing in Jakarta its first ever regional partnership. The product SuperO2 Sportivo GarudaFood now displays the logo of the club and five emblematic PSG players (among others Zlatan Ibrahimović and Thiago Silva). A television advertising campaign named "Super sports water" with the players of PSG was also broadcasted on Indonesian channels to support the launch of the new product. This seems to be just the beginning of a long collaboration between the club and GarudaFood. While contacts were initiated during PSG's summer tour of Asia (2014), one could imagine that the new partner will become, eventually, a top sponsor. "With time, the regional partnership can lead to a global partnership," Frédéric Longuépée clearly affirms. Other partnerships should be created, and our analysis leads us to believe that PSG can quickly become a global leader in regional sponsorships. Anyway, this is a "real" emerging trend in football which mainly involves the clubs. However, our analysis leads us to believe that the countries with a strong brand image (Spain, Germany, Brazil, France, England, etc.) may take over this question and develop new growth areas. For François Vasseur, "The globalization of football brands is a real issue, we actually think about regional sponsorship within the FFF. We have to see if our brand has the potential."

State sponsorship

Fan (2010) begins with the fact that the academic literature has developed considerably around the concept of the country brand since the early 2000s. Many states have thus associated with sports entities in a marketing perspective. In this context, state sponsorship can be defined as: a communication technique that is, for a state, to directly or indirectly create or sustain a sponsored entity and associate themselves through media to achieve marketing communication objectives. As a so-called classic sponsorship activity, the main objectives are cognitive, affective and conative.

In an article published in 2014, Chanavat and Desbordes analyzed the overall development strategy of Qatar, a tiny country in the Persian Gulf which has made sports a cornerstone of the development strategy of its brand image, and its effect on consumers and policy makers worldwide. Qatar sees strengthening its brand equity as a way to consolidate its diplomatic influence, and therefore to protect its independence. Overall, the sovereign wealth fund, Qatar Investment Authority,[12] through its branch dedicated to sports, Qatar Sports Investments, has developed a strategy of influencing sports based on the following major activities: the acquisition of professional sports facilities (Paris Saint-Germain and Paris Handball); the organization of recurring events (Doha Tennis Open, the Tour of Qatar, Qatar Masters golf, etc.) and one-time events (the 2006 Asian Games, the World Athletics Indoor Championships 2010, Handball World Championships in 2015, the world championships in Athletics 2019, the World Cup of Football 2022, etc.); the acquisition of television rights (Ligue 1, UEFA Champions League, etc.); the creation of an equipment manufacturer (BURRDA); contracting partnerships (FC Barcelona, the Prix de l'Arc de Triomphe, the Tour de France, etc.); the headhunting of sporting talents that are being paid through the nose (and development of a center of excellence such as Aspire or a center for medicine such as Aspetar, naturalization of athletes, sports safety with the ICSS, etc.); and the election of a Qatari atop a sporting body (failure of Mohamed bin Hammam to FIFA in 2011, etc.).

Overall, Qatar's strategy seems to go beyond the emirate itself to influence the entire international perception of the Middle East. The brand development of Qatar can make a tiny state, a diplomatic and economic reference for a region with powers like Saudi Arabia and the UAE. We therefore do not consider the PSG as a "dancer". Instead, this acquisition is part of a "real" global strategy (marketing, geomarketing and geopolitical). It is part of a process of investment all around in the industry, sports and media of Qatar. The only professional football club from the capital becomes the spearhead of their diplomacy, their quest for influence (Ratignier and Péan, 2011). So there are "real" marketing and economic interests for a country. The association of Qatar with the PSG has thus led to several partnerships in order to strengthen the association between the two entities: Ooredoo, QNB, QTA, Aspetar, BeIN Sports, etc. Football in general and professional sports entities with a powerful brand-capital are media that promote development (cognitive, affective and conative) and the internationalization of brands, whatever their nature, public, private, parastatal, etc. If other sports can be "used", football remains the most coveted territory of expression that allows the reach of a wide target audience (see Chapter 10 dedicated to the PSG).

Box 6.8 QTA communication campaign in Paris

In September and October 2014, the Tourist Office of Qatar (QTA) launched a major poster campaign in Paris and its surrounding areas, featuring the football and handball clubs of Paris Saint-Germain in multiple Qatari decorations. This poster campaign shows the players of the club in a variety of places and landscapes depicting the touristic diversity of the country and its many attractions. Deployed on the Champs-Élysées, Boulevard Saint Martin, Porte de Clichy and at the Roissy-Charles de Gaulle airport, this campaign displays the heart of a strong currency, in France, for Qatar tourism: the international exhibition of tourism in Paris, the UEFA Champions League match between Paris Saint-Germain and FC Barcelona and the Qatar Prix of the Arc de Triomphe, the most prestigious race in the world. Between tradition and modernity, picturesque landscapes and vibrant urban planning, the players of Paris Saint-Germain play their role as ambassadors of Qatar with many people passing these posters in Paris.

Source: http://www.psg.fr/fr/News/112002/Article-Cote-Club/68356/Campagne-d-affichage-QTA-a-Paris – Article published on October 7, 2014. Accessed April 20 2015.

Other countries are associated with clubs in the perspective of state sponsorship. Two examples illustrate this point. The owner of Manchester City is Abu Dhabi United Group, a group founded by Mansour bin Zayed Al Nahyan, the Prime Minister of the UAE, upon repurchase of the club in 2008. In this context, Etihad Airways, the national airline of the United Arab Emirates, is the number one partner of Manchester City. The Etihad Airways partnership with the English club includes sponsoring several activities: the shirt, the stadium, the academy and the training center. Other initiatives such as the recruitment of Patrick Vieira (former player and coach of the U21 of Manchester City FC) show the close relationship between the club and the sponsor.

Although Qatar "owns" the PSG, it is a partner of FC Barcelona. In the same style, Abu Dhabi owns Manchester City and wants to develop a special partnership with Real Madrid. According to AS, the work of modernizing the Santiago Bernabéu would cost about 500 million euros to Real Madrid. Accordingly, the club has decided to opt for the deployment of a naming rights contract for the enclosure that could be called "Abu Dhabi Bernabéu". The multinational Microsoft and Audi, at one time considered, would therefore be excluded.[13] In the same style, in 2015, Atletico Madrid signed a new partnership with Azerbaijan. The country has also established partnerships with other sports entities such as RC Lens and obtained the organization of the 2015 European Games in Baku. This fits into what Ferrand and Chanavat (2006) call a process of "territorial marketing events" supposed to develop the reputation or image of a territory.

Box 6.9 Etihad partnership strategy

Etihad recruits Patrick Vieira as an ambassador

The airline based in Abu Dhabi has hired the development manager of the Manchester City club to be its brand ambassador. The former footballer will work on a number of initiatives to increase awareness of Etihad Airways in the UK, but also in other key markets for the airline. Etihad Airways plans to use the credibility as well as sports and the reputation of the winner of the 1998 World Cup with the team of France. Patrick Vieira said: "In my official capacity as the Etihad Guest Ambassador, I always hope for more collaboration with numerous promotional initiatives planned for the future." Peter Baumgartner, Etihad Airways Chief Commercial Officer, added: "Etihad Airways already has a long-standing relationship with Patrick. We are delighted to further expand this relationship by welcoming among us our Etihad Guest Ambassadors."

Source: http://www.sportstrategies.com/actualites/marketing/244161-etihad-recrute-patrick-vieira-comme-ambassadeur – "Etihad recrute Patrick Vieira comme ambassadeur", published on March 12, 2014. Last accessed on April 20, 2015.

Box 6.10 The partnership between Atletico Madrid and Azerbaijan

Atletico Madrid sign a new agreement with Azerbaijan

The management of the Atletico Madrid has formalized a new agreement with Azerbaijan. The club Colchonero will promote the first European Games to be held in Baku in June 2015. Explanations . . . The management of the Atletico Madrid lifted the mystery on the change of the jersey sponsor made in the last Madrid derby played on Saturdays. The leaders of the Colchoneros formalized the signing of a new agreement with the Azeri government on the promotion of the first European Games to be held in Baku in June 2015. As a result of the major sponsorship agreement, jerseys mentioned "Baku 2015" during major matches of the return phase of the Liga BBVA 2014–2015. Registration will also be visible in all the Champions League matches of the Madrid club from the 8th finals of the competition. The collaboration started even before the formalization of the agreement because Atletico was already wearing a shirt sponsored by European Games in Baku in the derby win against Real Madrid. The commercial director of the European Games in Baku, Charlie Wijeratna, showed his satisfaction at the press conference to formalize the partnership. "Atletico Madrid is the current champion of Spain and one of the most recognized teams in the world. The presence of the Baku 2015 logo on the Atletico jerseys is an original way to ensure the promotion of the event and to give value to our brand," said the Business Manager of Baku 2015. Satisfaction was also noticeable on the part of the management of Atletico Madrid. "The first edition of the European Games is a crucial step in the development of sports on the continent. And we are pleased to be associated with the promotion of this event," then indicated Miguel Ángel Gil Marín, CEO of Atletico Madrid. Atletico Madrid tries to catch revenue behind the two giants of La Liga. Since 2013, Atletico Madrid has continued to strengthen these ties with the Azeri state. The Madrid club has already signed a first sponsorship agreement in January 2013 – a period of 18 months – with Azerbaijan to ensure the touristic promotion of its jersey. A partnership that was then reported at 12 million to Atletico. Regarding the agreement on the promotion of the European Games, the financial details were not disclosed. Nevertheless, this new agreement is the first on a long list that should punctuate the year 2015 for Atletico Madrid. Very behind in income in terms of Real Madrid and FC Barcelona, Atletico Madrid counts on an important development for its commercial revenue – until the inauguration of the new stadium – to continue to compete with the two giants of La Liga BBVA. Besides Azerbaijan, the leaders of Atletico also rely on the arrival of Wang Jianlindans in order to attract new Chinese partners. It has invested 45 million euros in the Madrid club to acquire 20% of the social capital. It should make important networks in China to find new partners allowing Atletico to significantly boost its commercial revenues.

Source: http://www.ecofoot.fr/atletico-madrid-accord-azerbaidjan-2015/ – "L'Atletico Madrid signe un nouvel accord avec l'Azerbaïdjan", article published on February 10, 2015 written by Anthony Alyce on ecofoot.fr. Last accessed on May 8, 2015.

The citizen sponsorship

We agree with Bayle and Mercier (2008) on the fact that, regardless of their excesses and ethical breaches, sports entities aim to implement alternative strategies and marketing communication tools in order to live up to the myth of sports ethics and to sustain the commercial potential linked to the values of sport. The economic crisis only reinforces a trend that began there about 15 years ago: brand development in the social sphere. For Bayle and Mercier (2008, p. 15),

> the concept of citizen sponsorship that has emerged in recent years is characterized by: – a spirit, relating to generosity, donations, and altruism; – A will, the will to make a move forward even if it is on a small scale of the society and of the environment; – concrete actions: which illustrate this spirit and this will.

The citizen sponsorship is considered like a sponsorship of meaning and content, which leans towards a form of sports sponsorship and echoes the CSR activities (see Chapter 9 dedicated to CSR activities). It is therefore beyond the utilitarian ethic to access social ethics by adopting a different communication strategy. Although this approach concerns of course commercial businesses, clubs and professional leagues are also affected by this in a civic sense. "In this context, the message of the sponsor consists in saying that the company is not only an economic actor, producer of wealth and capital accumulator, but also a social institution that participates in community life" (Tribou, 2007, p. 63).

FC Barcelona and Athletic Club Bilbao have long been two exceptions by refusing to sign jersey partnerships. This approach was intended to make the product both rare and exclusive. But since 2006, the UNICEF logo has been on the Barça jersey, first on the front and then on the rear of the shirt. Quite exceptional in terms of sponsorship, FC Barcelona will even pay 1.5 million euros to UNICEF for the name of the United Nations agency responsible for helping children in the world to be on the shirt of Catalans. Nike has also been innovative in its relationship with the club because together they designed and developed a textile line called "Mes" referring to the flagship citation of Barça written on the collar of each shirt: "Mes que un club" which means "More than a club". This is about a relationship between UNHCR (the UN agency for refugees) and the club. UNHCR implements programs dedicated to education and sport for refugee children in the world. More than a football club, Barça hopes to be seen as an organization with humanitarian values. The goal of this partnership is to give an image of a world citizen for the club and the Nike brand. This qualified operation of "citizen sponsoring" helped the Catalan club to see the number of its supporters increase worldwide, in addition to allowing the team to increase the sponsorship fees. The products are also distributed through the foundation of FC Barcelona, on the website of the UNHCR and in Nike Stores. The innovation in matters of communication that FC Barcelona introduced in 2006, although it remains imperfectly exploited today, will be a track to expand to other professional sports entities. This in a logic of "citizen sponsoring" increasingly used by brands.

Figure 6.8 Jersey of the FC Malaga and the Barça clubs, respectively associated with UNESCO and UNICEF, while also bearing the logo

Source: http://store.nike.com/fr/fr_fr/pd/2014–15-fc-barcelona-stadium-home-maillot-football/pid-1547286/pgid-10079280. Last accessed on May 8, 2015.

In the same style, FC Malaga club associated itself to UNESCO (United Nations Educational, Scientific and Cultural Organization).

In France, the clubs are at the initiative of several social actions that tend to improve their brand image. Particularly through a partnership between the UCPF, the LFP and the FDJ, a national platform for employment, called "Supporters of employment" has been put into place since the 2013–2014 season. François Vasseur concludes on this theme:

> The citizen sponsoring is a subject we begin to grasp at the FFF. All our partners are looking for meaning in their partnership, beyond visibility. The social section in the sponsoring activities is very important. Partners need to put a small stone there, which also gives the resonance.

Our analysis suggests that the concept of citizen sponsorship is to bring fans the answers to their daily life problems without necessarily soliciting in the logic of the consumer. In a saturated market, and with consumers versed in communication strategies, they reject the aggressive strategies. In any case, the creation of a powerful brand in sport seems to go through a strong social commitment, which can be expressed through sponsorship activities. Our analysis echoes the words of Boris Lafargue, responsible for marketing and media of the Toulouse FC, for who "we cannot have a football club with a strong brand if it is not engaged in society, it has become paramount."[14]

Box 6.11 The employment forum of FC Sochaux-Montbéliard

FC Sochaux-Montbéliard supporting employment

Pioneer in the field, FC Sochaux-Montbéliard organized a forum of employment with Pôle Emploi and the ADIE[a] Thursday, April 16, at Stade Bonal in the SUPPORTERS OF EMPLOYMENT program. Within the societal aspect of the partnership between the French Games and the Professional Football, a national platform for employment, christened SUPPORTERS OF EMPLOYMENT, was implemented during the 2013–2014 season by the clubs the UCPF, the LFP and the FDJ, with the collaboration of Pôle Emploi and ADIE. At the launch of the second season, MEDEF joined the platform Supporters Employment. Forerunner of this device with Bonal Appointment from 2009 to 2012, FC Sochaux-Montbéliard organized on April 16 at the Stade Bonal an employment forum with Pôle Emploi and ADIE. This day enabled employers and job seekers to meet during flash interviews. Nineteen enterprises were present to meet these 80 job seekers by appointment. Besides these companies, 20 partner booths (training, employment, technology research, interim agency, army) were available for job seekers who had not made an appointment in advance, and conferences were organized in the presence of the President of the FCSM, Laurent Pernet, and the coach of the professional workforce, Olivier Echouafni. As a reminder, the SUPPORTERS OF EMPLOYMENT platform has already been deployed this season with great success at Stade Oceane in Le Havre, at the Allianz Riviera in Nice at the Stade de Gerland in Lyon, at the Stade de l'Aube in Troyes, at the Stade Gaston-Petit in Chateauroux, at the Stade Marcel Picot of the AS Nancy-Lorraine, at the Stade of Lorient Road by Stade Rennais, at the Annecy Sports Park with Evian Thonon Gaillard FC, at the Etrat with AS Saint-Étienne and at the Stade de la Beaujoire with FC Nantes. After this new stage of the Stade Bonal with

FC Sochaux-Montbéliard, the SUPPORTERS OF EMPLOYMENT program will be organized on April 21 at the Costieres Stadium by the Nîmes Olympique, and on April 28 at the stadium Saint-Symphorien by FC Metz.

a. The Association for the Right to Economic Initiative, better known by the acronym ADIE, supports job seekers who want to start a business. It grants microcredits to people excluded from the labor market and the traditional banking system.

Source: http://www.lfp.fr/corporate/article/le-fc-sochaux-montbeliard-supporter-de-l-emploi-1.htm – "Le FC Sochaux-Montbéliard supporter de l'emploi", published on April 17, 2015. Last accessed on April 20, 2015.

The multiple sponsorships of sporting events

We must recognize that sponsorship operations have a plural character by essence. In general, a sports entity simultaneously is sponsored by several advertisers. This plurality recognized is also explained by the fact that a sponsor can engage with various entities during an event. On behalf of a single event, the proliferation of sponsorship contracts between sports organizations and advertisers, to which are added the shares of ambush marketing, may limit the effects sought by the sponsors. Indeed, when an organization is a partner of various co-sponsored entities and/or when an entity sponsored several partners in the context of an event, we speak of multiple sponsorships of sporting events (Chanavat, 2009; Chanavat and Desbordes, 2014a).

Box 6.12 Multiple sponsorship for a suit: the case of FC Barcelona-Nike-UNICEF-Qatar Airways

To illustrate the multiple sponsorships, we have chosen the example of FC Barcelona, whose sporting success and originality of communication are well established. Before 2006, only the brand of the equipment manufacturer was visible on the uniform of the club. Today, four brands of various types (FC Barcelona-Nike-UNICEF-Qatar Airways) are associated with the *blaugrana* jersey. The club FC Barcelona has allowed Nike to expand its sales of licensed merchandise internationally insofar as it is a club with a strong reputation. Indeed, its championship games but also Champions League are broadcast by many media sources in the world. Let us add that to the fact that the club is over 100 years old (it was created in 1899), which gives credibility to the brand and promotes its influence worldwide. For many years, Barça refused to have a sponsor for its jersey, to make the product both rare and exclusive. But since 2006, the UNICEF logo has been on the front of the jerseys for home games and away games. In addition, the club paid 1.5 million euros per year for UNICEF to affix its logo on textiles linked to the club. Nike also innovates in its relationship with the club because together they have designed and developed a textile line called *Mes*, referring to the flagship quote from Barça written on the collar of each shirt: "*Mes que un club*", which means "More than a club". Why has FC Barcelona never partnered for its jersey before 2006? "Because its president Josep Lluis Nunez had an excellent economic management", according to Jaime Gil Lafuente. "FC Barcelona became the richest club in the world without being an incorporated company!" This president defended the "exclusiveness" of the jersey for two reasons:

- Differentiation: to be the "only" club in the world that has a "clean" jersey;
- The preservation of the future: the president at that time explained to everyone that the jersey should be the last resort in case Barça comes to experience serious financial problems.

Was the partnership with UNICEF a surprise? Yes. Socios were expecting a mana that helps the club to pay its debts and a sponsor to increase its financial resources.

Officially, this sponsorship operation is valued as an investment of the brand FC Barcelona. Did this relationship with UNICEF change the perception of fans and club sponsors? According to Jaime Gil Lafuente, the answer is no. The club has become more popular only in winning titles (in 2009, Barça won six championships in which it participated).

Moreover, on September 24, 2011, the socios have ratified the partnership making the Qatar Foundation the new main sponsor of the Catalan club jersey from the 2011–2012 season (for an amount of 170 million euros over 5 years). Since the 2013–2014 season, Qatar Airways is now visible on the club's jersey.

In any case, the arrival of the Qataris to FC Barcelona, which implies a four-way relationship, has proven controversial. But it foreshadows the future of the sponsorship. Four logos, four brands, with different objectives, coexist on a football jersey: those of the club, the equipment supplier and of the partners. The innovation in matters of communication that FC Barcelona began in 2006 then developed in 2011, even if it remains imperfectly exploited today, is a track to use for other clubs and should feed innovative research on issues related to multiple sponsorships of sporting events.

Participatory sports sponsorship

Participatory financing (or crowdfunding) represents an alternative financing method for companies or individuals to raise funds for their project. It is a funding mechanism that provides the opportunity for each member of the community to invest a certain amount of money which, combined with that of other members, funds a project. In most cases, this device allows collection of sometimes very small amounts from a large number of people. This way allows many people to unite around a project. It brings together project promoters and public investors, mostly through online platforms. The conditions of participation offered by the project holder are known from the start. The public can invest according to levels of interventions defined by the project owner and is informed what their investment brings them. In light of the sustained economic crisis and contraction of angel investors (both in number of projects funded as well as in the amount invested), project leaders are becoming more likely to want to opt for an alternative solution which, if considered in the most professional manner, may represent a credible alternative to the research of funds. This phenomenon is growing in artistic circles, but also in the innovative entrepreneurship sector. It is not new to the extent that it has been in for several years the world of music, film and literature.

One of the highest profile transactions in participatory sports sponsorship was that of RC Lens. During the 2012–2013 season, in the absence of a main jersey partner, the club partnered with the crowdfunding platform My Major Company to enable supporters to become the next club sponsors. The club invited its supporters to vote for the messages they would have liked to see on the team jersey. Compensatory measures to the most generous contributors proposed by RC Lens could appear attractive (posing with the players on the official photo of the club, giving the kickoff for a game, sharing a day of training with the players and the staff, immersion within the team on game day, etc.). However, only 5,000 euros were collected while the club hoped for 250,000 euros within 90 days. The MonRCLens.com operation first initiative in the field of French professional football in participatory sponsorship has thus ended in failure due to lack of legitimacy with the Lensois public. Obviously, it was not the normal realm of My Major Company, which carries out projects with musical artists.

Thanks to social networks, sports organizations have developed their media power and therefore their power of attraction. And the sport has taken over this practice in recent years.

This new trend of sponsorship called participatory sports sponsorship (or community sports sponsorship) can be defined as the pooling of individual financial contributions to finance a sports-related activity. This new form of partnership allows professional and amateur sports projects, individual or team, to find the necessary funding in order to see the next day and to endure.

Unlike the conventional banking system, the philosophy of participatory financing is not only to take advantage of its investment, but to help and support a project leader to implement his idea.

Box 6.13 Participatory sponsoring of RC Lens and My Major Company

Football: RC Lens would have liked to be sponsored by its supporters, but the operation was a huge flop

Not having found a jersey sponsor, RC Lens proposed to its fans to contribute before each game in order to display a message on the jersey. The club envisioned to raise 250,000 euros, and raised only 5,000 euros . . .

The Lens supporters might be attached to their club, but they are not willing to spend money endlessly.

After failing to find a main sponsor for their jersey, the team of president Dayan had devised a unique system, called "MonRCLens.com". The plan was that before every game, the fans would give money. In exchange, they could suggest a logo or phrase that, if elected by the Internet users, could be on the back of the players during the match.

Before the match in Auxerre, we received "Get me wet!", "Lens-AJA: the L1 is has-been", "Niko, Luka, bet on us", among other jokes.

Despite these pranks, RC Lens did not have much success with this initiative, perhaps because Internet users did not see how they would benefit from the deal. Within a month, the club collected only 5,280 euros. It had hoped for 250,000 euros in 3 months . . .

The Blood and Gold club was associated with My Major Company, a website specializing in raising Internet funds.

Some singers had their first albums financed by Internet users who are then given benefits or advantages.

Source: http://www.lavoixdunord.fr/sports/foot-le-rc-lens-voulait-etre-sponsorise-par-ses-ia0b0n784845 – released on October 26, 2012. Accessed May 8, 2015.

While the acknowledgment of failure of the Lensois project leads us to question legitimately the effectiveness of the crowdfunding system in sport, it can be explained by the inappropriateness of the project on a cultural crowdfunding platform where contributors ignore the specific characteristics of the sport. However, there may be little since the development of specialized structures in sport: *Sportfunder*, etc.

Indeed, the Internet version of crowdfunding and social networks change dimension insofar as it seems to reach a much wider audience. Also, the first French platform of participatory sports sponsorship seems to be Sponsorise.me. This entity founded in 2011, a subsidiary of SportLab Group, will be able to count on a strong partner in its international development strategy. By increasing its capital, now valued at 10 million euros, the platform has attracted four foreign investors, including the Coca-Cola Group. Sponsorise.me is the first French startup backed by the Atlanta giant. The soft drinks manufacturer's participation in Sponsorise.me is estimated at 5%. Coca-Cola counts on Sponsorise.me to help innovate by continuing to support the athletes. Seventy percent of those participating in the Olympics could not practice their sport without subsidies, both in France, the United States or elsewhere. Sponsorise.me is compensated by a commission of 10% to 20%.

Sport is a very specific industry; it is different from the music and film industry. It does not lend itself to this type of practice because of the essence that constitutes it and because of the values upheld by its practitioners: effort, communication, solidarity, mutual help. With its positioning and legitimacy in sport, Sponsorise.me created the first crowdfunding platform specialized in sport. With the aim of imagining the sponsoring of tomorrow by finding new ways of financing and putting fans in the heart of the event. Thus, the concept of Sponsorise.me allows sports project owners to find funding from private individuals, associations, public bodies and companies.

In 2014, over 3,000 projects have been received in France, 70% funded and 1.2 million euros collected. One of the keys to success is based on the project manager's ability to monetize its community. Loïc Yviquel, president of the group Sportlab and co-founder of Sponsorise.me, estimates the global market at more than 200 million euros in 4 years. "Crowdfunding is growing 40% per year; we want to become the world leader in sport. By the end of the year, we plan to also open branches in Spain and the Benelux countries as well as in Rio for the Olympics,"[15] he announced. He concluded:

> These transversal projects are an effective and credible alternative to descending sponsorship. We acquired some legitimacy on the market and wanted to launch something innovative. With the web and social networks, it is easier to gather 10 times 1,000 euros, than 1 times 10,000 euros. Our vocation is to be open not only to athletes but also to clubs, federations, associations . . . small as well as big.

Thus, professional football is directly affected by this new device and is of particular interest in the context of the writing of this chapter dedicated to professional football. One of the main projects of Sponsorise.me, entitled "All behind OM", illustrates this trend. In 2013, OM had offered to some SMEs to obtain the status of "supporting companies" of OM for an amount ranging from 90 to 50,000 euros. The most creative on social media had the privilege to see its name on the shorts of the players during a match. This demonstrated the commitment of local businesses that support the OM (even if Orange was elected!). It was also to develop additional revenue for the club. It should be noted that the project was funded at 111% of the expected budget. "It is especially an image and development operation of our business file. We are not seeking a new jersey sponsor! That said, in a tough economy, it is a different and interesting way to seek additional sponsorship revenue," says Corinne Gensollen, director of OM operations.[16]

Our analysis suggests that participatory sports sponsorship is complementary to traditional sponsorship. However, it does not in any way replace it. Although this new form of sponsorship can still be a major source of revenue for sports structures, it embodies an interesting alternative that must gain in popularity.

For Bruno Belgodère, director of finance and marketing for UCPF, "The participatory marketing does not necessarily relate to money but rather gives a dynamic and creates the link."[17] This initiative allows sports clubs to find simple and temporary solutions to finance a particular project, allowing them to establish more links with their fans and be able to make reality from a dream project. Participatory sponsorship can thus be considered as a method of financing that involves fans at a time when the idea of *socios* is considered by clubs like AS Saint-Étienne (see Chapter 12 dedicated to AS Saint-Étienne for more information). "The participatory sports sponsorship is an interesting strategy. But it is perhaps not yet firmly rooted in the mentality of the French. We have projects such as la Place Verte but it takes time," explains Arnaud Jaouen, marketing director of the AS Saint-Étienne.[18]

This is a trend that is going to develop strongly in the area of sports sponsorship. "Sports sponsorship has, we believe, not yet taken advantage of the web, and we believe that crowdfunding will be a key to this new trend," said Loïc Yviquel. But how many clubs in the image of the AS Saint-Étienne or OM are able to mobilize a large community of fans?

In any case, our analysis highlights a great story to narrate to the public: an effective project, a strong network and limited counterparts are the key success factors of this new partnership.

Toward a full liberalization of the sponsoring market?

Overall the clubs of the various European football leagues want more freedom in terms of sponsorship to generate more additional revenues. However, they are not allowed to market any location of their official uniform. Since 2012, the LFP is the first league to promote the development of revenue in terms of partnership ending the restriction of six sponsors and the prohibition of the marketing of certain locations (right sleeve of the shirt, right leg and back of the shorts, etc.). By the 2012–2013 season, the AS Saint-Étienne marketed advertising space on the back of the shorts. This new rule will allow more entry tickets into the world of sports sponsorship and encourage the interest of new business partners.

Thus, through the company SponsorLive (www.sponsorlive.com), which is auctioning the shirts, signs and even the seats in stadiums, the ticket for a jersey sponsorship in Ligue 1 has proved possible for less than 10,000 euros. Evian Thonon Gaillard has put for sale the front of its jersey for the knockout stages of the 2013–2014 Cup League against Guingamp for 9,000 euros.[19] Against OL, the club Evian Thonon Gaillard is the first French club to have a sponsor on its socks. The deal was signed through the SponsorLive platform. The company Brake France was the first socks sponsor of Ligue 1. For Alain Roche, co-founder of SponsorLive:

> We look forward to this collaboration with the club Evian Thonon Gaillard, offering its sock spaces on the platform for all events until the end of the season. For a few thousand euros, all businesses have the opportunity to be visible for matches against the best teams in the championship such as PSG, OM and OL.[20]

The platform thus aims to help clubs compete in their financing, while offering to auction advertising space available on the shirt or shorts, for one or more games. The company then wants to work with the 5,000 advertisers known in the world of sports, but also with the 250,000 SMEs.

The sales system results in lower costs (10,000, 15,000, 30,000 euros) and would allow clubs to target a new population of SMEs. For Brieuc Turluche, the cofounder of SponsorLive,

> Until now, SMEs did not consider sponsorship as sponsoring a club costs money year-round and contracts are often signed for several seasons. With the platform, clubs will be able to pocket perhaps more by auctioning a space rather than sell it by the year. Example: A club sold a "pocket" (chest visibility of jersey) at a price of 150,000 euros a year.[21]

Steve Moradel, associate director of SponsorLive, said that

> SponsorLive can be a major player in the growth of the sponsorship revenues of Ligue 1 and Ligue 2. Thus, we can increase sponsorship revenue of clubs engaged with us by 10 to 15%. This is a very reasonable and prudent objective.[22]

If the liberation of the market for company sponsoring by the LFP market promotes economic development of clubs, the idea would be to go further in tackling the Evin law. This approach is advocated by the LPF, who proposed it to the government in its responsibility pact. The relaxation of this law would bring back the domestic market of new players that would create more competition. The report of the UCPF, dating from 2014, on the competitiveness of professional French football, explains in part weak sponsorship revenues for French clubs by banning advertising of alcoholic beverages and beer sales. It thus refers to this law. This is not the case in other European leagues which derive significant revenues from these goods. "In Germany, in addition to the sponsorship revenue, the sale of beer reported 40 million euros per year in the Bundesliga clubs" (UCPF, 2014, p. 9). On this subject, Mathieu Ficot, Economic Development Manager of LFP, says:

> [A]ll budgets from brewers escape the LFP. And this is not nothing: tens of millions of euros in Germany, in England. And for me, I do not have this money. Portugal and Belgium have brewers who are the title-sponsors of competitions. Yet insofar as it concerns public health, it seems complicated to call this into question.

Other European leagues aspire to restrict the regulatory framework of sports sponsorship. Also, since the 2014–2015 season, the Spanish club Atletico Madrid has distinguished itself by wearing sponsors on the socks of its players. The club, which has demonstrated innovation, was followed by others. Konami, through its football game PES 2015, is well visible on the socks of 14 clubs. This is the first "socks partnership" in the history of la Liga. This new device then allows the Spanish league to commercialize new locations on the official uniforms of its clubs.

In this process of liberalization of football sponsorship activities, Manchester United has proposed to the Executive Committee of the Premier League the idea of marketing a sponsorship space on the back of the jersey of the official uniform. Although the Steering Committee refused this measure, citing possible visual overdose with this initiative, it is actually a defense for some Premier League clubs. They fear that this would contribute to an imbalance in the sponsorship market in favor of the big teams in the championship. In other words, some professional sports organizations fear a withdrawal of their main partners in favor of more effective clubs (as a secondary sponsor). This reflection has meaning in the measure where this form of liberalization of partnership-spaces could paradoxically result in lower revenues for some less prestigious clubs. Although the European trend leans towards the liberalization of the market for sponsoring the official uniforms of football clubs, the Premier League resists this by maintaining a restrictive framework. Notwithstanding, the English league continues to generate the most revenue for sponsorship.

Conclusion

This chapter was intended to highlight the key elements dedicated to partnership strategies and initiatives in the world of professional football. Even if it does not offer a comprehensive set of activities for all stakeholders in this evolving sector, it has sought to combine scientific literature and case studies.

In the first section, the understanding of the genesis, the analysis of the different terminology related to partnership activities and the review of specific areas of application to the world of professional football led us to a proposed definition of the football sponsorship. The key success factors necessary for a successful sporting partnership, targets and objectives of the practice, were the subject of the second section of this chapter. There was also talk of the amounts invested in the discipline. Indeed, the amount of an "entry ticket" can vary significantly from one entity to another. The third and final section have, meanwhile, focused on the development of management practices and new trends in professional football. Brand activation initiatives were discussed. In addition, we have paid particular attention to the following activities: naming, ambush marketing, regional sponsorship, state sponsorship, citizen sponsorship, multiple-event sports sponsorship and participatory sponsorship.

If we have attached a particular importance to the illustration and analysis of sponsorship activities, one of the keys to this area is based on a strong position. This is to have the right regulator for the partner as a "true" story to tell to the consumer. The increasing sophistication of methods and strategies of sponsorship discussed makes sense only if each organization appropriates it, adapting it to its internal culture and the environment in which it operates.

But we had to make choices about professional sports entities and about the facets of sponsoring observed. Thus, the issue of licensing has not been addressed (see the different cases of clubs). OL has for example developed a multitude of outside-soccer and outside-sport activities, which has led to the expansion of the customer target. According to Thierry Sauvage, "OL innovated in this field with several licenses awarded."[23] The extension of the OL brand is illustrated in particular by developing a range of products and services unique to a football club: OL Café, OL Champagne, OL Taxi, OL Gourmet, OL Boissons (drinks), OL Coiffure (hairstyle), OL mobile by Orange, etc.

In addition, the problem of measuring the effectiveness of the partnership actions was only addressed briefly. But even if it is necessary to set up marketing initiatives, it is essential to know and to measure its impact. The challenge is for the sponsor to measure the impact related to its sponsorship activities to justify the amount invested. We can see a change in the behavior of advertisers in their approach to sponsorship. This maturity is reflected in professional measurement tools. In 1990, the effectiveness of sponsorship fallout was measured rather by the kilo of the Press Book. While the analysis of the visibility of a brand was, for example, manually measured by an individual with a stopwatch, new tools have appeared. Today, automated and highly sophisticated measuring tools were put in place. With the goal of optimization, advertisers usually refer to sports marketing agencies to guide them in their choice (see Chapter 4 dedicated to agencies). Some rationality is sought by business mentors to guarantee a certain profitability. However, calculating the profitability of a sponsorship action requires action. To decide whether or not to perpetuate a sponsorship policy, the issue of political choice in matters of communications is posed. Does it act to continue, to increase the sponsorship or, conversely, to focus on communication techniques whose effectiveness measurement is more known? Measuring the return on investment (ROI) constitutes a strategic tool to resolve issues internally and support decision makers about their choices in terms of communication. Many companies are therefore content to measure the effectiveness of their sponsorship from an estimate of the equivalent purchasing media fallout areas. Considered very simple, this form of measure is used by almost all advertisers. Billing methods can also be criticized. In fact, the duration of visibility of the sponsored brand logo is recognized, and then multiplied by the media purchase cost at the same time. This leads to fanciful values in media visibility fees. This questioning of the tools is explained in the measure where the media visibility is often partial, ineffective or overestimated, depending on the desired objectives. It seems that this measurement mode is very simplistic in wealth linked to the effectiveness of a sponsorship share since it gives no indication of how the operation is viewed from a qualitative point of view.[24]

Football activities highlight a proliferation of marketing initiatives and of innovative practices. Others may have been treated here to illustrate the vitality of sponsorship-related brands operating in the sector. Thus, in their book published in 2014, Marmayou and Rizzo stressed that the sponsorship transaction is not necessarily a "peaceful" operation. Between the desire of sponsors to optimize the partnership, and the desire of sponsored entities to draw a maximum of money out of it, the agreement is natural, but remains fragile. Especially fragile as it is meant to last. For example, the Twitter account WinamaxSport published Tuesday, March 24, 2015, a parodic image of the board game "Operation" becoming "Gourcuff Maboul" with the president of the OL Jean-Michel Aulas depicted as a surgeon and the logo of the Lyon club illustrated bottom right.[25] So, 3 weeks before the derby between Lyon and Saint-Étienne (April 19, 2015), the main partner of the AS Saint-Étienne, Winamax (poker site and sports betting) played the card of humor and provocation with a communication and marketing aim. Very active on social networks (see Chapter 11 dedicated to OL), the Lyon president Jean-Michel Aulas was quick to respond by requesting the intervention of the National Ethics Committee.

Figure 6.9 Tweet by WinamaxSport before the derby between Lyon and Saint-Étienne (2–2)

Source: https://twitter.com/WinamaxSport – Tweet by WinamaxSport 3 weeks before the derby between Lyon and Saint-Étienne (2–2) on March 24, 2015. Accessed May 8, 2015.

Football, a social phenomenon, is a sport that is characterized by its global reach and its omnipresence in the media: television, social networks, etc. In this context, players have realized the economic benefits they can derive from their reputation, their image or their affect. While sports clubs also claim rights to the sporting spectacle, they only have hardware support. Augmented reality, virtual 360-degree tours, mobile applications, etc., at the time of "all-digital" where social networks like Facebook, Twitter, Instagram, Pinterest and YouTube are everywhere, sponsors are increasingly using more digital tools in a marketing perspective. Whether to generate content, interact with consumer sporting events, communicate a message or create buzz, social media is now integrated into the partnership actions. Also, we are talking about "social media sponsorship", new means of communication for sponsoring brands.

In view of increased competition, sponsors have to exploit their rights by demonstrating originality with regard to activation. While a sponsor, like Nike, could previously choose sportsmen (the best in each discipline) in order to gain more visibility, the issue of measuring the brand image in this ever-evolving context is central today. Players are now highly involved in the marketing strategies of sports brands that ask them to speak to their communities through social networks. At the time of its passage of Nike at Warrior, the Belgian player of Manchester City Vincent Kompany made a video (available on YouTube) where he touts his new supplier. Is it a personal initiative of the player? Is this contractual between the athlete and the sponsor? In any event, the impact of the message is even stronger if it is relayed by the athlete. These elements are in line with the findings of Chanavat, Martinent and Ferrand (2009) on measuring the effectiveness of sports sponsorship. It is appropriate to strengthen ties in terms of image and affect between brands and sponsored entities with the aim of optimizing the partnership.

We have reviewed the techniques, objectives and resources dedicated to sponsoring in this sector. The panorama is quite comprehensive as we have interviewed and examined the activities of various stakeholders in the ecosystem of professional football. We bet that this chapter will contribute to the analysis of sponsoring activities in the world of professional football that is in perpetual mutation.

Notes

1 This study is based on the analysis of the six major european championships: Premier League, Bundesliga, Liga, Ligue 1, Serie A and Eredivisie.
2 A company appeared on the jersey of Ligue 1 team for 10,000 euros (for one match).
3 74 BC–8 BC
4 The August 1st, 2003 law n° 2003–709 (the "Aillagon Act") relative to patronage, associations and foundations, through its innovative provisions in the matter of quotas on opportunities for payment and increased "tax advantages" tied to amounts paid, which help to encourage, energize and give new impetus to the corporate sponsorship in France. Thus, this law was a game changer as it provided opportunities for brands to communicate via sponsorship.
5 For more information on the subject, the reader may refer in particular to the work of Chanavat (2009).
6 http://www.psg.fr/fr/Club/602002/Partenaires-et-Fournisseurs-Officiels – Data published on psg.fr. Last accessed on May 8, 2015 (see Chapter 10 dedicated to PSG for more information).
7 Interview conducted by Nicolas Chanavat on May 6, 2015, at the headquarters of the FFF.
8 Interview conducted by Nicolas Chanavat on May 6, 2015, at the headquarters of the FFF.
9 Interview conducted by Nicolas Chanavat on November 18, 2014, at the headquarters of the OGC Nice.
10 Interview conducted by Nicolas Chanavat on July 8, 2014, at the headquarters of ASSE.
11 Interview conducted by Nicolas Chanavat on November 18, 2014, at the headquarters of OGC Nice.
12 Qatar Sports Investments, an organization presided over by Nasser Al-Khelaïfi, aims to invest in sport worldwide to generate profit which will be reinvested in Qatari sport afterwards. Located in Doha, this organization is attached to QIA, Qatar Investment Authority, the soverign fund of the Emirate of Qatar,

which is worth more than 85 billion US dollars and presided by the emir and heir to the throne, Tamim ben Hamad Al Thani.

13 http://futbol.as.com/futbol/2015/01/28/primera/1422410145_462675.html – "El nuevo estadio pasaría a llamarse Abu Dhabi Bernabéu", an article by Tomás Roncero, published on January 28, 2015 by futbol.as.com. Last accessed on May 8, 2015.

14 Interview conducted by Nicolas Chanavat on February 18, 2015, at the headquarters of Toulouse FC.

15 L. Yviquel, Conference "Sport et Sponsoring: Les agences et leurs champs d'actions" conference organized on February 12, 2015, at the Université Paris-Sud by the 2014–2015 Master 1 MELS students for the Association des étudiants en management du sport d'Orsay (AEMSO) and supported by Nicolas Chanavat and Michel Desbordes. Moderator Bruno Fraioli. Orsay, 2015.

16 http://www.lefigaro.fr/sport-business/2013/03/05/20006-20130305ARTFIG00433-le-financement-participatif-gagne-le-monde-du-sport.php – Excerpt from the interview of Corinne Gensollen in the article titled "Le financement participatif gagne le monde du sport" published in lefigaro.fr on March 5, 2013. Last accessed on May 8, 2015.

17 Interview conducted by Nicolas Chanavat on October 10, 2014, at the headquarters of UCPF.

18 Interview conducted by Nicolas Chanavat on July 8, 2014, at the headquarters of ASSE.

19 *L'Équipe*, "Le foot aux enchères", October 24, 2013, written by Rachel Pretti (2013).

20 Interview conducted by Nicolas Chanavat and Michel Desbordes on May 5, 2015, at the headquarters of SponsorLive.

21 Ibid.

22 Ibid.

23 Interview conducted by Nicolas Chanavat on July 9, 2014, at the headquarters of OL.

24 See Chanavat (2009).

25 Transferred from Bordeaux to Lyon in the summer of 2010 for over 20 million euros and a salary estimated at 450,000 euros a month, Yoann Gourcuff has played 23 complete games in nearly five seasons. Saturday, March 21, 2015, at a loss to OGC Nice, he was injured again, for the 20th time.

Bibliography

Anne F., "La mesure de l'efficacité du sponsoring", *Revue Française du Marketing*, 138, 1992, pp. 123–136.

Bayle E. et Mercier S., "Sport et éthique: enjeux et outils pour le marketing sportif", *Revue Française du Marketing*, 219, octobre 2008, pp. 9–26.

Besson E., *Accroître la compétitivité des clubs de football professionnel français*, rapport au Premier ministre, 2008.

Bœuf J.L. et Leonard Y., *La République du Tour de France (1903–2003)*, Paris, Le Seuil, 2003.

Burton R., Quester P. et Farrelly F.J., "Let the game begin", *Marketing Management*, 7, 1, 1998, pp. 27–37.

Cegarra J.-J., La promotion par l'action – Analyse du parrainage de la course de l'Europe à la voile par la Commission des Communautés européennes, thèse de doctorat en sciences de gestion, Université Jean Moulin, Lyon III, 1987.

Chanavat N., Desbordes M. et Hautbois C., "How sponsors, sponsee and consumers imagine an 'ideal' sponsorship activation? Concrete responses with the case of the French Soccer Federation", Congress of the North American Society for Sport Management (NASSM), Pittsburgh (USA), 26–27 mai 2014.

Chanavat, N., Desbordes, M., et Renaud M. (2014). Naming et modularité des enceintes sportives: les clés de la réussite? *Jurisport: Revue juridique et économique du sport,* 142, pp. 41–45.

Chanavat N. et Bodet G., "Sport branding strategy and internationalisation: A French perception of the 'Big Four' brands", *Qualitative Market Research: An International Journal*, 12, 4, 2009, pp. 460–481.

Chanavat N., Desbordes M. et Ferrand A., "Faut-il avoir peur de l'ambush marketing?", *Jurisport*, 128, 2013, pp. 41–45.

Chanavat N. et Desbordes M., "Le parrainage sportif multiple événementiel: atouts, défis et conditions de succès", *Revue Gestion* (HEC Montréal), 38, 4, 2014a, pp. 27–36.

Chanavat N. et Desbordes M., "Towards the regulation and restriction of ambush marketing? The case of the first truly social and digital mega sport event: Olympic Games London 2012", *International Journal of Sport Marketing and Sponsorship*, 15, 3, 2014b, pp. 79–88.

Chanavat N., Étude de l'efficacité du parrainage sportif multiple événementiel: une application à trois entités sportives professionnelles et à un annonceur, thèse de doctorat en sciences du sport, Université Claude Bernard, Lyon I, 2009.

Chanavat N., Martinent G. et Ferrand A., "Brand images causal relationships in a multiple sport event sponsorship context: Developing brand value through association with sport sponsees", *European Sport Management Quarterly*, 10, 1, 2010.

Chanavat N., Martinent G. et Ferrand A., "Sponsor and sponsees interactions: Effects on consumer's perceptions of brand image, brand attachment and purchasing intention", *Journal of Sport Management*, 23, 5, 2009, pp. 644–670.

Chauveau A., "L'évolution du sponsoring sportif en France et en Europe", *Revue Française du Marketing*, 138, 1992, pp. 111–122.

Cornwell B.T., Weeks C.S. et Roy D.P., "Sponsorship-linked marketing: Opening the black box", *Journal of Advertising*, 34, 2, 2005, pp. 21–42.

Dambron P., *Sponsoring et politique marketing*, Paris, Éditions d'Organisation, 1991.

De Baynast A. et Lendrevie J., *Publicitor, publicité online & offline*, 8e édition, Paris, Dunod, 2014.

Deloitte, *Commercial Breaks, Football Money League, Sport Business Group*, 2015, pp. 1–40.

Derbaix C., Gérard P. et Lardinoit T., "Essai de conceptualisation d'une activité éminemment pratique: le parrainage", *Recherche et Applications en Marketing*, 9, 2, 1994, pp. 43–67.

Desbordes M., "Introduction: New directions for marketing in football", in M. Desbordes (ed.), *Marketing and Football: An International Perspective*, Oxford, Butterworth-Heinemann, 2007, pp. 1–15.

Desbordes M., Ohl F. et Tribou G., *Marketing du sport*, Paris, Economica, 1999.

Desbordes M. et Richelieu A., *Global Sport Marketing*, Abingdon, Routledge, 2012.

Dietschy P. et Clastres P., "Introduction: Le sport et l'histoire de la France contemporaine", in P. Dietschy et P. Clastres (éd.), *Sport, société et culture en France du xixe siècle à nos jours*, Paris, Hachette, 2006, pp. 5–7.

Dietschy P. et Mourat A., "Professionnalisation du football et industrie automobile: les modèles turinois et sochalien", *Histoire et sociétés. Revue européenne d'histoire sociale*, 18–19, juin 2006, pp. 154–175.

EY-UCPF, "Baromètre 2014 des impacts économiques et sociaux du football professionnel, Entre ombre et lumière", 2014, http://s.ucpf.fr/ucpf/file/201503/3e_Barometre_Foot_Pro_-_UCPF_-_EY_-_Mars_2015.pdf.

Fan Y., "Branding the nation: Towards a better understanding", *Journal of Place Branding and Public Diplomacy*, 6, 2, 2010, pp. 97–103.

Ferrand A., *Contribution à l'évaluation de l'efficacité du sponsoring événementiel d'image*, thèse de doctorat en STAPS, Université Claude Bernard, Lyon I, 1995.

Ferrand A. et Chanavat N., "Le marketing territorial événementiel", in J.-L. Chappelet (éd.), *Les politiques publiques d'accueil et d'organisation d'événements sportifs*, Paris, L'Harmattan, 2006, pp. 72–85.

Ferrand A., "La communication par l'événement sportif: entre émotion et rationalité", in A. Loret (éd.), *Sport et management*, Paris, Dunod, 1993, pp. 280–294.

Ferrand A., Torrigiani L. et Camps i Povill A., *Routledge Handbook of Sports Sponsorship: Successful Strategies*, London, Routledge, 2006.

Fleck-Dousteyssier N., *Effets du parrainage sur les réponses cognitives et affectives du consommateur envers la marque: le rôle de la congruence*, thèse de doctorat en sciences de gestion, Université de Paris-Dauphine, programme doctoral ESSEC, Paris, France, 2006.

Fuchs S., "Efficacité du parrainage et de l'*ambush marketing*: impact du contexte de communication sur la mémorisation des messages", Actes des journées internationales de recherche sur la communication marketing: communication "hors média", ICN, CEREFIGE, Université de Nancy, ICN, 2008.

Giannelloni J.-L., "L'influence de la communication par l'événement sur la nature de l'image d'entreprise", *Recherche et Applications en Marketing*, 8, 1, 1993, pp. 5–29.

Grohs R. et Reisinger H., "Image transfer in sports sponsorships – An assessment of moderating effects", *International Journal of Sports Marketing and Sponsorship*, 7, 1, 2005, pp. 42–48.

IEG, *International Events Group Sponsorship Sponsorship Report 1996*, Chicago, IEG, Inc., 1996.

IEG, *Performance Research 2014 Sponsorship Decision-Makers Survey*, 2014. http://www.sponsorship.com/IEG/files/7f/7f60c23c-43d6-4006-bc7d-2c32c5e83c1d.pdf.

IEG, *Sponsorship Spending Report Where the Dollars Are Going and Trends for 2015*, Chicago, IEG, Inc., 2015.

IREP – France Pub, *Le marché publicitaire français en 2014*, 2015, http://www.irep.asso.fr/_files/marche_publicitaire/CP_MPF_2014.pdf.

L'Équipe, "Le foot aux enchères", 24 octobre 2013, écrit par Rachel Pretti, 2013.

LFP–UCPF–IPSOS, *baromètre d'image des clubs professionnels de football*, 2015, http://s.ucpf.fr/ucpf/file/201502/Communique_Barometre_UCPF-LFP-IPSOS_-_24.02.2015.pdf.

Maltese L. et Danglande J.-P., *Marketing du sport et événementiel sportif*, Paris, Dunod, 2014.

Marmayou J.-M. et Rizzo F., *Les contrats de sponsoring sportif*, Paris, Lextenso Éditions, 2014.

McCracken G., "Who is the celebrity endorser? Cultural foundations of the endorsement process", *Journal of Consumer Research*, 16, 3, 1989, pp. 310–321.

Meenaghan T., "Sport sponsorship in a global age", in J. Amis et T.B. Cornwell (éd.), *Global Sport Sponsorship*, Oxford, Berg Publishers, 2005, pp. 243–264.

Nys J.-F., "La surenchère des sponsors dans le football", *Géoéconomie*, 3, 54, 2010, pp. 63–77.

Ratignier V. et Péan P., *Une France sous influence*. Quand le Qatar fait de notre pays son terrain de jeu, Paris, Fayard, 2011.

Repucom, *European Football Jersey Report 2014–2015*, 2015.

Repucom, *European Football Clubs Income Stream Report*, 2014.

Sporsora, *Les bonnes pratiques du sponsoring sportif*, 2014.

Tribou G., *Sponsoring sportif*, 3e édition, Paris, Economica, 2007.

UCPF, *Le décrochage*, novembre 2014.

Walliser B., L'efficacité du parrainage sportif au sein de la communication de l'entreprise, thèse de doctorat ès sciences de gestion, Université Pierre Mendès-France, Grenoble II, École Supérieure des Affaires, 1994.

Walliser B., "L'évolution et l'état de l'art de la recherche internationale sur le parrainage", *Recherche et Applications en Marketing*, 18, 1, 2003, pp. 65–94.

Walliser B., *Le parrainage – Sponsoring et Mécénat*, Paris, Dunod, 2006.

Wahl A. et Lanfranchi P., *Les Footballeurs professionnels des années 1930 à nos jours*, Paris, Hachette, coll. "La vie quotidienne", 1995, pp. 223–224.

Webography

http://www.emirates.com/fr/french/about/emirates-sponsorships/sponsorships.aspx Parrainages Emirates, publié sur emirates.com. Dernier accès 8 mai 2015.

http://futbol.as.com/futbol/2015/01/28/primera/1422410145_462675.html – "El nuevo estadio pasaría a llamarse Abu Dhabi Bernabéu", article écrit par Tomás Roncero, publié le 28 janvier 2015 par futbol.as.com. Dernier accès 8 mai 2015.

http://sportmedia.pmu.fr/communique/15548/Paris-Saint-Germain-Insider-David-decroche-job-de-reve-grace-au-PMU – "Paris Saint-Germain Insider: David décroche son job de rêve grâce au PMU", publié le 25 mars 2015. Dernier accès 8 mai 2015.

http://store.nike.com/fr/fr_fr/pd/2014–15-fc-barcelona-stadium-home-maillot-football/pid-1547286/pgid-10079280. Dernier accès 8 mai 2015.

http://volkswagen-fff.fr/operation-volkswagen/ – Dernier accès le 8 mai 2015.

http://www.ecofoot.fr/atletico-madrid-accord-azerbaidjan-2015/ – "L'Atletico Madrid signe un nouvel accord avec l'Azerbaïdjan", article publié le 10 février 2015 écrit par Anthony Alyce sur ecofoot.fr. Dernier accès 8 mai 2015.

http://www.emirates.com/fr/french/about/emirates-sponsorships/sponsorships.aspx Parrainages Emirates, publié sur emirates.com. Dernier accès 8 mai 2015.

http://www.forbes.com/pictures/mli45ellfg/2-cristiano-ronaldo-6/ – Données issues de l'étude intitulée *The World's 100 Highest-Paid Athletes 2014* écrite par Kurt Badenhausen et parue dans forbes.com le 11 juin 2014. Dernier accès 8 mai 2015.

http://www.forbes.com/sites/kurtbadenhausen/2015/03/11/david-beckham-banks-his-bigger-year-ever-with-earnings-of-75-million/ – Données issues de l'article intitulé "David Beckham Banks His Biggest Year Ever With Earnings Of $75 Million" écrit par Kurt Badenhausen et paru dans forbes.com le 11 mars 2015. Dernier accès 8 mai 2015.

http://www.francefootball.fr/news/Messi-la-tres-bonne-paie/545838 – Données issues de l'article intitulé "Messi, la (très) bonne paie" écrit par Roberto Notarianni et paru le 25 mars 2015 sur francefootball.fr. Dernier accès 8 mai 2015.

http://www.hyundai.fr/actualites/116 – "Hyundai vainqueur du trophée Sporsora 2015 pour la SociOL Room by Hyundai" publié le 10 février 2015. Dernier accès 8 mai 2015.

http://www.journaldunet.com/ebusiness/marques-sites/effet-streisand/bavaria.shtml – "Bavaria a éclipsé Budweiser grâce à l'effet Streisand" écrit par Benoît Méli le 1er mars 2011. Dernier accès 8 mai 2015.

http://www.lavoixdunord.fr/sports/foot-le-rc-lens-voulait-etre-sponsorise-par-ses-ia0b0n784845, publié le 26 octobre 2012. Dernier accès 8 mai 2015.

http://www.lefigaro.fr/sport-business/2013/03/05/20006–20130305ARTFIG00433-le-financement-participatif-gagne-le-monde-du-sport.php – Extrait de l'interview de Corinne Gensollen dans l'article intitulé "Le financement participatif gagne le monde du sport" réalisée par Olivia Detroyat et parue dans lefigaro.fr le 5 mars 2013. Dernier accès 8 mai 2015.

http://www.lfp.fr/corporate/article/le-fc-sochaux-montbeliard-supporter-de-l-emploi-1.htm – "Le FC Sochaux-Montbéliard supporter de l'emploi", publié le 17 avril 2015. Dernier accès 8 mai 2015.

http://www.nissan-idm.com/actualites/nissan-sponsor-officiel-de-l-uefa-champions-league – "Nissan, sponsor officiel de l'UEFA Champions League" publié le 5 janvier 2015. Dernier accès 8 mai 2015.

http://www.psg.fr/fr/Club/602002/Partenaires-et-Fournisseurs-Officiels – Données issues de d'une page Internet paru sur psg.fr. Dernier accès 8 mai 2015.

http://www.psg.fr/fr/News/112002/Article-Cote-Club/68356/Campagne-d-affichage-QTA-a-Paris – Article publié le 7 octobre 2014. Dernier accès 8 mai 2015.

http://www.psg.fr/fr/News/112002/Article-Cote-Club/70794/Ooredoo-lance-sa-campagne-globale-Fans-Do-Wonders – "Ooredoo lance sa campagne globale 'Fans Do Wonders'", publié le mardi 14 avril 2015. Dernier accès 8 mai 2015.

http://www.sportstrategies.com/actualites/marketing/244161-etihad-recrute-patrick-vieira-comme-ambassadeur – "Etihad recrute Patrick Vieira comme ambassadeur", publié le 12 mars 2014. Dernier accès 8 mai 2015.

https://twitter.com/WinamaxSport – "Tweet de WinamaxSport trois semaines avant le derby entre l'OL et l'ASSE (2–2) le 24 mars 2015". Dernier accès 8 mai 2015.

https://www.om.net/videos/172926/la-rodania-mobile-arrive-lom – "La Rodania Mobile arrive à l'OM", publié le 10 avril 2015. Dernier accès 8 mai 2015.

https://www.sponsorise.me/fr – Communiqué de presse de l'OM et de sponsorise.me non daté. Dernier accès 8 mai 2015.

7

THE OTHER FIELD OF PLAY

Football on social media

Boris Helleu

Favored by broadcast schedules adapted to Europe, the matches of the 2014 FIFA World Cup in Brazil generated an unprecedented number of viewers. In France, the five most watched television broadcasts of the year were the matches of the French national team in Brazil. The quarter-final against Germany, broadcasted at 18:00 on TF1, garnered 16.9 million viewers. Germany, the winner of the competition, broke two records right after the other for the largest amount of viewers. Their victory over the host country attracted 32.6 million viewers (87.8% were a part of the audience). Following that, there were 34.7 million viewers for the final against Argentina. According to Médiamétrie, about 90% of French, German, Spanish and English ages 4 and older watched at least 1 minute of a game live.[1] This World Cup was also the first of the post-digital era. Fans were not only in stadiums or in front of a television, but they were also on social media. According to Twitter, this mega sporting event has become the most commented on with 672 million tweets related to the event. The semi-final of Brazil–Germany holds the record for the most commented on sporting event with 35.8 million tweets.[2] Facebook also set a record for a sporting event: 88 million people generated 280 million interactions ("likes" and comments) related to the final. From June 12 to July 13 Facebook counted 350 million people who generated 3 billion interactions in relation to the competition.[3]

In 2014, "in France, the 5 biggest conversation peaks of 2014, in tweets per second, happened during the World Cup matches," said Christophe Abboud, director of communications for Twitter France.[4] The top 20 most popular French personalities on the microblogging platform included 4 players.[5] Antoine Griezmann, the young player for the French team, has made his entrance into the standings as the 32nd favorite sports player of the French. He even appears to be 8th for the 15–24 age group.[6] Having been on Twitter since November 2012, he is followed by 866,000 account holders. Also active on Facebook (2.4 million "likes"), Instagram (431,000 followers) and YouTube, he was elected digital sportsman for 2014 by *Sport Numericus*.[7] After the elimination of the French team in the quarterfinals, he expressed his disappointment and his confidence in the future on Twitter. Shared almost 26,000 times, this tweet was the second most retweeted in France during 2014.

The 2014 World Cup has confirmed the inclusive nature of the sports spectacle, but has also assessed its ability to engage the connected fans who react and share their feelings on social media. The digitalization of this mega event falls under #smsports. A hashtag and a portmanteau, #smsports "is used to delineate all uses, technologies and equipment, as well as the strategies

Figure 7.1 Antoine Griezmann's tweet published on July 4, 2014, after the elimination of France in the World Cup

and best practices, observed in the field of sports and digital technology" (Helleu, 2014, p. 173). Considering the wide variety of sports actors (fans, players, clubs, leagues, federations, sponsors, media), goals (dialogue and interactivity, branding, monetization, information, datatainment) and finally extent of means (the choice of devices and social media), we consider the diversity of issues shaping the field of #digisport: what do the athletes, teams and fans say on Twitter? How can advertisers extend their marketing strategies on social media? How does the second screen change the way one watches sports? These questions along with others are the subject of a recent academic investigation. By incorporating the uses and tools that delineate the #digisport field which did not exist 10 years ago, we must admit that the academic literature is currently being structured. However, it has the energy of its youth and finds expression in fertile land. The *International Journal of Sports Communication* (since 2008) and the newspaper *Communication & Sport* publishes original research, case studies, interviews with professional critics and reviews placing a large emphasis on social media. Both titles have released a special issue dedicated to the use of Twitter in sports.[8] Newspapers that are outside of the sports field have also seized on this issue. *Television & New Media* devoted a special issue to football during the World Cup in Brazil.[9] Adding to this are the contributions appearing in articles making reference to the fields of management research and sports marketing.

Filo et al. (2014) have also conducted a report. They identified and classified 70 articles published in academic journals of reference in the field of sports management.[10] Thirty-five articles under the category of "strategy" include contributions dealing with the use of social media by sports actors (organizations, athletes, brands). Twenty items are within the "operational" category, which classifies the contributions that explain how sports actors use social media every day. Finally, the last 15 articles were categorized as "user-focused", which analyze the motivations and purpose of the fans. Of the 70 articles, we identified only six whose object of study compiled data dealing with football (Antunovic and Hardin, 2012; Coche, 2014; Garcia, 2011; Ioakimidis, 2010; McCarthy et al., 2014; Pegoraro, 2010).

Finally Filo et al. (2014) identified three areas of development. First, noting that 52% of the analyzed articles did not clearly mention their theoretical foundation, they encourage a conceptualization effort. One can probably explain this gap by the speed at which the phenomenon has affected the management of sports organizations, the media coverage of the sporting event, and the communication of the athletes and the fan experience, which were all outlined in this case study. Then, Filo et al. (2014) observe that the articles essentially take hold of objects of study related to North America. They then encourage greater geographical diversity in particular to show how cultural factors affect the use of social media. Finally, the authors observe that, in 64% of studied articles, the methodology focuses on either the analysis, the content or the questionnaires. Considering the diversity of the means for collecting data and also the new possibilities offered by these platforms, the authors invite diversification.

This chapter does not fall completely within in the recommendations of Filo et al. (2014). Speaking to a diverse audience of academics, students and professionals, its objective is to make a report of football 2.0, identify good practices and highlight them with the academic literature. The challenge is that digital activity in football is dense, complex and changing. It is co-produced by a wide variety of actors creating ephemeral communities of interest at the mercy of interactions. This chapter will cover in four ways the digitalization of the principal actors in football: the fans, clubs, players and sponsors/media.

Box 7.1 Three key concepts

Social media: a technical solution allowing one to create an account to generate, share and comment on content within a community linked by common affinities. The best-known socio-digital networks used around the world are Facebook, Twitter, Instagram, Google+, LinkedIn, Snapchat, Tumblr, Vine, Tencent QQ, Qzone, Tencent Weibo, Sina Weibo, etc. They differ according to the preferred content generated (for example micro videos for Vine and photos for Instagram), geographical area (Tencent QQ, Qzone, Tencent Weibo, Sina Weibo are solutions equivalent to Twitter and Facebook for the Chinese market), or the management of subscriptions and subscribers and the extent of interactions depending on whether content or commenting are more popular.

Commitment: one can commit themselves to a contest, a wedding or a cause. The engagement can be a contract such as a kickoff. The concept therefore assumes semantic complexity referring to cognitive elements, affective and conative. In the field of social media, commitment is an implication defined by the methods of interaction between a fan and content. Does he like it? Does he share it? Does he comment on it? Analyzing the community of Cleveland Cavaliers fans (NBA), Pfahl et al. (2012) identify several opportunities for commitment involving the club, the players, and the coach speaking out.

Content: "Content is the King." The exclusiveness, relevance, consistency, form (text, images, videos) and the tone adopted define the quality of content and its ability to generate commitment (see Figure 7.2). Since the advent of Web 2.0, quality content can also be generated by fans. In this instance, one uses the terms UGC or FGC when speaking of user/fan-generated content.

Figure 7.2 Exchange of tweets between the official accounts of AS Roma and Manchester City during a group match of the Champions League in 2014–2015

The fan 2.0: the evolution of consumption patterns for the sports spectacle

"It's a whole new ball-game," said Jimmy Sanderson when highlighting the disruptive nature of new media in the sport (2011). Indeed, the consumption patterns of spectator sports have changed dramatically in a short time. In their book *The Elusive Fan*, Rein et al. (2006) identify three generations of the sports spectacle. The first (1900–1950) is characterized by sports consumption in stadiums relayed by the newspapers and the radio. The second generation (1950–1990) is that of televised sports show. The third (1990–2006) corresponds to the emergence of new information and communications technology, including the Internet. Since then, the interactive and participatory Web 2.0 and the success of mobile devices (smartphones and tablets) favored the deployment of services unknown until then. If Facebook and Twitter were created in 2004 and 2006, other social media has extensively been used by sports actors (Instagram, Vine, Snapchat or Google+) for less than 4 years. Continuing the reflection of Helleu and Karoutchi (2013), Rein et al. (2006) propose to consider a fourth generation that would be one of the digital experience. The fan is no longer a (tele)spectator passive to the limited sporting emotion characterized by the 90 minutes of a weekly game. He becomes a media of himself that speaks out. In the digital and experiential age, he is a consum'actor that can generate, comment or consume content related to his favorite team 7 days a week and 24 hours a day.

The annual report *Know the Fan: The Global Sports Media Consumption Report* allows for the characterization of this new fan. The report makes analyses in 16 major countries,[11] the most followed sports, as well their consumption patterns. According to this study, football remains the most popular sport in the world. Taking first place in nine out of the 16 studied countries and second in three other countries, football brings together around 466 million fans. The means of accessing the sports spectacle combines both traditional tools (television, radio, the printed press, the entrance ticket to the stadium) and new media (Internet, mobile devices, social media). In all of the markets analyzed, television remains the favored tool for consuming sports. For example, this is the case for 96% of French fans. Around the world, the report *Sports Consumption* observes an increase of sports consumption patterns on the Internet, mobile devices and social media, while radio and even the written press are losing momentum. In other words, the tablet replaces the remote, and the tweet replaces the text message. It is the same in stadiums where fans use their smartphone to write text messages, call friends, and connect to social media.[12] Of the 16 markets surveyed, France lags furthest behind in this practice. Twenty percent of French fans have connected activity in stadiums as opposed to 52% of Turkish fans. While televisions allow one to watch the game, social media allows one to live it. They also allow access to content (videos, content shared by a team or a player) or even the ability to generate it. In France, 74% of connected fans are using Facebook to follow the sport, 52% use YouTube, 17% use Twitter or Google+ and 8% use Instagram (summary of data outlined in Table 7.1).

Table 7.1 The consumption patterns of sports in France for 2014

Means used to consume sports
TV 96% Internet 53% Press 35% Stage 37% Mobile 30% Social media 21%
Content accessed on a second screen
Live Commentary 53% Video clips 24% Of reports 18%
Device used to follow the sport on the Internet
On a computer or a mobile: 50% On a mobile device: 30% (smartphone: 23% vs. tablet: 13%)
Social media used to track sports
Facebook 79% YouTube 52% Twitter 17% Google+ 17% Instagram 8%

Source: The 2014 Global Sports Media Consumption Report, Global Overview, directed by PERFORM, Kantar Media and Sport SportBusiness, 2014.

Médiamétrie confirmed this underlying trend showing that sport is engaging. In 2014, 27.8% of Internet users and 43.5% of users aged 15 to 24, equipped with a second screen, watched a television program while viewing social networks.[13] The first statistics of this social audience (Table 7.2) show that half of the most commented programs on Twitter are sporting events. Seven football matches (in dark gray) appear in the rankings.

In 2011, Bouchet et al. put forward a typology of spectators, classifying them by their sports consumption experience. The classification utilizes works dating 10 years back even though socio-digital media did not exist then. They consider a profile of the "interactive spectator" who is in search of entertainment, shared emotions and interactions with the spectacle. How to better define the fan 2.0? The latter seeks to satisfy, using new media and new technologies, desires inseparable from the sports spectacle: sharing his emotion, claiming "I was there!" capturing a moment. We can explain the emergence of a fan 2.0 by a congruent pairing of the sports spectacle and social media. The sport that is seen as a spectacle of uncertainty (Yonnet, 2004) whose main result is generating unpredictable emotions live. The sports spectacle, in essence, is therefore engaging. It calls for the reaction and sharing of emotion. It allows for social media,

Table 7.2 Sports on TV, a program that engages on Twitter[a]

Program	*Channel*	*Date*	*Hearing*	*Tweets*[b]
Final of the World Handball Championship in 2015	TF1 et BeIN Sports	01/02/15	419,000	189,000
Ligue 1 Lyon-PSG	Canal +	08/02/15	470,000	147,000
Super Bowl 2015	W9 et BeIN Sports	42,037	339,000	113,000
The Voice	TF1	24/01/15	397,000	105,000
The Hold	TF1	26/01/15	323,000	92,000
The 2015 Grammys	France 2	13/02/15	588,000	81,300
The Voice	TF1	31/01/15	414,000	81,000
Ligue 1 semi-final, Lille-PSG	France 2	03/02/15	400,000	71,000
Ligue 1 PSG-Caen	Canal +	14/02/15	268,200	69,900
Ligue 1 Saint-Étienne-PSG	Canal +	25/01/15	329,000	69,000
The Voice	TF1	07/02/15	391,000	67,000
Hands off my post	D8	04/02/15	297,000	66,000
New Star	D8	22/01/15	256,000	60,000
French Cup: PSG-Bordeaux	France 3	21/01/15	341,000	60,000
French Cup: PSG-Nantes	France 3	11/02/15	384,500	56,500
The Voice	TF1	14/02/15	347,500	53,300
Ligue 1 Monaco-Lyon	Canal +	01/02/15	309,000	43,000
Top Chef	M6	26/01/15	310,000	31,000
Taken	M6	19/01/15	263,000	30,000
Rugby RBS Six Nations Ireland-France	France 2	14/02/15	297,900	26,600

[a]Unique Audience (cover): number of unique Twitter accounts which have been exposed to at least one tweet related to the measured program.
[b]Tweets: number of tweets issued on a program.

Source: Médiamétrie Twitter TV ratings from January 19 to February 15 (http://www.mediametrie.fr).

which is the sharing of this emotion within a community of peers. Moreover, social media allows for simultaneity at a distance, as explained by Gantz (2013).[14]

We understand better why a football match is also a social event. Just before the last World Cup, France Twitter released the following data: more than two-thirds of French Twitter users use Twitter for something that relates to football, 29% of users follow a football club on Twitter and 44% tweet when a goal is scored.[15] Clearly, Twitter radically changes the relationship between a club and its fans as shown by Price et al. (2013) in an article titled "Changing the game? The impact of Twitter on relationships between football clubs, supporters and the media." And if Twitter is changing the rules of the game, will the same happen to other social media? How do clubs use them?

The digital activity of clubs

Professional football clubs have always used the information and communications technology to inform their fans and promote their partners. In doing so, they pursue traditional goals of relationship marketing (loyalty of the fans) and transactional marketing (selling tickets). Starting from 2000, Beech et al. observe that the Internet has been growing rapidly and has substantially disrupted the marketing strategy of the English Premier League clubs. They note that

> The recent use of the Internet by business and commerce world-wide has proliferated dramatically. Indeed, many commentators are now claiming that the technology is leading to a new era in marketing. Sports have not been immune to such rapid developments and are increasingly using the Internet as a medium through which clubs and teams can effectively communicate and establish stronger relationships with supporters.

Now, social media complements the official sites. Thus, in a decade, the marketing and sales strategy of clubs have passed from BtoB/BtoC to Business to Fans (BtoF). It is indeed necessary to appeal to a public that is certainly present at the stadium and in front of the television, but also on social media. Possessing a smartphone, these 2.0 fans (Sutera, 2013) generate content on their club (Kwak et al., 2010), which strengthens their identification with the club (Phua, 2010).

Table 7.3 shows the top 25 European football clubs on major social media platforms. Cumulatively, the total audience amounted to 679 million fans, three-fourths of which are on Facebook. As for the rest, there is Twitter (14% of the audience), Google+ (7%), Instagram (3%) and YouTube (1%). It is not surprising to see Real Madrid, FC Barcelona and Manchester United comprise the top. Similarly, Forbes ranked the three clubs as the most well-known European sports brands. Global brands even before the advent of the Web 2.0 (Bodet and Chanavat, 2010; Chanavat and Bodet, 2009; Hill and Vincent, 2006; Richelieu and Pons, 2006), these clubs use social media as tools to mobilize all the fans around the world. Cesar Garcia (2011) explains how the reputation of Real Madrid also points to a relationship marketing strategy aiming to conquer and retain fans worldwide. It points out that,

> Real Madrid's success in the use of social media has been to think of each fan as one person and not so much as the public or stakeholders. This approach has been particularly successful in promotions that have adequately contextualized creating genuine conversations among Real Madrid fans. . . . A good portion of Real Madrid's successful content creation in social media has been the freedom given to the players. Real Madrid is not only much more relaxed about this aspect than some Premier League clubs but also than most companies.

Table 7.3 The digital fan base of European football clubs, the top 25 on January 1, 2015

#	Team	League/ Country	Digital Reach	Facebook Likes... 01.01.2015	Twitter Follower... 01.01.2015	Google+ Follower... 01.01.2015	YouTube Subscriber... 01.01.2015	Instagram Follower... 01.01.2015
1	FC Barcelona	La Liga, Spain	122,225,393 2,225,780	80,831,873 1,154,720	26,648,432 508,278	7,541,577 130,606	1,615.049 32,302	5,588,462 399,874
2	Real Madrid	La Liga, Spain	114,454,528 2,910,358	79,993,590 1,655,439	21,368,938 622,451	5,816,837 156,263	1,634,437 30,100	5,640,726 446,105
3	Manchester United	Premier League, UK	74,815,422 2,299,985	63,345,261 1,272,276	4,745,633 616,590	4,343,587 241,145	0 0	2,380,941 169,974
4	Chelsea FC	Premier League, UK	53,314,173 1,545,857	39,848,940 1,103,387	5,666,296 200,359	5,839,680 143,156	393,521 6,369	1,565,736 92,586
5	Arsenal FC	Premier League, UK	41,795,457 1,152,206	31,572,689 699,644	5,197,579 279,759	3,362,185 112,238	177,513 12,467	1,485,491 48,098
6	Liverpool FC	Premier League, UK	33,879,080 758,700	24,642,066 455,259	4,087,411 149,183	3,771,615 113,967	313,171 3,057	1,064,817 37,234
7	AC Mailand	Serie A, Italy	32,007,989 657,659	23,892,931 300,851	2,493,970 193,482	4,645,910 126,777	257,423 2,603	717,755 33,946
8	FC Bayern München	1. Bundesliga, Germany	31,899,100 1,421,888	25,840,987 1,141,621	2,125,598 102,142	2,128,963 58,801	268,408 14,742	1,535,144 104,582
9	Manchester City	Premier League, UK	25,278,384 927,091	17,626,915 693,830	3,183,517 107,848	3,530,722 78,249	340,610 20,491	596,620 26,673
10	Paris St. Germain	Ligue 1, France	19,946,838 1,250,458	15,874,965 994,652	1,970,515 102,126	1,021,872 42,229	159,925 12,777	919,561 98,674
11	Juventus Turin	Serie A, Italy	19,795,490 809,340	15,735,820 639,276	1,804,399 58,321	1,234,129 55,462	314,341 4,864	706,801 51,417
12	Galatasaray Istanbul	SuperLig, Turkey	19,405,392 368,059	13,193,144 156,187	4,693,551 158,857	647,833 11,458	149,554 1,595	721,310 39,962
13	Fenerbahce Istanbul	SuperLig, Turkey	14,906,202 227,205	10,265,366 98,761	3,819,235 110,316	309,418 9,835	112,688 622	399,495 7,671
14	Borussia Dortmund	1. Bundesliga, Germany	14,547,618 446,614	11,794,711 343,501	1,414,001 41,990	892,744 27,352	91,009 2,871	355,153 30,900
15	Atlético de Madrid	La Liga, Spain	12,185,920 493,719	9,511,847 423,398	1,362,346 44,346	850,382 2,843	68,591 1,146	392,754 21,986
16	Tottenham Hotspur	Premier League, UK	7,435,961 246,009	5,961,293 203,147	989,034 24,882	219,002 14,536	92,255 2,722	174,377 722
17	Besiktas Istanbul	SuperLig, Turkey	7,208,215 167,607	5,743,423 110,166	988,271 44,802	429,448 9,995	47.073 2,644	0 0
18	Olympique Marseille	Ligue 1, France	5,853,041 173,870	3,985,451 113,468	1,247,248 49,467	545,981 4,957	36,099 777	38,262 5,201
19	F.C. Internationale	Serie A, Italy	5,801,143 210,352	4,599,306 162,817	753,873 31,782	108,785 3,680	141,250 1,230	197,929 10.843
20	AS Roma	Serie A, Italy	5,294,118 146,455	4,251,404 99,121	597,396 23,892	200,500 12,728	98,858 564	145,960 10,150
21	SSC Napoli	Serie A, Italy	4,034,889 205,976	3,291,675 82,509	478,654 16,923	104,036 3,534	42,533 857	117,991 102,153
22	Benfica Lisbon	Liga Zon Sagres, Portugal	3,610,829 60,124	3,065,173 36,843	345,917 15,976	95,731 2,299	52.175 1,100	51,833 3.906
23	FC Schalke 04	1. Bundesliga, Germany	3,189,117 72,218	2,451,883 43,443	355,448 12,296	214,021 10,353	46,687 461	121,078 5,665
24	Valencia CF	La Liga, Spain	3,086,855 89,089	2,233,496 76,700	491,311 4,104	287,148 2,237	18,113 670	56,787 5,378
25	FC Porto	Liga Zon Sagres, Portugal	3,058,566 149,915	2,580,149 129,160	349,999 15,981	4,560 195	39,700 1,192	84,158 3,387
		Total Number of Fans :	679,029,720	502,134,358	97,178,572	48,146,666	6,510,983	25,059,141
		Overall Change compared to previous month:	19,016,534	12,190,176	3,536,153	1,374,895	158,223	1,757,087

Source: Result-sport.de, Digital Sport Medien, January 2015, p. 18.

Digital strategy varies little from one major club to another. The goal is to motivate and satisfy its fans by generating regular and exclusive content. The clubs ensure the loyalty of fans and then try to monetize that audience. Pasi Lankinen, digital manager of FC Barcelona, said,

> We have expanded our number fans in our country and in Europe. Now we are looking at gaining a global, profitable fan base. Communicating values is more long-term,

talking about what we are and gaining more loyal fans, so that when you stop winning then something stays and they don't move to the next team that is winning. But to monetise – that is where the challenge is. The short-term goal is to monetise the emotion felt for the club. Commercial organisations have big budgets and purchasing clients, who they are trying to make into "fans" of their products. But we are trying to do the reverse, we are trying to use the emotion of fans to create clients and consumers – and not just viewers – around the world.

Winner of numerous awards for its activity on social media, the Catalan club has invested in social media,[16] launched mobile applications for its fans, set up on its website a hub for aggregating all of its accounts and connected its stadium. With very active players on social media, the club has created a #TeamFCB hashtag which disseminates its brand across different continents.

Noting that the clubs pursue relationship marketing objectives, Miranda et al. (2013) measured the effectiveness of clubs on Facebook. They use a measuring tool called the Facebook Assessment Index (FAI) to assess the quality of the clubs' pages. The FAI takes into account the popularity (number of fans), interactivity (number of comments, "likes" and shares) and content (photos, messages, games, offers), etc. The analysis focused on the major clubs in the Premier League, La Liga and NBA and NFL franchises. It shows that, on Facebook, three clubs are distinguished: FC Barcelona, Manchester United and Real Madrid. Already popular before the post-digital era, they were able to convert their popularity rating into "likes". If a positive reputation and notable prize list allows for the rapid acquiring of a digital fan base, their loyalty and involvement came about through the implementation of a coherent digital strategy.

From this point of view, the two Manchester clubs have different trajectories. Manchester United was late to the game in regards to social media. In 2011, the club had a Facebook page with 14 million "likes". Jonathan Rigby, marketing director for the Red Devils, said: "We were delayed on social media because we wondered a lot about the its use and efficacy for a football club. . . . There will be no Twitter account until we are convinced of the use we can make of it." Thus, Manchester United was the last of the English clubs to open an official Twitter account in July 2013, while the account of their rival Manchester City had already existed for 5 years. In less than an hour, the official account gathered 108,000 subscribers. Since then, the club has

Table 7.4 Facebook Assessment Index (FAI) pages of professional clubs

Rank	*Team*	*League*	*FAI*	*Popularity*	*Content*	*Interactivity*
1	Barcelona	La Liga	0.8718	1.0000	0.7500	0.8984
2	Manchester United	Premier	0.7104	0.7847	0.6875	0.6839
3	Real Madrid	La Liga	0.6425	0.8941	0.6250	0.5005
4	Miami Heat	NBA	0.4759	0.1911	0.5000	0.6327
5	Chelsea	Premier	0.4208	0.3924	0.6250	0.2599
6	Detroit Pistons	NBA	0.4091	0.0115	1.0000	0.1407
7	Minnesota Vikings	NFL	0.4023	0.0346	0.9375	0.1638
8	Manchester City	Premier	0.3973	0.1190	0.8125	0.2079
9	Aston Villa	Premier	0.3781	0.0250	0.8125	0.2186
10	Arsenal	Premier	0.3747	0.3260	0.5625	0.2408

Source: Miranda et al. (2013, p. 81).

become active on Instagram and Google+. In partnership with Google social media, Manchester United designed in March 2014 the operation Front Row that allowed fans around the world to be broadcast on the jumbotron at the Old Trafford Stadium. This can be seen as a joint commitment between local and global because everyone, wherever they may be, can encourage their favorite team at the stadium.

While Manchester United does not rush to speak out on social media, rival club Manchester City has put this at the heart of their strategy. They were anxious to quickly bring together a growing community of fans, driven by the revival of the club in the late 2000s and involving them by inviting them to generate content. Since 2010 for example, the club seeks the assistance of fans to co-produce an iPhone application according to their needs. This can also take the simple form of a photo contest on Instagram or the most elaborate form of a digitized collective memory. In August 2013, the club launched the collaborative program titled #citystories where fans share their memories and in this way write the history of the club. Gigliani Diego, head of marketing, media and development of fans said:

> Our online audiences are growing rapidly and we're always looking for new ways to engage our fans on a global level. We see this platform as the next step in user generated content because #Citystories allows our fans to produce their own content, tell their own story and share it with the world. We hope our fans love what we have created just for them.[17]

Since then, the club continued its digitization by becoming the first Premier League club to offer free wi-fi in its stadium. Finally, the goal of building and mobilizing a fan base seems to have been reached. In January 2013, Manchester City was crowned the best English club in regards to its use of Twitter according to data including the number of followers, the activity of players and also the commitment of the fans.[18]

In France, all of the Ligue 1 clubs have a Facebook account and a Twitter account. The digital fan base depends on the reputation of the clubs, their sporting performance, the size of the cities determining a number of potential fans, number of years on the social media platform and the development of resources on these accounts. Assessing the activity of sports actors on the Internet, the 2014 Web Sport Challenge report points out the little homogeneity Ligue 1 clubs share and a certain delay that characterizes them on Twitter and Facebook as compared to their European neighbors. The French professional football clubs, satisfied by the windfall of television rights, were not encouraged to develop other sources of income. The building of the sports brand, winning the loyalty of a fan and optimizing their match day experience have all long appeared as minor objectives, so much so that clubs have focused on their sports performance (such as qualifying on a continental scale or not being relegated) rather than on their sales and marketing strategies (interacting with the fans, becoming a popular brand and filling the stadium even in defeat). Therefore, the majority of French clubs have invested in a social media strategy without real content, but because everyone else is present on social media, it was necessary that they do so. The position of Community Manager was then given to a passing intern or was assumed by a person of the marketing-communications department in addition to his other tasks.

Now, the clubs are aware of the usefulness of social media to carry out conversational and experiential marketing strategies. Their approach is more daring, as evidenced by the proliferation of contests or their appeal to the fans to design a product. Active since 2009 on Facebook and Twitter, PSG has since expanded its digital mix to best meet their marketing objectives: the relationship with the fans, international brand development and maintaining it. The club has

Table 7.5 Digital audience of Ligue 1 clubs (February 2015)

Clubs	*Facebook*	*Twitter*	*Total*
PSG	17,160,254	1,979,738	19,139 992
OM	4,161,163	1,329,623	5,490,786
Monaco	2,136,233	428,000	2,564,233
Lyon	1,926,927	573,000	2,499,927
Lille	563,193	284,000	847,193
ASSE	539,134	293,000	832,134
Bordeaux	539,852	151,000	690,852
Toulouse	196,890	284,000	480,890
Rennes	283,999	127,000	410,999
Nantes	193,751	190,000	383,751
Lens	290,108	74,600	364,708
Bastia	165,258	155,000	320,258
Montpellier	167,888	145,000	312,888
Nice	122,129	124,000	246,129
Lorient	129,621	108,000	237,621
Guingamp	137,483	82,900	220,383
Évian	117,046	97,400	214,446
Reims	99,993	94,000	193,993
Caen	91,634	47,500	139,134
Metz	94,949	34,300	129,249

the largest digital fan base of France: nearly 2 million followers on Twitter, 17.1 million fans on Facebook, more than 1 million followers on Instagram and Google+, 72,600 on Vine and a presence on Chinese social networks.[19] The Twitter account is available in several languages (Swedish, Indonesian, Portuguese, Arabic, Spanish). Attentive to the match day experience of its customers/fans, the club has one Twitter dedicated to providing information and tips on how to follow the match at the stadium in the best conditions (@PSGStadium) and another dedicated to the dressing rooms, lounges and VIP areas (@ PSG_Hospitality).

Box 7.2 The digital strategy of Paris Saint-Germain by Michel Mimran, marketing director of the club

Like many clubs, Paris Saint-Germain is very active on social networks. I think football brands are relational brands, they are in direct contact with their public, their fans, their customers, which is a privilege that many brands do not have. Most brands pass through a distribution network. For us, we are lucky to be in direct contact with them and know them. Football is also a relational brand because customers are also in demand for this relationship. Unlike many brands whose product is somewhat neutral, football and the club we love represent a brand with which we want to be in permanent contact. It is the duty of clubs to meet this relationship. Before new technologies, there was not much to talk about, apart from the stadium and the mail. The arrival of new technologies has completely changed things. . . . The website disseminates information, it is not intended to create a space for community dialogue even though it can be considered as a forum space. This is a vertical relationship. The value of social networks, including Facebook, is to create a relationship. We wish to virtually create the same atmosphere that is found in the Parc des Princes. The brand communicates in a different way and fans react. It is a horizontal relationship . . .

For now we do not monetize our audience. As an exception, I can make the social media page available as a great partner for an ad, and although I offer it, I would not monetize. On Twitter, it's the same, it is rare that we tweet or retweet the advertisement of a partner. This is something that we very, very rarely do. The only way to monetize that audience for us is to ensure that a fan or follower enters the PSG database by sending us their contact details. The fan becomes a recipient of PSG offers for ticketing and merchandising. Converting a fan into client, that is effectively my job, but there we are in the third and final phase.

Source: http://www.sportbuzzbusiness.fr, "Facebook and Twitter to PSG – Interview with Michel Mimran, Marketing Director of Paris Saint-Germain", published on November 5, 2012, Sports Business Buzz. Last accessed February 15, 2015.

If monetization tools and strategies exist, for example, selling tickets or leading fans to the shops cannot be the principle objective of a presence on social media. Indeed, when a fan subscribes to the official account of a club to express his allegiance, it is awkward to say, "if you love me, buy me." Rather, social media serves to nurture a relationship with the fans and not to sell products to customers. But if the experience of the fan takes precedence over monetization, inducing an important, global and active digital fan base will only create additional value for clubs. In 2013, *Forbes* magazine attempted to link the estimated value of a sports club in Europe, just like in North American sports, to its digital fan base. Forbes notes that on its own the club FC Barcelona has more fans and followers than all 30 NFL franchises combined.[20] Can we then say that having 2 million fans, in the same way as the track record, reputation or even the essential players, is a resourceful item for a club? Scelles et al. (2013) conducted an exploratory analysis and concluded the pertinence of this connection. In other words, the more a team has fans, followers and subscribers on its social media, the more value it has.

What are the players saying on social media?

At the end of 2014, Cristiano Ronaldo has distinguished himself by becoming the first athlete to cross the 100-million fan mark on Facebook. He had already been the first to pass the 50 million mark in October 2012. Obviously, Ronaldo is a global star: a quarter of his fans come from Asia, in Africa he mobilizes over 14 million Facebook users and in France 2.3 million fans follow him. In addition, his Facebook page generates engagement: since 2009, he has more than 231 million likes, 9.8 million comments and 8.6 million shares. As shown in the following table, the fan base of this player on his three main social media accounts exceeds 155 million. He is also the most watched player on Twitter and the second most followed on Instagram. The agency Repucom considered him the most famous and "bankable" player in the world and estimated at 115,000 euros the cost of a Facebook post to please a sponsor.[21] The Golden Ball and the other 14 players listed in the following table are international stars who are mainly playing in the more popular clubs. However, many players speak out on social media. But why do fans appreciate them so much that they follow these players on social media? And what can it tell us?

Starting from 2010, Ann Pegoraro analyzed the use of Twitter by North American sports professionals. She sought to measure interactivity with the fans, conduct content analysis and see if athletes consider this platform as a marketing tool. She has collected and analyzed almost 1,200 tweets generated by 49 athletes in one week. The results suggest that athletes are anxious to meet the demands of the fans and also share elements of their personal life (daily and family life, parties, or even the weather). In this way, the fans would see Twitter as a way to develop a relationship with an inaccessible, famous sports star but also as a form of gratification. In a 2012 article titled "Why We Follow", Frederick et al. (2012) seek to identify specific motivations which cause a fan to follow an athlete. Feeling more than a simple admirer, belonging to a community of fans, obtaining more in depth information than traditional media, seeing photos and videos of the athlete (to possibly share with a celebrity) are often reasons mentioned. Witkemper et al. (2012) show that the motivation to follow an athlete is mainly due to the search for information and distraction (entertainment).

Table 7.6 presents the most followed players on major social media. Their fame, athletic excellence and seniority on these platforms explain the importance of their fan base. Lionel Messi is unique in regards to being absent from Twitter, but having an account on Tencent Weibo, the Chinese equivalent. In 2007, a Japanese person created the address @leomessi that the player ordinarily uses. Neymar is distinguished by his daily Instagram use. With over 15 million subscribers, he

Table 7.6 Top 15 most followed footballers on social media (survey, February 2015)

Rank	*Player*	*Club*	*Nationality*	*Facebook*	*Twitter*	*Instagram*	*Total*
1	Christiano Ronaldo	Real Madrid	Portugal	107,057,234	33,709,490	12,606,111	153,372,835
2	Lionel Messi	FC Barcelona	Argentina	78,187,241	n/a	10,322,056	88,509,297
3	Neymar	FC Barcelona	Brazil	51,846,551	16,973,077	15,645,929	84,465,557
4	Ricardo Kakà	Orlando City	Brazil	32,800,673	22,100,805	3,554,772	58,456,250
5	Ronaldinho Gaucho	Querétaro Fúbol Club	Brazil	30,405,742	11,630,602	2,934,281	44,970,625
6	Mesut Ozil	Arsenal	Germany	27,862,083	9,021,602	2,249,679	39,133,364
7	James Rodriguez	Real Madrid	Colombia	24,955,894	6,804,859	6,981,448	38,742,201
8	Wayne Rooney	Manchester United	England	26,023,416	10,741,907	1,855,981	38,621,304
9	Andres Iniesta	FC Barcelona	Spain	24,082,922	10,420,935	3,007,511	37,511,368
10	Gareth Bale	Real Madrid	Wales	22,965,842	6,220,836	4,942,659	34,129,337
11	Gerard Piqué	FC Barcelona	Spain	17,111,763	10,177,552	2,733,588	30,022,903
12	David Villa Sánchez	Melbourne City	Spain	16,023,552	6,935,033	1,115,868	24,074,453
13	Karim Benzema	Real Madrid	France	18,922,002	1,703,248	3,046,570	23,671,820
14	Luiz Suarez	FC Barcelona	Uruguay	11,404,273	4,522,336	1,879,755	17,806,364
15	Cesc Fàbregas	Chelsea	Spain	6,585,101	7,623,174	2,674,055	16,882,330

Figure 7.3 January 11, 2015, Francesco Totti celebrates a double by taking a selfie with supporters

is the most followed sports player within the photo sharing platform. He is second only to singers (Beyonce, Taylor Swift, Miley Cyrus, Nicki Minaj), icons of pop culture (Kim Kardashian, Selena Gomez, Kendall and Kylie Jenner) or Justin Bieber. While his account is particularly appreciated for his daily use and selfie sharing, the player also knows how to use it to communicate. It was on Instagram that he announced his transfer to FC Barcelona. The majority of the most followed players on social media aggregate a community which is based on its celebrity more than the quality of the content. They do not always directly manage their accounts as they sometimes assign it to their club, supplier or agent.

Thus, fans of smaller teams or those in search of authenticity and originality of tone prefer to follow the less famous players who they themselves are feeding their own accounts. Barthélemy Collin, manager of France Sports Twitter,[22] said:

> If I had to give them (sports actors) advice, I would tell them to be above all authentic in their relationship with their audience. The public wants to discover the person behind the athlete and Twitter precisely allows for this humanization. I recommend athletes to talk about what interests them the most, whether it's news, sports or not, but also to give the public a privileged access to the behind the scenes of competitions or exclusive content.

Then aren't the real stars of Twitter Felipe Saad, Pierre Bouby and Manu Imorou? These players interact with the fans, joke, comment on TV programs, and debrief their game. This usage reflects a mastery of the tool, while other players were taunted for their *fails*. In 2012, after his team's defeat against South Korea at the Olympic tournament, the Swiss player Michel Morganella took racist and discriminatory remarks to his Twitter account, which caused him to be excluded from the Olympic team.[23] Rio Ferdinand has been fined of 70,630 US dollars for retweeting a fan who tweeted racist remarks against another player.[24] Therefore, many clubs, leagues and federations enter into awareness or training in the proper use of social media by referring to a charter. For example, in 2012, the players of the English Football Association were made to sign a selected a code of conduct governing inter alia the use of social media. They then asked the players not to be critical on Twitter or Facebook, have no digital activity on the eve of a match and to even keep in mind that private content (message, image) may become public.

The players are not the only ones who tweet. In France, Jean-Michel Aulas, President of the Olympique Lyonnais has been registered on Twitter since September 2011.[25] Followed by more than 167,000 people, he opts for a tone sometimes serious, sometimes corrosive, not hesitating to share with fans of the club, taunt his opponents, referees and consultants or even express strong opinions to his players or staff in a style that combines emoticons and even texting. Jean-Michel Aulas reveals in this way his activity on Twitter:

> Twitter is currently the most relevant means for being true to the fans; it allows proximity. This is a direct way of communicating with the supporters and the critics as a matter of principle. In being directly anonymous, and showing them that I attach some importance to what they can say, it seems to me that one can change their mindset and they themselves a priori. I enjoy the exchange. I have been reproached at times for my tweets with supporters of Saint-Étienne and Marseille. I think they are often copies. There are never to insult. When I return to Paris, there are at least ten people on the train that came up to me and told me that I made them laugh on Twitter. And they were not supporters of the OL. Twitter is a suitable means, used with self-control and not too serious, to allow everyone to find a human face.[26]

Box 7.3 The point of view of Guilermo Ochoa (AC Ajaccio goalie from 2011 to 2014)

Digital-Football Marketing (D-F M): You are on Facebook and Twitter. Where do you get this interest in social networks?

Guillermo Ochoa (G.O.): Many fans are connected on social networks; it is important for me to be close to them and engage in discussion with them.

D-F M: Are the content and interaction with your fans managed by you?

G.O.: Yes, I manage my Facebook, Twitter and Instagram. I am a photographer on occasion (laughter).

D-F M: Do clubs take an important place in the formation and implementation of actions on behalf of the players on social networks?

G.O.: I think that before the start of each season, the club should train players in social networks. Explain that this can be good for their image. After that they should respect the choice of each player to be present or not on the Internet.

D-F M: Should clubs limit the use of social networks by an internal charter?

G.O.: Some content may only be reserved at the club, one should not communicate on the injuries or notifications of games or example. Players must have the freedom to post what they want, especially outside the football part.

D-F M: Between players, do you talk about the best practices on social networks?

G.O.: Between players we look at what is written and each other, we read the reviews of games and discussions with supporters. Then, sometimes we laugh at our photo content for example.

D-F M: In the future, should the players run their accounts on social media?

G.O.: The player must have a greater freedom of expression on the Internet in order to be original in their content. It is also always necessary that we continue to share with our fans.

D-F M: You tweet exclusively in your mother tongue. Does this limit your proximity to the fans of the ACA? On the other hand, does it help you keep in contact with your Mexican fans?

G.O.: When I departed from Mexico I left a lot of fans, so I give them news using social networks. It is quite normal and natural for them to follow my career. But actually, I do read the French messages and I do some tweets in French as well.

Source: http://marketingdigital-football.com, "G. Ochoa: 'I manage my Facebook, Twitter and Instagram'", published on September 3, 2013, Marketing Digital-Football. Last accessed February 15, 2015.

The digital activation of sponsors

In their 2014 book, Maltese and Danglade define activation as the "operational modalities of implementation of sponsorship on the field in order to connect the fans (or direct audience) with brand sponsors." Allowing for a potential investment into a large fan base, the advertisers of brands now carry out their strategy of classical communication through social media.

Advertisers of brands in football make an effort to develop important social devices in order to activate their partnership. Beyond classical visibility (jerseys or the jumbotron) that offer a sponsorship contract, brands are now able to invest, enliven and reward a community of fans. On the occasion of the World Cup final, the French team's partners such as Crédit Agricole and SFR made an effort to set up cross-channel operations which articulate both online and offline. The mobile operator, in line with its business, transmitted messages of encouragement with the hashtag #JPLB (I Poke the Blues). Messages generated by the fans were accessible on Twitter, Facebook and Vine, but also disseminated in the SFR space and the stadium's billboards. In its 40 years of presence in football, Crédit Agricole has also put the fan at the center of its digital activation. Capitalizing on User Generated Content, the bank launched on Twitter, Facebook and Instagram a photo contest (the footogram) with the winner earning a trip to Brazil during the World Cup.

Orange is regularly praised for the quality of its digital devices. Ranked first in the ranking of the Top 100 digital brands,[27] the telecommunications operator uses sports to promote its brands and demonstrate its expertise. For example, the M-Stadium project developed in 2010 by Orange Labs tests contactless technology for the customer experience on game night. Thanks to NFC (Near Field Communication), the ticket is dematerialized, and the client can receive exclusive content on his smartphone. If Orange is not "namer" of Ligue 1, they still have the broadcast rights for mobile devices and tablets. Therefore, the brand presents itself as the privileged partner of fans that seeks to bring them together within the platform of the 12ᵉ homme (12th man) created in 2011. Twenty male and female players make up the Orange Team and have been called into action in some of the brand's operations. The 12ᵉ homme intends to bring the spectacle to life in total immersion by means of a strong presence on social media (75,000 Twitter followers, 609,000 Facebook fans, 10,200 subscribers on Instagram and 2,950 on Vine). The 12ᵉ homme manages to associate itself with the major events of the Ligue 1. In March 2015, during a crucial match between Olympique Marseille (ranked 3rd) and Olympique Lyonnais (ranked 1st), the 12ᵉ homme selected fans of both clubs and pitted #TeamOL and #TeamOM against each other first in a video game match up, then in a treasure hunt. This was also an opportunity for promoting the latest innovations of the operator.

The recent activation hailed by industry experts places the fan once again at the center of the plan. The SociOL Room of Olympique Lyonnais, for its partner Hyundai, was awarded the Sporsora prize in 2015 for the best activation as well as the prize for the best digital sports activation at the 2014 Sport Numericus. The club and Hyundai invited their supporters to watch preeminent matches (Marseille, Monaco, PSG, Saint-Étienne) in a box so that they could share their behind-the-scenes experience on social media. The match day experience, conventionally divided into the before-during-after, is commented on by supporters of the OL who have the opportunity for an all access pass. From the arrival of the teams to the reactions after the match, they generate relevant and exclusive content. Digital activity can draw fans to the accounts of the main sponsor who will then initiate a relationship with these potential customers. For Vincent Bernard, director of marketing and communications for Hyundai Motor France:

> Today, it is necessary to be able to activate sports sponsorship. Activation means being able to use all of the means of communication at our disposal, being able to communicate to the general public, and operating in the traditional manner. It also means being able to get in touch with fans via a communication channel such as digital media. In other words, it is the free access to creativity. Digitalisation also makes it easy to measure our impact, having accurate figures demonstrating the effectiveness of our investments. It's a wonderful recognition for a major brand today which today is even a small company on the French market.[28]

For both the club and the brand, this operation can increase the number of fans and potential customers. The club estimates that the transaction will reach up to 2 million people per game.

Conclusion

Wishing to identify the challenges and good practices of football 2.0, this chapter is dedicated to exploring academic literature and case studies. Anxious to shed more light on the use of social media by the major players of football (fans, clubs, players and sponsors), we have been superseded in our analysis by previous stakeholders or trends that may constitute for the reader food for thought and further investigation. Therefore, we have not addressed the digital strategy of broadcasters. TF1, Canal + and BeIN Sports have noted that the viewer uses a second screen while watching TV. As a result, the chain BeIN Sports launched the #pureLive device which allows one to watch a game without commentary, but allows them to share their thoughts on social media. The content is in this way integrated onto the screen. Canal + would rather preserve the main screen and provide its viewers with additional content (angles, data, etc.) on a dedicated application.

We have not talked about the professional sports leagues or federations that supply accounts and pages dedicated to their various products. In this respect, the interested reader can refer to Helleu (2014), which detailed the digital strategy of the French Football Federation whose objective was to win back fans and rework its image.

We have not addressed the connected stadium, the new social media outlets which are sometimes adopted by sports actors (Snapchat, Meerkat or Chinese social media) or even the problems posed to rights holders when a goal is immediately displayed on social media. We have not addressed the issue of big data, of the quantified self and of connected objects in the management and preparation of professional teams.

Finally, we have not relayed fears, rejections or refractory objections. And perhaps this is where it is necessary to finish our examination of the way we live sports entertainment. Mark Cuban is a rich businessman who built a part of his fortune through the Internet. Mark Cuban tweets (2.7 million subscribers), posts on his Instagram account (197,000 subscribers) and writes a blog. Cuban, who is also the owner of the NBA franchise the Dallas Mavericks, details how he considers the field of the sports spectacle. His background would suggest that he would value an excessive digital experience of fan, yet he despises the use of smartphones during his team's games. He explains,

> I want it (the game) to be very participatory. I want it to be very social. I want it to be very inclusive. I want it to be memorable. . . . IMHO, that means eliminating as many of the "look down" moments in the game as I possibly can. Once you sit in your seat, the only time I want you to look down is to pick up the soda or beer you set down under your seat and maybe to check your phone to see if you got a text from the sitter or your buddy about where to meet after the game. I want you always looking up. Looking at the game and the entertainment in the arena. . . . I can't think of a bigger mistake then trying to integrate smartphones just because you can. The last thing I want is someone looking down at their phone to see a replay . . . . If you let them look down, they might as well stay at home, the screen is always going to be better there.[29]

From this point on, the question is whether the emotion is generated by the conversation or the match itself, as if the sports spectacle was only a pretext for promoting the digital experience in which the second screen would eventually become the first concern?

Notes

1 "La Coupe du Monde de Football 2014 a fait le plein de téléspectateurs et de records dans le monde", http://www.mediametrie.fr/eurodatatv/communiques
2 "Insights into the #WorldCup conversation on Twitter", Simon Rogers, https://blog.twitter.com/2014/insights-into-the-worldcup-conversation-on-twitter –
3 "2014 World Cup Breaks Facebook Records", http://newsroom.fb.com/news/2014/07/world-cup-breaks-facebook-records/
4 "L'année 2014 sur Twitter", Christopher Abboud, https://blog.twitter.com/fr/2014/lann-e-2014-sur-twitter
5 Data on December 9, 2014: 6th Samir Nasri (@samirNasri19), 14th Raphaël Varane (@raphaelvarane), 16th Thierry Henry (@ThierryHenry), 18th Paul Pogba (@paulpogba).
6 "Le Mag 40 des sportifs préférés des Français", TNS Sofres.
7 Sport Numéricus is a yearly event dedicated to the use of social media and new technology in sport.

8 *International Journal of Sport Communication*, Volume 5, Issue 4, December 2012, Special Issue: Changing the Game in 140 Characters: Twitter's Rising Influence in Sport Communication. *Communication & Sport*, Volume 2, Issue 2, June 2014, Twitter Research Forum.
9 *Television & New Media*, Volume 15, Issue 8, December 2014. Special Issue: Media and Sports Culture after World Cup 2014.
10 *Journal of Sport Management, Sport Management Review, Sport Marketing Quarterly, European Sport Management Review, International Journal of Sport Management and Marketing, International Journal of Sport Management and Sponsorship, International Journal of Sport Management, International Journal of Sport Communication, Communication & Sport, Global Sports Business Journal, Journal of Issues in Intercollegiate Athletics* et *Journal of Sport Administration & Supervision*, etc.
11 Australia, Brazil, China, Germany, France, Great Britain, India, Indonesia, Italy, Japan, Russia, South Africa, Spain, Turkey, United Arab Emirates, United States.
12 "PSV Eindhoven fans protest against introduction of Wi-Fi at stadium", *Guardian*, http://www.theguardian.com/football/2014/aug/18/psv-fans-protest-against-wifi-access.
13 "L'Année Internet 2014 : + d'écrans, + de contenus, + d'interactivité, + de complémentarité entre écrans", http://www.mediametrie.fr/internet/communiques/l-annee-internet-2014-d-ecrans-de-contenus-d-interactivite-de-complementarite-entre-ecrans.php?id=1213
14 "Fans are intellectually and emotionally vested in sports. It seems natural, then, for fans to want to share their expectations and responses with, at a minimum, like-minded others. . . . With modern technology, fans are able to watch and simultaneously communicate with friends 10 or 10,000 miles away."
15 Infography, "Restez dans le match cet été avec Twitter".
16 In May 2013, the clubs was rewarded by the Social Stars Awards in the category "sports clubs". Other nominees were Real Madrid, Chelsea FC and Manchester United.
17 "The club today announce details of a new fan engagement platform, #citystories."
18 "#TwitterLeagueTable", Lewis Wiltshire, https://blog.twitter.com/en-gb/2013/twitterleaguetable.
19 Mailman group gave PSG the 10th rank of the most efficient European clubs on chinese social media *in its Red Card report 2015*, http://www.mailmangroup.com
20 "Barcelona and Real Madrid Rule Social Media"
21 "Ronaldo vs. Messi: Qui est le plus 'bankable'?", http://repucom.net/fr/ronaldo-vs-messi-bankable/
22 "[Interview] Twitter, le plus grand terrain de sport"
23 On the 29th of July 2012 he tweeted: "Je fonsde out les coreen allez sout vous lebru. Ahahahhahahaahdeban zotre" which can be translated as: "I fuck all Koreans, go get burned, retards."
24 For more examples, see "When Players Do Twitter Wrong", Ghazi Akoubi.
25 On this topic, see Chapter 11 about Olympique Lyonnais.
26 See, "Comment Jean-Michel Aulas est devenu une star sur Twitter".
27 "TOP 100 du Rayonnement Numérique des Marques – Février 2015 – 5e édition" on lafactory-npa.fr
28 "Verbatims de la cérémonie des Trophées", Sporsora: http://sporsora.com.
29 "The Fan Experience at Sporting Events – We dont need no stinking smartphones!", published on December 24, 2011, by Mark Cuban at http://blogmaverick.com. Last accessed on March 1, 2015.

Bibliography

Antunovic D. et Hardin M., "Activism in women's sports blogs: Fandom and feminist potential", *International Journal of Sport Communication*, 5, 2012, pp. 305–322.

Beech J., Chadwick S. et Tapp A., "Surfing in the premier league: Key issues for football club marketers using the internet", *Managing Leisure*, 2 (5), 2000, pp. 51–64.

Bodet G. et Chanavat N., "Building global football brand equity: Lessons from the Chinese market", *Asia Pacific Journal of Marketing and Logistics*, 22 (1), 2010, pp. 55–66.

Bouchet P., Bodet G., Bernache-Assolant I. et Kada F., "Segmenting sport spectators: Construction and preliminary validation of the Sporting Event Experience Search (SEES) scale", *Sport Management Review*, 14 (1), 2011, pp. 42–53.

Chanavat N. et Bodet G., "Internationalisation and sport branding strategy: A French perception of the Big Four brands", *Qualitative Market Research: An International Journal*, 12 (4), 2009, pp. 460–481.

Coche R., "Promoting women's soccer through social media: How the US Federation used Twitter for the 2011 World Cup", *Soccer & Society*, 1, 2014.

Filo K., Lock D. et Karg A., "Sport and social media research: A review", *Sport Management Review*, 2014, http://dx.doi.org/10.1016/j.smr.2014.11.001. Last accessed on the 10 th January 2015.

Frederick E.L., Lim C.H., Clavio G. et Walsh P., "Why we follow: An examination of parasocial interaction and fan motivations for following athlete archetypes on Twitter", *International Journal of Sport Communication*, 5 (4), 2012, pp. 481–502.

Gaillard C., "Sur Twitter, il joue meneur", *L'Équipe*, October 28, 2014, p. 17.

Gantz W., "Reflections on communication and sport: On fanship and social relationships", *Communication & Sport*, 1 (1/2), 2013, pp. 176–187. Published online before print December 12, 2012.

Garcia C., "Real Madrid football club: Applying a relationship-management model to a sport organization in Spain", *International Journal of Sport Communication*, 4, 2011, pp. 284–299.

Helleu B., "La conversion digitale de la Fédération Française de Football. Tu ne m'aimes plus? Like moi !", in C. Hautbois (éd.), *Le Marketing des Fédérations Sportives*, Paris, Economica, 2014, pp. 169–185.

Helleu B. et Karoutchi M., "The internet, online social networks and the fan digital experience", in J. Beech et S. Chadwick (éd.), *The Business of Sport Management*, Harlow, Pearson, 2013, pp. 298–320.

Hill J.S. et Vincent J., "Globalisation and sports branding: The case of Manchester United", *International Journal of Sports Marketing & Sponsorship*, 7 (3), 2006, pp. 213–230.

Ioakimidis M., "Online marketing of professional sport clubs: Engaging fans on a new playing field", *International Journal of Sports Marketing & Sponsorship*, 12, 2010, pp. 271–282.

Kwak D.H., Kim Y.K. et Zimmerman M.H., "User- versus mainstream-media- generated content: Media source, message valence, and team identification and sport consumers' response", *International Journal of Sport Communication*, 10 (3/4), 2010, pp. 402–421.

"Le Mag 40 des sportifs préférés des Français", sondage de TNS Sofres effectué pour l'Équipe Magazine, réalisé du 10 au 13 décembre.

Mailman Group, *Red Card 2015: China Digital Football Index*, rapport édité par Andrew Collins CEO de Mailman Group, disponible surhttp://www.mailmangroup.com

Maltese L. et Danglande J.-P., *Marketing du Sport et événementiel sportif*, Paris, Dunod, 2014.

McCarthy J., Rowley J., Ashworth C.J. et Pioch E., "Managing brand presence through social media: The case of UK football clubs", *Internet Research*, 24, 2014, pp. 181–204.

Miranda F.J., Chamorro A., Rubio S. et Rodriguez O., "Real Madrid football club: Professional sports teams on social networks: A comparative study employing the Facebook assessment index", *International Journal of Sport Communication*, 7 (1), 2013, pp. 74–89.

Ozanian M., "The Forbes Fab 40: The World's Most Valuable Sports Brands 2014", Mike, publié le 7 octobre 2014 sur Forbes.com. Last accessed on the 10th of January 2015.

Pegoraro A., "Look who's talking – Athletes on Twitter: A case study", *International Journal of Sport Communication*, 3 (4), 2010, pp. 501–514.

Perform, *The Global Sport Media Consumption Report 2014, Global Overview*, Kantar Media Sport et Sport-Business, 2014.

Pfahl M.E., Kreutzer A., Maleski M., Lillibridge J. et Ryznar J., "If you build it, will they come?: A case study of digital spaces and brand in the National Basketball Association", *Sport Management Review*, 15, 2012, pp. 518–537.

Phua J.J., "Sports fans and media use: Influence on sports fan identification and collective self-esteem", *International Journal of Sport Communication*, 3 (2), 2010, pp. 190–206.

Price J., Farrington N. et Hall L., "Changing the game? The impact of Twitter on relationships between football clubs, supporters and the sports media", *Soccer & Society*, 14 (4), 2013, pp. 446–461.

Rein I., Kotler P. et Shields B., *The Elusive Fan: Reinventing Sports in a Crowded Marketplace*, New York, McGraw-Hill, 2006.

Richelieu A. et Pons F., "Toronto maple leafs vs football club barcelona: How two legendary sports teams built their brand equity", *International Journal of Sports Marketing & Sponsorship*, 7 (3), 2006, pp. 231–246.

Salmon Kurt, Nates Audencia et Kantar Sport, *Sport Web Challenge 2014*, étude disponible sur. http://www.kurtsalmon.com

Sanderson J., *It's a Whole New Ball-Game: How Social Media Is Changing Sports*, New York, Hampton Press, Inc., 2011.

Scelles N., Helleu B., Durand C. et Bonnal L., "What impacts of the globalization of a sport on the number of social media fans for professional sports clubs and on their value in the United States and in Europe?", *12th International Business & Economy Conference*, Caen, France, 2013, 9–12 janvier.

Sutera D., *Sports fans 2.0: How Fans Are Using Social Media to Get Closer to the Game*, Lanham, MD, Toronto Plymouth, UK, The Scarecrow Press, 2013.

Witkemper C., Lim C.H. et Waldburger A., "Social media and sports marketing: Examining the motivations and constraints of Twitter users", *Sport Marketing Quarterly*, 21, 2012, pp. 170–183.

Yonnet P., *Huit leçons sur le sport*, Paris, Gallimard, 2004, p. 66.

Webography

http://blogmaverick.com/2011/12/24/the-fan-experience-at-sporting-events-we-dont-need-no-stinking-smartphones/ – "The Fan Experience at Sporting Events – We dont need no stinking smartphones !", published on the 24th of December 2011 by Mark Cuban on his blog blogmaverick.com. Last accessed on the 1st of March 2015.

http://marketingdigital-football.com/g-ochoa-gere-mes-comptes-facebook-twitter-instagram/ – G. Ochoa: "Je gère mes comptes Facebook, Twitter et Instagram", published on the 3rd of September 2013 on Marketing Digital Football. Last accessed on the 15th of February 2015.

http://mashable.com/2012/08/24/fake-twitter-followers-sports/ – "10 Sports Twitter Accounts With a Shocking Number of Fake Followers", published on the 24th of August 2012 by Sam Laird. Last accessed on the 15th of February 2015.

http://newsroom.fb.com/news/2014/07/world-cup-breaks-facebook-records/ – "2014 World Cup Breaks Facebook Records", published on the 14th of July 2014 on Facebook information website. Last accessed on the 29th of January 2015.

http://purelyfootball.com/2015/01/when-players-do-twitter-wrong– "When Players Do Twitter Wrong" by Ghazi Akoubi, published on the 12th of January 2015. Last accessed on the 15th of February 2015.

http://repucom.net/fr/ronaldo-vs-messi-bankable/ – "Ronaldo vs. Messi: Qui est le plus 'bankable'?", published on the 1st of December 2014. Last accessed on the 15th of February 2015.

http://sporsora.com/index.php/association/item/2245-verbatims-de-la-ceremonie-des-trophees – "Verbatims de la cérémonie des Trophées" sur le site de Sporsora, published on the 19th of February 2015. Last accessed on the 21st of February 2015.

http://www.bbc.com/news/business-18065300 – "Barcelona uses new media to sell its brand to fans", by Bill Wilson. published on the 21st of May 2012 on bbc.com. Last accessed on the 15thof February 2015.

http://www.forbes.com/sites/kurtbadenhausen/2013/07/15/barcelona-and-real-madrid-rule-social-media/ – "Barcelona And Real Madrid Rule Social Media", published on the 15th July 2013 by Kurt Badenhausen. Last accessed on the 15th of February 2015.

http://www.theguardian.com/football/2014/aug/18/psv-fans-protest-against-wifi-access – "PSV Eindhoven fans protest against introduction of Wi-Fi at stadium", published on the 18th of August 2014 on the website of *The Guardian*. Last accessed on the 15th of February 2015.

http://www.ifop.com – "Observatoire des réseaux sociaux 2013 – vague 8", published on the 13th of December 2013. Last accessed on the 18th of February 2015.

http://www.lafactory-npa.fr/strategie-digitale-contenus/top100-rayonnement-numerique-edition5/ – "TOP 100 du Rayonnement Numérique des Marques – Février 2015–5e édition". Last accessed on the 1st of March 2015.

http://www.lequipe.fr/Football/Actualites/Le-numerique-nouvel-eldorado/522198 – "Le numérique, nouvel Eldorado?" published on the 16th of December 2014 on lequipe.fr by Jean Le Bail. Last accessed on the 15th of February 2015.

http://www.lequipe.fr/Football/Actualites/Twitter-la-methode-aulas/540976 – "Comment Jean-Michel Aulas est devenu une star sur Twitter", published on the 7th of March by par Alexis Danjon. Last accessed on the 15th of February 2015.

http://www.mcfc.co.uk/news/club-news/2013/august/city-stories-release – "The club today announce details of a new fan engagement platform, #citystories", published on the 19th of August 2013 on the official website of the club: http://www.mcfc.co.uk. Last accessed on the 10th March 2015.

http://www.mediametrie.fr/eurodatatv/communiques – "La Coupe du Monde de Football 2014 a fait le plein de teéléspectateurs et de records dans le monde", published on the 17th of July 2014. Last accessed on the 22nd of July 2014.

http://www.mediametrie.fr/internet/communiques/l-annee-internet-2014-d-ecrans-de-contenus-d-interactivite-de-complementarite-entre-ecrans.php?id=1213, "L'Année Internet 2014: + d'écrans, + de contenus, + d'interactivité, + de complémentarité entre écrans", published on the 19th of February 2015. Last accessed on the 19th of February 2015.

http://www.sportbuzzbusiness.fr/facebook-et-twitter-au-psg-interview-de-michel-mimran-directeur-marketing-du-paris-saint-germain.html – "Facebook et Twitter au PSG – Interview de Michel Mimran, Directeur Marketing du Paris Saint-Germain", published on the 5th of November 2012 on Sport Buzz Business. Last accessed on the 15th of February 2015.

http://www.sport-numericus.com – "[Interview] Twitter, le plus grand terrain de sport", interview with Barthélemy Colin published on the 7th of May 2014 on the website Sport Numéricus.

http://www.tns-sofres.com/communiques-de-presse/connected-life-2014-letude-qui-revele-les-usages-des-internautes-dans-50-pays – "Connected Life 2014: L'étude qui révèle les usages des internautes dans 50 pays", published on the 24th of September 2014. Last accessed on the 18th of February 2015.

https://blog.twitter.com/2014/insights-into-the-worldcup-conversation-on-twitter – "Insights into the #WorldCup conversation on Twitter", billet de Simon Rogers published on the 14th of July 2014 on the blog of Twitter. Last accessed on the 29th of January 2015.

https://blog.twitter.com/en-gb/2013/twitterleaguetable – #TwitterLeagueTable, published on the 11th of January 2013 by Lewis Wiltshire on the English blog of twitter. Last accessed on the 15th of February 2015.

https://blog.twitter.com/fr/2014/lann-e-2014-sur-twitter – "L'année 2014 sur Twitter", published on the 10th of december 2014 by Christopher Abboud on the blog of Twitter France. Last accessed on the 2nd of February 2015.

Result-sport.de, Digitale Sport Medien, January 2015, p. 18.

8

REGIONS AND PROFESSIONAL FOOTBALL CLUBS

What do sports brands and regional brands have in common?

Christopher Hautbois

Regional sports marketing, as defined by Hautbois and Desbordes (2008), is the field of research that studies how sports contribute, directly or indirectly, to the promotion of a region, understood here as a brand. In this area, major international sporting events and professional sports clubs (especially those belonging to high-profile sports) appear traditionally in the eyes of local policymakers or the general public as the best known and most effective conveyors. If a major international sporting event can allow the host country to benefit from strong media exposure for a short time, a professional sports club is often the "positive" megaphone of a region, usually a town, able to address the general public, potential tourists or business leaders seduced by the energy of the event a priori associated with the sports town. Professional sports are now largely globalized, which is certainly true in France as well as in Europe, North America and increasingly in the rest of the world.

Today, the region is less and less the "lifeless" venue of a professional sports club. The interconnectedness of a club and its region is often strong and available on the historical and economic, financial and strategic plans. As a result, regions engage themselves in their own brand-building logic. Consequently, we see the co-existence of two brands: that of the region and that of the professional sports club, both of which design a marketing strategy of their own. This chapter analyzes the strategic aspects of a cohabitation such as this. This raises, in particular, the issue of potential, respective advantages. To what extent does this cohabitation constitute a fruitful partnership for both parties? In other words, to what extent does the existence of a brand positively influences the development of the other? Conversely, in the case of a strong growth of both brands/entities, can one have a negative impact on the development of the other? In the most extreme case, can one of the two brands do damage to the other? These issues are addressed here by means of professional football clubs, particularly those of Auxerre, Bordeaux and Montpellier.

The sporting spectacle, the preferred medium of local brand building

City branding or regional marketing: a very recent field of analysis

Regional brand-building strategies are fairly recent since they were mainly developed in the 2000s. The work of Anholt (2005, 2008), Dinnie (2008), Florian (2002) or Maynadier (2010) discusses the concept of local branding. Another element indicating the organization of a theoretical field in this area is the establishment in 2004 of a scientific journal (*Place Branding and Public Diplomacy*) to bridge the conceptual gap linked to local brand building. Is a region a product like any other? Are the elements relating to the concept of a brand useful to the construction of a regional brand? If we stick to Keller's definition (1993),[1] a region or a city can actually be compared to a brand. Nevertheless, it must be qualified. "Most researchers are in agreement of accepting the idea that regional marketing can be likened to the marketing of a product while recognizing its specific nature" (Anttiroiko, 2014). Kapferer (2008) also adds that a

> city is first and foremost a human reality, local and immutable (which does not mean we cannot change it), rooted in a common history, culture and ecosystem. A local brand cannot be built without taking into account these factors. The construction of a territorial brand must be the result of a consultative process involving all key players in the region.

Therefore, a consensus emerges to say that a region can be seen as a product like any other, but nonetheless presents specificities.

The regions involved in place-branding desire to attract tourists or visitors, residents or businesses. To do this, public managers must pay attention to the attributes of the brand-region, its associated values, identity and overall reputation. Baker (2012) points out how difficult it is to improve the image of an area that has been perceived negatively for years. According to Morgan et al. (2011), regions that want to improve their image must be able to initiate a virtuous circle based on six interconnected elements: (1) tone (the local atmosphere, the attitude of the population, local heritage, testimonies about local life); (2) tradition (based on the local culture and history and a certain authenticity); (3) tolerance (being able to accommodate everyone in the same way regardless of race, region, origin, sexual orientation); (4) talent (being able to welcome all talents to strengthen the local economy, participate competitively in regards to tourism and promote a way of life and new ideas); (5) adaptability (being able to integrate new technologies but also striving to think differently – when in times of crisis, one has natural tendency to stay in a comfort zone and rest on its already dependable markets); and (6) testimonies (stories about the territory told by tourists, students, residents and businessmen who used to feel attracted to the territory).

The primacy of sporting events in the construction of local brands through sport

The literature mentions how sports can be one of the triggers of this virtuous circle. Related publications highlight the diversity of desired objectives (reputation, image, local economic development,[2] civic pride,[3] etc.), of the idea men (mostly local representatives), the used mediums (amateur, professional, leisure sport, spectator sports,[4] sports events[5]) and the importance given to sports (central or peripheral as defined by Michel, 1999) in the building of the regional brand or even its enrollment (short, medium or long term). We refer the reader to the works of Avraham (2000, 2004) on the effect of the region's image in media on the perceptions of tourists, the public opinion and the local inhabitants of the region. We refer the reader to the work of Berkowitz et al. (2007) on the opportunity presented by the Beijing Olympic Games to change the image of China. The work of Rein and Shields (2007) outlines brand building and development in newly industrialized nations, and the work of Chalip et al. (2003), Chen and Funk (2010), Chung and Woo (2009), Gibson et al. (2008) and Hede (2005) explains the impact the perception that the region is a tourist destination has on the intentions of the visit.

So, those are several variables that must be crossed to consider this issue as a whole. However, and although this diversity does exist in the literature, most of the work in regional sports marketing deals with the role played by major sporting events such as the Olympics or the World Cup in building these local brands, as evidenced by the references above. The aim of this chapter is to analyze the relationship specifically between a region and its professional football club. As amazing as it sounds, although there are many cities in the world known for their particular professional sports clubs, very few publications have focused on the importance of this type of structure regarding the building of a regional brand. This chapter therefore seeks to partially fill the gap. The reasoning behind choosing football in this context is based on several related arguments. Primarily, it is the most popular sport played in Europe. On the European continent, it is in this sport that professional clubs have both the greatest financial power and the strongest brands in a marketing sense. Accordingly, regardless of the sport itself, football, for these reasons, seems the best able to shed light on the local brand strategies which are based on professional sports club and the existing interactions between the regional, local brand (the city) and the sports brand (the professional club). It should also be noted that a region and a professional club have usually built a multifaceted relationship over the years: financial (the public community subsidizes its local club most of the time, respecting an ad hoc legal framework), in terms of the animation of the region (the presence of a professional football team is a unifying element for the local population whose region is trying to make good use of itself), infrastructure (these complex properties and sports arenas are mostly already owned and renovated by the community who puts them at the disposal of the clubs in exchange for an annual rent), etc. Regions and professional sports clubs, including football, already have important and ancient relationships. They now extend as a marketing angle, which theoretically questions the cohabitation of whether these two brands give rise to either competition or complementarity.

A study of three cases of cohabitation

Recall that the purpose of this chapter is to question from a strategic perspective the cohabitation of two brands (a regional brand on the one hand, the brand of a professional football club on the other) and more particularly the issue of potential, respective advantages. To what extent does this cohabitation constitute a fruitful partnership for both parties? To what extent does the existence of a brand positively influence the development of the other? In the case of a strong growth of both brands entities, can one have a negative impact on the development of the other?

A qualitative, non-statistically representative approach

The issues mentioned above are addressed through three parings between regions and clubs: Auxerre/AJA, Bordeaux/Girondins and Montpellier/MHSC. These three cases were selected "intuitively" given their supposed explanatory power and without consideration for any statistical representativeness. This work can be understood as an exploratory work done prior to further study. The topic here requires one to search ahead, to experience this problem on the field and to explore multiple cohabitation models. To further this research and move towards a more comprehensive analysis model, it would be necessary to carry out a thorough study of one of the European Football Championships examined in its entirety, or by performing a crossover study of European leagues while providing for each of them a representative cross-section of clubs.

A qualitative fact-finding survey was constructed for each of the three pairings. This led us to examine one or more representatives of the football club (mostly having a function relating to marketing, communication or development), one or more local representatives relating to external actors

Table 8.1 Table of interviewees

City	*Institution of the Interviewee*	*The Function of the Interviewee*	*Name of the Interviewee*	*Date of the Interview*
Montpellier	Agglomeration community	Former mayor – deputy in charge of sport until 2014	Jacques Martin	May 21, 2014
	Montpellier Town Hall Deputy	Mayor – deputy in charge of sport since 2014	Fabien Abert	May 27, 2014
	Regional Council Languedoc-Roussillon	Head of sports and events	Mathieu Anglade	May 23, 2014
	Montpellier Tourist Office	Director	Fabrice Cavillon	June 10, 2014
Bordeaux	Bordeaux City Deputy	Mayor – Deputy in charge of sport	Arielle Piazza	October 7, 2014
	Girondins of Bordeaux	Marketing Project Manager	Nicolas Descous	June 27, 2104
	Girondins of Bordeaux	In charge of community relations	Sylvie Pépin	August 8, 2014
	Board of Tourrism	CEO	Nicolas Martin	June 18 2014
Auxerre	Auxerre Mayor	Mayor's chief of staff	Marc Picot	June 23, 2014
	AJ Auxerre	Director of marketing and communication	Baptiste Malherbe	May 27, 2014
	Office of Tourism Auxerre and Auxerrois	Director	Valérie Thomas	June 18, 2014

(tourist office, chambers of commerce or industry) to these two entities, concerning these strategic relationships which play themselves out between each other. While maintaining this framework for the three cases mentioned, the interviewees were identified by cross-checking the information gathered through telephone from various local actors, designating in turn the people whom were deemed most relevant locally in relation to the subject of the research. Finally, Table 8.1 clarifies the function and affiliated institutions of the 11 interviewed actors.

The Montpellier Hérault Sport Club (HSC), a central element to a proactive approach of promoting a region through sports

Box 8.1 The personal information sheet of Montpellier HSC

Name of the president of the SASP: Louis Nicollin

Average attendance per match: 14,679 (2013–2014)

Number of Facebook fans: 158,832 (August 1, 2014)

Budget of the club: 75 million euros (2012–2013)

Budget breakdown: audiovisual rights (74%), sponsorship (10%), games revenue (7.5%), other (8.5%)

Total number of partners/sponsors: 12

Names of the partners in 2014: ONZEO, Wati B, Faun, U Stores, Nicollin Group, Dyneff, South of France, Languedoc-Roussillon, Montpellier Agglomeration, Nike, Mutual Sun, Beinsports.

High-performance sports, the first driving force of promoting a region

The collected data come together to position high-performance sports as a vehicle for promoting the history of the region. The place given to high-performance sports reflects a deliberate policy of the public sphere and one man in particular, Georges Frêche, Mayor of Montpellier from 1977 to 2004. "The strong will from Georges Frêche has imbued our city with a brand that places a high importance on sports," said Jacques Martin, Executive Vice President of sports in Montpellier until 2014. "There was originally a desire from Frêche to reawaken Montpellier using sports. . . . Today the sport is part of the city's DNA," confirms Fabien Abert, deputy mayor of Montpellier sports since 2014. For nearly 30 years, the town councilor has shaped this territory by making this high-performance sport its main showcase. Today, Montpellier is the French city which has the highest density of professional sports clubs, including the football club which was the 2012 champion of France and was used to convey a positive and dynamic image. It would be too simple and too fast-acting to find a causal relationship between the density of the top clubs in a given region and their excellent results with their political support, as hard as it is. But it is nevertheless the result of several years of investment into high-performance sports that is now amassing in the Montpellier territory and it is not a "coincidence", an opportunity which the region has decided to use as a showcase. Today, high performance sports are used as the commercial representatives. According to Fabien Abert, although "there are no specific communication plans of the city which can be linked to the good sporting results of professional clubs," sports are used as a means of communication and replaces in part the conventional, promotional and regional campaigns that may have been created by local decision-makers. For Fabrice Cavillon, the director of the tourism office in Montpellier, football is like "an interesting gateway which can put the country in the market for tourist destinations from South America". Fabien Abert estimates on his part that "the 13-players rugby club plays in the English Championship which can bring additional, foreign tourists." This approach is equally legitimized by the fact that there exists an unintentional solidarity between top clubs. The poor results of some are offset by the better results of others so that the region benefits from a common image of positivity thanks to sports. "What is important is to have repetition in the media," concludes Fabrice Cavillon.

The MHSC-Languedoc-Roussillon region: an original co-branding strategy

Professional sports, including football, helps promote a positive image of Montpellier and its suburbs. "When a team works well, we talk about the town. This generates undeniable media coverage," says Fabrice Cavillon. But in the case of this particular region, the partnership between these two entities goes beyond the point of considering a co-branding strategy. Marketing considerations, as illustrated in this book, conducted by professional football clubs lead these clubs to develop real branding strategies. It is thus up to the club management to identify the differentiating elements of their own structure in terms of image, value, message, etc. Regarding Montpellier HSC, this football club conducts a rather classical marketing strategy of its own that seems in the eyes of most of its leaders to contribute to the development of the club. Here, the originality is that the Languedoc-Roussillon region has simultaneously developed its own umbrella brand under the name "South of France" whose "mission is assisting companies in domestic and international markets but as an interface with buyers to promote regional expertise and be able to better advise regional entrepreneurs in a competitive approach" (www.suddefrance-developpement.com/fr). The goal is therefore to encourage economic activity in the region by supporting the involved companies and producers. Football leaders and economic actors, seeking

Figure 8.1 2014–2015 home jersey of MSHC

to promote their respective brands nationally and internationally (thus improving their sales), have been committed for 4 years to a sponsorship contract enabling the brand "Sud de France" to be visible on the front of the MHSC jersey. This partnership also has some of the attributes of a classic sponsorship deal. Thus, "by associating itself with the sport, the objective is to create likability for the Sud de France brand," explains Mathieu Anglade, the department head of high-performance sports and events in the Languedoc-Roussillon region. "By associating itself more precisely with football, the Sud de France brand is looking to expand its international visibility." But this partnership goes beyond a conventional sponsorship deal. For Mathieu Anglade, it is indeed a "co-branding approach based on the principle of a win-win partnership. Each brand really works to develop the other. For example, the association with MHSC contributes to the fact that the logo is beautiful and well received."

A model in constant evolution

The Montpellier/MHSC pairing constitutes a good example of coexistence that can be described as positive as it seems both rooted, as it is based on a common history, and beneficial to both parties. However, this model of cohabitation needs to be constantly looked at for several reasons. The first is the cost of public support in regards to high performance sports and to football in particular. As was said earlier, sports are the result of a strong political will materialized through financial support for nearly 30 years. But the community's objective today is to continue to support high-performance sports at the local level while not weighing too heavily on public finances. "The example of water polo is ultimately the example to follow in terms of a business model," says Fabien Abert. "Private partners and public partners come together to help develop the club which will help reduce the financial support of public authorities." Fabrice Cavillon adds that the 2010s will probably be a decade in which public authorities will without a doubt seek to "rationalize their financial commitments".

Second, the news shows each week that high-performance sports are not always the virtuous universe that one imagines. In 2012, the Paris match-fixing scandal, which has exposed the Montpellier handball team, is one example. In this case, Mathieu Anglade considers that "the statement was made well enough to explain to the public that the problem mainly emanated from some players and not from the club as a whole which was ultimately one of the victims of the scandal." Nevertheless, this case points out that high-performance sports cannot be of benefit when it comes to being of use in a communications strategy, including when it is a region that seeks to promote it. This is also causing the region to develop other promotional approaches. Fabrice Cavillon, director of the Tourism Office of Montpellier, confirmed that if, "high performance sports constitute a communication strategy of the region, it is not the only one. The history, culture and heritage have formed as a result of 5 or even 10 years of strong promotional strategies. They accompany and contribute to the general development of the city."

Finally, it is appropriate to put into perspective the supposed benefits of this cohabitation between brand(s), sport(s) and local brands as the numerical evaluations are lacking. On this subject, Fabrice Cavillon believes that "we have some data but it is not that formal." "We are more in the supposed economic impact," acknowledges Jacques Martin. In addition, for Fabien Abert, "the high-performance sport is useful for the image of the city but will not, in my opinion, be useful beyond. There is no impact on corporate activity and employment, although one can imagine that the city infrastructure will appeal to businesses." Therefore, the positive effects connected to this coexistence remain theoretical in part.

The Girondins of Bordeaux, the secondary lever of promoting the territorial brand

Box 8.2 Personal information sheet of Bordeaux

Name of the president of the SASP: Jean-Louis Triaud
Average attendance per match: 18,833
Number of Facebook fans: 465,491 (August 1, 2014)
Budget of the club: 71 million euros (2012–2013)
Budget breakdown: audiovisual rights (60%), sponsorship (14%), games revenue (10%), other (16%)
Total number of partners/sponsors: 8
Names of the partners in 2014: Kia, Puma, Orange, Pigeon, Cdiscount, Quick, Crédit Agricole Aquitaine, M6

The case of the Bordeaux/Girondins pairing complements the other two cases in this chapter. Indeed, as any professional football club, Girondins is constantly looking to consolidate their brand and make it stronger and more attractive, whether in France or abroad. For this, the club relies on several strengths, including that of their prize list. The club has notably won six league titles in France, four Coupes de France and three French League Cups. But the originality of this case lies in the fact that as strong as the sports brand is, it coexists with a regional brand, Bordeaux, which is now a global brand and the most powerful as of yet.

A regional brand with an international dimension

Chamard and Liquet (2009) propose a prototypical and categorical analysis of the French regions, based on a quantitative study conducted via an online questionnaire. Respondents had total freedom of the words they wished to associate with each region. Regarding Aquitaine, 10 items stand out in descending order of frequency: wine, burgundy, Basque, ocean, sea, moors, mountains, beach, sun, oysters. No mention related to the Girondins appears. The only sports-related term is "surfing". It should be noted that respondents were asked about Aquitaine and not Bordeaux. Therefore, it is almost normal that the word "Girondins" is not associated with Aquitaine.

Nevertheless, Nicolas Martin, director of the Bordeaux tourism office, confirms the communication strategies around which the regional brand operates:

> We have three main pillars. First, the wine. Bordeaux is the wine capital of the world. Then we have heritage. The city is designated as a UNESCO World Heritage site. Bordeaux possesses a heritage of the nineteenth century. . . . The third strategy is to keep in mind that Bordeaux is a port. It was even the first port in Europe in the eighteenth century. So today we try to develop our river tourism, such as cruises on the Garonne.

Mr. Martin also clarifies that these three pillars aim to promote the regional brand with clearly defined markets: "We have three markets undergoing consolidation: North America, Japan and Australia. We have two parallel markets of conquest: China and Brazil."

A few sports brands integrated into the strategy of the region

Since the "Bordeaux" brand is old and already possesses a high level of reputation and sympathy, local elected officials accept the idea that the professional football club is not, in this context, a representative of regional promotion. Nicolas Martin recalls that

> the Girondins were a medium used 15–20 years ago when the club was the best in France. Today, given the results, we do not really use them. This is something that is important for the radiance of the city but as part of a tourism promotion strategy, this is not, to date, a useful lever for us.

Nicolas Descous, responsible for marketing and events for the Girondins de Bordeaux, confirms that "we have an agreement with the city that provides a number of things. The club participates in events organized by the city such as the 'Quai des Sports'. The city also regularly requests the provision of some players for operations." The club is therefore involved in the life of the city, allowing the maintenance a win-win relationship between the two entities. Nicolas Martin confirms, however, that from a tourism point of view,

> the Médoc marathon and the Bordeaux marathon, which will be the first marathon to be run at night, will be interesting for us because people come from far away to participate in these trials. On the other hand, one does not come from far away to attend a Girondins match. Basically, football is secondary in our promotional strategy because football is secondary to our target markets. North America, Australia, China and Japan are not football countries. Brazil is of course a land of football, but the Girondins are not Barca so we cannot really rely on it.

Sylvie Pepin, responsible for External Relations and Protocol for the Girondins, adds that "the city relies on our club to forge ties with various local associations, with young people, etc." Arielle Piazza, deputy mayor in charge of sports in the city of Bordeaux confirms that "the club has expanded in recent years within the lives of Bordelaise, shopkeepers through the intermediary of different operations such as La Ronde des quartiers (Around the neighborhoods)." On the other hand,

> from a marketing point of view, the usage of our brand by the city is rather minor. Do not forger that Bordeaux remain a rugby town. The city uses the image of football as it

> does with rugby, basketball, etc. On the contrary, the Girondins are entirely integrated into the region and its image. The club displays for example the wine leaf on its jerseys.

The power of the "Bordeaux" brand and the difficulty of the Girondins to appear as a genuine international sports base are the two elements which give the regional brand the status of dominance over the sport brand without being detrimental to the latter. However, Arielle Piazza, deputy mayor of sports explains the role of professional sports in the promotion of the city: "when I welcome a foreign delegation, I give them a tour of the city, I have them enjoy the wine, but I'm also present the region by means of the Girondins."

AJ Auxerre, a longtime central element to the promotion of the territory, today of secondary importance

Box 8.3 Personal information sheet for AJ Auxerre

Name of the SASP president: Guy Cotret
Average number of spectators per game: 5,986
Number of Facebook fans: 60,711 (August 13, 2014)
Budget of the club: 11.6 million euros (2012–2013)
Budget breakdown: audiovisual rights (63%), sponsorship (16%), other (21%)
Total number of partners/sponsors: 8
Name of the partners in 2014: Airness, Trailers Louault, Vitrans, CG of the Yonne, JDPS, Yonne Republic, Elite Catering, Intermarché

Auxerre in this instance constitutes the third case of cohabitation between a regional brand and a sports brand. From a strategic point of view, this cohabitation is initially for the benefit of the territory and its reputation. Recent years have seen a rebalancing, even a reversal of the dynamic.

AJA, a showcase of the Auxerre territory

All the players interviewed are in agreement that for about 30 years, AJA has been a local institution and has allowed the city to escape the status of relative anonymity. The sports brand has been built over the years, often assisted by a brilliant sporting career. However, the size of the region (35,500 inhabitants, the 210th most populated French city[6]) has not predisposed the club to such a record which would point to a "permanent miracle" that the former president has alluded to when talking of sports scores. "The club has long been a conveyor of identity for the area," recalls Marc Picot, chief of staff for the mayor of Auxerre. Valerie Thomas, director of the Tourism Office of Auxerre, confirms,

> in the 1990s, the region used the AJA in order to promote itself. Auxerre still had 30 years of football behind it. There was talk of Auxerre on the radio every 15 days thanks to football and Guy Roux . . . All of this had an undeniably positive effect in terms of images . . . Thanks to this, many people thought that we were a big city with a significant draw for tourism.

Baptiste Malherbe, director of marketing and communication for AJ Auxerre has a more nuanced perceptions of the local decision making regarding the effects of the club:

> When AJA played in the European Cup, everyone thought it was great because it enhanced our products, Chablis for example, in the eyes foreign supporters . . .On the other hand, if we consider just the French championship, the opinion has been more mixed as football remains a sport considered as popular. Therefore, this was reflected on the image of the city by giving it a more popular image, fairly distant from the rather high-end image that elected officials wanted to give the city, given its heritage and its downtown which is quite nice architecturally.

Still, the football club has been an important driving force for the building of the regional brand, with even a perverse effect. "At the end we were too known for football. The problem was that it hid everything," says Valerie Thomas. This observation was the starting point of a regional desire to no longer exclusively focus its reputation strategy on the football club. The desire to build a genuine regional brand has led local actors to expand the possibilities.

Towards a reversal of the respective importance of brands

Today, the regional brand clearly aspires to emancipate itself from the sports brand, by choice, but also by default. Indeed, since AJA is playing today in Ligue 2, the media exposure which can benefit Auxerre is largely reduced. Valerie Thomas considers, "today it is obviously harder to use AJA in terms of media exposure because the club is in Ligue 2. AJA is integrated into the heritage but it is more difficult to rebound from the given results." Beyond this problem is also a desire to enrich the brand which guides local decision makers. Auxerre seeks to highlight its strengths in the cultural, historic and geographic sectors. For Valerie Thomas,

> the first strength concerns heritage. Auxerre is indeed a center of art and history, with an important historic and religious heritage. . . . The second strength is that of wine and gastronomy. The third approach is both river and green tourism. In every case, two of our strengths are our proximity and accessibility to Paris thanks to the A6.

If the local officials do not aspire to place AJ Auxerre in the heart of the communication strategy of the region, it also because of the changing economic model of professional football. "A lot of things have changed in the structure of the club," said Marc Picot. "Historically, AJA was a club with associative structure. . . .Today the club has a professional structure which is closer to other French professional clubs. The business model has undergone a change with outside investors." Thus, because of the financial self-management of professional football clubs on the one hand and the desire of local authorities to maximize their support to professional sports in general and professional football in particular, the city of Auxerre, over the years, rationalized its relationship with its club. "In the 1990s there was a strong fusion between the club and the city. . . . It was not necessarily very healthy," estimates Mr. Picot. This process no longer has AJA as the gravity center of local life and has given the club the local entity status among others. But if the club no longer establishes itself as the sole means for promoting the region, it nevertheless remains as an interesting opportunity. "Communicating through the club remains consistent for our town because it is small, therefore having one of the 40 French professional clubs is something that one quickly sees," concludes Valerie Thomas.

Conclusion

The objective of this chapter was to illustrate, using a qualitative, non-statistically representative approach, the notion of cohabitation between a sports brand and a regional brand. The sports brands were those of professional football clubs, while at the regional level, they were cities. The three case studies reflect different types of cohabitation that would be necessary to deal with in-depth through a more systematic study of pairings between professional clubs and regions. The case of Montpellier HSC is a good example of a win-win coexistence between a sport and a regional brand. The football club contributes to the promotion of the image of a region equally as much as the existence of the professional club is desired and supported by the local public sphere. The Auxerre case illustrates another form of cohabitation: that an important opportunity given to a smaller region initiates, through the results of its football club, a recognition process on the national and international level. This process is shelved for two reasons: the sharp decline of the club in terms of sports and the desire to promote the city through ways other than football. The case of Bordeaux constitutes a third form of cohabitation. One in which the initial power of the regional brand (does not) leaves a secondary role for the Girondins club which is promoting the brand.

In their own ways, these three cases illustrate the place that occupies a professional football club in their regional marketing strategy. They bring about several evaluations which are all avenues for future research. First, the place occupied by a professional football club within regional brand building is examined in terms of the local sporting context. Is the football club the sole representative of professional sports in the region? A territory may have even more of a tendency to invest in a football club if it is the only team which has professional status. Helleu and Durand (2007) analyze the phenomenon of metropolization in professional sports. On this basis, the brand building strategy can be different depending on whether the region has one product (only one professional club) or not. Another aspect relates to the choice of sports. What are the respective advantages of professional football clubs, basketball, rugby, handball, etc.? In a brand-building perspective, do they all have the same value? Are built brands stronger and more durable in soccer than in basketball? Are they equivalent? Even more broadly, what is the dominant criterium needed to build such a regional brand through a professional team: the sport? the type of strategy (exclusive via one club or many)? The profile of the city (is the construction of a regional brand through sports it possible no matter the size of the territory or only with a minimum number of people)? Finally, is there a French specificity in the matter which is explained by the traditionally important role of the public sphere in the animation of local and national regions, or is the logic of city branding eminent and applicable from one country to another? Further cases are in this way interesting to study. The case of Manchester, England, contains two professional football clubs and employs a very different logic of regional brand building. Additional interesting cases include that of Valencia in Spain, where the football club is considered as the best ambassador of the city, or conversely that of Birmingham in England, where the city considers the football club to be a restriction on the regional brand building (Hautbois, 2015).

Notes

1 "A brand can be defined as a name, term, sign, symbol or design or combination of them which is intended to identify the goods and services of one seller or group of sellers and to differentiate them from those of competitors."
2 See Eisenger (2000), Gratton et al. (2005) and Preuss et Alfs (2011).
3 See Maennig and Porsche (1999) about the World Cup in Germany.
4 See Agrusa and Tanner (2002).
5 See Westerbeek (2009).
6 Source: INSEE.

Bibliography

Agrusa J. and Tanner J., "The economic significance of the 200 Buy.com golf tournament on the Lafayette, Louisiana area", *Journal of Sport Tourism*, 7(1), 2002, pp. 6–24.

Anholt S., "Some important distinctions in place branding", *Place Branding and Public Diplomacy*, 1(2), 2005, pp. 116–121.

Anholt S., "Place branding: Is it marketing or isn't it?", *Place Branding and Public Diplomacy*, 4, 2008, pp. 1–6.

Anttiroiko A.-V., *The political economy of city branding*, New York: Routledge, 2014.

Avraham E., "Cities and their news media images", *Cities*, 17(5), 2000, pp. 363–370.

Avraham E., "Media strategies for improving an unfavorable city image", *Cities*, 21(6), 2004, pp. 471–479.

Baker B., *Destination branding for small cities: The essentials for successful place*, Portland, USA, Creative Leap Books, 2012.

Berkowitz P., Gjermano G., Gomez L. and Schafer G., "Brand China: Using the 2008 Olympic games to enhance China's image", *Place Branding and Public Diplomacy*, 3, 2007, pp. 164–178.

Chalip L., Green B.C. and Hill B., "Effects of sport event media on destination image and intention to visit", *Journal of Sport Management*, 17(3), 2003, pp. 214–234.

Chamard C. and Liquet J.-C., L'évaluation de l'image perçue des régions françaises, Colloque CNRS "Vivre du patrimoine", Corte, janvier 2009. http://imagesdesterritoires.univ-pau.fr/live/digitalAssets/78/78994_Pr__sentation_Corse_2009.pdf

Chen N. and Funk D., "Exploring destination image, experience and revisit intention: A comparison of sport and non-sport tourist perceptions", *Journal of Sport Tourism*, 15(3), 2010, pp. 239–259.

Chung W. and Woo C.W., "The effects of hosting an international event on country image: The 2008 summer Olympics case", *Working Paper*, 2009.

Dinnie K., *Nation branding: Concepts, issues, practice*, Oxford, UK, Butterworth-Heinemann, 2008.

Eisenger P., "The politics of bread and circuses: Building the city for the visitor class", *Urban Affairs Review*, 35(3), 2000, pp. 316–333.

Florian B., "The city as a brand", in V. Patteeuw (ed.), *City branding: Image building & building images*, Rotterdam, Nai publishers, 2002.

Gibson H., Xueqing Q. and Zhang J.-J., "Destination image and intent to visit China and the 2008 Beijing Olympic games", *Journal of Sport Management*, 22, 2008, pp. 427–450.

Gratton C., Shibli S. and Coleman R., "Sport and economic regeneration in cities", *Urban Cities*, 42(5–6), 2005, pp. 985–999.

Hautbois C., "Sport and city branding: How useful are the professional football clubs to brand European cities?", in S. Chadwick, N. Chanavat et M. Desbordes (ed.), *Handbook of sport marketing*, Londres, UK, Routledge (à paraître en 2015).

Hautbois C. and Desbordes M., *Sport et marketing public*, Paris, Economica, 2008.

Hede A., "Sports-events, tourism and destination marketing strategies: An Australian case study on Athens 2004 and its media telecast", *Journal of Sport Tourism*, 10(3), 2005, pp. 187–200.

Helleu B. and Durand C., "La métropolisation du sport professionnel en Europe et en Amérique du Nord: une approche comparative", *Mappemonde*, 88, 2007.

Kapferer J.-N., *The new strategic management*, Londres, UK, Kogan Page, 2008.

Maennig W. and Porsche M., "The feel-good effect a mega sports events", Recommendations for public and private administration informed by the experience of the FIFA World Cup 2006, *IASE/NAASE Working Paper Series*, 08–17, 1999.

Maynadier B., *Branding the city, une étude du marketing des villes*, Strasbourg, Éditions Universitaires Européennes, 2010.

Michel G., "Évolution des marques: approche par la théorie du noyau central", *Recherche et Applications en Marketing*, 14(4), 1999, pp. 33–53.

Morgan, N., Pritchard, A. and Pride, R. Destination branding: Managing Place Reputation Oxford: Butterworth-Heinemann, 2011.

Preuss H. and Alfs C., "Signaling through the 2008 Beijing Olympics, using mega sport events to change the perception and image of the host", *European Sport Management Quarterly*, 11(1), 2011, pp. 55–71.

Rein I. and Shields B., "Place branding sports: Strategies for differentiating emerging, transitional, negatively viewed and newly industrialised nations", *Place Branding and Public Diplomacy*, 3(1), 2007, pp. 73–85.

Westerbeek H.M., "The Amsterdam Olympic games of 1928 and 2028: Will city heritage inform legacy intent?", *Sport in Society*, 12(6), 2009, pp. 776–791.

9

CSR

A new strategic component for European professional football clubs[1]

Aurélien François and Emmanuel Bayle

Introduction: social responsibility in professional football – a deeply rooted but complex issue

Thanks to its exceptional popularity, professional football occupies a unique position in European sport. This is reflected in football's dominance of media sports coverage, especially since the emergence of private television channels in the 1980s, and the sport's extremely high earnings (Drut, 2014). In fact, the combined turnover of Europe's professional football clubs has grown constantly for more than 30 years, reaching almost 20 billion euros in 2013 (Deloitte, 2014). This focus on the commercial side of the sport has led to European professional football being seen by many people as a symbol of financial capitalism,[2] a view that is reinforced by the headline-making transfer fees and salaries that have resulted from clubs investing most of the television rights bonanza in players' salaries and transfers, especially since the Bosman ruling in 1995.[3] Nevertheless, professional football cannot be considered merely in commercial terms, as it is also a source of positive externalities for clubs' local areas and for society as a whole. In fact, by creating jobs, providing a focus for local identities, and acting as a vector for social cohesion, professional football has always demonstrated a form of corporate social responsibility (CSR). This chapter examines present practices in football CSR and suggests ways in which these practices may evolve.

Many attempts have been made to define the multifaceted concept of CSR. Here, we focus uniquely on one conception of CSR, that is, as a way for an organization to show it "has taken into account its responsibilities towards the different groups with which it interacts and gone further than its strict technical, legal, and economic obligations" (Gond and Igalens, 2010). This definition is imperfect, as it does not indicate the extent of a company's responsibilities, but it at least encourages CSR researchers to examine homogenous business sectors to determine why and how companies engage in CSR actions. Research into these aspects of CSR in sport organizations first blossomed in the mid-2000s, and several books on this topic have now been published (Bayle et al., 2011; Paramio-Salcines, Babiak and Walters, 2013; Rodriguez, Késenne and Garcia, 2009). Many of these studies focused on CSR within professional football, especially in the wake of Breitbarth and Harris's (2008) pioneering comparison of CSR across world football, which has inspired numerous studies of CSR by English (Anagnostopoulos, Byers and Shilbury, 2014; Anagnostopoulos and Shilbury, 2013; Walters, 2009; Walters and Chadwick, 2009; Walters and Tacon, 2010) and then European (Breitbarth, Hovemann and Walzel, 2011) football clubs. Although most of these studies embrace a proactive vision of CSR as a creator of value, few have examined new motivations for CSR initiatives that could come into conflict with those underlying the actions already being pursued by these organizations.

This issue raises other preliminary questions which we address in this chapter. Why do professional football clubs engage in CSR actions and what form(s) do these actions take? What benefits can clubs obtain from CSR actions and what are the pitfalls to avoid? CSR is currently a new aspect of clubs' strategies, but how sustainable will it be? We examine each of these questions in turn, drawing upon information provided by the many articles on CSR in European professional football that have appeared in recent years. We begin by benchmarking CSR initiatives in European football and then discuss the implications of CSR for the strategic management of clubs.

Benchmarking CSR initiatives within European football

The multifaceted nature of CSR makes it difficult to build an accurate understanding of how the concept has been embraced by sport organizations, which are themselves extremely varied, even within the field of professional sport. This diversity is exemplified by the professional football sector, which consists of clubs with very different organizational characteristics (stock ownership, size, statute, etc.) and strategic outlooks. In addition, CSR within European football only recently began to appear on the research agenda (Breitbarth and Harris, 2008), with few studies conducted before the early 2010s. All these considerations increase the value of benchmarking current CSR initiatives.

Overview of CSR practices by European clubs

As a first attempt to overcome this research deficit, in 2010 the *Union of European Football Associations* (UEFA) contracted Walters and Tacon (2011) to study CSR in European football. UEFA's research was followed by a number of private initiatives, such as the studies carried out by the Swiss company Schwery Consulting, whose *Responsiball* website, created in 2010, claims to be "[t]he first point of reference for responsible football clubs". These two initiatives indicate a desire to compare CSR engagement and practices across Europe (Box 9.1).

Box 9.1 Attempts to compare CSR initiatives across Europe

Walters and Tacon (2011) based their study on a questionnaire sent to Europe's 53 national federations and 730 professional football clubs. It examined current CSR practices, the determinants of engagement in CSR, difficulties in implementing CSR actions, and the choice of target stakeholders. Their report's[4] main conclusions were based on the 112 professional clubs that replied to the questionnaire.

This study facilitated other initiatives, such as *Responsiball*, whose objective is to highlight good practices in areas such as governance, local development, and the environment. In addition, *Responsiball* draws up league tables comparing the CSR engagement of professional clubs in European leagues whose national team took part in the last European Championship. Their latest report was based on 51 CSR indicators collated from the clubs' websites and adapted from international reporting standards (*Global Reporting Initiative*, ISO 20121)[5] (Responsiball, 2014).

Our analysis of CSR engagement by European professional football clubs and the ways in which this engagement is fulfilled is partly based on these studies.

On the singularity of the factors determining social involvement

The factors determining professional clubs' involvement in CSR have been a popular theme in sports management research (Babiak and Wolfe, 2009). Walters and Tacon (2011) devoted an entire section of their report to the reasons why European professional football clubs engage in CSR (Figure 9.1).

As Figure 9.1 shows, CSR involvement by European professional football clubs is most strongly influenced by external factors. For example, 63% of respondents stated that CSR actions were a response to the "seriousness of a social need", whereas only 18% admitted that the "profitability of the venture" was a very important or important factor. These results are in line with the findings of Babiak and Wolfe's (2009) study of CSR practices in North American sport,[6] which showed the primacy of external factors over internal factors in determining CSR initiatives. Nevertheless, the external factors identified by Babiak and Wolfe, most notably pressure from key external stakeholders (public authorities, sponsors, etc.) differ from those reported by Europe's professional football clubs. Strangely, encouragement from the football leagues does not feature among the reasons for CSR engagement,[7] and pressure, whether from public opinion (36%), special interest groups (25%), or government authorities (22%), was seen as less important in determining CSR initiatives than certain internal factors, most notably "the interest of the individual owner of your football club", which was considered important by 43% of respondents.

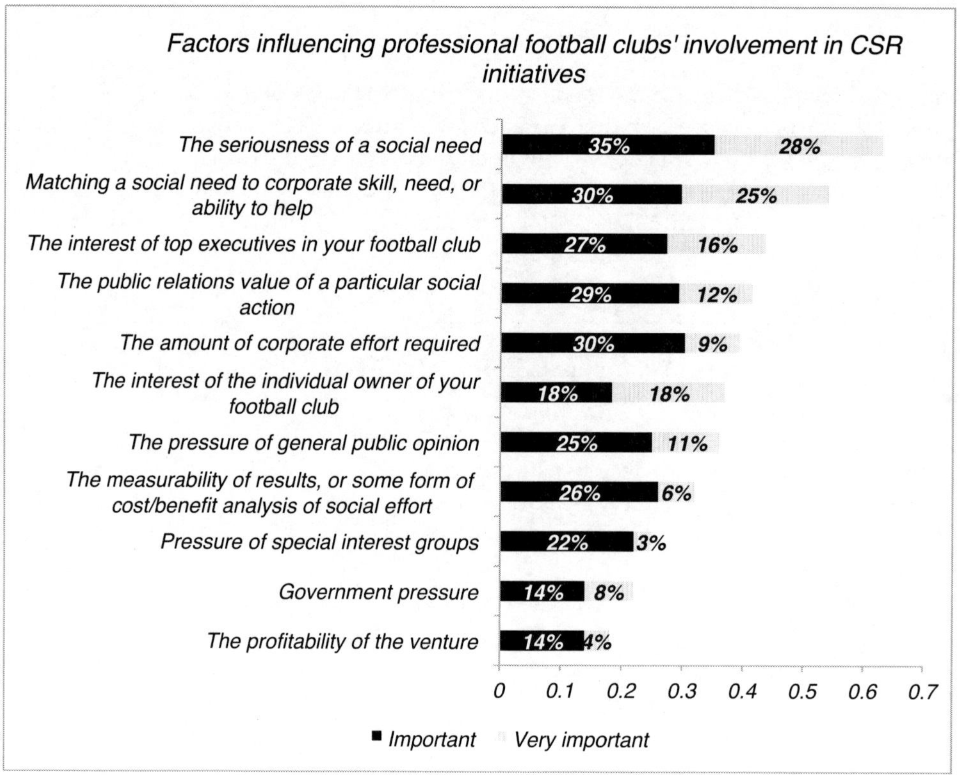

Figure 9.1 Factors seen as "very important" or "important" in determining CSR involvement by European professional football clubs

Source: Figure adapted from Walters and Tacon (2011).

Box 9.2

Going beyond the comparison with Babiak and Wolfe (2009), Walters and Tacon's results are similar to those reported for SMEs (Baumann-Pauly et al., 2013), which have similar characteristics (size and credit standing)[8] to football clubs. Considered corporate citizens, or even public enterprises, by some academics (Durand and Bayle, 2004), football clubs are also similar to SMEs in terms of their activities' impacts on local communities. However, despite their historic community roots (Lelore, 2011), the privatization of European football clubs during the second half of the 20th century, symbolized by the change from non-profit organizations to commercial enterprises, has forced them to (re)build their community dimension. Hence, clubs' CSR engagement must be analyzed in the light of the non-regulated liberalism in which European professional football has been caught up for the last 30 years. Consequently, many football clubs see CSR initiatives first and foremost as a way of improving their image (François, 2012).

The archetypal form of CSR: philanthropic socio-educational initiatives within the local community

CSR initiatives can be directed at three main areas – the local community, employees, and the environment. According to Walters and Tacon (2011), football clubs tend to focus on the first two of these areas and to neglect the third (Figure 9.2). The actions most frequently cited by club executives include establishing community educational and employment programs, supporting

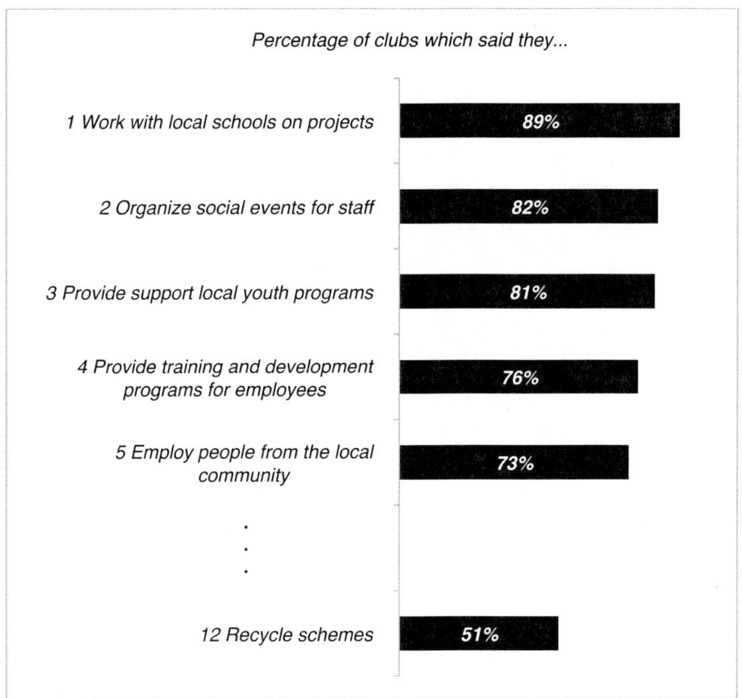

Figure 9.2 Main types of CSR actions undertaken by European professional football clubs

Source: Figure adapted from Walters and Tacon (2011).

training for administrative staff, and offering assistance with their staff's community projects. On the other hand, far fewer clubs engage in environmental initiatives. For example, even the most common type of environmental action reported in 2010 (recycle schemes) involved only half the clubs who replied to the questionnaire.

Since their very beginnings at the end of the 19th century, Europe's football clubs have been involved in social actions and education through sport (Lelore, 2011) and have therefore been widely supported by the communities in which they worked. Most initiatives have tended to be directed towards young people within the community and the clubs' employees, in other words, two groups of stakeholders with very close ties to the clubs. On the other hand, possible environmental initiatives have received much less attention. This is the case throughout professional sports, including in the United States, where CSR has strong cultural roots (Babiak and Trendafilova, 2011). In professional football, few clubs have assimilated the importance of environmental issues, and environmental impact analyses are carried out only for major events (Collins et al., 2007). The most recent Responsiball report (2014) confirmed this trend, as the 16 leagues (270 clubs) studied achieved much lower ratings (average of 8%) on Responsiball's environmental pillar than on the other two pillars (community and governance). An important reason for this is the high cost of environmental initiatives compared with the clubs' investment capacities, so even though environmental programs could provide clubs with substantial long-term benefits, such actions tend to be left to the public authorities, which own most clubs' stadiums.[9]

Contextualization of the clubs' CSR engagement: the British, German, and French models

Even though Walters and Tacon's (2011) conclusions are exceedingly informative as to the character and form of CSR undertaken by European professional football clubs, the quantitative nature of their study masks major differences between clubs and between countries. This limitation led us to examine how different national contexts affect CSR by examining CSR initiatives by clubs in England, Germany, and France, three of Europe's major football leagues. We chose these three countries as much for pragmatic reasons (access to data) as for the diversity of their CSR actions.

The English model: institutionalized, community-based initiatives

England has some of the most institutionalized CSR practices among European professional football clubs. This has been the case since the early 1990s, a period that saw major socio-economic changes (social exclusion and mass unemployment), the introduction of pay-to-view television channels, and the beginnings of government interest in CSR (Anagnostopoulos and Shilbury, 2013). Nevertheless, the institutionalization process is rooted in the way the British government exploited football clubs' long-standing commitment to social initiatives to help address some of the socio-economic problems affecting the country in the mid-1970s. The first community-based programs were introduced under Labour governments as part of the British tradition of clubs "giving something back"[10] to their host communities. These initiatives were intensified by Margaret Thatcher's Conservative government in the 1980s. At this time, English professional football was being poisoned by economic and social problems, especially hooliganism, which was finally brought under control following a concerted national effort. It was in this context that the *Football League*[11] and the Professional Footballers Association created the "Football in The Community" (FiTC) initiative in order to reconnect clubs to their local communities (Mellor, 2008). This government-supported program was first tested by six clubs in northwest England in 1986 and then gradually extended to all British football clubs (Walters, 2009; Watson, 2000). As a result, FiTC became the main channel through which clubs could express their CSR. In 1997, the Labour Party was returned to power with a new political agenda labeled the "Third Way". As part of its fight against poverty, the new government extended the scope of clubs' actions, initially focusing on counteracting social exclusion among the young before going on to address a wide range of issues, including health, education, security, and the revitalization of clubs' local areas (Mellor, 2008).

Although Brown et al.'s (2006) report on football and its communities recognized the role played by FiTC in the clubs' CSR engagement, the authors also noted the nebulous nature of the relations between clubs and their communities, most notably due to the lack of any separation between clubs' commercial and social practices. One of the report's recommendations was to implement FiTC measures through Community Sports Trusts (CST), which would be external to the clubs but steered by them (Box 9.3). Although some clubs had already done this before the report was published, the years following the report saw the widespread creation of CSTs. As well as being symbols of the institutionalization of CSR, CSTs mark the change from community-based socio-educational initiatives to a wider CSR engagement carried out with strategic aims.

Box 9.3 Community Sports Trusts

Community Sports Trusts (CST) are charitable organizations that go under a variety of names (CST, foundation, community education, and sporting trust) and which use sport as a vector for implementing CSR actions. CSTs have their own managerial boards, which adopt strategies independently from their associated football club, after which most CSTs are named (Walters, 2009). Creating a CST allows a club to delegate its CSR actions to a subsidiary organization. This strategy has several major advantages, but it also has a few drawbacks (Jenkins and James, 2012):

- Advantages:
  - Ensures the independence, transparency, and financial security of CSR causes;
  - Facilitates creating partnerships and improves the visibility of initiatives;
  - Increases the professionalism of the actions carried out.
- Drawbacks:
  - Separates the CSR function from a club's internal management;
  - Reduces engagement by a club's employees and makes it more difficult to measure benefits for the club;
  - Leads to criticism of the strategic independence, balance (commercial vs. social practices), and communication between CSTs and clubs.

Despite these drawbacks, numerous clubs have delegated their CSR actions to CSTs. As a result, the number of CSTs set up by Premier League and Football League clubs increased from 40 in 2009 to almost 90 in 2011 (Bingham and Walters, 2012).

The German model: a more comprehensive conception of CSR

The Rhenish business model is a form of social market capitalism that arose from Germany's 20th century corporatist model. One of its aims is to reconcile the short-term and long-term interests of stakeholders and, as such, it has been described as a "multiple partnerships" model. Rhenish companies, with public sector support, play a central role in pursuing the common interest, as defined by the State, and have made CSR an integral part of their activities. Consequently, they have only recently begun using the term CSR (Reiche, 2013), although this development often masks long-standing practices that arose from notions of paternalism, citizenship, and sustainable development (Breitbarth and Harris, 2008). In addition, the social rating system used to assess companies' CSR actions is likely to encourage them to increase their commitment to CSR. The resulting tendency for clubs and leagues in Rhenish countries to publicize their CSR initiatives effectively is reflected in the latest Responsiball report (2014), which places the Dutch (*Eredivisie*) and German (*Bundesliga*) leagues 2nd and 3rd among the 16 European leagues evaluated.[12] Their high scores are partly due to the greater attention paid to environmental issues, which means CSR initiatives are more global and not confined uniquely to social issues.

The *Bundesliga*, the league on which most of our observations are based, is indicative of the way Rhenish clubs approach CSR. First created as nonprofit associations, Germany's football clubs are still at the heart of local associative networks. In fact, under the 50+1 Act of 1998, any club wishing to create a commercial company to manage its professional activities must allocate more than 50% of shares to co-existing nonprofit associations (support associations, supporters' associations, etc.). By underlining the importance of the associative approach, this system has made the implementation of CSR initiatives by clubs more implicit. It has also protected clubs from takeovers by foreign investors, who are often criticized by local people who do not identify with the new owners or their management policies, including their social policies. As a result, German clubs have created strong links with large German companies (Adidas, Allianz, Bayer, Veltins, Volkswagen, etc.) as shareholders, equipment suppliers, or sponsors/"stadium namers", and most CSR initiatives are carried out in partnership with these companies. In this case, CSR is more the result of company paternalism through which certain clubs, in conjunction with their "big" private partners, go as far as creating centers for implementing social (education, social inclusion, etc.) and environmental programs (Breitbarth and Harris, 2008; Reiche, 2013). This approach differs from the English approach, which involves contracting out CSR to charitable organizations, although German clubs are starting to adopt the English model. The political dimension of these initiatives (Breitbarth and Harris, 2008) is underlined by the fact that by the 2011–2012 season two-thirds of *Bundesliga* first-division clubs had specific social institutions, most of which were foundations created by the clubs after the mid-2000s in partnership with governmental footballing bodies[13] (Reiche, 2013). This change, which has accelerated since 2010, must not mask the fact that even if philanthropic CSR initiatives remain embryonic and are less firmly rooted than in England, other issues, especially sustainable development, are given greater importance than they are in the UK. Many clubs carry out environmental actions as part of the German Football Federation's "Green Goal" program, created for the 2006 World Cup (Breitbarth and Harris, 2008). Similar programs are now obligatory for all World Cup host countries, which must take steps to reduce the event's environmental impact by examining issues such as water use, waste, energy, and transportation (Dolles and Soderman, 2010). This has led to a large number of environmental initiatives, such as encouraging spectators to use public transportation by offering reduced-price tickets to those who do so, promoting the use of renewable energies, introducing environmental management systems (e.g., Ecoprofit, Eco-Management and Audit Scheme), and reducing football clubs' carbon footprints (Reiche, 2013).

The French model: A hybrid model looking for an identity

CSR in French football lies at the crossroads between the English and German models. This hybrid position is primarily the result of the inchoate way French football achieved its current professional status. Originally nonprofit associations, France's football clubs began the transformation to for-profit enterprises by becoming "sports-based limited companies" in the 1980s. However, these companies were required to maintain links (contracts) with their historical associations, which continued to manage youth teams. In 2012, new legislation designed to further liberalize professional sport allowed football clubs to become standard commercial companies.[14] As research has shown (François, 2012; François and Bayle, 2014), this situation has tended to limit the extent of French clubs' CSR actions, with most actions being designed to show clubs' commitments to their local communities (Durand and Bayle, 2004). Despite this clear desire, CSR initiatives have remained embryonic due to the reluctance of club executives to embrace the notion of CSR and the difficulty of reconciling different types of action (associative, commercial, and public) (François and Bayle, 2014).

During the 1990s, as French professional football moved towards a more regulated form of liberalization than in other major European leagues (maintenance of a national directorate of management control, joint negotiation of TV rights, obligation to redistribute some of these rights to amateur sport), few attempts were made to institutionalize CSR. Hence, executives' claims that their clubs were inherently socially responsible were based on their associative heritage and the supposed socializing values of sport (Smith and Westerbeek, 2007). CSR actions were often carried out at the discretion of administrative and technical staff, especially players, and tended to involve publicizing general-interest and/or charitable associations, or providing these associations with financial support. However, a growing need to justify the public subsidies given to professional clubs led the French government to introduce new legislation (the 1999 "Buffet Act") requiring clubs to carry out "community-benefit missions" (*mission d'intérêt général* – MIG). MIGs tend to focus on training, education, social integration, social cohesion, and preventing violence in sports stadiums, but they have been criticized for being disproportionately expensive to the taxpayer compared with the content of projects (Cour des Comptes, 2009). In addition, studies have shown that the obligation to carry out such missions has led to a huge disparity between the quantity and/or quality of CSR initiatives and the level of CSR claimed by some clubs' executives (François, 2012).

Nevertheless, professional football clubs, which are becoming less dependent on direct public aid,[15] do carry their own social responsibility initiatives, in addition to their mandatory MIGs (UCPF, 2013). Most of the programs initiated by the 40 professional clubs that make up France's professional football league (LFP) target social and economic aspects of sustainable development, and they are increasingly being implemented as bilateral (club + private sponsor) and/or trilateral (club + local authority + private sponsor) partnerships. This type of CSR is typified by the "Supporters pour l'emploi" program, which helps out-of-work fans find jobs. "Supporters pour l'emploi" was created in 2013 by the LFP in partnership with a private company (La Française des Jeux), a public body (Pôle Emploi), and an "association of recognized public utility" (Association pour le Droit à l'Initiative Économique) and has now been implemented by around 20 first and second division clubs. As in the German model, French clubs are beginning to create specific bodies to carry out their CSR actions (foundations, endowment funds)[16] and although this approach is still marginal in France, it is likely to develop, as it has done in England.

Comparing these contexts shows differences in the roots and development of CSR in England, Germany, and France. In England, the importance of football clubs' impacts on their host communities during times of social and economic crisis legitimized the institutionalization of CSR.

In Germany, retaining the clubs' associative links, the involvement of large German companies, and the private construction of stadiums for the 2006 World Cup appear to have created a more general awareness of CSR. In France, the need to legitimize public subsidies, the increase in socially responsible sponsorship and patronage in order to counter football's negative public image (2010 World Cup scandal, ethical and financial misconduct by clubs, etc.), and a tendency to follow in the footsteps of other major European clubs appear to have triggered the development of socially oriented CSR. However, CSR in French football remains poorly institutionalized and is still searching for an identity. These differences between countries suggest that the effects of CSR on the governance of professional leagues and clubs will differ between these three models. In order to test this hypothesis, it is necessary to analyze the current and potential impact of CSR practices on the strategic management of clubs.

CSR and the strategic management of clubs

The second section of this chapter examines the issue of CSR from a strategic perspective. It highlights the beneficial effects of social initiatives on the long-term management of clubs, while underlining the difficulties involved in integrating CSR policies into a club's global strategy. In addition to giving clubs added legitimacy, CSR is a veritable strategic asset requiring careful management, although achieving this can be difficult. Football executives must reconcile the opposing needs of accomplishing short-term sporting objectives, often supported by substantial and risky financial investments in players, with the long-term construction of the club. Doing so raises a number of challenges.

The business case for CSR

In his review of theories of CSR, Lee (2008) noted the massive influx of work from the field of strategic management during the 1990s. This approach, combined with the concept of competitive advantage, led to the postulate that enterprises which have fully integrated CSR into their business strategy are likely to be more competitive than those whose CSR policy remains peripheral (Porter and Kramer, 2006). These studies, which took a functionalist or "business case" view of CSR, gradually resulted in profit maximization becoming a primary objective of CSR (Lee, 2008). Strategic management proved to be a very successful approach to analyzing CSR in professional football, as it highlighted the benefits a club could expect to obtain by taking account of its key stakeholders' interests (Breitbarth and Harris, 2008; Walters and Chadwick, 2009). Most studies analyzing CSR from this perspective were based on stakeholder theory, the dominant theory in CSR research and a core component of strategic management. According to stakeholder theory, enterprises should strive to satisfy the interests of both their shareholders and any other parties who may affect or be affected by the organization's decisions, and the best way to do this is by adopting a partnership approach (Freeman, 1984). Hence, the following sections examine CSR initiatives and their interactions with the numerous stakeholders involved as a potential resource for regenerating clubs' traditional economic models.

Managing a club's stakeholders

In the strategic management approach, stakeholder management is a crucial step in implementing CSR. According to Carroll and Buchholtz (2012), an organization should identify its key stakeholders, evaluate opportunities for meeting their needs, and involve them in implementing CSR initiatives. The supposed social nature of the sports business heightens the need for sport organizations to carefully manage stakeholders (Smith and Westerbeek, 2007). Realizing this, Breitbarth and Harris (2008) focused on CSR's potential for creating partnership value in European football. By mapping all the stakeholders involved in professional football, they were able to categorize them into three main types: national regulatory bodies, international sports institutions, and clubs' internal actors and commercial partners. Using a similar approach, we drew up a taxonomy of possible stakeholder contributions to a CSR policy intended to create value (Table 9.1).

This typology indicates several ways in which executives can initiate discussions with their stakeholders about the type of CSR strategy to follow. Although it is not a comprehensive list of stakeholders and even though it provides just one way of exploring possible contributions to implementing CSR, it offers clubs a framework for bringing together their often-disparate CSR initiatives into a more coherent social strategy and thereby changing their traditional economic models. In Europe, this approach to stakeholder management has led to the institutionalization of

Table 9.1 Possible contributions of stakeholders in professional football clubs to building CSR

Stakeholders	*Contribution in Terms of Resources*	*Possible Contributions to a CSR Strategy*
Executives	Managerial and relational skills for developing the club	Main decision-makers for choosing a CSR strategy – interface between the club and all its stakeholders
Shareholders	Provision of capital and proposals for strategic policy	Political power (voting rights at general meetings) to orient strategy towards more responsible management
Athletes and technical staff	Reputation (club's leading employees forming the heart of the offer)	Support for CSR actions (system of patronage) and personalities for external publicity
Administrative staff	Employees – human	Source of proposals for CSR actions (sponsors of social projects)
Sports institutions (leagues, federations, etc.)	Financial – legitimacy (authorization to take part in championships)	Assistance with actions by implementing national CSR programs and participation in CSR actions for local bodies
Social partners (unions)	Human – legitimacy	Participation in national CSR actions; integration of CSR into training programs for players in order to raise awareness of its importance
Private partners	Financial and relational	Provision of finance for social programs, drawing up of responsible partnerships and sharing experiences in the field of CSR (socially responsible sponsorship and patronage)
Local authorities	Financial and relational (political support)	Checks on how subsidies intended to improve living conditions in the local area are used (integration, social cohesion, etc.)
Supporters, season-ticket holders	Financial – fixed receipts from ticket sales	Source of proposals for CSR actions (sponsors of social projects), participation in actions; community linked to the club's identity
Spectators	Financial – variable receipts from ticket sales	Source of proposals for CSR actions (sponsors of social projects), participation in actions
NGOs – associations	Reputation and relational	Awareness raising for social causes and sharing of CSR skills with the club
Media	Finance and publicizing reputation	Responsible communication

Source: Table adapted from François (2012)

CSR through the creation of tools such as foundations and investment funds. In this way, CSR, in the form of social initiatives carried out by bilateral partnerships with private or public partners or by multiple partnerships (clubs/companies/local authorities), can lead clubs to redirect their business model. This has been the case for Olympique Lyonnais (Box 9.4).

Box 9.4 Institutionalization of CSR and changing Olympique Lyonnais' business model[17]

Social responsibility has always been part of Olympique Lyonnais' (OL) philosophy, even though the term CSR was never used before 2010. Since the 1990s, the clubs' CSR initiatives have focused on providing support to a group of charitable organizations. In 2007, OL Groupe decided to rationalize its CSR strategy by bringing together its disparate social actions. To do this, the group, six of its nine subsidiaries, and four of the club's private shareholders (Accor, Pathé, Cegid Group, Providis Logistique) created a corporate foundation called "OL Fondation". The foundation's total budget of 2 million euros for the period 2007–2012[18] consisted of a cash budget of 965,000 euros supplemented by match tickets and services provided by its members. A large part of this budget was invested in programs covering four themes (social insertion through sport, education, help to the ill or hospitalized, support for amateur sport). The foundation's life has since been extended, first in 2012 for a further 3 years and again in 2015, and the club has set up an endowment fund (sOLidaire) that can collect donations from any club supporter, rather than just from companies within the foundation.

After institutionalizing its CSR through these mechanisms, OL took a careful look at its global CSR strategy. In 2011, the group's board asked one of the club's two female administrators to head a specific CSR department. This was a first for a French sports club. In 2012 OL Groupe mentioned CSR in its annual report for the first time, presenting it as "one of the three pillars[19] on which Olympique Lyonnais has decided to build its development strategy" and "an integral component of the club at all levels (which) will take the form of solidarity programs and support for innovative projects". The reorientation of OL's corporate strategy was prompted by the building of a new stadium (Stade des Lumières), which also provided a catalyst for its new approach to CSR, under which OL Groupe has expanded its actions to cover five main areas: training and employability, diversity, wellness and health, support for amateur sport, and responsible behavior.

What are the expected benefits?

Viewed from a business case perspective, CSR provides an additional way of assessing a club's performance, alongside the classic criteria of sporting and financial results. According to this approach, CSR would be expected to have a substantial effect on performance in a number of areas. This is borne out by the impact on English football clubs of community initiatives (generally implemented via CSTs), which have been shown to have positive effects in the organizational (improving internal climate, increasing employee motivation), commercial (strengthening the club's brand and reputation, attracting new and better private and public partners, reducing tensions between economic and social objectives), and sporting (recruitment and training of young players, spectators identifying with local players, etc.) fields (Jenkins and James, 2012; Walters, 2009; Walters and Chadwick, 2009). Walters (2009) built on Smith and Westerbeek's

Table 9.2 Examples of potential benefits of partnerships between CSTs, commercial partners, and a football club

Community Sports Trust (CST)	*Commercial Partners*	*Football Club*
• Increased financial power • Ability to respond to social issues (health, education, and social inclusion) • Increased benefits in kind • Access to extra resources	• Resources for responding to CSR issues • Benefits in terms of reputation • Customer loyalty • Employee engagement • Creation of partnerships	• Reduction of tensions between commercial and social objectives • Better management of the club's reputation • Contribution to building a "community" brand • Increased ability to attract sponsors

Source: Table adapted from Walters (2009)

(2007) typology of attributes that make sport an implicit vector of CSR[20] in order to determine the potential benefits of CSR for English football clubs (Table 9.2).

Although benefits depend on the context in which programs are carried out and the reception initiatives are given by their target groups, they would appear to be transferable to other contexts. These potential benefits have been recognized by Europe's big clubs, which use CSR to strategic ends. FC Barcelona, for example, set up the largest cause-related marketing action in European football (Box 9.5), while the case of AJ Auxerre (Box 9.6) shows that much smaller and less famous clubs can still set up social initiatives with strategic aims, although these initiatives tend to be more modest and more local.

Box 9.5 The premises of a globalized, cause-related marketing program at FC Barcelona

The tripartite partnership between FC Barcelona, its equipment sponsor, Nike, and UNICEF (United Nations Children's Emergency Fund) is an example of cause-related marketing in which two nonprofit organizations worked together for their mutual benefit. In 2006, FC Barcelona, whose shirts had not displayed a sponsor's logo (except for that of the supplier) since 1899, offered UNICEF the opportunity to put its logo on the team's shirts at no cost to UNICEF. The club even went as far as donating 1.5 million euros to UNICEF. For FC Barcelona, this cost was more than offset by an improved sponsorship deal with Nike, the club's equipment sponsor, which increased its contribution from 15 million euros to 25 million euros to have its logo alongside that of UNICEF. Nike also joined FC Barcelona in carrying out social initiatives benefiting UNICEF.

All the partners in this three-way agreement gained strategic benefits. UNICEF obtained financial resources and publicity, Nike enhanced its brand image, and FC Barcelona expanded its markets and formed reservoirs of potential future players by being associated with actions in densely populated parts of the world. Nevertheless, this case also shows the huge marketing and sponsoring power of merchandising, as FC Barcelona ended its partnership with UNICEF in 2010 in favor of Qatar Sport Investment, which offered the club sponsorship of 165 million euros for the period 2011–2016, first via the nonprofit Qatar Foundation and then as part of a more classic partnership with Qatar Airways, which started in 2012.

Box 9.6 AJ Auxerre and the *Famille AJA* program[21]

AJ Auxerre (AJA), a moderate-sized club in a small city, has long claimed that social responsibility has been a natural element of the club's make up through its tradition of nurturing local talent. In the mid-2000s, increasing public disapproval of the darker side of the football business made AJA's executives realize they could no longer rely solely on football's presumed social values to show their club was socially responsible.

As a result, the club decided to become more directly involved in the *Famille AJA* program, which had been initiated by the president of one of the supporters' clubs in order to promote good citizenship among young fans. *Famille AJA*, which was granted an award by France's *Fondation du Football* in 2010, became a community association in 2011. AJA's executives began presenting the program as the heart of their social initiatives. By providing a few educators to organize the program on match days and offering young fans taking part in the program reduced-price tickets to matches, AJA strengthened its image as a caring club for little cost. In addition, the program, which still exists, helped increase attendance at AJA's home matches. (In 2011, the club's last season in French football's top flight, AJA had one of the lowest attendance rates in Ligue 1.)

The challenges of CSR management

Despite the benefits CSR initiatives can bring, social responsibility is a complicated issue for professional football clubs to manage due to their focus on short-term goals and the contradictions inherent to CSR. In addition, a club's failure to fully integrate CSR into its strategic management can lead to discrepancies between its words and its deeds, especially in cases where engagement in CSR is motivated primarily by a wish to affirm a club's legitimacy or to superficially meet the expectations of certain stakeholders, rather than a desire to effectuate deep-seated changes in the way a club is run (François, 2012; François and Bayle, 2014). Consequently, evaluating CSR practices is an essential preliminary step to carrying out actions that will blend into a club's management and be embraced by all their different departments (training, HR, marketing, etc.). CSR in the professional football of tomorrow is being shaped in the light of the latest trends and, most importantly, by stricter legislation aimed at institutionalizing the concept of CSR in sport.

From the difficult integration of CSR to strategic management

Studies based on an "integrationist" perspective that have attempted to reconcile CSR with an organization's performance have met with a degree of skepticism. Critics have focused on the inability of the integrationist approach to provide in-depth analyses of the cohabitation between commercial and social objectives and have underlined the risk of creating huge disparities between words and deeds. This is even truer in "hybrid" organizations such as professional football clubs, where these contradictory objectives are exacerbated. Sheth and Babiak (2010) highlighted these antagonisms in professional sport when they studied perceptions of CSR by executives of franchises in America's leading sports (American football, basketball, ice hockey, and baseball) and their clubs' CSR engagement.[22] On comparing their results with Carroll's (1979) model of CSR, which ranked economic responsibilities as the most important factor governing CSR engagement, followed by legal, ethical, and philanthropic responsibilities, Sheth and Babiak found an inversion in the established order, with their respondents claiming to give greater weight to ethical and philanthropic considerations than to economic and legal responsibilities. In addition to this result, which reflects the hybrid rationales at work in professional sport, they also found a slightly negative relationship between the declared level of CSR engagement and sporting performance.[23] In other words, the more executives perceived their clubs as being socially responsible, the less likely they were to be victorious. Hence, strong CSR engagement appears to consume human, material, and financial resources which could have been invested in other aspects of performance, thereby disturbing the balance between a club's priorities. This conclusion, if it were found to apply to professional football, would create serious doubts about the ability of executives to incorporate CSR into their club's management.

One suggestion for overcoming this drawback is to carefully evaluate clubs' CSR policies in order to determine which actions should be given priority (François, 2012, Breitbarth et al., 2011). Many clubs fail to carry out such evaluations when drawing up CSR strategies, even though they should be the cornerstones of these strategies. In 2008, the president of the G14,[24] Jean-Michel Aulas, spoke about the biggest challenges facing European professional football in the years to come, saying (G14, 2008):

> In particular, we need to improve our measurement and evaluation of our social and community investments. By working more closely with our partners and by seeking out best practice from within and beyond the sporting world, we can hope to continually improve the strategic use and effectiveness of our work.

Given this tendency to overlook the *ex ante* (i.e., pre-implementation) evaluation of CSR strategies, few academics have attempted to draw up models for assessing CSR policies. Breitbarth et al.'s (2011) CSR measurement model for European football clubs, drawn up on the basis of interviews with executives from German, English, and Swiss clubs and their main stakeholders involved in implementing social initiatives, is one of the rare exceptions to this rule. The most important result of this research was the formulation of a "balanced scorecard" as a way of taking into account new performance indicators based on a club's economic, ethical, and political responsibilities. However, Breitbarth et al. (2011) realized that their scorecard was not universal, as CSR strategies depend on a club's characteristics and its executives' vision. This pioneering study has been followed by the creation of other evaluation tools, such as the "societal panoramas" drawn up by governing bodies within European football, which may provide sources of inspiration. In France, for example, the national federation publishes an annual societal panorama of French football, and the LFP published a panorama of social and community actions by French clubs for the 2012–2013 season (UCPF, 2013) (Box 9.7).

Box 9.7 Multiplication of social reporting initiatives in French football

The *Societal Panorama of French Football,* the first edition of which was published in June 2011 by the *Fondation du Football*, evaluates community engagement and efforts to promote sustainable development by every actor in the football world, including national governing bodies, leagues, districts, and clubs, both professional and amateur. Its assessments of social engagement, social cohesion, accessibility, sustainability, and economic activity paint a picture of federal football's (national federation and professional football) social impacts.

Similar evaluations of France's professional football league (LFP) have been carried out since 2010, initially via the "Foot pro" barometer, which was drawn up by Ernst & Young at the initiative of the Union of Professional Football Clubs (UCPF). "Foot pro" measured the economic and social impacts of the activities of the 40 football clubs within the LFP. The final section of its last report covered clubs' social engagement, solidarity, and community-mindedness (UCPF, 2012). Since 2013, UCPF has expanded its presentation of social initiatives by producing a specific, 50-page document highlighting the most notable programs.

What future for CSR in the professional football of tomorrow?

Although dissenting voices have questioned the ability of CSR to regulate the highly commercial world of modern professional football, changes in standards and legislation could lead to an increase in socially responsible initiatives and contribute to their institutionalization. Some executives see UEFA's Financial Fair Play (FFP) regulations as a hindrance to sporting competiveness,[25] but they should not weigh negatively on clubs' CSR engagement. In fact, FFP is designed to ensure a balance between income and expenditure on "football operations", excluding expenditure in areas such as developing young players and community development, which can legitimately be considered part of CSR. Similarly, FFP could provide a way of initiating or expanding a CSR strategy, as it should curtail at least certain aspects of the financial misconduct that has sometimes blighted professional football (Durand and Dermit, 2013). In fact, FFP could lead to a change in clubs' business models by encouraging them to give greater weight to training and slowing the galloping inflation in salaries. The actual effects of FFP will only become clear over the next few years, as the regulations did not fully come into force until the 2015–2016 season. Nevertheless, certain clubs have already anticipated this new orientation by investing substantial sums in training and, most importantly, by making training an important part of development.

Finally, CSR, which originally involved voluntary and discretionary initiatives by organizations, is starting to become mandatory. At the moment, legislation goes no further than requiring very large companies to publish information about how they take into account the social and environmental consequences of their activities.[26] However, new legislation making CSR obligatory for professional sports organizations, especially football clubs, could see the light of day. In France, a recent white paper[27] reiterated the need to reassess professional sport's economic model. Measures envisaged include an obligation for professional clubs to set up endowment funds and/or foundations to carry out socio-educational and community sport actions, which is generally the first step in implementing a CSR policy. Even if its lead author admits that this white paper will almost certainly be substantially revised,[28] the new guidelines it would like to impose foretell a potential cultural revolution. Consequently, the clubs with the least advanced social policies will have to rethink their CSR strategies and increase their efforts.

Conclusion

CSR does not concern only private companies, and the concept is gradually being transposed to all types of organization. In the case of European professional football clubs, CSR has become increasingly important as a result of the public's growing distrust of the football business due to certain clubs showing disdain for sporting ethics and the reporting of numerous cases of match

Table 9.3 Main sources for the data used

	Documents	*Description*
Primary data (mostly interviews carried out in France)	*AJA:* - **Baptiste Malherbe** – marketing & communication manager - **Alain Hébert** – president of Famille AJA *OL:* - **Jean-Michel Aulas** – CEO of OL Groupe - **Laurent Arnaud** – general secretary of OL Fondation	• Interview about the social representations of AJA's executives. • Interview about the Famille AJA program and its links with AJA. • Interview about the group's global strategy. • Interview about how OL Fondation and the sOLidaire endowment fund function.
Secondary data (benchmarking reports for CSR initiatives in Europe)	- Report of the G14: "Community engagement. Insights into the contribution of European club football" - UEFA report "Corporate Social Responsibility in European Football" by G. Walters and R. Tacon - Responsiball reports – founded by Schwery Consulting - Reports of the FC Barcelona foundation	• 2008 report, drawn up in partnership with *Business in The Community*, on social initiatives taken by the 18 clubs in the G14. • 2011 report drawn up on the basis of questionnaires about CSR sent to 53 national federations and 730 football clubs in Europe. • 2013 and 2014 reports ranking CSR initiatives by European football leagues. Available at the *Responsiball* website. • Succession of reports from the foundation. The latest, for 2013–2014, can be accessed at http://foundation.fcbarcelona.com/

fixing, betting fraud, violence, and corruption, etc. At the end of this chapter, we discussed ways in which CSR can impact the strategic management of clubs by encouraging them to consider new ways of evaluating performance. To achieve this, clubs must integrate CSR into their overall strategy and ensure their commitment to CSR is reflected in their deeds and not just their words.

More generally, well-designed CSR initiatives by professional football clubs and institutions could help address many of the great social challenges facing the modern globalized world. CSR has become a powerful tool for revamping football's image, which has been severely tarnished in recent years by the scandals reported by today's all-pervasive and increasingly powerful media. More importantly than this cosmetic function, CSR also has the potential to become a regulating influence on football by steering the sport away from the controversial behaviors that are threatening the long-term future of the global game[29] and thereby silence its detractors. For this to happen, football's international and national regulating bodies must either ensure there is substance behind each club's CSR initiatives or make concrete initiatives obligatory. Doing this is essential if football is to convince skeptics who see CSR as an instrument for protecting the current system, rather than a way of inducing deep-seated change.

Notes

1 The authors would like to thank Paul Henderson for his help translating this chapter.
2 As shown by two phenomena unique to professional football. First, there is a long history of clubs being floated on the stock exchange, starting with Tottenham Hotspur in 1983. A second, more recent phenomenon, is the third-party ownership of players by private investors, who obtain a return on their

investment in the form of interest payments from clubs and from capital gains realized on each player's future transfers.

3 For example, Real de Madrid bought Cristiano Ronaldo from Manchester United in June 2009 for 94 million euros and is thought to have paid Tottenham Hotspur 100 million euros for the Welsh winger Gareth Bale (see *L'Equipe*, September 4, 2013).

4 Available at http://www.sportbusinesscentre.com/wp-content/uploads/2012/08/CSR2.pdf.

5 ISO 20121 is a management standard aimed at minimizing the social, economic, and environmental impacts of events (for details, see http://www.responsiball.org/).

6 This study involved analyzing eight interviews with executives from North American sport franchises and internal documents produced by sports clubs (web articles, reports, etc.).

7 The absence of the influence of the football leagues from Walters and Tacon's (2011) list of 11 possible reasons for CSR engagement is surprising given the league's normalizing power with respect to CSR initiatives (especially in the United Kingdom – see section 1.2.1.).

8 The EU defines SMEs as enterprises with fewer than 250 employees and an annual turnover of less than 50 million euros or less than 43 million euros of assets on the balance sheet.

9 In 2008, only 17% of 1st division clubs in Europe owned their stadiums, while 65% of them rented their stadiums from local authorities and 18% rented them from third parties (UEFA, 2010).

10 The term "giving back" expresses the philanthropic ideal that is such a strong part of Protestant culture, so much so that successful individuals often feel a moral obligation to help their communities (stewardship).

11 The Football League was created in 1888, making it Europe's oldest football competition. In 1992, the 1st division was replaced by the Premier League, with the lower divisions subsequently being renamed the Football League Championship (2nd division), League One (3rd division), and League Two (4th division).

12 Both ahead of England, which lies in 4th place. The previous year, Germany had been given a social responsibility score of 51%, making it the highest rated league in Europe.

13 For example, the oldest of these institutions, the *Fritz Walter Foundation*, was set up in 1999 by Kaiserslautern in partnership with the German Football Federation (*DFB*) and the state of Rhineland-Palatinate.

14 Article 10 of Act n°2012–158 of February 1, 2012, aimed at strengthening sports ethics and the rights of sportspeople. This legislation allows commercial companies managing the professional sections of football clubs to become limited companies, limited-liability companies, or simplified joint-stock companies.

15 Subsidies provided by local authorities to Ligue 1 clubs as part of MIGs accounted for just 2% of these clubs' budgets. This sum does not take into account service contracts or indirect financial assistance (stadium rental at below-market rates, possibility of waiving the tax on entertainment events, etc.), which makes local authorities essential stakeholders for the stability of clubs' accounts.

16 In 2014, three clubs (Paris, Lyon, and Toulouse) created corporate foundations, while three other clubs (Lyon, as a complement to its foundation, Marseille, and Montpellier) set up endowment funds.

17 Box drawn up on the basis of interviews with Jean-Michel Aulas, CEO of OL Groupe, and Laurent Arnaud, secretary of OL Fondation.

18 During its first 5 years of existence, a corporate foundation must allocate at least 150,000 euros to a program of multi-annual actions aimed at financing projects in the general interest.

19 The other two pillars listed in the club's internal documents are a strong economy and durable training.

20 These authors identified seven characteristics that make sport an implicit vector of CSR: mass media distribution and communication power, approach with young people, positive health impacts, social interaction, sustainability awareness, cultural understanding and integration, and immediate gratification benefits.

21 Box drawn up on the basis of interviews with Baptiste Malherbe, AJA's marketing and communication manager (now general manager), and Alain Hébert, the founder of the *Famille AJA* initiative.

22 Sheth and Babiak combined qualitative and quantitative methods by using a questionnaire containing both open-ended and closed-ended questions. They sent questionnaires to 122 directors or community relations managers from all the professional franchises in America's four leading sports. Thirty-one questionnaires were returned, and 27 were useable.

23 Sheth and Babiak (2010) obtained a correlation coefficient of –0.329 between level of engagement evaluated by the 27 franchise executives and the percentage of victories by the franchise.

24 Organization set up in 2000 by 14 rich European clubs. Its membership expanded to 18 clubs before it was disbanded in 2008.

25 See "Le fair-play financier, frein ou rebond ?", article by Jérôme Touboul published in *L'Equipe*, April 10, 2014.

26 For further details, see the European directive on non-financial reporting, passed on September 29, 2014.

27 White paper n°711 of July 2014 with the aim of renovating relations between local authorities and professional clubs and modernizing the economic model of professional sport.

28 Semi-structured interview with Senator Michel Savin, the lead author of the white paper, carried out on January 15, 2015.

29 Here, we are thinking of forthcoming international competitions such as the 2022 World Cup, to be held in Qatar, which has been controversial due to suspicions of collusion with certain European countries during its attribution and the poor treatment of workers hired to build the stadiums required for the competition.

Bibliography

ANAGNOSTOPOULOS C., BYERS T., SHILBURY D., Corporate social responsibility in professional team sport organisations: Towards a theory of decision-making, *European Sport Management Quarterly*, 14(3), 259–281, 2014.

ANAGNOSTOPOULOS C., SHILBURY D., Implementing corporate social responsibility in English football: Towards multi-theoretical integration, *Sport, Business and Management: An International Journal*, 3(4), 268–284, 2013.

BABIAK K., TRENDAFILOVA S., CSR and environmental responsibility: Motives and pressures to adopt green management practices, *Corporate Social Responsibility and Environmental Management*, 18, 11–24, 2011.

BABIAK K., WOLFE R., Determinants of corporate social responsibility in professional sport: Internal and external factors, *Journal of Sport Management*, 23(6), 717–742, 2009.

BAUMANN-PAULY D., WICKERT C., SPENCE L.J., SCHERER A.G., Organizing corporate social responsibility in small and large firms: Size matters, *Journal of Business Ethics*, 115(4), 693–705, 2013.

BAYLE E., CHAPPELET J-L., FRANÇOIS A., MALTESE L., *Sport et RSE. Vers un management responsable?* Bruxelles: De Boeck Editions, 2011.

BINGHAM T., WALTERS G., Financial sustainability within UK charities: Community sport trusts and corporate social responsibility sponsorships, *Voluntas: International Journal of Voluntary and Nonprofit Organizations*, 24(3), 606–629, 2012.

BREITBARTH T., HARRIS P., The role of corporate social responsibility in the football business: Towards the development of a conceptual model, *European Sport Management Quarterly*, 8(2), 179–206, 2008.

BREITBARTH T., HOVEMANN G., WALZEL S., Scoring strategy goals: Measuring corporate social responsibility in professional European football, *Thunderbird International Business Review*, 53(6), 721–737, 2011.

BROWN A., CRABBE T., MELLOR G., BLACKSHAW T., STONE C., *Football and its communities*. Final report for the Football Foundation, 2006.

CARROLL A.B., A three dimensional conceptual model of corporate performance, *Academy of Management Review*, 4(4), 497–505, 1979.

CARROLL A.B., BUCHHOLTZ A.K. *Business & society: Ethics, sustainability, and stakeholder management* (8th ed.). Mason, USA: South-Western Cengage Learning, 2012.

COLLINS A., FLYNN A., MUNDAY M., ROBERTS A., Assessing the environmental consequences of major sporting events: The 2003–2004 FA Cup Final, *Urban Studies*, 44(3), 457–476, 2007.

COUR DES COMPTES., *Les collectivités territoriales et les clubs sportifs professionnels*, Rapport public thématique, Paris, 2009.

DELOITTE., *A premium blend*, Annual Review of Football Finance: Highlights, 2014.

DOLLES H., SODERMAN S., Addressing ecology and sustainability in mega-sporting events: The 2006 football World Cup in Germany, *Journal of Management & Organization*, 16(4), 587–600, 2010.

DRUT B., *Economie du football professionnel*. Paris: La Découverte, 2014.

DURAND C., BAYLE E., Soutien de la sphère publique locale aux clubs sportifs professionnels: le retour du club citoyen? In S. Cueille R. Le Duff & J-J. Rigal (Eds.), *Management local, de la gestion à la gouvernance*, Paris: Dalloz, pp. 211–231, 2004.

DURAND C., DERMIT N., La régulation du sport professionnel en Europe: le fair play financier de l'UEFA, annonciateur d'une révolution culturelle? *International Review on Sport and Violence*, 7, 74–89, 2013.

FRANÇOIS A., *Les pratiques de RSE des clubs sportifs professionnels français: vers un nouveau modèle de légitimation*, PhD thesis, University of Burgundy, Dijon, 2012.

FRANÇOIS A., BAYLE E., Analyse des pratiques de RSE des clubs sportifs professionnels français, *Revue de l'Organisation Responsable*, 9(2), 5–20, 2014.

FREEMAN R.E., *Strategic management: A stakeholder approach.* Pitman: Boston, 1984.

G14, *Community engagement: Insights into the contribution of European club football*, Business in the Community, 2008.

GOND J-P., IGALENS J., *La responsabilité sociale de l'entreprise.* Paris: Presses Universitaires de France, 2010.

JENKINS H., JAMES L., *It's not just a game: Community work in the UK football industry and approaches to corporate social responsibility.* Cardiff: The ESRC Centre for Business Relationships, Accountability, Sustainability and Society, 2012.

LEE M.-D.P., A review of the theories of corporate social responsibility: Its evolutionary path and the road ahead, *International Journal of Management Reviews*, 10(1), 53–73, 2008.

LELORE E., Le club de football professionnel comme moteur de l'action socio-éducative en Europe: définition des publics et modalités d'action. In G. Robin (Ed.), *Football, Europe et régulations.* Villeneuve d'Ascq: Septentrion, pp. 133–144, 2011.

MELLOR G., The 'Janus-faced sport': English football, community and the legacy of the 'third way', *Soccer & Society*, 9(3), 313–324, 2008.

PARAMIO-SALCINES J. L., BABIAK K., WALTERS G., *Routledge handbook of sport and corporate social responsibility.* Londres: Routledge, 2013.

PORTER M.E., KRAMER M.R., Strategy and society: The link between competitive advantage and corporate social responsibility, *Harvard Business Review*, 84(12), 78–92, 2006.

REICHE D., Drivers behind corporate social responsibility in the professional football sector: A case study of the German Bundesliga, *Soccer & Society*, 15(4), 475–502, 2013.

RESPONSIBALL., *Responsiball ranking 2014.* The fourth annual social responsibility ranking of football leagues in Europe, 2014.

RODRIGUEZ P., KÉSENNE S., GARCIA J., *Social responsibility and sustainability in sports.* Oviedo, Spain: Oviedo University Press, 2009.

SHETH H., BABIAK K., Beyond the game: Perceptions and practices of corporate social responsibility in the professional sport industry, *Journal of Business Ethics*, 91(3), 433–450, 2010.

SMITH A.C.T., WESTERBEEK H.M., Sport as a vehicle for deploying corporate social responsibility, *Journal of Corporate Citizenship*, 25, 43–54, 2007.

UCPF, *Stade critique. Clubs en difficulté, filière en croissance. 2ème baromètre "Foot pro" – Impacts économiques et sociaux*, Paris, 2012.

UCPF, *Cœurs de clubs. Actions citoyennes et sociales des clubs professionnels de football. Panorama 2013*, Paris, 2013.

UEFA, *The European club footballing landscape: Club licensing benchmarking report financial year 2008*, Nyon, Suisse, 2010.

WALTERS G., Corporate social responsibility through sport: The community sports trust model as a CSR delivery agency. *Journal of Corporate Citizenship*, 35, 81–94, 2009.

WALTERS G., CHADWICK S., Corporate citizenship in football: Delivering strategic benefits through stakeholder engagement, *Management Decision*, 47(1), 51–66, 2009.

WALTERS G., TACON R., Corporate social responsibility in sport: Stakeholder management in the UK football industry, *Journal of Management & Organization*, 16(4), 566–586, 2010.

WALTERS G., TACON R., *Corporate social responsibility in European football.* A report funded by the UEFA Research Grant Program, 2011.

WATSON N., Football in the community: What's the score? *Soccer & Society*, 1(1), 114–125, 2000.

PART III

Case studies from Europe's "Big 5" and emergent professional football leagues

The third part illustrates the strategies and types of operations of European professional clubs through nine concrete cases, while the strategic development of Asian football leagues are addressed in the last two cases. They can be considered as the many implementations of marketing principles mentioned previously. Clubs that have been studied represent a wide range of possible configurations: German, English, Spanish, French and Italian clubs, more or less important in terms of budget or number of fans, national, European or global standing, etc. Chapter 10, from Nicolas Chanavat and Michel Desbordes, studies the marketing aspects of the PSG and especially its globalization strategy since the arrival of QSI in the capital of the club. Along these lines, the OL development strategy is the subject of Chapter 11. Certain marketing aspects of the Parc Olympique Lyonnais' and the "Grand Stade" are the subject of special attention. Chapter 12 deals with marketing logic deployed by AS Saint-Étienne. It focuses on the issue of operationalization of marketing innovations that create value for the club. Written by Verónica Baena, Chapter 13 focuses on the role of sport as an agent of social change and of performance marketing through the case of Real Madrid. Analysis of the brand management strategy of Borussia Dortmund is the subject of Chapter 14, written by Gerd Nufer, André Bühler and Sarah Jürgens. Another German case studies the VfB Stuttgart branding image and examines the purchasing behavior of its fans. This takes place in Chapter 15 by Jens Blumrodt. The analysis of the marketing strategy of ACF Fiorentina, based on the power of the local identity of the city of Florence, is in Chapter 16, written by Patrizia Zagnoli and Elena Radicchi. Then James Kenyon and Guillaume Bodet address the issue of fan support via social media by examining the case of Liverpool FC. In Chapter 18, Claude Boli reveals, through the case of Manchester United, how the establishment of the history of a club can become one of the bases of its economic success. Then, the focus of the cases changes to discuss the development of emergent football leagues. In Chapter 19, Dongfeng Liu explains how the development of professional football is coming as a response to the social development of China. In the final chapter, Yoshifumi Bizen and Shintaro Sato present the structure and strategies set forth by the J League (Japan).

10

TOWARDS A GLOBALIZATION OF THE BRAND PARIS SAINT-GERMAIN

Nicolas Chanavat and Michel Desbordes[1]

Paris Saint-Germain (PSG) generated 474.2 million euros in revenues during the 2013–2014 season. Also the club is, for the second consecutive year, 5th among the 20 most powerful football clubs in the world (Deloitte, 2015) and feeds legitimate ambitions, both sporting and economic. One must recognize that, since the acquisition of the club by Qatar Sports Investments (QSI) in June 2011, PSG has entered a new era and has set in motion a strategy to compete with the biggest sports brands in the world. This is to make PSG a powerful professional sports entity, like the great American franchises such as the New York Yankees or the major European football clubs such as Real Madrid, or some Formula 1 teams such as Ferrari. Moreover, it would be the same for the club to become a brand of entertainment expected to exceed the strict framework of sport.

In this context, the main strategic objective of the PSG is to become a global brand. If sporting success is a precondition regarding the globalization of the PSG brand, it is insufficient. Also, the marketing strategy deployed by the club is the capital for its development. This strategy is based on two key themes: a change in branding and a diversification of growth. Note that the PSG has considerable economic means to fulfill its purpose and promote its development.

With a marketing unit, the number of human resources more than doubled since the arrival of QSI, the club shows its capacity for innovation, especially in marketing. The international dimension is now in the DNA of the club and the integrated logic of globalization in various marketing initiatives proposed by the club. Indeed, the internationalization of the brand PSG is the major strategic focus of the club. The slogan "Dream Bigger" adopted by the club testifies to this. The idea is to encourage fans to be more into the club's history since its "beginning". In 2013, the arrival of David Beckham to PSG created an extraordinary craze. This acted as a key step for the globalization of French football and the PSG brand: the club passes its national leader status to that of an international player.

This chapter aims to illustrate the fundamental elements associated with the PSG marketing strategy and its operational versions: the creation of a sports brand, internalization of strategic business and marketing, the launch of the brand BeIN Sports, the creation of a new visual identity, the acquisition of brand-athlete, setting a new innovative partnership strategy, internationalization of the brand strategy, the PSG foundation development, diversification of PSG products, the deployment of a digital strategy, the launch of a training program, etc. The implementation of the club brand globalization strategy is the theme of this chapter and in particular the object of our analysis.

Box 10.1 Awards and brief history of Paris Saint-Germain

Paris Saint-Germain FC was created on August 12, 1970. The first team of Saint-Germain-en-Laye, which had just established its place in the National league (former Ligue 2) allowed the new brand PSG to emerge at a high level of competition in 1970–1971. It was a total success; PSG won the championship "National" and celebrated its first anniversary in the first division. Although the club had won titles in the past, PSG has entered a new era and set in motion a strategy to compete with the major brands of sport in the world since the acquisition of the club by QSI in June 2011. Building on the larger budget in Ligue 1 and the European five, PSG is now one of the most successful clubs of France and it got the most beautiful prize of French football in recent years: won the European Cup, five league titles in France, nine Cups of France, five League Cups and four Trophies of Champions. During the 2014–2015 season, the club achieved an unprecedented four victories in France and in the major European leagues: Championship of France, Cup of France, League Cup and Trophy of Champions. As a multisport club, it features a handball section that rivals the best European teams, and a women's football section, one of the most powerful in France. The arrival of QSI coincides with the excellent results of recent seasons and the marketing structure of the club. PSG distinguishes itself then by innovations in marketing, especially in an international perspective.

Sources: Interview with Frédéric Longuépée, Deputy General Manager in charge of business and PSG club website: http://www.psg.fr. Accessed February 20, 2015.

Box 10.2 The personal information sheet of Paris Saint-Germain

Name of the President of SASP: Nasser Al-Khelaïfi

Number of subscribers: 32,500

Number of fans on Facebook: almost 20 million (May 2015)

Average attendance per match: 45,672 (capacity of Parc des Princes: 47,929)

Budget of the club: 480 million euros

Total income from operations: 474.2 million euros

Distribution of revenue: match day (63.1 million euros, 13.3%), TV rights (83.4 million euros, 17.58%), sponsoring and licensed products (327.7 million euros, 69.10%)

Name of partners in 2015: Emirates, Nike, Ooredoo, QNB, Aspetar, BeIN Sports, Orange, Citroën, PMU, Huawei, GDF Suez, Panasonic, Nivea Men, Coca-Cola, Man, Puressentiel, McDonald's, MoneyGram, Go Sport, Aurel BGC, Hublot, Viagogo, Hugo Boss, EA Sports.

Source: Qualitative Interview with Frédéric Longuépée, Deputy General Manager in charge of PSG commercial activities.

What strategic objectives and what organization for the Paris Saint-Germain from QSI?

The ambitious project led by QSI PSG is to build an international brand in the sport: one of the most recognized and most admired sports brand around the world. In this context, four objectives were defined by the club (2014–2015 season), given the constraints imposed by the UEFA and its singularities. First, the club obviously must give priority to sports results and wishes to continue its climb. The renovation of the Parc des Princes is a secondary objective. The design and establishment of a training center and an academy in the Paris region represents a third priority for the club. Finally, the club wants to continue the strong growth in its turnover. For this, the business and marketing club are to be strengthened. Although multiple targets are distinguished, our analysis focuses on marketing aspects of projects and especially on issues of internationalization.

PSG, an ambitious club integrated into QSI

On April 11, 2006, the trio Colony Capital, Butler Capital Partners and Morgan Stanley have spent 26 million euros payable in four annual installments to buy PSG from Canal +. If the Qataris were willing to become shareholders of the club at that time, it is in 2011 that QSI would become the new owner of the PSG. Nasser Al-Khelaïfi, then appoined CEO, shows very clearly the strategic objective of the club: "On entering the capital of PSG, the ambition of QSI was clearly expressed: build a big European club that radiates globally the image of Paris and thus gives pride to all its passionate fans." After renouncing, in September 2011, its contract with Sportfive, which manages its sponsorship activities, the club management has imposed methods inspired by the great American franchises. Therefore, PSG is fully part of the elite European sports brands, and it plays a leading role in the international influence of Ligue 1. The club has also become multisport (football, handball) in the goal of enriching its brand equity. More than a club, QSI seems to want to build a sport entity based on the Barcelona model. This ambition is expressed through the new name given to Paris-Handball, which became PSG Handball. It is therefore necessary to talk about brand-franchise. PSG became a brand whose name and image could be exploited by other professional sports structures from the Paris region belonging to QSI. Overall, the sports scores of the club enrich its image and help to acquire a legitimacy as a brand club over time, suggesting that the club may be in the midst of a strong economic development.

The former owners and leaders: what legacy for the club?

Since the 1970s, the previous owners (Daniel Hechter, Francis Borelli, Canal +, Colony Capital, etc.) have met with economic difficulties in managing the club that has, every time, led to its resale. In any case, the ownership of a football club rarely proves lucrative, the hazard posed by sports results helping to make this particularly risky. If sporting success is a key element that enables a professional sports organization to enter a virtuous circle, it does not guarantee significant revenues (sponsorship contracts, merchandising, etc.). However, it promotes the development of awareness and image, and it affects consumers with regard to the club. These elements allow the increase in the number of fans who consume more of the club brand. These economic returns are essential to the extent that they allow more sporting success and the ability to cope with the inflation experienced by the market players. However, sporting success is more complex without several quality players. The idea is to strengthen the PSG brand and to achieve and find substantial and innovative growth drivers, abstracting sports results. However, the acquisition of financial stability has, until the arrival of QSI, still been lacking for the successive leaders of the club.

Before the club's acquisition by QSI, PSG ended the Ligue 1 championship in an honorable fourth place. However, the club's image remains that of a difficult club management: a waltz of presidents, a waltz of coaches, financial deficit and difficult relationships with supporters, etc. In 1991, Canal + invested in PSG, and Michel Denisot became president-delegate of the club. The broadcaster aimed to revive the excitement around the league by opposing an adversary to the Olympique de Marseille, which dominated at the time. This prosperous period symbolized by the victory in the Cup of Winners Cup in 1996 seems far away. Further still seem the 1980s during which Francis Borelli, the "president-supporter", cheered his men across Europe. In 2006, the club had become a real money pit, Canal + gave all of its MTP shares to the Franco-American trio Colony Capital (US), Butler Capital Partners (French) and Morgan Stanley (US). Colony Capital became the main shareholder and was represented by Sébastien Bazin, a Frenchman at the head of Colony Europe, who struggled to stabilize the finances of the club and decided to sell just 5 years later. Beyond the financial aspects, the club went through a period of crisis characterized in particular by the death of a young man on the sides of the match PSG vs. Hapoel Tel Aviv in November 2006. In 2010, considering the repeated violence and the deaths of a supporter near the Parc des Princes, Robin Leproux, then president of the club, decided to implement a set of measures to fight against the violence around PSG. This resulted in a reshuffle of the stands. The Auteuil and Boulogne stands are no longer open to memberships. This terminated the existence of supporters' associations. Aware of the need to restore the club's branding, QSI logically continued this strategy, which seemed to favor the emergence of a new fan target: families and a female audience. In any case, the results are there: "PSG has spent 4 years in the main hotbed of violence linked to football in France with one of the quietest stadiums of the country where no violent act was recorded for the first half of the 2014–2015 season." If several key measures of Leproux's plan, like the random placement in corners, are still applied today, we can observe that it has been relaxed for the 2015–2016 season: "the change of subscribers will benefit the next season with the ability to lend their membership card, on the condition that the recipient of the loan is identified, which was not the case since the 2010–2011 season." This change concerning the loan of membership cards directly addresses a new problem for the club: a lower attendance. While the club broke its record of subscribers (32,500) during the 2014–2015 season, and officially had the best attendance in the league (95%), the bleachers of the Parc des Princes looked sparsely filled at times. This is what is called the "no show". Just like other big European clubs such as Liverpool FC, PSG is working on this issue. "It is the role of the clubs organizing the sale, like viagogo for example. We must ensure that the seats are occupied. And that someone who wants to come in the place of someone who cannot come can come," explained Frédéric Longuépée, Deputy General Manager in charge of PSG business. Obviously, although the arrival of QSI in 2011 helped "save" the PSG, the Qataris seem to have received a lukewarm reception in France instead.

PSG, pillar of a diplomacy through sport for Qatar?

Chanavat and Desbordes (2014) highlight the overall development strategy of Qatar, a tiny Persian Gulf country, which has made sport a cornerstone of its strategy to develop its brand image, and its affect on the consumers and policy makers worldwide. With an area of only 11,586 km^2, the emirate of Qatar has become one of the richest countries in the world thanks to its hydrocarbon resources. The existence of a historical paradox between the small territory, the demographic weakness of a population and its importance on the world geopolitical scene make Qatar the object of analysis, desire and intrigue to international observers. From 1995 to 2013, Qatar was headed by the Emir, Sheikh Hamad bin Khalifa Al Thani,[2] who provided the country with a new constitution and established the Al-Jazeera channel to increase awareness of the emirate. Qatar seeks to enhance its brand equity internationally linked to sport, a way to consolidate its diplomatic influence and therefore to protect its independence. As we mentioned earlier, the sovereign fund, Qatar Investment Authority, through its branch dedicated to sport, Qatar Sports Investments, has developed a strategy of influence through sport based on the following major activities: the acquisition of professional sports facilities; organizing recurring and one-time events; the acquisition of television rights; the creation of a supplier; contracting partnerships; hunting for gold sports skills; and the election of a Qatari atop a sporting body (see Chapter 6 dedicated to sponsoring). Overall, the strategy of Qatar seems to go beyond the emirate to influence the entire international perception of the Middle East. The brand development of Qatar can make a tiny state a diplomatic and economic reference to a region with powers like Saudi Arabia or the United Arab Emirates. Our analysis echoes that of Champagne (2012, p. 73), former director of international relations of FIFA: "sport provides an additional platform in Qatar to influence, to exist altogether. And also unable to exercise hard power, the Qatari leadership has beautifully managed to place his country on the map of world sport." From a sociological perspective, Camy (2014, p. 310), meanwhile, says that

> even if we can agree on the role of major sporting events in international relations strategy ("soft power" that one also referred to as "power sport") of Qatar, sport development beyond the project of a form of diplomacy. This is good, we think, an original mode of modernization of a society, a large part of which is part of a concerted plan.

In any event, if it still seems difficult to measure the effectiveness of this new strategy based on sports marketing, the redemption of PSG by Qatar is the centerpiece of the device. In other words, we do not consider the PSG a "dancer". Instead, this acquisition is part of a "real" strategy (marketing, geo-marketing or geopolitical) overall. It is part of a process of investment in all directions, industrial, sports and media of Qatar. The only professional football club from the capital becomes the spearhead of their diplomacy, their quest for influence (Ratignier and Pean, 2011). Also, since the 2011–2012 season, PSG has its Aspire facilities in Doha to practice during the winter break.

In summary, the sport in general and PSG in particular find themselves at the center of the diplomatic strategy of Qatar. Investments seem to serve a cause less noble than the love of the sport: the image of the emirate and soft power. Thus, for some, like Beau and Bourget (2013), the image of wealthy savior without afterthought of Qatar begins to falter.

For the organization of a multisports club under construction

If QSI wishes to make PSG a global sports brand, it must legitimize and lend credibility to its project. Indeed, the credibility of a brand requires above all the legitimacy of its "founders". On June 30, 2011, Qatar Investment Authority bought all the MTP shares owned by the company Colony Capital for 76 million US dollars. On November 4, 2011, Nasser Al-Khelaïfi became the new CEO of the club. The choice of the new leader of the PSG was a particularly important issue for Qatar as the emirate suffers from a controversial image. Nasser Al-Khelaïfi exudes an image of seriousness, professionalism and simplicity supposed to symbolize Qatar. If the club has experienced crises (the Leonardo case, incidents on the Trocadero during the celebration of the championship of Ligue 1 in 2013, Zlatan Ibrahimović's insults towards a referee in 2015, etc.), Nasser Al-Khelaïfi seems to have kept his calm and answered the press poise and serenity, never showing any concern or any anger. Upon arrival, he has set ambitious targets. He has spent for that considerable financial resource made available by the new shareholders of the club: 100 million euros to recruit players in summer 2011. Obviously, the creation of a reassuring leadership seems to be a lever of legitimization and acceptance. If obtaining the membership of supporters is necessary to achieve, construct and accept a sports project, the choice of leaders is of strategic importance. Indeed, they are a direct link between the owners of the club and the fans, and they convey the image of the club around the world. On October 7, 2011, QSI announced that Jean-Claude Blanc was appointed Deputy CEO of the club. Philippe Boindrieux is, meanwhile, deputy director in charge of the administration and Frédéric Longuépée deputy director in charge of commercial activities.

QSI's ambition is to make PSG a great sports club "The PSG brand is strong enough for it to exist in the future in new territories and in other sports," said Frédéric Longuépée. If the men's football is and will remain the number one vector, the brand extension of the club has already begun. On June 4, 2012, QSI acquired PSG Handball. The club then recruited 10 international players, including three French Olympic champions and the world's best player

Figure 10.1 The multisport organization of PSG

Source: Paris Saint-Germain, the 2013–2014 Annual Report, 2014, pp. 64–65.

at the time, the Dane, Mikkel Hansen. With substantial financial resources, the handball team continues to grow, which should lead to the European summits. Note that this arrival was analyzed as a means of development of a handball championship for France. In terms of basketball, the rapprochement between Paris-Levallois and PSG could lead to a sale of the club to PSG or taking of equity. This diversification strategy seems consistent with a view to compete with other big clubs like FC Barcelona, which has five professional sections (football, basketball, handball, roller hockey and futsal), which have all won at least one European Cup. In addition, the women's section of the football club is not set aside. The new owners of the club invest to build a team capable of competing with the best teams. The goal of the women's section is the same as for the men's soccer team. These compete with OL to head the Championship and qualify for the Champions League. Although there may be connections between different Facebook pages, between the websites or through joint events, partnership strategies entities prove to be different. The three teams are distinguished by the nature of their sponsors.

The club is structured around 14 departments. Our analysis shows that this organization is heavily commercial and markets as if they exist in no other club than Ligue 1. If the men's football logically groups the most people in the club (68 and 114 professionals in training), there are eight different entities in the sports organization of the PSG.

In addition, the club is organized around several legal entities: SASP PSG, PSG Merchandising, PSG Foundation, SE Sports and Events and PSG support association. The organization of the club is singled out by the internalization of all its activities. The 2013–2014 annual report of the club further refers to the continued rapid growth in all economic and commercial indicators (number of subscribers, merchandise sales and hospitality) demonstrating its performance and attractiveness. Our analysis thus shows a strong appeal for PSG.

For an internalization of strategic business and marketing

Sports results of the club are a crucial element in the development of the PSG brand. If for this sport cell PSG has been considerably structured, the club has committed its parallel reform on marketing and commercial efforts to optimize revenue. This burden falls to Frédéric Longuépée. He explains,

> [We want] to become one of the biggest sports brands in the world. To achieve this, we need ambitious results, we need to win the League of Champions as soon as possible; the club must have a lot of talent. It remains in parallel, it is important to create the conditions for long-term success. From an income statement perspective, the acquisition of players, and the depreciation that go with it, are expenses that eventually become difficult to absorb.

Arriving in early 2012, it is under the direct responsibility of Jean-Claude Blanc, who runs the club, except for the sports part. The sales, 70-people strong (35 in 2011), includes "seven activities: ticketing, hospitality, partnerships, licensed merchandise, international development, marketing and operational implementation (production)", explains Frédéric Longuépée. An organization that seems to approach the standard of the major North American franchises. As we mentioned at the beginning of the 2012–2013 season, PSG and SportFive separated and ended their exclusive relationship. The new strategy of the club leads in fact to directly support the development of its revenues and internalize the marketing of its marketing and hospitality rights. Only television rights are managed collectively by the LFP. The decision to internalize (and not pay a commission to the agency) makes sense at a time when the club is changing. This strategy seems otherwise legitimate to the extent that the club wants to control its image. The control of the image is the cornerstone for the success of building a brand. "We are structured like the Anglo-Saxons, everything was strategically internalized. We are the only masters on board," says Frédéric Longuépée on this point.

What role(s) for BeIN Sports?

BeIN Sports is a subsidiary of Al-Jazeera chaired by Nasser Al-Khelaïfi. It was launched in 2012 in France, the United States and Indonesia. Although the entity, controlled from Paris, is directed by Florent Houzot, it was led and initiated by Charles Biétry, iconic former leader of sports writing at Canal +. Since its launch, BeIN Sports has hired several journalists, and Canal + has acquired the television rights to several major events. While we can highlight a plethora of football competitions, the channel has offered the rights for the NBA, for tennis and for cycling events. The BeIN Sports strategy is distinguished by an attractive offer of a monthly subscription fee (11 euros initially, then 12 and 13 euros), reflecting a desire of market penetration. The offer proposes that the chain has the advantage of being non-binding, while that of Canal + requires a commitment of 1 year. There were a million subscribers within 6 months after its launch. And the growth in rights does not cease to grow even today. According to Canal +, previously having a quasi-monopoly on the market, BeIN Sports disrupts the market, to the extent that financial resources have enabled it to acquire many television rights. In any case, its launch has been very badly perceived by Canal +. Indeed, from its start in 1984, the sport is one of the two pillars of the Canal + offer (the other being the cinema). The chain is investing huge sums in sport to acquire a maximum of television rights. In particular, it modernizes the setting of images and relies on the largest sports writing in European broadcasting. Canal + has quickly become synonymous with the sports fans on television. If Canal + has "prospered" from November 1984 to May 2012, no real direct competition (the attempts of Orange or TPS having failed quickly), the arrival of BeIN Sports upsets the French sports television landscape. Indeed, subscribers pay only for "consuming" the sport, while the subscription to Canal + also allows you to discover each month 30 recent films never seen on TV, original series in France, documentaries, etc. But it must be between 35 and 40 euros depending on subscriptions to watch sports on the encrypted channel (excluding promotion).

While broadcasting rights are increasing, one can emphasize that the two chains are closely following their loss leader that is football: programming similar programs with similar schedules, sharing the broadcasting of Ligue 1, Bundesliga and Série A. Moreover, the Premier League remains the exclusivity of Canal + and the Liga BBVA the exclusivity of BeIN Sports. In this framework, one can imagine a "battle" between the two chains over rights on football, a struggle which should also be intensified to other disciplines. For example, the BeIN Sports handball offensive is a response to the acquisition of rights to Formula 1 by Canal +. But if the development of BeIN Sports is studied in this chapter dedicated to PSG marketing, this is because of the proximity between the channel and the club. Indeed, it has maintained a strong link between the two entities to suggest that BeIN Sports is an important image vector for the club whose leaders also have control, to the extent that they are indirectly the leaders of the chain. Although BeIN Sports does not have the TV rights to all meetings of the PSG, one can highlight that the chain multiplies reports on players or club leaders. This is to bring exclusive content with original reporting. Obviously, the "use" of the chain is beneficial for the club. It promotes a preferential and "controlled" media exposure. This tool is therefore involved in the building of the PSG brand desired by QSI. Simultaneously, the development of the PSG brand and the interest that the club raises in respect of sports fans favor the increase in BeIN Sports subscribers. The backstage access to PSG is an issue of the economic and editorial "war" that engages BeIN Sport and Canal +.

Towards a (re-)building of the PSG brand

The slogan "Dream Bigger" reflects the process of changing the PSG image. The brand equity of the club is strengthening the seasons and sporting achievements. In this sense, the feat of the PSG against Chelsea (two goals each) in the quarter-finals of the Champions League (2014–2015 season) feeds the club's branding. Brand strategy implementation is based mainly on a controlled communication, the backing of the club's image to that of the city of Paris (a club at the height of the energy of the capital and of Qatar), the conceptualization of a new logo and visual identity or acquisition of brand-athletes. These elements are designed to move towards a rapid internationalization of the PSG brand and increase the growth.

A legitimate project, a new image, a controlled communication

As noted above,with the arrival of QSI, the brand image of PSG is controversial and its legitimacy seems contested: financial difficulties, fan violence, results in half-tone, etc. In any event, this does not seem to be in line with the prestige of Paris. The goal is to establish a strong brand, able to limit the effect of contingent sports results on the economy and the club's branding. In this context, the first challenge seems to be to legitimize: legitimize the leaders to legitimize a project. Therefore, the issue of local and national roots seems to assume a working image of owners, but also the club. QSI seeks to "control" its communication.

The construction of the PSG brand is distinguished insofar as it is at the crossroads of several topics (marketing, communication, political, diplomatic and societal). Given the extensive media coverage of the club's takeover by the Qataris, communication has rapidly been established as a major challenge for the new leadership. Although PSG has always been a media and publicized club, its takeover by the American Colony Capital in 2006 had not attracted much interest. Therefore, it is the economic means of the new owners which seem to have fueled media interest around the takeover of the club and the attainment of a majority shareholding by Qataris. More than a club, QSI wants to build, as we have discussed, a sports entity based on the Barcelona model. This ambition is expressed through the new name given to the Paris-Handball, which became PSG Handball. It is therefore necessary to talk about brand-franchise. The acquisition of the handball product allows the PSG brand to conquer other target audiences sometimes skeptical about football. PSG has become a brand whose name and image could be exploited by other professional sports structures from the Paris region belonging to QSI. If other clubs allowed the PSG brand to develop its reputation and image by diversifying, they would benefit in return from the reputation of the brand and its resources. It is therefore necessary for QSI to make a football club a brand club, but especially a multisport globalized-brand franchise.

The operationalization of the club's strategy and investments have allowed it to go in the right direction and change of dimension. The initial objective was to be champion of France, and now it is to win the Champions League. Communication overall remains very controlled, with little affect. If it tries to create a story (storytelling), those told by PSG can appear too smooth. Moreover, the image and communication of Nasser Al-Khelaïfi were entrusted to Jean-Martial Ribes, head of the agency Ketchum Pleon France. They are managed independently of the club. Nasser Al-Khelaïfi's communication strategy appears to be that of discretion insofar as it is usually only in the great moments, especially when the image of the club, but more that of Qatar, are being questioned. For example, although he had not spoken for months before the cameras, he stopped his silence following the controversial statements of former sporting director Leonardo, but especially just after the publication of the dossier of France Football "the Qatargate" in January 2013. For the first time, Nasser Al-Khelaïfi responded to reporters, not in English, but in French. Obviously, the choice of Nasser Al-Khelaïfi has given a modern face, serious and credible to the Qatari project. It therefore allows a counter-balance to the sometimes controversial image of Qatar. This standardization is even more important that Nasser Al-Khelaïfi seems to have acquired a significant weight in the French sport. Beyond his work on behalf of the PSG, he led the chain BeIN Sports and was a member of the union executive committee of the "Clubs de Football Professionnels" (UCPF).

On July 13, 2011, Nasser Al-Khelaïfi appointed Leonardo as sporting director. This was the first important decision on his arrival. The Brazilian has legitimacy in the world of football and therefore a network. While Leonardo left the club in July 2013, it seems that QSI allowed PSG to alleviate some of the difficulties that PSG has had in the past in recruiting players and to bridge the gap with other leading teams. The network of Leonardo is particularly Brazil and Italy. Also the club recruited several players from Italian clubs in the first months: Jeremy Menez (AS Roma), Momo Sissoko (Juventus), Thiago Motta (Inter Milan), Salvatore Sirigu (Palermo) and Javier Pastore (Palermo). Later, he obtained the transfer of two stars from AC Milan that allowed the club to change dimension: Zlatan Ibrahimović and Thiago Silva. The idea is to lend credibility to the club at all levels. Indeed, at both the sporting and administrative level, the QSI recruitments allow credibility for the brand club in the eyes of those involved in football globally.

These items tend to characterize the PSG as a club with an ambitious project, not as a dancer for Qatar. We must recognize that the strong men of the club, given their professional accomplishments and their communicative qualities, promote the construction of the club's branding. However, even if the club is highly publicized, it is still "young" in the market of European football clubs.

Paris, number one asset of the club brand

The PSG represents the most exposed French club to the media. Degorre and Touboul (2009, p. 205) explain this, highlighting the rivalry developed around the news of the club between two newspapers: *L'Équipe* and *Le Parisien*. But the club wants to go further. Also, "[b]ecoming a great brand is successful when speaking to everyone, not just captivated fans, and to open our natural field, leaving *L'Équipe* and *Le Parisian*," explains Frédéric Longuépée.

The local presence of the PSG requires a reconquest of the fans of the Île-de-France. This building of the brand requires the approximation of the PSG image with that of the city it represents, Paris. The objective is thus to capitalize on the brand image of the city to develop the club. This affiliation with Paris resulted from the arrival of QSI with the establishment of panels in the colors of PSG in the streets of the city. The communication campaign around the slogan "Let us dream bigger" attests to this. Thus, 2,500 JC Decaux billboards of the Île-de-France relayed three visuals where players of the PSG were associated with three symbols of Paris: the Louvre Pyramid, the Arc de Triomphe and the Eiffel Tower. In addition, the campaign also went on digital media, in the press and in MK2 cinemas of the Île-de-France, via the broadcast of a short video.

This strategy aims to recall that the PSG is the club of the city. "People will always need to dream. The beauty of this club resides in the alliance between the words 'Paris' and 'football', which is infinitively strong," explains Frédéric Longuépée. It is addressed to all Parisians. Alongside the sporting project, there is a brand project. To do this, the club quickly measured the interest of appropriating everything that represents the city of Paris. "One of the club's flagship assets is Paris. It has the ability to mobilize all of Paris and to use social networks to create a buzz," he adds. Although PSG has always been the Paris Club, it has not always been seen as the height of the prestige of the city. One can question the identification of the Parisians with the club. In any event, the affect developed towards the city was not expressed through their commitment to the club. The development of a successful team at the European level, combined with the arrival of star players and global icons, have promoted the club brand building and the number of fans, team performance; the qualifications obtained have, in turn, legitimized and given credibility to the project of QSI. However, the Parisian identity should be strengthened particularly through the training center, the renovation of the Parc des Princes or building a new relationship with the fans.

The desire to join the city of Paris is also expressed through the creation of a new logo.

Figure 10.2 Communication campaign under the slogan "Let us dream bigger"

A logo and visual identity rethought and marketed

The club's foundation date no longer appears on the logo of the PSG. QSI can also be used for all sections of the sports brand. In other words, it is not only the logo of the PSG football club, but that of the sports brand. Dated 2013, the evolution of the PSG logo marks a milestone in the implementation of the construction strategy and internationalization of the PSG brand. The club seems to adopt a visual identity, which highlights its values, its city and its history. It reflects its strategy and is part of the impetus to raise the Parisian club to the rank of an inescapable global brand and sport, to get it into the circle of the most recognized global franchises. This visual identity seems to carry with it a dream. This is a dream that Paris embodies worldwide. The city of Paris is the heart of the identity of the club, it is supposed to infuse its strength, its ethical aspirations (freedom, the quest for perfection, demand, etc.) and aesthetic (beauty, elegance, etc.). If the new logo reflects the lofty ambitions of the internationalization of the PSG, it would not, however, break with its origins. The new logo thus has some changes.

The cradle, supposed to remember the birth of Louis XIV in Saint-Germain-en-Laye, was not necessarily evocative. It logically disappeared in favor of the lily, symbol of French royalty. The date of creation of the club in 1970 is also removed to the extent that it does not compare with other competitors' clubs like Manchester United (1878), Juventus (1897), Bayern Munich (1900) or Real Madrid (1902). If the size of the Eiffel Tower, the Paris icon, is reduced, it is refocused to enter the heart of the logo. The name of Paris, global icon, is now larger and holds, alone, the top of the logo. The name of Saint-Germain, meanwhile, was disconnected from Paris and moved to the bottom for readability. Moreover, the red and blue, traditional club colors are preserved, but the blue is made more intense to be Parisian blue. As for the red, it's brilliant to stand in contrast. A golden key is added, symbol of excellence. Universally the logo gives all the communications that have the ambition of the brand. More than ever, the PSG seeks to associate its image with that of Paris. Frédéric Longuépée explained the reasons for the change: "The idea is to assert Paris, to be related to the extraordinary values of this city. The required values, respect and elegance. We wanted to put Paris in the heart of this logo with a reworked aesthetic."

In the same dynamic, in summer 2012, the club staged, with the Eiffel Tower in the background, the signing of Zlatan Ibrahimović when he arrived at the club.

The marketing impact of players

The international dimension of PSG recruitment proves interesting in a marketing perspective. Although the football skills of the players seem indispensable, their image and the effect of the fans on them are undeniable assets. For the 2014–2015 season, PSG has a staff of players from seven different countries in addition to France: Argentina, Brazil, Ivory Coast, Italy, the Netherlands, Sweden and Uruguay. All foreign players who constitute the football team are international, like Zlatan Ibrahimović, a true icon in his country and captain of the Swedish national team. The diversity of the geographical origin of the players is an asset for the development of the PSG brand. Moreso than "big" players, the sums of money, sometimes very substantial, engaged in transfers allow the club to develop true ambassadors with global reach, often well beyond their countries of origin.

These items legitimately lead us to believe that PSG is based on a strategy inspired by galactics (The Zidane and Pavones), established by Florentino Perez when he chaired the club for the first time between 2000 and 2006. The strategy is to find an alchemy between grown players (like Francisco Pavon) and galactics, the best players of the moment (as Zinédine Zidane). Thus, Florentino Pérez has recruited a super star every season. Luis Figo arrived in 2000, Zinedine Zidane in 2001, Ronaldo in 2002, David Beckham in 2003 and Michael Owen in 2004. Of these, only Beckham has never won the Ballon d'Or. While this strategy has proven to be a total economic success, sports scores of Real Madrid have not been as high as the expectations (Kase et al., 2007). From 2003 to 2007, the club did not win any major title; a phenomenon not experienced since 1954. This failure of policy of Pérez, under fire from critics, sounds the alarm. He resigned in 2006. This strategy seems to have been taken up by other clubs like Chelsea (Abramovich) and Manchester City (Sheikh Mansour bin Zayed Al Nahyan). In short, athletes are presented as marketing tools to facilitate trade with a specific market. It is thus for clubs to recruit international players according to their marketing profile, represented by their potential in terms of merchandising and the interest they generate in the media (Chanavat, 2009). This strategy has been adopted particularly with Asian players like Junichi Inamoto for Arsenal FC or Park Ji-Sung for Manchester United (Desbordes, 2007).

Obviously, the arrival of Zlatan Ibrahimović has allowed the club to change dimension. Adored in Sweden, his country of origin where a special stamp has been available since 2014, he played and won titles in the biggest European clubs: Ajax, Juventus, Inter Milan, FC Barcelona and AC Milan. Given his charisma and his media provocations, Zlatan Ibrahimović is an icon that goes beyond sport. His biography, *I Zlatan* (Ibrahimović and Lagercrantz, 2013), is a bestseller. Better yet, since 2012 the name of the athlete has been a neologism in popular culture, embodied by the word "Zlataner". If his character is perceived as arrogant, it only gives rise to numerous parodies, his arrival has been a double feat. Furthermore, the aim is first to legitimize and lend credibility

Figure 10.3 New PSG logo since 2013

to the project QSI vis-à-vis the French targets and also to encourage the internationalization of the PSG brand. However, the Swede, considered irascible, arrogant and sometimes in bad faith, seems to have succeeded in converting metropolitan Parisianism opposite to the expectations of its leaders. If the slightest of his acrobatic feats spread around the world via Internet, his outbursts follow the same path.[3] In any case, one may legitimately ask whether the club can afford to ignore such an attack on its image, even with such a prestigious "guilty" star player? Although Zlatan Ibrahimović is also very popular in China, he has no Weibo account and his fans have no media to express their support.

While Zlatan Ibrahimović is a big name in sport that speaks to football fans around the world, David Beckham is a name that speaks to everyone. PSG was able to strike a blow in the history of French football. Thus, on January 31, 2013, the arrival of David Beckham to PSG aroused a passion hitherto never seen in France for a football player. This is a further step in the globalization of French football and globalization of the PSG brand. In other words, beyond the sporting aspect, the arrival of the superstar player takes part in the overall strategy of commercial expansion and marketing. Only 37 years old, the Briton continues to be the most famous footballer, especially in Asia and North America. At the time of the announcement of the signing of David Beckham, PSG instantly gained 5,700 Twitter followers and 23,591 Facebook fans, and more than 150 journalists[4] attended the press conference. One result: the club has sold 400,000 jerseys in 2012–2013, an increase of 60% over the previous year. However, the club is still far from Real Madrid, Manchester United or FC Barcelona in the field, with over a million sold garments. Also, in a marketing perspective, the best brand that has joined PSG in recent years remains David Beckham, recruited for only 5 months from January to May 2013 because of his brand image. Although David Beckham has no longer been considered one of the best players in the world for many years, he remains one of the icons of the sport and was a definite marketing advantage. The Briton maintains an "immaculate" picture: beautiful, friendly, intelligent and smiling. An image that is worth being the highest paid footballer in the world at the time of signing the contract with PSG. In addition, the first game played by David Beckham (PSG vs OM) broke audience records. Of the 40 cameras positioned around the field by Canal +, one has been specifically pointed on the Englishman: the "Beck cam". This craze surrounding the athlete, together with his late career under the jersey of PSG, has brought unprecedented media exposure to PSG.

As Frédéric Longuépée explains,

> The values of PSG: elegance, aesthetics, etc., the lack of complaining to the referee, etc. This must be reflected at all levels of the club. It is important to be aware of when recruiting some players over others. Since they are more or less likely to stick to the brand values that one tries to promote.

His words echo the factors mentioned above. By acquiring PSG, QSI was also interested in the characteristics of the city of Paris: luxury, fashion, etc. Which player best embodies these strengths? From the perspective of brand development, David Beckham seemed to be the perfect person. Especially since the salary of the Englishman was donated entirely to a charity that defends children. When David Beckham arrived in Paris, it was the meeting of two international brands: on one side a glamor footballer, on the other the most eternal romantic city of the world. This co-branding will be beneficial for a third mark, PSG. Thus, our analysis is consistent with the results of the study by Yu (2005), based on David Beckham, demonstrating the use of a brand-athlete with the view to increase the number of fans of a club, but also in achieving marketing goals. To the extent that the Englishman is not moving to PSG, the club must find other solutions, particularly from the perspective of overall brand development.

For a rapid internationalization of the club

The internationalization of the sport is mainly due to the maturation of the traditional markets of Western Europe and North America (Desbordes, 2007). Indeed, the major goal of professional sports entities (ESP) is based on a logic of globalization (Chanavat, 2009). From an international perspective, the strategies deployed by the NBA and the Premier League are an example in this regard. In French football, this approach is illustrated by the will of the LFP to compete every year for the Champions Trophy abroad.

As we have mentioned several times, it is necessary to raise PSG to become a global sports brand. If PSG has developed several initiatives in the context of going strategically towards being international in the last 15 years, the club globalization process coincides with the arrival of QSI in the equity of the club. Moreover, the central strategy of the club is now based on this process of internationalization.

Although athletic achievement remains a necessary condition for globalization of the club, its financial strength supports its development. It is therefore necessary for the club to continue its economic growth to achieve its objectives. As we have seen, buying star players has strengthened the club's image. However, obtaining titles and exploits on the European scale are essential elements to strengthen the club's brand equity, to pass a course and get a place at the top of the elite of European and global professional sports organizations (Chanavat and Bodet, 2009). Building a global brand requires the setting in motion of a globalization strategy. It is actually not possible to become a great sports brand without being international. The passage of a national brand to a global brand requires a greater presence and better brand recognition worldwide. What levers can PSG use? What are the determinants of success in the globalization of the brand?

Our analysis and previous studies (Kerr and Gladden, 2008; Chanavat and Bodet, 2009; Richelieu, 2011) highlight two types of determinants of the performance in terms of globalization of the brand: internal and external determinants.

Table 10.1 Analysis of the determinants of success in the internationalization of PSG[a]

Determinants	
Internal Determinants	*External Determinants*
1. A story and a powerful legacy (records, iconic players and coaches, powerful symbols, legendary matches and events, etc.)	1. Ownership of the club by fans through fan sites and social networking
2. Strong current attributes (fans, players, coach, president, sports arena, show quality, etc.)	2. A reputed league and powerful brand equity
3. An efficient communications system (website, TV channel, presence on social networks, etc.)	3. A strong rivalry between clubs
4. Sports activities rooted in foreign markets (organization of tournaments and exhibition games, presentation of new players, development of partnerships with clubs, opening of schools, training centers or academies, etc.)	4. Country of origin renowned in sports represented by the club
5. Economic and societal activities rooted in foreign markets (opening of community programs, sponsorship of regional development, store openings, etc.)	5. Television broadcasts in several countries
6. Co-branding activities (a range of licensed products, development of partnerships with stars)	
7. Development of strategic international partnerships (supplier, international companies)	

[a]This analysis focuses only on male football.

Internal determinants

In regards to internal determinants, our analysis highlights several elements.

THE HISTORY AND HERITAGE OF THE CLUB

Titles: we have seen, although the club was founded in 1970, it has already provided a record including a Cup of Cups in 1996 and several national titles. During the 2014–2015 season, PSG won all hexagonal competitions of the season to achieve an unprecedented national quadruple victory in France and in the major European leagues: Championship of France, Cup of France, League's Cup and Champions' Trophy. However, the Champions' League victory remains indispensable. Chelsea FC has made an impact by winning the European title for the first time by beating Bayern Munich on penalties in 2012.

Iconic players played for PSG: Anelka, Ayache, Baratelli, Bats, Beckham, Bianchi, Dahleb, Jean and Youri Djorkaeff, Fernandez, Ginola, Guérin, Lama, Leonardo, Le Guen, Makélélé, Pauleta, Raí, Ricardo, Roche, Ronaldinho, Simba, Simone, Susic, Valdo, Weah, etc.

Iconic coaches: Fontaine, Houiller, Jorge, Fernandez, Halilhodzic, Ancelotti were also on the club's bench.

Strong symbols: the city of Paris and the Eiffel Tower are important assets for the club. Unsurprisingly, these have been part of the new logo of PSG since 2013. Qatar is also strongly committed to the club's image.

Legendary games and events: beaten 3–1 at the Santiago Bernabéu in the first leg, PSG snatched its qualification in the semifinals of the UEFA Cup (1992–1993), winning at the end of a crazy game against Real Madrid (4–1) and a goal from Kombouaré. In 2015, PSG wrote a beautiful page in its history at Stamford Bridge by getting a historic draw on the lawn of Chelsea. Led twice, at 10 against 11 (following the expulsion of Zlatan Ibrahimović), players showed heart and pride pulling off a monumental qualification for the quarterfinals, with a goal by Thiago Silva at the end of extra time.

THE CURRENT ATTRIBUTES[5]

The fans: although, since 2010, the Leproux plan has been implemented to fight against violence around the PSG, it also ended the existence of supporters' associations. In this context, the Parc des Princes has lost much of its atmosphere. In a general view, the sound level of the sports arena has decreased since the implementation of this plan and the atmosphere seems a little less warm,[6] as QSI endures since the emergence of a family clientele. "When I go to the Parc des Princes, I'm fascinated to see more and more families, children and fun. When it resonates, it's 45,000 people who have a good time," said Mathieu Ficot, Economic Development Manager of the LFP.[7] These elements lead us to talk to more spectators and supporters of PSG rather than absolute fans. Obviously, it seems so legitimate that PSG put in place a strategy to "warm up" the atmosphere of the Parc des Princes, without necessarily going through the "reformation" of fan groups.

The players: PSG has a workforce of players from eight different countries: Argentina, Brazil, Ivory Coast, France, Italy, the Netherlands, Sweden and Uruguay. If almost all the players who make up the team are international, a "local" star issue of the Parisian training center could contribute to the development of the PSG brand.

The coach: Unai Emery is a Spanish retired footballer who played as a left midfielder, and the current manager of French club Paris Saint-Germain FC. He also possesses a strong array of skills. Moreover, he is perceived to go on to win titles at PSG and to improve the club's image.

The president: Nasser Al-Khelaïfi exudes an image of seriousness, professionalism and simplicity which is supposed to symbolize Qatar. A trusted man of Sheikh Tamim bin Hamad Al Thani because he is loyal and faithful to him, he is considered an ambassador for his country.[8] He presides as chairman for the Qatar Sports Investments Board and directs BeIn Media Group, which issues BeIn Sport. In addition, he was named Qatar Minister "senior executive", that is to say, without specific assignment.

The sports arena: it is certainly the Achilles heel of the PSG. Even if we find children and women at the Parc des Princes and that the atmosphere is good, it lacks a stage. While the PSG wants to become one of the biggest European clubs, it operates in a stadium whose capacity is two times lower than that of its competitors. For example, the Camp Nou of FC Barcelona is equipped with 99,354 seats. The interaction of the audience and the players represents the soul of high-level football, the reciprocal impact from one to the other. If an audience can wake a team up, the performance of a team can make the audience fall asleep.

The show quality: with the best attack in the home league, the show is usually guaranteed at the Parc des Princes. The collective offensive armada of PSG combined with the individual talent of the players contributes to this.

AN EFFICIENT COMMUNICATION SYSTEM

Website and social networks: the club has a website available in eight languages: English, Spanish, Portuguese, Arabic, Chinese, Indonesian, Korean and French. The "fan base" of the club is made up of nearly 20 million fans on Facebook,[9] nearly 2 million followers on Twitter, more than a million followers on Instagram, etc. PSG is one of the first clubs in the world and the first French club to have opened accounts on Asian social networks.[10] We can count 12 Facebook pages in eight languages, nine Twitter accounts, six apps and four platforms. PSG relies heavily on digital medias to strengthen the image and attachment to its brand. Its digital arsenal allows it to share emotions with the community.

The TV channel: PSG TV is a digital channel available on the club website or on YouTube for free, thanks to a short advertisement broadcast before each subject. However, matches and summaries are reserved for subscribers. The supporter can therefore have daily free access to players.

SPORTS ROOTED IN FOREIGN MARKETS

The organization of tournaments and exhibition games: the club has increased the preseason tournaments in the last few years in North America, Sweden, Asia, etc. We also take note of stays in Qatar during the winter break (Qatar Winter Tour).

The presentation of new players: Lucas arrives in Doha December 31, 2012, during the winter break of Parisians and is presented to the media on January 1, 2013, in the presence of Nasser Al-Khelaïfi and Leonardo.

The development of partnerships with clubs: the City Football Group is a holding company created to manage the relationships between different clubs linked to Manchester City: New York City and Melbourne City. If no such partnership currently exists for PSG, the question of such a device may arise.

The opening of schools, training centers and academies: the club opened academies in France, El Jadida (Morocco), New York, Doha, Rio, Gurgaon (near New Delhi) and Bangalore. Thus, the PSG Academy is part of the development strategy of the brand abroad. Since 2014, the club moved to India when the Indian Super League was launched. To launch this program, PSG has partnered with an agency specializing in sports marketing, Sports Roots. The official ambassador of the PSG, the former player Pedro Miguel Pauleta, was present to initiate the operation of the club in India.

ECONOMIC AND SOCIETAL ACTIVITIES ROOTED IN FOREIGN MARKETS

The opening of societal programs: social responsibility programs are implemented by the PSG Foundation outside of French borders. For example, it helped to form a football championship for

850 children in the NCR of Delhi. Residents of the Orphanage of Bernoussi from Casablanca, invited by the PSG Foundation, could, in turn, attend a workout for footballers, and even participate alongside players of the club.

The development of regional sponsorship: it is an innovative approach to segmentation and regionalization partnerships, which is a growing trend in football, to be considered for the clubs. PSG aims to develop additional revenue by developing customized and innovative partnerships for each specific market. It should measure the market opportunities with the goal of developing effective initiatives and of optimizing this new economic resource (see Chapter 6 dedicated to sponsoring).

The opening of stores: on December 31, 2013, a localized store in the Villaggio mall in Doha, on the Aspire complex, was inaugurated during the Qatar Winter Tour. As part of this dynamic, the network of stores worldwide is expected to strengthen rapidly. Indonesia, China, the United States and Brazil could be part of the selected countries.

CO-BRANDING ACTIVITIES

A range of licensed products: PSG has developed a wide range of heterogeneous products ("Blue" socks of the brand Happy Socks at 10 euros, with the S. T. Dupont pen for 235 euros). We can also note a partnership with the Colette boutique, rue St-Honoré in Paris.

The development of partnerships with celebrities: the co-branding strategy has been expanded to other types of stakeholders (athletes and personas). One can cite the example of Serena Williams, who posed with the shirt of the PSG, Rafael Nadal or Brazilian Ronaldo who gave the kick-off at Parc des Princes. This allows the transfer of components of image and "positive" affects towards consumers who are not necessarily supporters of PSG.

DEVELOPMENT OF STRATEGIC INTERNATIONAL PARTNERSHIPS

The equipment: although a partnership with Burrda Sport, supplier of QSI, could be considered, international development of the PSG cannot materialize without the help of a powerful supplier. Nike, established everywhere and having a strong image among the younger generation, is thus a partner of PSG. A key advantage as the club sells more and more shirts in the world.

International companies: PSG favors premium brand partners congruent with its internationalization strategy. It has demonstrated its expertise in this area by signing several strategic partnerships with global sponsors (see next section).

External determinants

Although the analysis of internal determinants for the club highlights the performance of the club in internationalization, our study of external determinants seems more measured.

OWNERSHIP OF THE CLUB BY FANS THROUGH FAN SITES AND SOCIAL NETWORKING

Many communities of supporters, which set up at the initiative of fans themselves, have grown for several years. This is a way to get involved in the life of the PSG outside of club meetings. For example, the PSG Community is a team of enthusiasts grouped together to create a community of fans in Paris.

> The purpose is mainly to share with you the news, analyses and celebrate with you while following our team. You will not miss any of the news of the PSG, and we will

offer you the exclusive and participatory content via interviews and surveys. You are welcome on our website and we invite you to respond to us or through the comments of the site or on social networks.

A REPUTED LEAGUE AND POWERFUL BRAND EQUITY

The 2014 report from the Union of Professional Football Clubs (UCPF) on the reasons for the large athletic and economic "drop" in French clubs highlights four major obstacles to their development: severe disability (payroll, disadvantageous employers and taxes, restriction on sponsorship), sporting erosion (exodus of the best French players, etc.), an economic competitiveness at half-mast (television rights, sponsorship revenue, match days, the number of small subscriptions, naming in its infancy, etc.) and fragile finances (under-capitalization, revenues to develop, etc.).

While the attractiveness of three major European leagues (England, Germany, Spain) generate strong revenues, the league's operating income was a deficit of 274 million euros (2013–2014). France therefore spends more than it earns. Moreover, France ranks only sixth in the UEFA index. However, France gravitates towards an overall financial balance. These are the products of mutations (transfers) and the intervention of shareholders (write-offs) that explain this result that must be qualified, however, insofar as sales of overseas players, if they provide immediate resources, constituting in the long-term an athletic weakening weighing on economic development.

In any event, although the brand equity of Ligue 1 is in development, it is not comparable with that of the English or Spanish leagues. However, PSG has partly helped to take some audiences in Ligue 1 in some countries such as Sweden, Italy and Brazil.

A STRONG RIVALRY BETWEEN CLUBS

If there is a real rivalry today between PSG and Olympique de Marseille, the PSG-OM match remains primarily a marketing shock. In the early 1990s, French football was limited to a single club: OM. The rivalry was then trumped by Canal + who sought a poster to promote and develop "their" championship. It seems that the rivalry has therefore been created under the leadership of Bernard Tapie and Michel Denisot. Although this PSG-OM rivalry has ended up settling in time, historic rivalries remain in Ligue 1 such as ASSE-OL and Lille-RC Lens.

A COUNTRY RENOWNED IN SPORTS REPRESENTED BY THE CLUB

France hosted the 11th FIFA World Cup and won on July 12, 1998, which seems far away. The LFP–UCPF–IPSOS barometer (2015) image of professional football clubs confirms the strong bond of Ligue 1 and Ligue 2 with the French, which place these championships at the head of the sports shows. This survey establishes football as a favorite sport of the French (before tennis and rugby): 17 million are interested and 14.5 million follow it regularly, 36% (+2 points versus last season) and 31% (+3 points) of the national population. Also, if football is generally developed in France, it represents a real "religion" and is part of the culture in some countries, such as Spain. A French club happens to arouse the interest of its fans 2 hours a week, while in Spain, it is more than 2 hours a day![11]

BROADCASTING IN SEVERAL COUNTRIES

The meetings of Paris Saint-Germain always arouse more interest in France, but also internationally. The "classico" between Olympique Marseille and PSG on April 5, 2015, for example, was broadcast by 41 channels in 167 territories on all continents. In the first leg, the distribution was 160 territories.

For an activation of catalysts

The catalysts examined promote the analysis of several strategic dimensions of PSG in matters of internationalization. Once endowed with all these levers of action, the challenge consists of activating it in the right place at the right time. For if PSG today represents a powerful media, it remains a SME.

According to Frédéric Longuépée,

> We cannot attack entire countries because they would disperse themselves and spend a lot of money. The challenge therefore is to cross a set criteria. Where is the club broadcasted? What is the competition in front of us? What is the potential of fans in the market in question likely to buy PSG? To decide to put our energy in one area rather than another, one will go where, to an amount of energy equivalent, the results will be the most convincing.

So it seems logical that before conquering markets such as Russia or China, the club will expend energy where its chances of success are greatest, to the extent that success will bring more success. The Asian market offers economic development prospects and attractive business in particular to develop the sale of licensed products. Thus, Manchester United began to use the South Korean Ji-sung Park like an ambassador, to develop a specific relationship with Asian consumers (Hill and Vincent, 2006).

As mentioned, the digital tools of the club (the web platform and e-commerce, social networks, etc.) are well developed in different languages. It is appropriate that the information means something to an Indonesian or Brazilian fan for the product to be available in the geographic area of said fan. Once the brand strategy is defined, it is essential that any variation is consistent. This is not an easy exercise in the football sector, given the over-hype of some clubs like PSG. If every club has a brand equity of its own, internationalization strategies may appear to be similar to the extent that the clubs have a brand based in particular on the performance, sports scores, world stars, etc. In any case, the logic of internationalization seems endless as the territories to conquer are numerous and of diversified initiatives. Our analysis echoes that of Frédéric Longuépée for whom

> the internationalization of the brand is an endless story. Markets to conquer will always be there. When PSG develops the digital side of its business, it opens its academy, when we will have extended the actions of the Foundation in the main countries, we will go to other countries because a country that has not broadcasted us will end up doing it; we will attract the interest of other brands in other countries, etc. I'm not sure that there is an end to this development.

Is it not proper of large brands?

For a global and innovative partnership strategy

The club has operated several levers in a context of globalization. The partnership strategy of PSG occupies a special place for this.

Reducing the number of partners, increasing quality, developing more revenue

In early 2000, PSG was associated with over 70 brands. It now has over 24 partners, and not all are highlighted via the lighted sign at Parc des Princes. Since the arrival of QSI, PSG has significantly redesigned its partnership relations. It is now important for the club to develop an ambitious partnership strategy. Building on the power of its brand, PSG continues to develop its partnership program by giving an increasingly international scope. If the number of partners has decreased (46 in 2011–2012 to 26 for the 2014–2015 season), the revenue generated has been multiplied by 3.7 over the same period to 56 million euros. According to the club's official website, one can observe, for the 2014–2015 season, the 24 partners of PSG, which are divided into five levels:

- Four top sponsors (Emirates, Nike, Ooredoo, and QNB) for an estimated 5 to 25 million euros;
- A major partner (Aspetar);
- Four official partners (BeIN Sports, Orange, Citroën, PMU, Huawei) for an estimated 1.2 to 1.5 million euros;
- Eight official suppliers (GDF Suez, Panasonic, Nivea Men, Coca-Cola, Man, Puressentiel, McDonald's, MoneyGram) for a sum estimated between 0.7 and 1 million euros;
- Six official labels (Go Sport, Aurel BGC, Hublot, Viagogo, Hugo Boss, EA Sports) for a partnership of 0.4 to 0.5 million euros.

In 3 years, the average value of a contract generally costs about 300,000 euros to 3 million euros. This change fits into the overall development strategy of PSG, which aims to become a sports brand recognized internationally. However, we analyzed that sponsors have a major role for a club that claims a status change, and that has to incarnate the elegance of the city of Paris in order to earn its international reputation. This is called the congruence: by partnering with luxury brands, a club can change the perception of consumers. The relationship between PSG and its partners seems clearly strengthened. If this visibility at meetings constitutes an interesting element, enlargement of the rights granted by the PSG for more engaging brand activations with regard to fans appears as the new keystone device of the club. Overall, if the sponsors are willing to pay more, there are fewer of them, they have more visibility and are better able to activate their partnership, and thus optimize their rights (see paragraph on enabling PSG below).

The international dimension of the club's partnership program is illustrated also in the Qatar Winter Tour. This helped mobilize the regional partners around a platform of activations to the fans and to recall the important role of sport in promoting Qatar. PSG widely disseminates its brand and its values throughout the Middle East and in Asia and South America, where its radiation should take a new dimension in the years to come. Our analysis shows that, following the consolidation of the relations maintained by the club with its partners, PSG, global and prestigious brand, continues to exert a stronger attraction of power in the economic sphere. The club wanted to reduce the number of sponsors and search for others at a high level. Overall, our analysis highlights that the club wants to partner with prestigious brands. However, it is not because a partner is going to offer a lot of money that it will be systematically accepted. PSG is innovative insofar as it is a force of proposal in terms of brand activation. The club has thus multiplied the original initiatives with its partners, especially involving social networks. In this context, the club has attracted some multinational and has renegotiated existing contracts to its advantage. Nike is now a partner of PSG for an estimated annual budget between 20 and 30 million euros (until 2022) against 6.5 million euros before 2014. While the club was struggling to find sponsors, PSG reversed the balance of power. To some extent, it can choose its partners. In any case, if the club wishes to associate with premium partners, it remains obliged to generate maximum revenue from the perspective of Financial Fair Play. Also another form of partnerships (licensing) has developed to enhance the sale of products (crackers, etc.). These new forms of partnerships developed with brands that are not necessarily "high standing" could parasitize the PSG brand that advocates elegance.

A new form of partnership: the sponsoring state

QTA is the entity in charge of tourism development in Qatar and its promotion abroad. After the 2010–2011 season, PSG made official the signing of a unique partnership with the organization. Indeed, it is neither a classic sponsorship deal nor a naming contract, but a contract based on the image: one between Qatar and the PSG. In other words, this new form of partnership falls within "nation branding". The idea of associating the image of a nation with the image of a football club had in fact been unprecedented. Although the precise amount of this 5-year contract has not been disclosed, the club said that it was a contract innovative in character as to aim to promote a territory and not a business. The contract would have allowed PSG to pocket 150 million euros in the first year and would reach 200 million in subsequent years. The partnership "record" has sparked controversy. The "Direction Nationale du Contrôle de Gestion" (DNCG) said it validated this. Indeed, the balance of accounts seems to be the only requirement of the DNCG. However, the financial fair play of the UEFA has reassessed the contract. The amount of the partnership has been discounted by half to comply with market values. If the contract was considered legitimate and rational by the UEFA, it was considered out of touch for the market.

While sponsoring this state makes sense, given the strategy of Qatar discussed above, it also helps to highlight to everyone (including the UEFA) that QTA is an active, lucrative and innovative partnership "using" PSG as a true marketing tool. The entertainment program developed since the 2014–2015 season by QTA reveals this. It results in a communications campaign featuring footballers and handballers of the club visible on the Champs Elysées, the Renaissance Theatre facade of the Boulevard Saint-Martin, the Porte de Clichy and the Roissy Charles de Gaulle airport. Exhibits include Zlatan Ibrahimović, staged at the Fort Al Zubarah, Mikkel Hansen before the buildings of Doha, Luc Abalo at Barzan Tower, Javier Pastore in the Qatari desert, Thiago Silva before the Doha skyline and Daniel Narcisse at the cultural village of Katara. Players are thus considered ambassadors of the country they

Figure 10.4 GTA communication campaign with football players and handball players from PSG

all visited during the last tour of the club, the Qatar Winter Tour and Qatar Handball Tour. This seems to also illustrate the many facets of the country that oscillates between tradition and modernity. This agreement shows the importance of PSG in the strategy of Qatar. It also demonstrates the strength of PSG and contributes to its brand globalization strategy mentioned above.

The regional sponsorship, a new stage

The regional sponsorship faces a double challenge. It first generates additional economic resources to a club. This form of partnership promotes the globalization of the club brand on specific territories. This new trend of sponsorship can be defined as a partnership activity expected to sell image rights for a professional sports entity locally, within a specific territory by segmenting markets. The report published by Repucom "European Football Clubs Income Stream Report" (2014) examines the 20 most powerful European clubs, which combined have about 5 billion euros of revenue. Beyond the usual growth drivers, the study highlights a growing trend towards the exploitation of regional partnerships and highlights several elements. For the 2013–2014 season, the study identifies 84 regional sponsorship deals for the 20 studied European clubs, which corresponds to an additional income of 54 million euros. Nearly 60% of this amount was developed by Manchester United, which represents 32 million euros (38 for partnerships). In terms of number of partnerships, following are Chelsea FC (13 partnerships), Barcelona (11), Arsenal FC (8) and Manchester City FC (6). Asia seems to be the most appropriate market for this form of sponsorship of a new kind, with 47 contracts in total. Next come Europe (15), Africa (10) and South and Central America (4). Thailand appears to be the most active country with 17 partnerships.

English football has pioneered this form of sponsorship program. Manchester United has developed since 2008 a partnership making the brand of vodka Smirnoff its drink partner in Pacific Asia. Also, with 20 contracts, finance is the sector that invests the most in this type of contract, followed by telecommunications (16) and food (11).

This is a "real" emerging trend in football. The results of the study show that Manchester United remains the leader in regional partnerships. On this specific strategy, the club generates 350% of income more than the runner, FC Barcelona. If Manchester United currently dominates the regional sponsorship market, PSG clearly wants to profit from this.

PSG has logically signed in 2015 its first regional partnership in Indonesia with the Indonesian food group GarudaFood.

The new beverage group, SuperO2 Sportivo, became the official water of the club in Indonesia, where PSG has over 2 million fans on Facebook (for its local fans, the PSG has developed a version in Bahasa Indonesia on the official site). Frédéric Longuépée, present for the formalization of the partnership, explains:

> In November 2013, the website of the club was available in Indonesian, with the idea of opening a market which has an extraordinary potential of football fans. Today, there are as many Indonesian fans as French fans on Facebook. When we saw that, we decided to invest by spending time there and by reaching out to brands. And 6 months later, we landed a partnership. This is the example of Jakarta and GarudaFood.

The PSG has measured the opportunity to position themselves in interesting territories in terms of number of subscribers on Facebook (62 million in Indonesia) and where matches are broadcast (especially by BeIN Sports and Channel B). This example illustrates the international expansion strategy developed by PSG. The club takes another step in its international expansion. The product SuperO2 Sportivo from Garuda Food will now display the logo of the club and five iconic PSG players (including Zlatan Ibrahimović and Thiago Silva). TV advertising signed "super sports water" with the players of PSG is also broadcast on Indonesian channels to support the launch of the new product. This seems to be just the beginning of a long collaboration between the club and GarudaFood. While contacts were initiated during the summer tour of PSG in Asia (2014), we could imagine that the new partner will become, in the long-term, a top sponsor. "The regional partnership can effectively lead to a global partnership in the long-term," says Frédéric Longuépée. Other partnerships should be created and our analysis leads us to believe that PSG can quickly become a global leader in matters of a regional sponsorship program.

What operational variations for the business strategy of the PSG?

This second section examines several PSG operational marketing initiatives: the development of social actions with the PSG foundation, diversification of licensed products, the introduction of an innovative naming of the Ooredoo training center, the deployment of digital activities and digital implementation of a training program and the deployment of innovative brand-activation programs. They fit together, overlapping most of the time, with some logic already discussed in the first section of the chapter.

The PSG Foundation: between social responsibility and an international dimension

Founded in 2000, the PSG Foundation has entered a new era under the presidency of Nasser Al-Khelaïfi. One can observe a tripling of the subsidy granted by the club and the establishment of an endowment fund allowing it to double the number of its shares. This program has three objectives: provide professional projects for unemployed youth without training, offer sport to children in social, educational and cultural difficulties, and bring comfort to suffering children. The 2013–2014 annual report points out that since its creation, the Foundation has supported 120 young people from 18 to 25 years old and has allowed them to enter the profession while training social activists. On the occasion of 260 annual operations, the Foundation wants to convey the values of solidarity, tolerance and respect for others for the growing number of children in the Île-de-France.[12]

PSG was the first club in French football to set up a foundation, and it continues to innovate with this issue. Thus, it was the first to extend its actions while becoming a real citizen. Although the SASP of the PSG has not received any municipal subsidy since 2012, a grant from the City of Paris to the PSG Foundation is awarded each year (450,000 euros in 2014, 230,000 in 2015) in particular to support the creation the first school "Red and Blue". Thus, the colors of the club, located in the 19th arrondissement, offers a mix of academic support and physical activity. On the 15th anniversary of the PSG Foundation, a gala evening and an auction were held at the Pavillon Gabriel, near the Champs-Élysées on January 27, 2015. Together with the PSG team, many personalities from political, sports, entertainment and media backgrounds were present (Anne Hidalgo, Michel Drucker, Harry Roselmack, Jamel Debbouze, Marcel Desailly, Jean-Pierre Papin and Brahim Asloum). During this dinner, an auction was organized, and its proceeds went to the PSG Foundation and its work on behalf of sick children. In total, 19 lots were offered for sale, including the first jersey of David Beckham on PSG, rackets from Rafael Nadal, Roger Federer and Novak Djokovic (24,000 euros for the pack of three), and a replica of the Givenchy embroidered sweater worn by Beyoncé (16,000 euros) during her visit in September to the Parc des Princes. The co-branding developed with foreign stars thus proves beneficial from a societal perspective. The lots were sold for almost 255,000 euros (191,800 euros the year before). Since 2015, the Foundation has had operations in India by partnering with the Khel Khel Mein

League Cup in New Delhi. This project has seen 500 children from poor districts of the city compete in a big tournament. Upon arrival, QSI has strengthened civic engagement of the club.

The social responsibility of the company seems to become progressively more of an essential component for the strategy of European professional football clubs. For François and Bayle (2014), the adoption of certain CSR practices in professional sport is part of the superficial logic of legitimization and compliance, without any deep change in the administration of the clubs (François and Bayle, 2014). Meanwhile, the strategy of PSG seems singular with a unique international dimension. Our analysis wishes to emphasize an increase in social actions and their promotion. The development of the foundation internationally is explained and makes sense given the willingness of globalization for the PSG brand.

For a diversification of the PSG brand

Generally, revenue from the sale of related products account for a small percentage of revenue for the club; however, they support the development of its brand image. According to Frédéric Longuépée,

> The merchandising of football clubs is between 5 and 10% of the activity. This is what merchandising represents for the PSG, it aims to grow in the same proportion. However, it must continue to support the development of the club from an economic perspective.

Overall, the sales generated by merchandising has grown steadily and has amounted to 28.6 million euros. Our analysis shows that PSG continued its development strategy to rely on more efficient distribution and offer its fans a diversified offer. In addition, the 2013–2014 annual report stresses that the physical distribution network is still the main source of income with a 15% increase of its turnover. While the 2013–2014 annual report says the jersey of PSG remains the star product with 152,000 items sold (25,000 more than the previous season), revenues generated by the sale in France of branded products recorded Nike, accordingly, a 50% growth.

Licensed products must be consistent with the club's branding to the extent that they are supposed to be developed. Also the club wants the distribution of these products to be controlled. The strategy implemented by the PSG is supported for example by the creation of a partnership with Go Sport, a European leader in the distribution of sporting goods, creating a Pop Up Store on the ground floor of Galeries Lafayette on boulevard Haussmann, or the highlighting of the official store on the Champs Elysées. The development of sales locations and a richer range of licensed products have strengthened again the club's merchandising activity this season. Indeed, to accompany the international influence of the brand, two new stores were opened. The first real concept store is located within the grounds of Galeries Lafayette. The second store, located in the Villaggio Mall in Doha, was inaugurated at the last Qatar Winter Tour. Given the privileged relations with Qatar, it illustrates the international expansion strategy of the club. The extension of the range of licensed products was diversified with the "home" range offering towels, bathrobes, slippers, cups and decorative objects in the effigy of the club. Not surprisingly, the Champs Elysees boutique is the primary setting in which the PSG brand "shines". The club also has two shops (at Parc des Princes and Orly Airport) and two franchises in the Île-de-France: Belle Thorn and O'Parinor. These shops are an answer to the question of local presence and internationalization issues of the brand. Obviously, the store network in the world is expected to strengthen rapidly in cities like Beijing, New York, Rio and New Delhi because of the attractiveness of the brand and the dynamic tourism in these areas. PSG extends its reach to consumers of sporting events around the world via its online store, as well as with major brands attracted by its image. With an increase of 17.7% in its turnover to reach 5.3 million, the e-commerce platform seems to play an important role in the expansion strategy of the brand abroad. The 2013–2014 annual report shows that 12% of orders were made abroad with a main destination being the United States.

Finally, one can notice a proliferation of licenses. Although the products developed in the gaming, toy or edition industry allow it to cover more categories of products successfully, one can legitimately question the relevance of certain partnerships (as with Eurosnack for aperitif biscuits). Note that a program of "licensing" specific to Scandinavia, Japan and the Middle East has been developed. Overall, we went from 6 to 15 international licenses of that type, which represents more than a quarter of the overall portfolio. If several prestigious international brands are now associated with PSG through co-branding operations, we can highlight two activations to illustrate the successful strategy of the PSG. First, the launch of the Ultimate Box with Microsoft and the launch internationally of the first PSG fragrance with S. T. Dupont. Others were to follow.

Similarly, within the boundaries of art and fashion, PSG has partnered with others. The club is a partner of the Colette concept store, offering a range of products bearing the image of the club and which has been met with a tremendous success. With the prospect of becoming a brand outside the strictly sporting sphere, PSG speaks on topics not necessarily instinctive for a football club. "For example the opening of a photo exhibition of PSG players at Buddha Bar (in January 2015). And one can speak without overdoing it. This is a signal and an expression that is not natural for a club," said Frédéric Longuépée. Other actions taken by the club aim to reach a wide audience. "When one signs a partnership with Hugo Boss, one makes sure that the fittings of players take place at the store on the Champs and that Paris Match is present. It allows to stage the players dressed in costume and not in football wear in a magazine like Paris Match," he said.

This desire for diversification is also reflected in partnerships with prestigious brands. Frédéric Longuépée added,

> When one renovates the Parc des Princes hospitality spaces, one makes a call to the designers who have worked in large hotels or palaces, because they are going to know what to do, and beyond the revenues, it makes a message on the positioning of the club.

The club envisions developing a joint creation (a pastry) with Lenôtre. It makes sense to the extent that the customer that goes into the outlets of this brand at the Porte d'Auteuil or anywhere in the world is not necessarily the one that goes to the Parc des Princes. In addressing a population increasingly large, the PSG will enter the subconscious of the population and become a separate brand. Since the results are random, and you do not build a brand starting at the top, PSG is working on the rest: the conditions of success for when the results arrive. This is for the commercial and marketing cell to work on what it can control. "When the team wins, it is necessary that the conditions are met. Whether in France, Europe, Indonesia and Brazil. For that we take an international proportion that meets the goal of becoming a major international sports brand," explains Frédéric Longuépée. A large popular brand must be given access to all targets. The football stadium remains indeed one of the only places able to meet all occupational categories, all religions, in search of the same emotion.

Towards a new form of naming: The Ooredoo training center

According to Chanavat, Renaud and Desbordes (2014, p. 42), "the naming consists of selling the name of a sports stadium to a sponsor brand over a long period." Initiated in the last 30 years in North America, the practice of naming stadiums was particularly developed in Germany,

England and the Netherlands. In France, although the practice has existed for many years in sailing, motorsports and cycling, the development of naming stadiums is relatively recent. If it is possible to "rename" an existing installation, assuming it was deeply renovated, the amount of the agreement will generally be lower. The naming is, for the sponsors, a communication technique to significantly impact cognitive (image and reputation), affective (brand loyalty) or conative (purchase) reactions of the consumer sporting spectacle. These effects are reinforced in view of the long-term partnerships, which is one of the keys to a successful sponsorship.

The activity of naming does not constitute in itself an innovation. However, the idea to attach for the first time the name of a business partner to one of its sports infrastructure makes PSG an innovative club in the matter. Thus the famous "Camp des Loges" was renamed "Ooredoo Training Center", named after the Qatari phone company that will sponsor the club until 2018, for 13 million euros per year. Insofar as the Parc des Princes is the property of the City of Paris and the club wants to develop new revenue sources, other such partnerships should be created. "New infrastructure of PSG will be named in important places of PSG in the stadium. It was the desire to tell stories and we are in active research to tell them," concludes Frédéric Longuépée on this point. These elements lead us to believe that this form of naming is a development tool that should inspire other professional sports facilities.

What digital activities for the club?

The 2014 edition of *Digital Sport Challenge* devoted to the use of French athletes in terms of social media and Internet strategy highlights that

> the sports sector in France has still not received its fair value and social networks remain a highly dynamic field in which the truth of a day is not that of the next day. Each player has the possibility to rapidly evolve his share of voice or market provided he invests in his interface, the usability of his website, his web animation device at large, or simply that he manages to "make a buzz" through his communication campaigns on Facebook, Twitter or on other channels.

In this context, the use of digital media by professional football clubs is booming (see Chapter 7 on football social media). If social networks were generally integrated into the digital strategy of the clubs, some professional sports facilities are much more innovative and efficient than others in this regard. The official websites of clubs are no longer sufficient, and clubs are increasingly active in the social media world with Facebook, Twitter, Pinterest, Instagram, Deezer and Dailymotion.

The struggle between the major football clubs in Europe finds ever new variations. Since 2013, they now compete on Sina Weibo, Tencent Weibo and Renren, the Chinese social networks that bring together 591 million users. According to François von Zedtwitz, cofounder of Shankai Sports, the company based in Beijing who advised the Parisian club in this digital conquest, success in this area also requires maximum responsiveness. "The PSG was the first European club to have posted on Chinese social networks with condolences to the victims of the earthquake in Sichuan. The next morning the local newspaper put a section of its sport section: Thanks, Paris Saint-Germain."[13]

With a strong digital budget, the PSG, very active on social networks, has deployed innovative digital communication devices that have met great success with fans. Although, since 2009 (with Facebook and Twitter), the primary objective was to inform the fans about the club news, digital media has become a multi-function which allows the club to meet different marketing objectives. In other words, it allows the club to communicate, inform, animate, retain, conquer, share, sell, entertain and internationalize. In view of construction and globalization of the PSG brand, the digital arsenal of the club allows it to share emotions with the community. The fan base of the club is made up of, as we mentioned, nearly 17 million fans on Facebook, nearly two million Twitter followers and more than a million followers on Instagram, etc. PSG is also one of the first clubs in the world and the first French club to have opened accounts on Asian social networks. Also the number of fans has increased significantly in Brazil in recent years, given the strong Brazilian delegation in the team and the presence of a community manager in Brazil who specifically manages the Portuguese network. PSG logically capitalizes on its "foreign players" active to develop its brand. This explains the fact that the first fan community on Facebook is not in France, but abroad. Frédéric Longuépée says,

> For 3 ½ years we started with 500,000 Facebook fans, which is indicative of the appetite of the market for a club. 80% of fans were French 3 years ago. Today we have 17 million fans (far from the 80 million of Spanish clubs) and the largest increase in clubs. 85% of them are foreigners today.

The heart of the digital art can be distinguished into two sides: the entertainment and animation in real time. The only French football club to offer its fans a free gaming experience, the PSG offers various applications like #PariStories that allows one to relive the game through the eyes of the fans. This immersive digital platform developed with the help of Google and the AKQA agency reinvents the replay and groups the content generated by the fans. Another example will demonstrate how the PSG is at the forefront of innovation on the issue of digital: SoLive. This is a tool that allows PSG to graphically live tweet, which is reminiscent of the #PureLive application of BeIN Sport. When live tweeting a meeting, it is important to be responsive and to be the first to announce an event and become Top Tweet. The Top Tweet is going to ride the wave and generate more tweets. Previously, two alternatives were available to the club: tweeting a text in real time to be the first or to tweet an image to produce quality content. With SoLive, the community manager is able to achieve both simultaneously to the extent that the tool creates graphic tweets in real time and shares them together.

The Parc des Princes has become a "trendy" place in Paris, and David Beckham has contributed to this a lot. The development of this facet of the club brand is reinforced through social networks. For example, #ParisMeltingSpot is a social hub of digital influencers from the worlds of fashion, media, cinema or any other person with a significant social audience. These influencers are invited by the PSG (and its partners), receiving gifts and living an exceptional game experience.

This device can generate high value-added tweets of people who are not necessarily sports fans. This device again shows the consistency of PSG in its marketing operationalization. PSG aims to become a brand of consumer entertainment and to develop its scope and audience. Other actions such as the one proposed on the occasion of Valentine's Day or the opposition to Chelsea could be developed here. If PSG communication generally proves a success, innovative and distinctive, the PSG activities on the social web seem to have enough inspiration to other professional sports structures, other sports brands, and even entertainment.

Inexpensive and quickly profitable, it also allows you to link with fans around the world, who, far from the club, can not necessarily go to the games. The digital media will extend the brand experience (before, during and after the match) and create a link between the different teams that make up the sports brand; the visual identity of these pages is very close, if not similar. Thus, the online store site brings together all the licensed products of the brand (www.boutiquepsg.fr). The digital tools enable fans to access additional information, access backstage drives and take new players. Interactivity has been reinforced by the proliferation of contests. In any event, through social networks or PSG TV, the club shows its determination to become a proper media. The development of digital strategy seems logical insofar as the web happens to be the ideal tool to transcend distances and cross borders. The PSG can no longer afford to do a simple "tour" during the pre-season, in which only occasional contacts are made, and had to set up a real digital strategy. Meanwhile, the arrival of wi-fi at the Parc des Princes should, in turn, be an important step in the digital experience of the club's fans.

Towards a training program

The idea of making PSG a great club is not just through the purchase of players. It is necessary to rely on a high-performance training center. Thus, Nasser Al-Khelaïfi admits he dreams of finding the new Lionel Messi. The performance of the training center is a central issue in the PSG development strategy that would once again draw inspiration from the Masia, the FC Barcelona training center. Training players gives the possibility for the club to reduce transfer costs and to participate in the creation of its image. The fans usually develop a particular affect against players from the training center. For example, Mamadou Sakho has been one of the favorite players of the fans before being transferred to Liverpool. He was akin to a form of "supporting player" of the team. Conversely, non-club-trained players, if they can express their attachment to the club, do not generally react the same way. Players typically develop a particular affect towards their first club to which they dedicate a form of recognition.

It is necessary for the club to become one of the best training centers in the world. The project appears to be credible to the extent that the Paris pool is one of the richest in Europe in terms of young players. However, too many young people in the region currently pass through the net and will be trained outside of Paris. Paul Pogba, born in Seine-et-Marne, for example, was trained in Le Havre. In other words, it is for the club to develop a high-performance training center and not to let out talents from Ile-de-France. Although the problem is not new, the leaders seem to want to give themselves the means for their ambitions. They wish thereby to strengthen their team of "scouts" to scrutinize the largest number of world regions. This local involvement is an important foundation for the construction and the globalization of the PSG brand. This approach also allows the club to be in line with the requirements of the UEFA. This requires that at least four club-trained players be retained on the list of the 25 players of the team selected to compete in the Champions League matches.

It seems necessary for PSG to develop a training model for the professional team fueled by talent trained at the club and the Academy. The PSG academies, developed over several years in France and in the world, are used to disseminate the PSG brand and know-how in terms of football education. It is more of a leisure education than an education at the training center. However, Frédéric Longuépée states that "the club does not forbid identifying kids in Rio, Doha and Bangalore where it has opened an academy. This is not a financial issue but the development of the brand."

A club with a wealth of original brand activations

We have discussed above, the sponsors of the PSG have made still more engaging brand activation programs vis-à-vis supporters. Note that the first television advertising campaign involving PSG players to sponsor, Nivea in this case, proved to be very efficient. The impact on sales was found to be twice the average advertisement carried by the men's care brand. Additionally, partners have been particularly active on digital platforms with a goal of achieving loyalty. These activations help attract new fans to the club and to lead the community of sponsors around the PSG. The title of "Official Label" represents a new marketing product allowing the use of branding and PSG symbols. The activations with fans are numerous, such as "Citroën Golden Barre" (animation at halftime of Ligue 1 matches with an accurate animation) and "Happiness football club" (Coca Cola allows young players to play Escort Kids and accompany the players when they enter the field), and some seem "truly" innovative.

Two examples we illustrate are the innovative side of activations developed by PSG and its sponsors. In the case of Center Parcs, the brand has decided to innovate by exploiting an idea previously little used in sports partnership. To understand the activation is to understand the positioning and signing of Center Parcs, namely "Nature is fun." This position comes with very unique event activations around activities all year round in the heart of intact nature, present in parks. From a marketing perspective, Center Parcs has decided to activate its partnership with PSG using the gardener Club, Jonathan Calderwood, elected gardener of the year in the Premier League (2009 and 2012). Jonathan Calderwood is thus at the heart of Center Parcs' media

Figure 10.5 PMU brand activation with PSG INSIDER

Source: http://www.psginsider.fr https://www.facebook.com/PMUOnParie – Facebook Page of the INSIDER on April 16, 2015.

campaign and a video in which we learn that the Paris Saint-Germain sends its best element to give the kickoff Ateliers Foot PSG at the Center parks.

Furthermore, from February 23 to March 15, 2015, PMU, the official sponsor of the PSG, activated sponsorship with the club by launching an unprecedented recruitment for a dream "job". Through the program "Paris Saint-Germain Insider", a fan was offered the opportunity to stay behind the scenes of PSG for a month. Accustomed to activations "Money can't buy" (see Chapter 6 dedicated to sponsoring), PMU and PSG therefore permitted a supporter of the club to follow the daily operations of the club. The insider could immortalize special moments and share them with the community of fans via social networks. The fan has been transformed by a panel of the PSG and PMU employees and has participated in various events: a training at the Ooredoo training center closest to the staff, a face-to-face meeting with Blaise Matuidi, a trip to the Stade Velodrome and the game OM against PSG, PSG vs Lille in a VIP match on the field and a Paris Live Poker tournament. This is an innovative tool for activating the PMU sponsor. Indeed, after the defeat of PSG 3 goals to 1 against Barcelona in the quarter-final (first leg) of the Champions League from 2014 to 2015, one could read the following message on behalf of the tweeter insider: "3–0 at the Nou Camp, we believe in it!" #onpariebypmu.

Conclusion

The objective of this chapter was to provide a specific explanation and analysis of the marketing strategy deployed by the PSG. We had to choose the activities to be observed. From this point of view, this work does not claim to be exhaustive, but it was exhaustive to observe the main marketing areas for development of the club and their operationalization. Since the arrival of QSI and Nasser Al-Khelaïfiin in 2011, the main strategic goal is to make PSG a great European club, a sports brand with a global reach in the image of Paris. Frédéric Longuépée explains,

> The goal of PSG is to be the only club, of the most watched sport in the world, in one of the most iconic capitals of the world. It is a most considerable asset that does not have other football clubs. There are two clubs in Rome, two in Madrid and six in London. And one in Paris. We believe we have the potential to become this great international sports franchise.

If the budget is a prerequisite for a successful club, it does not necessarily guarantee victory (the club's budget should amount to 530 million euros for the 2015–2016 season). In any case, the success of a professional football club requires significant marketing deployment beyond a sports cell. For Frédéric Longuépée, "there must be a willingness to invest in the invisible." To do this, PSG consists of some 14 departments, mainly polarized on trade issues and marketing. Overall, the strategy of the club is based on two key dimensions: a change in branding and diversifying growth.

The first section of this chapter was to explain the overall context of the QSI version of the PSG club. The extension of the club brand aims to make PSG a great sports club, structured in the Anglo-Saxon manner, in which strategic activities are internalized. BeIN Sports, a subsidiary of Al-Jazeera chaired by Nasser Al-Khelaïfi, was launched in 2012 in France, and it promotes a preferential media exposure of the club. Overall, the club's brand strategy is based on a controlled communication, the idea of PSG as a club from the city of Paris, the conceptualization of a new visual identity and the acquisition of a brand-athlete. The slogan "Let us dream bigger/Dream

Bigger", the evolution of the logo and the changing position of David Beckham seem to mark a milestone in the implementation of the PSG brand-building strategy. These elements feed its rapid internationalization, a strategic central focus of the club, based on two types of levers (internal and external). The performance of PSG in matters of globalization is mainly based on an excellent communication system, sporting, economic and social activities rooted in foreign markets, co-branding activities, the development of strategic international partnerships, etc. Sponsors play a major role as to a club status change. Also the global partnership strategy and innovation of the club distinguishes itself by a reduced number of partners, increasing their standing and revenue. The innovations of the club with regard to sponsorship (state sponsorship, regional sponsorship), and they demonstrate marketing power and contribute to its globalization strategy.

Several operational marketing initiatives were discussed in the second section of this chapter: the development of social actions with the PSG foundation, diversification of licensed products, the introduction of an innovative naming with the Ooredoo training center, the deployment of digital media and digital activities, the implementation of a training program and the deployment of innovative brand activation programs. Others could have been treated. It is to note that PSG relies heavily on the digital image and to strengthen its commitment to its brand and share emotions with its community. In this context, the network of physical stores worldwide is expected to increase rapidly.

PSG does not otherwise cease to innovate and work for new projects. Two examples illustrate this. The first is related to the Parc des Princes, a stadium which should have a warmer atmosphere, without necessarily reshaping the fan groups. This is the Achilles heel of the club. PSG, who does not own its stadium, is constrained by its infrastructure. However, the club has a long lease of 30 years, with a rent of 1 million euros per year. In this context, it may invest in itself through its renovation. Like all great clubs, PSG wants to make its stage assets and invest 75 million in a first renovation for Euro 2016. Thus the development of ticketing and lodging is a major asset for the club. Furthermore, "complete" display changes the relationship established between supply and demand. Although the Parc des Princes offered more seats than it had requested and showed therefore a very low selling price, today the difficulties fans face to find seats have increased the price thereof. As Frédéric Longuépée analyzed,

> When you are looking to fill up a stadium, you start working on strong games since the effort is lower than working on weak matches. When you want to buy a ticket for a strong game that is full, it means a priori that the club generates interest . . . and so I might want to be a partner and to go and buy a ticket.
>
> The more something is rare, the more value it has. In 2015, at the PSG–Barcelona match in the quarterfinals of the Champions League, a ticket was sold on eBay for 2,700 euros.[14]

Overall, the club has many arguments from the perspective of its development. However, the stadium is a major problem for the club. Indeed, the Parc des Princes, if renovated, will have a limited capacity (47,000) compared to the Camp Nou of FC Barcelona (98,000), the Bernabéu in Madrid (81,000), Arsenal's Emirates Stadium (60,000) and the Allianz Arena in Munich (75,000). Although the PSG stadium is a "good point", it is not in line with major European teams, which has implications on revenues.

Second, it would be necessary for the club to develop a museum that would enable consumers to experience the brand in a unique manner. Although the concept of the museum is nothing new, the club would like to have the visitor (re)live a unique experience with the brand. The idea is to enjoy the impact of Paris on tourists worldwide. Although PSG is not, unlike Paris, the first tourist destination of the world, the club could attract more tourists visiting the museum. In any case, Paris constitutes an asset and a strength of PSG brand equity. In this regard, Frédéric Longuépée explains that

> The PSG experience is a project for the future, to expand the brand throughout the year. The captivated fans looking to prolong the experience by purchasing licensed products, it makes sense to extend the experience with a different experience by immersing themselves in the PSG adventure through an audio, video, or olfactory experience.

A PSG Hall of Fame around the Parc des Princes tracing the history and presenting the best players in the club could also be created. This would be like the project already developed by Jean-Claude Blanc at Juventus.

Our analysis highlights the consistency of deployed marketing actions to structure and develop the marketing aspects of the club in a logic of globalization. However, although all the club's marketing arsenal is undoubtedly part of the references, the consecration of the globalization strategy of the brand necessarily requires an extraordinary sporting achievement that only a Champions League victory would seem to allow.

Notes

1 The authors would like to thank all the people interviewed for this research. Special thanks goes to Frédéric Longuépée, vice director in charge of the commercial activities for PSG, for his help and for making himself available.
2 His son, Tamim ben Hamad Al Thani, has been the new emir of Qatar since June 25, 2013.
3 R. Bourel and H. Penot, "Et si Ibra devenait encombrant?", *L'Équipe*, March17, 2015, p. 6.
4 P.-É. Minonzio, "PSG, des ambitions sans frontières", *L'Équipe*, July 1, 2013, p. 22.
5 Information related to the 2014–2015 season.
6 http://www.lequipe.fr/Football/Actualites/L-ambiance-aucune-influence/532296 – Excerpt from the article "L'ambiance n'a-t-elle aucune influence sur les résultats?" published in lequipe.fr, January 30, 2015. Last accessed on April 15 2015.
7 Interview conducted by Nicolas Chanavat on December 3, 2014, at the headquarters of the LFP.
8 http://www.challenges.fr/sport/20150310.CHA3742/nasser-al-khelaifi-un-ambassadeur-bis-au-service-exclusif-du-qatar.html – Excerpt from the article "Le vrai visage de Nasser al-Khelaïfi, patron du PSG et ambassadeur bis du Qatar" published in challenges.fr on March 12, 2015. Last accessed on April 15, 2015.
9 Ces chiffres datent d'avril 2015 et devraient continuer à augmenter. Le club comptait un million de fans au début de la saison 2012–2013.
10 L'agence Mailman, dans son rapport Red Card 2015, classe le PSG au 10e rang des clubs européens les plus efficaces sur les médias sociaux chinois, http://www.mailmangroup.com
11 LFP–UCPF–IPSOS, baromètre d'image des clubs professionnels de football, 2015.
12 Paris Saint-Germain, *Rapport d'activité 2013–2014*, 2014, p. 57.
13 Excerpt from P.-É. Minonzio, "À la conquête du Web chinois", *L'Équipe*, September 30, 2013, p. 24.
14 http://sport24.lefigaro.fr/le-scan-sport/business/2015/03/30/27004–20150330ARTFIG00086-des-places-a-2700-euros-pour-psg-barcelone.php – excerpt from the article "Des places à 2 700 euros pour PSG-Barcelone" published on March 30, 2015, on the website http://sport24.lefigaro.fr – Last accessed on April 16, 2015.

Bibliography

Beau N. et Bourget J.-M., *Le vilain petit Qatar. Cet ami qui nous veut du mal*, Paris, Fayard, 2013.

Camy J., "Société sportive et 'sport power': la famille régnante Al-Thani et le système sportif du Qatar", in E. Bayle (ed.), *Les grands dirigeants du sport*, Louvain-la-Neuve: Belgium, De Boeck, 2014, pp. 295–312.

Champagne J., *La diplomatie sportive du Qatar, instrument d'une nouvelle notoriété internationale*, Paris, Géoéconomie, 2012.

Chanavat N., *Étude de l'efficacité du parrainage sportif multiple événementiel: une application à trois entités sportives professionnelles et à un annonceur*, thèse de doctorat en sciences du sport, Université Claude Bernard, Lyon I, 2009.

Chanavat N. et Bodet G., "Sport branding strategy and internationalisation: A French perception of the 'Big Four' brands", *Qualitative Market Research: An International Journal*, 12, 4, 2009, pp. 460–481.

Chanavat N. et Desbordes M., "Le parrainage sportif multiple événementiel: atouts, défis et conditions de succès", *Revue Gestion (HEC Montréal)*, 38, 4, 2014, pp. 27–36.

Chanavat N., Renaud M. et Desbordes M., "Naming et modularité: les clés de la réussite?", *Jurisport*, 142, 2014, pp. 37–41.

Degorre D. et Touboul J., *La folle histoire du PSG, des origines à nos jours*, Paris, Éditions Prolongations, 2009, p. 205.

Desbordes M., "Introduction: New directions for marketing in football", in M. Desbordes (ed.), *Marketing and Football: An International Perspective*, Oxford, Butterworth-Heinemann, 2007, pp. 1–15.

François A. et Bayle E., "Analyse des pratiques de RSE des clubs sportifs professionnels français", *Revue de l'Organisation Responsable*, 9(2), 2014, pp. 5–20.

Ibrahimović Z. et Lagercrantz D., *Moi, Zlatan Ibrahimović, Mon histoire racontée à David Lagercrantz*, Paris, Éditions Broché, 2013.

Kase K., Urrutia I., Marti Sanchis C. et Opazo M., "The proto-image of Real Madrid: Implications for marketing and management", *International Journal of Sports Marketing and Sponsorship*, April 2007, 8(3), pp. 212–233.

Kerr A.K. et Gladden J.M., "Extending the understanding of professional team brand equity to the global marketplace", *International Journal of Sport Management and Marketing*, 3, 1/2, 2008, pp. 58–77.

Nye J., *Soft Power: The Means to Success in World Politics*, New York, NY, Public Affairs, 2004.

Ratignier V. et Pean P., *Une France sous influence*. Quand le Qatar fait de notre pays son terrain de jeu, Paris, Fayard, 2011.

Richelieu A., "L'internationalisation des marques d'équipes de sport", in M. Desbordes et A. Richelieu (ed.), *Néo-marketing du sport. Regards croisés entre Europe et Amérique du Nord*, Bruxelles, De Boeck, 2011, pp. 25–42.

Yu C., "Athlete endorsement in the international sport industry: A case study of David Beckham", *International Journal of Sports Marketing and Sponsorship*, April 2005, 6(3), pp. 189–199.

Webography

http://fr.fifa.com/fifa-world-ranking/ranking-table/men/index.html – Données issues du classement mondial FIFA/Coca-Cola et paru dans fr.fifa.com le 9 avril 2015. Dernier accès le 16 avril 2015.

http://sport24.lefigaro.fr/le-scan-sport/business/2015/03/30/27004–20150330ARTFIG00086-des-places-a-2700-euros-pour-psg-barcelone.php – données extraites de l'article "Des places à 2 700 euros pour PSG-Barcelone" paru le 30 mars 2015 sur le site http://sport24.lefigaro.fr – Dernier accès le 16 avril 2015.

http://www.challenges.fr/sport/20150310.CHA3742/nasser-al-khelaifi-un-ambassadeur-bis-au-service-exclusif-du-qatar.html – Extrait de l'article intitulé "Le vrai visage de Nasser al-Khelaïfi, patron du PSG et ambassadeur bis du Qatar" écrit par Jérôme Lefilliâtre et paru dans challenges.fr le 12 mars 2015. Dernier accès le 15 avril 2015.

http://www.lequipe.fr/Football/Actualites/L-ambiance-aucune-influence/532296 – Extrait de l'article intitulé "L'ambiance n'a-t-elle aucune influence sur les résultats?" écrit par Yann Sternis et paru dans lequipe.fr le 30 janvier 2015. Dernier accès le 15 avril 2015.

http://www.lequipe.fr/Football/Actualites/Le-psg-assouplit-legerement-le-plan-leproux/543837 – Extrait de l'article intitulé "Le PSG assouplit légèrement le plan Leproux" et paru dans lequipe.fr le 19 mars 2015. Dernier accès le 22 mars 2015.

http://www.psg.fr/fr/Club/602002/Partenaires-et-Fournisseurs-Officiels – Données issues d'une page Internet parue sur psg.fr. Dernier accès le 4 mars 2015.

http://www.psgcommunity.fr – Dernier accès le 16 avril 2015.

http://www.psginsider.frhttps://www.facebook.com/PMUOnParie – Page Facebook de l'INSIDER le 16 avril 2015. Dernier accès le 16 avril 2015.

Studies, documents and press releases

Deloitte, *Commercial Breaks, Football Money League, Sport Business Group*, 2015, pp. 1–40.

France Football, Extrait de l'article intitulé, "PSG-Qatar l'histoire secrète du mariage", rédigé par Philippe Auclair et Éric Champel et paru dans France Football du 28 janvier 2015, p. 18.

Kurt Salmon, Sport Web Challenge 2014, regards a` 360° des acteurs du sport sur internet, 2014, pp. 1–52.
L'Équipe, Extrait de l'article intitulé "À la conquête du Web chinois", rédigé par Pierre-Étienne Minonzio et paru dans L'Équipe du 30 septembre 2013, p. 24.
L'Équipe, Extrait de l'article intitulé "Et si Ibra devenait encombrant?", rédigé par Renaud Bourel et Hervé Penot et paru dans *L'Équipe* du 17 mars 2015, p. 6.
L'Équipe, Extrait de l'article intitulé "PSG, des ambitions sans frontières", rédigé par Pierre-Etienne Minonzio et paru dans L'Équipe du 1er juillet 2013, p. 22.
LFP–UCPF–IPSOS, baromètre d'image des clubs professionnels de football, 2015.
Paris Saint-Germain, *Rapport d'activité 2013–2014*, 2014.
Repucom, Emerging Giants, 2005, p. 7.
Repucom, European Football Clubs Income Stream Report, 2014.

11

THE PARC MULTIFONCTIONNEL OLYMPIQUE LYONNAIS AND THE "GRAND STADE"

At the heart of the OL Groupe's marketing strategy

Nicolas Chanavat and Michel Desbordes

The professional Olympique Lyonnais (OL) club became an Anonymous Professional Sports League (a form of incorporation) in 2002, with a budget of 115 million euros, the third highest budget in Ligue 1 for the 2014–2015 season (Les Echos, 2014). Since 1999, the club has been owned by OL Groupe, a finance company specializing in sports management, owning various portions of capital in several business subsidiaries. This is a precursor model in France developed around five activity products: ticket sales, partnerships and advertising, marketing and television rights, products pertaining to the diversification of the brand, and player trading. In this context, the Olympique Lyonnais devised a structured strategy plan based on five approaches. As for other professional sports clubs, the principal objective of the club consists of increasingly satisfying its actual consumers (spectators and partners) while attracting new ones. However, one element differentiates Groupe OL: the mobilization of the marketing evolutions and technologies for revolutionizing consumption. In this perspective, it must be recognized that the multifunctional Olympique Lyonnais Park represents a unique project.

The OL Groupe represents the first and only French football club to construct a 100% private sports arena, to benefit from economic and operating profits. Imagined as a true "lieu de vie" (living space) at the heart of a multi-activity complex open 365 days a year, the "Grand Stade" hopes to combine comfort, interactivity, and security in the vision of facilitating exchange and conviviality for any type of event. These elements impart the club with a specific issue from the point of view of its development and marketing strategy.

Several semi-structured interviews constitute the framework of this chapter which concerns the marketing strategy adopted by the Olympique Lyonnais and its operationalization. These include, in particular, responding to the following questions: what are the strategic approaches and operational implementations for the OL Groupe? What about the modification of branding and the internationalization of the club? What is the role and social responsibility for the businesses regarding the development of the club? What is the true role of the women's branch in the global strategy of the OL Groupe? In what way does the group diversify itself? How does training factor into in OL's marketing logic? In what way do the Park and the "Grand Stade" projects impact the global strategy of developing the club? How does the OL envisage the marketing experience and the digitalization of client relations? Overall, our analysis provides evidence that OL Groupe's strategy and its marketing initiative constitute an innovative example; a benchmark in the context of both French and European professional football. Also, certain marketing aspects of the Parc Olympique Lyonnais and of the "Grand Stade" are the object of special attention.

Box 11.1 Prize lists and a brief history of the Olympique Lyonnais

If the OL was founded in 1950, it had to wait until 2002 before winning its first championship of France. In this way, the Olympique Lyonnais, for the greater part of its history, has been a "middle of the pack" club, without exceptional, athletic performance. The club reached its height during the 2000s, where its domination of French football permitted them to obtain a number of records. They won, for example, seven consecutive titles as champion of France. The OL represents today one of the most successful clubs in France and possesses one of the most decorated prize lists in 21st century French football: seven Champion of France titles, five Coupes de France, one Coupe de la Ligue and seven Champion League trophies.

Since the middle of the 2000s, the OL has proclaimed itself a pioneer in both French and European women's football. The female section holds one of the most decorated European prize lists: nine champion of France titles, five Coupes de France, two Champion League and one World Championship.

Sources: Qualitative interviews with Thierry Sauvage, general manager of the OL and Didier Kermarrec, director of development for the OL and the club website : http://www.olweb.fr. Last accessed on April 22nd, 2015.

Box 11.2 The personal information sheet for the Olympique Lyonnais

Name of the SASP president: Jean-Michel Aulas
Number of season ticket holders: 12,200
Number of fans on Facebook: close to 2 million (April 2015)
Average number of spectators per match: 34,414 (capacity of Gerland: 41,044)
Budget of the Club: 115 million euros
Total revenue from businesses: 120.5 million euros
Distribution of revenue: sponsoring/commercial (15.8%), marketing rights and television (46.6%), ticket office (10.8%), brand products (13.4%), trading of players (13.4%)
Name of partners in 2014: Adidas, Hyundai, Veolia, Oknoplast, Intermarché, Cegid, MDA, Renault Trucks, BeIN Sports, Orange

Sources: Qualitative interviews with Thierry Sauvage, general manager of the OL and Didier Kermarrec, director of development for the OL and the club website

What are the strategic approaches and operational implementations for the OL group?

OL Group, presided over by Jean-Michel Aulas, organized itself around the professional club of the Olympique Lyonnais. Generally, it relies on the training and the recruitment of elite players and the creation of projects permitting growth and the diversification of club revenues. Taking into account its specific features, five approaches are defined: the high level of the professional club, the anticipation of the development of women's football, the capitalization and the know-how of the OL Academy, the exemplary nature of the business' social responsibility and the innovation of the private Park and "Grand Stade" projects. Although several developmental approaches distinguish themselves, the Park and "Grand Stade" projects constitute the major, strategic approach and anchoring point to the entire marketing strategy of the Groupe and the club.

The OL group, a development of diversified activities

In 2014, a year before the opening of the "Grand Stade", OL Group planned to continue the reorganization of its income statements and to register itself with the orientations of the financial fair-play rule put in place by the UEFA. This concept is based, both middle and long term, on the two fundamental pillars that are the OL Academy and the Park and the "Grand Stade" projects, as well as on the sustainable development of women's football. The OL Groupe presents itself as "a leading player in the entertainment and media sectors in France". The development of diversified and innovative activities is engraved in the DNA of the OL brand. In this context, the strategic marketing vision put in place within the OL Groupe illustrates that clubs do not only address supporters exclusively interested by the sporting spectacle. From a marketing perspective, the club aims to access the largest number of consumer products and OL services, and in this way evolve its sales' offers by adapting itself to the expectations of consumers.

The organization and the activity of the OL brand

The OL Group is structured around the professional club of the OL presided over by Jean-Michel Aulas since 1987. Since its creation in 1999, the group based its development on a precursor model around five complementary activities: ticket sales, partners and advertising, marketing rights and television, products of diversification of the brand, and player trading. Overall, the Groupe is made up of a holding company, whose actions are rated on Euronext Paris (compartment C), as well as 10 operational subsidiaries (see Figure 11.1)

If the OL Groupe logically controls the SASP Olympique Lyonnais, which manages the football club's professional committee, it has developed additional, independent activities, offering new commercial opportunities: "OL Voyages" (vacations and moving), "OL Merchandising" (licensed merchandise), "OL Association" (football stadiums), "OL Restauration" (food service industry), M21 (advertising items), "OL Organisation" (events and seminars), "OL Images" (audiovisual production) and AMDL (medical academy). Even if these subsidiaries are primarily concerned with the sporting event, the media, and entertainment, they are also part of complementary trades which generate additional revenue. Thus, the OL Groupe has built its strategy on an economic model aimed at acquiring its financial means through the development of the OL brand, and the diversification of both its activities and revenues. This unprecedented structure in French football since the 2000s has been dictated in large part by

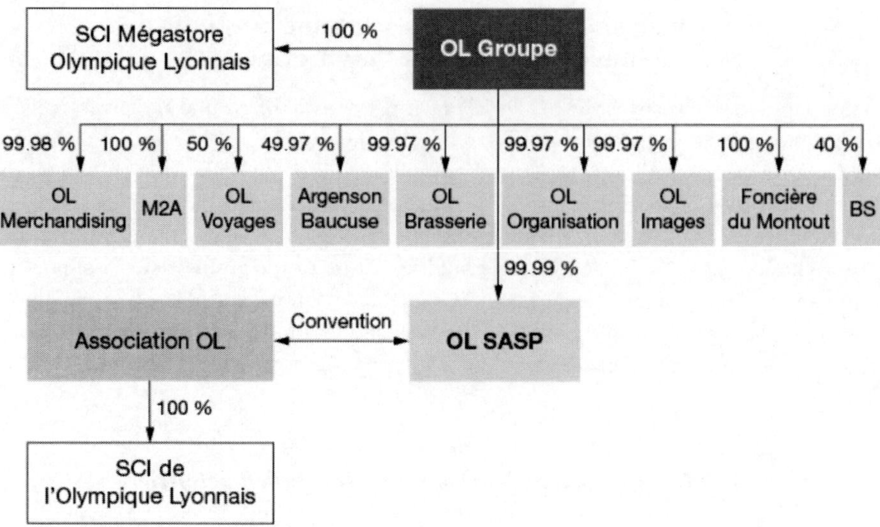

Figure 11.1 Organization of Groupe OL on June 30, 2013 (links between holding companies and subsidiaries)

Source: Olympique Lyonnais, Document de référence, *OL Groupe, 2009–2010*, 2010, p. 15.

Box 11.3 "Foot: Pioneers of listing, the English clubs now shun the stock market"

First to enter the stock market, in the 1980s, 20 years before the Olympique Lyonnais, the English football clubs have experienced contrasting fortunes and some left the public market, being bought by foreign billionaires. Listed since 1983, Tottenham followed Sheffield United, then Sunderland and Leeds United in 1989, before a gust of inductions in the middle of the 1990s was triggered by a lucrative agreement on the rights of television retransmission with the BSkyB television package. Within years, Manchester United, Chelsea, Arsenal, and Newcastle came to fill the ranks, while abroad, certain Italian and Turkish clubs, along with the Ajax of Amsterdam and the Bourussia Dortmund (Germany), followed suit. Created in 1992, the DJ Stoxx Football Index has in this way included up to 33 clubs from 17 different countries (23 today). But its performances have proved to be deceiving, with incessant fluctuation and a lower profitability than the market. "While the pretext for the IPO has often been the construction of a new stadium or a shopping center, English clubs have mostly used their stock income to recruit new players," which expands their massive salaries as explained by the economist Michel Aglietta in 2008. In the Review of Economic Policy (*Revue d'économie politique),* he additionally deplores the difficulty to determine the "fundamental value", of these companies, who "fluctuate with the sports results, the form and the moods of the players, their relation with the coach and with the president." After the effervescence of the 1990s, the trend was reversed when certain stars of the Premier League passed into the hands of foreign investors, like Chelsea, bought in 2003 by the Russian, Roman Abramovitch, and then Manchester United, taken again in 2005 by the American Malcolm Glazer. Summarizing this movement alone, Manchester City, went public in 1995, was released in 2007 after its acquisition by the former Thai Prime Minister, Thaksin Shinawatra, before the latter resold the club in 2008 to Sheikh Mansour, a member of the ruling family of Abu Dhabi, which multiplies players' purchases. After the withdrawal in late 2009, Birmingham City, which was taken over by the Hong Kong millionaire Carson Yeung, does not remain a popular club on the main market of the London Stock Exchange, and those who remained on the stock exchange are now relegated to a market dedicated to SMEs, such as the Alternative Investment Market. Among the few remaining clubs, there are clubs with very variable size, elite clubs like Arsenal or Tottenham, and more obscure formations such as Watford. Although the English example calms the stock exchange fervor in Europe, where its latest major introduction is with the French club, Olympique Lyonnais in February 2007, the stock exchange appeals from now on to other continents; following the Accra Hearts of Oak, champion of Ghana, which entered the stock market in May 2010. Nonetheless, for Michel Aglietta, football remains "structurally" problematic for an investor: faulty management, "absence of financial supervision" by the UEFA, exorbitant salaries and "the proliferation of intermediaries unregulated and penetrated by the mafias".

Source: http://www.lepoint.fr/sport/foot-pionniers-de-la-cotation-les-clubs-anglais-boudent-desormais-la-bourse-03-02-2011-135269_26.php – Article titled "Foot: pionniers de la cotation, les clubs anglais boudent désormais la Bourse", published in lepoint.fr on February 3, 2011. Last accessed April 22, 2015.

the desire to access public savings (the possibility of being publicly traded). This motivation has been guided 100% by the necessity to finance one stadium. But the debt capacity has been insufficient, given the group's equity. Therefore, they had to consult the constitution of the OL Groupe which could be subject to an IPO, contrary to a "classic" football club in France. This introduction took place in 2007, more than 30 years after the English clubs. Although this stock market listing is still controversial since no European club as a whole has managed to keep its price of introduction, football structurally being in deficit, it constitutes the only path for president Jean-Michel Aulas. Globally, the stock market listing allowed for the raising of funds needed for the construction of the club's new stadium. In any case, no matter what the cause, the arrival of the presidency of Jean-Michel Aulas allowed the club to experience a major economic and marketing leap forward.

Jean-Michel Aulas, a pioneer of sportainment and social networks?

The notion of *sportainment*, a contraction of sport and entertainment, symbolizes the marriage between the sport, the spectacle, and the money. This trilogy climaxed in the advent of sport-spectacle and of sport business in the perspective of maximizing the experiences of consumers of the sporting event. We speak thus of the fan experience. If the sports competition constitutes the DNA of the event, the fan is located at the center of these concerns, which has consequences in terms of interactivity, activation, or animation. This approach seems to be in tune with the vision of professional sports in which Jean-Michel Aulas immediately subscribed from the beginning of his presidency. Beginning in 1987, the Gerland Stadium was temporarily equipped with a giant screen and fireworks for the whole season. "Revolutionary measures" in the world of football from the end of the 1980s gave way to, little by little, a fierce determination, from the part of its sportainment precursor in France, to be able to exploit its own spectacle. The idea of the creation of a private stadium has progressively grown in the spirit of Jean-Michel Aulas, which illustrates the concept of sportainment. In 2007, he subsequently launched the project "OL Land", which should be finished sometime during the 2015–2016 season with the construction of a new generation stadium, which will include recreation centers, business centers, restaurants and hotels, etc.

On April 29, 2009, Jean-Michel Aulas was named the most striking leader in French sports in the 2000s in receiving the award of "Sport Business Personality of the Decade 1998–2008" ("Personnalité Sport Business de la décennie 1998–2008"). Beginning with the launch in 1987 of his plan "OL Europe" he promised to make the OL a European club in the span of 4 years. Provided with a budget of around 17 million francs (2.5 million euros) for the 1987–1988 season, the club professionalized itself rapidly, notably in the manner of marketing (François and Bayle, 2014, pp. 359–376). Jean-Michel Aulas appeared to have a precise idea of the organization and management of a club that he seemed to have always considered, in a pragmatic way, under the entrepreneurial prism:

> For me, a football club is a business in which there is an industrial part: the structure which manages the footballers, with, on one side, the training center, where one produces the footballers, and, on another side, the professional team, which "produces" the results. At the head of this training center, there must be an engineer, the Technical Manager, who is the trainer. This industrial tool will allow for the construction of an economic model, founded on the ability to a exploit a brand, to negotiate the rights of television, to a generate licensed products.
>
> *(cited by François and Bayle, 2014, p. 362)*

Also, if Twitter seems to have become the preferred method of communication for numerous athletes, it is also used by certain leaders, such as Jean-Michel Aulas, who had as many as 188,000 followers in April 2015.

The performance of the professional team, showcase of the OL brand

The first strategic approach defined by the OL Group consists of making the professional team's performance a genuine showcase of the club-brand. Under the marketing angle, this approach is based on two major issues. On one hand, it is about internationalizing the team with a view to promote the OL brand. On the other hand, it is about reinforcing the modification processes of the club's brand image through advocating more for "family values, solidarity and the youth".

An internationalisation of the club-brand

It should be noted that the club appears to have a longevity and regular sporting performances compared to some major foreign clubs (Real Madrid, Arsenal, or Manchester United) to the extent that the OL club's flag participates regularly in the European games. Since 1997–1998, the club has participated in its 18th season of the Europe Cup ("Coupe d'Europe"), including 12 consecutive Champions League, the most prestigious of continental competitions. OL Groupe is the French club that has played the most European matches. They total 212 (107 wins) since its first march against the Italian club, Inter Milan, on December 10, 1958. From an international perspective, after having been a part of G14, an organization of the most important clubs of Europe, until its dissolution in 2008, the OL Groupe is one of the founders of the European Association of Clubs (European Club Association). Would the OL therefore be an "international club"?

The globalization of clubs, and more generally of the sport, can essentially be explained for three reasons: the economic necessity, the new businesses opportunities, and the transformation of the sport (Richelieu, 2011). In this way, "the teams and the sporting events are in competition with a series of other entertainment options for capturing the discretionary dollar or the euro of the consumers" (Richelieu, 2011, p. 26). Although this competition initially took place at the local level, it has become international, particularly through the means of new technologies (television, satellite, Internet, etc.). To respond to a domestic market, which is reaching saturation, the steps towards globalizing the club-brand seems the most obvious approach for sports structures with strong reputation or those evolving in high-profile leagues. One such approach targets a triple objective: strategic, economic, and media-friendly.

Overall, the club has turned itself strategically towards the rest of the world for about the past 15 years. This is reflected by its international team's strong overseas presence and the coming together of international sport structures and partners. If several French clubs had this drive, a true approach of globalization of the brand would have to be integrated, like the strategy of the OL.[1] For Thierry Sauvage, the Technical Director of the OL: "The internationalization of the club does not date from yesterday. The OL has also innovated on these questions." The OL is a club which has exported itself for years. "The long trips are a part of the club's development program," explains Jean-Michel Aulas. One observes that the Lyonnaise teams multiplied the number of these long trips after the club became a real business. The tour to the island of Maurice in May 1998, which was done to formalize the signature of Vikash Dhorasoo, appears as the first of a long series. In May 2000, "The Sonny Anderson generation" took its residence in Guadeloupe. It was a sign of the club's international marketing development. It seems that the participation at the Peace Cup organized in South Korea in 2003 (finalist), 2004 (finalist), and 2007 (winner) revealed itself to be a trigger/catalyst for the internationalization of the club-brand. This idea was shared by Thierry Sauvage: "This international approach has been carefully considered. The professional team's participants at the Peace Cup, since 2003, have proved themselves to be hardworking." The participation at this competition without a doubt favored the development and the reputation of the club-brand in Asia. The club has for a long time put in place initiatives overseas: the tour of Israel in 1977, the stay in Ivory Coast in 1968 on the occasion of the "Lyonnaise week of Abidjan," and these are a part of the real strategy at the end of the 1990s. Thanks to the titles obtained, the club has had multiple invitations which were entirely paid for by the host: the anniversary of Partizan Belgrade (Serbia) in 2008, the Sporting Lisbonne (Portugal) in 2010, the confrontation with the Juventus Turin (Italy) in the depths of Calabre (Italy) in 2010, or the celebration of the Genk title (Belgium) in 2010. The winter tours, in particular in North Africa (Tunisia or Morocco), also contributed to the internationalization of the club. To the extent that the professional team plays a crucial role in the globalization of the OL brand, other initiatives have ensued. In 2012, which marked the defining moment of the North American tour for the French Clubs, the Champions Trophy was won by Olympique Lyonnais, who faced Montpellier on the New York Red Bulls' field. The approach of the club is henceforth that of the Professional Football League, which supports the promotion and globalization of Ligue 1 by organizing the Trophy of the Champions abroad for several years (Canada, Tunisia, Morocco, the United Sates, Gabon, and China in 2014). In 2013, Lyonnais went again to New York to face Thierry Henry's Red Bulls.

Although the reputation of Ligue 1 still seems limited, several French clubs have international ambitions and wish to develop global partnerships and achieve closer relations with foreign clubs. The OL has demonstrated its know-how, regarding this matter, with its several strategic partnerships: partnerships with clubs from foreign countries (Brazil, Japan, the United Arab Emirates, etc.), partnerships in China (with the federation of football and the press group Titan), and partnerships with major, international sponsors (Adidas, Hyundai, etc.). The OL's relation with the South Korean conglomerate Hyundai demonstrates its international proactivity. This approach is also favored by the purchase of foreign players. In this sense, during the summer of 2014, the

South Korean attacker Kim Shin, for example, signed a contract with the OL. Moreover, for years, the professional team's friendly matches are exclusively played against foreign clubs. Thus, the OL was opposed to playing against the clubs of Debrecen VSC (Hungary), FC Copenhaguen (Denmark), Chakhtiar Donetsk (Ukraine), and FC Sevilla (Spain) during the 2014–2015 preseason. Finally, although the preseason tours and the friendly matches represent the establishment of contact for conquering the foreign market, the clubs still needed to develop successful digital strategies. OL accumulated in this way the greatest number of supporters in China via social networks. The official club website is accessible in several different languages: Korean, English, Mandarin, and also French. In effect, one of the keys to the club's marketing strategies concerns the understanding of the "satellite fan": the overseas spectator/supporter (Kerr and Gladden, 2008; Chanavat and Bodet, 2009). Given these characteristics, the club seems to have adopted a structured and high-performing globalization strategy inspired by the great European clubs like Real Madrid or Manchester United.

In the direction of "family values, solidarity and the youth"?

Today, branding constitutes the most important asset for a sports structure (Bauer, Sauer and Schmitt, 2005). In this way, every sports organization possesses a brand and it is in their interest to develop their brand equity through a marketing approach (Ferrand and Torrigiani, 2005). If for a long time the emphasis and resources of the club were centered around ticket sales, the emphasis today is focused on the brand. This is achieved by reinforcing the emotional connection between the club and the fans (Richelieu, 2011).

The professional team is young and carries significant capital gains. For the 2014–2015 season, a large majority of the professional team's players are from the training center. The Olympique Lyonnais has also extended the contracts of a number of new players formed by the club (Nabil Fekir, Rachid Ghezzal, Mathieu Gorgelin, Lucas Mocio, Mour Paye, Corentin Tolisso, Mohamed Yattara, or Mehdi Zeffane), thereby strengthening its strategic orientation, which privileges the players formed in its training center. Additionally, the performances of Nabil Fekir, OL's real discovery in the 2014–2015 season (voted highest prospect at the UNFP Trophies ceremony) or that of Alexandre Lacazette (voted best player), both symbolize the great quality of Lyonnaise's formation and training center.

In a strategic perspective, this tendency, which has been developed for several years, faces a double objective. It is, on one hand, to maximize the club's payroll and, on another hand, to participate in the construction of the club's new image. Overall, the studies show that the marketing dimension or the *business* of professional clubs reveal itself to be an important dimension of these clubs' brand equity for the supporters of French and English clubs (Bodet and Chanavat, 2010, pp. 55–66). In this context, although in the 2000s the image of the OL brand was characterized generally by the following semantic elements ("club business", "stock market listing", "money"), it seems to have modified itself in recent years. Paradoxically, the attachment to the general public with the regard to the OL brand seems to have also strengthened itself following the end of the club's reign as champion of France and the takeover of Paris Saint-Germain. Today, the capital's club assumes the role of a "rich club".

In any case, the arrangement of a new sports organization since the successive arrivals of Rémi Garde and Hubert Fournier to the technical direction of the professional team is not without consequences for the OL brand. In fact, these administrators, former players of the club, seem to personify the renewed success of the OL founded on the loyalty to the club's original values. If this is, of course, to reinforce the cohesion and the confidence within the professional group, there seems to exist a real impact on the brand's image regarding partnerships and the general public.

The development of women's football

Since the middle of the 2000s, OL has been a pioneer of both French and European women's football. In 2008, the male and female teams each won the league and the cup (*le doublé coupe-championnat*), a first in the history of French football. The development of women's football in this way is represented as the second strategic approach of the club. From a marketing perspective, the performances of the women's team intend to favor in particular the OL brand's globalization and reinforce the club's societal initiatives.

Concerning the branding plan, "The female section is an integral part of the DNA for the Olympique Lyonnais club," explains Thierry Sauvage. The budget allocated by the OL for women's football gives the female players a professional status. At the same time, its principal competitors remain reserved on this subject. Also, the women's team has earned itself a unique prize list in less than 10 years thanks to an ambitious development policy. This strong, "avant-garde" professionalization, based on the recruitment of the best French and foreign players, proved itself decisive as evidenced by the team's sporting results at the national and European levels. For both the club and French football as a whole, the success of the women's team is historic. In the words of Jean-Michel Aulas,

> The three titles in 2012 (Champion of France, Coupe de France, and the second consecutive title in the UEFA Champions League) along with the Champion of the World title won in Japan in November 2012, has rewarded their avant-garde policy which has been developed for some years.[2]

Our analysis is in agreement with François and Bayle (2014), which highlights that this success story allows OL to boast women's football as one of the five strategic approaches at the center of a project much more social than it was before. This is explained by a number of failures of the previously, more business-oriented project: the delayed "Grand Stade" project whose share price sharply decreased since its introduction, relative failures of the OL brand in terms of merchandising and licensing fee sales, and questionable player trading since the end of the 2000s. The logic of engaging in women's football can be generalized in four points, economic opportunity, new lines of communication, reinforcement of the brand's globalization approach, and the new strategic approach centered on a societal project. Indeed, it is also to strengthen the internationalization of the OL brand with the recruitment of foreign players (Japanese, Swedish, Norwegian, American, etc.). "Young Asian players also come to integrate the training center" concludes Thierry Sauvage. In essence, the development of marketing synergies proves itself interesting for the club. OL explains its engagement in the development of products for women's football through three key elements:

1. a growing popular appeal;
2. a breath of fresh air in French football;
3. the expression of its businesses' social responsibilities, in particular around the defense of equality.

In any case, if the development of women's sections can be considered a strategic approach of clubs, its impact remains relatively moderate.

Training, a prioritized strategic focus for the club

If training is presented as the third strategic focus of Groupe OL, it seems to more so situate itself at the heart of its strategy with a capitalization on the training center, whose more than 70% of potential capital gains from actual players on June 30, 2013, come directly from players formed in the OL Academy (compared to around 46% on June 30, 2012, and 38% on June 30, 2011). Through a marketing and communicational angle, the Olympique Lyonnais chose to bank on its training with the desire that its young players coming from the Academy symbolize the club's values and know-how and favor the development of the attachment to the club-brand. Historically at the heart of the club, the OL Academy turns itself towards the pursuit of excellence. This logic is evidenced by Jean-Michel Aulas:

> The training of players represents a strategy marked by a perpetual pursuit of excellence, for the guys and the girls alike, so that the Olympique Lyonnais stays one of the reference points in regards to not only training but also education.

This tendency is confirmed by the strong European position of the OL Academy, which remains in second place, after FC Barcelona and before Real Madrid. Indeed, it is the second European club in regards to its training as it supplies players currently developing in the first division of one of the five largest European champions of football (Italy, Spain, Germany, England, and France). A permanent recruiting ground of talent feeds these leagues. Karim Benzema, Hatem Ben Arfa, and Loïc Rémy (three players who have confirmed their potential by playing in their heyday against major European clubs for several years) are, for example, pure products of Lyonnaise training.

On June 11, 2014, the club was once again crowned the best youth club and first in training in the rankings Direction of National Training (DTN) of the French Federation of Football (FFF) by the National Commission Paritaire de la Convention Collective Nationale des Métiers du Football. This ranking seems to reward the policy carried out by the club in regards to training and reinforces the club in its strategic directions. The OL Academy shows itself to be in this way essential for the club's global strategy and the OL brand. On June 30, 2013, the market value of the players according to Transfermarkt, reevaluated for young players, still remains very high around 120 million euros, generating a net worth evaluated at 37.4 million euros (including contracts held for sale), for a potential capital gain in sales above 80 million euros. "The *savoir-faire* of the Academy also looks abroad, putting partnerships in motion, notably in China and in Lebanon," concludes Thierry Sauvage.

Modeled on Arsenal, which usually recruits young players whose talent is not known internationally, "the production plant" therefore represents a reliable and prioritized strategic focus for OL.

The social responsibility of the business, at the junction of the strategic axes of group OL

The concept of the business's social responsibility (RSE), developed throughout the second half of the 20th century in the United States, represents the implementation of the principles of sustainable development in businesses. The European Commission defines this concept as "The voluntary integration of social and environmental concerns with business operations and interaction with stakeholders" (European Commission, 2001, p. 7). Overall, the exercise of the RSE in professional clubs seems to have, above all else, assumed a cosmetic character marked by a weak integration of the RSE within their global strategy (Bayle, Chappelet, François and Maltese, 2011; François, 2012). However, the fourth strategic approach clearly defined by Groupe OL deals with the development of the business's social responsibility. It seems to be situated at the crossroads of the organization's strategic approaches. If OL presents several singularities, then it distinguishes itself from other French clubs given its strong societal dimension. Although these ethics seem to have been always figured among the pillars of the club, the Olympique Lyonnais chose to base its development strategy on the RSE. In other words, this strategy seems to have found itself at the heart of the Olympique Lyonnais strategy through its priority engagements in the domains of training, employability, support of amateur sports, health prevention, promotion of diversity, and responsible behavior. The club showcases itself as a precursor in this way. Didier Kermarrec, director of OL Development, emphasizes that "it is not an industry phenomenon. A significant structural investment has been made for years within the club regarding RSE. The Sports Initiative in the city, for example, has been put in place since 1999."

The societal engagement shared by male players, female players, the management, the supporters and the partnerships has materialized itself for several years through a dedicated structure: OL Foundation. It is the first of its genre in France. This entity was created in 2007 to accompany target projects and actions of general interest through three areas of intervention: integration through the sport, education and help for sick and hospitalized people. This showcases that the creation of this organization came in continuation of the driving sponsorship policy established by Olympique Lyonnais for several years and partnerships arranged with associations who possess the legitimacy and the competence for carrying out projects of general interest such as "Sport dans la Ville" (Sports in the City), "Handicap International", "Docteur Clown" (Doctor Clown), "Huntington Avenir" (Huntington Future), "l'Asup Brésil" (Asup Brazil) or "Terr'Active" (Active Earth). This is for the foundation to grant them the financial means to promote these initiatives. The foundation's activities are essentially based on the mobilization and the involvement of male players and female players in partnerships to enhance and highlight the supported projects. In August, 2012, the foundation's business was extended for 3 years with the notable addition of three major partners "Sport dans la Ville" for the integration aspect, "Footvaleurs" (football values) for the educational aspect, and "le Centre Léon Bérard" as help for sick or hospitalized people. Bernard Lacombe, president of the OL Foundation, declares that, "The primary objective was to affirm the will of Olympique Lyonnais and to engage itself sustainably on social actions and devote significant financial resources to them" (OL Fondation, 2013, p. 7).

A symbol of the club's attachment to the values of respect and solidarity, the development of an authentic RSE policy whose direction was entrusted to an administrator of OL Groupe has been put in place since the 2012–2013 season. A committee as well as a CSR board of directors was created, and action plans were declined in each of its domains, with the arrangement of CSR referents within different Groupe services and subsidiaries, responsible for relaying this policy throughout the organization. Sidonie Mérieux, president of the Olympique Lyonnais CSR committee, emphasizes that,

> The activity developed by the OL Foundation is perfectly adequate with the CSR policy that we wish to deploy and which articulates itself around two fundamental strategies: pragmatism and efficacy. The desire for social impact is at the heart of its concerns and the partnerships with actors such *as Sport dans la Ville or the Centre Léon Bérard perfectly* reflect the role that we wish to take on for allowing these associations to develop their project. In the continuation of this policy which has been put in place for six years within the OL Foundation, we hope to construct a RSE strategy which will permit us to a have a more global approach and unite all of the club's components together around strong, shared values.
>
> *(OL Fondation, 2013, p. 4)*

Proof of the efficiency and media coverage of the club in this matter, OL Foundation was rewarded the Oscar of Sponsorship ("l'Oscar du Mécénat") on July 3rd, 2014 during the 29th Oscars Ceremony organized by l'ADMICAL (Association for the development of industrial and commercial sponsorship). This reward confirmed the dynamic which the Olympique Lyonnais has been engaged for 10 years and constitutes a stage of RSE construction which will be reinforced by the Cité de l'Innovation Sociale of the "Grand Stade". The reward exemplified the business's societal impact on its territory/area. This is clear evidence that the club has proved itself a precursor regarding CSR and its new initiatives should see the light of day with the "Grand Stade" project. "We are working on the creation of a home employment, an unprecedented initiative for a professional football club," declares Thierry Sauvage. This would be to "conceive and to develop individualized, accompaniment programs and to re-classify unemployed people for promoting the development of jobs and business creation," he stated.

Overall, the initiatives imagined by OL regarding CSR seem to target a triple objective: legitimize OL's entrepreneurial activities within its local environment, show citizen engagement in the eyes of public authorities in a perspective of medium term (issues related to the construction of the "Grand Stade"), and rationalize the social policy around a limited spectrum of themes (François, 2012). While, initially, the idea to be open to the community was the fruit of a social sensibility of the leaders, the integration of the RSE as a pillar of club development seems to come mainly from external factors. Copied from either the classic business sector or inspired from major European clubs, the social actions arranged by OL allow it to face external pressures from the club environment. There is clear evidence that, even if the foundation and the CSR committee do not have ambition to be marketing tools, the societal initiatives carried out by the club seem to favor the club's brand-equity. François (2012) highlights that it is especially true that OL could be challenged in its local environment, taking into account the essence of its business, professional football, described by a part of society. Finally, it should be emphasized that this RSE strategy is linked to relationships developed with local authorities. Typically, the Olympique Lyonnais Parc and the "Grand Stade" would never have seen the light of a day without public institutions. It appears, thus, logical to "give back to community" through the lens of an CSR policy.

The "Parc Olympique Lyonnais" and the "Grand Stade", central pillars to the marketing strategy

The "Parc Olympique Lyonnais" and the "Grand Stade" projects constitute OL Group's central and fundamental strategic approaches. In a marketing plan, this complex wishes to get ahead of the needs of customers by offering them optimal conditions at the spectacle. Globally, the club wants to make the stadium a communal space where the public can gather for the general public as much as for *business*. The added values of the new sports arena are comfort, interactivity, and security, which aims to facilitate the exchange and conviviality for all types of spectacles. Serving as more than a stadium, the innovative complex wants to become a space of exchange and socializing. It has as its goal to reunite teams and facilities allowing multiple activities. This place of exchange mobilizes the marketing evolutions and technologies for "revolutionizing" consumption.

A multi-activity complex for responding to the needs of all

It must be recognized that the "Parc Olympique Lyonnais" and the "Grand Stade" represent a unique project. Imagined as a place of life, this multifunctional complex open all year round combines the centers of training and professional football, hotels, office buildings, day care centers, a medical center, reception rooms, and amphitheaters of the "Grand Stade" (cf. frame 14.4). It is a modern and unique complex which combines events dealing with sports, culture, leisure, business, entertainment, relaxation, and spectacle. The slogan, "Le Parc Olympique Lyonnais, for all, all year" visible on the club's website,[3] effectively translates the general idea of the new complex. Outside of football matches, consumers can utilize this multi-activity park throughout the year:

> On the inside of the stadium, there will be 3,000 m² of office space for OL. On the outside, there will be a youth center, hotels and offices for outside companies. It is a park of 44 hectares, which we wish to create daily activities. The objective is that people from the urban area can walk it, with restaurants, shops, the museum, and a bicycle path. We want to create a social and economic activity every day. Xavier Pierrot, Stadium Manager of the OL.[4]

Regarding marketing strategy, this ensemble responds to the needs of different public goals: families, supporters and economic partnerships. Indeed, these various activities, designed for supporters on match days and the overall public all year round, will also be available to companies as part of incentive events, seminars, etc. Overall, if the complex was designed to respond to the different consumer needs, it was also desired to be a response to the needs of businesses with la Cité des Entreprises (the City of Enterprise) and incentives. The Olympique Lyonnais offers an innovative partnership. It allows to associate businesses with one of the biggest "Leisure-sports-spectacles" projects in Europe, to benefit from a strong visibility and to be a part of new partnership models.

The "Grand Stade" will possess several components: the headquarters of the OL Groupe, space for restaurants, innovative retail spaces, a museum, etc. In this way, the club hopes to offer a unique shopping experience to its customers. The site of the Mega Store will combine the best of OL and Adidas: 730 m² dedicated to the latest trends, technological advice, animations, and the latest innovation. A living center, open all year round, social places (themed bars), and *entertainment* (game space) associated with the OL store, will notably enliven the stadium before matches.

As for the museum, modeled on either Real Madrid, Manchester United, or Bayern Munich, it hopes to assemble collections which recount the history of the club, as well as its present and future ambitions. The "OL Museum" will not be a simple conservatory of the club's history. Rather, its mission is to highlight the practice of sport though discovering the sports excellence of the region through exhibitions. "In the unique setting of the Park and the 'Grand Stade', the

Figure 11.2 The multi-activity complex of the Parc Olympique Lyonnais and the "Grand Stade"

Source: website of the club: http://www.olweb.fr. – Last accessed on August 13, 2014.

museum's objective is to have people discover the history of the OL, from its creation in 1950 to nowadays," declares Jean-Claude Jouanno, president of the Steering committee (COPL) for the museum and the stadium.[5]

> The museum articulates itself around large themes: 1) The spirit of the Olympique Lyonnais; 2) The prize list; 3) The club's big names; 4) From Gerland Stadium to the "Grand Stade"; 5) Innovation and football.
>
> *(OL Museum, 2014, p. 3)*

Finally, a City of teaching and assistance in job creation (CENACLE) will have an integral part in the project of the Park and the "Grand Stade". This project places itself in an innovative approach, between the non-profit sector and the for-profit sectors, which combine the sharing of human resources and necessary finances to the sustainability and development of the link between social and professional. CENACLE's objective is to support and guide the carrying out of projects of non-profits having an economic, social and socially unifying impact.

A new generation stadium for a new economic model

Jean-Michel Aulas made accessibility to his team's stadium the base for the new economic model to which he aspires. He explains,

> Arsenal did it in London with Emirates Stadium, Bayern did it in Munich with Allianz Arena. Copenhagen has also done it with Parken Sport. Bayern's example shows that a club can pay off the cost of its stadium in close to ten years, and ultimately it will generate revenue for the club owner. . . . Me, I am an entrepreneur, I am willing to take risks in which OL will be able to gain back 100% of its resources. Lyon is the second biggest metropolis in France and we are the premiere French club in the European Top 20. And in the Top 20, there are only two clubs that do not own their stadium.[6]

Indeed, compared to other clubs such as Arsenal FC (Emirates Stadium) or Bayern Munich (Allianz Arena), OL decided to base its future development on a Grand Stadium. Despite the renovations started for the 1998 World Cup, Jean-Michel Aulas judged Gerland Stadium, constructed in 1926, dilapidated and too small (40,000 seats). The first archives making mention of a new stadium project in OL's internal documents date back to 2004 (L'Équipe, 28 mars 2013, p. 6).

The Parc Olympique Lyonnaise is based on an innovative economic model. If clubs have equipped themselves with new sports installations, Olympique Lyonnais represents the first, and to this day, the only French football club to construct a 100% private stadium to benefit from the economic and operating profits. OL's main objectives consists of becoming a popular meeting place in France and Europe and to allow the group to become a major actor in sports and advertising with diverse events and a varying schedule all year round.

The finalization of financing the "Grand Stade" throughout the summer of 2013, for a total amount of 405 million euros, enabled the start of construction work in July 2013 with an objective to finish it by the 2015–2016 season. The total project expenses include the cost of construction, the project management fees, land acquisition, development, education, fees, and financing costs. This complex, following the example of other modern stadiums located in major European cities, is expected to generate new growth and sustainability of the OL

Groupe revenues, with an additional annual revenue target of at least 70 million euros at least 5 years after the opening of the stadium. This complex therefore possesses a strong economic ambition and seems to pursue an economically responsible approach. At the time, it is pursuing a management strategy of territory and economic development of the region. Indeed, if the "Grand Stade" is supposed to yield a profit for the club, the entire arena can also have a real impact on the whole Lyonnaise urban population. Jean-Michel Aulas (Olympique Lyonnais, 2012, p. 2) declares,

> The construction of the "Grand Stade", which aims to be a benchmark in sustainable development, prolongs the Group's strategy in this area and contributes to the development of Grand Lyon and East Lyon therefore making Lyon the grand European metropolis it claims to be.

This large metropolitan structure at the forefront of innovation allows Lyon to host the largest events of 2016 European Championship, for which they are a candidate to host an opening match and a semifinal. If this project reflects the desire of the club to innovate and develop new economic revenues, it is also an answer to the necessity for the French sport, to equip itself with modern sport structures responding to the needs of consumers regarding accessibility, capacity, and quality of reception. Within the construction of this marketing strategy, the OL Group has with this space a particular asset: its capacity to propose an innovative offer adapted to the needs of actors comprising its economic and institutional environment.

We have not here uniquely chosen prestigious and flagship stadiums: the last two stadiums from Table 11.1 show that one can have quality enclosures for a reasonable cost.

The first section served to study the club's strategic plan based upon five approaches: the professional football team's high ranking, the anticipation which came with the development of women's football, the capitalization on the OL Academy's know-how, the exemplary nature of the business social responsibility, and the innovation of the Park and "Grand Stade" private projects. While certain marketing aspects have been addressed, two specific operational ranges of the club's marketing strategy are the subject of the second section. Other activities could have been studied.

Table 11.1 Characteristics of some major European stadiums

Stadium	*Residing Club*	*Year of Commissioning*	*Capacity*	*Number of VIP Seats*	*% VIP Seats/Total*	*Overall Cost (in euros)*	*Cost of Construction per Seat (in euros)*
Wembley Stadium	English football team	2007	90,000	17,000	20.7%	1.082 billion	12,027
Stade de France	France football team France XV rugby team	1998	81,338	8,100	10%	364 million	4,475
Emirates Stadium	Arsenal FC	2007	60,000	9,240	15.4%	557 million	9,216
Stade Cornella-El-Pratt	Espanyol of Barcelona	2009	40,500	2,500	6.1%	65 million	1,604
Commerzbank Arena	Eintracht Francfort	2006	51,500	3,500	6.8%	126 million	2,446

Operational ranges of the marketing and commercial strategy

Starting from his assumption of power in 1987, Jean-Michel Auras has professionalized the marketing and commercial aspects of the club. Although many human resources are now working on these questions, given the multitude of activities and entities that compose the OL Groupe, the strengthening of marketing initiatives prove itself necessary to the development of the club, specifically in the perspective of the Park and "Grand Stade" projects. Two directions can illustrate the singular marketing operationalization put in place by the club. The first has to do with the diversification of OL products. The development of experiential marketing and the digitalization of client relations is the subject of the second.

The extension of the OL brand, a major characteristic of the OL Groupe

For a professional sports structure like OL, the extension of the brand consists of reducing financial incertitude through engaging itself in atypical and innovative marketing logic. The concept of brand stretching or the extension of the brand started in the 1980s. It consists of an entity exploiting the power of its brand (reputation, image, effectiveness, etc.) acquired on the market to conquer new ones. In other words, it is meant to import a brand name known to consumers in a universe that is not originally theirs. The club extends the prestige associated with its name to new categories of products or services. In fact, facing an uninterrupted continuation of brands, it is proven that the consumer researches that which is familiar. And one finds the names which one recognizes. Thus, professional sports teams generally possess a very high rate of recognition. The motivation is often financially based to the extent that this strategy avoids the creation of a new brand, which is expensive in terms of marketing efforts.

A successful brand extension policy consists of legitimizing itself in the eyes of consumers. In this perspective, positioning itself in a connected universe can represent a sizable asset to the extent that the brand continues to address the same customer base and communicate through the same media. On the other hand, investing in a segment already disputed over while distancing oneself from its original domain doesn't always have an immediate effect. It's also about not letting one's guard down under the pretext that one will be carried by a strong brand. Overall, if the brand's extension strategy involves possessing a reputation already sufficiently established, its success is based primarily on three criteria: the new product or service should be in coherence with the brand's identity; the product should bring added value compared to the current competitors on the market; and the brand's central values should be legitimized and accepted within the new category of products or services. In the case of OL, if the stated goal consists of bringing supporters closer to the club, a brand's bad licensing policy or extension can "lead to situations of rejection and discontent on the part of the public and consumers" (Bouchet and Hillairet, 2009, p. 49). While there always exists the risk of brand dilution through multiplying the references in all directions, the peripheral revenues generated by OL's licensing demonstrate that a professional football club can generate additional economic revenue thanks to the power of its brand. In this way, OL, a club branded by excellence, has developed a multitude of activities outside football and outside sports, which has produced an extension of the target customer (cf. Table 11.2). In addition to the developed subsidiaries which concern various, diverse customers, the club commercializes licenses via OL Merchandising. The Lyonnais club has in this way multiplied the source of non-sport revenues and imagined an innovative sports merchandising strategy for a strategy of excessive diversification. The OL brand's extension has presented itself as the development of a range of products and services which are unique for a football club: OL Coffee, OL Champagne, OL Taxis, OL Gastronomy, OL Drinks, OL Haircut, OL Mobile by

Table 11.2 Activities and extensions of the Groupe OL brand

Name of the Entity	*Sector of Activity*	*Characteristics*	*Clients/References*
OL Images	TV channels and broadcasting	OLTV, programs fully dedicated to club life (nearly 1 million subscribers). A production structure performing many exclusive programs (films, documentaries, etc.).	TF1, Canal +, Adidas, L'Équipe TV, Pathé, EA Sports, Krys, Accor, TCL, Walibi, banque palatine, Lou Rugby.
OL Merchandising	Licensed products from the OL brand	Control of all of the activity from design to distribution. Sales promotion and corporate gifts.	Renault Trucks, Merial, Marchal, Toupargel, Stal, Veolia
M2A	Advertisement	Supporting clubs in custom sports merchandising (football, rugby, cycling). Support for companies' communication about sport.	Carrefour, BASF, Pathé, Société Générale, Standard de Liège, EA Sports.
OL Event/ Organisation	Organization, event planning, seminars et security	Support for logistics and security events, entertainment and shows. Ticket management. Seminar organization.	OL
Stages OL	Football training camps	Organizing football camps during the school holidays at two sites: Tola Vologe and Hauteville.	Children, girls or boys. Experts courses (8-/11-year-olds). Leisure courses (10-/17-years-old).
OL Voyages	Travel and business travel organization	Answer all the needs and choices of travel, business travel, holidays for companies and for individuals.	ASVEL, Lou Rugby, FFVB, Clermont Foot Auvergne, RCF, DRAC Rhône-Alpes, fédération française de Taekwondo.
OL Restauration	Restauration	Association to renowned groups to create places of conviviality and hospitality. The Argenson at Gerland. OL Brasserie, at the Saint-Exupéry airport.	Large public, companies, and individuals
FIFA Medical Center	Health	Innovative structure recognized for the quality of medical experts and researchers and associates, FIFA's label of excellence for the Medical Centre	Players

Source: Olympique Lyonnais (2012).

Orange, etc. The club has even developed licenses with beauty salons for men and in the domain of food products such as Saint-Marcellin cheese, dumplings, or fresh pasta. Other innovative products, such as strings OL were also sold by the club. In any event, if a brand's extension is more likely to be successful when it concerns products and services close to the initial sector, OL group has invested in new territories and taken advantage of its brand's power in diversified business sectors. If this approach is not without risk of brand dilution, it also allows entering new markets located outside its core business. Generally, it is to insure the development of the Group by enhancing the club's brand equity and generating new revenues which are necessary for the club's development. To conclude this point, while it seems as if the creation of the holding and development of various activities were intended to make money, this plan has also proved the Group's solidity, with regard to financial markets gaining access to the stock exchange listing in 2007, and successfully completing the Park and "Grand Stade" projects.

Towards a development of experiential marketing and the digitalization of client relations

"Experiential marketing is everywhere" (Schmitt, 1999, p. 53). For nearly 30 years, experiential marketing has represented an innovative approach for businesses and brands in the perspective of responding to the needs of consumers, creating and maintaining a competitive advantage (Caru and Cova, 2006; Tynan and Mckechnie, 2009, pp. 501–517). Sports clubs are no exceptions. However, if the services play an increasingly important role in the modern sports industry, there are few studies on the impact of experiential marketing on the behavior of the sports spectator.

The stadium is considered as a profit center in its own right in the economic and marketing development of a club. It's about making the infrastructure evolve to place the sports spectator at the heart of the club. This connected stadium project raises several challenges: bringing (back) the public to the stadium, generating supplementary revenues, applying new technologies to the world of sports, and bringing to life an enriched experience to consumers. Overall, if the connected arena should allow a fan to enjoy a rich experience with strong emotions, it should also guarantee both quality of information and comfort. Essentially, the stadium 2.0 aims at responding to the needs of sports spectators: interactivity before, during and after the event. Also, the OL's future stadium wishes to offer an experience to the spectators in proposing connected services. The last generation of Services 2.0, such as the delivery of food and drink orders to the spectator's seat, slow motion multi-cameras, social games and networks, paperless ticketing, cashless payments, or dynamic displays of sponsors express the will of the club. This is meant for the club to create a new stadium, at the cutting edge of technology, to the service of sports performance, adapted to the television spectacle, secured and automated while handling the flow of spectators achieved through the means of a modern ticket. This stadium contains numerous innovative concepts and tools, "365 days a year" suites and diverse partnerships. Overall, it is to offer a unique experience (promotions, photos, replays, interactive games, ticket office, live video, etc.) previously unseen to the consumers through offering them innovative, connected services: 25,000 simultaneous wi-fi connections, 300 connected IPTV screens,[7] 120 multi-platform access points, two giant screens, paperless ticketing, 350 connected and interactive points of sale, etc.

The digitalization of client relations for a club like OL seems to take into consideration the rapid evolution of fan needs. In this context, one can identify two principal issues: the desire for immediate gratification and the need for recognition. It's necessary for the club to make an effort to encourage this sentiment of the "individual consumer". In today's day and age, the spectator wants to have a privileged status. He wishes to have access to everything, everywhere, even in a stadium of 60,000 people. The advent of new technologies seems to have reinforced the desire for immediate gratification within the fan. In other words, he wants to benefit from the same services that he has access to at his house: access to slow motion replays, ability to order from his seat, access to statistics, access to additional content, etc., while being in the sports arena. Vincent-Baptiste Closon,[8] the OL marketing director declares

> Overall, the digital technology has an effect on the entire customer experience. From the spectator who is at their home and has the intention to buy a seat at the match to the fan that is in the stadium or the one who just left.

From the point of view of responding to the needs of the public, the club rose to the challenge of satisfying the desire for immediate gratification and accessibility. The digitalization of OL client relations seems in this way to take into consideration the rapid evolution of fan needs. In this manner, a "Grand Stade" spectator will begin the digital technology experience from the booking of his seat *via* the Internet. Paperless ticketing will allow the fan to follow on their smartphone the directions to their seat or parking spot through geolocation. The "Grand Stade" spectator will be able to see match statistics, relive the action in real time (thanks to the Stadium Vision[9] software program) from other perspectives, or vote for the player of the game. Geolocation will allow the public to quickly find an entrance into the stadium, to order a drink or a sandwich without leaving their seat, and to pick up their order to the closest refreshment area through paying with their smartphone.

In the same dynamic, the stadium must integrate nearly 300 screens, allowing fans to post messages on Facebook or Twitter, which are then displayed on large screens near the field. The stadium is also equipped with an adjustable press box with a minimum capacity of 200 posts, two studios for TV sets, giant screens measuring around 72m², etc. This living space, open all year round and every game day, has been designed to host seminars and conventions and will be equipped with hospitality structures offering 6,000 VIP seats, 900 of which are situated in 105 private boxes. Two "business clubs" with a capacity of 1,250 will be created. As mentioned previously, the "Grand Stade" will also house the 730m² OL store, the travel agency "OL Voyages", OL Organization, and the Group's commercial and marketing services. Xavier Pierrot assures,

> As for the stadium 2.0, we have two partnerships which are Orange and Cisco. In the future stadium, there will be 3G and 4G connections, yet also 25,000 simultaneous Wi-Fi connections, so that spectators can order from the refreshment area directly from their seat and view statistics or slow-motion replays on their smartphone.

Based on the assumption that "the consumer assumes power," businesses and notably professional clubs should adapt their organization. Indeed, consumers' new behaviors have changed the paradigm of customer relations. If France possesses a very good brand culture, this is to the detriment of a true culture of the client. Unsurprisingly, in the sector of professional sports and stadiums, the American model proves itself to be a precursor. "We have benchmarked American franchises in order to be efficient regarding customer relations in the perspective of the new complex," explains Thierry Sauvage. If OL is based on foreign experiences, its approach of digitalizing client relations seems to remain innovative in France and Europe.

Conclusion

This chapter's goal was not to offer an exhaustive compilation of the strategic objectives and their operational implementations, but to highlight the fundamental elements on the matter. Overall, the medium and long-term strategic objectives of the OL Group aim to pursue its development of products and services in order to respond to demand and to enhance the satisfaction of its actual consumers while attracting new ones. The OL Group has developed around five activities: ticketing, partnerships and advertising, marketing and television rights, products which diversify the brand, and player trading.

The club's strategy strives to reinforce its high level with the professional team, developing women's football, capitalizing on the know-how of the OL Academy, supporting the social responsibility of businesses and innovating with the Parc and "Grand Stade" projects. The first section analyzed this strategy's five approaches from a marketing perspective. It has proved that the creation of the complex is situated at the center of the Group's global marketing strategy and impacts its marketing logic. OL's future complex will offer an experience to the spectators through offering connected services. These latest generation 2.0 services express the club's desire to develop a stadium experience. Overall, it is meant to combine comfort, interactivity and security to facilitate exchange and conviviality for all types of spectacle.

Two marketing initiatives developed by the club were dealt with in the second section of the chapter. They truly symbolize OL Group's initiative since the end of the 1980s. The first dealt with the extension of the OL brand. The development of experiential marketing and the digitalization of client relations throughout the connected stadium are the subject of the second initiative. Other initiatives, only slightly or not addressed, prove themselves to be interesting in the view of achieving the club's objectives. Two examples allow us to illustrate our point. The first concerns the digital technology strategy developed outside the sports arena. In the image of the most powerful club brands, OL accumulates the greatest number of its supporters in China via social networks. Thus, the OL published on its Tencent Weibo account a greeting card in Mandarin for the Chinese New Year. This approach falls in line with the brand's globalization strategy previously dealt with. In fact, in regards to conquering the Chinese market, European clubs can no longer afford to tour preseason, which are only periodic encounters. They must develop genuine digital technology strategies. The club's official site can be accessed in several languages. In the same vein, the club has developed "SociOL Room". This digital technology activation involves strengthening fan engagement through social networks on the night of the match through offering exclusive content put forward by the community managers, supporters of the club, and guests of Hyundai (sponsor of OL) in order to discover what really goes on behind the scenes of the stadium and to share the inside experience with the community #teamOL. In addition, in April 2015, during the derby against Saint-Étienne, the faces of 12 Lyonnais fans appeared on the jerseys of OL players. As part of this operation, #Le12emeGone, the 12 winners were invited to experience the match in the stands of the Gerland stadium and received a collector's jersey of the player they supported during the match.[10]

The second initiative concerns the question of sponsoring. If the amount of partnerships represents a relatively important part of the club's global budget, the *naming* of the "Grand Stade" will constitute an element which can determine the success of OL's new economic model. If it possible to "rename" a preexisting facility, with the theory that it has been profoundly renovated, the amount of agreement will be generally lower (Bolotny and Gouze, 2008). The modernization of infrastructures and naming constitute essential levers for economic and sport competitiveness of French professional sport's structures. (Chanavat, Renaud and Desbordes, 2014, pp. 37–41). As a proof of its importance, the question of naming is managed directly by Jean-Michel Aulas. It should be noted that in addition to the stadium, the training center and the Parc will be subject to naming. Thus, in April 2015, the OL president confirmed that a naming contract will be drawn up for the future training center with the insurance company Groupama.[11]

No matter what, OL's global strategy and its marketing operationalization constitute an innovative example and a benchmark in the current context of French and European professional football, especially in the perspective of financial fair-play which should, according to Thierry Sauvage, "put the church back into the center of the village."

Notes

1 Interview conducted by Nicolas Chanavat on July 9, 2014, at the headquarters of OL.
2 Olympique Lyonnais, Plaquette OL Groupe, *Nous sommes OL Groupe*, 2012, p. 2.
3 http://www.olweb.fr/fr/club/grand-stade-fiche-descriptive-169.html – published on olweb.fr. Last accessed on April 22, 2015.

4 http://www.footmercato.net/ligue1/info-fm-plongee-dans-le-grand-stade-de-l-ol-ce-bijou-en-plein-chantier_125638 – Excerpt from the article titled "Plongée dans le Grand Stade de l'OL, ce bijou en plein chantier", published in FootMercato.net on March 3, 2014. Last accessed on April 22, 2015.
5 Interview conducted by Nicolas Chanavat on May 13, 2015, in the headquarters of the Départemental Olympique et Sportif du Rhône.
6 http://www.lesechos.fr/01/07/2013/LesEchos/21468-077-ECH_jean-michel-aulas——-le-football-francais-peut-entrer-dans-un-cercle-vertueux – htm – Excerpt from an interview of Jean-Michel Aulas titled "Le football français peut rentrer dans un cercle vertueux" publihsed in leschos.fr on July 1, 2013. Last accessed on April 22, 2015.
7 *Internet Protocol Television.*
8 http://www.lesechos.fr/thema/0203672437932-video-la-digitalisation-de-la-relation-client-vue-par-vincent-baptiste-closon-olympique-lyonnais-1028611.php – Excerpt from the interview of Vincent-Baptiste Closon titled "La digitalisation de la relation client vue par Vincent-Baptiste Closon – Olympique Lyonnais", published in leschos.fr on June 29, 2014. Last accessed on April 22, 2015.
9 Also used at the *Staples Center* in Los Angeles.
10 http://www.olweb.fr/fr/article/felicitations-aux-12-gagnants-le12emegone-67813.html – Excerpt from the article entitled "Ils auront leur selfie sur le maillot de l'OL pour le Derby!" published on olweb.fr on April 7, 2015. Last accessed on April 22, 2015.
11 OLTV, interview of Jean Michel Aulas, April 13, 2015 – olweb.fr. Last accessed on August 13, 2014.

Bibliography

Bauer H.H., Sauer N.E. et Schmitt P., "Customer-based brand equity in the team sport industry", *European Journal of Marketing*, 39, 5/6, 2005, pp. 496–513.

Bayle E., Chappelet J.-L., François A. et Maltese L., *Sport et RSE. Vers un management responsable?*, Bruxelles, De Boeck, 2011.

Bodet G. et Chanavat N., "Building global football brand equity: Lessons from the Chinese market", *Asia Pacific Journal of Marketing and Logistics*, 22(1), 2010, pp. 55–66.

Bolotny F. et Gouze G., "L'Exploitation des enceintes sportives, modèles économiques, optimisation commerciale et sécurité juridique", *Les Échos Études*, février 2008.

Bouchet P. et Hillairet D., *Les marques de sport – Approche stratégique et consommation sportive*, De Boeck, Brussels, Collection Management & Sport, 2009.

Caru A. et Cova B., "Expériences de consommations et marketing expérientiel", *Revue Française de Gestion*, 162, 2006, pp. 100–113.

Chanavat N. et Bodet G., "Experiential marketing in sport spectatorship services: A customer perspective", *European Sport Management Quarterly*, 14, 4, 2014, pp. 323–344.

Chanavat N. et Bodet G., "Sport branding strategy and internationalisation: A French perception of the 'Big Four' brands", *Qualitative Market Research: An International Journal*, 12, 4, 2009, pp. 460–481.

Chanavat N., Renaud M. et Desbordes M., "Naming et modularité: les clés de la réussite?", *Jurisport*, 142, 2014, pp. 37–41.

Ferrand A. et Torrigiani L., *Marketing of Olympic Sport Organisations*, Champaign, Human Kinetics, 2005.

François A., Les pratiques de RSE des clubs sportifs professionnels français. Vers un nouveau modèle de légitimation?, Thèse de doctorat, Université de Bourgogne, Dijon, 2012.

François A. et Bayle E., "Jean-Michel Aulas: un précurseur pragmatique", in E. Bayle (ed.), *Les grands dirigeants du sport*, Belgium, De Boeck, 2014, pp. 359–376.

Kerr A.K. et Gladden J.M., "Extending the understanding of professional team brand equity to the global marketplace", *International Journal of Sport Management and Marketing*, 3, 1/2, 2008, pp. 58–77.

Richelieu A., "La construction stratégique de la marque dans le monde du sport", in M. Desbordes et A. Richelieu (ed.), *Néo-marketing du sport. Regards croisés entre Europe et Amérique du Nord*, Bruxelles, De Boeck, 2011, pp. 11–24.

Schmitt B., "Experiential marketing", *Journal of Marketing Management*, 15(1–3), 1999, pp. 53–67. doi:10.1362/026725799784870496.

Tynan C. et Mckechnie S., "Experience marketing: A review and reassessment", *Journal of Marketing Management*, 25, 2009, pp. 501–517. doi:10.1362/026725709X46182.

Webography

http://blogs.lesechos.fr/echosdataviz/le-budget-previsionnel-2014–2015-de-la-ligue-1-a14925.html – Données issues de l'article "Le budget prévisionnel 2014–2015 de la Ligue 1", rédigé par Jean-Marie Colomb et paru dans le blogs.leschos.fr le 7 août 2014. Dernier accès le 22 avril 2015.

http://www.footmercato.net/ligue1/info-fm-plongee-dans-le-grand-stade-de-l-ol-ce-bijou-en-plein-chantier_125638 – Extrait de l'article intitulé "Plongée dans le Grand Stade de l'OL, ce bijou en plein chantier", rédigé par Jahed Mkhlouf et paru dans FootMercato.net le 3 mars 2014. Dernier accès le 22 avril 2015.

http://www.lepoint.fr/sport/foot-pionniers-de-la-cotation-les-clubs-anglais-boudent-desormais-la-bourse-03–02–2011–135269_26.php – Article intitulé "Foot: pionniers de la cotation, les clubs anglais boudent désormais la Bourse", paru dans lepoint.fr le 3 février 2011. Dernier accès le 22 avril 2015.

http://www.lesechos.fr/01/07/2013/LesEchos/21468–077-ECH_jean-michel-aulas-–-le-football-francais-peut-entrer-dans-un-cercle-vertueux – .ht – Extrait de l'interview de Jean-Michel Aulas intitulée "Le football français peut rentrer dans un cercle vertueux" réalisée par Romain Gueugneau et David Barroux et parue dans leschos.fr le 1er juillet 2013. Dernier accès le 22 avril 2015.

http://www.lesechos.fr/thema/0203672437932-video-la-digitalisation-de-la-relation-client-vue-par-vincent-baptiste-closon-olympique-lyonnais-1028611.php – Extrait de l'interview de Vincent-Baptiste Closon intitulée "La digitalisation de la relation client vue par Vincent-Baptiste Closon – Olympique Lyonnais" parue dans leschos.fr le 29 juin 2014. Dernier accès le 22 avril 2015.

http://www.olweb.fr/fr/article/felicitations-aux-12-gagnants-le12emegone-67813.html – Éléments issus de l'article intitulé "Ils auront leur selfie sur le maillot de l'OL pour le Derby !" paru sur olweb.fr le 7 avril 2015. Dernier accès le 22 avril 2015.

http://www.olweb.fr/fr/club/grand-stade-fiche-descriptive-169.html. – Titre d'une page Internet parue sur olweb.fr. Dernier accès le 22 avril 2015.

https://twitter.com/JM_Aulas – Tweet de Jean-Michel Aulas après la victoire de l'OL le 31 juillet 2014 face à Mlada Boleslav. Dernier accès le 22 avril 2015.

https://twitter.com/JM_Aulas – Tweet de Jean-Michel Aulas après le derby entre l'OL et l'AS Saint-Etienne (2–2) le 19 avril 2015. Dernier accès le 22 avril 2015.

Studies, documents, and press releases

Commission européenne, *Livre vert. Promouvoir un cadre européen pour la responsabilité sociale des entreprises*, 2001.

L'Équipe, Extrait de l'article intitulé "Le stade, son grand projet", rédigé par Vincent Duluc et paru dans *L'Équipe* du 28 mars, 2013, p. 6.

OL Fondation, Fondation d'entreprise, *Rapport annuel d'activité, 2012–2013*, 2013.

OL Museum, Projet OL Museum, Note de synthèse stratégique, Comité de Pilotage (COPIL), document non publié, 17 juin 2014, p. 3.

Olympique Lyonnais, Document de référence, *OL Groupe, 2009–2010*, 2010.

Olympique Lyonnais, Document de référence, *OL Groupe, 2012–2013*, 2013.

Olympique Lyonnais, Plaquette OL Groupe, *Nous sommes OL Groupe*, 2012.

Television

OLTV, interview with Jean-Michel Aulas, Monday, April 13, 2015.

12
THE "GREEN FANDOM"
At the heart of the marketing plan of the Association Sportive de Saint-Étienne

Nicolas Chanavat and Michel Desbordes[1]

The Association Sportive de Saint-Étienne (AS Saint-Étienne or ASSE) had the seventh-largest budget in Ligue 1 for the 2014–2015 season. In the season 2013–2014, the club got 60 million euros in revenue and spent about 70 million euros. The ASSE has a structural deficit. If the club is resigned to sell some of its best players every year to balance its books, its new marketing strategy aims to generate 10 million euros of revenue. Also, the club envisions a new economic model based on diversification of its revenues. The club foresees a strategy in line with its budget. After 5 years of outstanding athletic growth (from 17th to 4th place), only economic development seems to be able to guarantee the sustainability and maintain the ASSE at the European level (in the top five of Ligue 1). The strategic vision is to move from a "family" club to reach "regional/national" and to a backbone club to rest on a historical pedestal and of rich values specific to the ASSE.

In this context, the club aims for a threefold objective. First, it aims to give a European dimension to the ASSE. Second, it acts to unite and meet the expectations of large public target priorities (families and supporter groups), individuals (viewers, subscribers, friends of the non-local club) and economic partners. Finally, the idea is to use three levers of growth around the matches. Two strategic axes were determined to attain these goals. The first axis allows the establishment of a retention strategy aiming toward the different targets of the club. Strengthening the commitment to the ASSE brand and the "modernization" of the image of the club, in the view of giving it a European scope, constitutes the second strategic area of the club.

Rich from several competitive advantages, the club has a very powerful brand equity. But the ASSE suffers from a lack of economic means that hinders its growth. Yet, the club displays a willingness to innovate to find new sources of growth and develop its image. The "musée des Verts" that opened in December 2013 is a good example. Thus, since 2014, marketing constitutes a transversal department within the club. The fans are in the DNA of the ASSE and are at the center of its marketing plan. The choice of the slogan of the subscription campaign "our strength is you," attests to this.

Box 12.1 Charts and brief history of the Association Sportive de Saint-Étienne

The professional football club of the ASSE was founded in June 1933 by Pierre Guichard, CEO of Casino, within an industrial and working region. This is the French club that is the most successful in history, with 10 league titles in France, six victories in the French Cup, a League Cup and finally a Champions League. The golden age of the ASSE was mainly between 1964 and 1982 when, for almost 20 years, the club dominated the French football. At that time, the ASSE was chaired by the iconic Roger Rocher, pioneer of television broadcasting, innovative marketing and merchandising in French professional sports. Roger Rocher proves to be a builder for the professionalization of sport business in France, one of the precursors of the development of a real sports show business in France. The only club to wear the star symbol of 10 titles of champions of France, the ASSE is a popular professional sports entity with an exceptional potential audience, and it has a powerful brand. The good sports results of recent seasons coincide with the development of innovative marketing initiatives for the precursor club in this matter. Also, the ASSE is the first French football club to have founded a museum in 2013.

Source: Qualitative interview with Arnaud Jaouen, marketing director of the ASSE and website: http://www.asse.fr – Last accessed on April 25, 2015.

Box 12.2 Personal Information Sheet of the Association Sportive de Saint-Étienne

Name of the President of the Supervisory Board: Bernard Caiazzo
Name of the President of the Executive Board: Roland Romeyer
Number of subscribers: 18,023
Number of fans on Facebook: close to 600,000 (April 2015)
Average number of spectators per match: 32,000 (capacity of Geoffroy-Guichard: 42,000)
Budget of the club: 49 million euros
Total income from operations: 60 million euros
Distribution of revenue: sponsoring/advertising (14 million, 23.3%), TV rights (32.8 million, 54.7%), ticket sales (8.7 million, 14.5%), other products (4.5 million, 7.5%)
Names of partners in 2014: Adidas, Winamax, Crédit Agricole, Orange, Groupe Casino, Desjoyaux, St Once, Markal, Despi, Bewell Connect, Triangle Acting, BeIN Sports, Cigaverte

Source: qualitative interview with Arnaud Jaouen, marketing director of the ASSE.

With primary data, this chapter deals with the adopted marketing strategy of the club and its operationalization. Although the goals and strategic directions of the ASSE are examined, special attention is paid to the operationalization of marketing innovations that create value for the club: the member card, "le musée des Verts", "la Place Verte", the brand activations "money can't buy", "Le Chaudron Vert", "ASSE Cœur Vert", etc.

The strategic objectives and directions of the Association Sportive de Saint-Étienne

The ASSE aims principally for a threefold objective: to attain a European dimension, to integrate and respond to the expectations of priority targets (public, collective, individual and corporate) and operate three levers of growth around the games. Increasing the number of seats sold constitutes the first lever. This necessitates expanding the attendance to family and relatives. The club hopes to reach an attendance of 32,000 in 2015, 33,000 in 2016 and 34,500 in 2017. The second lever is aimed at increasing attendance at the stadium by encouraging a desire to "revisit". Finally, the lengthening of the time spent in the stadium or in the proximity and increasing the consumed leisure on the day of the game is the third lever. To achieve these objectives, two strategies, evoked in the introduction, emerge. They are found at the center of the club's new development strategy, mainly concerning its marketing strategy (AS Saint-Étienne, 2014).

For a marketing strategy integrated to the global strategy

In matters of finance, of transfer and of global development strategy, each French club functions in its own manner. While some clubs have the economic means to spend large sums of money on the transfer market, almost all clubs must organize differently. For the ASSE, the training, the salary cap and the trading of players proves to be necessary. Obviously, it seems that despite a limited budget, the club has the willingness to set up a transversal and innovative marketing strategy. Therefore, each developed activity responds to a marketing problem. In any event, there is a "real" marketing logic for the long-term. The ASSE marketing initiatives can generate additional revenues while respecting the image of the brand and the tradition of the club.

Organization, objectives, and global strategy and salary of the club

Pioneer in matters of television broadcasting, of innovative marketing and of merchandising in professional sports, Roger Rocher proves to be a builder for the professionalization of sport business in France. The professional structure of the club became "Société Anonyme Sportive Professionnelle" (French incorporation structure for sport organizations) in 2003. In 2006, Bernard Caiazzo is joined by Roland Romeyer, and they form between them a co-presidency. On January 27, 2010, as part of a revision of the club's organization chart, based on the German model, Bernard Caiazzo became president of the newly created Supervisory Board and Roland Romeyer president of the new Executive Board of which the functions are operational. If the organization of the two-headed presidency of the ASSE has been criticized in the past, it is proving very successful (with time). For several seasons, the club seems to constantly progress as well in the sporting plan as the economic. The definition of the missions and the complicity between Bernard Caiazzo and Roland Romeyer contribute a lot to this result. "President Romeyer has strong regional roots. He is present daily and has seen the club since his childhood," affirms Arnaud Jaouen.[2] On June 29, 2010, Dominique Rocheteau, iconic former player of the club in the 1970s, was considering taking the deputy chairman position of the Supervisory Board before taking the athletic coordinator position[3] in December 2011. The success of the organization of the ASSE seems to be based on the performance of the trio Caïazzo-Romeyer-Rocheteau that returns a very positive image full of seriousness, organization and reflection. The coach Christophe Galtier also represents one of the cornerstones of the club. Besides being a tactician, he is also a skillful communicator and leader of men. He is an open, honest and competent coach. He is in line with his players and in line with the values advocated by the club. By consequence, everthing is going well and the club's foundations are solid.

The fact of working for the long term, the fineness of the overall strategy as well as the diversity and complementarity of the profiles and skills of the leaders (former athlete, entrepreneur, etc.) appear to be an asset in regards to the economic and sporting success of the club. This direction symbolizes the wisdom more than the exuberance. It demonstrates that a club can be efficient without paying excessive salaries. Indeed, since the restructuring in 2010, the overall strategy of the club distinguishes itself notably by its singular policy based on the logic of the salary cap. This is an anti-deficit model based on a simple reasoning: it is not suitable to spend money that it does not have. Essentially, as in a conventional business, there are, for the players, a part of fixed salary and a variable portion based on sports results. The remarks of Roland Romeyer testify:

> As in businesses, the salesmen have a fixed income. The guy who works well, he earns more. We built our salary grid on this model. A fixed salary of 90,000 euros and a maximum of 40,000 euros in variable income. That way, I can look everyone in the eye, there is no difference in salary as there was before in the locker room. It creates jealousy, and that necessarily reflects on the results.[4]

The strategy rests furthermore on the formation of players, which is one of the club's pillars. "The integration of young players, trained at the club, within the professional group, is something vital for us," explains Dominique Rocheteau. Within 3 years, the idea would be to have 80% of the workforce resulting from the formation. It is for this reason that the club became in 2012 owner of the training center of the Etrat (6.2 million euros of acquisition and 3.8 million euros of renovation). The ASSE is preparing for the future by focusing on training instead of buying 10 million euros' players.

As mentioned previously, the club envisions a threefold objective. First, it acts to give a European dimension to the ASSE. For this, the strategic plan (2014–2016) of the club is clear. In sporting terms, it acts to pursue the current momentum in settling itself for the long-term in the "top five" of Ligue 1 and ensuring annual participation in the Europa League. With the economic plan, the club aspires for a strong growth in its turnover. So it comes to pass from 20 to 30 million euros within 3 years (also stated for the 2016–2017 season).[5] This growth should promote the preservation of its player capital and ensure its player sporting competitiveness. Second, it should unite and meet the expectations of priority targets. Finally, the idea is to use three levers of growth around the games. How? Two strategic directions were clearly highlighted by the club. The first direction is to develop a retention strategy by conquering all the targets. The strengthening of the commitment to the ASSE brand and the modernization of its image in the goal of giving it a European dimension constitute the second.

A changing economic model: the marketing of the athletic service

After 5 years of exceptional athletic growth (from 17th to 4th place), only the development of the club's financial resources seem to be able to guarantee its athletic sustainability. Also the club is envisioning a new economic model.

"If I spend 10 to 20 million, the club does not sell more players. The idea is to benefit from a more competitive team," explains Arnaud Jaouen.[6] Also the role of marketing within the club is to be able to generate additional revenues in line with the business strategy for having a competitive team over several years. Beyond the financial windfall from the anticipation of the call to offer the television rights, the club must multiply its sources of revenue. If this new deal increases the share of television rights for the clubs, it should not stop their approach in researching subordinate sources of revenue. Also, the club envisions 70 million euros of revenue, outside of player sales in 2016. "In this case, the club is no longer found in the obligation to sell players. If it succeeds, it will change the European competitiveness of the ASSE," says Bernard Caiazzo.[7] Therefore, marketing initiatives prove to be truly indispensable in regards to the sustainability of the club. And the marketing and economic performance should prevent the best players from being sold annually. It comes as a challenge for the club's marketing department that wants to serve the sporting unit. "The new stadium of 42,000 seats and all of our marketing initiatives, 'Le Chaudron Vert', merchandising, etc. should allow these 2 years to generate 10 million euros in additional revenue," concluded Arnaud Jaouen on this subject.

Although the Verts expanded their workforce every season, these operations occur generally at a lesser cost. For several years, the club remained true to this strategy. Thus, since the return of the ASSE in Ligue 1 (season 2004–2005), the balance of transferred players is positive. The club has spent 115.1 million euros to buy players and has had sales of 139.3 million euros, representing a profit of 24.2 million euros. Although *mercatos* 2004–2005 and 2009–2010 have proven unprofitable, since 2010–2011 the club is always beneficial. This period corresponds to the return of the club in the top 10, with the appointment of Dominique Rocheteau as vice president in 2010 and then sports advisor, and with the prolongation of the contract of Christophe Galtier. Since 2010, the ASSE bought players for 44.5 million euros, focusing on players in Ligue 1 such as Stéphane Ruffier, Romain Hamouma, Franck Tabanou or Benjamin Corgnet. Its budget is limited, and ASSE opts for player loans as during the 2013–2014 season with Joshua Guilavogui and Benoît Trémoulinas who could similarly get back into the race for the 2014 World Cup with the French National Football Team. The purchase of players in 2011–2012 (15.6 million euros) and in 2013–2014 (16.5 million euros) is financed through the sale of players. High performance in matters of trading players for several seasons, the club earned 81.8 million euros since 2010. Given a profit of 37.3 million euros including the sale of club-trained players to large European clubs: Kurt Zouma (Chelsea for 15 million euros), Joshua Guilavogui (Atlético Madrid for 10 million euros) and Faouzi Ghoulam (Naples for 5 million euros). Other players that went through the club were resold such as Pierre-Emerick Aubameyang (Borussia Dortmund for 13 million euros), Dimitri Payet (Lille for 9 million euros) and Blaise Matuidi (Paris Saint-Germain for 8 million euros). This strategy makes the ASSE one of the most successful French clubs with regard to trading players.

Overall, following the organization of a mega event like the World Cup of FIFA or the Euro of the UEFA, the affluence increases from 15% to 20% in the stadiums of the host country (Drut and Szymanski, 2014). Therefore, we can legitimately think that the Euro 2016 is going to promote the French clubs with a higher rate of stadium attendance. The chosen project for the renovation of the Geoffroy-Guichard stadium seems clearly beneficial in regards to the economic development of the ASSE. The cost of the work for the stadium, whose capacity can reach 42,000 seats, amounts to 71.8 million euros. The stadium has two bleachers with 8,000 seats each, or the largest in France. The stadium can accommodate new services, sports and cultural events (rugby, concerts, etc.) and in addition to the meetings, the lounges are capable of hosting forums, seminars, conferences, etc. The fact that the city of Saint-Étienne is hosting Euro 2016 could also allow the ASSE to attract new economic partners. The renovation of the stadium should allow the club to increase its revenues, particularly in sales of tickets, perfectly meet the EU strategy and must "initiate internationalization strategies", affirms Philippe Lyonnet, the communication director of the ASSE.[8]

If the club always had a direction for its communication, it is "really" with a marketing unit since the arrival of Arnaud Jaouen to the club in 2014. Although few human resources are working on these issues, the reinforcement of guidance marketing proves to be necessary to the development of the ASSE. "It acts to incorporate the various profit centers. So that they work together. The idea is to embed all future products," explains Arnaud Jaouen.[9] We acknowledge an expansion of marketing innovations integrated into the overall strategy of development of the club. "In every public project there is a marketing vision that allows progress on an internal matter requested by the presidents," he added.[10] In other words, each operationalization marketing refers to a marketing problem.

In this context, the event strategy of the club is closely linked to the marketing initiatives developed by the club. This does not require media buying. As Arnaud Jaouen explains,

> We developed the first museum for a French team: that created a buzz. It's the same for summer internships, the new hotel-restaurant "Le Chaudron-Vert", the new memberships, the initiatives of "ASSE Coeur-Vert" with Roland Romeyer who went to Paris by bicycle for the final of the Coupe de la ligue (League Cup) in 2013, or even with brand activations like "the 12th man".[11,12]

For marketing integrating the different profit centers of the club

It would be good to make a distinction between the sports and the marketing in a professional football club. The marketing cell of a club should be considered as a separate company. "It starts from the principle that we are a service company and that it is necessary to create products that correspond to the needs. The athlete is the icing on the cake. It is the shell of the ASSE but, as a marketer, the idea is to make the sport sometimes abstract," explains Arnaud Jaouen.[13] At the ASSE, the marketing division led by Arnaud Jaouen has a mission to develop together all the club's profit centers (excluding TV rights and sports cell), licensed merchandise, museum, ticket sales, sponsoring and advertising, "ASSE Cœur-Vert", "Chaudron-Vert" course, etc. In any case, the club promotes a multiplication of growth and advocates cross-marketing for the club's profit centers.

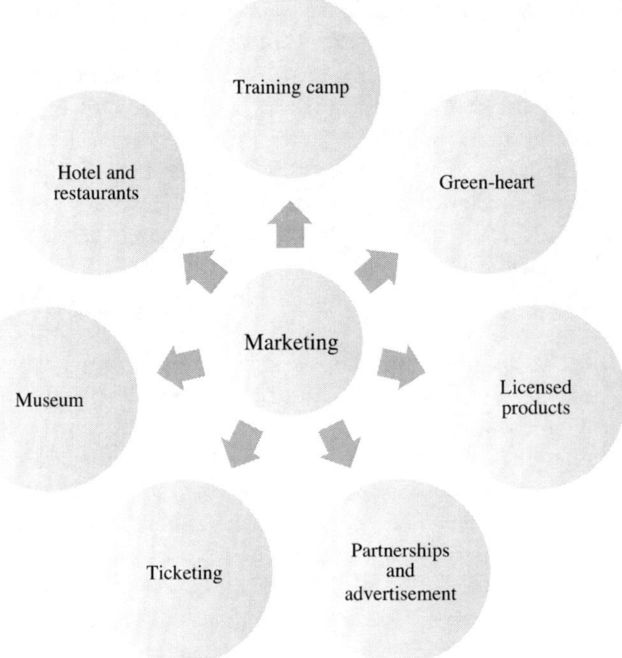

Figure 12.1 Cross-marketing for the profit centers of the ASSE

In order to "climb in power, a club must define itself in a true marketing sense", stresses Arnaud Jaouen.[14] One of the keys of success of the club's marketing initiatives seems to find itself in the union of different clusters. Also marketing is seen as a transversal department within the club. For this, it is also necessary to involve all the company employees to carry out this strategy. However, without paradox, when envisioning a new initiative, the marketing orientation "needs the point of view of the leadership, the president and the sports side on certain actions", continues Arnaud Jaouen.[15]

Overall, the question to ask is, "What is this going to generate for me in terms of additional revenue and how to sustain them?" explains Arnaud Jaouen. Professionalization and the development of the club's marketing require the rethinking of the organization and the structure, to make it a show, and to innovate as a goal to make a buzz and to be covered by the media. In summary, the key success factors of the marketing division of the ASSE are the establishment of a well-structured internal organization, the defining of a global vision for the medium- or long-term (and not a short-term vision), and the prioritization of actions. The fact of having a team permanently settled in the top rankings also promotes the construction of a strategic vision in the medium term and permits work on more expensive brand activation levels. For Arnaud Jaouen, "if everyone still has a lot of ideas, the implementation is another thing. We must find and implement a marketing device that is at the center of the business agenda," he concludes.[16]

The ASSE and the SportFive agency signed in July 2010 a long-term partnership agreement. Also the club has outsourced its marketing rights until 2023. This agency can prospect for all profit centers: museum, etc. About this partnership, Bernard Caiazzo says,

> The ASSE should be both a regional, national, and international club. SportFive is going to help the club grow while generating new resources, which will give the means of our ambitions. New partners will come to join the club in a win-win relationship.[17]

This contract covers the management of the integrity of all commercial rights of the club: sponsorship, public relations, advertising support, media support and events. The agency also brings its expertise to the club as part of the renovation project of the Geoffroy-Guichard stadium, the stadium hosting the Euro 2016. Overall, for a club, the role of a sports marketing agency like SportFive consists of finding new partners to retain the organization of the operations of public relations and events. SportFive holds the position as the European leader in the commercialization of sports marketing rights, including those of many football clubs. The agency has the objective to bring together right holders and advertisers and to provide them with expertise as well as the tools adapted to meet their specific needs in several areas:

- Marketing: communication strategies of the brand, product innovation, research of new visibility supports;
- Market research: media impact study, affinity study, general information on sponsorship and football;
- Development stadium/consulting: optimization of stadium space.

The tendency is to make "tailored" solutions to companies that each have different communication objectives. If the agency holds an expertise in matters of sports marketing, it possesses a sizeable customer base at the national level: Olympique Lyonnais, RC Lens, OGC Nice, etc. One can therefore legitimately pose the question whether the company is necessarily and primarily "to push" the ASSE close to advertisers. Moreover, the agencies are not always proposals. If the boards offer a plan of visibility and public relations, they should go further. The agencies (and therefore the clubs) have to propose to sponsors of brand activations that can "make a difference" and generate a return on investment on the brand in terms of reputation, image, attachment and sales. For Arnaud Jaouen, "This requires a product innovation, working on new concepts."[18]

Developing loyalty and conquering the different targets of the club

The strategic vision consists of moving from a "family" club to a "regional/national" club, unifying the European influence, while resting on a historical foundation and the rich and specific values of the ASSE. The club would like to translate this strategic vision into customer vision. In fact, promise made to the customer is formalized on the strategic plan of the club: "I'm not a spectator or supporter but a socio of the ASSE who is genuinely committed to the club and I am proud" (AS Saint-Étienne, 2014). In this context, the first axis is the establishment of a retention strategy conquering nearly all the different targets of the club.

Towards a segmentation of the offer

Marketing segmentation is the action of dividing a population (supporters) into homogeneous subsets according to various criteria (demographics, etc.). The chosen segmentation criteria must allow one to obtain population segments of sufficient size. Segmentation allows for differentiated marketing actions based on segments and for eventually proposing a suitable specific offer.

Strategic marketing vision implementation within the ASSE illustrates the manner of which the clubs segment their offers and no longer addressing only "traditional supporters". In a marketing perspective, the club aims to reach new audiences and do so to regularly evolve its offerings to match consumer expectations. The segmentation of the ASSE is to satisfy (1) the general public (fan groups (associations), individual subscribers, viewers (local and regional populations)), friends of the club (geographically dispersed, families/ teenagers); (2) business to business (local businesses, domestic investors).

In its 2014–2016 strategic plan, the club's marketing department distinguishes seven priority targets grouped into two families. For the general public target, several sub-goals are identified by the marketing department of the club. This acts to create a single and "true" community of "partners' supporters" led by the club. Regarding the individual subscribers, the club wants to retain the loyalty of current supporters and attract new ones to reach 50% occupancy rate of

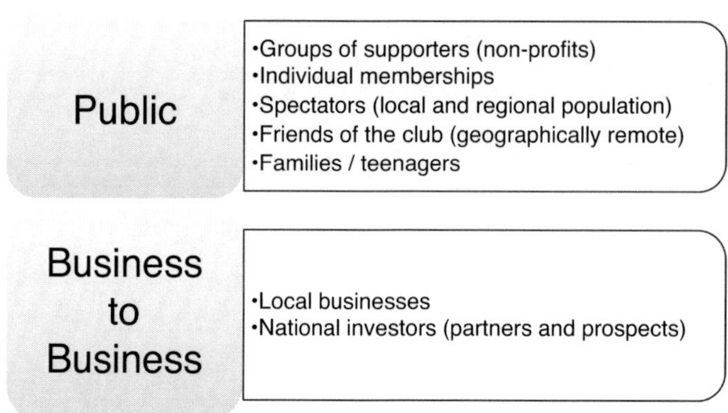

Figure 12.2 The priority targets of the ASSE (*Strategic Plan 2014–2016*)

the stadium (2014–2015 season: 20,000; 2015–2016 season: 22,000). For the target "spectator", its about creating "THE place" for meeting the ASSE fortnightly. About the target "friends of the club", the ASSE has the will to strengthen a strong and lasting bond with the fans of the club at a national level. Finally, "families and children" are a favored target. The idea is to develop all business lines, an offer "tailored" for this high-potential target because these are the future consumers of the brand. Several marketing initiatives are devoted to it: green family subscription, operation teenager, summer internship, launch of the ASSE Kid's Club with a new mascot, logo and positioning, etc. The goal is to create a daily encounter with the participant (AS Saint-Étienne, 2014).

The supporter, the "socio" in the center of the club's marketing device

> Our idea is a model of socios like the German one. In France, we cannot do as in Spain with the public. It would take a stock market approach. It would be nonsensical. It is not to make money for shareholders but to unite, step by step, our potential supporters. It is the goal of the membership card. We are aiming for 100,000 cards within 5 years. In France, it is innovative.
>
> Bernard Caiazzo[19]

Although the atmosphere tends to cool down in the stadiums, there remain some fans with who it is good to follow football, passionate fans. In addition, although there is no football culture as in France as in England, Argentina, Spain or Germany, certain stadiums are worth the trip, including Geoffroy-Guichard. The ASSE has over 220 sections of fans spread throughout the country, nearly 2 million supporters in France, and the club's website is very powerful: second in terms of attendance (after l'Olympique de Marseille). Thus Étienne supporters appear in the "Top 10" of the world's best audiences.[20] Arnaud Jaouen says, "The pride of the ASSE is represented by its supporters. They are at the heart of marketing device. We see them everywhere. It is by fans that we can happen to grow revenue".[21] Composing an important part of the club's DNA, fans thus find themselves at the center of the club's marketing concerns. The fans are the pride of the club!

From a marketing perspective, the 2014–2016 strategic plan highlights two prerequisites. First, customer knowledge. It acts as an essential prerequisite for implementing a retention and conquest strategy and to ensure the consistency of devices over all business areas for a 360° vision. This requires the creation and characterization of a database of customers and prospects. The "My ASSE" program aims thus to qualify the customers of the club. The second prerequisite concerns the control and security. As Arnaud Jaouen declares,

> We cannot work permanently on the club's image without mastering all the features and actions carried out on behalf of the club and without guaranteeing the security. It is necessary to know the consumer and to have a global vision. That's the key.[22]

In other words, a professional football club has to be able to identify the needs of its customers today. The club must initially address the fans (business to consumer), before worrying about the business to business. There must be a real logical and consistent marketing for the midterm to ramp up. "The development will go through an increase in turnover with supporters to create value and upgrade B-to-B packages. In other words, more of the club's image will be developed, the more we create value in B-to-B packages," adds Arnaud Jaouen.[23]

The ASSE seems to want to assimilate the clubs built around a large community of supporters. German clubs unite powerful communities that generate significant financial resources. In the measure where the strength of the club is its community of supporters, the ASSE could become very long term, a club of "socios", in order to sustain this strong bond between the fan and the club. "Me, my goal, anyway, is to one day have a very successful stadium with people who are all members of the ASSE", explains Arnaud Jaouen. "We must eventually have a customer vision that tells us this: I am not a mere spectator or supporter but a socio of the ASSE which engages in the club and I'm proud," he continues.[24] These remarks underscore the central place occupied by fans in different growth drivers of the ASSE. The goal consists of bringing together the maximum amount of supporters and their favorite club. In each of its steps, the club keeps the same line and transmits the various values advocated by the ASSE and dear to the fans.

This requires commercial actions, knowledge of the expectations and needs of the fans. This is for the club to conquer new targets with products and services that meet their needs. If the club seeks profit, it wants above all to create a strong story with its supporters. Supporters who, not surprisingly, have an important place in le musée des Verts. These elements echo Arnaud Jaouen: "The marketing development of the club comes from the general public target. In other words, it is through the support that we happen to grow the revenue of the club."[25] If the proximity between the club and the fans is old, the anchor also comes from the strategy implemented by the current management. Arnaud Jaouen affirms,

> At PSG, we go to see a show, but there is more sense of belonging to the ASSE. At the PSG, I dream about sports but not about the closeness that I am going to have with my clients. It is the reverse with the ASSE. A club president like Romeyer goes to the fans to tell them. The pride of the ASSE is represented by its supporters. The supporter is at the heart of the marketing device. We see it in everything.[26]

The increase in the number of subscribers is a common objective of the clubs. Two elements, however, singularize the context of the ASSE: the power of its brand image and the fervor of its supporters.

Modernization of the image and the strengthening of commitment to the brand ASSE

The strengthening of the commitment to the ASSE brand and the modernization of the club's brand image refers to the second strategic area of the club. Five dimensions are highlighted in the strategic plan (2014–2016) for the marketing department to achieve this: the proximity, the ambassadors, the museum, the charity and the modernization of the club's brand image (Association Sportive de Saint-Étienne, 2014).

Figure 12.3 Campaign subscriptions of the ASSE for the 2014–2015 season

The brand image, a major force of the ASSE

Keller (1993, p. 3) defines the concept of image as "the perceptions about a brand as reflected by its brand associations held in the memory of the consumer". From a marketing perspective, the most important thing is not the real image, but the perceived brand image. The club chose to convey the image of a unifying club and a European influence without "forgetting" its local and regional ties. For the club, it is not about hiding the past. During the 1970s, the ASSE, on the "outside", had more supporters than the home team. Several factors explain this popularity: the origin of the players and the 50 sections of "Membres Associés". The geographical position of Saint-Étienne is also decisive. Located in the southeast, the city has the characteristics of a northern city. Above all, the European course starts at the moment when media coverage of sports becomes a television issue. Two programs are emerging: "Stade 2" and "Téléfoot". The working culture of the club and the city is, furthermore, appreciated by the laborious France. The ASSE shines on the international stage, especially as French sports are going through dark years.

Since the European course of 1975–1976, the "green fever" has spread throughout France. The day after the final of the European Cup in 1976, the "Verts" of Roger Rocher parade on the Champs-Élysées and are received by the President of the Republic. The vanquished have conquered the hearts. A blue-white-red line appears on the jersey of the ASSE: it is now the club of all the French! The media interest is considerable, applications for the European cup matches are at record levels (200,000 for the ASSE versus Liverpool!) and merchandise sales are exploding. The ASSE switches to the "modern" football. Under the leadership of Under the leadership of Roger Rocher, the club is at the origin of the phenomenon of "remote fandom" that consists of supporting a team far from one's place of residence (Lestrelin, 2010). Overall, even today, the "green brand" has an image and a powerful and unique brand equity in the minds of consumers of sports entertainment. Indeed, France seems to like the "Verts". If it acts as an affirmation often delivered based on a vague feeling, fed by nostalgia and a genuine popularity, the results of the IFOP-Canal + (2014)[27] survey place the ASSE at the head of the most popular clubs in France. The managing editor of France Football (2014), Gerard Ejnès, believes that "good results inevitably have an influence but the quality of the show is also taken into account". He adds that

> The Verts have always been in the heart of the French. There is an expectation but above all a very strong desire to love this club. The ASSE has a history. It has indicated it in recent months with the opening of the museum that has seen a huge success. It is not a coincidence. People want to find the Verts at the highest level. If, one day, the ASSE shined in the League of Champions, there would be a considerable national momentum, like no other club because the true nostalgia is about the ASSE and the team of France in 1998.

These words echo the works of Charroin and Chanavat (2014) that put in perspective the power of the club. Indeed, the ASSE now represents more than just a club. It is a sports brand with an image and a powerful brand equity. Now, whether through a victorious prize list, tradition, local or foreign star players or management, on the field and off, a sports club must pay particular attention to its image. Being the only club to wear the star symbol of 10 league titles in France,[28] the emblem of the ASSE is, obviously, one of the most prestigious in French football. In any case, the issue of the club's branding is of fundamental importance for partners, the media, the club and its audience.

The five strategic dimensions

Five points are clearly distinguished in the 2014–2016 strategic plan of the club:[29]

- The proximity: to create dreams and to make the players available to create a desire, offering exclusive experiences like "money can't buy" (exclusive workouts at Geoffrey Guichard, trips with players, etc.);
- The ambassadors: to rely on opinion leaders, club glories, former iconic players;
- The museum: to capitalize on the success of this place of worship, of pilgrimage, to make it the "display cabinet" of the club and to better exploit its business potential, while bringing together all the products of the club (in 5 months, more than 30,000 visitors for a turnover of more than 200,000 euros, including 43,000 euros from B to B);[30]
- The charity with "ASSE Cœur Vert": an action that must continue to develop and to exploit media including sports challenges (e.g. Roland Romeyer traveled to Paris on bike for the final of the League Cup in April 2013[31]), auction sale transactions (e.g. the sale of pieces of square posts of the final of the Cup of Europe in 1976), a charity gala dinner, activities for the benefit of local associations;
- The modernization of the image of the club with (1) the evolution of the graphic design, and (2) the development with the new supplier, Le Coq Sportif, capitalizing on the DNA of the brand (AS Saint-Étienne, 2014).

The first section had the goal to study the objectives and strategic directions of the club. The wealth of the marketing initiatives of the club is discussed in the second.

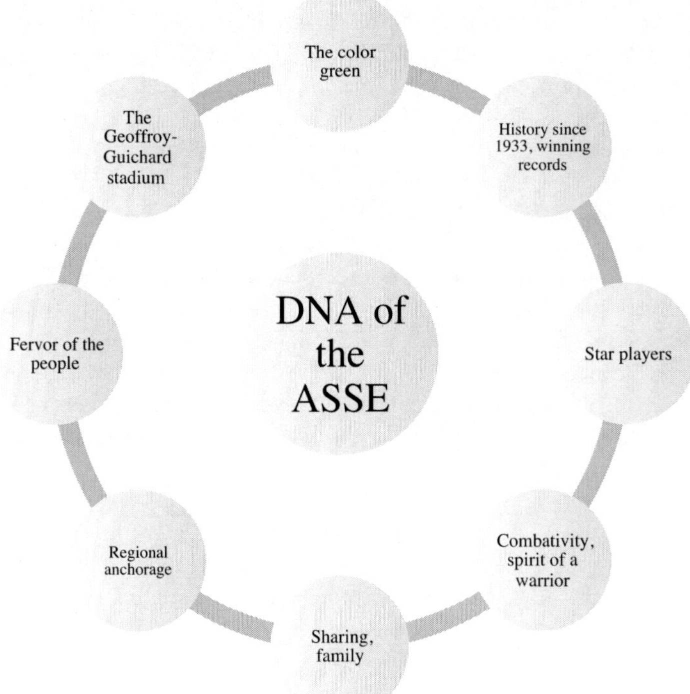

Figure 12.4 The DNA of the brand ASSE (Strategic Plan 2014–2016)

Operationalization of marketing innovations: create novelty to create value

The awareness of the necessary club marketing development is not new. Since the 1960s, under the presidency of Roger Rocher, the club strives to promote the development of non-sporting revenue (television rights, sponsorship rights, merchandising, etc.). Thus, the club of the ASSE is becoming a spectator sport company and the first French professional sports entity considered to be a sports brand in itself. The ASSE, under the presidency of Roger Rocher, is considered to be a builder club that has contributed to the professionalization of sport business in France. A pioneer in matters of television broadcasting, marketing innovation or merchandising in professional sports, the ASSE is now a professional sports entity with a powerful and unique brand image (Charroin and Chanavat, 2014). The club wishes to pursue this innovative approach. Arnaud Jaouen says,

> In order to create value the ASSE brand must stand out from others. It is necessary to create novelty to create value for the brand. For all these products to succeed it is necessary that the marketing and the communication work hand in hand. But it's not easy. We talk about sports marketing, corporate communications and product communication. It is necessary to not mix different discourses. It must be as transparent as possible. It is worth it to have a global brand vision.[32]

Several guidelines that illustrate the "creative" operationalization implemented by the club are addressed in the following order: the creation of le musée des Verts, the development of a participatory marketing project named "La Place Verte", the establishment of a CRM system with the advent of the member card, the development of digital communication, the acquisition of an establishment "Le Chaudron Vert" and the deployment of societal actions with the creation of the association "ASSE Cœur-Vert".

"Le musée des Verts": Product image or growth drivers with respect for tradition?

Marketing operationalizations of a professional football club must meet a real long-term marketing logic. The ASSE marketing initiatives can generate additional revenues while respecting the brand image and the tradition of the club. The creation of the museum illustrates this perfectly. The club museum, inaugurated Friday, December 20, 2013, welcomed over 60,000 (40,000 after 7 months) visitors in its first year of operation while the club hoped for 45,000 at best. The ASSE is the first French football club to open a museum. Driven by the Loire General Council, the creation of this exceptional space of 800m^2 meets the desire of the club to use its history to promote its values and to satisfy the passion of all its fans. It is part of the renovation of the stadium Geoffroy-Guichard, supported by Saint-Étienne Métropole. This project expresses a common desire to perceive a unique museum complex around a legendary football club. The museum is located at the Geoffroy-Guichard stadium. It acts as a true strength for the club.

Although the museum can be primarily considered to be a product image that would generate talk about the club or arouse curiosity, it is also a significant growth driver. The words of Arnaud Jaouen attest: "The museum generates 20,000 euros in sales per month. It's not nothing".[33] More specifically, the museum is part of the upgrade of marketing packages. It is going to be able to create new additional content by offering for example a tour of the stadium in addition to a museum visit in order to attract new visitors. On the occasion of the first anniversary of the museum (in December 2014), the club has proposed a tour of the museum with the purchase of a ticket for a match. Although the museum is new, and many marketing products have yet to be implemented, several operations have already been performed. "Ambassadors of the museum are commissioned there, and autograph signings are taking place there. All this in order to talk about the club, the museum and thus to bring it to the world," said Arnaud Jaouen.[34] The museum can relive the glory years of the club, and thus live the green passion. The club proposes special operations towards its partners. According to Arnaud Jaouen, these act as

> private visits led by the conservative Philippe Gastal who has a memory of an elephant, he knows by heart the story of the Verts. It is a real plus for a museum visit with cocktails in the temporary exhibition room and private tour of the museum on the history of the Verts. The trend is towards a balance between revenue from B to B and B to C.[35]

In a marketing perspective, a satisfaction survey was developed to better understand the consumer. After only 6 months of activity, a study revealed that 21 nationalities were represented and that 97% of visitors wanted to come back. "This is why we must create new products and not cease to innovate," concludes Arnaud Jaouen on the subject.[36]

Towards a development of participatory marketing

> The fan will have the opportunity to have his name on a paved stone and to have a presence for life in the Geoffroy-Guichard! The idea would be to build this between the museum and the shop. 75,000 paved stones are envisioned. The goal is to make participatory marketing at first while a few months later to then make a licensed product. If one does not subscribe, one can have their paved stone for life, next to the legend of their choice.
>
> Arnaud Jaouen[37]

Thanks to marketing and crowdfunding, the ASSE and Saint-Étienne Métropole are planning to create "La Place Verte". This acts as an area totally dedicated to the history of the club and its supporters. Even if not yet at the stage of "project", the ASSE dreams of completing a "plaza", giving homage to its glories and its supporters. This acts to take advantage of the renovation of the Geoffroy-Guichard stadium in preparation for the Euro 2016, in order to create this space. Based on the "Hollywood Walk of Fame", the club Étienne would like to create "La Place Verte" between the museum and the shop, dedicated to the history of the club and the supporters. The idea would be to allow loyal fans to put their name alongside the legends of the ASSE, while buying a paved stone. Although this project has the ability to strengthen the sense of belonging to the club, it remains a marketing device that may develop additional revenue for the club. At the time of the interview

Figure 12.5 The project "La Place Verte"

Figure 12.6 The paved stones with the names of fans next to legends

with Arnaud Jaouen, it was to market the spaces as paved stone blocks (see Figure 12.5): a paved stone for 99 euros, a paved stone next to a legend for 199 euros. "Logically over 2,300m² could therefore be available to the club, there will be a hundred thousand paved stones,"[38] explains Roland Goujon, the vice president of Saint-Étienne Métropole in charge of sports.

To conclude this topic, Arnaud Jaouen adds that

> a person who spends 100 euros for a paved stone, this is a person who can be a "socio" one day. This is a real test to know whether we eventually can become "socio". If it works, it would be one of the only French clubs to succeed with a capital opening and to go with this model.[39]

What digital activities for the club?

From a marketing and communicational perspective, the work of redesigning the site recently led by the club has developed a new version of the official website in September 2014. The official website is able to maintain a daily link with all the fans. To inform as accurately and as regularly as possible is a service that the club wants to make since it publishes most often very specific information. Eight people make up the club's communications department. The ASSE administers and develops content for eleven types of communication: three websites (asse.fr, museedesvert.fr, asse-kids.fr), a monthly magazine (*Maillot Vert*), a TV channel (Onzéo), a Dailymotion channel, a match program of a 16-page insert in the regional newspaper *Le Progrès*, a monthly business letter, an official Facebook page, an official Twitter account and an official Instagram account.

The new version of the website is particularly notable in responsive design. A platform is available on smartphones and tablets. More content is posted there. Beyond the professional team, the club will give more visibility: (1) to other teams (women and those of the training center), and (2) business activities (ticket sales, merchandising, etc.). Today, the site generates between 250,000 and 300,000 unique visitors per month and nearly 10 million page views, which places the club among the top 3 clubs in Ligue 1. The audience is fueled by the popularity of the club, but also by its ability to produce content. If the digital audience of a club is necessary, it must be monetized, either from official partners, or from local advertisers, whereas asse.fr can be perceived in Rhône-Alpes and Auvergne as a medium endowed with a large audience. A coupling of the club's communication materials is proposed. Philippe Lyonnet explains,

> Besides the website we also have a match program inserted in the regional newspaper *Le Progrès* and distributed with 100,000 copies. In addition, we send a weekly newsletter to 100,000 email addresses. Thus, the regional broadcasters can mount a comprehensive communication plan based on our different media. This new approach allows us to better use our digital media.

If the audience of the official site of the club is increasing, it is not specifically correlated to sports results. Philippe Lyonnet further explains,

> Recently, the newsletter News Football Tank prepared a comparison of progressions of the Facebook communities of the clubs of Ligue 1. This study shows that the ASSE recorded a net gain of 280,000 Facebook fans in a year. This sharp increase is exclusively organic because we do not conduct advertising campaigns for the acquisition of fans. We have an editorial strategy focused on content to create ever more connections with our fans.

"The online ticket sales represents 60% of revenues from activity, while 25% of licensed products are from the online shop run entirely by the club," he adds. Clubs wish thus to disassociate sports and economic results. A powerful marketing strategy seems necessarily "validated" and "stimulated" by good sporting results. In regard to the development of digital strategies in professional sports, one can legitimately ask: to what extent do social networks fit into the digital strategy of the club? Some of the content published on the official website is relayed on social networks of the club. Social networks, constituting audience intersections, are able to energize the audience of the official site thanks to viral phenomena. Social networks promote interactivity with the community of fans. They allow a club to take the pulse of fans, while interacting with them more easily. If some players of the ASSE are very active on Twitter, we find that former players of the club continue to regularly comment on current events of the ASSE: Pierre-Emerick Aubameyang, Joshua Guilavogui or Bafétimbi Gomis. Philippe Lyonnet concludes on this subject that, in the image of other clubs and sports federations, players under contract with ASSE

> can of course speak freely on social networks while respecting the values and image of the club. The club's communications department is on standby. And our door is always open to provide some guidance. Generally, all our players are imbued by this spirit of conviviality that animates the club.

The new member card: between CRM and development of the largest community of fans in France?

The development of the new club website was accompanied by the implementation of a major project: the member card. For Arnaud Jaouen, "the membership card enables one to 'trace' consumers and qualify them."[40] The club thus hopes to create the largest community of fans in France. The objective of the club card is to bring together all components of the club ASSE in a single and unique community. If there is a segmentation between the different categories of fans, it acts to bring together all of the club's supporters. Through this card, the fans have an account on the official website, and their points are assigned to each of their purchases in the club's profit centers. They also enjoy great discounts. Then, with the accumulated points, they can participate in events and experience unique moments within the club, "events money cannot buy."

The ASSE member card is regularly highlighted on the club's official website. The project was launched in autumn 2014, and the club had 18,000 members as of January 2015. The club website has generated about 60% of subscriptions.

The marketing department of the ASSE, led by Arnaud Jaouen, has made the establishment of a database of supporters one of the priorities of the marketing of the club. This is what one calls a basic CRM (Customer Relationship Management).[41] This system includes all the tools and techniques for capturing, processing and analyzing information on customers and prospects

Figure 12.7 The member card of the ASSE (left) highlighted on the website of the club (right)

to retain them by providing the best service. The launch of this new card enables one to better understand the needs of the fans in order to optimize certain profit centers. The card therefore enters in the scope of the CRM strategy of the club. Different profit centers, shop, ticket office, museum, etc., are able to obtain a lot of information. In matters of CRM, the goal is not to collect information, even if this represents the basic condition, but instead to treat it in depth. It is to know "who buys what" to learn more about the fans and get closer to them. This translates to offering proposals consistently and in line with the fan's needs. For Arnaud Jaouen, "At the marketing level, the goal of course is to be able to qualify these people."[42] In other words, the ASSE member card was created to know the buying habits of members and thus to meet their needs and offer them personalized offers. As Arnaud Jaouen explains,

> Today I am capable of telling you in 2 months that Mr. Durand has spent 200 euros at the shop, 50 euros at the online shop, he went twice to the museum and that he ate at the Chaudron Vert three times and, behind, to be able to in words, propose offers responding to his desires.[43]

Largely inspired by Real Madrid, this member card, launched in late 2014, is becoming one of the main strengths of the marketing department of the ASSE. It is going to be able to provide much information on the characteristics of the members and therefore the consumers of the brand ASSE.

The membership card equally allows the fans to strengthen their sense of belonging to the club and thus their loyalty. With this card, there exists a real program of qualification, loyalty and personalization. The public part is very interesting for the club as it allows for a personalization of the offer. This card seems to have become an indispensable tool for the club. "At a football club level we must perfectly know our customers, in order to also be able to offer them additional services," explains Arnaud Jaouen.[44] The card also becomes a stake for sensitizing more partners. Indeed, the club may argue more with its partners, given the information on the fans of which the club has and can use to generate interest. This adds value to the partnerships of the ASSE. "Tomorrow I'll be able to tell Mr. Citroën 'Here among my members I have X percent that wish to change vehicles within 6 months', so it is interesting to become a partner of the club," concludes Arnaud Jaouen on this aspect.[45]

The fact that there are two offers for the card allows the club to reach the maximum amount of fans. The ASSE member card is free. The Premium ASSE member card costs 20 euros. It targets more regular supporters, the subscribers. This card will allow the member to enjoy exclusive and personalized offers. As for the premium member, he will notably have the right, at the time of acquisition of the card, to visit the museum, as well as preferential rates on the products of the club shop. The premium card furthermore offers a seat for the club's home game: everything is done to bring the fans to the heart of the ASSE! Thus, there exists a logic of customer loyalty with this premium member card, but also a recruitment search with the free card. To get a little more word of mouth about their membership card, the club has drawn a Premium member ahead of the ASSE versus PSG (January 25, 2015) and gave him, just before kick off, a C1 vehicle in partnership with Citroën. As with any loyalty card, when a member makes purchases in profit centers of the club, it accumulates points which, subsequently, give access to a catalog of products (from an autographed jersey to a simple keychain). It also will make unique experiences for fans.

"Le Chaudron Vert", the crossroads of fans

From a development perspective, the ASSE has acquired the property "Le Chaudron-Vert". Located two blocks from the Geoffroy-Guichard stadium, it is now the official bar-restaurant-hotel of the club. To the extent that the increase in time spent in the stadium can prove to be complicated, the club develops initiatives to spend more time with its fans around Geoffroy-Guichard. For Arnaud Jaouen, "Le Chaudron Vert is a hotel-restaurant which is now the official restaurant of the ASSE. This is 'the place to be' before and after the game."[46] This acquisition seems to fit into the loyalty program: it can accommodate fans who are not from the region and give them, the time of a weekend, an experience in the heart of the club. This establishment gets into the marketing plans of the club since it is able to develop new growth drivers. Although it remains largely a product image, it allows a valuation of different packages offered. These elements echo Arnaud Jaouen, who points out that the

> club may propose new formulas, with a total immersion in the world of Verts: a match ticket, a museum ticket, a stadium tour, a lunch at the Chaudron Vert, the hotel Chaudron Vert to welcome them and they leave the next day.[47]

In the end, the ultimate goal for the club is to make this establishment the place to go for all lovers of the club, before and after the game. Without necessarily being a very lucrative profit center, the Chaudron Vert therefore constitutes a product image for the club, which will bring the fans and generate the flow around the club. The idea is to provide an "official" space that can accommodate the fans. Overall, the purchase of this property promotes the idea of having a consumer experience with the brand ASSE.

To give the inaccessible to fans: towards brand activations "money can't buy"

As we have just mentioned, the ASSE is willing to share with its fans unique experiences with the closest players and the club: to give a kick on the lawn, to get on the player's bus, to participate in training with the players, to get in the plane with the players to go to a match, etc. The initiative "money can't buy" offers consumers the unattainable. Literally, these act as events that money cannot buy. If, for the sponsor, the idea consists of promoting and activating its partnership, this type of device proves to be beneficial for many stakeholders in sports events:

- The rights holder (club, federation, etc.) that is able to give its fan a unique experience and create buzz;

- The sponsor that manages to activate its rights in an innovative manner;
- The sports marketing agency that works to meet the needs of a rights holder and an advertiser;
- The customer who will experience an extraordinary moment;
- The community of supporters who can identify the fan-win.

Also the ASSE, its marketing agency SportFive and Orange have given the opportunity to a fan of the "Verts" of an unforgettable moment that illustrates the will to innovate the club and the ability to create a marketing buzz. "Initially, the club suggests an innovative device and asks SportFive to work on the concept and to offer brands," says Arnaud Jaouen.[48]

On the occasion of the 38th and final day of the Ligue 1 championship (2013–2014 season), Orange, through its digital platform the 12th man, allowed a football fan to realize his dream. The best proposals are retained and conducted by the brand. The campaign named "I Have a Dream" is able to make many happy. Arthur, a fan of the ASSE, was able to fulfill his dream: to pitch his tent and to camp overnight in the stadium of his favorite club, Geoffrey-Guichard, in Saint-Étienne. Upon his arrival at the stadium, he is welcomed by an Orange team player who is also emblematic of the ASSE: Jérémie Janot. First surprise for the fan who met the former goal keeper of the ASSE. After a night in the "Chaudron", the Turk Mevlüt Erdinç brought the croissants of Étienne to the fan and shared his breakfast with him. So that the dream continues, the fan attends the ASSE match against Ajaccio, where his team wins 3–1. This weekend will remain unforgettable for Arthur, who had a chance to see his dream come true. We must recognize that this marketing initiative is distinguished from the usual brand communication around football. The human is emphasized here. The business dimension is clearly shelved, which may explain its success. Orange succeeds in activating its rights as the partner of the ASSE in a clever way to create a memorable experience for the consumer.

Packages and partner activations should be revaluated. The brand activation is not just related to the visibility of the billboards in a sports arena. To truly "emerge", it is necessary (1) to activate by customer databases, (2) set up contests, and (3) use the digital network. The club needs to develop a reflection in matters on social networks. This acts as an indispensable strategic direction to create an international community. Although it is necessary to have a community, it seems essential to answer the question: "how to profit?"

"ASSE Cœur Vert": For an innovative CSR

Building on the brand image and the values held by the green people, the ASSE has created an associative structure "ASSE Cœur-Vert". It is chaired by Dominique Rocheteau and directed by Lionel Potillon (former club player). The central objective of this entity is to promote various activities of general interest, particularly in the fields of solidarity, sports, the environment and sustainable development. "ASSE Cœur-Vert" also has four sub-objectives: encouraging solidarity in face of illness and disability, developing citizenship, preserving the environment and promoting amateur sports. The club has furthermore created a website dedicated to this association to give more visibility to its social actions. In this context, the ASSE mobilizes its professional players, all its teams and all its communication tools to enable partner associations of "ASSE Cœur-Vert" to succeed in their charitable actions, "we have once a month two players who go to the hospitals to see sick children, etc," declares Arnaud Jaouen.[49] Alongside these initiatives, the club is looking for new partners who, through this association, could develop concepts in line with sustainable development, citizenship and disability for example.

In 2013, the entity "ASSE Cœur-Vert" supported 100 associations, organized or accompanied 200 activities, distributed 212,000 euros and offered 5,000 game seats.[50] In 2014, to mark the 38th anniversary of the final of the Champions League (May 12, 1976), "ASSE Cœur-Vert" organized, in partnership with eBay, an auction of pieces of mythical square goal poles from Glasgow to benefit two charities: the League against Cancer and Santa Claus Monday.[51] In April 2015, in partnership with the UN, the club organized a match against poverty, which pitted the All-Stars team of the ASSE "aux amis de Zidane". The revenues of this match were donated to associations selected by Cœur-Vert. Like the museum, "ASSE Cœur-Vert" proves to be a powerful image tool in line with the marketing strategy of the club.

Conclusion

This chapter was intended to highlight the marketing strategy of the ASSE. It proves that it is integrated into the overall strategy of the club, which has three major objectives: to give a European dimension to the ASSE, to unite and meet the expectations of priority targets and to operate three levers of growth around the games. Two strategic areas have been identified: the establishment of a retention strategy encompassing different targets of the club and the strengthening of the commitment and the "modernization" of the club's branding. If our analysis shows that the success of the organization of the ASSE is based on the performance of the triumvirate Caïazzo–Romeyer–Rocheteau, management of sports cells led by Christophe Galtier will remain a centerpiece. While marketing initiatives bloom for the club, their success seems closely linked to sports results. The sports policy should be related to the image the club wants to develop and the expectations of the fans. "Now you know, we can have a fabulous pool of supporters, but if the results are not there, the size of the community will decrease," affirms Arnaud Jaouen.[52] The image of a club depends on its sporting results, which will impact the membership (or not) of fans and partners.

Our analysis suggests that the introduction of a salary cap, trading of players and training are integrated into the overall strategy of the club development and contribute to its economic and sporting success. While the club has a structural deficit, the new marketing strategy of the club aims to avoid the best players being sold annually. Thus, since 2014, marketing is considered a transversal department of the club profit centers. Several marketing innovations identified in this chapter continue the creation of novelty and value: the creation of the "musée des Verts", the development of a participatory marketing project named "La Place Verte", the establishment of a CRM system with the advent of the member card, the development of digital activities, the acquisition of an establishment "Le Chaudron Vert" and the deployment of social actions with the creation of the association "ASSE Cœur-Vert". The club is working on many tracks and a willingness to innovate on a multitude of projects: customer experience, ticket sales, merchandising, partnering, development, etc. In terms of merchandising, the club could for example extend its product range to reach all populations. In any case, other initiatives and arrangements could have been treated in this chapter.

Two examples allow us to illustrate our point. The first relates to the partnership strategy. One must recognize that the ASSE is not a "cleaving" club. Its brand equity enables it to attract many sponsors. During the 2014–2015 season, the club has attracted a partner listed in the exchange, le Groupe Visiomed and its Bewell brand, connected leaders in the health sector. Le Coq Sportif has also been selected as the new club equipment manufacturer (for the 2015–2016 season). Although this sponsor was not the most economically advantageous, it finds itself fully in line with the values advocated by the ASSE. In its image, the equipment represents a French brand that can develop. There is therefore a structural partnership that makes sense for both the club and for the sponsor. The marketing success also depends on good relations with partners in signing long-term contracts with them. Signing such agreements can "create stories" with partners and thus offer them different brand activations. And it is these activations that allow, among others, the retaining of the fan. Our analysis leads us to believe that Le Coq Sportif would be heavily involved in this type of innovative partnership by developments such as naming of a profit center of the club.[53] Although the ASSE has known seven different suppliers in its history, Le Coq Sportif is one with which the club won the most titles (1969 to 1984). The legend of Les Verts in the 1970s and the final of the European Champion Clubs' Cup against Bayern Munich happened with the French equipment manufacturer. Adidas, on the contrary, is sponsoring a multitude of professional sports structures and does not necessarily customize for the club. One can contest, for example, that the club's jersey is not deeply "worked" from one season to another.

The second concerns the issue of the club internationalization. If the club ultimately wants to develop a website in several languages like those of PSG or Lyon, a lasting presence on the European scene is required. Obviously, although the globalization of the brand is interesting in absolute terms, it first passes through a perpetuation of sports results. The purchase of foreign players (iconic) may also allow the club to gain an international reputation and community. However, we can highlight for example that the purchase of the player Daisuke Matsui by the ASSE did not "explode" the Asian market of the club. This episode was even considered a "flop" for Konica Minolta. Today, the ASSE has recruited several players from Asia younger than 17 years. If the posting of a blog has been offered, it should be careful and show above all the qualities of the players. Moreover, the development of agreements and synergies with foreign clubs so that one can speak of the ASSE internationally seems essential.

In conclusion, our work highlights the need for each marketing initiative to be linked to a global issue of the club. Not surprisingly, the fan is at the center of concerns and the club's marketing device. The relationship between the ASSE and its fans proves to be the engine of choice and of the objectives set by the club. It is crucial for the ASSE to be closer to its fans by going directly to their meeting. In a marketing perspective, the club wants to retain and "qualify" its customers, which requires significant work on the CRM. These elements echo the words of Arnaud Jaouen, which highlight two key factors of success within the club's marketing success "to qualify the customer and above all humanize the relationship between the fan and the club".[54]

Notes

1 The authors wish to thank the people interviewed for this research. Special thanks to Bernard Caiazzo, president of the ASSE Supervisory Board, Arnaud Jaouen, marketing director of the ASSE and Philippe Lyonnet, communications director of the ASSE, for their assistance and their availability.
2 Interview conducted by Nicolas Chanavat on July 8, 2014, at the headquarters of the ASSE.
3 Until now adviser to the president Roland Romeyer, he is particularly responsible for the training center of the unit of supervision and observation of players and post-training.
4 http://www.le10sport.com/football/ligue1/asse/mercato-asse-lasse-doit-elle-revoir-sa-strategie-pour-ruffier-139353 – Excerpt from the Roland Romeyer interview in the article titled "Mercato – ASSE: L'ASSE doit-elle revoir sa stratégie pour Ruffier?" Le10sport.com published on March 14, 2014. Last accessed on April 25, 2015.
5 Association sportive de Saint-Étienne, Confidential and unpublished documents provided by Arnaud Jaouen, *Plan stratégique ASSE 2014–2016*, 2014.
6 Interview directed by Nicolas Chanavat on July 8, 2014, at the headquarters of the ASSE.
7 http://www.butfootballclub.fr/1585367-asse-caiazzo-leve-le-voile-sur-les-objectifs-financiers-du-club/ – Excerpt from the Bernard Caïazzo interview in the article titled "ASSE : la stratégie économique

des Verts pour briller en Europe" published at butfootballclub.fr September 17, 2014. Last accessed on April 25, 2015.

8 http://www.ecofoot.fr/interview-philippe-lyonnet-directeur-communication-asse/ – Excerpt from the Philippe Lyonnet interview titled "Interview exclusive de Philippe Lyonnet, directeur de la communication de l'ASSE" directed by Anthony Alyce and published at ecofoot.fr on January 22, 2015. Last accessed on April 25, 2015.

9 Interview conducted by Nicolas Chanavat on July 8, 2014, at the headquarters of the ASSE.

10 Interview conducted by Nicolas Chanavat on July 8, 2014, at the headquarters of the ASSE.

11 The 12e homme (12th man) initiative is described in the second section of the chapter.

12 Interview conducted by Nicolas Chanavat on July 8, 2014, at the headquarters of the ASSE.

13 Interview conducted by Nicolas Chanavat on July 8, 2014, at the headquarters of the ASSE.

14 Interview conducted by Nicolas Chanavat on July 8, 2014, at the headquarters of the ASSE.

15 Interview conducted by Nicolas Chanavat on July 8, 2014, at the headquarters of the ASSE.

16 Interview conducted by Nicolas Chanavat on July 8, 2014, at the headquarters of the ASSE.

17 http://www.lagardere.com/centre-presse/communiques-de-presse/communiques-de-presse-122.html&idpress=4731 – Excerpt from the Bernard Caïazzo interview in the press release titled "L'AS Saint-Étienne confie la gestion de ses droits commerciaux à SPORTFIVE (Lagardère Unlimited)", published at lagardere.com on July 2, 2010. Last accessed April 25, 2015.

18 Interview conducted by Nicolas Chanavat on July 8, 2014, at the headquarters of the ASSE.

19 L'Essor Affiches Loire, Excerpt from the Bernard Caïazzo interview in the article titled "L'économie verte: le nouveau but", written by Xavier Alix February 20, 2015, p. 20.

20 http://www.sofoot.com/top-10-les-meilleurs-publics-du-monde-172939.html – Data derived from the article "Top 10: les meilleurs publics du monde", written by Régis Delanoé and published at sofoot.com on October 21, 2013. Last accessed on April 25, 2015.

21 Interview conducted by Nicolas Chanavat on July 8, 2014, at the headquarters of the ASSE.

22 Interview conducted by Nicolas Chanavat on July 8, 2014, at the headquarters of the ASSE.

23 Interview conducted by Nicolas Chanavat on July 8, 2014, at the headquarters of the ASSE.

24 Interview conducted by Nicolas Chanavat on July 8, 2014, at the headquarters of the ASSE.

25 Interview conducted by Nicolas Chanavat on July 8, 2014, at the headquarters of the ASSE.

26 Interview conducted by Nicolas Chanavat on July 8, 2014, at the headquarters of the ASSE.

27 Performed every 6 months with Canal +, this survey is able to highlight changes in the popularity rating of the clubs. This national survey is more representative in that it only asks people who are interested in football. They are therefore real connoisseurs of football who expressed their feelings, as people who have seen the games.

28 The star of l'Olympique de Marseille represents the victory of the club in the European Cup in 1993.

29 Some initiatives such as the museum, the concept of "money can't buy" and "ASSE Cœur Vert" are further detailed in the second section of this chapter.

30 A mandate was established with SportFive to generate new revenues with business to business with an annual target of €120,000.

31 Roland Romeyer, co-president of Saint-Étienne, who had bet he would do the route Saint-Étienne–Paris by bicycle if his team reaches the final of the Cup during the 2012–2013 season. He completed a journey of over 500 kilometers with a green jerseys squad for the "Défi ASSE Cœur-Vert". This initiative was deemed successful. Very widely followed by the media, it has raised €42,000 for two associations: Mécénat chirurgie cardiaque and Life Priority.

32 Interview conducted by Nicolas Chanavat on July 8, 2014, at the headquarters of the ASSE.

33 Interview conducted by Nicolas Chanavat on July 8, 2014, at the headquarters of the ASSE.

34 Interview conducted by Nicolas Chanavat on July 8, 2014, at the headquarters of the ASSE.

35 Interview conducted by Nicolas Chanavat on July 8, 2014, at the headquarters of the ASSE.

36 Interview conducted by Nicolas Chanavat on July 8, 2014, at the headquarters of the ASSE.

37 Interview conducted by Nicolas Chanavat on July 8, 2014, at the headquarters of the ASSE.

38 http://www.francebleu.fr/infos/saint-etienne/saint-etienne-une-place-verte-cote-de-geoffroy-guichard-1847998 – Excerpt from the Roland Goujon interview in the article titled "Saint-Étienne: une place Verte à côté de Geoffroy-Guichard", directed by Mathilde Montagnon and published at francebleu.fr on October 13, 2014. Last accessed on April 25, 2015.

39 Interview conducted by Nicolas Chanavat on July 8, 2014, at the headquarters of the ASSE.

40 Interview conducted by Nicolas Chanavat on July 8, 2014, at the headquarters of the ASSE.

41 It acts as the customer relationship management (CRM).
42 Interview conducted by Nicolas Chanavat on July 8, 2014, at the headquarters of the ASSE.
43 Interview conducted by Nicolas Chanavat on July 8, 2014, at the headquarters of the ASSE.
44 Interview conducted by Nicolas Chanavat on July 8, 2014, at the headquarters of the ASSE.
45 Interview conducted by Nicolas Chanavat on July 8, 2014, at the headquarters of the ASSE.
46 Interview conducted by Nicolas Chanavat on July 8, 2014, at the headquarters of the ASSE.
47 Interview conducted by Nicolas Chanavat on July 8, 2014, at the headquarters of the ASSE.
48 Interview conducted by Nicolas Chanavat on July 8, 2014, at the headquarters of the ASSE.
49 Interview conducted by Nicolas Chanavat on July 8, 2014, at the headquarters of the ASSE.
50 http://www.asse.fr/fr/Club-2/Saison-2014–2015/Asse-coeur-vert-8 – Title of an Internet page published at asse.fr. Last accessed on April 25, 2015.
51 Each piece, 6-cm long, is numbered from 1 to 38. The starting price is set at €760.
52 Interview conducted by Nicolas Chanavat on July 8, 2014, at the headquarters of the ASSE.
53 Today, there exists only one example of *naming* of a training center in French football: Ooreedo for the PSG.
54 Interview conducted by Nicolas Chanavat on July 8, 2014, at the headquarters of the ASSE.

Bibliography

Association Sportive de Saint-Étienne (2014). Confidential and unpublished documents, communicated by Arnaud Jaouen, Strategic Plan 2014–2016.

Charroin P. et Chanavat N., "Roger Rocher, Président de l'Association Sportive de Saint-Étienne (ASSE) des années 60–70: un visionnaire bâtisseur", in E. Bayle (ed.), *Les grands dirigeants du sport*, Brussels: Belgium, De Boeck, 2014, pp. 113–134.

Drut B. et Szymanski S., *The private benefit of public funding: The FIFA World Cup, UEFA European Championship and attendance at host country league football*, http://www.soccernomics-agency.com/wordpress/wp-content/uploads/2014/04/The-private-benefit-of-public-funding.pdf, avril 2014.

Keller K.L., "Conceptualizing, measuring, and managing customer-based brand equity", *Journal of Marketing*, 57, 1993, pp. 1–22.

Lestrelin L., *L'autre public des matchs de football. Sociologie des supporters à distance de l'Olympique de Marseille*, Paris, EHESS, Collection En temps et lieux, 2010.

Webography

http://www.asse.fr/fr/Club-2/Saison-2014–2015/Asse-coeur-vert-8 – Title of an Internet page at asse.fr. Last accessed on April 25, 2015.

http://www.butfootballclub.fr/1585367-asse-caiazzo-leve-le-voile-sur-les-objectifs-financiers-du-club/ – Excerpt from the Bernard Caïazzo interview in the article titled "ASSE: la stratégie économique des Verts pour briller en Europe" published at butfootballclub.fr on September 17, 2014. Last accessed on April 25, 2015.

http://www.ecofoot.fr/interview-philippe-lyonnet-directeur-communication-asse/ – Excerpt from the Philippe Lyonnet interview titled "Interview exclusive de Philippe Lyonnet, directeur de la communication de l'ASSE" directed by Anthony Alyce and published at ecofoot.fr on January 22, 2015. Last accessed on April 25, 2015.

http://www.francebleu.fr/infos/saint-etienne/saint-etienne-une-place-verte-cote-de-geoffroy-guichard-1847998 – Excerpt from the Roland Goujon interview in the article title "Saint-Etienne: une place Verte à côté de Geoffroy-Guichard" directed by Mathilde Montagnon and published at francebleu.fr on October 13, 2014. Last accessed on April 25, 2015.

http://www.lagardere.com/centre-presse/communiques-de-presse/communiques-de-presse-122.html&idpress=4731 – Excerpt from the Bernard Caïazzo interview in the press release titled "L'AS Saint-Étienne confie la gestion de ses droits commerciaux à SPORTFIVE (Lagardère Unlimited)" published at lagardere.com on July 2, 2010. Last accessed on April 25, 2015.

http://www.le10sport.com/football/ligue1/asse/mercato-asse-lasse-doit-elle-revoir-sa-strategie-pour-ruffier-139353 – Excerpt from the Roland Romeyer interview in the article titled "Mercato – ASSE: L'ASSE doit-elle revoir sa stratégie pour Ruffier?" published at le10sport.com on March 14, 2014. Last accessed on April 25, 2015.

Studies, documents and media

Association sportive de Saint-Étienne, confidential and unpublished documents provided by Arnaud Jaouen, *Plan stratégique ASSE 2014–2016*, 2014.

France Football, Sample results of the IFOP-Canal + (2014) survey in the article titled "Baromètre du Foot français", written by Gérard Ejnès and published in *France Football* on June 3, 2014.

L'Essor Affiches Loire, Excerpt from the Bernard Caïazzo interview in the article titled "L'économie verte: le nouveau but", written by Xavier Alix on February 20, 2015, p. 20.

13

I CAN'T HELP FALLING IN LOVE WITH MY TEAM

Active engagement in social initiatives as a driver of fan commitment in sports

Verónica Baena[1]

Introduction

Supporters' fervor gives rise to an irrational rather than a rational economic way of consuming football (Rodriguez-Pomeda, Casani and Alonso-Almeida, 2015). Therefore, from a marketing perspective, the distinction between fans (those who are highly identified with the team, coach, players, etc.) and spectators is crucial. In view of that, good marketing plans have to focus on and accentuate the connection between the followers and their team to get advantage of such emotional attachment. However, only recently researchers have started to address the understanding of the brand-supporter relationship or fan commitment (Wallace, Buil and De Chernatony, 2014; Baena, 2016).

More specifically, among the different constructs, the emotional attachment towards a brand appears to be recent (Albert, Merunka and Valette-Florence, 2009; Bergkvist and Bech-Larsen, 2010). First investigations concerning the self-expressive brand construct dealt with the definition and conceptualization of the construct. This connection can be established through the symbolic representation of the ideal past, present or future self of the customer (Markus and Nurius, 1986). Later, Ahuvia (2005) stated that the loved objects play a decisive role in the understanding of how a person sees herself or himself. This concept is very important for sport marketers as through the representation of the current self, brands may cultivate one's self by mirroring the customers' identity, beliefs and values. Subsequently, a self-expressive could be defined as "the consumer's perception of the degree to which the specific brand enhances one's social self and/or reflects one's inner self" (Carroll and Ahuvia, 2006; p. 82). This construct is nowadays considered a higher-order construct including multiple cognitions, emotions and behaviors, which consumers organize into a mental prototype. It includes but goes beyond brand attachment and self-brand connection. That is, the determination of self-expressive brand is divided into two aspects. On one side the inner self, appealing to how a consumer sees himself. On the other side, the social self, which determines the contribution of the brand towards the image of the consumer in his or her social environment (Batra, Ahuvia and Bagozzi, 2012).

Sport marketers should also notice that we operate in a global society, and people are nowadays more aware of firm's actions in terms of social problems (Mattera and Baena, 2014).

Accordingly, corporate social responsibility (CSR) has become increasingly prevalent in the sport industry. For instance, Nelson Mandela's averment that sport can change the world holds much ideological sway. In addition, former United Nation Secretary-General Kofi Annan once commented that he was interested in the power of football to teach lifelong lessons about playing against others rivals, not enemies (Smith and Westerbeek, 2007). This is because sport can spread understanding and tolerance through the introduction of new cultural values in fun and interactive ways. In particular, literature has identified a positive association between the efficiency of a firm and the way it invests in CSR to create and enhance a sustainable competitive advantage (Jones, Felps and Bigley, 2007). Implementing CSR actions is also positively associated with the company's brand awareness (Mattera, Baena y Cerviño, 2014). We then may argue that sports CSR takes the perspective that teams are members of the society, who are expected to support the communities in which they operate (Mazodier et al., 2016). Unfortunately, little academic attention has been paid to the relevance of fans' understanding and involvement of the socially responsible initiatives implemented by their clubs as an important constituent of emotional attachment towards the team.

In an attempt to shed light on this topic, the present study analyzes whether socially responsible actions carried out by sport teams are able to increase community involvement and have an impact on fan commitment. The role of brand communities (through website and social networks) to inform supporters about the CSR actions carried out by their team, as well as the followers' engagement in such social initiatives (by working as a volunteer on charity matches, funds donation in social campaigns promoted by the team, etc.) is also considered. To achieve this goal, we focus on the Real Madrid F.C. in general and particularly, on the Real Madrid Foundation.

Box 13.1 History and trophies of the Real Madrid

Founded in 1902 as the Madrid Football Club, the team has traditionally worn a white home uniform ever since. The word Real (royal in Spanish) was conferred to the club by King Alfonso XIII of Spain in 1920 together with the royal crown in the emblem. The team has played its home matches at Santiago Bernabéu Stadium in downtown Madrid since 1947. In December 2014, Real Madrid had won 32 "Ligas" (national league trophy), 19 "Copas del Rey" (as the national cup in Spain is called), 10 European Championship titles, 3 Intercontinental Cups trophies, 2 UEFA SuperCup trophies, as well as 1 Club World Cup, among others. Because of this exceptional number of titles, Real Madrid was named "FIFA Club of the Century" in 2002. Real Madrid is also allowed to wear a multiple-winner badge on their jersey during UEFA Champions League matches as the club won more than five European Cups. Added to this, on 23 December, 2000, Real Madrid was awarded with the recognition of FIFA Club of the 20th century. More recently, it received the FIFA Order of Merit in 2004.

With regards to brand value, Manchester United, Real Madrid, and Bayern Munich have traditionally been the most successful sports teams in Europe. Particularly, in 2010, *Forbes* estimated Real Madrid's worth to be approximately US$1,323 million, ranking them second after Manchester United. Nevertheless, Real Madrid has recently usurped Manchester United's long-held title as the most valuable soccer team in the world. More specifically, the season 2012–2013 marks the first time since Forbes began tracking the value of soccer teams in 2004 that Manchester United has not ranked first. Therefore, Real Madrid is worth more than any team in the world. A fact that is especially notable in a period of crisis in Europe.

Furthermore, Real Madrid has realized the importance of the brand and grasped the ability to market in a way not seen anywhere else in the world of soccer. In particular, this football team is one of the most recognizable brands in sports and is among the top three teams of the world in terms of followers and engagement in social media. With some of the world's greatest players on the field, Real Madrid exemplifies that team value is also based on brand management. For example, the fusion of the potent Real Madrid brand with equally powerful global football superstars such as David Beckham and Cristiano Ronaldo was a profitable decision. Specifically, once the two famous footballers started to wear the Real Madrid jersey, the club was able to dramatically increase the price paid by their major corporate sponsors.

Source: official website of the club: http://www.realmadrid.es

Box 13.2 History and awards of the Real Madrid Foundation

This entity is near 20 years old and one of the largest sports education institutions in the world. Specifically, in Spain, more than 10,000 people have benefited from 124 projects developed by the Foundation through its Social Sport Schools. In the world, the team's Foundation has opened near 400 Social Sport Schools in 70 countries with more near 50,000 direct beneficiaries.

These academies are not scouting outposts aiming to find the next Cristiano Ronaldo or Gareth Bale, but educational centers funded by the Real Madrid Foundation and its partners. Specifically, the Foundation's main goal is to encourage values inherent in sport and use the latter as an educational tool. Because of that, the Foundation received in 2007 the Plaque from the COE (Spanish Olympic Committee) in recognition of "its extraordinary social work". It has also been awarded with the International Award for Solidarity in Sport, for the "School united by the peace of football (Israel and Palestinian Territories)" program, as well as the Corporate Social Responsibility Award from the Football Is More Foundation, which was created by S.D. Prince Constantin von und zu Liechtenstein to promote development and peace through football.

A highlight of the season 2013/2014 was the inauguration of the integrated sports and cooperation project, with includes two schools, one for football and the other basketball for Romanian gypsy children living in the "El Gallinero" slum. The social sports school project for young people in Vilcávaro (Madrid) in an unique example in Europe of public–private cooperation using sport as a tool for insertion, education and solidarity. The project has the support of both the City Council of the Madrid Regional Institute for Resettlement and Social Integration and several private companies. It includes a football and basketball school, as well as a supplementary program for transportation, food, health and hygiene for children at extreme risk of social exclusion. At the 2014 annual awards of the European Club Association (ECA), this initiative was named the best social project, and the Real Madrid Foundation got the prize for the Best Community and Social Responsibility Program.

Source: Real Madrid Foundation Annual Report 2016/2016 and the official website of the club's foundation: http://www.realmadrid.com/en/about-real-madrid/foundation

Table 13.1 Identity Card of Real Madrid

Name of the Chairman: Florentino Pérez
Number of subscribers: 67,000 people
Number of Facebook fans: +80 million
Average number of spectators per match: 72,834 people (capacity of Santiago Bernabéu: 81,044 people)
Budget of the club: €540 million
Total income: €603 million
Distribution of revenue: marketing (32%), broadcasting (29%) membership dues, ticketing and stadium revenue (25%), revenues from friendly matches (14%)
Name of sponsors: Adidas, Emirates Airlines, IPIC, Bwin, Mahou, Audi, Microsoft, Coca Cola, BBVA, Nivea Men, STC, Samsung, Solán de Cabras, NBAD, Sanitas, Tecate, FUD and Ooredoo.

Source: Real Madrid Group Management Report 2016/2016 and the official website of the club: http://www.realmadrid.es

Table 13.2 Identity Card of the Real Madrid Foundation

Name of the Chairman: Florentino Pérez
Name of the Managing Director: Julio González
Number of Facebook fans: + 4 million
Average number of beneficiaries: + 50,000 beneficiaries at over 360 social sports schools in 70 countries.
Main Benefactors: Fundación Mapfre, Endesa, Microsoft, La Caixa, Google, Banco de Desarrollo de América Latina, Banco Santander, Barclays Foundation, Banco Espirirto Santo, ACS Foundation, Sanitas, HSBC, BBVA Foundation, Banco Popular, MMT, Halcón Viajes, Congo Trade Company, Emirates, Iberia Airlines, El Corte Inglés, Spanish Red Cross, Colgate – Palmolive Spain, and the Spanish Olympic Committee.

Source: Real Madrid Foundation Annual Report 2016/2016 and the official website of the club's foundation: http://www.realmadrid.com/en/about-real-madrid/foundation

The combination of the aforementioned factors made Real Madrid the appropriate brand to choose for this study, representing a leading organization in sports, marketing, and CSR.

Sport as a useful vehicle in the employment of CSR

During the 21st century, consumers distrust of many corporate entities is high, with the misdeeds of a few tainting the marketplace for the rest. For instance, headline-making companies such as Enron, Arthur Andersen or Merrill Lynch have triggered a rapid shift in how companies are viewed both legally and by the public at large (Walker and Kent, 2009). Therefore, having a clear understanding of CSR is critical in the evaluation of every organization.

While numerous definitions and interpretations of the concept of CSR have been offered, the general consensus would be that it represents a set of actions that appears to further some social good, extend beyond the explicit pecuniary interests of the firm (McWilliams, Siegel, and Wright, 2006) and are not required by law (Mattera and Baena, 2014).

Regarding sport, it plays a significant role. Particularly, sport allows for development of several initiatives to extend to groups where traditional development schemes tend not to reach. The ability of sport to reach out to communities that are particularly marginalized by traditional development initiatives, as well as its capacity to create partnership among institutions that would not normally work together, should also be highlighted (Levermore, 2010). Moreover, sport can spread understanding and tolerance through the introduction of new cultural values in fun and interactive ways. The link between participating in sport and positive health benefits is well established too (Walters, 2009). In short, sport offers substantial potential for community return (Smith and Westerbeek, 2007)

This has resulted in the integration of CSR into the strategic management of some teams to deliver a number of benefits that can ultimately create and enhance a sustainable competitive advantage for the club. For example, highly identified game attendees may look for the socially responsible activities of teams to reinforce their engagement towards the club. Besides, CSR associations have a strong and direct impact on supporters' attributions, which in turn influence brand evaluations, and purchase intentions (Baena, 2016).

Likewise, when customers are affectively committed to an institution, they identify themselves with the club's vision and values, and in turn, they are interested in its growth (Patwardhan and Balasubramanian, 2011). Similarly, followers with strong team engagement are more likely to buy related products and spread positive information about the club. They also offer their opinions and suggestions to help the brand, as well as participate in company-sponsored activities (Kim et al., 2008). Nevertheless, for such commitment to be acknowledged by fans, supporters need to be made aware of such social issues (Mazodier et al., 2016). In short, effective communication with stakeholders, and especially the team's followers, is critical to enable the team's brand to derive value from such social investment.

The Real Madrid Foundation exemplifies this discussion as it exists thanks to the collaboration of many different agents (both public and private institutions), but also thanks to the support from thousands of *Madridistas* (Real Madrid supporters) who wish to reinforce their commitment with the club. Specifically, as Florentino Pérez – Chairman of Real Madrid – argued,

> [A]ll Real Madrid supporters should feel proud of the Real Madrid Foundation battle against poverty and injustice. The work of its Foundation increases every day because it has proved to be a guarantee of quality and its huge commitment to its social project. . . . The Foundation constantly received the support of many organizations and people that wish to contribute their solidarity. A message that must be conveyed to the entire society.[2]

Besides, Real Madrid's figures all support and promote the team's CSR activities whenever they can. All these actions help to increase the emotional attachment the followers have towards Real Madrid as well as their identification with the club, creating a shared social identity, as discussed in the next section.

Social marketing as a tool to get affection and support in sports

As stated, the club is well aware of the importance of its message reaching all the entities and people that lend or may lend their support, and society as a whole. To achieve this goal, it is essential that detailed information about every single initiative undertaken by the Real Madrid Foundation is made known. Specifically, the team has attempted to develop involvement activities as part of a broader CSR initiative, which can also be used to increase and maintain the bonds between the club and the community. In this sense, the following vehicles are used to help spread the word about its social initiatives:

i. *Magazine.* A quarterly publication, the magazine has a circulation of near 10,000 copies. It provides information on prominent national and international projects and contains a heritage section with stories and images of Real Madrid. Recipients of the magazines are the patrons, associate members and sponsors.
ii. *E-Newsletter.* It is a monthly publication that informs members and associates of the most important Real Madrid Foundation events.

iii. *Annual Report.* They provide a detailed record of the activities and projects developed by the Foundation Real Madrid. It is published in both English and Spanish and includes an evaluation of the economic management and audit. The Annual Report shows the solidarity challenges that have been consociated during the season.
iv. *Publishing.* Through the publication of books, Real Madrid describes the club's history as the values that characterized the institution.
v. *Realmadrid.com.* This website hosts the Foundation's own webpage. It receives more than 10 million visits per month and publishes information of its most important events and activities.
vi. *Social Networks.* As a part of its effort to increase its level of support as much as possible, the Real Madrid Foundation has a strong presence on Facebook and Twitter. Particularly, the Foundation has over 4 million followers on Facebook, which makes this Foundation the most followed charitable sport institution worldwide.

Real Madrid also collaborates with many individual athletes who have set up charitable foundations (i.e., the Rafael Nadal Foundation). In addition, it organizes special events with the collaboration of famous stars to get funds for a charitable purpose. The concert organized by Real Madrid in June 2016 at the Santiago Bernabéu to pay tribute to Spanish singer Plácido Domingo and celebrate his 75th birthday could serve as an example. In particular, as stated by the Chairman of the team – Florentino Pérez – during the presentation of the event, "Plácido

HISPANIC WORLD

VOLVER A "HISPANIC WORLD"

Florentino Perez announces concert for Placido Domingo at Bernabeu

SOCCER REAL MADRID | 09 de diciembre de 2015

G+1

Spanish tenor Placido Domingo delivers her speech during the presentation of "Placido en el alma" charity concert at Santiago Bernabeu stadium in Madrid, Spain, 9, December 2015. EFE

Figure 13.1 Tribute and charitable concert to the Maestro Plácido Domingo at the Santiago Bernabéu Stadium

Source: http://hispanos.servidornoticias.com/309_hispanic-world/3504381_florentino-perez-announces-concert-for-placido-domingo-at-Bernabéu.html. Last accessed on March 18, 2016.

Domingo is one of Real Madrid's foremost ambassadors and this will be an extraordinary event that recognizes the exceptional career of a true great. . . . The Santiago Bernabéu is and will always be his home." Profits will be donated to the Real Madrid Foundation academies in Mexico, of which Plácido Domingo is a great proponent. By doing so, the team increases the number of potential (direct and indirect) beneficiaries as well as the engagement with the team.

Experiential marketing

The omnipresence of sport has prompted the elevation of teams as influential members of the global community (i.e., issues such as education, social values, etc.). Accordingly, top clubs are currently addressing social issues and act in a responsible manner with community-based sports organizations. Such initiatives may take the form of athlete volunteerism, educational initiative, charitable donations and community initiatives, all of which aim to provide assistance to the local communities in which the sporting club operates (Mazodier et al., 2016).

Likewise, sports programs and events provide a natural and non-political arena where partners can meet up to strengthen the interaction of business, NGOs, civil society and political institutions. Specifically, Real Madrid's social initiatives are carried out in nearly 400 socio-sporting schools located in 70 countries of Europe, America, Africa, the Middle East and Asia, helping more than 60,000 people either directly or indirectly. To achieve this goal, volunteers and collaborating members play a crucial role. In particular, as shown in Figure 13.2, the Real Madrid Foundation is mostly aimed at

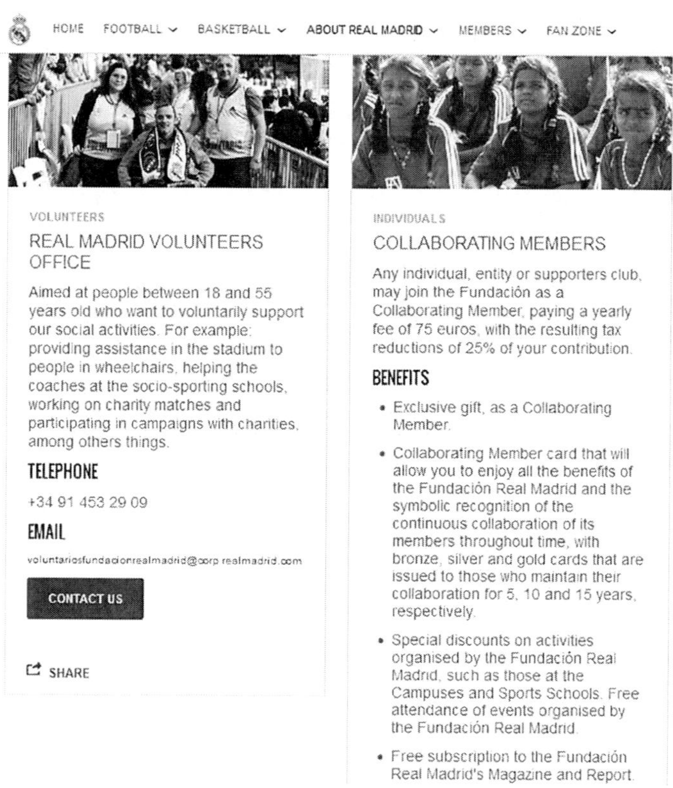

Figure 13.2 Real Madrid Foundation website informs supporters how to help people

Source: Real Madrid Foundation website. Last accessed on March 23, 2016.

people between 18 and 55 years old, who want to voluntarily support social activities like providing assistance in the stadium to people in wheelchairs, helping the coaches at the socio-sporting schools, or working on charity matches and participating in campaigns with charities.

Any individual, entity or supporters club may also join the Foundation Real Madrid as a collaborating member, paying a yearly fee of €75. Collaborators also receive an exclusive gift as a Collaborating Member as well as Collaborating Member Card. Special discounts on activities organized by the Foundation Real Madrid, such as those at the Campuses and Sports Schools, are also offered in conjunction with free attendance of events organized by the Foundation Real Madrid and free subscription to the Foundation Real Madrid's Magazine and Report.

The above-mentioned actions aim to get followers immersed in the team's social experiences. In this sense, having a prosocial agenda means having a powerful marketing tool that may build and shape the team's status (Walker and Kent, 2009). That is, through CSR programs, sport teams can further enhance their position in the society, which positively affects fan attraction, commitment and social identification (Walters, 2009). Membership in a social group also strengthens community cohesion and drives a strong feeling of commitment to the brand (Pronschinske, Groza and Walker, 2012). Thus, getting involved in the actions carried by the team to get social welfare in the communities in which the club operates may help followers to feel part of this social community and enhance its identification with the team (Gruen, Summers and Acito, 2000).

Moreover, the Real Madrid Foundation facilitates the social integration of immigrant children and their families through the joint practice of football and complementary education programs

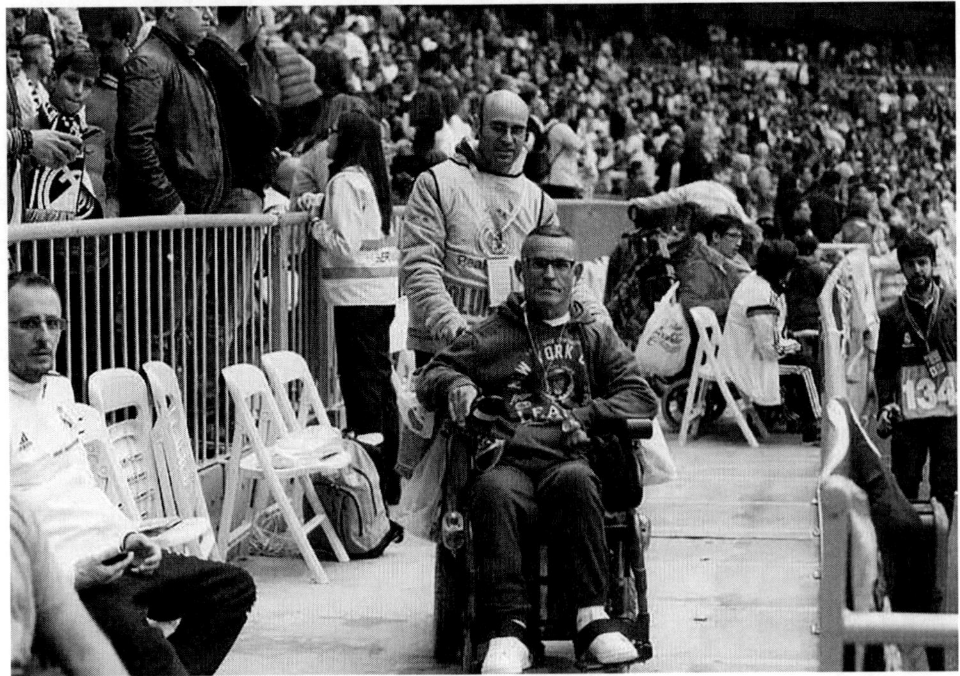

Figures 13.3a and 13.3b Volunteering in the Real Madrid Foundation

Source: Real Madrid Foundation Newsletter, N° 51, p. 44.

Figures 13.3a and 13.3b (Continued)

worldwide. The new football clinic opened in Panama in late 2015, which involved children aged between 5 and 17, illustrates how educational activities are important for Real Madrid. More specifically, part of the revenues serve to finance the three social sports schools operated by the Real Madrid Foundation in the country, located in Panama City and the towns of Chitré and Tolé, that are attended by more than 500 children. Emilio Butragueño, Real Madrid's Director of Institutional Relations, was on hand to officially present this clinic. During his visit to the country, Butragueño was received by Lorena Castillo de Varela, the first lady of the Republic of Panama, at the Presidential Palace, who said: "I'm grateful to you for sharing this time with us; I know that the lessons our children will learn will have an impact on every single one of them, and will help them to be better citizens."[3]

According to the above discussion, it has to be noted that funding for all those social projects also comes from the club and includes the charitable matches, the Foundation's annual gala or special events organized in which it instills values to be emulated by society. Corporate partnerships are also a major source of the Foundation's resources, however. For instance, every year, the Real Madrid Foundation organizes the Corazón Classic Match at the stadium Santiago Bernabéu. Particularly, Real Madrid Leyendas and Liverpool Legends played each other in a charity game in 2015. Ticket prices were set at €5, €10 and €15, and all the proceeds went towards buying educational materials for more than 20,000 children at risk of exclusion as part of the Promoting Educational Success program by the Spanish Red Cross. The social target was more than exceeded, thanks to the huge crowd that went to enjoy the outreach match. Most funds were used for education and sports programs at shelter homes and juvenile detention centers for minors under state care. On top of the proceeds obtained from gate receipts, a significant donation was also made by El Corte Inglés (Spanish retail chain), in addition to the many anonymous fans who did their bit by sending a charity text message. Support also came from the Fundación SEUR, which provided its logistics services for the delivery of the materials, ensuring they arrived at their destination in perfect condition, as depicted in Figure 13.5.

Figure 13.4 Emilio Butragueño and Lorena Castillo, the first lady of Panama, with students of the social sports schools

Source: Real Madrid Foundation Newsletter, N 51, p. 19.

Figure 13.5 Handover of school materials to families after the 2015 Corazón Classic Match

Source: Real Madrid Foundation Newsletter, N1 51, p. 21.

Overall, sports fans are becoming more conscious and demanding commitment with society (Mattera and Baena, 2014). By doing so, teams have to build long-term relationships with the wider society (Lichtenstein, Drumwright and Braig, 2004) and make an effort to keep supporters informed about the social initiatives carried out. This is associated with the idea of creating memorable experiences (Bodet, 2016). More specifically, when supporters identify closely with a team, a sense of connectedness ensues, and they begin to define themselves with the club (Mael and Ashforth, 1992). They then become vested in the successes and failures of such an organization (Lings and Owen, 2007), which drives a greater sense of belonging to a community (Eisingerich and Rubera, 2010).

In other words, individuals internalize the values and beliefs of the community as their own through membership in a social group, creating a shared social identity (Gruen, Summers and Acito, 2000). The feeling of identification and commitment to the brand is discussed in the next section.

Methodology

In an attempt to test the role of CSR as a driver of fan commitment in sports, an online survey was created and administered on the survey platform www.surveymonkey.com from March till April 2016. Participation was solicited among undergraduate students from the university of the author via e-mail, which provided a direct link to the survey and stated the academic nature of the present research. This produced a total of 83 participants aged between 18 and 25 years, resulting in a mean age of 21 years.

To avoid any kind of bias, respondents had to first state if they consider themselves Real Madrid fans. Only those who affirmatively answered the above question were invited to complete the survey. As all of the items were configured as mandatory in order to move on to the next question, the problem of missing values was not an issue in this study.

After completing the first survey, participants were invited to follow the Real Madrid Foundation (through the official website and social networks) for a month. By so doing, we attempt to understand the difference between the predictive and real impact of updating the fans about the CSR actions carried out by the club. The purpose is to analyze whether this positively affects social identification and fan engagement towards the club. To achieve this goal, respondents, after having followed the Real Madrid Foundation for 2 months, were asked to repeat the survey that they filled out at the beginning of this research. An open question was also provided to invite respondents to talk about this experience. An average mean test was then conducted to support or reject the following hypotheses:

H_0 (null hypothesis): There is no difference in means.
H_1 (alternative hypothesis): There is a difference in means.

Regarding the variable measurement, Carroll and Ahuvia's (2006) concept of self-expressive brand (SELF-EXPRESSIVE) was combined and adapted to sports. In particular, the word "brand" was replaced by the word "club" to clarify the context for the respondents. It was measured through Likert-type scales, consisting of the 5 points from strongly disagree to strongly agree. The example of Eisingerich and Rubera's (2010) work was followed to assess the social image (CSR). Nevertheless, a slight adaptation was required. Particularly, the word "brand" was replaced by "Real Madrid" to clarify the context for the respondents. The effect of word-of-mouth (WOM), understood as a non-digital way of engaging with a brand, was

Table 13.3 Measurement of variables

Self-Expressive Brand – Adapted from Carroll and Ahuvia (2006)
This brand symbolizes the kind of person I really am inside.
This brand reflects my personality.
This brand is an extension of my inner self.
This brand mirrors the real me.
This brand contributes to my image.
This brand adds to a social "role" I play.
This brand has a positive impact on what others think of me.
This brand improves the way society views me.
CSR – Adapted from Eisingerich and Rubera (2010)
I consider Real Madrid as a socially responsible brand.[a]
Real Madrid is more beneficial to society's welfare than other soccer teams.[a]
Real Madrid does not contribute something to society (items were reverse coded).[a]
Word of Mouth (WOM) – Adapted from Carroll and Ahuvia (2006)
I have recommended this club to lots of people.
I "talk up" this club to my friends.
I try to spread the good-word about this club.
I give this club tons of positive word-of-mouth advertising.
Active Social Engagement (ASE) – Own elaboration
I attend the social events organized by the Real Madrid Foundation.[a]
I serve as a volunteer for the Real Madrid Foundation.[a]
I participate in the social initiatives performed by the Real Madrid Foundation.[a]
I donate funds to the Real Madrid Foundation.[a]

[a]Answer scale: 1 = not at all; 2 = slightly; 3 = quite; 4 = extremely.
[b]Answer scale: 1 = never; 2 = sometimes; 3 = usually; 4 = always.
[c]Answer choice: 1 = yes; 2 = no.

considered. As shown in Table 13.3, the variable was surging from the study of Carroll and Ahuvia (2006), although adapted to the sport environment, similar to the prior items. Finally, the active engagement and fan participation in the co-creation of such social practices (EXPERIENTIAL) was assessed through the following items "I attend the social events organized by the Real Madrid Foundation", "I serve as a volunteer for the Real Madrid Foundation", "I participate in the social initiatives performed by the Real Madrid Foundation", and "I donate funds to the Real Madrid Foundation".

Data analysis

Reliability for each of the factors was obtained using the calculation of a Cronbach's alpha coefficient. In particular, the Cronbach's alpha coefficients ranged from 0.74 to 0.83, thus providing support of internal consistency. Reliability is also evidenced by the fact that the lowest composite reliability value is well above the suggested level of 0.70 (Fornell and Larcker, 1981). Likewise, as shown in Table 13.4, the Average Variance Extracted (AVE) coefficients were computed. Values always were well above 0.50, as required to evidence convergent validity.

Table 13.4 Reliability and validity test

Self-Expressive	Cronbach's Alfa (whole scale)	AVE	Composite Reliability
	0.765	0.581	0.818
CSR	Cronbach's Alfa (whole scale)	AVE	Composite Reliability
	0.741	0.617	0.875
Active Social Engagement	Cronbach's Alfa (whole scale)	AVE	Composite Reliability
	0.795	0.615	0.897
WOM	Cronbach's Alfa (whole scale)	AVE	Composite Reliability
	0.834	0.631	0.910

Table 13.5 T-student tests for equity of means results

VARIABLES	*Mean*	*Standard Deviation*	*95% Confidence Intervale of the Difference*		*t-student*	*Significance (p-value)*
			Lower	*Upper*		
Self-Expressive Brand	0.0769	1.4979	−0.8282	0.9821	0.185	**0.086**
CSR	0.5455	0.9342	−0.0822	1.1731	1.936	**0.082**
WOM	0.5385	1.05	−0.0961	1.173	1.849	**0.079**
Active Engagement	0.0833	1.0836	−0.6052	0.7718	0.266	**0.005**

Results

As stated, after having tested the reliability and validity for each of the variables considered in this study (SELF-EXPRESSIVE BRAND, CSR, ACTIVE SOCIAL ENGAGEMENT and WOM), an average mean test was conducted to check whether there is no difference in means (null hypothesis). Results are shown in Table 13.5.

As the sample findings are unlikely, given the null hypothesis, we can reject the null hypothesis. Typically, this involves comparing the p-value to the significance level (95%), and rejecting the null hypothesis when the p-value is less than the significance level. Therefore, since the p-value for every single variable considered in this study is lower than the significance level (0.05), we can reject the null hypothesis and support the alternative hypothesis (there is a difference in means).

In short, our finding reveal that updating the fans about the CSR actions carried out by the club positively affects their social identification and commitment towards the brand (SELF-EXPRESSIVE and WOM). Social image (CSR) and social commitment (ACTIVE ENGAGEMENT) were positively affected as well.

Discussion

Literature has suggested the importance of the strength of connection followers hold towards sport brands (Kunkel, Funk and Hill, 2013). Specifically, highly involved fans are more likely to watch the sport brand live or via media, buy merchandise and positively evaluate sponsors of sports brands (Lings and Owen, 2007). Then, getting supporters involved towards the brand leads to increased income for the team (Bergkvist and Bech-Larsen, 2010). In other words, when a consumer identifies closely with a club, a sense of connectedness ensues, and he or she begins to define himself or herself with the sport entity (Mael and Ashforth, 1992). This is crucial for every sport entity, as fans identification with their team may condition their behavior (Rodriguez-Pomeda, Casani and Alonso-Almeida, 2015).

Besides, we operate in a global society, which implies that people are nowadays more aware of firm's actions in terms of social problems (Mattera and Baena, 2014). Under this scenario, traditional marketing may not be enough to impact the club's followers. Therefore, new concepts like experiential marketing and brand communities should be further investigated to determine its influence on fan commitment. In an attempt to shed light on this topic, the present study focuses on the Real Madrid Foundation. This exists thanks to the collaboration of many different agents (both public and private institutions), but also thanks to the support from thousands of Real Madrid supporters, who wish to reinforce their commitment with the club and expect a serious involvement in society from their sport brand. Moreover, the Real Madrid Foundation is the most followed charitable sport institution worldwide.

Regarding the above discussion, as Florentino Pérez – Chairman of the Real Madrid F.C. – argued,

> all Real Madrid supporters should feel proud of the Real Madrid Foundation battle against poverty and injustice. The work of its Foundation increases every day because it has proved to be a guarantee of quality and its huge commitment to its social project. . . . The Foundation constantly received the support of many organizations and people that wish to contribute their solidarity. A message that must be conveyed to the entire society.[4]

In short, the club is well aware of the importance of its message reaching all the entities and people that lend or may lend their support, as well as society as a whole.

According to the obtained results, it is essential to provide detailed information of all the social initiatives undertaken by the team, as part of a broader CSR initiative. This can be useful to increase and maintain the bonds between the team and the fan community. Specifically, our findings demonstrate the appropriateness to implement a brand management strategy to assess customer's perceived ethicality and incorporate it as a part of the integrated marketing plan. Particularly, the club's engagement to social causes becomes a factor to take into account when building sports brand and team identification. Real Madrid Foundation exemplifies this discussion. In particular, as Julio González said,

> thousands of boys and girls see Real Madrid as a reference model that accomplishes the expectations generated by the team tradition and colors. . . . The Real Madrid Foundation is an outstanding symbol of the club and unites all Real Madrid supporters. Therefore, they can proudly say that Real Madrid has achieved success far beyond the football field.

That is, "Real Madrid Foundation is the proof of fact that using our will, we (the team) can achieve anything. The Foundation show there is not any (caring) challenge unattainable to Real Madrid."[5]

Besides, Real Madrid

> is fully aware that its strength, power and prestige must focus of fighting inequality and above all, the injustice affecting the most vulnerable, the boys and girls that need

> us, wherever they are, because for Real Madrid, in the area of solidarity, there are no border.[6]

For that reason, the club runs regular "sports camps" for children around the world while also working in prisons and hospitals and with immigrants and individuals with physical or learning difficulties. Moreover, Real Madrid focuses on social welfare and integration by cooperating with both public and private agents; helping more than 80,000 people either directly or indirectly in 70 countries of Europe, America, Africa, the Middle East and Asia. As shown in this study, fan engagement in such initiatives may help to reinforce the followers commitment with the club, which in turn may drive self-expressive brands.

The extensive use of information and communication technologies made by the Real Madrid in order to attract a worldwide audience, as well as transmit corporate values and ideas, should be also noted. From its very inception, the team has always encouraged groups of fans (*peñas blancas*).[7] Additionally, online brand communities allow organizations to better communicate to their followers and establish rich relationships in which the fans become heavily involved with the organization (Muniz and O'Guinn, 2001). In other words, the value of developing a sense of community around the sport team is eminent (Grant, Heere and Dickson, 2011). This discussion aligns with prior literature on the Social Identity framework, which posits that individuals internalize the values and beliefs of the community as their own through membership in a social group, creating a shared social identity (Tajfel, 1978).

Our results also confirm the fact that followers like to build consumer-brand relations, talk about this with their peers, and be active in the creation of their own experience instead of common spectators.

Conclusions

According to the Social Identity Theory, individuals identify themselves to varying degrees with different social groups. In so doing, they adopt the norms and values of the group. Then, the individual's self-identity becomes defined by the group, and they experience the group's successes and failures as their own (Lings and Owen, 2007).

Based on the above framework, this work has demonstrated that CSR activities carried out by the team positively influences the followers' commitment towards the brand. Particularly, keeping fans updated about such charitable activities help to increase the bonds between the club and their supporters. Moreover, through CSR programs that allow fans active participation, sport teams can further enhance their stature in the society, which will positively affects emotional attachment towards the brand. In words of one of the correspondents,

> Volunteering with the Real Madrid Foundation is a chance to stand shoulder to shoulder with those who are in need of our help – an opportunity to get involved in an effort underpinned by a commitment to solidarity. As a volunteer, I have participated in a wide range of projects organized by the Real Madrid Foundation (i.e., providing assistance to people with disabilities at football and basketball matches and offering support to immigrant children at social sports schools). There is nothing more rewarding than helping others. At the Real Madrid Foundation, we believe that by all working together we can build a better world.

This work also provides readers with an overview of the current state of brand engagement in sport marketing, which could help researchers interested in gaining further insight into this topic. Furthermore, the strategy of Real Madrid, a leading organization in sports, marketing and CSR, has been discussed, which adds incremental value to the literature.

Finally, the present study attempted to provide various practical implications. In particular, it is our hope that our results may serve marketers as a guide to their future strategic plans. The example of Real Madrid could be then used as a standpoint for other sports teams to engage in social commitments and use these as a basis for their marketing strategy. In doing so, the team will not only create significant benefits for the communities that the club collaborate with, but also position the sports brand as a socially committed one. In addition, as shown in this study, social practices create a strong link between fans and the sports brand, which ensures a long-lasting relationship between the team and the supporters. Then, for sports marketers working in highly competitive business environments where customer relationships, retention and loyalty are paramount, our findings can aid in the elaboration of an efficient marketing mix in a global market.

We conclude this work by pointing out some limitations and offering suggestions for further research. First, similar to the other online surveys, the sample in this study includes only those people who were willing to answer the questions in the survey, and this causes limitation. Another limitation of the study is the methodology. In particular, we have applied an analysis which is limited to less than 1 year in the club's life. It would be interesting to widen this time span with new observations to test the existence of discontinuities. Then, we propose this as a further research avenue.

Notes

1 The author wishes to thank Emilio Butragueño, Director of Institutional Relations of Real Madrid, and Julio González, Managing Director of the Real Madrid Foundation, for their support and availability.
2 Letter from the Chairman of Real Madrid, Florentino Pérez, published in the Real Madrid Foundation's Annual Report 2014/2015.
3 Interview published in the Real Madrid Foundation Newsletter, N1 51 (2015).
4 Letter from the Chairman of Real Madrid published in the Real Madrid Foundation's Annual Report 2015/2016.
5 Julio González (Managing Director of the Foundation Real Madrid) was interviewed by the author the 21st of November, 2015.
6 Florentino Pérez, Chairman of Real Madrid. Foundation Real Madrid Annual Report 2015/2016.
7 They act as private clubs that organized trips to other stadiums when Real Madrid plays away, fraternity meals, etc. They actively collaborate with the team in the co-creation of many initiatives carried out by the team, most of them socially oriented.

Bibliography

AHUVIA, A. (1993) *I love it! Towards an unifying theory of love across diverse love object*, Ph. Dissertation. Northwestern University, Evanston, Illinois.

AHUVIA, A. (2005) "Beyond the extended self: Loved objects and consumers' identity narratives", *Journal of Consumer Research*, 32(1), 171–184.

ALBERT, N., MERUNKA, D. and VALETTE-FLORENCE, P. (2009) "The feeling of love towards a brand: Concept and measurement", *Advances in Consumer Research*, 36, 300–307.

BAENA, V. (2016) Analyzing online and mobile marketing strategies as brand love drivers in sports teams: Findings from real Madrid, *International Journal of Sport Marketing & Sponsorship*, 17(3), 202–218.

BATRA, R., AHUVIA, A. and BAGOZZI, R. (2012) "Brand love", *Journal of Marketing*, 76(March), 1–16.

BERGKVIST, L. and BECH-LARSEN, T. (2010) "Two studies of consequences and actionable antecedents of brand love", *Journal of Brand Management*, 17, 504–518.

BODET, G. (2016) "Experiential marketing and sporting events", in S. Chadwick, N. Chanavat and M. Desbordes *Handbook of Sports Marketing*, Chapter 16, pp. 222–231. Routledge Taylor & Francis Group Publisher. New York.

BÜHLER, A. and NUFER, G. (2016) "Relationship marketing in sports: Building and establishing long-standing relations in the business of sports", in S. Chadwick, N. Chanavat and M. Desbordes *Handbook of Sports Marketing*, Chapter 15, pp. 207–221. Routledge Taylor & Francis Group Publisher. New York.

CARROLL, B. and AHUVIA, A. (2006) "Some antecedents and outcomes of brand love", *Marketing Letters*, 17, 79–89.

CHANAVAT, N. and BODET, G. (2009) "Internationalisation and sport branding strategy: A French perception of the Big Four brands", *Qualitative Market Research: An International Journal*, 12(4), 460–481.

DUTTON, J. and DUKERICH, J. (1991) "Keeping an eye on the mirror: Image and identity on organizational adaptation", *Academy of Management Journal*, 34(3), 517–554.

EISINGERICH, A. and RUBERA, G. (2010) "Drivers of brand commitment: A cross-national investigation", *Journal of International Marketing*, 18(2), 64–79.

FORBES (2013) "Top Forbes' Social Media Rankings". December, 2013.

FORNELL, C. and LARCKER, D. F. (1981) "Evaluating structural equation models with unobservable variables and measurement error", *Journal of Marketing Research*, 18(1), 39–50.

FOURNIER, S. (1998) "Consumers and their brands: Developing relationship theory in consumer research", *Journal of Consumer Research*, 24(4), 343–373.

GRANT, N., HEERE, B. and DICKSON, G. (2011) "New sport teams and the development of brand community", *European Sport Management Quarterly*, 11(1), 35–54.

GRUEN, T., SUMMERS, W. and ACITO, F. (2000) "Relationship marketing activities, commitment and membership behaviors in professional associations", *Journal of Marketing*, 34(3), 34–49.

HOLLIS, N. (2008) *The Global Brand: How to Create and Develop Lasting Brand Value in the World Market*, Milward Brown, New York.

IOAKIMIDIS, M. (2010) "Digital marketing of professional sports clubs: Engaging fans on a new playing field", *International Journal of Sports Marketing & Sponsorship*, 11(4), July, 271–282.

JONES, T. M., FELPS, W. and BIGLEY, G. A. (2007) "Ethical theory and stakeholder-related decisions: The role of stakeholder culture", *Academy of Management Review*, 32(1), 137–155.

KIM, J., CHOI, J., QUALLS, W. and HAN, K. (2008) "It takes a marketplace community to raise brand commitment: The role of online communities", *Journal of Marketing Management*, 24(3/4), 409–431.

KUNKEL, T., FUNK, D. and HILL, B. (2013) "Brand architecture, drivers of consumer involvement, and brand loyalty with professional sport leagues and teams", *Journal of Sport Management*, 27, 177–192.

LEVERMORE, R. (2010) "CSR for Development Through Sport: examining its potential and limitations", *Third World Quarterly*, 31(2).

LICHTENSTEIN, R., DRUMWRIGHT, M. and BRAIG, M. (2004) "The effect of corporate social responsibility on customer donations to corporate-supported nonprofits", *Journal of Marketing*, 68(October), 16–32.

LINGS, I. and OWEN, K. (2007) "Buying a sponsor's brand: The role of affective commitment to the sponsored team", *Journal of Marketing Management*, 23(5/6), 483–496.

MAEL, F. and ASHFORTH, B. (1992) "Alumni and their alma mater: A partial test of the reformulated model of organizational identification", *Journal of Organizational Behavior*, 13, 103–123.

MARKUS, H. and NURIUS, P. (1986) Possible selves. *American Psychologist*, 41(9), 954–969.

MATTERA, M. and BAENA, V. (2014) "Getting brand commitment through internet and mobile sports marketing: An insight on Real Madrid football team", in S. Chadwick, N. Chanavat, and M. Desbordes *Strategies in Sports Marketing: Technologies and Emerging Trends*, Chapter 13, pp. 203–218. Ed: IGI Global, Pennsylvania, EE.UU.

MATTERA, M., BAENA, V. and CERVIÑO, J. (2014) "Investing time wisely: Enhancing firm's brand awareness through stakeholder engagement in the service sector", *International Journal of Management Practice*, 7(2), 126–143.

MAZODIER, M., PLEWA, C., PALMER, K. and QUESTER, P. (2016) "Achieving corporate social responsibility through sponsorship", in S. Chadwick, N. Chanavat and M. Desbordes *Handbook of Sports Marketing*, Chapter 22, pp. 317–326. Routledge Taylor & Francis Group Publisher. New York.

MCWILLIAMS, A., SIEGEL, D., and WRIGHT, P. (2006) "Corporate social responsibility: Strategic implications", *Journal of Management Studies*, 43, 1–18.

MUNIZ, A. and SCHAU, H. (2005) "Religiosity in the abandoned Apple Newton brand community", *Journal of Consumer Research*, 31(4), 737–747.

MUNIZ, A. and O'GUINN, T. (2001) "Brand Community", *Journal of Consumer Research*, 27(4), 412–432.

NETBREEZE (2013) *Report*. Available at https://api-reports.netbreeze.ch/report [Accessed: 12 Mar 2015].

PATWARDHAN, H. and BALASUBRAMANIAN, S. K. (2011) "Brand romance: A complementary approach to explain emotional attachment towards brands", *Journal of Product & Brand Management*, 20(4), 297–308.

PHUA, J. (2010) "Sports fan and media use: Influence on sports fan identification and collective self-esteem", *International Journal of Sport Communication*, 3, 190–216.

PRONSCHINSKE, M., GROZA, M. D. and WALKER, M. (2012) "Attracting Facebook 'fans': The importance of authenticity and engagement as a social networking strategy for professional sport teams", *Sport Marketing Quarterly*, 21, 221–231.

RODRIGUEZ-POMEDA, J., CASANI, F. and ALONSO-ALMEIDA, M. (2015) "Emotions' management within the Real Madrid football club business model", *Soccer and Society*, 1(3), 1–14.

SHIMP, T. and MADDEN, T. (1988) "Consumer-object relations: A conceptual framework based analogously on Sternber's triangular theory of love", *Advances in Consumer Research*, 15, 119–135.

SMITH, A., and WESTERBEEK, H. (2007) "Sport as a vehicle for deploying corporate social responsibility", *Journal of Corporate Citizenship*, 25, 43–54.

TAJFEL, H. (1978) "The social identity theory of intergroup behavior" in S. Worchel and W. Austin "*Psychology of Intergroup Relations*", pp. 7–24. Nelson Hall. Chicago.

VINCENT, J., HILL, J. S. and LEE, J. W. (2009) "The multiple brand personality of David Beckham: A case study of the Beckham Brand", *Sport Marketing Quarterly*, 18(3), 173–180.

WALKER, M., and KENT, A. (2009) "Do fans care? Assessing the influence of corporate social responsibility on consumer attitudes in the sport industry", *Journal of Sport Management*, 23, 743–769.

WALKER, M., KENT, A., and VINCENT, J. (2011) "CSR communication among professional sport organizations: Stakeholder information and involvement strategies", *Sport Marketing Quarterly*, 19, 125–131.

WALLACE, E., BUIL, I. and de CHERNATONY, L. (2014) "Consumer engagement with self-expressive brands: Brand love and WOM outcomes", *Journal of Product & Brand Management*, 23(1), 33–42.

WALTERS, G. (2009) "Corporate social responsibility through sport: The community sports trust model as a CSR delivery agency", *Journal of Corporate Citizenship*, 35, 81–94.

ZAGNOLI, P. and RADICCHI, E. (2016) "Sports marketing and new media: Value co-creation and intertype competition", in S. Chadwick, N. Chanavat and M. Desbordes *Handbook of Sports Marketing*, Chapter 20, pp. 277–298. Routledge Taylor & Francis Group Publisher. New York.

14

THE MANAGEMENT OF FOOTBALL BRANDS

Brand identity management illustrated by Borussia Dortmund

Gerd Nufer, André Bühler and Sarah Jürgens

Box 14.1 Club history and awards

The "ball game" club Borussia Dortmund 09 (abbreviated Borussia Dortmund, BVB, or BVB 09) is one of the German clubs with the best sporting results in men's football: in addition to eight German championships and three victories in the German Cup, BVB won the 1966 European Cup Winners' Cup (making it the first German club to win a European Cup), and in 1997, the Champions League, at the same time as the Intercontinental Cup.

The club has over 116,700 members.

Since November 1999, the section of licensed players Borussia, Team II, as well as the "youth", are integrated into the Dortmund GmbH & Co. This company, has been present in 'SDAX index since June 23, 2014.

Honors

Internationally

- Winner of the Champions League in 1997
- Finalist of the Champions League in 2013
- Winner of the European Cup Winners' Cup in 1966
- Finalist of the UEFA Cup in 1993 and 2002
- Winner of the Intercontinental Cup in 1997
- Finalist of the UEFA Super Cup in 1997

Nationally

- German Champion in 1956, 1957, 1963, 1995, 1996, 2002, 2011, 2012
- Vice-Champion of Germany in 1949, 1961, 1966, 1992, 2013, 2014
- Winner of the German Cup in 1965, 1989, 2012

- Finalist of the German Cup in 1963, 2008, 2014
- Winner of the German Super Cup in 1989, 1995, 1996, 2013, 2014
- Indoor German Champion in 1990, 1991, 1992, 1999
- West German Champion in 1948, 1949, 1950, 1953, 1956, 1957
- Champion of Westphalia in 1947

Box 14.2 Sales and revenues of Borussia Dortmund 2013–2014

Sales: 223.78 million euros
Profit for the year: 10.55 million euros
Revenue matches: 40.52 million euros
Advertising revenue/sponsorship: 73.0 million euros
TV rights revenues and other media: 81.44 million euros
Commercial/merchandising/restore revenue: 19.55 million euros

Brands are everywhere in the sports business. The importance of brands depends not only on the different functions that brands play in the sports field based on supply and demand, but also the financial value that brands now account for in sports organizations. In the context of the commercialization and professionalization of sport, a global visibility of the brand is becoming increasingly more important to sports organizations. Hence the need for brand management which should be comprehensive and systematic.

Despite a growing awareness of the importance of the management of trademarks at the club level, there is a significant delay regarding the professional management of the brand within the Bundesliga clubs. So far, the principles of brand identity management were rarely applied, and most clubs have given up, despite a high economic potential, the ability to create competitive advantages in economic terms, but also in sports terms. In this chapter, we will study the success factors of the management of brand identity of professional football clubs from the actual case of Borussia Dortmund.

Brands in sport

First we will show how, in sport in general and in football in particular, brands can be built and perpetuated through brand management (Bühler and Schunk, 2013).

The weight of brands in sport

The importance of the brand to a sports club is emphasized by Jorge Valdano (former sports director of Real Madrid) and recalled in the study of Mohr and Merget (2004, p. 106): "Every club is a brand with products marketing. Now what is happening on the ground is no longer the only important thing. The image of the club is paramount."

Table 14.1 Presentation of the interviewees

Functions of the Interviewee	*Date, Time and Place of the Interview*
General manager Commercial Service/Marketing: CSR/Tickets/Managing supporters 1. FSV Mainz 05	2014 49 min (17:00–17:49) Club Headquarters
Journalist and documentary filmmaker	2014 1 h, 57 min (10:30–12:27) Colourfield tell a vision GbR, Dortmund
CEO of the city-marketing company (CMG) Framework for Dortmund agency	2014 1 h, 17 min (14:00–15:17) Dortmund Agency
Director of the Dortmund agency	2014 1 h, 17 min (14:00–15:17) Dortmund Agency
Head of Marketing and Public Relations, Evonik Industries (main sponsor of BVB)	2014 18 min (18:30–18:48) Restaurant in Essen
Senior Account Manager Borussia Dortmund to the Sportfive agency	2014 1 h, 4 min (12:00–13:04) Club Headquarters
Director of Marketing and Sales Department, Borussia Dortmund	2014 39 min (10:00–10:39) Club Headquarters
Commentator for football matches and sports journalist	2014 24 min (20:00–20:24) Plazamedia GmbH, Ismaning
German footballer, former captain of Borussia Dortmund	2014 34 min (12:15–12:49) Hotel Salon Elisabeth, Kirchberg (Tyrol, Austria)

Indeed, beyond revenues, clubs have increasingly more vocation to act as a commercial enterprise in the market. Because sport should, too, confront the fundamental issues in terms of the economy and resist competition to ensure at least the meager resources from ticket sales and sponsors. That's why the clubs now assign an important role in their own exhibition as a sports brand and in its commercial value.

That said, the purpose of professional sports brands proves quite comparable to the objectives set by the companies operating in other economic areas: appropriate use of the brand must prove economically profitable or long-term. The economic importance of brands in sport was highlighted by Gladden and Milne (1999) and also by Bauer, Sauer and Schmitt (2004). Their studies accurately measure the significant impact of club brands on their economic success. But for club officials, it is important to distinguish, at least partially, between economic success and athletic success and therefore also to use the stabilizing function of trademarks. Thus, many clubs give to this increasing importance in the operation of their own brand whose wise use must ultimately be profitable or long-term. It is precisely in the field of sport that this theory makes sense. The flagship clubs of the Bundesliga show how one can put forward its own sports brand by leveraging the strengths of the brand: Borussia Dortmund puts emotion at the center of its brand with the slogan "Echte Liebe" ("Real Love"), while Bayern uses "Mia san mia" (listed on the shirt of this club), a phrase that expresses the Bavarian self-confidence. With Bayern holding the record for German league titles, this slogan became the authentic brand message.

If one looks internationally, the flagship clubs in Germany had to take better care of their own brand, for other European clubs already make huge efforts to conquer new markets. Thus Bayern seeks, for example, to set up in Asia as the Federal Handball League did the same in the United States (Handelsblatt, 2005, 2009). In recent years, several Bundesliga teams were able to increase the value of their brand significantly. The British rating agency Brand Finance has, in 2014, estimated the value of the FC Bayern brand at 896 million dollars, following internationally Real Madrid with 768 million dollars, then Manchester with 739 million dollars and Barcelona with 622 million dollars. But these examples are rather the exception than the rule, because the brand value of most sports clubs is very low and often hardly measurable. Moreover, one can also ask how sports clubs are actually perceived as brands, and what type of brand do they represent?

The types of brands in sport

The place of its own brand among the competition is the cornerstone of successful brand management. On this subject, many industries and services have a custom to start with market research before making any decision regarding trademarks. This is where we compare its own product or trademark to other branded products to establish a rank. In doing so, it shows different classes or product classifications. In this way, we can define each brand in relation to others based on specific criteria. Through such analysis, the market becomes more transparent, not only for producers, but also for consumers.

For what concerns the sports field, it is essentially the one that offers a product that takes advantage of its own position, and of the relationship with other brands within its market. Through scientific analysis and ranking of brands groupings, officials of sports brands, at first, the means to identify the clubs to which they are able to compete on equal terms. Then they can try, from the conclusions reached will be to continue to systematically develop their own brand. This involves repositioning measures and the awareness that the brand has acquired a dominant position on the market.

An important step in this process is the classification of various types of brands in the various sports leagues. Note that, in the minds of many fans, there is a clear representation of some sports clubs. Thus, one readily cites FC Bayern München as the team that holds the championship record, while clubs like Borussia and Schalke 04 are considered workers' clubs. But the media also frequently classifies the clubs as tradition clubs, club-cults or clubs created from scratch (Süddeutsche Zeitung, 2011; Südwestpresse, 2011). Yet in the sports business, there is not, unlike in other sectors, a division to comprehensive and systematic brands. Although the theme of the sports brand and of the management of sports brands is more and more important in research and academic publications (e.g., Bauer, Exler and Sauer, 2005; Couvelaere and Richelieu, 2005;

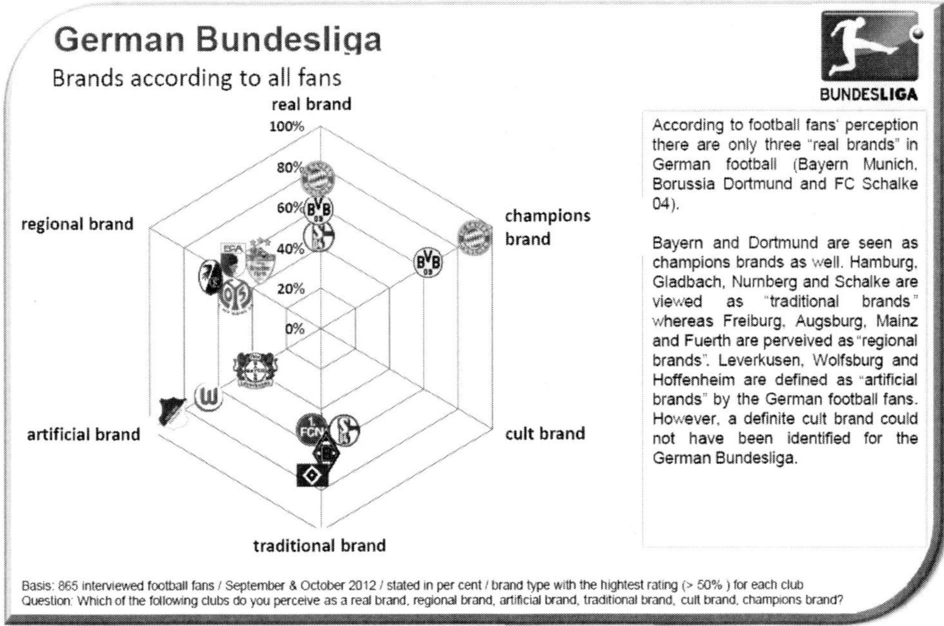

Figure 14.1 Overview of the Bundesliga brands (brand perception by football fans)

Source: Bühler, Scheuermann and Nufer (2013, p. 11).

Mohr and Merget, 2004; Schilhaneck, 2011; Welling, 2005), there is no generally accepted definition of what a sports brand is and what characteristics make a sports organization a real brand. At the same time, more and more clubs, federations and athletes consider themselves a brand, but without presenting evidence of proper management. While in other economic areas there are clear brand classifications (e.g., in the automotive industry with subcategories such as high-end, mid-range, compact), one looks in vain for a homogeneous classification in the economic market of sports.

A study by Bühler and Scheuermann (see Figure 14.1) tried to fill in this gap. Starting from the concept of a brand defined by Burmann, Meffert and Koers (2002, p. 6), who speak of a brand as a "well-defined image, firmly rooted in the consumer's subconscious or other groups concerned with the brand", it was possible, through a survey of 4,678 German fans and 58 clubs of the major German football, handball, basketball and ice hockey leagues, to identify five types of brands (Bühler and Scheuermann, 2014; Bühler, Scheuermann and Nufer, 2013)

- The champion brand (brand attributes: athletic and economic domination of the club, polarizing effect, great enthusiasm or rejection from the fans)
- The historic brand (brand attributes: many sporting successes in the past, always enjoys a good reputation and knows how to attract sympathy from the supporters of other clubs)
- The cult brand (brand attributes: possesses an extraordinary character of exclusivity, a crowd of hardcore fans, also enjoys great popularity from the supporters of other clubs)

- The "made" brand (brand attributes: club created from scratch, no established tradition, few supporters looking to quickly buy sporting success through significant investments)
- Local/regional brand (brand attributes: local heroes, unconditional supporters, mainly in its own region, is less popular in other regions).

In the Bundesliga, FC Bayern München, Borussia Dortmund and FC Schalke 04 are clubs perceived as true brands, associated with known and recognized brand attributes. Borussia Dortmund, for example, has impressively all the attributes of a positive brand representation: the BVB is perceived, both by fans of the club and by all the interviewed fans, as a brand champion, cult brand and historic brand. This image of the brand is based partly on brand attributes which fall between the tradition and on the recent sporting successes, and also on specific marketing activities at the club. The current campaign with the slogan "Real Love" could, in the long term, position the BVB as a cult brand. Dortmund is comparable to SC Freiburg, it is a relatively small club among the competitors in the Bundesliga, but its brand is considered as having a potential, as a regional brand, with authenticity and credibility. For cons, the TSG 1899 Hoffenheim and the VfL Wolfsburg give the impression that they want to confirm their position of a "manufactured" brand. As the position of "brand champion, cult or historic" seems unlikely in the absence of sufficient sports results or essential brand attributes, these clubs may be classified as a "regional" brand. Overall, the study of brands from 2012–2013 confirms what has been observed for years in the professional leagues of sport: many collective sports clubs take themselves for a brand, but few of them are perceived this way. This discrepancy between the image that one makes of its own brand and the image that is perceived by others can be explained in different ways, for example, in the case where club officials overestimate largely or if they do not communicate enough on the strengths of the brand. Ultimately, many clubs lack the foundations for management for a systematic global brand. This is due to a lack of resources and/or expertise. But it may be otherwise; some cases – admittedly few – prove this: Borussia Dortmund tries for example to position itself as a cult brand with the slogan "Real Love", for which the brand is perceived less dependent on sporting results. FC St. Pauli has already reached this goal to the extent that the club is perceived in German football as THE brand regardless of the league in which the club plays (Bühler and Scheuermann, 2014; Bühler, Scheuermann and Nufer, 2013).

Identity brand management

Identity management of the brand is, according to Meffert, Burmann and Koers (2002, p. 30), "a process of internal and external management for a cross-functional sharing of all decisions and all measures taken to develop a strong brand identity".

This definition shows that the internal and external orientation is an essential component of identity management of the brand. It is therefore necessary to go beyond the initial strategy directed only to external demands and to replace the perspective "inside-out" by the "outside-out" perspective. Identity brand management is responsible for the planning, execution, implementation and control of all the steps taken to develop the final image (Meffert, Burmann and Kirchgeorg, 2011; Meffert, Burmann and Koers, 2002). In this case, it is to find the correlation between the image that one has of oneself (brand identity) and the image that others have (image) of a company (see Figure 14.2).

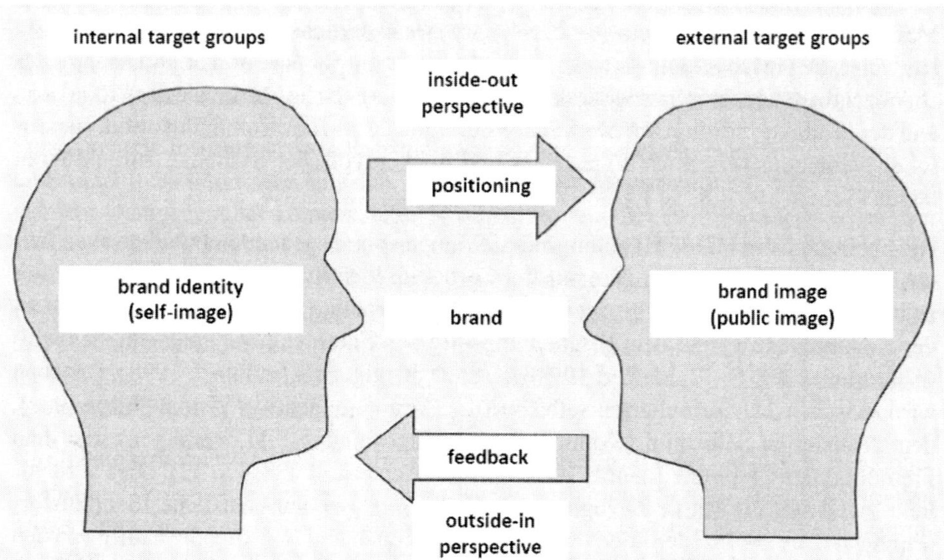

Figure 14.2 Model of the identity management of the brand

Source: Burmann and Meffert (2005, p. 52).

Under the management of the club brand, it is important to consider heterogeneous internal groups (e.g., coaches, players, trainers, managers), but also external groups (e.g., fans, mass media, sponsors, marketing agencies). As for identity brand management concerning groups and their interdependencies, it is particularly well suited for professional sports clubs (Schilhaneck, 2008; Welling, 2005).

Brand identity as a basis for brand management

The brand identity, which is the essence as well as the brand, is the basis that can provoke the applicant's emotion and identification. Burmann and Meffert (2005, p. 49) characterize the identity of the brand as a "comprehensive and compelling set of features of a brand that distinguish itself from the others". Thus, it represents the subjective image of the company. The brand identity is therefore considered as the sum of the characteristics that give the brand its absolute specificity and that it should represent, first internally and then externally. What is important is to identify the profile of the relevant treatment of the customer that the brand will identify and that will become a brand promise.

Specialists differentiate between the immutable identity and other features that change over time (including Esch, 2012; Kapferer, 2008). Aaker and Joachimsthaler (2009) define the sustainable features as the "core of the brand" and the features that may change as "a broader identity". The football clubs turn out to be, in general, very heterogeneous target groups. For heterogeneous groups, the central identity should be designed broadly enough so that it can match all the groups concerned. It remains essential that the core is compatible with additional attributes of the enlarged identity. Using the marketing potential, one can clarify the ambitions of the brand in a catchy slogan.

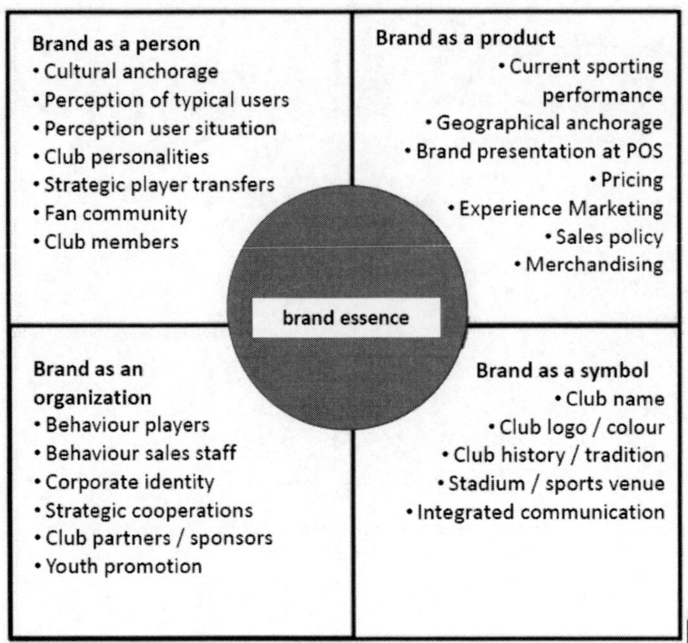

Figure 14.3 The components of the identity of the club brand

Source: Schilhaneck (2008, p. 131).

Considering the stated above, we can divide the identity components into four types: "the brand as a product", "the brand as an organization", "the brand as a person" and "the brand as a symbol". Building a brand identity is illustrated by the Figure 14.3.

The central identity reflects the values, content and features that are at the heart of the brand. This core is reflected in the features mentioned above and becomes accessible to customers. The brand identity of football clubs mainly depends on the product, that is to say, the game provided, including all the required additional services. In this context, sports scores as well as the attractiveness of the game play a key role in the perception of the brand.

The victory and attractiveness are components that depend mainly on the players and the coach. They influence the brand identity through their behavior on the field, but also through the media and the public. In collaboration with everyone involved in the clubs, they constitute the organizational dimension of brand identity. Thus, for example, the identity of the Borussia Dortmund brand is based on existing management skills. Because of this aspect, "service provider" of the discipline, there is a profound interweaving of corporate identity and brand identity.

Personality characteristics depend on the representation of typical users (e.g., FC St. Pauli and its alternative social environment) and situations of use (e.g., the Allianz Arena, which facade shines in three colors). In this context, we must emphasize the importance of supporters who, through their behavior and consumption of products, influence the way the club is perceived from the outside. The behavior and the number of supporters impact the atmosphere of the stadium. Thus, the community of fans is for the duration of the match a component of the brand. Moreover, cultural roots (e.g., carnival and FC Köln) are a source of fundamental identity as part of the personal dimension. The feeling of belonging to a specific region can then be transferred to the club; the cultural point of view is well established in the region. This shows how football clubs generally develop first as local brands. But thanks to media marketing, some clubs can position themselves as national brands even internationally. These are obviously mostly the clubs with the best sporting results that succeed.

The sporting successes are also the starting point of the history and tradition of the club; these are key elements of the symbolic dimension. Thus, one still calls to this day the team Mönchengladbach the "Eleven foals". This nickname was given to them for their very casual play style and their good sporting results in the 1970s. Moreover, the symbolic dimension is reinforced by the name, logo and colors of the club.

Brand identity, brand image and brand positioning

Brand identity, brand positioning and brand image are intertwined. While the brand identity depends on the image one has of one's own business, branding is a function of how others see the brand. The brand image is composed of many subjective impressions of customers who will then merge into a global representation of the brand. It can be defined as the representation of a brand which is firmly entrenched, concentrated and rewarded in the subconscious of representative target groups (Burmann and Meffert, 2005).

The basic principle for the development of a brand image is the brand awareness. The external target group should be able to recognize and locate the brand. While the brand identity is actively developed by football clubs, brand image only develops after some time as a reaction to the brand management activities practiced by the club. Targeted branding can be developed by the communication of the brand identity designed internally. To do this, one identifies the components of the identity of the brands that are particularly relevant to the target group and that distinguish the best brand from the competition. Then the features are highlighted by the positioning of the brand and are transposed into concrete measures, both internally and externally. Positioning means the transposition of identity into marketing potential (Burmann, Welling and Schade, 2008). The brand image finally provides guidance on the successful transmission of identity through brand positioning on the market. The link between identity, positioning and brand image is illustrated in the Figure 14.4.

The identification of the target group with the brand is established by the degree of convergence between brand identity and brand image. This convergence is also important for the establishment of a lasting relationship between the brand and the customer. The more marketing potential meets customer expectations and is integrated into the daily behavior of the promoters of the brand and employees, the more this relationship is durable (Burmann and Blinda, 2006).

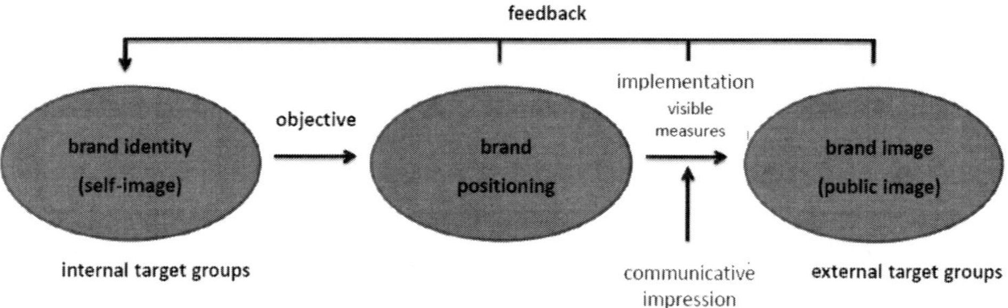

Figure 14.4 Brand identity, brand positioning and brand image

Source: Esch (2012, p. 91).

Success factors of brand identity management

The value and power of the brand is the main criteria to measure the effectiveness of brand management, and factors of success will be heard concepts that contribute to the progression of these two values. Concerning the identification of growth factors, we will take into account both general concepts that could be applied to the management of a club, as well as specific peculiarities in the management of sports brands (Jürgens, 2014; Jürgens and Nufer, 2015).

The identification of the brand objectives will be the starting point of brand management. The objectives of the brand management must be modeled in a clear and verifiable manner on the objectives of the company. They are the basis for a thorough and continuous control of the brand's success. In the management of a football club, this success can hardly be separated from sporting success. The brand perception actually depends on the quality of play and on the sports performance of the team. Therefore, a control system, large and complex, will be a success factor.

Brand management should be closely linked to the management of the company so that action can be tracked and accompanied centrally. To take coordinated action requires that the responsibilities in the implementation of the brand strategy at the management level be clearly defined. Brand managers should have the full support of the company management to be able, if necessary, intervene when a crucial decision must be made. However, it is not only the brand managers, but all employees who must play a key role in brand identity management. Thanks to the positioning of the brand, we can make a brand promise that must be reflected in the daily behavior of employees who become brand ambassadors. It is on this condition that we can build a strong and sustainable brand.

A successful brand positioning should be oriented to the target groups, differentiated and credible, and limited to a small number of characteristics that make an impact. For football clubs, it has both challenges and opportunities. Because of sporting regulations, regional roots and thus a strong emotional connection of fans with their "club", the positioning possibilities are severely limited; but this limitation also provides the ability to highlight, thanks to a brand promise, the specific characteristics of the club to clearly distinguish its own brand from other brands.

To be able to create an accurate picture, one has to consider the strength and continuity of the brand in addition to positioning and internal and external orientation. The starting point is the core of the brand identity from which marketing measures flow. In connection with the construction, management and direction of the brand, the football clubs are responsible for developing existing bases of the club's brand through targeted measures to strengthen the brand over time. Examples of brand consolidation measures include a structured management of customer loyalty, a successful cobranding and commodification as a brand management tool. Through these instruments, brand awareness can be increased and enrich the brand of the club with advantageous and original associations. In addition, it can help to neutralize any negative associations.

Customer loyalty management plays a key role in the brand management of the club, although we can usually count on a continued commitment from the club supporters. As the results on the pitch are uncertain, and therefore it can affect the relationship with the fans, it is particularly important to build a net-work and to maintain it over time. Due to the heterogeneity of the groups involved, a structured management of customer loyalty nevertheless proves complex and requires a thorough analysis of needs. Cobranding and commodification are, for the football clubs, an essential component of brand management. Consumers have a dual role because they can be considered as savvy : on one hand, fans are brand ambassadors are, and on the other hand, they are the key players to represent the club. Therefore, commodification offers opportunities to increase brand awareness and have a targeted impact on the brand image. We must also use cobranding as a brand management tool by considering not only the sponsors as a funding

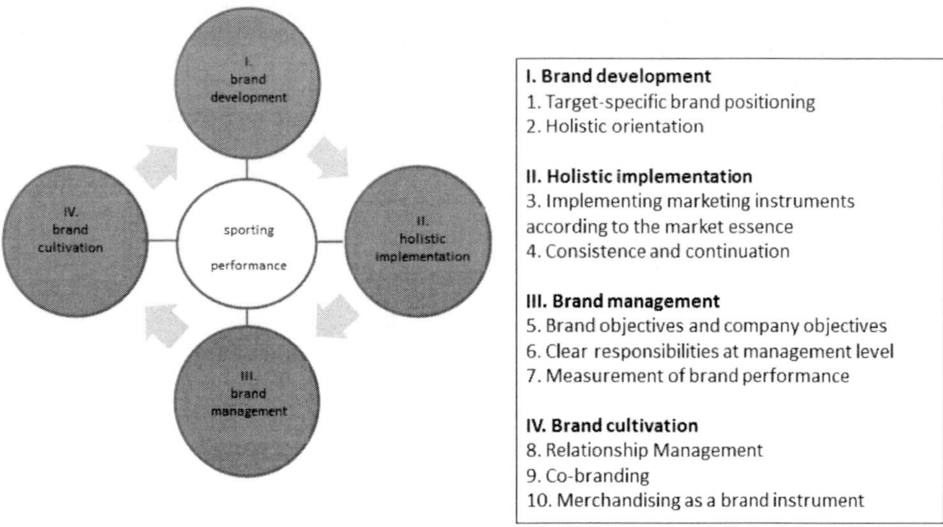

Figure 14.5 Interaction of factors of success

source, but also as brand partners. Through these marketing partnerships, the brand can be enriched by additional associations since an image return transfer takes place on the club's brand.

Basically, these success factors can enter four areas: brand building, the overall implementation, the steering of the brand and the sustainability of the brand.

Overall, if one wants to practice a compelling brand management, one cannot neglect any of these four areas. Figure 14.5 shows the relationship between the identified success variables.

Brand management analysis of the Borussia Dortmund brand

Now we will check if the brand management success factors of a club also play a vital role in practice, or how well they are actually taken into account by professional football clubs. In this perspective, we will validate the 10 factors for success in the practice of the Bundesliga's club, Borussia Dortmund (Jürgens, 2014; Jürgens and Nufer, 2015).

Situation at the beginning

Borussia Dortmund is one of the biggest football clubs and top performers in Germany. The management of everything related to professional sport has been entrusted to an LLC: KGA, publicly traded, which guarantees transparency for interested individuals. Due to a severe financial crisis in 2005, Borussia Dortmund, after near-bankruptcy, has made a paradigm shift. To consolidate the success of the club in a sustainable way, officials are remembering what has characterized Borussia Dortmund since its creation: good management as a basis for sustainable success. In the years that followed, the BVB managed to introduce major restructuring. In addition, from 2008, there is a new philosophy of sport developed by the coach Jürgen Klopp, promising a "hurray-football" with young players, with which they can identify. Subsequently, there was a revival in sporting and economic terms, so that the club became the German champion in 2011 and even won, in 2012, the double Cup/Championship. In 2013, the BVB became vice-champion

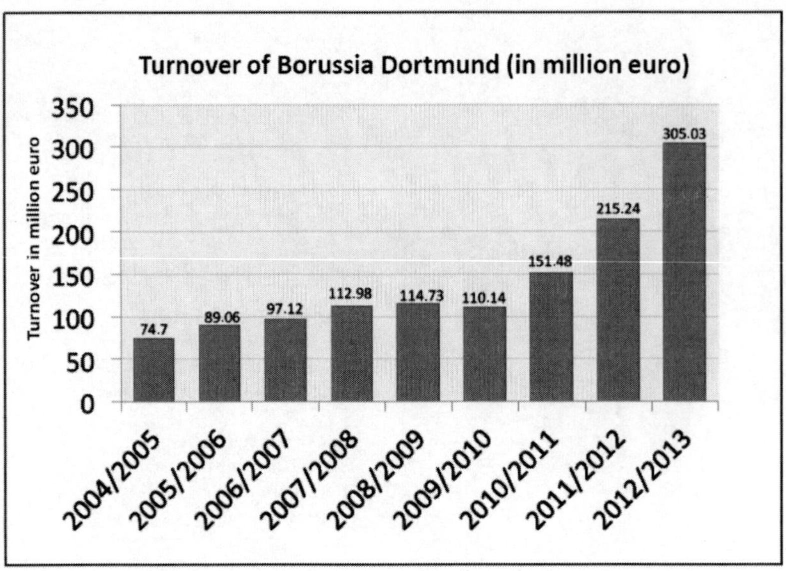

Figure 14.6 Sales for the development of the business Borussia Dortmund

Source: Borussia Dortmund, turnover, 2005–2013.

and found itself in the finals of the Champions League by the UEFA. Thus the financial statement of the club was able to present a record turnover of 305.03 million euros. During the 2013–2014 season, the club retained its title of vice-champion and reached the finals of the German Cup. As shown on the Figure 14.6, the company's turnover on Borussia Dortmund was multiplied by more than four since the 2004–2005 season to the 2012–2013 season (Borussia Dortmund, 2013).

Details of the approach

For a practical validation, the identified success factors are confronted with the practical experience and technical knowledge of experts. To ensure scientific objectivity in this study, the Borussia Dortmund club has been studied from different aspects. Various experts were initially contacted in writing to participate in the study. Once the researchers partnering for the interview were designated, we defined the guidelines for the interviews. From May 23 to July 11, 2014, there were 10 interviews conducted with 11 experts (in one case, there were two interviewees).

A more accurate presentation of the various interviewees can be found in Table 14.1.

The expert interviews were exploited using the synthesis of qualitative analysis. Interviews with experts focused mainly on the following issues.

- What is the impact of the 10 factors of the brand management success of the club in practice? Are they enforced by Borussia Dortmund and, if so, to what extent?
- How to reconcile growing commercialization in professional football and club tradition, as part of the brand identity?

A quantitative study of the representation of the Borussia Dortmund brand image completes the qualitative survey. The objective of this quantitative approach was to know if the positioning in the club has a positive impact. If this is the case, the identity of the brand (image seen by itself) is reflected in the image (image seen by others). For this purpose, respondents from May 5 to May 9, 2014, gave their personal vision of the club. The sample consists of 557 people from different age groups with interest in football (77% men, 23% women). The study was published on the Facebook pages of fans of all Bundesliga clubs, encouraging participation of fans from very different clubs. There were 25% of respondents who indicated that Borussia Dortmund was their favorite club.

Validation of success factors

The objective of the brand-building process initiated in 2008 was to ensure that the economic gains are less dependent in the short-term onsports performance. From the 2007–2008 season to the 2012–2013 season, Borussia Dortmund was able to increase its total turnover by nearly 170%. In this context, the question is what part the measures taken to manage the brand played in the growth of revenues? Nevertheless, it is difficult to assess the effects of marketing activities regardless of sports scores. The significant increase in earnings in these areas, as well as significant improvement in visibility in the media, are indications that, in addition to sports scores, we could achieve a better perception of the brand. This is underscored by the fact that, in recent years, Borussia Dortmund has won several awards for the brand. One can cite, for example that the brand BVB was deserved an award (2012) for the best managed sports brand in Germany or the Marketing Prize of Sport (2014) for the campaign "From Dortmund with love" as part of the final of the Champions League in London in 2013.

Brand building

BRAND IDENTITY, POSITIONING AND BRAND PROMISE

As part of the management of their brand, football clubs may strengthen the influence of their brand by defining a brand identity ("Who are we?"), and by positioning itself based on that ("How do we want to be perceived?"). We can further refine the brand's profile by highlighting the essence of the brand identity into a brand promise (Claim).

It is in this light that Borussia Dortmund has launched, in collaboration with the XEO agency of Düsseldorf, a comprehensive study of brand identity. Through a survey of internal actors, such as employees, the coaching staff, the players, as well as the sales manager and the management team, one was able to highlight the image of the brand viewed from the inside of the club. The Borussia Dortmund brand was analysed : "Intensity", "Authenticity", "Cohesion" and "Ambition" emerged, as well as "live football" (Heitfeld, 2014). This phenomenon does not affect the fans in the stadium. The aim of the brand is to educate as many people as possible who need to feel solidarity with the Borussia Dortmund. This broadening of the sphere of influence must not be at any cost: we must remain faithful to the fundamental brand to keep the principles of sympathy and authenticity.

From the core of the brand, "Intensity" directly follows the brand promise "Echte Liebe". As part of this qualitative study, 36% of people interested in football were able to correctly name the brand promise "Echte Liebe", and there were 74% among those who consider the Borussia

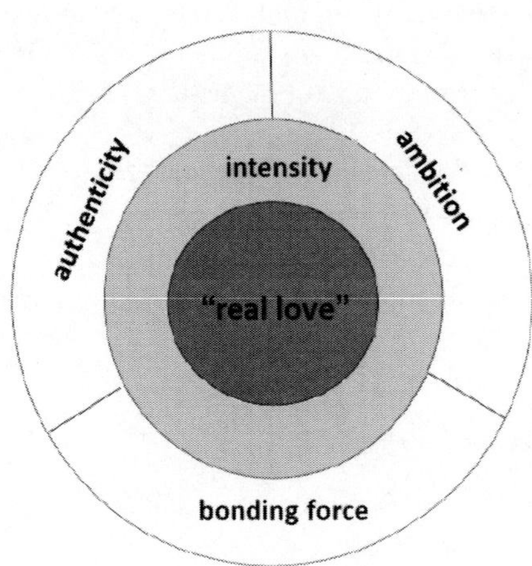

Intensity
Through our intensity, we create incomparable football events.

Authenticity
Through our authenticity, we provide people with deep faith and real love.

Bonding force
Through our bonding force our club becomes the home and family for many people.

Ambition
Through our ambition, we reach big goals and sporting performance.

Figure 14.7 Brand identity of Borussia Dortmund

Source: Woisetschläger, Backhaus, Dreisbach et Schnöring (2012, p. 22).

Dortmund as their favorite club. This promise is valid both for the fans as well as the club and therefore does not seem a pure "marketing claim".

Figure 14.7 summarizes the essential elements of Borussia Dortmund's brand identity.

The lesson is that Borussia Dortmund has developed a clear brand identity. The correlation between the subjective image (brand identity) and the objective image (the brand) guarantees the credibility of the brand. We now ask ourselves whether the subjective image of Borussia Dortmund corresponds to its objective image.

BRAND IMAGE

As part of the quantitative survey, 76% of people interviewed and interested in football answered that they had an accurate image of the brand Borussia Dortmund. There were even 91% among those who considered the BVB as their favorite club. This confirms the emotional dimension, tradition, ambition and skill that we associate with the brand Borussia Dortmund. In addition to the key qualifier that is "Ambition" (83%), the core of the brand "Intensity" (75%) and the adjective "Authenticity" (76%) occupy a similar place in the perception of respondents. Only the word "bonding force" (58%) is relegated a little further behind the other elements of brand identity (see Figure 14.8).

Interviews with experts nevertheless confirm that in Dortmund, and even throughout the Ruhr,[1] there is a strong relationship between the fans and the club. The BVB incarnates a particularly high degree of loyalty. And this concept that does not "talk" may explain the results of the survey. Experts interviewed on the fundamental values of the club often cited the concepts of group membership and solidarity, two closely related concepts of the concept of loyalty.

The large capacity of loyalty in the club indicates that the image of the brand BVB corresponds to the desire of identification of supporters. Regarding differentiation, the study "Types of Brands in the German Professional Sport" concludes that BVB brand could differentiate from

Top-2-box: "applies fully" + "applies mainly"

Attribute	%
Familiarity	51
Innovation	49
Easiness	45
Bonding force	58
Sustainability	51
Emotionality	84
Uniqueness	56
Tradition	75
Sympathy	83
Ambition	63
Internationality	83
Down-to-earthness	78
Authenticity	59
Trustworthiness	76
Expertise	64
	80

0 20 40 60 80 100

Question 10: Please state which attributes you think apply to Borussia Dortmund. Your personal perception of the club is therefore important.

476 respondents with interest in national football (stated in %)

Figure 14.8 Characteristics of the BVB image

Source: Jürgens and Nufer (2015, p. 17).

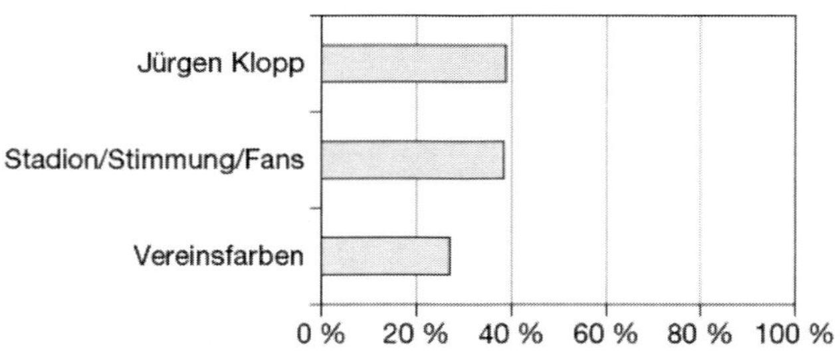

Figure 14.9 Top 3 spontaneous associations with Borussia Dortmund

Source: Jürgens and Nufer (2015, p. 18).

Bayern Munich brand. This also applies to other brands of Ruhr clubs like Schalke 04 (Bühler, Scheuermann and Nufer, 2013, p. 12). Stefan Heitfeld stresses that four BVB brand attributes (Strength, Loyalty, Ambition and Authenticity) are also claimed, at least in part, by other clubs, but Borussia is clearly distinguishable from other clubs regarding the valuation of these characteristics (Heitfeld, 2014).

The brand consists of many collected impressions, which are collected in a global representation. To identify factors that arrive first in the perception of the club, we asked the participants of the quantitative study to cite three elements they spontaneously associate with Borussia Dortmund (Figure 14.9).

The analysis revealed a correlation between brand identity and branding for Borussia Dortmund. It is from this that we can generate some credibility in brand management. Only brand differentiation with respect to other area clubs can be accentuated even more. But an artificial demarcation would not be compatible with the "Truth" attribute. The brand promise "Echte Liebe" is in tune with the emotional nature of the club and its place in the city of Dortmund, but it also represents a permanent challenge for the BVB. It is therefore important to constantly adapt its behavior to the brand identity by complying with a discipline.

EMPLOYEES AS BRAND AMBASSADORS

As part of the overall brand management, employees act as ambassadors of the brand by externally representing the values of the club. Many are the players of BVB – whether they grew up in Dortmund or not – like Marco Reus, Kevin Großkreutz and Neven Subotic who are part of the club and even the Ruhr. That is why there is a strong identification of the fans to the players of the club. All employees and players benefit from training concerning the brand at which one teaches the distinctive character of the brand. Sebastian Kehl stresses that "each of us obviously try to internalize the brand Borussia Dortmund, that is to say: What is the club? How does it live? How do we manage the relationships within the team while respecting each other? What image are we giving . . . ?" (Kehl, 2014).

Furthermore, one has established for players of BVB, from the brand identity, a valid code of conduct for all levels, from professionals to young teams. This code requires an unconditional commitment on the ground, enthusiasm at all times, a lot of ambition and mutual support. In addition, each player must put 100% of his abilities to the team's service and take responsibility regardless of the game.

Off the field too, it exerts an influence on the brand image. Each interview with club officials weighs on the brand perception and must, therefore, be in line with the strategy chosen by the club. The compatibility of coach Jürgen Klopp with the brand is underlined in a study group of Nymphenburg. In its "Limbic Map", the group compared the "value space" of the BVB to that of Jürgen Klopp. Based on this analysis, we can judge how a coach or manager corresponds to the concerned club. When the match of value space between the club and the coach is not proven, it will be difficult to credibly represent the club. According to the study done internally, the BVB embodies these values: friendship, family, loyalty and homeland security. Jürgen Klopp not only embodies all these values, but he adds more flexibility, friendliness, open-mindedness and humor. The transfer of this image with these qualities to the BVB is no stranger to the valuable asset that represents the Jürgen Klopp Club (Bühler, Häusel and Nufer, 2013; Neveling, 2013).

In summary, we can say that the internal and external orientation of brand management with employees as ambassadors of the brand is a critical success factor in brand management of professional football clubs. Officials, like the team itself, embody the BVB brand identity. Jürgen Klopp plays the role of brand ambassador and reinforces its authenticity. Through the contract which runs until 2018, this component of authenticity of the Borussia Dortmund brand is ensured for another few years.

Global transposition

The experts considered that the continuity and strength in brand management, as well as refocusing all marketing activities on the heart of the brand, were critical success factors. The club officials, who, on average, remain in office long enough, embody the stability of the staff. Jürgen Klopp has been coach of Borussia Dortmund since 2008. Hans-Joachim Watzke, commercial director of the club, started in 2001 as treasurer, and BVB sporting director Michael Zorc joined the club in 1978 as a young player. In addition, Reinhard Rauball was again re-elected to the post of president of the club in 2014. According to Kehl (2014),

> It is staff stability and leadership behavior, which run the management thread. The officials help to create a clear line, in tune with the heart of brand that will reach outward with the positioning and communication. The links between the different sections of Borussia Dortmund have significantly tightened. . . . [I]t must transmit a union image and corporate culture.

Despite the importance of continuity and solidity, it acts to maintain its relevance to the brand and develop it in accordance with its definition. Currently, Borussia Dortmund is still in the development stage of the brand, so the penetration, brand building and clarification of the profile are of paramount importance. That is why change is not really appropriate.

Steering of the brand

As part of the validation of the success factors concerning the steering of the brand, it is considered in Borussia Dortmund that brand management constitutes an essential component of corporate management. The brand identity serves as guideline for decision making in critical areas of business development, including the research for sources of income and for sponsors. Brand management does not only reduce the dependency on sports performance, it stimulates the brand indirectly. Therefore, the company's objectives and those of the brand are closely related. It is difficult to establish a prognosis for the brand's success because economic success depends on sports performance. This is why it happens that assumptions, guided by intuition, concerning developments in brand perception contribute to poor decision making. Controlling ensures the rationality of decisions, provides timely information on changes and offers the opportunity to redress the balance by quickly taking concrete measures.

Unlike the emphasis on brand controlling, the results of the qualifying survey highlight that this instrument is underdeveloped at present in the Bundesliga. BVB's brand controlling is primarily addressed by the implementation of studies on everyone. It would be necessary to constantly make evaluations so as to bring about developments and to implement them. To ensure better controllability and improved adjustability of the brand's success, we need to refer to a system of internal criteria for the club. For the establishment and management of brand activities, we need brand managers. Experts confirm that clear responsibilities regarding the brand and its effects on the management play a key role in the success of the club. In the guidelines for the management of the company Borussia Dortmund, the brand management is central.

In summary, it can be concluded that all the criteria for the steering of the brand highlighted play a role in the life of the BVB club. The potential of a strict controlling of the brand is, for the moment, not yet fully exploited in this sector.

Sustainability of the brand

COMMODIFICATION

In 2014, the total turnover of the commodification of the BVB totaled nearly 32 million euros. In 2015, the club sold for the first time more than 400,000 jerseys. All fans of a club are the ambassadors of the club's brand. It is in this context that the multiplier effect interferes. This is why the sale of products may not only generate profits, but may also display the brand of the club towards the outside.

Thus, when choosing products, club officials ensure first and foremost the quality, and second, that the product is appropriate to the target group and in line with the club's brand. To verify this, the BVB provides an analysis of the compatibility with the club's own brand identity. One then gives to the licensees of the club strict guidelines for the practice of the brand.

Overall, Borussia Dortmund offers more than 822 items to fans. This places the club at position number 3 last season, behind Bayern München and the no. 1 FC Nürnberg among the clubs offering most products (the range is from 150 products – FC Augsburg – to 1,100 products – FC Nürnberg). However, Borussia Dortmund has no plans to expand the range; the tendency would be rather to implement a strategy which is not too ambitious. Thus Borussia Dortmund recently reported that during the 2014–2015 season, it intended, for the first time in several years, to give up an additional winter jersey. Prices of home jerseys and of flocking remain unchanged for the third consecutive year.

The results confirm the hypothesis according to which the commodification represents, in addition to the objective of generating profits, a central instrument for managing the football clubs brand. A policy of targeted products, centered on the core and brand identity, is able to increase brand awareness and also make it more attractive and more meaningful to customers. Borussia Dortmund has a wide range of products for its supporters, the specific target group. In this way, it responds to the desire of fans to see their well-recognized brand and at the same time reduces the multiplier effect. However, we must strive to keep an overall view of the range and to practice a product and price policy based on brand values. If not, the authenticity of the club advocated towards external communication could suffer.

PARTNERS OF THE BRAND

In recent years, sponsorship has become one of the main sources of income for Borussia Dortmund. The BVB has 55 sponsors distributed as follows:

- *Main sponsor*: Evonik
- *Custodian of the rights to the name of the stadium*: SIGNAL IDUNA
- *OEM*: Puma
- 12 BVB Champion partners
- 17 BVB partners
- 23 BVB partner products

The number of partners indicates that the BVB club favors the quantity and diversity in the selection of sponsors. Compared to BVB, FC Bayern has for example only 27 partners to whom it can, therefore, offer greater exclusivity. The objective of the BVB is a lasting collaboration with partners, which appears in the duration of contracts with Signal Iduna (until 2021), Puma (2020) and Evonik (2025). Profits from sponsorships totaled in 2014 to about 69.3 million euros, and they will pass in 2015 the bar of 70 million euros.

It can be concluded that effective co-branding, designed as brand partnerships, can contribute to effective brand management. It is true that only a few professional football clubs can afford to select potential partners based on synergies within their brand. Because of the economic development from the previous years, Borussia Dortmund was able to choose its partners even after reciprocal image transfer.

MANAGEMENT OF THE RELATIONSHIP WITH THE FANS

For Borussia Dortmund, the management of customer relations is the management of relationships with supporters. As indicated by the club, 6.6 million people with an interest in football cite Borussia Dortmund as their favorite club, and 27 million Germans sympathize with BVB. In the context of the management of the relationship with the fans, do not forget that, in general, supporters demonstrate great loyalty to their "club". Borussia Dortmund has over 100,000 members and 54,000 permanent subscribers. For home games, the club recorded the largest attendance at the European level: 80,482 for the 2012–2013 season. And for away matches, the quota of tickets allocated to the club is regularly fully exhausted. Similarly, the significant increase in earnings from commodification in recent years (over 285% from 2008 to 2013) is an indicator of the deep attachment of the fans and their identification with Borussia Dortmund. However, Carsten Cramer recognizes that there is still room for improvement in terms of customer loyalty.

"The CRM subject . . . is unfortunately still a flaw in our company. We know too little about our supporters" (Cramer, 2012). This is an explicit reference to the problem of data protection, hence the need for active membership from the fans; this complicates the management of the retention of well-targeted customers (Cramer, 2014).

The results confirm that a structured management of customer loyalty is a success factor in brand management of professional football clubs. This analysis shows that Borussia Dortmund followed in this area. It is true that there is a need to catch up, both in building a fans file and in thinking about the appropriate discourse to hold.

Conclusion

Giving less importance to the correlation between sports results and indirect support of these results, brand identity management provides football clubs with the opportunity to generate substantial advantages.

This analysis aimed to validate the critical success factors of brand identity management by studying the case of a Bundesliga club, Borussia Dortmund. In examining the four key areas, Construction of the Brand, Global Implementation, Management of the Brand, and Sustainability of the Brand, we analyzed 10 success factors in total:

- General architecture,
- Solidity and continuity,
- Clearly defined competencies at the management level,
- Differentiated brand positioning adapted to the target group,
- Implementation of marketing instruments depending on the core of the brand,
- Commodification as a brand management tool,
- Loyalty management of customers,
- Measure of brand success,
- Brand objectives and business goals,
- Cobranding.

Results from our qualifying study show that these success factors are essential in the practice of the BVB club. In this club, the brand identity is consistent with the brand image, which has helped to develop a clearly defined brand image. Coach Jürgen Klopp, the stadium, including the South Stand, the fans, the atmosphere, as well as the yellow and black colors all seem to have an important place in the perception of Borussia Dortmund. This is why these associations should be encouraged. Although the brand is similar to brands of other Ruhr clubs, an artificial demarcation is not desirable. For the progressive enrichment of original associations, it can strengthen its own position. The first aspect is a different cultural anchor that can feed different histories of the cities concerned. In terms of customer loyalty management and control of the brand, it still remains inclined to Borussia Dortmund growth potential in order to advance sustainable development. Using the brand identity, the measures taken by the club must be constantly verified in view of their compliance with the club's brand. It acts in this case to stay true to its own line. BVB identity of brand management can serve as a practical model for the other Bundesliga clubs which still have potential for improvement in this area.

Borussia Dortmund is evaluated by officials not only in terms of economic and sporting success, but also how the two factors are handled. This is inherent to the club's identity, which is also reflected in the brand promise "Real Love", in the core of the brand "Intensity" as well as in essential skills "Cohesion", "Authenticity "and "Ambition". If you want to play in the big leagues, you cannot do it without marketing or professionalization. It is important to find a good balance between the commodification of the brand and the club's own tradition. When the football match is secondary, it deals with increasing sales, and the limits of marketing seem affected. Unlike other sectors, the clubs are not managing customers, but fans who want to be treated as such. Sometimes they criticize and influence certain measures taken by the club. The brand promises "Real Love", and therefore officials have an ongoing challenge for their actions. That is why we must not lose sight of the sustainability of the brand and the questions arising about the activities concerning the brand identity.

Notes

1 Polycentric urban area in North Rhine-Westphalia, Germany.
2 Clubs located in the Ruhr region within North Rhine-Westphalia, Germany.

Bibliography

Aaker D.A. and Joachimsthaler E., *Brand Leadership*, New York, Simon & Schuster, 2009.

Bauer H., Exler S. and Sauer N., "Brand Communities im professionellen Teamsport", *Thexis*, n° 3, 2005, pp. 11–15.

Bauer H., Sauer N. and Schmitt P., "Die Erfolgsrelevanz der Markenstärke in der 1. Fußball-Bundesliga", *Wissenschaftliches Arbeitspapier*, Working Paper n° W75, Institut für Marktorientierte Unternehmensführung, Universität Mannheim, 2004.

Borussia Dortmund, Geschäftsbericht 2012/2013, Dortmund, 2013.

Borussia Dortmund, Geschäftsbericht 2013/2014, Dortmund, 2014.

Brand Finance, The Brand Finance Football 50 Report 2014, London, 2014.

Bühler A., *Professional Football Sponsorship in the English Premier League and the German Bundesliga*, dissertation, Berlin, Germany, 2006.

Bühler A., Häusel H.G. and Nufer G., "Neuromarketing im Sport", in G. Nufer et A. Bühler (Hrsg.), *Marketing im Sport: Grundlagen und Trends des modernen Sportmarketing*, Erich Schmidt Verlag, 3. Aufl., Berlin, 2013, pp. 417–444.

Bühler A. and Nufer G., *Relationship Marketing in Sports*, Londres, Elsevier/Butterworth-Heinemann, 2010.

Bühler A. and Nufer G. (Hrsg.), *International Sports Marketing: Principles and Perspectives*, Berlin, Erich Schmidt Verlag, 2014.

Bühler A. and Scheuermann T., "Kult, Tradition, Champions, Lokale Helden und Retorte – Eine empirische Markenklassifizierung im Sport", in H. Preuß, F. Huber, H. Schunk and T. Könecke (Hrsg.), *Marken im Sport*, Wiesbaden, Springer Gabler, 2014, pp. 125–143.

Bühler A., Scheuermann T. and Nufer G., "Markentypen im deutschen Profisport – Ergebnisse eines empirischen Forschungsprojekts zur Markenwahrnehmung in den deutschen Teamsportligen", *Nachspielzeit – Die Schriftenreihe des Deutschen Instituts für Sportmarketing*, n° 3, 2013, 3–23.

Bühler A. and Schunk H., "Markenmanagement im Sport", in G. Nufer and A. Bühler (Hrsg.), *Marketing im Sport: Grundlagen und Trends des modernen Sportmarketing*, 3. Aufl., Berlin, Erich Schmidt Verlag, 2013, pp. 117–146.

Burmann C. and Blinda L., "Markenführungskompetenzen – Handlungspotenziale einer identitätsbasierten Markenführung", *LiM-Arbeitspapier*, n° 20, Universität Bremen, 2006, 157–178.

Burmann C. and Meffert H., "Theoretisches Grundkonzept der identitätsorientierten Markenführung", in H. Meffert, C. Burmann et M. Koers (Hrsg.), *Markenmanagement. Identitätsorientierte Markenführung und praktische Umsetzung*, 2. Aufl., Wiesbaden, Gabler, 2005, pp. 37–72.

Burmann C., Meffert H. and Koers M., "Stellenwert und Gegenstand des Markenmanagements", in H. Meffert, C. Burmann et M. Koers (Hrsg.), *Markenmanagement – Identitätsorientierte Markenführung und praktische Umsetzung*, Wiesbaden, Gabler, 2002, pp. 3–16.

Burmann C., Welling M. and Schade M., "Führung von Sportvereinsmarken", *USP Menschen im Marketing*, n° 3, 2008, pp. 14–15.

Couvelaere V. and Richelieu A., "Brand Strategy in Professional Sports: The Case of French Soccer Teams", *European Sport Management Quarterly*, n° 5, 2005, pp. 23–46.

Cramer C., "BVB 09, Echte Liebe. Die Faszination der Marke Borussia Dortmund", Präsentation beim Marketing-Club Düsseldorf e.V., 2012, abgerufen von: http://www.marketing-club.net/medien/club-tv/videos-2012/echte-liebe-die-faszination-der-marke-borussia-dortmund.html (Zugriff: 27.03.2014).

Cramer C., *Direktor Vertrieb und Marketing Borussia Dortmund,* personal interview by authors, Dortmund, 30.05.2014.

Esch F., *Strategie und Technik der Markenführung*, München, Vahlen, 2012.

Gladden J.M. and Milne G.R., "Examining the Importance of Brand Equity in Professional Sports", *Journal of Marketing*, n° 1, 1999, pp. 1–22.

Handelsblatt, "DFL will Milliardenmarkt Asien weiter erschließen", *Handelsblatt Online*, 2005, http://www.handelsblatt.com/sport/fussball/nachrichten/dfl-will-milliardenmarkt-asien-weiter-erschliessen/2561928.html (Zugriff: 06.10.2012).

Handelsblatt, "Handballer zielen auf den US-Markt", *Handelsblatt*, 24.09.2009, p. 16.

Heitfeld S., "Senior Director Team Borussia Dortmund bei Sportfive, persönliches Gespräch", *Dortmund*, 27.05.2014.

Jürgens S., *Erfolgsfaktoren der identitätsorientierten Markenführung am Beispiel von Borussia Dortmund*, Master Thesis, Munich Business School, Munich, Germany, 2014.

Jürgens S. and Nufer G., "Erfolgsfaktoren der identitätsorientierten Markenführung am Beispiel von Borussia Dortmund", in *Nachspielzeit – Die Schriftenreihe des Deutschen Instituts für Sportmarketing*, 2015–3.

Kapferer J., *The New Strategic Brand Management: Creating and Sustaining Brand Equity Long Term*, Londres, Kogan, 2008.

Karlowitsch E. and Michaelis M., *Merchandising als Marketinginstrument und Einnahmequelle – Eine ökonomische Analyse der Potenziale von Klubs der 1. Fußball-Bundesliga*, Westfälische Wilhelms-Universität, 2005.

Kehl, Sebastian, interview with authors Gern Nufer and André Buhler.

Meffert H., Burmann C. and Kirchgeorg M., *Grundlagen marktorientierter Unternehmensführung*, Wiesbaden, Gabler, 2011.

Meffert H., Burmann C. and Koers M., *Markenmanagement – Grundfragen der identitätsorientierten Markenführung*, Wiesbaden, Gabler, 2002.

Mohr S. and Merget J., "Die Marke als Meistermacher – Strategische Markenführung im Sport", in K. Zieschang and C. Klimmer (Hrsg.), *Unternehmensführung im Profifußball*, Berlin, Erich Schmidt Verlag, 2004, pp. 103–120.

Neveling E., *Jürgen Klopp – Echte Liebe*, München, Copress Sport, 2013.

Nufer G., *Ambush Marketing im Sport: Grundlagen – Strategien – Wirkungen*, Berlin, Erich Schmidt Verlag, 2010.

Nufer G., *Event-Marketing und -Management. Grundlagen – Planung – Wirkungen – Weiterentwicklungen*, 4. Aufl., Wiesbaden, Gabler, 2012.

Nufer G., *Ambush Marketing in Sports: Theory and Practice*, Londres/New York, Routledge, 2013.

Nufer G. and Bühler A. (Hrsg.), *Management im Sport: Betriebswirtschaftliche Grundlagen und Anwendungen der modernen Sportökonomie*, 3. Aufl., Berlin, Erich Schmidt Verlag, 2012.

Nufer G. and Bühler A. (Hrsg.), *Marketing im Sport: Grundlagen und Trends des modernen Sportmarketing*, 3. Aufl., Berlin, Erich Schmidt Verlag, 2013.

Schilhaneck M., *Zielorientiertes Management von Fußballunternehmen – Konzepte und Begründungen für ein erfolgreiches Marken-und Kundenbindungsmanagement*, Wiesbaden, Gabler, 2008.

Schilhaneck M., "Markenmanagement im Sport", in G. Nufer and A. Bühler (Hrsg.), *Marketing im Sport: Grundlagen, Trends und internationale Perspektiven des modernen Sportmarketing*, 2. Aufl., Berlin, Erich Schmidt Verlag, 2011, pp. 117–141.

Süddeutsche Zeitung, "Fußball: 1860 vor der Insolvenz, Bangen um eine Kultmarke", 2011, http://www.sueddeutsche.de/sport/fussball-vor-der-insolvenz-bangen-um-eine-kultmarke-1.107371 (Zugriff: 06.10.2012).

Südwestpresse, "Holger Stanislawski: Keiner muss uns lieben", 2011, http://www.swp.de/ulm/sport/fussball/ueberregional/Bundesliga-Hoffenheim-Stanislawski; art1157834,1268442 (Zugriff: 06.10.2012).

Welling M., "Markenführung im professionellen Ligasport", in H. Meffert, C. Burmann and M. Koers (Hrsg.), *Markenmanagement*, 2. Aufl., Wiesbaden, Gabler, 2005, pp. 496–522.

Woisetschläger D.M., Backhaus C., Dreisbach J. and Schnöring M., *Fußballstudie 2012 – Die Markenlandschaft der Fußball Bundesliga*, Technische Universität Braunschweig, 2012.

15

BRAND IMAGE IMPACTS ON SPECTATORS' PURCHASE BEHAVIOUR

The German football club VfB Stuttgart

Jens Blumrodt

Being present at a Bundesliga championship match (The German Football League, or the German Football Championship) means watching matches in stadiums which are chock-a-block full up to 90%[1] or more of their capacity. These matches are broadcast in restaurants and hotel reception areas on the small screen.

At this very moment, a certain thought springs to mind. Football has become *salonfähig,* a German expression which illustrates the intrusion of football into upper-middle-class households. Sport activity has been integrated into daily life. The Deutsche Fußball Bund (DFB, the equivalent of the British Football Federation) is the biggest sports association in the world with more than 6.85 million members.[2] The French and Germans get worked up about football in different ways. Whilst French football clubs have difficulty filling their stadiums, the number of spectators in the 2. Bundesliga (second German league) is equal to that of the 1st French League.[3] One of the explanations for this phenomenon is the "stadium experience".[4] The difference in the quality of stadium has been the subject of government as well as Federation reports. The Ligue has created committees during all great international events so as to obtain detailed report on new stadiums and renovated stadiums. Reports, as well as our own observations in this book, emphasise that stadiums are becoming multifunctional infrastructures, which can be transformed into show halls, with shops, boutiques, conference halls, club museums, as well as restaurants. Germany took advantage of the World Cup in 2006 to launch a big renovation project for its stadiums. They are bigger and more recent than French stadiums, and the spectator is close to the pitch. Sportainment has become the rule.

The match is sold as much via the sponsoring as via merchandising. Clubs can considerably increase their revenues through means other than television rights, that is "stadium" rights and "marketing" rights. Spectators present in the stadium are at the centre of our consideration. One central question shall guide the approach to the case of VfB Stuttgart e.V.: *What are the stadium experience elements which influence the supporters' purchasing behavior?*

We chose VfB Stuttgart e.V. for different reasons. In this club, the chairman and the board define the strategies of the club brand. As regards the number of employees (200), it is of average size and belongs to the professional football 1. Bundesliga. This club is a national brand with an international recognition. The case of VfB shall be presented in the form of four parts, the first of which shall briefly state the club profile, the second shall provide a framework for observing the spectators, the third shall reflect the club's brand image and its impact on the brand-capital and the last shall summarize if VfB is a case to be followed.

Box 15.1 Track record and brief history of VfB Stuffgart e.V.

The track record of VfB Stuttgart e.V. relates first to its history and its importance as a sports association. It is among the biggest sports associations in Germany and is the biggest in the region of Bade-Wurtemberg. Created in 1893, the most important section is that of professional football whose first team has – with the exception of two seasons – always played in the Bundesliga. The club's official colours, white and red, are worn during home matches. The white shirt has a red shield on the front on which the name of the main sponsor is written, the Mercedes Benz Bank. The shorts and socks are white. The VfB Stuttgart Club is found at the top of the football competition table. Its sport track record is confirmed by being five times champion of the Bundesliga (1950, 1952, 1984, 1992, 2007), four times vice-champion (1935, 1953, 1979, 2003), its triple champion title (1954, 1958, 1997) and triple second title (1986, 2007, 2013) in the Liga Cup and the DFL super cup champion in 1992. Its international track record is the place of vice-champion in the European Cup (Cup of Cups, 1998)

Source: Qualitative interviews with Steffen Lindenmaier, spokesman and Bernd Wahler, chairman of VfB.

Box 15.2 VfB Stuttgart e.V. data sheet

Chairman of the SASP: Bernd Wahler
Number of season ticket holders: 27,500
Number of Facebook fans: 500,000
Average number of spectators per match: 55,400 (Capacity of the Mercedes-Benz Arena: 60,441)
Club budget: 116.5 million euros
Budget distribution: sponsoring 20%, media 33%, tickets 30%, spin-off products 17%
Total number of products: 19
Sponsors: 34
Name of main ("premium") partners in 2014: Mercedes-Benz, Puma, Krombacher, Würth, Fanuc, EnBW, Gazi Kärcher
Key success factor: Counting on sport performance

Source: Qualitative interviews with Steffen Lindenmaier, spokesman and Bernd Wahler, chairman of VfB.

Box 15.3 Presentation of Bernd Wahler, Steffen Lindenmaier and Ulrich Ruf

Bernd Wahler: Chairman of VfB, 57 years old, in office since 2013.

Steffen Lindenmaier: Communications and media relations director of VfB, 35 years old, in post since 2012.

Ulrich Ruf: Financial director at VfB, 59 years old, in post since 1980.

Club profile

VfB Stuttgart e.V. (United for Games of Movement Stuttgart e.V.), created in 1893, has 45,032 members and proposes different sporting disciplines such as athletics, fistball, hockey and table tennis. The leading team is the professional football team, but also there is a second division team, amateur teams, as well as a training centre. Like many of the professional German football clubs, VfB has remained *eingetragener Verein* (e.V.), an associative, non-profit making club.

The club blatantly displays its "good management and its superb business results", the pride of the chairman, Ulrich Ruf (Financial and Management Director).[5] The association has nonetheless externalized a certain number of subsidiaries, acting as independent profit centres. VfB Stuttgart e.V. is in the majority of cases 100% owner of these subsidiaries (see Figure 15.1.)

A business section also appears on the club's Internet page, which lists the different options for business collaboration with VfB Stuttgart Marketing

Multinationals like Mercedes-Benz, Total or even Coca-Cola are among the biggest sponsors, as well as medium-sized companies with local roots, such as Hofmeister (shop supplies). The Communication Manager for VfB, Steffen Lindenmaier, confirms the club's ambition with regard to sponsoring as "showing everyone that the club has local roots, but that its charisma is well and truly international". Besides this, main partnerships with their associated marketing rights packages "are a whole range of very effective promotional activities which our sponsors profit from", continues Ulrich Ruf. There are other forms of sponsoring around the club. "Reha Welt", the rehabilitation and recovery centre, a business subsidiary of the club, is installed in the Carl Benz Centre. The training centre (Jugendakademie) was set up in 2007 and includes 22

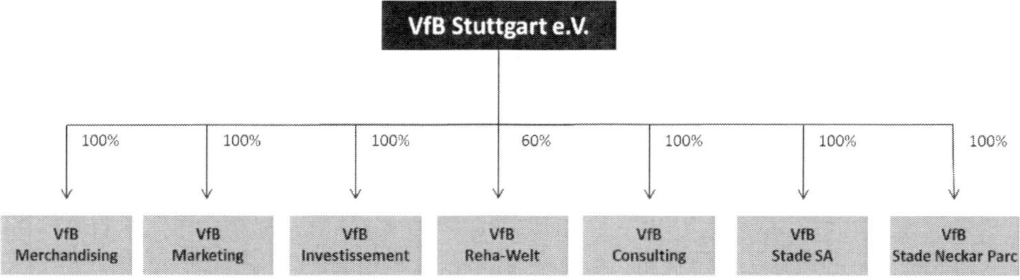

Figure 15.1 Organisation of VfB Stuttgart e.V. and its different subsidiaries

Source: VfB STUTTGART e.V., Reference document, Annual Financial Report 2013, p.5. *(Jahresabschluss VfB Stuttgart 1893 e.V. au 31.12.2013)*

young people who train as well as participate in school activities within the club. They have their own playing fields. It recruits future recruits within the football school whose associative activity is based on different football sport sections. Sponsors can also support other structures of the club. There is the "VfB Fritzle Club", which represents the festive part of the club, particularly with the mascot that brings children to different sport events, organizes birthdays and animates the stadium during home matches.

The club is strongly rooted in the town and the region (Land) of Baden-Wurtemberg. The town of Stuttgart has more than 600,000 inhabitants and the club attracts around 55,400 spectators on average per home match, which corresponds to an attendance rate of around 90% during the last few seasons. The atmosphere is intense before and after the match, "it's a family event where friends and the whole family meet for the event. The food in our catering/hospitality areas with their sausages, pretzels and other drinks, are part of the evening. A small trip around our official boutique is for many spectators part of the experience," emphasizes Steffen Lindenmaier. "What is felt when one comes to the match, is a festive and convivial atmosphere," he adds.

This proximity, because of its environment, nevertheless goes beyond the framework of the matches. The club is also committed very actively to many social activities whose main characteristic is the involvement of young people. These activities are often supported by public or private bodies. They concern in particular support for clinics in their fight against pediatric cancer, illiteracy, drugs and violence. VfB "has due to its popularity, an attraction for children that few other bodies can guarantee. Our commitment is also financial," explains Chairman Bernd Wahler.

The club is resolutely orientated towards youth and family. Its desire is to deliver an event for everyone in which football plays the central role. Championship matches are for professional clubs a part of the budget that have a strong potential for growth, and managers are aware of this. If French clubs have a marked dependence as regards television rights, German clubs have been showing for years more balanced budgets for sales and tickets (Deloitte, 2012). Stuttgart is hardly exceptional to the rule. The very low amount of television rights[6] for the budget of clubs in 1. Bundesliga is thus compensated for by two other factors: ticket sales and business elements.[7]

Spectators are important for the stadium atmosphere, and they also play a crucial role in the club's financial survival.

The operational framework for examining spectators

The public benefits from the club's services on the day of the match. The supporters belonging to fan clubs have the most outstanding places. They have specific places in the stadium and represent around 10% of the spectators. There are VIPs who have access to particular services, like places closer to the pitch and different catering/hospitality arrangements. Some are able to follow the match whilst holding a business meeting. In Germany, they represent in general 10%–15% of the spectators. In VfB stadium, business seats and VIP boxes places represent 15%.[8] If these audiences are important for the atmosphere or even the revenues, they are not the essential source of income from ticket sales. Occasional spectators or season ticket holders fill up the majority of the stadium and also deserve our attention. They are however less well known than the fans and the VIPs for which clubs have more specific information. It is this very public which falls within the framework of this observation, and whose behaviour the club wishes to influence. It tries to affiliate it, to bring it to the stadium to incite it to buy a season ticket and to push it to buy spin-off products, for a stadium supporter must also be equipped with a full range of club products.

It is recognised that knowledge of the brand influences our perceptions and our behaviour (Keller, 1993),[9] and we also know that in the field of sport and in the context of football in

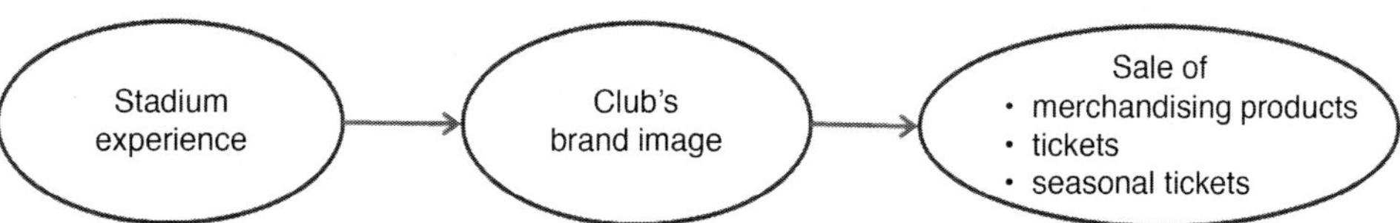

Figure 15.2 The impact of the "stadium" experience on purchase behaviour[10]

particular, the club's brand image alone acts directly on spectator's behaviour (Ross, 2006).[11] The brand image is a set of emotional and rational representations linked to the club. Since it is impossible to read spectators' thoughts, a deeper knowledge of the experiences which form the club's image is required. Within the framework of this approach, a certain number of factors can be listed if they form the brand image (Blumrodt, Desbordes, Bodin, 2013).[12] This approach can be applied to all clubs. The answer to the central question would indicate in the first place which factors make up VfB Stuttgart's club brand, and second, what are the factors which influence spectator purchase behaviour (see Figure 15.2).

Stadium experience can enhance club's image and than bring more revenues such as merchandising product sales, ticket sales, season ticket sales.

So as to list these elements and determine their impact, an observation framework should be set up (Cooper, Schindler, 2010).[13] This includes a conceptual approach, which helps identify the key factors of the club image. These factors must be tested by observing their influences on spectator behaviour. The observation framework then calls upon statistical measurements directly applying the conceptual framework.

At the end of the 2013 season, a series of studies was set up and interviews were carried out, recorded and analysed with 10 spectators.[14] The results were compared with the data supplied by the literature, and a questionnaire was developed from this base. This questionnaire was pretested on the club, adapted one last time, and the final questionnaire was administered to 364 people. It contained three parts, of which the first was aimed at spectator behaviour, the second, brand image and the last spectator profile. Other interviews were carried out in 2014 with the communications and finance departments as well as the club Chairman.

VfB Stuttgart e.V.'s brand image

Analyses were carried out using IBM SPSS 20. The first phase reflected the descriptive statistics. It was observed that the audience present in the stadium was not a homogenous group of spectators (see Table 15.1).

The stadium welcomes a young audience. In fact, 60% of those interviewed were between 16 and 39 years old, 35% between 40 and 59 years old and 5% over the age of 60. It has a female presence, like all German stadiums. Women are more present in VfB Stuttgart's stadium (over 25%) than in stadiums in France (around 10%): "It's a secure stadium with a superb atmosphere. I like coming here with my boyfriend," explains a female supporter.

Socioprofessional categories are more diversified, indicating in this way that football reaches a wider population. The data averages correspond to statistics of the Ligue and the Bundesliga.[15] The second phase of exploratory analysis includes factorial analysis (FA),[16] with a reduction of items[17] whose end objective consists in listing the most important to reflect the club's band image. As a general rule, three items play a role on the brand image, also called factor (F), (see Figure 15.3).[18]

Table 15.1 Profile of VfB Stuttgart spectators

	VfB Stuttgart		
Sex	f_o	**%**	**Cum %**
Man	272	74.7	74.7
Woman	92	25.3	100.0
Total	364	100.0	
Age			
16–39 years	215	59.1	59.1
40–59 years	125	34.3	93.4
60 and over	24	6.6	100.0
Total	364	100.0	
(CSP) Socioprofessional categories			
Executives, managers and CEOs	56	15.4	15.4
Employees	99	27.2	42.6
White- and blue-collar workers	44	12.1	54.7
Self-employed	41	11.3	65.9
Retired	16	4.4	70.3
Housewife/husband	11	3.0	73.4
Pupils, students, apprentices	74	20.3	93.7
Unemployed	1	0.3	94.0
Others	15	4.1	98.1
N/A	7	1.9	100.0
Total	364	100.0	

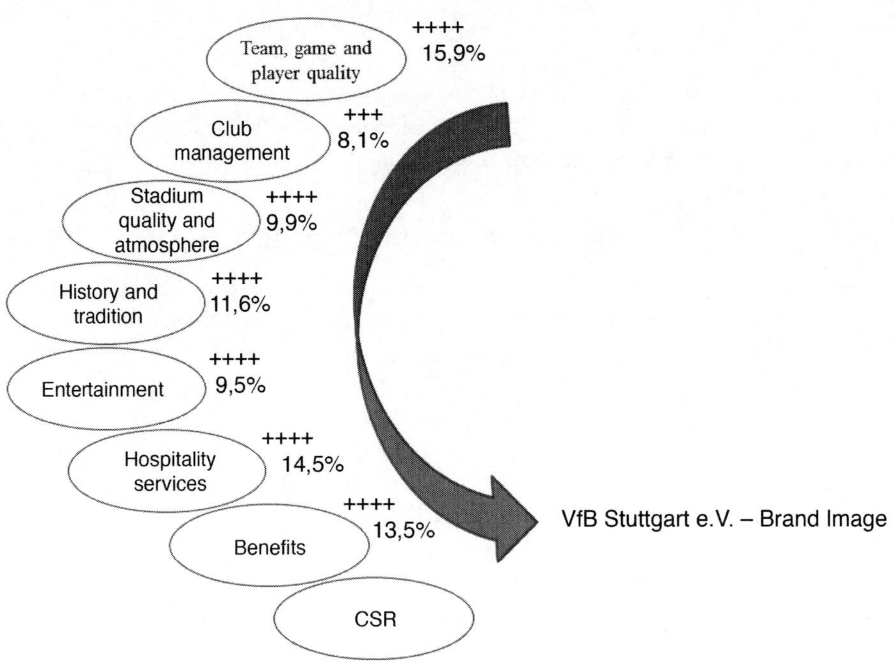

Figure 15.3 VfB Stuttgart's club brand image

Eight factors are consequently listed on a scale of one (----) to eight (++++). The factors obtained excellent averages whose contribution to the overall image (indicated in percentage) varies from factor to factor. The two first, team, game and player quality, as well as Club Management concern attributes relating to products (Blumrodt, Bryson, Flanagan, 2012; Keller, 1993). Attributes are characteristic traits of the product and are necessary ingredients to insure the funny aspects of the product or service. These factors include, within the framework of sportainment, sporting and managerial elements.[19] Surprisingly, they do not affect the club's image, even if the sporting component is primordial.

The second block of factors, or category, concerns peripheral services: stadium quality, history and tradition, side attractions and catering/hospitality services. Peripheral services are aspects which are exterior to the product or service with regards to purchase or consumption. The assessment shows their importance for VfB, and their cumulated percentage (45.5%) is superior to that of the first attributes (24%).[20]

The third category is that of benefits. These are personal values that the consumer attaches to the product or service attributes. In other terms, these are elements that the consumer considers as being beneficial for themselves, such as family outings or outings with friends. People also go to the stadium for escapist reasons, to express themselves or to sing. They want to be accepted as club supporters and be proud of their club, in short, they wish to live a whole range of emotions.[21]

The fourth and last category is that of the brand's attitudes. It reflects the brand's overall evaluation and includes the following items: The club is a unique brand, worthy of trust, and it evokes positive feelings. Elements such as that of social responsibility of the company (CSR) are part of this. This is the club's social commitment, its involvement in the regions and its honesty, instruction of young players and humanitarian actions. This obtains the highest score as a factor.[22] Purely football orientated elements (attributes related to the product) only get second place (24% of the AVE), whilst factors which are not related to the product are in first place (peripheral services: 45.5%). CSR obtained a score which is higher than that of F1 (team, game and player quality), and is the third attribute in the brand image. If sporting performance is a crucial element for the development of the team image from that of a local team to an international team (Couvelaere, Richelieu, 2005),[23] it seems however, to be in some way already acquired for clubs with a national, or even international, image such as that of VfB (Chanavat, Bodet, 2014).[24] This can be illustrated by using the example of a brand recognised all over the world such as Coca-Cola. Although Coca-Cola is first and foremost a fizzy drink, its world-wide presence, due to publicity campaigns, sponsoring and its Internet presence, ensures another image with consumers. This brand represents a lot more than a drink. It's a simple and universally pertinent theme, which affects all other communications of the brand: happiness. VfB is more than just football. It is also synonymous with amusement, snack bars and community commitments. These elements even gain the upper hand in the club's image, thus confirming a multi-faceted vision which goes well beyond a simple football game. Among these elements, a certain number of attributes influence the spectator's behaviour.

The third phase of the analysis, the regression analysis, establishes the link between independent variables, spectator and dependent perceptions, and purchase behaviour. It indicates the predictability of behaviour (purchase of a season ticket, merchandising products and several visits to the stadium for non-season ticket holders). A certain number of statistical indications[25] are inherent in this step. Table 15.2 summarises the behaviour of spectators in relations to their perceptions,

Table 15.2 Impact of brand image on purchase behaviour

Purchase / *Categories*	*Season Tickets*	*Spin off Products*	*Revisits*
1st Category **Attributes related to the product**		✓1	
2nd Category **Peripheral services**	✓1	✓2	✓1
3rd Category **Benefits**	✓2		✓2
4th Category **Attitude/CSR**	✓3	✓3	✓3

and these are grouped into categories. Results confirm that the behaviour of consumers depends on the brand image and that different categories influence the behaviour of the purchase of a season ticket and spin-off products. These categories are indicated by order of importance (see Tables 15.1–15.4). The sale of tickets to non-season ticket holders at the stadium is also an indicator of brand image.

Several observations can be made:

- Purchases can be explained in relation to the impact of the different categories.
- It's always a set of categories which lead to purchase.
- The attributes related to products do not impact the purchase of a season ticket or even revisiting the stadium.
- The CSR category and attributes which are not linked to the product are omnipresent.
- The category linked to the product explains the purchase of spin-off products.

The three types of purchase behaviour are different in nature. A large part of the purchases can be explained by the club's brand image. Literature on the subject has highlighted the link between a club's brand image and its brand capital (Bodet, Chanavat, 2010;[26] Gladden, Funk, 2002). The brand equity then impacts the consumer behaviour (Ross, Russell, Hyejin, 2008).[27] It is over the last few years that academic and managerial research have taken an interest in corporate responsibility in the context of sport (Bayle, Chappelet, François, Maltese, 2011):[28] "It is incontestable that VfB is more than just a football team. I think it is important that a club gets involved in the life of its town and that it sets up projects with hospitals, for example", says a supporter. If the clubs commitment to society requires well-defined managerial approaches (Kihl, Babiak, Tainsky, 2014),[29] return on investment can be a pertinent question (Walker, Kent, 2009).[30]

In present research, a conceptual framework has been set up and has been confirmed. It is applied to all the clubs whose brand image we aspire to evaluate. Even if these images are different, they will evolve nevertheless within this framework. The element of social responsibility is a full-part brand image and impacts spectator behaviour. Our contributions tie up to some extent this new approach and complete the brand image of a professional football sport club.

If we have observed the link between the "stadium" experience, club image and spectator behaviour, it still remains to be determine if VfB is an example to be followed.

VfB Stuttgart: An example to be followed?

If the majority of elements of the image are perceived in an extremely positive manner, a slight criticism remains in relation to the club's management.[31] Marketing in sport depends all too often on the team's performance and sport results (Mullin, Hardy, Sutton, 2014). VfB has succeeded in throwing off this dependency and has successfully bet on other strengths. These elements are controllable because of the club management. The management can control the quality of the services and their organisation around the stadium.

Different categories influence spectator behaviour and consequently have an impact on the brand capital. Buying spin-off products does not lead to the same behaviour as buying a season ticket. Attachment to a team is visible because of these products. The increase in attributes linked to the sport aspect increases the purchase of spin-off products. However, other parameters also come into play. Sport performance is at this point the most important category. The composition of the image enables other categories to influence the purchase of season tickets, and it also predicts that they will go back to the stadium. The most important factors are peripheral services, benefits and the club's community commitment. These elements are, in these cases, judged to be more important than the attributes related to the product.

People come to the stadium to eat and have a good time with their friends or family. The club's audience is composed of young people and women. To summarise the club's image in a few words, it should be borne in mind that: "social commitment, youth training, faultless services and sport performances" make of it a "a club where you feel good and have a good time" as one supporter puts it. Unlike clubs with a local or regional image, the sport aspect takes second place as regards purchase decisions (Blumrodt et al., 2012). Sport performance is not so much put to one side, but it is a factor, among others regarding image and purchase behaviour. This club has acquired a recognised sport level among supporters, which is based on all the members of the team, and the real stars who come from the training centre: "I adore the players who are faithful to the club, such as Cacau, but my preference is for sportsmen who come from the training center such as Timo" (Testimony of a VfB supporter).

It is in this respect that the club is an example to be followed. It has succeeded in

- Turning social commitment into a strategic axis;
- Delivering faultless services;
- Putting on family entertainment;
- Attracting more women;
- Turning its stadium into a good work tool.

Do you need to have a multifunctional stadium to obtain such a diversified image? This is a typical chicken and egg question.[32] Let us say that the club has been able to take advantage of its stadium's modernisation by improving peripheral services whilst maintaining sporting performance. The stadium ensures a good proximity to the game. It is comfortable and offers privacy, in particular when it comes to the toilets, which is an aspect picked up on in the testimonies of female supporters.

> A football match which goes on for some time, during the break it's a race to the food outlets and the toilets. But the infrastructure is clean – between you and me, the men no longer borrow our toilets, you don't have to wait. The club has done well.
>
> *(Testimony of a German female supporter)*

Whilst it may be that such a testimony is considered merely anecdotal, it is not the only one to have underlined the importance of a certain comfort and privacy in a crowd situation at a football match.[33] VfB concentrates on spectators, supporters, members and partners. VfB's perpetual consideration is "courage and fidelity",[34] practiced at the every level of the club. "Our players and employees are courageous and faithful toward the public, the club is also towards its partners," says Steffen Lindenmaier. This fidelity is shown in terms of hard cash. A German supporter spends in the stadium vicinity on average five times more money per match than a French supporter (Blumrodt, 2011).[35]

At the present time, the club has the status of an association, composed, whilst remaining owner, of different subsidiaries with a business status (LLC). Discussions are underway about how to develop the status of the club's professional section into an economic model whereby the association framework of the club would exist alongside shareholders, which is synonymous with a commercial company (Drut, 2014).[36] The club would make the search for profit co-exist more clearly with sport success (Dietl, Franck, 2007).[37] The chairman, Bernd Wahler emphasises that

> The organisation of our first team no longer matches the ideals of an association. In the future, separation of the two entities is a necessity. Just look at the results table for the last season. Nearly all the associative clubs have finished in the bottom half. The last association to become German Champion was VfB. We consider that the status of a stock company as being the most suitable. As regards this separation, Daimler AG has already declared itself to be interested in developing existing partnerships.

This decision is to be taken "whilst bearing in mind the aspirations of club members, because the club exposes its decisions to public scrutiny."

Were the Chairman's words a vision of the future? This could be believed, since financially, the club lost its place among the 30 richest clubs in Europe during the 2013–2014 season (Deloitte, 2012; 2015)[38] and as of 2014–2015 it was, halfway through the season, relegatable because it was at the bottom of the division table. Financial manna related to transformation into a LLC is expected and would give the club a breath of oxygen allowing it to take on new talent under contract. There is however no single plan which would guarantee clubs' financial and sporting success. But only five clubs out of the 18 in the 1. Bundesliga have not yet externalised their professional section (FC Schalke 04, 1. FSV Mayence 05, SC Fribourg, SC Paderborn and VfB Stuttgart). This economic model is doomed to disappear because the correlation between league table position and legal status is too obvious. Three of the five aforementioned clubs are at the end of the league table in season 2014–2015.

The four German clubs in Deloitte's Top 30 in 2015 have different statuses and profiles. VfB Stuttgart, with its strong association bias and its potential shareholders, could find inspiration in F.C. Bayern's economic model. This club is based on a popular shareholdership, where F.C. Bayern Munich e.V. (association) is the main shareholder of F.C. Bayern Munich AG (FCB-SARL). The mother association holds 75% of the shares. The remaining shares (each at 8.33%) are held by the FCB's long-term partners (Adidas AG, Audi AG, and Allianz SE).[39] This option would allow VfB to be faithful to its past status and to find a more suitable economic model enabling the attraction of big financial investments.

Notes

1 http://www.cahiersdufootball.net/article-un-modele-allemand-4876 – The figures indicated refer to the 2012–2013 season. They appeared in the article "Un modèle allemande: L'air du temps est à la Germania-mania. Derrière cette vogue, il y a les fondations solides de clubs qui résistent à la crise . . . et respectent le football." Last accessed February 10, 2015.

2 http://www.dfb.de/verbandsstruktur/mitglieder/ – This is the official site of the DFB presenting the association and its different subsidiary companies. Last accessed February 10, 2015.

3 This observation is the result of a comparison of data provided by the Ligue: http://www.lfp.fr/ligue1/affluences/journee – and the DFB: http://www.dfb.de/bundesliga/statistik/zuschauerzahlen/ Last accessed February 10, 2015.

4 http://www.lfp.fr/uploads/fichiers/2014_04_07_Presentation_LFP_etudes_stades.pdf?org=tinymce – Public studies of the stadiums of Ligues 1 and 2, March 2, 2014. Last accessed February 10 2015.

5 The quotations indicated are based on qualitative interviews carried out with the club management on December 12, 2014.

6 The Bundesliga is far behind, the broadcasters only paying 675 million euros in comparison to the Ligue whose television rights are worth 748 million euros, close behind the Spanish Liga (750 million euros), and far behind Italy (960 million euros) and England (1,200 million euros) (Mosnier, 2014).

7 Four German teams appear in the top 30 richest football clubs in Europe in 2013–2014: FC Bayern Munich (3rd place), BV 09 Borussia Dortmund (11th place), Schalke 04 (14th place) and Hambourg SV (28th place). Their Internet sites are indicated as a reference in the web resources. Only two French clubs appear in the list: Paris Saint Germain and l'Olympique de Marseille. These statistics highlight the very important place that revenues other than television rights have.

8 These data were provided by Steffen Lindenmaier.

9 Keller, K.L., Conceptualization, measuring, and managing customer-based brand equity, *Journal of Marketing*, 57, 1–22, 1993.

10 This conceptual framework is based on the work of Blumrodt et al. (2012).

11 ROSS, S.D., A conceptual framework for understanding spectator-based brand equity, *Journal of Sport Management*, 20, 22–38, 2006.

12 BLUMRODT, J., DESBORDES, M., BODIN, D., Professional football clubs and corporate social responsibility, *Sport, Business, Management: An International Journal*, 3, 3, 205–225, 2013.

13 COOPER, D.R., SCHINDLER, P.S., *Business Research Methods* (11th ed.), Singapore, McGraw-Hill, 2010.

14 Regarding this matter, before the match, spectators were invited to participate in interviews on the club's promises. They were occasional spectators or season ticket holders who were mitting to this. They all wanted to give their opinion about the match.

15 DFB (2014) and LFP (2014).

16 Factorial analysis in the Anglo-Saxon meaning of the term is used to reduce the number of variables towards the most important in relation to the number of latent variables. In other words, the results obtained indicate a percentage over the club's overall image.

17 The items are key words which appear as questions in the questionnaire. Thirty questions concern brand image.

18 Each factor (F) has a certain place in the club's overall image, the average variance extracted (AVE after the varimax rotation was 86% and is here recalculated over 100%). The reliability (Cronbach's alpha coefficient α) is satisfactory (> 0.7). The Kaiser-Meyer-Olkin (KMO) sampling precision measurement is also high (> 0.5). The items do not appear directly in the statistical data so as to ensure a better legibility.

19 The *F* factor: *Team, game* and *player quality* with its different items (*Is*): team and game quality, team success, fidelity of the team to its fans, player quality, star players, international success. F: *Club management* and its *Is*: trainer quality, club management and Chairman's commitment.

20 *F: Stadium quality and atmosphere* and its *Is*: modern state of the stadium, stadium personality and atmosphere, stadium location; *F*: *History and tradition* with its *Is*: Club's long history, Club history is a successful one, the Club is historically part of the 1. Bundesliga; *F: Entertainment* with its *Is*: giant screen contributing to the atmosphere, cheerleaders, commentators, sound and other forms of entertainment; and the *F: Catering/hospitality services* with its *Is*: politeness of staff, efficiency of services, catering/hospitality quality

21 Attribute *F*: *Benefits* and its *Is*: outing, escapism; emotion relating to the game, peer acceptance.

22 Attribute *F*: *CSR* and its *Is*: commitment to the region, openness and honesty of the club, corporate responsibility, youth training and security.

23 COUVELAERE, V., RICHELIEU, A., Brand strategy in professional sports: The case of French soccer teams, *European Sport Management Quarterly*, 5, 1, 23–46, 2005.

24 CHANAVAT, N., BODET, G., Experiential marketing in sport spectatorship services: A customer perspective, *European Sport Management Quarterly*, 14, 4, 1–22, 2014.

25 Logistic regression analysis is a binomial regression tool determining whether the independent variable explains a large part of the variation of the dependent variable (Malhotra, Birks, Wills, 2012). The different

factors were recalculated into categories which are listed in the first column. This form of logistic regression indicates the probability that an event shall take place for a person. The results can be read in SPSS in the form of blocks. Exp (B) was over 1, indicating in this way that the results shall increase (Field, 2013). The Cox and Snell R-Square as well as the Nagelkerke R-Squared indicate that the growing predictive variable increases the probability that the even and the purchase behavior shall occur. All the predictability percentages are greater than 75%. FIELD, A., *Discovering Statistics Using SPSS* (4th ed.), London, Sage, 2013.

MALHOTRA, N.K., BIRKS, D.F., WILLS, P., *Marketing Research: An Applied Approach* (4th ed.), Paris, Pearson Education, 2012.

26 BODET, G., CHANAVAT, N., Building global football brand equity: Lessons from the Chinese market, *Asia Pacific Journal of Marketing and Logistics*, 22, 1, 55–66, 2010.

27 ROSS, S.D., RUSSELL, K.C., HYEJIN, B., An empirical assessment of spectator-based brand equity, *Journal of Sport Management*, 22, 3, 322–337, 2008.

28 BAYLE, E., CHAPPELET, J.L., FRANÇOIS, A., MALTESE, L., *Sport & RSE: Vers Un Management Responsable?*, Bruxelles, Groupe De Boeck, 2011.

29 KIHL, L., BABIAK, K., TAINSKY, S., Evaluating the implementation of a professional sport team's corporate community involvement initiative, *Journal of Sport Management*, 28, 324–333, 2014.

30 WALKER, M., KENT, A., Do fans care? Assessing the influence of corporate social responsibility on consumer attitudes in the sport industry, *Journal of Sport Management*, 23, 6, 743–769, 2009.

31 The coach was already very criticized when we did our interview.

32 The principle of organisational recursion by which the product or the ultimate effect becomes the prime element and prime cause (Morin, 1977).

MORIN, E., *La méthode, tome 1: La nature de la nature*, Paris, Éditions du seuil, 1977.

33 An observation which stands out very clearly from the IPSOS study: http://www.lfp.fr/uploads/fichiers/2014_04_07_Presentation_LFP_etudes_stades.pdf?org=tinymce – LFP, Public studies of Ligues 1 and 2, March, 2014. Last accessed February 10, 2015.

34 Translation provided by the author: "furchtlos und treu".

35 BLUMRODT, J., *L'attractivité du football français. L'image de marque des clubs à l'épreuve*, Sarrebruck, EUE, 2011.

36 DRUT, B., *Economie du football professionnel*, Paris, Editions La Découverte, 2014.

37 DIETL, H, FRANCK, E., Governance failure and financial crisis in German football, *Journal of Sports Economics*, 8, 6, 662–669, 2007.

38 In the Deloitte report (2012), Stuttgart is still in 27th place (Deloitte, *The Untouchables. Football Money League, Fan Power*, London, Publié, 2012). Although the club VfB Stuttgart e.V. has succeeded in increasing its budget from 95.5 to 116.5 million euros (information: Steffen Lindenmaier), it has lost its place in the top 30 richest clubs in Europe (*cf.* Deloitte, *Football Money League 2015: Commercial Breaks*, London, Published, January 2015).

39 This information appears on the site of Bayern F.C. http://www.fcbayern.de/de/club/fcb-ag/organe/ – Last accessed February 10, 2015, and it has been translated by the author.

40 http://www2.deloitte.com/uk/en/pages/sports-business-group/articles/deloitte-football-money-league.html – All Deloitte reports are available through this link. Last access on 10 February 2015.

Bibliography

BAUER, H.H., STOKBURGER-SAUER, N.E., EXLER, S., Brand Image and Fan Loyalty in Professional Team Sport: A Refined. Model and Empirical Assessment, *Journal of Sport Management*, 22, 205–226, 2008.

BAYLE, E., CHAPPELET, J.L., FRANÇOIS, A., MALTESE, L., *Sport & RSE: Vers Un Management Responsable?* Bruxelles, Groupe De Boeck, 2011.

BLUMRODT, J., *L'attractivité du football français. L'image de marque des clubs à l'épreuve*, Sarrebruck, EUE, 2011.

BLUMRODT, J., BRYSON, D., FLANAGAN, J., European Football Teams' CSR Engagement Impacts on Customer-Based Brand Equity, *Journal of Consumer Marketing*, 29, 7, 482–493, 2012.

BLUMRODT, J., DESBORDES, M., BODIN, D., Professional Football Clubs and Corporate Social Responsibility, *Sport, Business, Management: An International Journal*, 3, 3, 205–225, 2013.

BODET, G., CHANAVAT, N., Building Global Football Brand Equity: Lessons from the Chinese Market, *Asia Pacific Journal of Marketing and Logistics*, 22, 1, 55–66, 2010.

CHANAVAT, N., BODET, G., Experiential Marketing in Sport Spectatorship Services: A Customer Perspective, *European Sport Management Quarterly*, 14, 4, 1–22, 2014.

COOPER, D.R., SCHINDLER, P.S., *Business Research Methods*, (11e éd.), Singapore, McGraw-Hill, 2010.

COUVELAERE, V., RICHELIEU, A., Brand Strategy in Professional Sports: The Case of French Soccer Teams, *European Sport Management Quarterly*, 5, 1, 23–46, 2005.

DELOITTE, *The Untouchables: Football Money League, Fan Power*, London, Publié, 2012.[41] http://www2.deloitte.com/content/dam/Deloitte/uk/Documents/sports-business-group/deloitte-uk-deloitte-football-money-league-2012.pdf – Dernier accès le 10 février 2015.

DELOITTE, *All to Play for Football Money League*, London, Publié, 2014. https://www2.deloitte.com/content/dam/Deloitte/uk/Documents/sports-business-group/deloitte-uk-deloitte-football-money-league-2014.pdf – Dernier accès le 10 février 2015.

DELOITTE, *Football Money League 2015: Commercial Breaks*, London, Publié, janvier 2015. http://www2.deloitte.com/content/dam/Deloitte/uk/Documents/sports-business-group/deloitte-football-money-league-2015.PDF – Dernier accès le 10 février 2015.

DIETL, H., FRANCK, E., Governance Failure and Financial Crisis in German Football, *Journal of Sports Economics*, 8, 6, 662–669, 2007.

DRUT, B., *Economie du football professionnel*, Paris, Editions La Découverte, 2014.

FIELD, A., *Discovering Statistics Using SPSS*, (4th ed.), London, Sage, 2013.

GLADDEN, J.M., FUNK, D.C., Understanding Brand Loyalty in Professional Sport: Examining the Link between Brand Associations and Brand Loyalty, *International Journal of Sports Marketing & Sponsorship*, 3, 67–91, 2001.

GLADDEN, J.M., FUNK, D.C., Developing an Understanding of Brand Associations in Team Sport: Empirical Evidence from Consumers of Professional Sport, *Journal of Sport Management*, 16, 54–81, 2002.

Keller, K.L., Conceptualization, Measuring, and Managing Customer-Based Brand Equity, *Journal of Marketing*, 57, 1–22, 1993.

KIHL, L., BABIAK, K., TAINSKY, S., Evaluating the Implementation of a Professional Sport Team's Corporate Community Involvement Initiative, *Journal of Sport Management*, 28, 324–333, 2014.

MALHOTRA, N.K., BIRKS, D.F., WILLS, P., *Marketing Research: An Applied Approach*, (4e éd.), Paris, Pearson Education, 2012.

MORIN, E., *La méthode, tome 1: La nature de la nature*, Paris, Éditions du seuil, 1977.

MOSNIER, M. Droits TV: La L1 vaut autant que la Liga mais beaucoup moins que la Premier League, 4 April 2014, http://www.eurosport.fr/football/ligue-1/2013-2014/droits-tv-la-l1-vaut-autant-que-la-liga-mais-beaucoup-moins-que-la-premier-league_sto4201121/story.shtml – last accessed 10F ebruary 2015.

MULLIN, B.J., HARDY, S., SUTTON, W.A., *Sport Marketing*, (4th éd.) Champaign, Illinois, Human Kinetics, 2014.

ROSS, S.D., A Conceptual Framework for Understanding Spectator-Based Brand Equity, *Journal of Sport Management*, 20, 22–38, 2006.

ROSS, S.D., HYEJIN, B., SEUNGUM, L., Assessing Brand Associations for Intercollegiate Ice Hockey, *Sport Marketing Quarterly*, 16, 2, 106–114, 2007.

ROSS, S.D., RUSSELL, K.C., HYEJIN, B., An Empirical Assessment of Spectator-Based Brand Equity, *Journal of Sport Management*, 22, 3, 322–337, 2008.

WALKER, M., KENT, A., Do Fans Care? Assessing the Influence of Corporate Social Responsibility on Consumer Attitudes in the Sport Industry, *Journal of Sport Management*, 23, 6, 743–769, 2009.

Webography

http://www.bvb.de/ – Site officiel du BV 09 Borussia Dortmund. Dernier accès le 10 février 2015.

http://www.cahiersdufootball.net/article-un-modele-allemand-4876 – Titre d'une page Internet parue sur le football allemand ("Un modèle allemand"). Dernier accès le 10 février 2015.

http://www.dfb.de/bundesliga/start/ – Les statistiques du DFB (Zum Statistikenbereich). Dernier accès le 10 février 2015.

http://www.dfb.de/verbandsstruktur/mitglieder/ – Il s'agit du site officiel du Deutscher Fußball Bund. Dernier accès le 10 février 2015.

http://www.eurosport.fr/football/ligue-1/2013-2014/droits-tv-la-l1-vaut-autant-que-la-liga-mais-beaucoup-moins-que-la-premier-league_sto4201121/story.shtml – Article intitulé "Droits TV: La L1 vaut autant que la Liga mais beaucoup moins que la Premier League" rédigé par Martin Mosnier et paru dans eurosport.fr le 4 avril 2014. Dernier accès le 10 février 2015.

http://www.fcbayern.de/ – Site officiel du FC Bayern de Munich. Dernier accès le 10 février 2015.
http://www.hsv.de/ – Site officiel du HSV. Dernier accès le 10 février 2015.
http://www.lfp.fr/uploads/fichiers/2014_04_07_Presentation_LFP_etudes_stades.pdf?org=tinymce – Etudes publics des stades Ligue 1 et Ligue 2 mars 2014. Dernier accès le 10 février 2015.
http://www.lfp.fr/uploads/fichiers/2014_04_07_Presentation_LFP_etudes_stades.pdf?org=tinymce – LFP, Etudes publics des stades Ligue 1 et Ligue 2. Mars, 2014. Dernier accès le 10 février 2015.
http://www.schalke04.de/s04/index.html – Site officiel du Schalke 04. Dernier accès le 10 février 2015.

Appendix

Interview guide

Interviews with the public were carried out during the week of April 28 to May 3, 2014. To do this, VfB let us use its premises. The interviews were filmed. The interviewees were quite at ease and in no way bothered by the presence of the camera or the two interviewers. So as to guarantee a certain dynamic, we proceeded with individual interviews as well as interviews in small groups. Twenty people were questioned during this period (15 men and 5 women). All the interviewees wanted to talk about their club, give their opinion and recount all they knew about it. We therefore imposed semi-guided interviews to guarantee coherent discourse. All the participants attended VfB Stuttgart matches on a regular basis.

Some, in particular, were season ticket holders who were present at all the home matches. Interviewees names were listed, and the interviews were re-transcribed within 24 hours following the interview. Below is the outline of the questions asked by the interviewers.

Introduction and basic information

1. How long have you been coming to VfB matches? How many matches did you go to last season? How do you find the public?

   Do you follow VfB's news? How do you do this: television, newspapers, Internet or any other means?

Transition and main body of questions

2. For what reasons do you come to the stadium instead of watching the matches on the television?
3. What does VfB Stuttgart represent for you?
4. What do you think of the quality of the players? What do you think of the quality of VfB's game? What do you think of the training of young players?
5. What does the trainer represent for you? Is the club well managed?
6. Do you know anything of the club's history? Are the club's past successes important for you?
7. What is the atmosphere like in the stadium during a match? Is the stadium well managed? Is it well located?
8. Is it possible to eat well in the catering/hospitality outlets?
9. How does the club get involved in community life (town, region)?

The duration of the interview was limited to 45 minutes. The data were processed using NVivo software. The answers illustrate our claims regarding VfB Stuttgart e.V., and the inquiry also produced qualitative reasoning. This process is above all useful in generating the content of questions and helping to formulate different questions.

16

THE ACF FIORENTINA MARKETING

The strength of local identity

Patrizia Zagnoli[1] and Elena Radicchi

1. Evolution of the club

The Fiorentina professional football club is one of the A Series Italian teams, and it is substance and symbol of a strong identification with the city. Florence, a medium-sized town and "heart of the Italian Renaissance", has this unique professional football team whose primary asset is its fans.

The Fiorentina was created on August 26, 1926, through fusion of two local clubs: Libertas and Club Sportivo Firenze. The Fiorentina's club color started out as white and red, but in 1929, it became purple ("viola") and from that point on, the team became known as "I Viola".[2] In its early years, the Marquess Luigi Ridolfi was its President, and in 1931, he managed to insert the club in the A Series, the football top division, which well reflects the city's historical sense of importance.

In 1937–1938, the Fiorentina lapsed back into B Series, but in the 1950s, it became one of the most important Italian football teams, and, after a rather unsuccessful period, it won its first national championship in 1955–1956. Also, it did well on a European level, reaching the finals in 1956–1957 and winning the Cup of the Cups in 1961. In the 1960s, the Fiorentina continued its success with the second national championship in 1968–1969, with Nello Baglini as its President, a businessman from Pisa who moved to Florence.

In the 1980s, the Fiorentina continued to do well under the patronage of the Pontello family, owners of important construction companies in Florence, who had been its major shareholders for a decade. Economic problems began to trouble the team's solidarity, and it had to sell some of its best players, such as Roberto Baggio, who went to play for Juventus, much to the anger of the local fans. The strong local identification of the team with its fans meant an important stakeholder lobbying role. The club therefore was induced to sell its majority shares to the Cecchi Gori family, a Florentine businessman active in the emerging sector of private television (Telemontecarlo) and the films production and distribution. Cecchi Gori's enthusiasm as owner and "fan among fans", saw the return of the Fiorentina to the A Series in 1992, emerging from the B Series where it played in 1991–1992. During the rest of the 1990s, the team remained in the A Series and also in the Champions League, where they passed the first rounds and almost made it into the quarter finals after having defeated in home games excellent teams such as Valencia and Manchester United, and having conquered Wembley Stadium.

At the beginning of the new millennium, financial and judiciary vicissitudes plagued Vittorio Cecchi Gori: losing out in the competition with Silvio Berlusconi in the world of television and cinematographic production, he started to have more and more difficulty in paying for excellent players, and his business bankruptcy caused the closing of the Fiorentina. On August 1, 2002, the Fiorentina disappeared from the national football panorama. On the same day, in the light of many initiatives, demonstrations, parades and efforts by fans and Florentine citizens during the week prior to the bankruptcy, the Mayor of Florence and his Councilor for Sport won the deliberation of the Federal Council of the Italian Football Federation (FIGC), which authorized the establishment of a team which was "representative of the city of Florence". Out of this deliberation was born a new club, the Fiorentina 1926 Florentia Srl, whose President was the Mayor of Florence. In the days immediately following this action, there were frenetic meetings regarding attribution of the newly founded club to another owner. The Mayor and his Sport Councilor explored every avenue to find a local entrepreneur – which was a decided preference of the citizens and fans. However, in the context of progressive globalization, it was not possible to identify a local businessman who could sustain the economic costs of a team of this high level, so the club was ceded to the emerging Della Valle fashion industrial group. Della Valle's family company, based in Marche Region in Central Italy, an area specialized in traditional sectors such as leather, shoes and clothing manufacturing, was able to promote its brand internationally. Moreover, the combination of its products and the ownership of the football Florentine team would be ideal to prompt the top-quality image of their fashion leather.[3]

The property of the Fiorentina, up until its economic failure in 2002, was characterized by strong connections and deep roots in the local context – these being expressions of fans and also of local entrepreneurship.

The rebirth of the club, instead, involved local institutions which promoted and guaranteed the entrance of the entrepreneur Della Valle, the first non-Florentine owner. Although the Viola fans might have desired a local "patron" to be a reassurance to them, after the failure of the Fiorentina, Diego Della Valle assumed a role as "savior" of the team, restoring it to its fans and its city. Although Della Valle was not a native Florentine, he succeeded in attaining the consensus of the city in a dialectic and collaborative atmosphere with fans, institutions and managers.

The period of 2002–2004 was fundamental to the process of restructuring the team and the club, with a crucial passage to save its name, its brand and its trophies which were to be auctioned off.[4] The bankruptcy of the team had altered the symbols which were important to the fans, with modifications in the color of the team uniform, which had become white with only a small amount of purple border, and the team name which had become Florentia Viola. Della Valle's actions exhibited not only his respect and care for the fans who were hurt by the loss of their sport heritage role, but also his desire to preserve the team's history which for the Florentines and local institutions was a kind of "public asset". The redemption of the Fiorentina symbolism meant not losing the patrimony of values embedded in the team name, undoubtedly linked with the city itself.

On the other hand, investment in the football team has also a strategic promotional significance for the industrial group. Besides gaining the "unconditional love of the Florentines", Della Valle won the sympathy of Italian football fans worldwide. The Fiorentina crisis was closely followed in the press, and so its rescue caused an international media buzz, promoting the image of a family company capable of combining managerial innovation and marketing with the Italian quality of traditional manufacturing. Florence is well known internationally for its beauty and the superb quality of its artisans in many sectors, including leather. The combination of these traditions of quality manufacturing in which the Della Valle family was involved and the city's football team helped to diffuse the brand names of TOD's and Hogan worldwide. In 2002–2003, the Fiorentina played in the C2 Series championships. The unexpected jump into the B Series in 2003–2004 surprised the managers who found they were running a team which was unprepared for the level of game they were required to play. The objective became to work on technical aspects to form a team "which would be second to no one".

The entrepreneur Della Valle, with his high-quality fashion products, wanted his football team also to occupy a top position which would personify its city. The team needed to express a first-class role, meaning to climb quickly into A Series, which it managed to do in 2004.

The period of 2005–2010 was the second phase of the evolution of the Fiorentina. In these years, the club owners wanted to enhance the value of the "team-product". The club, fans and citizens all awaited excellent playing: nevertheless, technical results and winning capability required significant financial investments. These objectives were not sustained by adequate means since the club's strategy was to be "self-financing", with parsimonious investments in new players, by enhancing internal grassroots strategies and at the same time acquiring young technical resources at "zero parameter", who were later transferred to other teams with resulting significant capital gains.

The beginning of this second phase coincided with one of the most difficult periods for the team, which became involved in the "Calciopoli" football scandal. The team had 19 penalty points when entering the 2005–2006 season. With the exception of two championships as protagonist, the 2008–2009 and 2009–2010 seasons were disappointing, staying in the lower half of the classifications. The initial choice to consolidate the technical project was carried out with a low-profile strategy of players acquisition and selling off the "big" names,[5] which was strongly criticized by an important number of fans. Disenchantment between fans and owners increased so much that supporters began to doubt that the Della Valle group, already well known at a global level for the high-quality image of its leather goods, was anymore strategically interested in the ownership of Fiorentina.[6]

The Municipality of Florence played a decisive role in confirmation of the team's identity with its city and as a prelude to its launch by reinforcing the "partnership" between the club and the city itself, allowing projects for restructuring the stadium and renewing the contract for use of the sport facilities.[7] In 2011, with the entrance of the Municipality government in the team's Board of Directors, the relationship between local stakeholders and the club was further consolidated. This was the beginning of a "new path" in managing the Fiorentina. New investments in qualified human resources were made in the club and the technical aspects were reinforced: the team began to gain a strategic business role within a diversified industrial group (Figure 16.1).

In the last 3 years (2012–2015), the Fiorentina club has undergone progressive organizational and management restructuring, assigning a decisive role with regard to marketing processes to the newly subsidiary Firenze Viola S.r.l., a social denomination that expresses the renewed

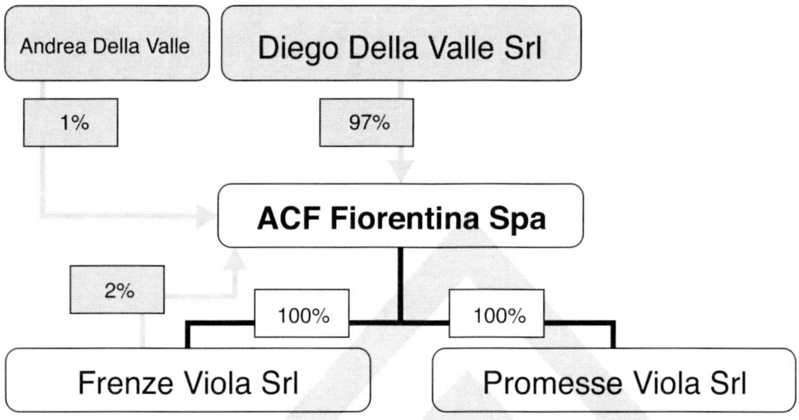

Figure 16.1 Organizational structure of the ACF Fiorentina

Source: ACF Fiorentina (2013).

confirmation of the identity between city and team. Local stakeholders and fans, involved in a complex network of relationships (see §. 2.1, 2.2, 2.3), continue to play a role of privileged "spokespersons" who are able to influence sport results and management decisions of the club.

The marketing project of Firenze Viola S.r.l. included the enhanced stadium experience (§. 3), the implementation of relational marketing strategies which involve supporters by the new fan membership card (§. 4), and the development of sponsors and partners relationships of exchange and collaboration (§. 5). New multimedia and interactive technologies play an important strategic role in the communication of the club (§. 6, 6.1, 6.2): the subsidiary Promesse Viola S.r.l. launches a new project of internationalization of the Fiorentina brand (§. 7), promoting football in good growth-potential markets.

Box 16.1 Palmares and the history of the ACF Fiorentina

In its early years, the Marquis Luigi Ridolfi was the President of the Fiorentina, and in 1931 he managed to insert the club in the A Series, the top division of football which reflects the city's historical sense of importance. In 1937–1938, the Fiorentina lapsed back into Series B, but in the 1950s, the team became one of the most important Italian football teams, and after a rather unsuccessful period, in 1955–1956, it won its first national championship and did well also on a European level. In the 1960s, the Fiorentina continued its success with the second national championship in 1968–1969, with Nello Baglini as its President, a businessman from Pisa who transferred to Florence. In the 1980s, the Fiorentina club continued to do well under the guidance of the Pontello family, owners of important construction companies in Florence, who were major shareholders for a decade. Economic problems began to trouble the team's solidarity, and the team had to sell some of its best players. The strong local identification of the team with its fans meant that these latter began to play an important stakeholder lobbying role. The club therefore was induced to sell its majority shares to the Cecchi Gori family, a Florentine businessman active in the emerging sector of private television (Telemontecarlo) and the production and distribution of films. During the 1990s, the team remained in the A Series and also reached the Champions League.

At the beginning of the new millennium, the Fiorentina went bankrupt and disappeared from the national football panorama. In 2002 the club was reinstituted through efforts of local institutions and citizens who ushered in the entrepreneur Della Valle, the first non-Florentine owner. In the 2002–2003 football season, the team played in the C2 Series championships. Its unexpected promotion to the B Series in 2003–2004 surprised the managers, who found themselves with a team which was not prepared for such a level of playing. Their objective then was to work on technical aspects, to reconstruct a team which would play at the highest levels. The owners worked to get the team promoted quickly into the top classification, and in 2004, the Fiorentina returned to the A Series.

Between 2005–2010, investment by the owners was designed to enhance the "team-product". This phase coincided with one of the most difficult periods for the Fiorentina, which was involved in the "Calciopoli" football scandal, and it entered the 2005–2006 season with 19 penalty points. With the exception of two championships, the 2008–2009 and 2009–2010 seasons were disappointing, with the Fiorentina in the lower half of the classifications. Since 2012, thanks to new investments in qualified human resources and reinforcements of a technical nature, the Fiorentina reached the highest positions of the classifications and participated in the Europe League.

Source: http://www.violachannel.tv. Last accessed February 2, 2015.

Box 16.2 ACF Fiorentina statistics

President of the ACF Fiorentina Spa: Mario Cognigni
Name of the Honorary President: Andrea Della Valle
Number of season ticket holders (2014/2015): 22,300
Number of Facebook fans: 1 million
Average number of spectators per match: 32,057 (2013–2014), (stadium capacity: 46,389)
Total profit from activities: 121 million euros
Earnings allocations: sponsors/advertisements (10.3%), TV rights (37%), tickets (8%), merchandising (0.5%), transfer of players (27.5%)
Names of sponsors in 2014: Save the Children, Joma, Banca CR Firenze, Volkswagen, Sky, Sammontana, GSport, Tim, I Gigli, Betclic.it, MetaEnergia

Source: http://www.violachannel.tv. Last access 27 February, 2015, and ACF Fiorentina, 2012–2013 Budget.

Box 16.3 Managers interviewed

Sandro Mencucci: CEO, Responsible for the International Fiorentina Project
Maurizio Francini: Stadium Manager
Tommaso Bianchini: Business Analyst
Martino Ferrari: Manager of Sponsorship and Marketing
Angelo Venturi: Social Media Manager

2. The role of local stakeholders

2.1 Local community and institutions

The Fiorentina football club is the focus of a network of relationships among fans, spectators, coaches, managers, institutions, the media and sponsors which all interact with each other to implement the "product-game".

Football is not only the most popular sport in the city, but Fiorentina is the unique A Series football team so that all citizens of Florence are united in their relationship with "I Viola". Florentines are traditionally proud of their city and have strong emotional ties to it, which helps in the identification of the team with the city and vice versa.

The local community feels that the Fiorentina is "their" team, and have internalized the strong and unusual identification of the city with the team, unlike other of the A Series Italian football clubs. The local community shares the emotions, joys, struggles and disappointments with their team. Although most citizens do not attend games nor follow them on television, they express interest in the ups and downs of the club, pay a lot of attention to the local posters which are exhibited on the streets at newspaper stands, showing a deep emotional tie with the Fiorentina's successes and losses.

At a critical time such as the club's bankruptcy, Florentines supported the team with collective emotional demonstrations (Le Bon, 2004):[8] even under adversity, the participation and identification of citizens with the Fiorentina helped to reinforce local feelings about the "collective Viola identity". The local community, therefore, represents a fundamental intangible support for the club: the strong collective identification between citizens and team, the cohesion even during the team life enhanced the "rescue" and development of the club.

Due to the active pressure of citizens, local institutions carried out key roles for the club which were manifested in two crucial steps for the life of the Fiorentina:

- In 2002, when the club closed down, Florence's Mayor and his Councilor of Sport, after a lot of pressure from fans and all citizens, carried out a mediator role with the judiciary sportive authorities (Tar and the FIGC),[9] resulting in the rescue of the club which was deemed a local "heritage". Notwithstanding its bankruptcy, the club was assigned on paper to the city of Florence, an essential precondition for finding a new owner, an effort in which the Municipality played an active role.
- In 2011, there was another confirmation of the special closeness between the team and the city, with its entrance in the Board of Directors by the Vice Mayor, Councilor for Sport and President of the City Council. The entrance of local institutions in the governance of the team was a strong message: the Municipality became a decisive stakeholder for the permanence of the ownership in the team and helped it achieve progressive qualification of a technical and competitive nature, as vividly hoped for by citizens and fans.

The "agreement" which tied the Della Valle group to local stakeholders, fans, city and institutions is continually reinforced up to a recent decision by the Municipality government to approve a project to construct a new stadium owned by the Fiorentina. This project was included among the public works considered of public utility by the City Council.

2.2 Viola spectators and season-ticket holders

The Fiorentina games emerge as the only "event" able to attract tens of thousands people in Florence. The fan community is variegated and deserves a specific description since it is remarkable in the city's context. In this section we will analyze the "unorganized" Viola fans, who follow the games either by watching them on television or by attending them live (spectators and season ticket holders), whereas organized fans clubs will be described in the next section. Some fans fulfill both roles: season ticket holders and organized fans; and spectators and organized fans.

Now that football can be watched on digital television, the number of "virtual" spectators who follow the Fiorentina games has increased through subscribers to Sky Pay TV and Mediaset Premium.[10]

The number of spectators who go to live home matches has been constant over the last seasons,[11] in which the Fiorentina in terms of live audience[12] has achieved a place among the first six teams of the Series A championships.

The heart of the fan community of Fiorentina is comprised of those who are season tickets holders, and thus express their enthusiastic attachment to the club.

The fans' affection for the Fiorentina brand, for the "purple shirt" and for the city's team is rather unusual within the Italian and European football scene. Some authors (Mullin, Hardy, Sutton, 2000; Lago, Baroncelli, Szymanski, 2004) reveal the important economic worth of a virtuous circle which is created between success on the field supporting the team. A club's ability to make profits (through ticket sales, membership cards, merchandising, etc.) depends largely on the fans' satisfaction.

The local city-team identity also has brought to life some aspects which are a counter-tendency: usually if a team does not do well on the field, supporters tend to abandon or neglect it. In the case of the Fiorentina, however, the ties between the team and the city are tight, even when the team is defeated or produces mediocre results or even when the team company collapsed. Following its bankruptcy in the 2002–2003 season, the newly born team was pushed back into the C2 Series. However, there were still almost 17,000 season ticket holders in that period, notwithstanding the low classification.

Devotion to the team also emerges during actual moments of "turbulence" and crisis which characterize Italian football. Even though the live presence of spectators at football games has gone down by 9.5% in the last 10 years on a national level, the active participation of Viola fans has actually increased by 36% (Lega Calcio, 2015).

Also the group of season ticket holders is stable, between 22,000 and 23,000 each year (ACF Fiorentina, 2015).[13] These could be defined as "hard-core fans" (Kotler, 2006) who remain constantly loyal to the team even if it does not win on the field.

Fiorentina fans can be considered a "tribe" with components sharing an "affective impulse" (Maffesoli, 2004) for their city's team, a passion which creates a strong territorial link between the city, the club and its fans. Although in recent years the number of supporters located outside of Tuscany has increased, the community of fans is "geographically marked".

As emerged from previous research carried out by the authors on the basis of the season ticket holder database (Zagnoli, Radicchi, Fanti, 2004) and from recent interviews with the club managers, there is a strong "Viola collective identity" that underlines the relevant territorial origin of membership ticket holders fans. Of these, 50% live in the city of Florence, with a further 37% in the Florentine metropolitan area. This overall 87% of season ticket holders confirms the very strong "territorial identity" between fans and team (Figure 16.2).

Although there has been growth in the number of women, Viola fans are predominantly men, aged between 25 and 44, and they have supported the "Viola" for a long time.[14] They can be divided into three socio-demographic profiles: core fans (25–44 years old), young people (6–24 years old) and seniors (over 65).[15] The socio-cultural level of fans is mainly middle class, but with a continual increase in the number of fans in the upper-middle class. These "wealthier" stay in the Tribuna, the stadium "aristocratic" area, which was restyled by the club to enhance services appealing to this particular target of fans who are willing to pay a premium price for tickets and membership cards.[16]

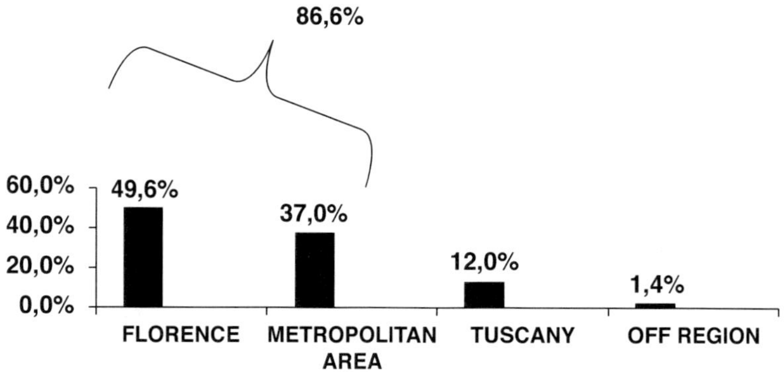

Figure 16.2 The collective Viola identity

2.3 Organized fans: the network of Viola Clubs

The organized community of Fiorentina fans is a composite network of micro-groups, a sort of "tribal constellation" (Cova, 1997) (Figure 16.3). An analysis of the manifold components of this constellation reveals that a large number of fans are organized into so-called Viola Clubs.

Although there are some Viola Clubs diffused throughout Italy and even internationally (such as in Scandinavia, Malta, etc.), most members of Viola Clubs are rooted in the Florence metropolitan area, confirming the identity between fans and city.

The number of fan clubs who are organized autonomously is small, with the majority being affiliated with associations which have played an active supportive role in the football club's policies. The most important associations are the Centro Coordinamento Viola Club (ACCVC), which comprises about 220 smaller clubs, and the Associazione Tifosi Fiorentini (ATF) with 30 fan clubs. Altogether these form a network of about 50,000 supporters, with slightly less than half of these individuals being season ticket holders.

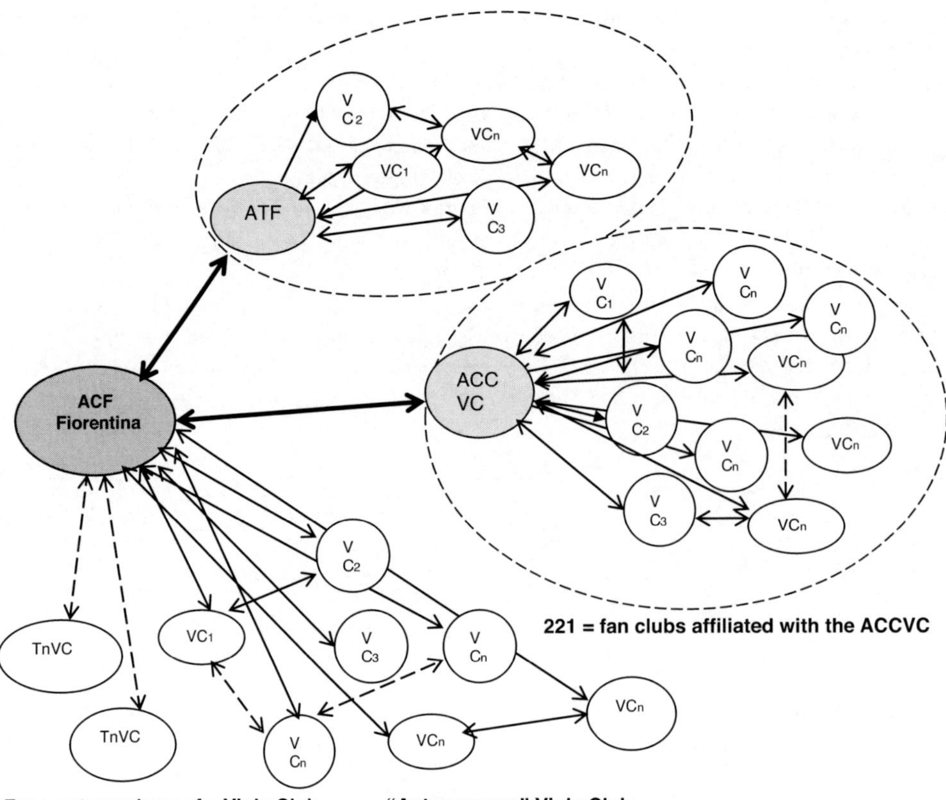

Figure 16.3 Network of ACF Fiorentina fan clubs

In addition to coordination of the Viola Clubs,[17] these associations play a crucial role in supporting the team, even in difficult situations such as the club's failure. The rebirth of Fiorentina occurred thanks to the strong stimulus of the fans, supporters and citizens,[18] so that the Viola Associations became directly involved in negotiations and pressured the appropriate local institutions.[19]

The fan clubs, defined as a kind of "partner" (Zagnoli, Radicchi, 2010, p. 1544), express a very high level of cooperation and "control" on decisions taken by the football club; therefore, they "condition" its strategies. The group of partners can be defined as "rule setters", being particularly opinionated fans who are willing to lobby and express publicly their positions through open letters to the presidents and managers and through the press, radio interviews, blogs and websites. These means all help to involve the entire community of fans and citizens, but are also able to promote direct contact with club officials and local institutions.[20]

The behavior of the Fiorentina fan clubs network is distinguished by a high level of freedom of opinion and action towards the club, but also by its inclination to be "propositively open". At the same time, the clubs acts towards groups of fans with dialogue and negotiation, inviting them to participate in workshops, round table discussions and other types of meetings involving stakeholders such as local administration, local police, etc.

The most recent phase of the Viola Clubs' life cycle has overcome the emergency situation, which characterized the first years following the Fiorentina's bankruptcy. Since 2011 fans, owners and local administration have developed friendly relationships. Therefore, the organized groups of fans have consolidated their approach by maintaining direct relations with the club and local institutions, with the aim of keeping their focus on football as a "joyful sporting event".

There is a small group of fans who can be defined "contrarian" (Zagnoli, Radicchi, 2010, p. 1546): if they do not approve the football club decisions, they are openly critical and manifest their opinions through blogs, social networks and fans websites (§. 4). The threat of this type of behavior is greatly amplified by the use of the new media which contribute a "viral diffusion" (Wilson, 2000) of strong emotions which then enter into a vicious circle, given the tendency of fans to share online experiences with friends, relatives, acquaintances, and thus to influence the social and sporting atmosphere.

3. The strategy of creating an emotional experience at the stadium

The first President of the Fiorentina club, the Marquess Ridolfi, promised a new stadium to the club, which was designed by the engineer Luigi Nervi and inaugurated in 1931.[21] The structure was very modern with innovative elements such as steel-reinforced concrete construction, external helical stairways and a covered Tribuna. It is still today a "national historic monument" and strong symbol of local identity. The stadium's architectural features have made it fairly complicated to renovate for new infrastructural needs introduced at the beginning of the new millennium and have impeded the chances of enhancing it as a marketing tool for the club.[22]

Between 2005 and 2007, the stadium was renovated in response to national and European directives, with the introduction of pre-filtering areas, electronic throughways, closed-circuit cameras, protective barriers between sections and separating the playing field from the spectators.[23]

Since 2008 local institutions, the Fiorentina club and officials responsible for public order, in collaboration with the University of Florence,[24] have been working on a project to gradually "demilitarize" the stadium and eliminate some of the barriers which were erected. This project has symbolic and educational scope with the intention of restoring a family-friendly climate in the stadium and with the object to give fans more responsibility: for the first time in 2012, the metal barriers in one of the sections (Maratona) were eliminated and replaced by a plexiglas railing.

Figure 16.4 Rendering of the renovated Tribuna of the Artemio Franchi Stadium

Source: ACF Fiorentina, 2015.

The club, strengthened by its renewed collaboration with Florence's Municipality, in the last 3 years began a process of enhancing the facility from new perspectives. The stadium started a progressive alteration in its functions, slowly evolving through laborious and respectful grafting onto the original structure, to offer an environment which would satisfy diversified customers' needs, connected not only to the direct attendance of sporting events, but also to gain other commercial interests.

In the summer of 2013, the Tribuna, a section of the stadium which was traditionally considered for the "elite", was restyled (Figure 16.4) by substituting the existing seats with ergonomic and easily accessible purple armchairs and by removing the barriers separating the spectators and the playing field. This reorganization continued to maintain the overall seating capacity of the stadium at 46,389 places.

The main objective of the club is to offer intense live participation to fans by increasing their overall comfort and providing an emotional experience (Pine, Gilmore, 2000) for supporters and partners (§. 5).

The stadium becomes the pivot of promotional and marketing activity, not just in relation to the matches but by offering a complex mixture of additional services suitable for multiple target customers. Special attention has been dedicated to business clients: installation of renovated VIP areas equipped with meeting rooms, restaurants, catering capabilities, etc., besides 19 Sky boxes. The press area and the Tribuna for authorities have been reorganized, as well as the hospitality areas designed to facilitate and enhance the relationships with sponsors and partners. The stadium was transformed into a constant accessible meeting point for institutions and in a desirable location for special events of Fiorentina partners who could thus offer their clients a special experience.

The segment of users-fans, in addition to the renovated Tribuna and Maratona, could look forward to implementation of a highly technological infrastructure with built-in wi-fi connection and other features which would transform the Artemio Franchi into a connected stadium. The main objective is to encourage fans to remain in the facility for as long as possible, partly by increasing the commercial offerings and services inside of it. The involvement of fans could be enhanced with constant access to club contents published on social networks (Twitter, Facebook, Instagram, etc.) before, during and after the match.

4. The fan card: From "monitoring device" to marketing opportunity

The need to strategically manage the activities carried out in sport facilities, together with the introduction of rules for preventing violence, and the application of Remote Frequency Identification (RFid) tickets, prompted the introduction of the "fan card". The fan card has been obligatory for all the Italian football clubs since the 2010–2011 season.[25]

There was excellent cooperation in Florence between the club and local institutions in the effort to actively involve fans and encourage their engagement. The city was an ideal environment in which to experiment the fan card "Orgoglio Viola" (Viola Pride) introduced in 2010. The smart card contained the individual fan's demographic information, but was not just an instrument for managing security access to the stadium: it also offered some additional services to fans. It could be set up as a prepaid and rechargeable debit card capable of purchasing not only tickets, but products and services from stores and the Internet, and to make withdrawals and deposits at zero cost.[26]

In 2014, the project of the fan card was augmented by being transformed into the "InViola Card", becoming an "explicit tool of relational marketing", involving fans in a new consumer experience. The InViola Card can be acquired in various ways[27] by the different target users (citizen-supporters, season-ticket holders and Viola Club members), who can gather points and exclusive benefits. The prizes have a strong emotional appeal: such as a team uniform with the name, number and signature of a favorite player, other official gadgets, tours of the Stadium, visits to sport centers and participation at the team's summer training camp.

Through the "InViola Card", more than 70,000 fans of the Fiorentina are offered a series of additional services which have been created in collaboration with partners and sponsors (banks, public institutions, mass media, online ticket agencies, etc.) and designed to maximize the fans' involvement, loyalty and entertainment. The card is not a payment tool because some of the fan clubs did not wish to have this service, as they felt it implied economic exploitation (§. 5). Instead, it provides a membership opportunity, and in the near future, thanks to the installation of wi-fi in the stadium, it can be utilized for new services such as reserved seats, automatic ticket buying and "cashless" purchases within the stadium.

The fan smart card also provides the club with an opportunity to gather data about its users (demographic, socio-economic, psycho-graphic and behavioral information) to update the fans database with useful elements to segment them, and to develop customized services dedicated to differentiated targets. The club has therefore, in the last 3 years, implemented an interesting strategy of Customer Relationship Management capable of enhancing one of its crucial assets, that is fans.

This approach involves a mix of information sources such as the season ticket holder database, the Fiorentina Point stores, official ticket sellers, the InViola Card and the social networks of the club (primarily Facebook and Twitter) which carry out a complementary role in the supporters' data management. This set of information regarding fans provides a foundation upon which both to offer additional one-to-one services targeting the special needs of loyal fans and to provide knowledge to sponsors and partners who are also consumers of products and services themselves.

5. Relationships with companies: from sponsorship to partnership

The Fiorentina marketing strategy is based on the development of a specific and new approach in its relationships with companies (suppliers, distributors and sponsors) from mere "brand exposure" to a real partnership activity. Up until the 2011–2012 season, the strategy was mainly oriented to provide advertising space (billboards, moving billboards along the playing field, backdrop interviews, athletic clothing, websites, etc.) to middle-sized firms. Often the stakeholder was an entrepreneur-fan who was part of the club local network, and being motivated by emotional attachment to sport and football, he invested in communication through the Fiorentina to obtain high visibility of his brand or products.

In the last 3 years, the choice of sponsors and partners has the goal of repositioning the Fiorentina brand name outside of an only local context. A "selective" strategy was carried out to attract medium- and large-sized companies of national and international reputation. The manifold transactions developed with companies generated both a progressive increase in income deriving from partnerships,[28] but also reinforced the team's brand name.

Compared to the traditional ways of dividing sponsors into categories such as main sponsor, technical sponsor, official sponsor, today the club uses a wide array of sponsorship typologies, such as, for example, top sponsor (Banca CR Firenze, BetClic.it), automotive partner (Volkswagen), marketing and advertising partner (GSport), TV sponsor (Sky) and technological partner (Kiocera, Hisense). Then, there is a further categorization of commercial sponsors into platinum, gold and silver.[29]

Interactions among the Fiorentina club and industrial, commercial, service and media sponsors can be classified from exchange relationships to collaboration and cooperation agreements (Figure 16.5). For example, the club has developed an exchange agreement with the Sky television network and brand licensors in which the object of the transaction is respectively ceding the rights to broadcast sports events and license to implement and commercialize Fiorentina brand name products.

Although the intention of the Fiorentina, from the very beginning of its relationship with Della Valle, was to couple its brand with companies positioned in the middle-to-high range of the marketplace,[30] only recently has the club begun to have true collaboration with these businesses – not just logo and brand-name exposure – but the pursuit of specific, complementary objectives,

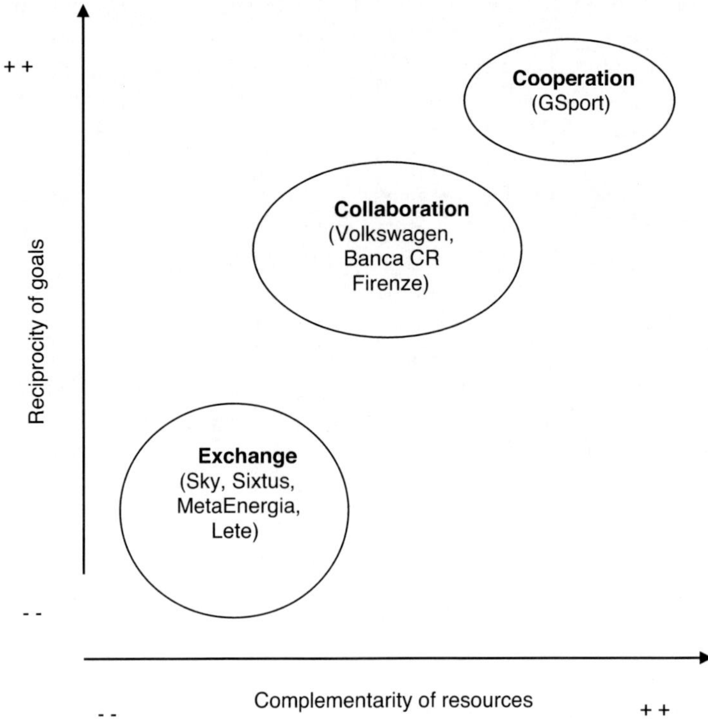

Figure 16.5 Partnerships between the ACF Fiorentina and companies

by sharing resources, skills and activities. This strategy has intensified with the enhancement of the Fiorentina brand name at a national and international level: partners are interested in pursuing various goals (image and name recognition, economic, marketplace or services benefits, etc.) promoting different levels of collaboration with a real co-marketing value (Zagnoli, 1991; Zagnoli, Radicchi, 2011), such as in the case of Volkswagen sponsorship.

This partnership between the Fiorentina and the German firm helped to increase the brand awareness of Volkswagen coupling with the team name, confirming its position in the market and reaching new groups of consumers. At the same time, the club, by tying its name to a respected and popular automotive brand, found that the international exposure increased its scope.

A sponsorship agreement with a cooperative value is the partnership with GSport, an Italian advertising sport agency. The common objective was to increase the number of firms interested in collaborating with Fiorentina. The partners achieve this common goal by sharing their resources and skills.[31] On one side, the Fiorentina would make available its facilities (stadium and sport center), its brand name and values such as sport, fair play, history, culture, etc.; on the other side GSport has specialized competences to manage the hospitality areas in the stadium to develop additional services for business partners, even using B2B structured activities (incentive services,[32] planning of so-called unconventional initiatives, etc.).

During the phase of the owners' new efforts towards the team, the different partnership patterns witnessed a great variety of agreements of exchange and collaboration, characterized not only by the relative complexity of the transactions, but by fairly brief timeframes (2–3 years). These sponsorships confirmed the strong role of the local identity: with some local firms such as the Banca CR Firenze and Sammontana, the Fiorentina has had continuing sponsorship relations for almost 10 years.

The role of supporters is also crucial, and the club was induced to listen to the opinions of organized fans. For example, when the "InViola Card" was launched (§. 4), notwithstanding the possibility of connecting it to a circuit of prepaid credit cards sponsored by a local bank, the fans were opposed to the commercial use of the card. Fans refused to set up this smart device as a bank card, because it was perceived as being imposed for strictly financial reasons: "not much to do with football but a lot to do with business".[33] This confirms the "lobbying role" of Viola fans who do not wish to be exploited for marketing goals of the club, so the new InViola Card (§. 4) does not have the financial attributes of the earlier one.

6. New media in the marketing and communication strategies of the ACF Fiorentina

6.1 Official club media channels

In 2013, the ACF Fiorentina Club significantly restyled its official web channel,[34] www.ViolaChannel.tv, with the goal of reinforcing the marketing relationship between club and fans. The new multifunctional design of the website offers contents, pictures, videos, interviews, real time statistics, games.

Although the website had higher-quality graphics and design, it was still rather "dispersive and not very engaging".[35] Therefore the management activated new direct connections with fans through social networks (Table 16.1) to raise the number of visitors. Especially the Facebook page and Twitter, filled with messages from the athletes which are posted directly to the site, and the albums of photographs published on Instagram[36] and Flickr, register a consistent number of loyal fans. You Tube, on the other hand, is stalled, even though one of the objectives is to launch it through online videos.

Links to the main social platforms create emotional connection through photographs and highlights offering an "exclusive" point of view of the athletes' life,[37] with the goal of boosting a sense of identification between supporters and champions. Given the constant expansion of mobile devices,

Table 16.1 Official social media of the ACF Fiorentina

Type of social media	*Number of fans, pictures, views or followers*
Facebook	1 Million Friends/1,282,135 "Likes"
Twitter	265,000 Followers
Instagram	48,400 Followers
Google+	36,939 Followers
LinkedIn	892 Followers
Flickr	24,449 Pictures
YouTube	2,087,117 Views/visualizations

especially among the youngest fans, the club has developed a specific app for the iPhone and Android, called "ViolaChannel", enabling fans to learn the latest news in real time, to look at images and videos, leave messages online and share news and comments on Twitter, Facebook and Instagram.

Offering interactive services through social media enhances the interaction between fans and the club, increasing brand loyalty through digital content, which keeps the fans' interest in and passion for the team alive, before, during and even long after the game is over. The potential growth of visits to the website could also allow the club to offer visibility and exposure to sponsors and partners, thereby becoming a multimedia platform on which specific co-marketing initiatives with other companies can be developed.

6.2 Communication channels managed by fans

The capacity of football to bring people together through the strong link between fans and their team is manifested by the Fiorentina club also through implementation of websites which are run by supporters rather than the club itself. We should call attention to the www.fiorentina.it[38] site, which is the self-proclaimed "site of Viola fans", born in 2001 and the second result to appear on Google search engine after www.ViolaChannel.tv.

The fiorentina.it domain immediately brings to mind a link between the club and the identity among the city, fans and team, allowing the multiplication of web contacts. Moreover, the intensely active participation of fans on unofficial websites through discussion forums and the publication of articles and comments all augment the number of visits and visualizations.

Fan channels comprise a direct communication avenue within the fan community and serve as tools by which supporters and Viola Clubs express dissent, judgments, evaluations and comments through virtual participation in activities pressuring club managerial decisions.

Fiorentina fan websites are not only an instrument for information, but also permit exchanges among loyal supporters through forums, in addition to Facebook pages. These applications reinforce the already intense interactions among users-fans who take on the role of main actors and "organized pressure groups" on the web.

The existence of online fan pages confirms the strong "autonomy" of the collective Viola identity, reinforced, for example, by the decision to sell advertising space on the website to local branches of national and international brands.[39]

Fan websites, therefore, are communication channels which lie outside the club's management and through them, supporters can activate autonomous relationships with other fans, the local community and citizens, as well as with a network of partners and companies which are often in direct competition with those selected by the football club. This particular propensity for self-management is an expression of local anthropological characteristics reflecting a need to carry out a role as independent stakeholder.

The unofficial websites also constitute a distribution channel of products and gadgets acquired by loyal fans so as to express their sense of allegiance to the club. In the past, some fan clubs registered the "Indiano" brand to place on a low-cost line of merchandising sold through the www.fiorentina.it site. As the Fiorentina gradually became more structured and began to introduce products at a more reasonable price in the "Nato Viola" (Born Purple) shop, the website started to sell accessories, sports clothing, T-shirts, etc. with the Fiorentina brand. Therefore, the fans' website became an official sales point alongside the official distribution channels of the club such as Fiorentina Point, Fiorentina Store and www.ViolaChannel.tv.

The activities implemented by fans on www.fiorentina.it, such as local sponsorships, discussion forums, sale of products, etc., have enormously increased the user traffic in comparison with the club's official portal. The renewed endeavors of the club's owners reinforces the fans' loyalty, even if the fans are proud of the independent maintenance of their own site.

The www.fiorentina.it fan website exhibits staunchly Diego Della Valle's choice to enter into politics with the denomination "Noi italiani" ("We Italians"),[40] confirming not only the synchrony of the fans with the club, but also their shared leitmotif centered on local identity, the strategic asset of Fiorentina and financial Group's marketing strategy.

7. Internationalization of the ACF Fiorentina brand

Up until now, as happens with many football teams in the top divisions, the main occasion of visibility and knowledge of the Fiorentina brand outside of its national context has been participation in the European Championships,[41] besides organization of promotional tours in foreign countries where the club has challenged other teams in friendly matches.[42]

In the last 5 years a new and sophisticated blueprint for expanding and diffusing the Fiorentina brand on a global level has taken place. The current strategy involves two primary objectives: to reinforce the supply chain of foreign sources for procurement of athletes; and to potentiate the global popularity of the Viola brand by positioning the "football product" on specific and selected markets such as the USA, India, Switzerland, China, and Japan.

For example, in 2007 the "International Development Program" was started in California, in a rich, technologically advanced context, with an ample international and Latin American presence, where although football was not yet as popular in the USA as baseball or American football, it nevertheless was receiving growing attention and was in a phase of expansion. The Viola Club, strengthened by a distinctive competence in the training of young football players on a technical-tactical level as well as educational and cultural,[43] exported a formative model which involved first of all, American coaches, and then a network of 70,000 kids and young people in the San Francisco area who had a chance to train following the "Fiorentina method". This strategy implies, first of all, achievement of finding young athletes who could eventually become future champions. On the other hand, it was also a means of promoting the Viola brand in California, a state with many immigrants from Tuscany who especially love Florence. The kids who had the privilege to participate in this program felt that they were real "Fiorentina footballers". Certainly the strong feeling of identification with the Florentine team and the attachment to the Viola brand are sources of affirmation of the team's merchandising in a context in which fan loyalty is manifested, much more than in Italy, through the purchase of a replica jersey and/or other official team products.

The partnership begun in 2014 with Pune FC, a new Indian Super League (ISL) team playing in the first Indian division, is an example of a resource-seeking strategy. The Indian club became a sort of academy in which young players were trained according to methods and training techniques well-honed in the world of Italian football. The Fiorentina is participating in the process of establishing the Indian team by furnishing coaches, technical staff and some athletes, thus transferring its expertise, skills and football know-how, to reinforce the potential development of the new Indian franchise. Thus, new talents from India could sometime in the future play with the Fiorentina at a reasonable cost.

This collaboration also fulfills the Viola Club's intention of amplifying its market in an "emerging" country such as India where the popularity of football is growing and the economic returns have potential, with estimates of a market of more than a billion fans. Expansion of the Fiorentina brand in India favors the creation of new business opportunities in the world of sport, commerce and tourism respectively for the owner group's products and for the city of Florence, which are inextricably connected.

An initiative in Ascona, Switzerland, in 2014, involved implantation of the established Fiorentina's grassroots managerial model as part of the "International" project as well. In this case, the primary aim was to capitalize on the distinct competence of the Fiorentina in the technical and educational preparation of young players, placing the football "product" in a market where it has the potential of expanding both technically and commercially.

8. Concluding remarks

The research carried out and data analyzed confirm that the Fiorentina is a team which is firmly based on and has a close connection with its home city and fans. If this club had been able to count on local economic stakeholders capable of operating on an international level, it would have remained Florentine in its ownership, management and sponsors, having the maximum expression of the strengths of name and role characterizing Florence: a city which symbolizes Italy in its rich history of being the magnificent heart of the Renaissance, first capital of the united Italy in 1865 and home of the cultural origins of the Italian language.[44]

Nevertheless, the Della Valle group, first non-Florentine owner of the team, after several years of adjustment and with the involvement of the Municipality of Florence in the Board of Directors, has managed to create a process of strategic and organizational reinforcement of the club. In harmony with the new political group Noi italiani ("We Italians") promoted by the entrepreneur-owner, the Fiorentina has become a central asset in the strategic business diversification of the Della Valle group.

The marketing project is enriched by the functions and activities managed by the subsidiary Firenze Viola S.r.l. with internationalization strategies to position the team and club's image and brand outside the "city's walls", while at the same time maintaining the historical heritage of the city and strong local identity which outline the relationships among team, club, institutions and fans.

Even though the club underwent a series of difficulties – the bankruptcy, then its rebirth, the uncertainty of whether Della Valle would maintain his "patron" role of Fiorentina, remaining in Florence – the club's identity of shared values with the city and local community has been never compromised. The owners' managerial choices reinforced these values: a new season of commitment confirmed the significant role played by local actors in a context based on the relationship with various stakeholders able to trigger a virtuous circle (Figure 16.6), which has sustained the team in all of its evolutionary stages.

The heaviest arrows connecting the three circles in the upper part of Figure 16.6 synthesize the system of relationships between supply and demand which play a key role in the club's strategy: Institutions, Fans and Club.

Institutions not only provide the team with sport facilities, but influence organizational and marketing decisions regarding the club through participation in its governance by representing the common "feelings" of citizens and fans.

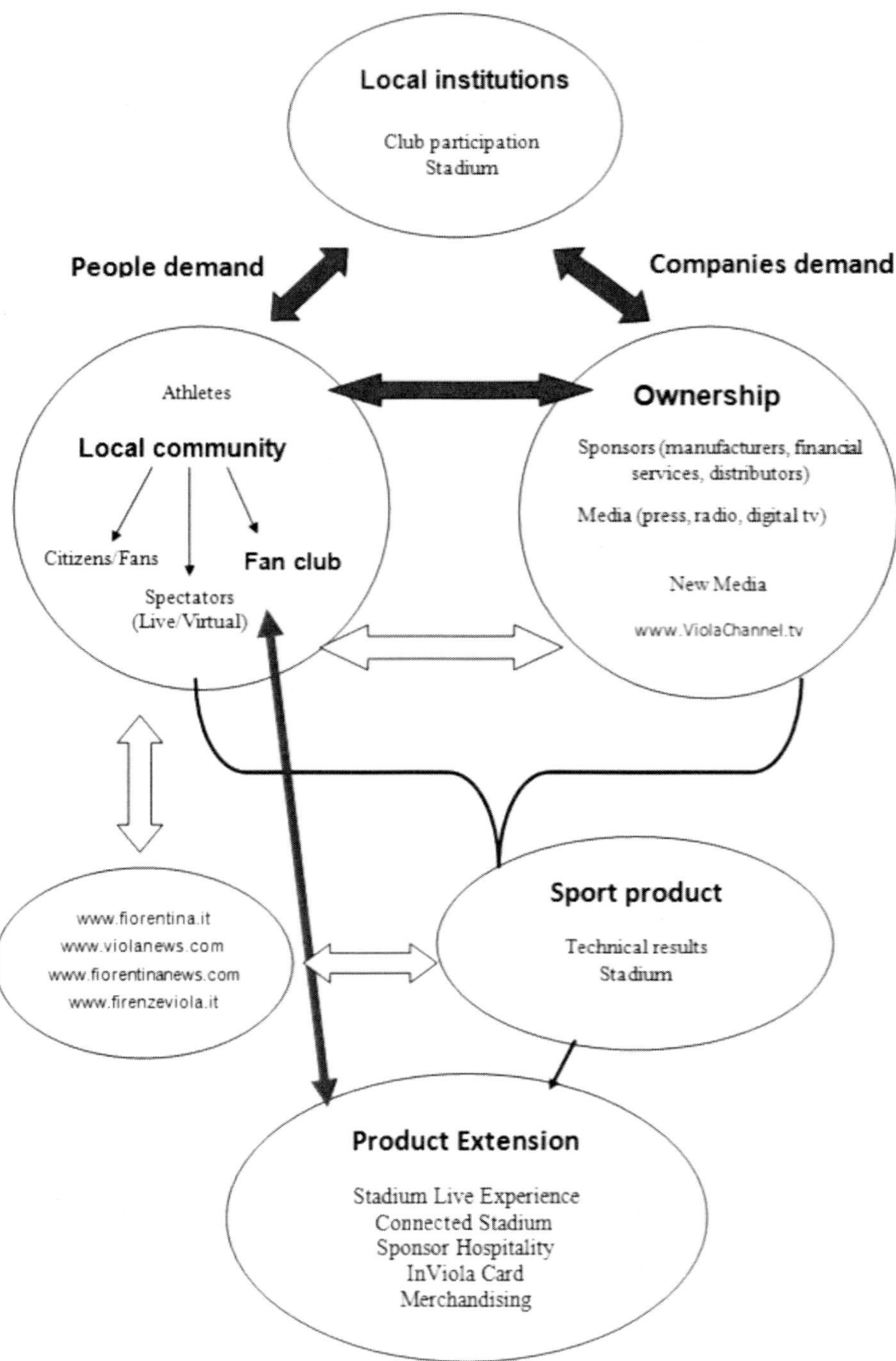

Figure 16.6 The creation of value in the ACF Fiorentina

The Ownership, after various periods of fluctuating involvement in the club, has progressively taken on a more determined approach in negotiating with institutions and is sometimes prompted by fans who claim a protagonist role in representing local community's wishes. The system of relationships is encouraged by the Viola fan community – local community which provides emotional support, spectators who participate both at live events and through the media, and fans organized into Viola Clubs – who perceives the team as being fully entitled to the city cultural, historical and social heritage. All of these elements sustain and motivate the team, with constant encouragement to play their best.

The strong collective Viola identity and the activism of the fan community are even evident in the use of multimedia and interactive communication channels developed and managed by the fans themselves. The www.fiorentina.it website is not run by the club, but by supporters (as shown by the direct arrow in Figure 16.6), and is a discussion platform through which the local community, its citizens and organized fans can speak out openly without being inhibited, providing both criticism and support of the team. These communication instruments reinforce the intensity of relationships within the network of loyal fans. The continuous flow of comments, information, products and content enhances the increased traffic on the websites managed by fans which also feed the official social media.

The official portal, www.ViolaChannel.tv, connected to social networks which it executes and updates, is followed by thousands of visitors. Another initiative launched in 2014, the "InViola Card", is a good example of relational marketing which, by offering services and other benefits, attracts and involves not only fans, but also sponsors, partners and local suppliers, thus consolidating the ties between the city and its team.

The marketing strategy of the Fiorentina aims at offering an excellent product from a technical-sportive perspective. Although the Viola fans are always enthusiastic about their team, even when it gives mediocre results on the pitch, the search for success and good entertainment will trigger both emotional involvement of the fans as well as fame for the team, which also reflects well on the city at a national and international level.

In recent years, the owners have pursued technically ambitious objectives, and the team has achieved excellent results both in national and European championships. The fans' satisfaction with a winning team further reinforces the sense of belonging to the city.

Like all top football clubs, the Fiorentina has activated strategies of product extension which increase the emotional appeal of the sport venue and boost the experience of the live match. Although the stadium in Florence has innumerable architectural features which are typical of a "historical monument", it has also been given a new role by being furnished with additional services designed not only to further satisfy the fans, but also to appeal to and target new and diversified "consumers". The historical stadium is a catalyst for the development of commercial and marketing collaborations with sponsors and partners, with the idea of acquiring new sources of revenue to sustain the financial autonomy of the club. In the meantime, there is a negotiation process towards building a new multifunctional stadium, with the blessing of the municipality, which would be located near the Florence airport and the main Italian highway.

The Fiorentina case is indicative of the rather common conditions today where local identity is challenged by the needs of globalization.

The Fiorentina team, like many others in Italy, "belongs" not only to the owners, but above all, to the whole citizenship. The changes which have occurred due to the economic crisis as well as due to fiscal and financial rules and regulations have meant that funds permitting local, qualified "patrons" to own a team have become scarce.

The happenings of this football team are emblematic of the challenges which local institutions must face, with many issues connected to global competition evolution, fairly incompatible with preserving "desirable attributes of identification" beloved by citizens and fans.

Notes

1 Although this chapter is the result of a shared research work, Patrizia Zagnoli wrote parts 1, 2.1, 2.2, 2.3 and Elena Radicchi wrote sections 3, 4, 5, 5.1, 6.2, 7. The conclusions, §. 8, were a mutual collaboration.
2 Some people maintain that this color "belongs" to the city of Florence because Florentine alchemists in the 1300s created the purple color artificially.
3 Diego Della Valle is owner, President and CEO of TOD's S.p.a., which is a luxury fashion industry comprising TOD's, Hogan and Fay. Florence has been recognized internationally as the fashion capital of Italian quality products. Moreover, Della Valle, strong promoter of the Italian identity, put a stake participation on Coliseum in Rome to progressively restore the whole building.
4 May 15, 2003, Della Valle participated in a public auction to acquire the previous Club, paying 2.5 million euros for the brand name, denomination, social colors and trophies of the AC Fiorentina.
5 For example, famous champions such as Frey and Montolivo were sold to Genoa and Milan, respectively.
6 *Il Sole 24 Ore*, "Contestati dai tifosi i Della Valle pronti a lasciare la Fiorentina", August 8, 2011.
7 On January 25, 2010, the city of Florence and ACF Fiorentina agreed that the club could use the Artemio Franchi stadium and surrounding area, which belongs to the municipality. This agreement, valid till 2016, allows the use of stadium for matches as well as surrounding areas for training, the so-called "Campini". The agreement also stipulates the architectural restoration of the sports center, with the addition of new hospitality areas inside the stadium (§. 3).
8 For example, the name of the Club was changed in 2002, following bankruptcy, to "Fiorentina Viola". For the first time in almost 100 years the historical name of the Club "AC Fiorentina", describing the history and home of the team, changed for legal reasons and to guarantee discontinuity with the previous management. The active participation was manifested not only by fans, but the entire city, influencing decisions of the new owners who in 2003 acquired the historical "brand" of the Club and its colors, to maintain at least with the name the continuity of the team of "Florence" (§. 1).
9 FIGC stands for Federazione Italiana Giuoco Calcio (Italian Federation of Football).
10 In the 2012–2013 season, the mean number of spectators for a single match on digital TV (Mediaset Premium) and digital satellite (Sky) was 23,812. *Source*: Centro Studi Lega Calcio, 2014.
11 Since the 2010–2011 season, the mean number of spectators at the stadium has constantly increased, being more than 32,000 in 2014–2015. *Source*: Centro Studi Lega Calcio, 2015.
12 In the 2013–2014 season the classification of the first six teams with highest mean number of spectators was: (1) Internazionale FC: 46,246; (2) Napoli FC: 40,632; (3) AS Roma: 40,436; (4) AC Milan: 39,874; (5) Juventus FC: 38,328; (6) ACF Fiorentina: 32,057. *Source*: Centro Studi Lega Calcio, 2014.
13 In the 2014–2015 season, the Fiorentina registered 22,300 season ticket holders (ACF Fiorentina, 2015).
14 The fans demonstrate their devotion to the team over the long term: there are generations of season ticket holders, from grandparents, to fathers, to sons, to grandchildren.
15 Zagnoli P., Radicchi E., Fanti D., *L'identità collettiva viola. Analisi socio-economica degli abbonati della ACF Fiorentina*, Università di Firenze, Giugno, 2004.
16 In the last 3 years, notwithstanding the economic crisis, the prices of tickets and season tickets in the Tribuna have gone up by a mean of 20%. For the 2014–2015 season, the cost of a season ticket in this section ranges from 2,950 euros for the Tribuna VIP to 525 euros for the external Tribuna, where visibility of the playing field is slightly reduced compared to central seats. Prices are also slightly different for different age groups (kids under 18 and under 14).
17 The main activities carried out by the associations in regard to the single Viola Clubs are, for example, ticket and season ticket sales support, transport organization, information management and communication with fans, and organization of convivial social activities in the local context.
18 In the months preceding the closing of the club, fans, through the press and other local media, managed to inform the entire city of the financial collapse going against the Fiorentina. They also organized initiatives designed to increase contestation, such as a demonstration in downtown Florence in April, 2001 (more than 30,000 fans participated), the boycott of the season ticket campaign, the presentation of a civic list "Florence for the Fiorentina" at the administrative elections of the club 2002. *Source*: Interview with Filippo Pucci, President of the Centro Coordinamento Viola Club (ACCVC).
19 Legal operations were also crucial, such as judiciary briefs carried out by some representatives of the Viola Club to express their disagreement with the decision made by the Florentine Court, the FIGC and the Lega Calcio (Football League), denouncing a "sick" football system diffused among several professional championship teams, which were not penalized as much as the Fiorentina. *Source*: Interview with Stefano Sartoni, ex-President of the "Collettivo Autonomo Viola" fan club.

20 *Source*: Interview with Valter Tanturli, President of the "Associazione Tifosi Fiorentini" (Association of Florentine Fans) (ATF).
21 The "City Stadium" (*Stadio Comunale*) was called this until 1993 when, following restructuring works for the World Soccer (Football) Cup "Italia 90", it was renamed "Artemio Franchi" after the legendary President of the Italian Football Federation and former Sport Director of the Fiorentina.
22 Law Decree of February 24, 2003, n. 28 "Urgent measures to combat violent activities at sporting events"; Law Decree of August 17, 2005, n. 162 "Further measures to combat violent activities at sporting events"; Ministerial Decree of June 6, 2005, "Video surveillance of structures and rules for the emission, distribution and sale of tickets for access to stadiums of a capacity of more than 10,000 people during football games".
23 The "Artemio Franchi" stadium is divided into four sections: the Maratona for "lukewarm" fans, the *aristocratic* Tribuna, the Curva Ferrovia and the Curva Fiesole, heart of the most *hard-core loyalist* Viola fans.
24 The Master's Degree in Sport Management at the University of Florence promoted this project with seminars and meetings dedicated to this topic, and the participation of students who worked on this project for their degree thesis.
25 The project of a fan card, launched in 2004 by the National Observatory of Sporting Events by the Interior Ministry, was born out of the understanding that security at sporting events, and especially football, could not disregard efficacious organizational efforts to prevent violent fans from taking action since repressive measures are not sufficient prevention. A fan card provides an electronic record of the participation of every fan in various aspects of the game; it helps reduce falsification of season tickets and helps manage the flow of spectators rapidly and easily. Its effective application and diffusion took 7 long years of work.
26 http://firenze.repubblica.it/cronaca/2010/06/08/news/arriva_la_tessera_del_tifoso_stamani_la_presentazione-4652414/ "Arriva la tessera 'Orgoglio Viola'. Chi non la attiva non fa l'abbonamento", ("The Viola Pride membership card is here. No season tickets without activating it"). firenze.repubblica.it, June 8, 2010. Last access December 12, 2014.
27 The "InViola Card Gold" is the smart card for season ticket holders and those who wish to participate in transfers. The "InViola Card Member" is a fidelity card which allows its owner to accumulate points through purchases to use in certain stores. It is also possible to put tickets on this card for stadium games. The "Temporary InViola Card" is a temporary card substituting the membership card. The "Virtual InViola Card" is the digital version of the card which can be downloaded onto a smart cell phone through the App InViola Card. The InViola e-Card can be activated by registering on the official Fiorentina website through either a virtual card or the actual physical card. *Source*: http://www.inviola.violachannel.tv/inviola-card.
28 From 2012 to 2013 revenues generated by sponsorships increased by 7%. *Source*: ACF Fiorentina, December 31, 2013.
29 http://www.violachannel.tv.
30 For example, in 2005 the Fiorentina selected TOYOTA as a *main sponsor*. In those years, the Della Valle family had a special market objective relationship with Japan in terms of its TOD'S brand of clothing.
31 http://it.violachannel.tv/sponsorship.html.
32 These events and organized initiatives in the football venue includes dinners, business tournaments and tours of the stadium to areas not normally open to the public, by which partners of the football Club can develop relationships with their clients and suppliers.
33 Firenze Today, "Sconti in banca con la tessera del tifoso ma gli ultras non ci stanno", ("Discount at the bank with the fan card but the ultras don't like it"), July 6, 2011.
34 Dal 2008 *www.ViolaChannel.tv* has replaced the previous web site *www.acffiorentina.it*.
35 Interview with Angelo Venturi, Social Media Manager.
36 The Fiorentina was the first Series A team to activate an official profile on Instagram (instagram.com/acffiorentinaofficial).
37 For example, the publication of the photo of the player Giuseppe Rossi during his first training practice after many months of absence due to a knee injury was an exclusive on Instagram.
38 It is necessary to cite three unofficial websites such as *www.violanews.com*, founded in 2001, *www.fiorentinanews.com*, born in 2002, and *www.firenzeviola.it*, published online in 2007.
39 For example, the Tuscan Ford and Honda dealerships, and the online betting site Star Casinò, etc.
40 http://www.fiorentina.it/it/news/articolo.54.23923/diego-della-valle-e-la-politicasarebbe-pronto-il-simbolo-noi-italiani.html "Diego Della Valle e la politica . . . c'è il simbolo: 'Noi Italiani'" ("Diego Della Valle and politics . . . the symbol is "'Noi Italiani'"), fiorentina.it, January 27, 2015.

41 The UEFA Cup in 2007–2008, the Champions League in 2009–2010 and recent successes in the European League (2013–2014 and 2014–2015). Last access February 2, 2015.
42 For example, the summer tour of the Fiorentina in England, UAE and China in 2011 and in South America in 2014.
43 In regard to this, the Fiorentina School Project began in the 2013–2014 school year. This initiative is aimed at training young athletes from the Fiorentina grassroots, combining educational instruction with sport attitude development. *Source*: http://www.fiorentinaschool.it.
44 The Italian language has its origins in literary Florentine of the 1300s as utilized by the poets and writers Dante, Petrarch and Boccaccio, and became the official national language of the united Italy in 1861.

Bibliography

CHANAVAT N., BODET G., Experiential marketing in sport spectatorship services: A customer perspective, *European Sport Management Quarterly*, 14/4, 323–344, 2014.
COVA B., Community and consumption: Toward a definition of definition of the linking value of products or services, *European Journal of Marketing*, 31/3, 297–316, 1997.
DESBORDES M., RICHELIEU A., *Global Sport Marketing*, Routledge, Abingdon, 2012.
KOTLER R., ARMSTRONG G., *Principles of Marketing*, 13th Edition, Pearson Education, New York, 2010.
KOTLER P., KELLER K.L., *Marketing Management,* 1st Edition, Pearson Learning Solutions, 2006.
LAGO U., BARONCELLI A., SZYMANSKY S., *Il business del calcio. Successi sportivi e rovesci finanziari*, Egea, Milano, 2004.
LE BON G., *La psicologia delle folle*, Seconda Edizione, TEA, Milano, 2004.
Lega Calcio, Annual report from the Italian Fedration, Roma, 2015.
MAFFESOLI M., *Il tempo delle tribù. Il declino dell'individualismo nella società post-moderna*, Guerini e Associati, Milano, 2004.
MULLIN B., HARDY S., SUTTON W., *Sport Marketing*, 3rd Edition, Human Kinetics, New York, 2000.
PINE J., GILMORE J.H., *L'economia delle esperienze*, Etas Libri, Milano, 2000.
WILSON J.R., The six simple principles of viral marketing, *The Web Marketing Today*, 70, 2000, http://www.practicalecommerce.com/articles/100366-viral-principles.
ZAGNOLI P., *I rapporti tra imprese nei settori ad alta tecnologia. Il caso della Silicon Valley*, Giappichelli, Torino, 1991.
ZAGNOLI P., La tessera del tifoso: valenze sociali, culturali ed economiche, Convegno Internazionale *La prevenzione della violenza negli stadi: la tessera del tifoso*, Firenze, 27 Giugno, 2007.
ZAGNOLI P., RADICCHI E., The football fan community as a determinant stakeholder in value co-creation, *Sport in Club*, 13/10, 1532–1551, 2010.
ZAGNOLI P., RADICCHI E., *Sport Marketing e Nuovi Media*, Franco Angeli, Milano, 2011.
ZAGNOLI P., RADICCHI E., FANTI D., *L'identità collettiva viola. Analisi socio-economica degli abbonati della ACF Fiorentina*, Università di Firenze, Giugno, 2004.

Studies, official documents and press

ACF Fiorentina 2015, annual report, not published, available online.
Law decree of February 24, 2003, n. 28 "Urgent measures to combat violent activities at sporting events"; Law decree of August 17, 2005, n. 162 "Further measures to combat violent activities at sporting events;" Ministerial decree of June 6, 2005, "Video surveillance of structures and rules for the emission, distribution and sale of tickets for access to stadiums of a capacity of more than 10,000 people during football games."
IL SOLE 24 ORE, "Contestati dai tifosi, i Della Valle pronti a lasciare la Fiorentina", (Opposed by fans, Della Valle ready to leave the Fiorentina), August 8, 2011.

17

SUPPORTER ENGAGEMENT THROUGH SOCIAL MEDIA

A case study of Liverpool Football Club

James Kenyon and Guillaume Bodet

Introduction

Since the launch of the first recognisable social network in 1997, SixDegrees.com,[1] the proliferation of social media has brought about significant change in how people use the Internet,[2] such that commentators are suggesting an 'immense transformation' of the 'media landscape' has now taken place.[3],[4] Referred to as "a group of Internet-based applications that build on the ideological and technological foundations of Web 2.0"[5,6], social media is comprised of "highly interactive platforms via which individuals and communities share, co-create, discuss, and modify user-generated content [UGC]".[7] Whether they be collaborative projects (e.g., Wikipedia), blogs and micro blogs (e.g., Twitter), content communities (e.g., YouTube), social networking sites (e.g., Facebook), virtual game worlds (e.g., World of Warcraft) or virtual social worlds (e.g., Second Life),[8] UGC provide the basis upon which the majority of these social media platforms operate.[9] For example, microblogging site Twitter, one of 'largest players' in social media,[10] enables users to create short communications, limited to 140 characters and referred to as 'tweets', "that are published to the user's stream of updates which can be followed and subsequently 'unfollowed' by others".[11] Alternatively, a social network, which often has more functionality, like Facebook for example, allows users to create and update profiles, to post and share text comments, photos and videos, to exchange private messages, and alerts users as to when other connections update their profiles, and post and share their own content. According to Boyd and Ellison, what makes these social media platforms unique, "is not that they allow individuals to meet strangers, but rather that they enable users to articulate and make visible their social networks" (i.e. a user's lists of connections).[12] Since their introduction, social media sites have become well established and now maintain universal appeal, especially among younger Internet users,[13] in what is an increasingly connected online world. For example, Twitter averaged 236 million monthly active global users during the last quarter of 2014;[14] Facebook averaged almost 1.4 billion in the same period.[15] For many users, social media habits have become integrated into 'daily practices',[16] and the number of people communicating via social media has long since overtaken the number communicating via email:[17]

> Consumers of all ages interact with [social media] content on mobile devices, PCs, kiosks, at home, at play, at events, at work, on holiday or when travelling – in just about any situation – in much greater, and ever increasing numbers than before.[18]

Having not just increased the number of ways in which users can communicate with each other, social media also facilitates direct and indirect communication between users and organisations, the latter of which maintain social media pages and profiles for their brands, services and products.[19] Thus social media comprises, according to Baird and Parasnis, "enormous potential for companies to get closer to customers and, by doing so, facilitate increased revenue, cost reduction and efficiencies".[20] In this respect, and when considered in the context of the social experience and tribal characteristics of football spectatorship,[21,22,23,24] for professional football clubs that appropriately engage with social media, it offers the potential to "build meaningful relationships [with supporters] through opportunities for communication, interaction, and value".[25] Thus with the widespread popularity of social media, its potential for worldwide dissemination of messages (resulting in the potential to raise awareness of a club), the considerable volume of UGC it produces, and its potential to develop 'meaningful relationships',[26] professional football clubs (and, more generally, other sports teams) are engaging with a variety of social media platforms "in new and innovative fashions"[27] aimed at strengthening connections with the existing supporter-base and expanding it further. Given the possibilities that social media offers then, and its relatively low costs,[28] it is now regarded as a key marketing communication tool for professional football clubs.[29]

The literature base pertaining to marketing, social media and professional football clubs is growing.[30] In 2014, McCarthy and colleagues[31] published a research paper which aimed to explore the challenges and opportunities involved in managing brand presence and supporter relationships through social media engagement for professional football clubs in the UK. The authors adopted a multiple case study approach, combining desk research and semi-structured interviews, and focusing on two clubs each from the 2010/2011 EPL (Bolton Wanderers and Newcastle United) and the 2010/2011 Football League Championship (FLCH) (Leeds United and Nottingham Forest). Thematic analysis of the collected data resulted in the identification of three main issues relating to club social media use (control of conversation, fan engagement and commercialisation) and four key perceived benefits (content, interaction, community and revenue generation). Building upon the findings of this piece of research then, the aim of this chapter is to explore the social media strategy of Liverpool Football Club (LFC) utilising the same methods employed by McCarthy et al. (2014).[32]

Box 17.1 Winning record and brief history of Liverpool Football Club

Liverpool Football Club is one of two professional football clubs based in the Northwest English coastal city of Liverpool (the other being Everton Football Club). The collective achievements of these two clubs render the city one of the most successful in English football,[33] and "among the most famous in the European game".[34] Liverpool F.C., the more successful of the two clubs, since being founded in 1892, have amassed 18 league championships, seven FA Cups and eight League Cups in domestic English competitions. In addition to this relatively impressive domestic record, Liverpool F.C. are the most successful English club to have participated in European competitions, having won five European Cups, three UEFA Cups and three UEFA Super Cups. The club's most recent European Cup triumph – a UEFA Champions League victory against Italian club A.C. Milan in 2005, who they beat on penalties after coming back from being 3–0 down at half-time – resulted in the club being awarded the trophy permanently and receiving the *UEFA Badge of Honour* for multiple winners of the competition,[35] a privilege bestowed to only three other clubs throughout Europe: Réal Madrid, A.C. Milan and Bayern Munich. Yet despite such an illustrious history, the pinnacle of which is considered to have come between 1975 and 1990 when the club dominated English football, winning 11 of their 18 league championships and four of their five European Cups, Liverpool have not won a league championship since 1990 when the top division in England was then known as the Football League First Division; that is, the club have yet to win an English Premier League title since the competition's inception in 1992 (they have been runners-up in the competition on three occasions – 2001–02, 2008–09 and 2013–14).

Box 17.2 Quick facts on Liverpool Football Club

Owner: Fenway Sports Group, USA (John Henry is the principal owner)
Chairman: Tom Werner
Number of season-ticket holders: 24,500[36] (Anfield capacity: 45,522)
Number of followers on Facebook: 24+ million[37]
Average number of spectators per game: 44,671[38],[39] (98%)
Club revenue: 264,234,000 euros[40],[41]
Revenue breakdown: matchday (22%), broadcasting (31%), commercial (47%), other operating income (<1.0%), grants (<1.0%)
Club expenses: 322,275,000 euros
Total number of partners/sponsors: 21

Name of partners in 2014: Standard Chartered (banking and financial services, main club sponsor), Warrior (sporting goods, kit supplier), Garuda Indonesia (airline, official training kit sponsor), Carlsberg (beverages, official partner), Vitality Health Life (insurance, official partner), Vauxhall (automotive, official partner), Dunkin' Donuts (food and beverage, official partner), Thomas Cook Sport (hospitality and tourism, official partner), Subway (restaurants, official partner), Gatorade (sports drinks, official partner), Jack Wolfskin (outdoor clothing & camping equipment, official partner), MBNA (banking and financial services, official partner), Maxxis (tire manufacturers, official partner), Barbados Tourism Marketing Inc. (hospitality and tourism, official partner), EA Sports (video games, official partner), Konica Minolta (electronics, official partner), InstaForex (financial services, official partner), Honda (automotive, regional marketing partner – Thailand), MONO Group (digital media, regional marketing partner – Thailand), Xolo (smartphone manufacturer, regional marketing partner – India) and Courts (retail, regional marketing partner – Malaysia & Singapore)[42]

Sources: The Liverpool Football Club and Athletic Ground Limited, *The Liverpool Football Club and Athletic Ground Limited – Directors' Report and Financial Statements.* Liverpool: The Liverpool Football Club and Athletic Ground Limited, 2013. http://www.liverpoolfc.com/corporate/partners – Titre d'une page Internet paru sur liverpoolfc.com. Last access date: February 15, 2015.

Box 17.3 Presentation of Fernando Maisonnave

Fernando Maisonnave: digital engagement co-ordinator, in post since October 2014

An LFC case study offers a valuable addendum to the research undertaken by McCarthy et al. (2014) in light of the club's size, history of success, and domestic and international support.[43] LFC can indeed be considered a much 'larger' club, in many respects, than any of the case study clubs investigated by McCarthy et al. (2014).[44] For example, of those case studies, LFCs nearest competitor in terms of scale, Newcastle United (NUFC), generated less than half the revenue of LFC in the 2012/2013 EPL season (NUFC 111.9 million euros/ LFC 240.6 million euros[45]). The club have also won significantly fewer honours than LFC over the course of their relative histories (refer to Table 17.1) – NUFC's last major honour was won in a FA Cup victory in 1955. From a marketing-industry perspective, NUFC are ranked 19 places lower than LFC in the *2014 Brand Finance® Football 50*[46] (NUFC ranked 27th with a brand value of 75 million euros/LFC ranked 8th with a brand value of 345 million euros[47]). Only in terms of live spectatorship might NUFC be considered larger than LFC, with an average attendance for the 2013/2014 EPL season of 50,395[48] (96.2% of St. James' Park's capacity of 52,404) compared with LFC's average attendance of 44,671[49] (98.1% of Anfield's capacity of 45,522). However, these figures should be considered within the context of Anfield's limited capacity compared to its major rivals[50] and compared to relative and existing demand for tickets – for example, LFC's official waiting list for season tickets was reported to contain more than 70,000 people in 2011.[51] Long been considered by the club to be an inhibiting factor in its overall development,[52] in December 2014 work began on increasing the capacity of Anfield to around 54,000, with the expansion due to be completed in the summer of 2016.[53,54] Spectatorship aside, and perhaps the most important consideration in terms of the focus of this chapter and the McCarthy et al. (2014) research, is the comparison between the clubs' relative number of connections on social media platforms: LFC's is significantly greater than NUFC, with the former currently maintaining a following of approximately 24 million followers on Facebook[55] and 4.3 million followers of its UK & Ireland Twitter account alone[56] (excluding 21 international accounts) compared with the latter's approximately 1.5 million followers on Facebook[57] and 546,000 followers on Twitter.[58]

Beyond these direct comparisons between LFC and the McCarthy et al. (2014) case study clubs, and further alluding to its stature in English and European football, LFC were, until recently, part of the 'Big Four' or 'Sky Four', referring to a period of dominance in the EPL throughout the 2000s maintained alongside Arsenal F.C. (AFC), Chelsea F.C. (CFC) and Manchester United (MUFC)[59,60] – LFC finished outside the top quartet in the EPL only twice between the 1999–2000 and 2008–2009 seasons. The club was also "a member of the transnational, commercially orientated (now defunct) pressure group G14",[61] which operated between 2000 and 2008 before being replaced by the more inclusive European Club Association. With that in mind then, one of the objectives of this chapter, which, as stated, builds on the research of McCarthy et al. (2014), is to offer insight into the issues relating to social media strategy facing LFC, a club whose "long-standing worldwide status as a successful and glamorous football club",[62] offers the potential to present some unique challenges and opportunities in how social media is managed,

Table 17.1 LFC's major club honours compared to the case study clubs of McCarthy et al.'s (2014) research

Club	*League Titles*	*FA Cups*	*League Cups*	*European Cups/ Champions League*	*UEFA Cups/ EUROPA League*	*UEFA Super Cup*	*Total*
Liverpool	18	7	8	5	3	3	44
Total	*18*	*7*	*8*	*5*	*3*	*3*	*44*
Newcastle United	4	6	0	0	0	0	10
Nottingham Forest	1	2	4	2	0	1	10
Bolton Wanderers	0	4	0	0	0	0	4
Leeds United	3	1	1	0	0	0	5
Total	*8*	*13*	*5*	*2*	*0*	*1*	*29*

in the case of engaging with the club's large domestic and international following online. Given the remit of this publication, and the fact that the literature pertaining to the area has been very recently reviewed in the McCarthy et al. (2014) publication, the remainder of this chapter is thus split into the following sections. The first section will outline the development of social media at LFC and discuss the evolution of the roles and responsibilities involved in its management. The second section of this chapter will present the findings of the LFC case study using the McCarthy et al. (2014) publication to inform the structure of these discussions: it will discuss the main issues relating to club social media use, those being control of conversation, fan engagement, and commercialisation. It will also expand on the work of McCarthy et al. (2014) by discussing issues related to measuring the impact of social media engagement. The final section will summarise the key findings of the case study.

LFC's social media strategy

Developing responsible roles

Somewhat supporting the assertion that football clubs in the UK were sluggish in fully engaging with supporters via meaningful social media activity,[63] the installation of relevant positions within the organisational structure of LFC responsible for social media is a relatively recent development. With that in mind, such roles, and their constituent responsibilities, are constantly evolving. The role of *Digital Engagement Co-Ordinator* (DEC) for example, that is, the role of the interviewee of this case study, was first appointed at LFC in October 2014. The responsibilities of the role preceding its creation, however, the *Online Communities Manager* (OCM), developed and expanded as the increased resource demands resulting from meaningfully engaging with the club's domestic and global fan base online increased with proliferation of social media use.[64] First appointed in January 2014, the OCM was initially responsible for maintaining and moderating the online forums and message boards that were part of the club's official website. This role then quickly evolved to include promoting campaigns (domestic/international and commercial) and producing content for the club's official social media outlets. With the need then to assess the impact of such online campaigns and content, both for the club primarily, but also for the club's commercial partners, the DEC role was developed to include such responsibilities and those of the OCM role it replaced. The role, in its current state then, is comprised of the following responsibilities:

- Contributing to the club's domestic-oriented social media output (including the creation of targeted social media strategies, content and campaigns)
- Managing and supporting teams to assist with the delivery of international online fan engagement via social media platforms
- Supporting the press office and retail departments in delivering digital content related to player interviews, kit launches and merchandise, events featuring club 'legends' and other press-related engagements
- Moderating the club's official website forums and other fan areas of www.liverpoolfc.com.
- Delivering the digital requirements of the club's commercial partners
- Researching and analysing data pertaining to the club's digital performance

The DEC works alongside a Website and Social Media team and an International Development team located within the club's Digital Media Department. While the former is responsible for the club's primary social media outlets based in the UK and Ireland market, the latter is responsible for the club's international social media channels. Although the DEC, Website and Social Media team and International Development team currently work largely independently of one another and report directly to the club's Digital Media Officer, further exemplifying what is a continually evolving environment,[65] a Social Media Manager will soon be installed into the club's organisational hierarchy, directly above the DEC, consolidating the strategic and managerial responsibilities of social media engagement. While the DEC is not directly responsible for any employees from a management perspective, there are a team of 'volunteer consultants' who report to the DEC. Volunteer consultants are supporters of the club (a requirement) who primarily fulfil two roles. First, these individuals are responsible for running the club's international social media sites (translating relevant content from the club's main social media outlets, generating and posting unique content, and moderating comments and replies to posts). These fans report both to the DEC and the head of the International Development team. Second, another team of volunteer fans, who report to solely to the DEC, are responsible for moderating the club's official online fan forums and message boards; an issue that will be discussed in greater detail later in this chapter.

Career profile

Liverpool Football Club's current DEC is a Brazilian national. Graduating with a Bachelor's degree in Computer Science in 2004, the DEC was then employed in the IT departments of an international steel producer (as an IT Executive) and of a financial services provider (as Senior IT Officer) – both based in Brazil – for nearly 8 years following graduation. Alongside this employment the DEC graduated with a Master's degree in Business Administration and Management in 2007, and later, a Postgraduate Diploma in Football Management and Sports Studies in 2012. It was the latter that led to the DEC then moving to the UK in 2012 to study on the University of Liverpool's *Football Industries MBA* (FIMBA). Delivered by the University's *Football Industry Group* (FIG)[66] and partnered with The Football Association (and to a lesser extent, UEFA), this postgraduate degree focuses on the business of football and promoting professionalism and professional development in the industry.[67] It was the highest-ranked football-specific Master's course in SportBusiness International's postgraduate sports course rankings of 2013,[68] in which it placed 13th overall in the top 25 sport management courses from universities around the world, in what according to the publication is "the industry's only authoritative ranking of the sector of sports management education".[69] As part of the FIMBA, the DEC engaged in an informal placement with LFC, which involved assisting the club with making some initial steps in engaging with the club's international online fan base. During this placement, the DEC was able to draw on previous experience and skills amassed during an extensive education and employment background in IT and 'digital systems', alongside fluency in Portuguese, Spanish and English. What it offered the DEC, alongside the FIMBA, was an opportunity for professional experience in the football industry. Upon graduating in 2013, the DEC then took up more formal, full-time employment with LFC as a team leader and contributor for the club's Brazilian and Portuguese social media channels. It was this role that led to the appointment as OCM, and then in turn to the interviewee's current role as DEC for LFC.

Social media portfolio

Although LFC's official UK and Ireland-based Facebook and Twitter accounts were established at the beginning of 2009, the club's international social media programme wasn't formally launched until November 2012. Prior to this, the club generally only utilised social media to engage in domestic UK & Ireland-based markets and (by-default) English-speaking countries (with the exception being a Brazilian/Portuguese-based official Twitter account launched in July 2011, and managed by the interviewee). The primary aim of this new international programme was, and still remains, to better engage with the large numbers of club supporters based in countries outside of the United Kingdom and Ireland: "to open a conversation with international fans . . . in their own language" (interview). At present, in addition to Liverpool F.C.'s official UK and Ireland-based social media accounts (Twitter, Facebook, Sports Yapper, Pinterest, Fancred, Google+ and Instagram), the club also maintain 40 official internationally oriented accounts on various social media sites (refer to Table 17.2), the majority of which post and create content in the language from where the account originates and/or the geographical market the account is aimed at. There are currently (aside from the domestic accounts mentioned above) 21 Twitter accounts, 12 Facebook accounts, two Instagram accounts, an account with Russian social network site VK (widely regarded as a "Russian Facebook"),[70] and accounts with Chinese social networking sites Sino Weibo (which combines functionality from multiple social media platforms), Tencent Weibo (akin to Twitter) and Weixin (a mobile text and voice messaging communication service). It is also worth noting that aside from these main (front-facing) domestic and international social media accounts, there are sub-departments and elements from within the LFC company structure that maintain their own official Twitter accounts. For example, @LFC_Help, the club's customer service department (7,000 followers); @MightyRed_LFC, the club's mascot (7,500 followers); @LFC_PR, the club's public relations team (10,200 followers); @LFCFoundation, the charitable arm of the club (28,600 followers); and @LFCTV, the official account of the club's TV channel (196,000 followers). Although it is very possible (and likely) that many supporters maintain multiple accounts across various social media platforms,[71,72] each individual 'Follow' or 'Like' represents one point of contact, with the resulting figure then, across all of the club's main social media accounts, equalling almost 40,000,000 points of contact to manage (refer to Table 17.2).

Table 17.2 LFC's main accounts held on social media platforms and current number of 'followers' (rounded off to the nearest 100)

Regions, Countries and Languages	*Official Twitter Account*		*Official Facebook Page*		*Official Instagram*		*Other*	
Arabic[2]	✓	79,200	✓	No specific country data available				
Australia and New Zealand[1]	✓	24,400	✓					
Bangladesh[2]	✓	11,000	✓					
Brazil and Portugal[2]	✓	24,000	✓		✓	1,200		
China[2]							✓	Sina Weibo (2,229,500), Tencent Weibo (1,037,000) and Weixin (no data)
France[2]	✓	17,000						
Finland[2]	✓	2,100						
Greece [2]	✓	3,100						
India[1]	✓	61,600	✓					
Indonesia[2]	✓	130,000	✓					
Italy[2]	✓	2,700						
Japan[2]			✓					
Malaysia[2]	✓	16,200						
Norway[2]	✓	6,600						
Pakistan[1]	✓	7,900						
Poland[2]	✓	3,200						
Russia[2]							✓	VK (49,800)
Spain[2]	✓	39,700	✓					
South Africa[2]	✓	18,300						
South Korea[1]	✓	6,600	✓					
Thailand[2]	✓	62,700	✓		✓	12,300		
Turkey[2]	✓	24,600						
UK & Ireland	✓	4,240,000	✓		✓	1,300,000	✓	Sports Yapper (600), Pinterest (1,170,400), Fancred (3,300), Google+ (4,205,400)
USA [1]	✓	57,000						
Vietnam [2]			✓					
Total	21	4,837,900	12	24,953,400	3	1,313,500	4	8,696,000

[1]International account (English language)
[2]International account (local language)

Social media strategy issues

In the following section, the perceptions of LFC regarding the issues and challenges associated with utilising social media to engage with the club's supporter base are outlined.

Control of conversation

Supporting the findings of McCarthy et al.'s research, in which the case study clubs were "concerned about the control of conversations associated with the club, and also, ultimately in the brand identity and image",[73] LFC are similarly concerned with such control on official social media channels. An important consideration, however, is, as discussed, that communication concerning the club has now ceased to be produced by football clubs exclusively, but is increasingly produced by fans through UGC on social media platforms.[74] It is necessary, therefore, to distinguish between the issues concerning the control of conversations from the perspective of club-created social media output (brand identity) and that of the fans through UGC (brand image). For LFC, club-created social media output is wide-ranging. It comprises, but is not limited to the following: match previews and reviews, match-day squad announcements, live match updates, transfer and contract announcements, behind-the-scenes insights, general club announcement and club press releases, interactive polls and votes (e.g., Figure 17.1), interviews with playing and non-playing staff, details of competitions, offers on club merchandise, content delivered on behalf of commercial partners, links to the club's other social media platforms, details regarding pre-season friendly tours, and the occasional comment on football-related events in the media. Content, in the form of posts, updates and/or shares, combines text, images, videos, interactive elements and hyperlinks, with supporters usually free to comment and respond directly to any and all of this content. In terms of the control of conversation, club generated content is, as much as is possible, aligned with the club's values, tradition and history, similar to the findings of McCarthy et al. (2014). However, genuine opportunities to incorporate these elements into communications are less frequent than one might initially anticipate. With a high proportion of the club's social media content, at present, relating to events in and around match days – for example, live in-game, minute-by-minute updates, match day squad announcements, etc. – combined with the nature of social media, that is communication

Figure 17.1 Interactive poll from LFC's official Facebook account exploring supporter associations, 6 September 2012

Figure 17.2 Example of an in-game live update tweet, 13 April 2015

of short and concise informative messages, for posts such as that presented below (Figure 17.2), it is not always possible for communications to covey club's values, tradition and history. Wherever it is possible though, the club attempt to communicate via social media platforms in a way that is dignified, inclusive, and engenders fans' perceptions that they are all part of the 'LFC family' (interviewee). This is a key strategic aim of LFC's approach to social media – that they are regarded as a 'family club' (interviewee). But not in the traditional sense that the club is 'family friendly' – that is welcoming to women or children – which, as a side note, it is generally considered to be anyway,[75] but more so in the sense of communicating to the club's supporters, wherever they are located around the world, that they are all part of the 'LFC family':

> Everyone is welcome, regardless of . . . race, religion, . . . gender and everything else. . . . [W]e try to make fans feel like they are a part of the [LFC] family.
>
> *(interviewee)*

Given that this is, by now, a relatively well-established social media strategy,[76] it is not surprising then that the biggest challenge in terms of control of conversation isn't so much club-created communications, but similar to the findings of McCarthy et al. (2014), it is in the supporter responses to social media posts and their online discussions on official forums; it is in the UGC.

Unlike the four case study clubs in the McCarthy et al. (2014) paper, LFC have formally allocated resources within the club's structure to monitor UGC across their portfolio of social media. However, it is possible that, in the years since McCarthy et al. (2014) actually conducted their research (2010), the case study clubs have since installed relevant roles with similar or scaled-down versions to that of LFC. Yet for LFC, even with their considerable resources, the club concede that it is "nearly impossible to moderate 100% of what's posted [online]" (interview), such is the volume of UGC that club-generated communication can instigate.[77] One club-generated post on Facebook, for example, can prompt hundreds, if not thousands of reply comments from individual Facebook users (both supporters and non-supporters), which in turn can prompt more reply comments from other users, thus exposing a snowball-effect-nature of social media communication. It is the club's moderators, predominantly comprising the aforementioned volunteer consultants, who have the job of deciding on the types of user comments that are inappropriate for publication on the club's numerous official online channels. Areas of responsibility, in terms of moderation for the club, include: the online forums and comments sections of the official LFC website; a dedicated area of the website which documents club supporters' online social media activity, titled #theKOP;[78] and, the messages, comments and replies on posts on official social media channels. In terms of openness, LFC maintain that social media engagement should allow "fans total freedom to say what they want to say" (interview), while concurrently attempting to remain congruous with the values, history and traditions of the club. What this mainly involves is the removing of UGC from official online spaces which is considered overtly abusive, insulting, discriminatory, objectionable or contains inappropriate language. Although definitive numbers were not available, the interviewee speculated, anecdotally, that between 10% and 15% of messages and comments which are reviewed by moderators across the social media portfolio are removed. Supplementing this official club moderation, there is also the option for fans to report comments they deem inappropriate to moderators, who then decide whether any action is required.

It is important to highlight at this point that LFC maintain that they do not remove comments that are merely regarded as negative or unfavourable towards any aspect of the club or its staff, as long as they are appropriately toned (i.e. not overtly abusive, insulting, etc.), and there was no evidence to suggest that such censorship had occurred; although such evidence is regarded as difficult to obtain.[79] But the number of messages that did require action from moderators was very much affected by the team's on-pitch performance; that is, when LFC win and the supporters are happy, posts and comments tend to be, overall, more positive than when the team lose (especially if they have lost more often than not over a number of matches), when a higher proportion of comments and posts tended to express dissatisfaction with the performance of the team, individual players and/or non-playing staff in *inappropriate* ways. During these times, supporters even resort to inappropriately expressing dissatisfaction with and posting abuse at one another; such UGC is also usually removed. For negative and unfavourable content that is not removed, it is worth referring to the literature here, according to which, social media specialists 'have attained near-consensus' that the 'most appropriate method' of handling such content is 'to attempt to respond in as positive a manner as possible'.[80] However, there are two immediately apparent problems with LFC attempting to adopt such a strategy. First, as mentioned above, even with relatively substantial resources available to LFC, the club are unable to read every individual user-generated message, comment and reply posted across the club's social media portfolio. Second, the question of how the club responds to certain negative and unfavourable comments can be somewhat complicated. For example, a negative post concerning an element of customer service that a user has experienced would be relatively simple to respond to (so long as it is seen by the club), compared to, say, a negative comment concerning the performance of the team in a particular game. It is just not possible, or even practical, to respond to negative or unfavourable UGC relating to performance, and just like the research conducted by McCarthy et al. "in order to tap into the passion of fans", the club recognise that "it is necessary to accept that views expressed by fans will not always be what the club wants to hear".[81]

Fan engagement

Contrary to the research conducted by McCarthy et al., who found that among their case study clubs "there was no real effort to know the customer [fan]" through social media engagement (2014: p. 192), LFC have attempted to address this issue, in the context of their worldwide fan base, through the launch of their international social media programme; the belief here being that supporters respond more positively to content that tailored specifically to them.[82] Principally, this involves engaging fans in their own language (e.g. the @LFCFrance Twitter account), but going beyond just directly translating UK-oriented content from the club's main social media channels. For example, but proving an exception to this general rule of international accounts publishing in the local language, the @LFCIndia Twitter account publishes Tweets in English, yet illustrates instead some alternative ways in which the club engages with specific supporter groups via social media. For example, marking occasions that are relevant to international supporters (e.g. commemorating local holidays; see Figure 17.3), advising followers on venues that broadcast games (Figure 17.4) or 'celebrating' non-football-related sporting achievements (e.g. cricket), and thus attempting to engage with the fan base through their country's more popular interests (e.g. cricket is the national sport in India). Quite simply, the idea here was "to start a conversation with [Indian-based supporters], and try to find other ways of reaching them, not

Figure 17.3 @LFCIndia tweet concerning Independence day in India, 14 August 2014

Source: http://twitter.com/LFCIndia.

Figure 17.4 Tweets and posts advising supporters where they can watch LFC games

Source: http://twitter.com/LFCIndia (top) / http://www.facebook.com/IndiaLFC/ (bottom).

always speaking about football, but other matters that are relevant to the people" (interview). International football fixtures and competitions also offer opportunities for the club to communicate uniquely relevant content via international social media channels. For example, during the 2014 FIFA World Cup, there were numerous official LFC social media accounts based in those countries represented in the competition (e.g. Brazil, France, Spain, United States, etc.). Thus the club was able to produce specifically tailored World Cup content for these countries' supporters and their teams (for example, see Figure 17.5); an undertaking that is made easier by a competing nation containing an LFC club player – for example, Mamadou Sakho and the French national team (for example, see Figure 17.6). Practicalities and specific examples aside, overall what this social media strategy facilitates, primarily, is the formation of country and/or language-specific

Figure 17.5 @GreeceLFC announces to fans the squad for their 2014WC game against Côte d'Ivoire

Source: http://twitter.com/GreeceLFC.

Figure 17.6 @LFCFrance tweet mentioning Mamadou Sakho and the French national team

Source: http://twitter.com/LFCFrance.

online communities whereby the aim is to engender a greater sense of belonging to, and increase supporter identification with LFC:

> One of the main objectives of launching international social media is to make these fans feel part of the club, feel part of the family . . . having a voice, and . . . bringing their ideas or their insight in to the club. . . . [T]he perception of the club, sometimes is a bit different depending on the country . . . but as a whole, [from our perspective] the fans feel LFC as a family club.
>
> *(interviewee)*

With reference then to the club's domestic supporter-base, there are challenges with engaging those fans via social media platforms who, geographically, are located closest to LFC. This potentially may result in these fans having "lived alongside the club for many, many years, so they know what is happening with the club. . . . They [are more likely to] go to matches" (interviewee). There is, however, an appreciation that these fans may feel like they've been "put aside" in favour of the club concentrating on growing their international fan base:

> It is a challenge indeed, it is. . . . [W]e don't want to make local fans feel put aside, because these fans are core to the club: they live in the city, they've been . . . growing and living with Liverpool all of their lives. . . . We see, unfortunately, . . . local fans complaining sometimes about Liverpool trying to reach fans worldwide. . . . It's tricky because . . . all of them are Liverpool fans and we want them [all] to feel part of the family. So maybe, we're trying to reach international fans because it's harder for them to feel part of the club, to feel part of the [LFC] family. They aren't here, they aren't in Liverpool, they can't go to Anfield to watch matches so . . . maybe that's the reason

> we're trying harder to reach them and why we're focussing a bit more on them than our local fans. But that doesn't mean we don't value our local fans. We do value them, we know they are core to the club, it's just . . . tricky sometimes.
>
> *(interviewee)*

Some of the comments contained within this quote are consistent with the findings of Bridgewater[83] (2010), who suggests that supporters located closest to a club's home ground often consider themselves 'better' or more 'loyal' than those who are located further away.[84] Thus presently, a major concern and challenge for LFC is engaging the local fan base in such a way that is mindful of these findings, and of supporter views, without compromising the effectiveness of the club's international social media programme. The research of Garcia[85] may offer some guidance here on working to overcome this challenge. Having interviewed marketing executives from the Réal Madrid Football Club, the author describes how, when developing their online marketing strategy, positive relationships with fans are cultivated with the club through relying on, and responding to, fan feedback. The danger here is that if LFC fails to engage sufficiently with their locally based fans, then they will instead turn to alternative unofficial sites to satisfy their communication needs;[86] a concern that was similarly raised in the findings of the McCarthy et al.'s (2014) research.

Commercialisation

Another increasingly important strategic objective for LFC is that the club effectively supports its commercial partners via its social media output. A challenge here is presented in the fact that commercial partners are, in general, making increasing demands of clubs in reference to communicating their brands via social media; indeed, promotion of an organisation, or its products and services, on official club social media platforms is something that commercial partners are regularly trying to leverage when they enter into relationships with clubs. The challenge then is that the relationship between fans and the club is not perceived as being overly commercialised. Thus, similar to the findings of McCarthy et al., LFC are very much aware that fans "may consider social media as their space (private or public)"[87] (2014: p. 194), and consequently the danger, from the club's perspective, is that in over-commercialising users' 'space', the relationship with fans is adversely affected. Furthermore, highlighting an issue that was not uncovered in the McCarthy et al. (2014) research, LFC are also attuned to the fact that certain social media platforms allow users as young as 13 years old to register for accounts, and consequently this is a consideration in how social media communications that advertise partners services and products are toned: "[W]e have to be careful . . . because we have children and youngsters [who engage with LFC's social media] . . . [we] try to be careful with what is posted" (interviewee). This is a particularly important consideration when posting social media content on behalf of the club's commercial partners whose products and services are not be suitable for under 18s (for example, gambling companies). Such content, then, needs to sufficiently meet the requirements of the partner, while at the same time, not seen to be unduly encouraging those who are too young – "but that's one of our challenges at the moment" (interviewee).

Assessing social media impact

An issue that wasn't raised in the McCarthy et al. (2014) research is related to assessing the impact of social media engagement. Though a potential reason for this may lie in the relative adolescence of the case study clubs' social media strategies when McCarthy et al. (2014) conducted their research (2010), coupled with the limited resources that these clubs allocated to its management. For LFC, however, assessing the impact of their social media engagement is firmly rooted within the club's social media strategy, supported by formally allocated staffing resources. Yet while that may be the case, the club do admit that formal performance indicator measures are far from fully developed. Currently, social media performance is quantitatively measured on post views, likes, comments and shares in relation to the 24M fans the club has on Facebook. For example, the proportion of post likes against number of views it gets provides LFC with some insight into how club-generated content is being received. LFC also continually and quantitatively evaluates its own social media performance against what it considers to be the club's main competitors (in a social media sense). In the UK, these are considered to be 'biggest clubs' in the EPL: Arsenal FC (41.8M Facebook fans),[88] Chelsea FC (41.8M),[89] Manchester City FC (18.8M)[90] and Manchester United FC (64.5M).[91] Everton FC (2.0M)[92] are also considered a competitor, but more from a regionally geographic perspective. Reflective then of LFC's global thinking in terms of its social media strategy, the club also regard Barcelona FC (82.7M)[93] and Réal Madrid FC (81.7M)[94] as competitors. The DEC described how the club "try to benchmark [social media] performance against what these other teams are doing and how they are engaging fans on social media" (interviewee). This might involve, for example, comparing how fans respond to club-generated content on the LFC Facebook page, the Réal Madrid Facebook page and the Barcelona FC Facebook page on a specific match day. The ultimate aim being to ascertain the type of content that fans respond more positively to, and thus determine whether any improving adjustments can be made to the club's own content, based on what these other teams are posting and how their respective fans react. This might relate to the visual configuration and presentation of new content and the utilisation of 'creative ideas' for its posting. What the club are not currently doing is qualitatively scrutinising the types of comments and replies that fans are posting in response to club-generated content to gauge their views and opinions. Although UCG is reviewed by the club's moderators (the DEC and volunteer consultants) the reason for doing so is, as stated, to ensure that it maintains an appropriate tone (i.e. is not abusive, insulting, discriminatory, etc.). But this is a lot less time-consuming than examining UGC to determine whether it is positively or negatively oriented, or if it can be qualitatively themed. Doing so might also require further training and skills development for volunteer consultants, who may not be familiar with, for example, content analysis. Yet although these challenges exist, LFC regards the incorporation of qualitative approaches to assessing social media impact as 'the next step' in developing their formal performance indicator measures; at the time of the interview, they were just unsure (or potentially unwilling to discuss) how they were going to enact this.

Conclusion

Social media then – and, more broadly, the development of new media technologies (for example, mobile communications and the live streaming of football matches) – have changed the manner in which professional sport is produced, marketed, delivered and consumed.[95,96] The result, Cleland proposes, is that "the creation of multiple platforms on the Internet has allowed for more 'active' football fans . . . to engage in everyday asynchronous discussions".[97] Such discussions – a large proportion of which are conducted via social media platforms – combined with the prospect that social media offers in terms of fans being able to communicate directly with clubs, have "transformed [fans] from mere content consumers into content producers".[98,99] As a result of the shift in communications concerning clubs, from what traditional media offered fans (one-way communication from the club to the supporter via TV, press releases, etc.) to what social media offers (two-way communication between fans and the club via multiple online platforms) "[t]he power has been taken from those in marketing and public relations by the individuals and communities that create, share, and consume blogs, tweets, Facebook entries, movies, pictures, and so forth."[100] The purpose of this chapter then was to explore elements of the social media strategy of LFC – a club who maintain a "long-standing worldwide status as a successful and glamorous football club"[101] – and highlight some of the issues relating to club social media use in attempting to develop meaningful relationships with supporters. The findings of this research provide insights for football clubs in responding to the challenges and opportunities posed by social media. It is worth highlighting, however, that when interpreting these insights, one has to be mindful that social media output (in terms of content) and performance (in terms of positive engagement) is markedly influenced by the performance of the team. Thus, on occasion, it's not about innovative new approaches to engaging with fans, or producing creative content, but merely "staying in line with what is happening on the pitch" (interviewee). Sometimes, fans can respond negatively to posts that are not "in sync" with their feelings, particularly when the team is not winning. Thus implementing "innovative" ideas when the team is losing is usually met with a larger degree of opposition "as a way of compensating for what is happening on the pitch" (interviewee). Thus, even when the team is winning, new and creative ideas for social media need to be introduced gradually, and they are best introduced when there is "momentum on the pitch" (interviewee).

Notes

1 BOYD D. M., ELLISON N. B., Social network sites: Definition, history, and scholarship, *Journal of Computer-Mediated Communication*, 13, 210–230, 2008.

2 HENNIG-THURAU T., MALTHOUSE E. C., FRIEGE C., GENSLER S., LOBSCHAT L., RANGASWAMY A., SKIERA B., The impact of new media on customer relationships, *Journal of Service Research*, 13(3), 311–330, 2010.

3 MANGOLD W. G., FAULDS D. J., Social media: The new hybrid element of the promotion mix, *Business Horizons*, 52(4), 357–365, 2009.

4 WALLACE L, WILSON J., MILOCH K., Sporting Facebook: A content analysis of NCAA organizational sport pages and Big 12 Conference Athletic Department pages, *International Journal of Sport Communication*, 4, 422–444, 2011.

5 KAPLAN A. M., HAENLEIN M., Users of the world, unite! The challenges and opportunities of social media, *Business Horizons*, 53(1), 59–68, 2010.

6 BERTHON P. R., PITT L. F., PLANGGER K., SHAPIRO D., Marketing meets Web 2.0, social media, and creative consumers: Implications for international marketing strategy, *Business Horizons*, 55(3), 261–271, 2012.

7 KIETZMANN J. H., HERMKENS K., MCCARTHY I. P., SILVESTRE B. S., Social media? Get serious! Understanding the functional building blocks of social media, *Business Horizons*, 54(3), 241–251, 2010.

8 KAPLAN A. M., HAENLEIN M., Users of the world, unite! The challenges and opportunities of social media, *Business Horizons*, 53(1), 59–68, 2010.

9 DART J., New media, professional sport and political economy, *Journal of Sport & Social Issues*, 38(6), 528–547, 2012.

10 *ibid*, p. 531.

11 PRICE J., FARRINGTON N., HALL L., Changing the game? The impact of Twitter on relationships between football clubs, supporters and the sports media, *Soccer & Society*, 14(4), 446–461, 2013: p.448.

12 BOYD D. M., ELLISON N. B., Social network sites: Definition, history, and scholarship, *Journal of Computer-Mediated Communication*, 13, 210–230, 2008: p.211.

13 KAPLAN A. M., HAENLEIN M., Users of the world, unite! The challenges and opportunities of social media, *Business Horizons*, 53(1), 59–68, 2010.

14 http://www.statista.com/statistics/282087/number-of-monthly-active-twitter-users/ – Title of an Internet page from statista.com. Last accessed February 15, 2015.

15 http://www.statista.com/statistics/264810/number-of-monthly-active-facebook-users-worldwide/ – Title of an Internet page from statista.com. Last accessed February 15, 2015.

16 BOYD D. M., ELLISON N. B., Social network sites: Definition, history, and scholarship, *Journal of Computer-Mediated Communication*, 13, 210–230, 2008.

17 PRONSCHINSKE M., GROZA M. D., WALKER M., Attracting Facebook "fans": The importance of authenticity and engagement as a social networking strategy for professional sport teams, *Sport Marketing Quarterly*, 21(4), 221–231, 2012.

18 WOODCOCK N., GREEN A., STARKEY M., Social CRM as a business strategy, *Journal of Database Marketing & Customer Strategy Management*, 18(1), 50–64, 2011.

19 ZWICK D., DIETERLE O., The [e-]business of sport sponsorship. In J. M. Amis and T. B. Cornwell (eds.), *Global Sport Sponsorship*. New York: Berg, 127–146, 2005.

20 BAIRD C. H., PARASNIS G., From social media to social customer relationship management. *Strategy & Leadership*, 39(5), 30–37, 2011: p.30.

21 DART J., New media, professional sport and political economy, *Journal of Sport & Social Issues*, 38(6), 528–547, 2012.

22 DE KNOP P., HOYNG J., *De Functies en Betekenissen van Sport*. Tilburg: Tilburg University Press., 1998.

23 DIONSIO P., LEAL C., MOUTINHO L., Fandom affiliation and tribal behaviour: A sports marketing application, *Qualitative Market Research: An International Journal*, 11(1), 17–39, 2008.

24 TAPP A., CLOWES J., From "carefree casuals" to "professional wanderers": Segmentation possibilities for football supporters, *European Journal of Marketing*, 36(11/12), 1248–1269, 2002.

25 WILLIAMS J., CHINN S. J., Meeting relationship-marketing goals through social media: A conceptual model for sport marketers, *International Journal of Sport Communication*, 3, 422–437, 2010: p.436.

26 *ibid.*

27 CORNISH A. N., LARKIN B., Social media's changing legal landscape provides cautionary tales of "Pinterest" to sport marketers, *Sport Marketing Quarterly*, 23(1), 47–49, 2014: p.47.

28 MICHAELIDOU N., SIAMAGKA N. T., CHRISTODOULIDES G., Usage, barriers and measurement of social media marketing: An exploratory investigation of small and medium B2B brands, *Industrial Marketing Management*, 40, 1153–1159, 2011.

29 ARGAN M., ARGAN M. T., KÖSE H., GÖKCE S., E-CRM applications of soccer teams as a strategic tool: A content analysis of English Premier League and Turkish Super League, *Journal of Sport Management Research*, 4, 1–11, 2013.

30 E.g. ARGAN ET AL., (2013); CLELAND (2013); CORNISH & LARKIN (2014); DART (2012); EAGLEMAN (2013); PRICE, FARRINGTON & HALL (2013); PRONSCHINSKE, GROZA & WALKER (2012).

31 MCCARTHY J., ROWLEY J., ASHWORTH C. J., PIOCH E., Managing brand presence through social media: The case of UK football clubs, *Internet Research*, 24, 181–204, 2014.

32 Data was collected through desk research and a semi-structured interview with a responsible individual from LFCs digital media team. Thematic analysis was conducted on the data collected.

33 As of January 2015, the collective achievements of clubs in London (13 in the EPL/Football League divisions) equate to 65 trophies from the following competitions: league championships (First Division/EPL), FA Cups, League Cups, European Cups/Champions League, UEFA Cups/EUROPA League and the UEFA Super Cup. The collective achievements of Liverpool F.C. and Everton F.C (the only two clubs in the city of Liverpool) equate to 58 trophies garnered from the same competitions.

34 RICHARDSON K., ROOKWOOD J., Partnerships, provision and product: Examining the modern football in the community programme – a case study on Everton Football Club, *Journal of Qualitative Research in Sports Studies*, 2(1),161–174, 2008: p.163.

35 "Subject to a licence being granted by UEFA, multiple winners of the UEFA Champions League (three consecutive times or a minimum of five times) may wear a multiple-winner badge on the free zone of the left shirt sleeve which should be placed above the UEFA Respect badge . . ." (UEFA, *Regulations of the UEFA Champions League 2012–2015 Cycle: 2014–1015 Season*. Nyon: UEFA, 2014, p.32).

36 Approx. for EPL season 2014–2015 (Pearce, 2014).

37 Correct in January 2015.

38 EPL season 2013/2014.

39 Fifth highest for EPL season 2013/2014 behind Man. Utd. (75,207), Arsenal (59,487), Newcastle Utd. (50,395) and Man. City (47,080) (SOURCE).

40 THE LIVERPOOL FOOTBALL CLUB AND ATHLETIC GROUND LIMITED, *The Liverpool Football Club and Athletic Ground Limited – Directors' Report and Financial Statements*. Liverpool: The Liverpool Football Club and Athletic Ground Limited, 2013.

41 Converted at a rate of £1 = 1.28 euro (correct in January 2015).

42 http://www.liverpoolfc.com/corporate/partners – Title of an Internet page published on liverpoolfc.com. Last accessed February 15, 2015.

43 ROOKWOOD J., MILLWARD P., We all dream of a team of Carraghers: Comparing "local" and Texan Liverpool fans' talk, *Sport in Society*, 14, 37–52, 2011.

44 "[I]n terms of attendance at matches, size of fan base and revenue" (McCarthy et al., 2014: p.188).

45 DELOITTE SPORTS BUSINESS GROUP, *All to Play for: Football Money League.* Manchester / London: Deloitte LLP, 2014.

46 "[P]ublished by Brand Finance plc [the Football 50] is the only study to analyse and rank the top 50 most valuable football clubs by brand value" (Brand Finance, 2014: p.2).

47 BRAND FINANCE, *Brand Finance® Football 50.* London: Brand Finance, 2014.

48 http://www.worldfootball.net/attendance/eng-premier-league-2013–2014/1/ – Data from an Internet page "Premier League 2013/2014 – Attendance – Home matches", from worldfootball.net. Last accessed February 15, 2015.

49 *ibid.*

50 At the time of writing, Anfield is the sixth largest stadium in England (not including Wembley) behind Old Trafford, 75,635; Emirates Stadium, 60,272; St. James' Park, 52,405; Stadium of Light, 49,000; and, City of Manchester Stadium (a.k.a. Etihad Stadium), 46,708

51 Liverpool Football Club (2011). Latest news – Season Ticket waiting list. *Liverpool Football Club Official Club Website* [online]. Available at: http://www.liverpoolfc.com/news/latest-news/season-ticket-waiting-list (accessed 14th January 2015).

52 "We [the club] have said consistently that if Liverpool is to continue to compete at the very top level of the game then future expansion [of Anfield] is an absolute necessity" (LFC Press Release cited in BBC News, 2000).

53 http://www.theguardian.com/football/2014/dec/04/liverpool-new-main-stand-anfield-corporate-seats — Data from the article "Liverpool defend rise in corporate seats in new £114m Anfield main stand", written by Andy Hunter and published at theguardian.com, December 4, 2014. Last accessed February 15, 2015.

54 http://www.theguardian.com/football/2014/sep/23/liverpool-granted-planning-permission-for-phase-one-of-anfield-redevelopment – Données issues de l'article "Liverpool granted planning permission for phase one of Anfield redevelopment", written by Andy Hunter and published at theguardian.com, September 23, 2014. Last accessed February 15, 2015.

55 http://www.facebook.com/LiverpoolFC – Profil officiel de Liverpool FC sur Facebook. Last accessed February 15, 2015.

56 http://twitter.com/LFC – Official Twitter account of Liverpool F.C. Last accessed February 15, 2015.

57 http://www.facebook.com/newcastleunited – Official Facebook profile of Newcastle United F.C. .

58 http://twitter.com/NUFC – Official Twitter account of Newcastle United FC sur Twitter. Last accessed February 15, 2015.

59 BERLIN, P., Money, money, money: The English Premier League. In R. Steen, J. Novick and H. Richards (eds.), *The Cambridge Companion to Football.* Cambridge: Cambridge University Press, 121–135, 2013.

60 BODET G., CHANAVAT N., Building global football brand equity: Lessons from the Chinese market, *Asia Pacific Journal of Marketing and Logistics*, 22(1), 55–66, 2010.

61 ROOKWOOD J., MILLWARD P., We all dream of a team of Carraghers: Comparing "local" and Texan Liverpool fans' talk, *Sport in Society*, 14, 37–52, 2011: p.40.

62 *ibid*, p.40.

63 MCCARTHY J., ROWLEY J., ASHWORTH C. J., PIOCH E., Managing brand presence through social media: The case of UK football clubs, *Internet Research*, 24, 181–204, 2014.

64 HENNIG-THURAU T., MALTHOUSE E. C., FRIEGE C., GENSLER S., LOBSCHAT L., RANGASWAMY A., SKIERA B., The impact of new media on customer relationships, *Journal of Service Research*, 13(3), 311–330, 2010.

65 PRICE J., FARRINGTON N., HALL L., Changing the game? The impact of Twitter on relationships between football clubs, supporters and the sports media, *Soccer & Society*, 14(4), 446–461, 2013.

66 http://www.liv.ac.uk/management/football/ – "The Football Industry Group (FIG) – University of Liverpool Management School", published at liv.ac.uk. Last accessed February 15, 2015.

67 http://www.liv.ac.uk/study/postgraduate/taught/football-industries-mba/overview/ – Title of an Internet page published on liv.ac.uk. Last accessed February 15, 2015.

68 SPORTBUSINESS INTERNATIONAL, University challenge: Sport business international's 2013 postgraduate sports course rankings, *Sport Business International*, 189, 78–100, 2013.

69 *ibid*, p.80.

70 For example, http://www.theguardian.com/world/shortcuts/2013/aug/02/vk-russian-facebook-edward-snowden-nsa – Data from the article "Edward Snowden: Pass Notes – VK: The 'Russian Facebook'

that has offered Edward Snowden a job", from theguardian.com, August 2, 2013. Last accessed February 15, 2015.

71 This could mean, for example, supporters following the club both via their own Facebook and Twitter accounts. It might also be possible that supporters follow various language-based accounts within one social network platform; for example, following the UK & Ireland-based and the France-based Twitter accounts.

72 http://pewinternet.Org/~/media//Files/Reports/2013/Social%20Networking%202013_PDF.pdf – Données issues de l'article "Social Media Update 2013", written by Maeve Duggan & Aaron Smith and published at pewinternet.org, December 30, 2013. Last accessed February 15, 2015.

73 MCCARTHY J., ROWLEY J., ASHWORTH C. J., PIOCH E., Managing brand presence through social media: The case of UK football clubs, *Internet Research*, 24, 181–204, 2014: p.191.

74 BRUHN M., SCHOENMUELLER V., SCHÄFER D. B., Are social media replacing traditional media in terms of brand equity creation? *Management Research Review*, 35(9), 770–790, 2012.

75 http://www.theguardian.com/lifeandstyle/2013/jul/19/football-clubs-on-the-ball – Données issues de l'article "Which football clubs are the most family friendly?", written by Mike Herd and published at theguardian.com, July 19, 2013. Last accessed February 15, 2015.

76 For example, a search on Twitter of #LFCFamily presents many thousands of user-generated tweets that contain this term.

77 BRUHN M., SCHOENMUELLER V., SCHÄFER D. B., Are social media replacing traditional media in terms of brand equity creation? *Management Research Review*, 35(9), 770–790, 2012.

78 http://www.liverpoolfc.com/fans/thekop/thekop-home – Title of an Internet page published on liverpoolfc.com. Last accessed February 15, 2015.

79 DEKAY S. H., How large companies react to negative Facebook comments, *Corporate Communications: An International Journal*, 17(3), 289–299, 2012.

80 *ibid.*

81 MCCARTHY J., ROWLEY J., ASHWORTH C. J., PIOCH E., Managing brand presence through social media: The case of UK football clubs, *Internet Research*, 24, 181–204, 2014.

82 WOODCOCK N., GREEN A., STARKEY M., Social CRM as a business strategy, *Journal of Database Marketing & Customer Strategy Management*, 18(1), 50–64, 2011.

83 BRIDGEWATER S., *Football Brands*. Basingstoke: Palgrave MacMillan., 2010.

84 ROOKWOOD J., MILLWARD P., We all dream of a team of Carraghers: Comparing "local" and Texan Liverpool fans' talk, *Sport in Society*, 14, 37–52, 2011.

85 GARCIA C., Réal Madrid Football Club: Applying a relationship-management model to a sport organization in Spain, *International Journal of Sport Communication*, 4, 284–299, 2011.

86 BOYD D., GOLDER S., LOTAN G., Tweet, tweet, retweet: Conversational aspects of retweeting on Twitter. *Document présenté à la Hawaii International Conference on System Sciences (HICSS)*, January 5–8, Kauai: The Grand Hyatt Kauai Resort & Spa, 2010.

87 MCCARTHY J., ROWLEY J., ASHWORTH C. J., PIOCH E., Managing brand presence through social media: The case of UK football clubs, *Internet Research*, 24, 181–204, 2014: p.194.

88 http://www.facebook.com/Arsenal – Official Facebook profile of Arsenal FC. Last accessed February 15, 2015.

89 http://www.facebook.com/ChelseaFC – Official Facebook profile of Chelsea FC. Last accessed February 15, 2015.

90 http://www.facebook.com/mcfcofficial – Official Facebook profile of Manchester City FC. Last accessed February 15, 2015.

91 http://www.facebook.com/manchesterunited – Official Facebook profile of Manchester United FC. Last accessed February 15, 2015.

92 http://www.facebook.com/Everton – Official Facebook profile of Everton FC. Last accessed February 15, 2015.

93 http://www.facebook.com/fcbarcelona – Official Facebook profile of FC Barcelona. Last accessed February 15, 2015.

94 http://www.facebook.com/RealMadrid – Official Facebook profile of Réal Madrid FC. Last accessed February 15, 2015.

95 DART J., New media, professional sport and political economy, *Journal of Sport & Social Issues*, 38(6), 528–547, 2012.

96 SANTOMIER J., New media, branding and global sports sponsorship, *International Journal of Sports Marketing & Sponsorship*, 10(1), 15–29, 2008.

97 CLELAND J., Racism, football fans, and online message boards: How social media has added a new dimension to racist discourse in English football, *Journal of Sport & Social Issues*, 38(5), 415–431, 2014: p.246.

98 BERTHON P. R., PITT L. F., PLANGGER K., SHAPIRO D., Marketing meets Web 2.0, social media, and creative consumers: Implications for international marketing strategy, *Business Horizons*, 55(3), 261–271, 2012: p.263.

99 FUCHS C., *Social Networking Sites and the Surveillance Society*. Salzberg: Unified Theory of Information, 2009.

100 KIETZMANN J. H., HERMKENS K., MCCARTHY I. P., SILVESTRE B. S., Social media? Get serious! Understanding the functional building blocks of social media, *Business Horizons*, 54(3), 241–251, 2010.

101 ROOKWOOD J., MILLWARD P., We all dream of a team of Carraghers: Comparing "local" and Texan Liverpool fans' talk, *Sport in Society*, 14, 37–52, 2011: p.40.

Bibliography

ARGAN M., ARGAN M. T., KÖSE H., GÖKCE S., E-CRM applications of soccer teams as a strategic tool: A content analysis of English Premier League and Turkish Super League, *Journal of Sport Management Research*, 4, 1–11, 2013.

BAIRD C. H., PARASNIS G., From social media to social customer relationship management, *Strategy & Leadership*, 39(5), 30–37, 2011.

BERLIN P., Money, money, money: The English Premier League. In R. Steen, J. Novick and H. Richards (eds.), *The Cambridge Companion to Football*. Cambridge: Cambridge University Press, 121–135, 2013.

BERTHON P. R., PITT L. F., PLANGGER K., SHAPIRO D., Marketing meets Web 2.0, social media, and creative consumers: Implications for international marketing strategy. *Business Horizons*, 55(3), 261–271, 2012.

BODET G., CHANAVAT N., Building global football brand equity: Lessons from the Chinese market, *Asia Pacific Journal of Marketing and Logistics*, 22(1), 55–66, 2010.

BOYD D. M., ELLISON N. B., Social network sites: Definition, history, and scholarship, *Journal of Computer-Mediated Communication*, 13, 210–230, 2008.

BOYD D. M., GOLDER, S., LOTAN, G. Tweet, tweet, retweet: Conversational aspects of retweeting on Twitter. *Document présenté à la Hawaii International Conference on System Sciences (HICSS)*, 5–8 janvier, Kauai: The Grand Hyatt Kauai Resort & Spa, 2010.

BRIDGEWATER S., *Football Brands*. Basingstoke: Palgrave MacMillan, 2010.

BRUHN M., SCHOENMUELLER V., SCHÄFER D. B., Are social media replacing traditional media in terms of brand equity creation? *Management Research Review*, 35(9), 770–790, 2012.

CLELAND J., Racism, football fans, and online message boards: How social media has added a new dimension to racist discourse in English football, *Journal of Sport & Social Issues*, 38(5), 415–431, 2014.

CORNISH A. N., LARKIN B., Social media's changing legal landscape provides cautionary tales of "Pinterest" to sport marketers, *Sport Marketing Quarterly*, 23(1), 47–49, 2014.

DART J., New media, professional sport and political economy, *Journal of Sport & Social Issues*, 38(6), 528–547, 2012.

DEKAY S. H., How large companies react to negative Facebook comments, *Corporate Communications: An International Journal*, 17(3), 289–299, 2012.

DE KNOP P., HOYNG J., *De Functies en Betekenissen van Sport*. Tilburg: Tilburg University Press., 1998.

DIONSIO P., LEAL C., MOUTINHO L., Fandom affiliation and tribal behaviour: A sports marketing application, *Qualitative Market Research: An International Journal*, 11(1), 17–39, 2008.

EAGLEMAN A. N., Acceptance, motivations, and usage of social media as a marketing communications tool amongst employees of sport national governing bodies, *Sport Management Review*, 16(4), 488–497, 2013.

FUCHS C., *Social Networking Sites and the Surveillance Society*. Salzberg: Unified Theory of Information, 2009.

GARCIA C., Réal Madrid Football Club: Applying a relationship-management model to a sport organization in Spain, *International Journal of Sport Communication*, 4, 284–299, 2011.

HENNIG-THURAU T., MALTHOUSE E. C., FRIEGE C., GENSLER S., LOBSCHAT L., RANGASWAMY A., SKIERA B., The impact of new media on customer relationships, *Journal of Service Research*, 13(3), 311–330, 2010.

KAPLAN A. M., HAENLEIN M., Users of the world, unite! The challenges and opportunities of social media, *Business Horizons*, 53(1), 59–68, 2010.

KIETZMANN J. H., HERMKENS K., MCCARTHY I. P., SILVESTRE B. S., Social media? Get serious! Understanding the functional building blocks of social media, *Business Horizons*, 54(3), 241–251, 2010.

MANGOLD W. G., FAULDS D. J., Social media: The new hybrid element of the promotion mix, *Business Horizons*, 52(4), 357–365, 2009.

MCCARTHY J., ROWLEY J., ASHWORTH C. J., PIOCH, E., Managing brand presence through social media: The case of UK football clubs, *Internet Research*, 24, 181–204, 2014.

MICHAELIDOU N., SIAMAGKA N. T., CHRISTODOULIDES G., Usage, barriers and measurement of social media marketing: An exploratory investigation of small and medium B2B brands, *Industrial Marketing Management*, 40, 1153–1159, 2011.

PEARCE, L., Tomas Berdych taking the tweet approach. *Sydney Morning Herald.* Retrieved 19 September 2014, from http://www.smh.com.au/sport/tennis/tomas-berdych-taking-the-tweet-approach-20140109-30kge.html.

PRICE J., FARRINGTON N., HALL L., Changing the game? The impact of Twitter on relationships between football clubs, supporters and the sports media, *Soccer & Society*, 14(4), 446–461, 2013.

PRONSCHINSKE M., GROZA M. D., WALKER M., Attracting Facebook "fans": The importance of authenticity and engagement as a social networking strategy for professional sport teams, *Sport Marketing Quarterly*, 21(4), 221–231, 2012.

RICHARDSON K., ROOKWOOD J., Partnerships, provision and product: Examining the modern football in the community programme – a case study on Everton Football Club, *Journal of Qualitative Research in Sports Studies*, 2(1), 161–174, 2008.

ROOKWOOD J., MILLWARD P., We all dream of a team of Carraghers: Comparing "local" and Texan Liverpool fans' talk, *Sport in Society*, 14, 37–52, 2011.

SANTOMIER J., New media, branding and global sports sponsorship, *International Journal of Sports Marketing & Sponsorship*, 10(1), 15–29, 2008.

TAPP A., CLOWES J., From "carefree casuals" to "professional wanderers": Segmentation possibilities for football supporters, *European Journal of Marketing*, 36(11/12), 1248–1269, 2002.

WALLACE L, WILSON J., MILOCH K., Sporting Facebook: A content analysis of NCAA organizational sport pages and Big 12 Conference Athletic Department pages, *International Journal of Sport Communication*, 4, 422–444, 2011.

WILLIAMS J., CHINN S. J., Meeting relationship-marketing goals through social media: A conceptual model for sport marketers, *International Journal of Sport Communication*, 3, 422–437, 2010.

WOODCOCK N., GREEN A., STARKEY M., Social CRM as a business strategy, *Journal of Database Marketing & Customer Strategy Management*, 18(1), 50–64, 2011.

ZWICK D., DIETERLE O., The [e-]business of sport sponsorship. In J. M. Amis and T. B. Cornwell (eds.), *Global Sport Sponsorship*. New York: Berg, 127–146, 2005.

Webography

http://news.bbc.co.uk/1/hi/sport/football/800749.stm – Data from the article "Liverpool set to leave Anfield", published in BBC.co.uk, on June 22 2000. Last accessed on February 15 2015.

http://pewinternet.Org/~/media//Files/Reports/2013/Social%20Networking%202013_PDF.pdf – Data from the article "Social Media Update 2013", written by Maeve Duggan & Aaron Smith and published in pewinternet.org, on december 30 2013. Last accessed on February 15 2015.

http://twitter.com/LFC – Official profile of Liverpool FC on Twitter. Last accessed on February 15 2015.

http://twitter.com/NUFC – Official profile of Newcastle United FC on Twitter. Last accessed on February 15 2015.

http://www.facebook.com/Arsenal – Official profile of Arsenal FC on Facebook. Last accessed on February 15 2015.

http://www.facebook.com/ChelseaFC – Official profile of Chelsea FC on Facebook. Last accessed on February 15 2015.

http://www.facebook.com/Everton – Official profile of Everton FC on Facebook. Last accessed on February 15 2015.

http://www.facebook.com/fcbarcelona – Official profile of FC Barcelona on Facebook. Last accessed on February 15 2015.

http://www.facebook.com/LiverpoolFC – Official profile of Liverpool FC on Facebook. Last accessed on February 15 2015.

http://www.facebook.com/manchesterunited – Official profile of Manchester United FC on Facebook. Last accessed on February 15 2015.

http://www.facebook.com/mcfcofficial – Official profile of Manchester City FC on Facebook. Last accessed on February 15 2015.

http://www.facebook.com/newcastleunited – Official profile of Newcastle United FC on Facebook. Last accessed on February 15 2015.

http://www.facebook.com/RealMadrid – Official profile of Réal Madrid FC on Facebook. Last accessed on February 15 2015.

http://www.liv.ac.uk/management/football/ – "The Football Industry Group (FIG) – University of Liverpool Management School", published in liv.ac.uk. Last accessed on February 15 2015.

http://www.liv.ac.uk/study/postgraduate/taught/football-industries-mba/overview/ – published in liv.ac.uk. Last accessed on February 15 2015.

http://www.liverpoolecho.co.uk/sport/football/football-news/liverpool-fc-reveal-season-ticket-6858841 – Data from the article "Exclusive: LFC reveal season ticket prices for 2014/15 campaign", written by James Pearce and published in liverpoolecho.co.uk, on march 20, 2014. Last accessed on November 17 2014.

http://www.liverpoolfc.com/corporate/charter – published in liverpoolfc.com. Last accessed on February 15 2015.

http://www.liverpoolfc.com/corporate/partners – published in liverpoolfc.com. Last accessed on February 15 2015.

http://www.liverpoolfc.com/fans/thekop/thekop-home – published in liverpoolfc.com. Last accessed on February 15 2015.

http://www.liverpoolfc.com/news/latest-news/season-ticket-waiting-list Données issues de l'article "Latest news – Season Ticket waiting list", published in liverpoolfc.com, on July 1st 2011. Last accessed on February 15 2015.

http://www.statista.com/statistics/264810/number-of-monthly-active-facebook-users-worldwide/ – published in statista.com. Last accessed on February 15 2015.

http://www.statista.com/statistics/282087/number-of-monthly-active-twitter-users/ – published in statista.com. Last accessed on February 15 2015.

http://www.theguardian.com/football/2014/dec/04/liverpool-new-main-stand-anfield-corporate-seats – Data from the article "Liverpool defend rise in corporate seats in new £114m Anfield main stand", written by Andy Hunter and published in theguardian.com, on December 4 2014. Last accessed on February 15 2015.

http://www.theguardian.com/football/2014/sep/23/liverpool-granted-planning-permission-for-phase-one-of-anfield-redevelopment – Data from the article "Liverpool granted planning permission for phase one of Anfield redevelopment", written by Andy Hunter and published in theguardian.com, on September 23 2014. Last accessed on February 15 2015.

http://www.theguardian.com/lifeandstyle/2013/jul/19/football-clubs-on-the-ball – Data from the article "Which football clubs are the most family friendly?", written by Mike Herd and published in theguardian.com, on July 19 2013. Last accessed on February 15 2015.

http://www.theguardian.com/world/shortcuts/2013/aug/02/vk-russian-facebook-edward-snowden-nsa – Data from the article "Edward Snowden: Pass Notes – VK: The 'Russian Facebook' that has offered Edward Snowden a job", and published in theguardian.com, on August 2 2013. Last accessed on February 15 2015.

http://www.worldfootball.net/attendance/eng-premier-league-2013–2014/1/ – Data from the article "Premier League 2013/2014 — Attendance – Home matches", and published in worldfootball.net. Last accessed on February 15 2015.

Studies, documents and press releases

BRAND FINANCE, *Brand Finance® Football 50*. London: Brand Finance, 2014.

DELOITTE SPORTS BUSINESS GROUP, *All to Play for: Football Money League*. Manchester / London: Deloitte LLP, 2014.

THE LIVERPOOL FOOTBALL CLUB AND ATHLETIC GROUND LIMITED, *The Liverpool Football Club and Athletic Ground Limited – Directors' Report and Financial Statements*. Liverpool: The Liverpool Football Club and Athletic Ground Limited, 2013.

SPORTBUSINESS INTERNATIONAL, University challenge: Sport business international's 2013 postgraduate sports course rankings, *Sport Business International*, 189, 78–100, 2013.

UEFA, *Regulations of the UEFA Champions League 2012–2015 Cycle: 2014–1015 Season*. Nyon: UEFA, 2014.

18

MANCHESTER UNITED

The capitalized history, from the 1960s to today

Claude Boli

For the last 20 years, the image of the English football club Manchester United has been closely linked to the economic strength of football. Manchester United is definitely the first club in the world to transform its successes on the field into an extraordinary commercial success. The achievements of the Frenchman Eric Cantona, the Englishman David Beckham, Portugal's Cristiano Ronaldo or the Welshman Ryan Giggs have helped to establish a successful, appealing and also glamorous reputation for the team, especially abroad.

While Manchester United has obtained mediocre results in recent years, the club continues to seduce and multiply sponsorship contracts (Chevrolet, Adidas, etc.) and happens to be the most efficient in terms of regional sponsorship in Asia and Europe. The team from Northern England has become a true benchmark in commercial policy, a paradigm of football business largely criticized by journalists and unenlightened observers of English society. Indeed, a whole range of decisions, including the construction of private boxes (1964), the creation of a museum (1986), being listed on the stock market (1991), the partnerships with leading global companies and the conquest of the Asian market through tours (2000) constitute the elements of a unique sports institution. The excessive, global media coverage of football and its leading teams feeds into the spectacular accounts.

However, reducing football's extraordinary success solely to economic data is too simplistic. An analysis such as this lacks other highly determinant elements which help one to understand the place of football in British society and the way in which a club establishes itself as an entity larger than sports. To better understand the uniqueness of a club, it is necessary to understand the complexity of the phenomenon through the fields of social history, sociology and sports economics. Rendering a page of contemporary England by using a football club as an analytical guide is the route that we wish to take (Boli, 2004).

This chapter aims to reveal how the creation of a club history became one of the foundations of Manchester United's economic success. The analysis enlarges on the club's history from the late 1950s, with "the Munich air disaster of February 1958," to the recent period, starting with the purchase of the club (2005) by the captain of American industry Malcolm Glazer. Three aspects will be analyzed. First, we will see what are the exemplary brands of a club. Then, we will follow the process of creating the Manchester United myth. Finally, we will highlight how the sports institution established itself as a genuine economic entity.

Box 18.1 A brief history of Manchester United

In 1878, the employees of the railway authority *Newton Heath Lancashire and Yorkshire Railway* founded a local branch dedicated to football. Its beginnings were laborious but the club progressed through adopting professional status (1885) and making notable changes in administration (company formation and the recruitment of a secretary-manager in 1892). Major economic difficulties due to poor results lead to bankruptcy. In 1902, a rich local brewer, famous for his philanthropic inclinations, allowed for the survival of the sports institution. The club changed its name to Manchester United. In the first decade of the 20th century, MU (Manchester United) shined in the league and in the Cup (FA Cup). Their first title was won in 1907, and their first Cup victory 2 years later. The opening of the Old Trafford stadium, a huge stadium of unparalleled modernity, confirmed the ambition of the club. The brilliant performances of players such as Billy Meredith and Charlie Roberts accentuated the club's popularity. In 1920–1930, the economic collapse threatened the club's survival. Once again, the club used a local investor to avoid liquidation. Manchester United narrowly avoided being relegated to the third division. The years 1940–1950 resemble the revival of the *reds*. Under the leadership of the Scottish coach Matt Busby, the club once again found its splendor. In February 1958, the football world was in turmoil. A serious plane crash decimated part of the team. Duncan Edwards and Tommy Taylor, high hopes for English football, were killed returning from a European Cup match. Ten years later, the first victory of an English team in the European Cup of Champion Clubs permitted Manchester United to be "reborn". George Best, Bobby Charlton and Denis Law were the most emblematic of this generation of players. In 1974, the club encountered the humiliation of the second division, then found its vigor in the early 1990s. Since then, Manchester United has generated as much talk for its sporting achievements as for its astonishing economic profits thanks to a commercial policy which has become a benchmark of excellence.

Box 18.2 Manchester United's facts and figures

Name of the co-chairmen: Avram Glazer and Joel Glazer
Number of members: nearly 200,000
Number of fans on Facebook: 60 million (November 2014)
Average number of spectators per game: 75,530 (2013)
Budget of club: 510 million euros
Overall income: 544 million euros
Distribution of revenue: game day (135.8 million euros, 25%), television rights (170 million euros, 31%), sponsoring and licensed maerchandise (237.8 million euros, 44%)
Name of the partners in 2015: Chevrolet, Nike, AON, Abengoa, Aeroflot, Aperol Spritz, Bulovbxula, Bwin, Casillero del Diablo, DHL, Epson, KamaGames, Kansai Paint, Nissin Foods Group, Singha, Swissquote, Toshiba Medical Systems, Yanmar [a]

[a] *Sources:* Manchester United annual report 2015 and other.

Box 18.3 Martin Edwards, chairman of Manchester United, and Maurice Watkins, a lawyer and director of the club in 1991

Martin Edwards:

"In 1991, we wanted to make renovations to the stadium, especially to the Stretford End bleachers. We knew that we had to restore that part of the stadium: Stretford End was not meeting the safety standards, and Trafford City Council told us that we would not get building permits, unless it were for important work. We knew we had to find one way or another, because the amount of work amounted to more than 10 million pounds. And at that time, we did not have this sum of money in the bank. One way to raise money was through the stock quote, because we could get the money from shareholders. The contribution of the shareholders amounted to 6 million of the 10 million pounds. There were other reasons as well and they were much more personal. I was the majority shareholder, but I had no idea of the value of my stocks because there was no market. The stock quote allowed me to measure the financial value of my stocks."[a]

Maurice Watkins:

"I think the quotation was a great help, it raised money to finance improvements to the Stretford bleachers. It also provided a wider range of investors. At its inception, entering the stock exchange enabled Martin Edwards to readjust his financial affairs, particularly the enormous capital invested in the club that he wanted to grow. The listing was the only solution. I think the current solid position of Manchester United is connected to the formation of the Premier League and equally to the introduction of the club in the stock market. This gave a financial strength and credibility which attracted investors to fund major development projects."[b]

[a]Interview with Martin Edwards, October 22, 1999, Old Trafford, Manchester, Office of Directors.
[b]Interview with Maurice Watkins, November 7, 1996, law firm, Boot Street, Manchester.

Manchester United: an exemplary case

Compared to the history of the rise of football in the major cities of London, Birmingham and Glasgow in the 1880s, Manchester was well behind. The popularity of football came relatively late. Locally, the rivalry between Manchester United and Manchester City was based on sporting criteria with extraterritorial dimensions that reoccurred in the 2000s. Here we were far from the religious oppositions which are found between the two Glasgow clubs, the Celtics (Catholic) and the Rangers (Protestant). The representation of the club, and in particular the social engagement, offer a unique look at the club from across the channel. The inclination to sports mingles with the moral obligation for social action.

A city that became the capital of football

Despite the choice of the city as a place for important meetings during the historical phases of the game's institutionalization (formalization of its professional status and the elite champion's league), the interest in football remained low. However, social factors facilitated its implementation. The economic and political position and improvement of living conditions, particularly in the areas of health[1] and transportation, had little impact on the development of professional football. The weight of a large population of male workers and the extraordinary change caused by the railroad, which facilitated the movement of people and therefore matches between different teams, seems somewhat influential. Despite this potential, the city was not shaken by the excitement of football in nearby locations. Insensitivity to football was noticed by the lack of leaders in the groups that institutionalized the game on a national level (*Football Association, Football League*) and also in the group that established and administered football at the regional level, the *Lancashire Football Association*. The low degree of social recognition of football in the eyes of major sports promoters was the cause of a relatively late passion. Sports such as cricket, golf, tennis, rugby and rowing had the support of local leaders, because they were closer to their worldly and elitist vision of sport. Two other elements can be added to this reasoning.

The first element can be explained by the lack of individual holders of cultural and economic capital willing to share the virtues of sports education through the promotion and development of football, as was the case in nearby locations. At Turton FC, near Bolton, the foundation of the club in 1871 resulted from the work of John and Robert Kay, former students of the Harrow public school and members of a prestigious local family. The origin of the Bolton Wanderers in 1874 is linked to the collaboration of Thomas Ogden, a schoolteacher at Chris Church, impressed by the *dribbling game* played by Turton FC, and JF Wright, the vicar of the church Christ Church. The formation of Darwen FC in the late 1870s benefited from the contributions of the Walsh brothers, former students of Harrow and sons of Nathaniel Walsh, a local rich manufacturer. The creation of the Blackburn Rovers in 1874 was also due to the efforts of former public school students, the Marlboroughs. In Manchester, the development of football did not benefit from the contribution of iconic personalities wishing to pass on a football competency inherited from elite institutions.

The second element can be explained by the relative timidity of the sport coming from the little interest given by the sports reporting of the time from eminently valued newspapers. The respectable local daily of the time, *Manchester Guardian*, preferred to open its columns with the *rugby Union* clubs (Rugby 15), rowing or cricket as opposed to reporting on the progress of football. Even when the popular success of football, during the mid-1880s, forced journalists of the *Guardian* to devote a few lines to football, its professionalism was regularly criticized.

It was not until the 1910s where a change occurred in the perception of football in the hierarchy of sports. The success of the two major clubs, Manchester United and Manchester City, in domestic competitions (*FA Cup*, champion's league) imbued the city with the rank of a major football locality. In 1909, Manchester United won its first Cup (FA Cup) in the Crystal Palace stadium in front of 71,000 spectators. The return to their city was a triumph. Thousands of fans flocked to the train station and the Town Hall Square to welcome their heroes. The event was copiously illustrated and reported in the columns of *Manchester Evening News*,[2] representing a historic moment for the city in the same way as the 1857 art exhibition in Manchester, which had a great impact (almost 1.6 million visitors) in the perception of the city as one in a full economic and cultural boom.[3] The greatness of the club helped to strengthen its reputation. In 1910, the construction of the Old Trafford stadium of Manchester United provided more recognition to the city and the club and placed them among the elite. The cost of construction was 60,000 pounds. The architecture was the work of Archibald Leitch, the best stadium designer of the time. The stadium included elements never before seen in a sports locker room: a massage room, a gym, a billiard room and a tea room.[4]

Gradually, football became the dominant sport. However, its elite status was spurred by the exploits of the talented gentlemen of the Lancashire Cricket Club, who built the Old Trafford neighborhood (the stadium site of Manchester United and the pitch for the Lancashire Cricket Club), a historical bastion for England's two most popular sports. The presence of a royal authority for the first time (George V) during the final of the Cup in 1914 provided a wider reputation to football in popular circles.

In the interwar period, the popularity of football did not budge. At Manchester, in 1923, Manchester City moved to Maine Road, a stadium similar to the mythical Wembley (the stadium for the national team). The stadium's capacity is estimated to hold between 80,000 and 90,000 spectators, making it the largest stadium in England. Nationally, the media's fervor for football increased tenfold. In 1926, for the first time, the final of the *Cup* was broadcasted (on tape delay) on the radio. Thousands of Lancashire homes listened in on the match between Manchester City and the Bolton Wanderers. The same year, Billy Meredith, star player of *City,* then *United,* made a notable appearance in *Ball of Fortune*, the first film with a football star. Ten years later (in 1936), the BBC offered excerpts from the league match between Arsenal and Everton. During the years 1940–1950, despite the austerity and extensive damage caused by the war (in 1941, part of the Manchester United Stadium was destroyed by German bombing), football enjoyed unprecedented success. The period was called the Golden Age because of the impressive number of spectators at matches. On December 27, 1949, a record was made. For the day of the championship, there were 1,272,155 spectators. Between 1946 and 1960, Manchester United was the club that hosted the largest number of spectators (45,000 on average) (Boli, 2004, p. 419; Taylor, 2008, p. 192). The loyalty of the spectators was related to the spectacle offered by the team that relied on an offensive and very spectacular gameplay. In 1968, Manchester United won the European Cup of Champion Clubs, allowing the club to belong to the elite of mythical teams, also positioning the city as a place marked by its passion for football. In the mid-2000s, the return of Manchester City to the forefront of the national and European level reinforced the idea of a city where football became a mark of distinction, a product that truly radiates internationally.

United-City: a sports rivalry

For over a century, the rivalry between Manchester United, created in 1902 by a rich local brewer, and Manchester City, which was founded in 1894 and came from a religious institution, is one of the characteristics of large English cities. Like London, where multiple elite teams coexist (Tottenham, Chelsea, Arsenal, West Ham, Crystal Palace, Queens Park Rangers, etc.) or Birmingham (Birmingham City, Aston Villa, West Bromwich Albion, Wolverhampton) Manchester City is marked by matches between the Red Devils and the Blues. An important feature of the passion for football, matches which oppose two local clubs are defined as *derbies*.[5] Beyond the sporting challenge, these meetings reveal both the position of sports at the time and how each club wants to be seen.

If there is a place where it is necessary to have knowledge of the city's social history and of the clubs' historical development, it is also necessary that there are methods of distinction between the different clubs. The now classic blueprint of rivalry based on religious aspirations between the two Glasgow clubs (Glasgow Rangers Protestant/Celtic, Catholic), which has been masterfully studied by Bill Murray,[6] cannot be applied to the case of the two Manchester clubs. Despite the "charm" of this simplification, the rivalry between Manchester

United and Manchester City is not based on a religious separation. The rivalry is primarily sports related. From the first moments of confrontation, conquering the local public became a priority. To achieve this, the clubs had to recruit the best players of the champion's league. In the 1890s, the aura of Manchester City went far beyond that of Newton Heath (ancestor of Manchester United, founded in 1878). The Blues had Billy Meredith, the "Welsh wizard", on their team. The public rushed to admire his technical prowess. At the end of the 1899–1900, 1900–1901 and 1901–1902 seasons, respectively 15,510, 17,135 and 16,825 fans on average attended Manchester City's matches, then in the first division. Meanwhile, Newton Heath, in the second division, attracted on average 6,175, 5,480 and 4,500 spectators for each match.[7] The Blues' strong position was confirmed by its first victory in the Cup in 1904, which was the first victory for a Manchester-based club. To catch up, the chairman of Manchester United, John Henry Davies, upset club organization by recruiting in 1903 James Ernest Mangnall, one of the industry's most famous secretary-managers. One of the decisions that he made was recruiting (very controversially) some of Manchester City's best players, including Billy Meredith. The arrival of these players allowed Manchester United to win prestigious titles (champions in 1908 and 1911, winner of the Cup in 1909). Here began the supremacy of Manchester United. While both clubs were massively followed by local supporters, the performances of Manchester United began to be noticed beyond English borders. In Scotland, and in both Ireland and Northern Ireland, the success of the Red Devils became known. Until the mid-1930s, when Manchester United experienced the humiliation of the second division, Manchester City was seen as the "second club in the city". The league title obtained by Manchester City in 1937 while United finished in second to last place marked the return of the Blues. But it didn't last long. The return of the war sees once again a clear domination of the Reds. The arrival of the young coach Matt Busby (former Manchester City player) profoundly changed the image of Manchester United. He imposed new visions for the club: a training policy, participation in the new European Cup launched by the French newspaper *L'Equipe*, a systematic approach to training, and an appetite for spectacular play. Between 1945 and 1970, Manchester United surpassed its opponents, including Manchester City. The success of the different generations of players trained by Matt Busby fascinated football observers. Domestically, the club won several titles, which included a number of young players trained by the club. Internationally, three of Manchester United's players received the award that recognized the best European player, the *Ballon d'Or* France-Football: Scotland's Denis Law (1964), England's Bobby Charlton (1966) and Ireland's George Best (1968). The drawing power of the club was inevitably changed. This period corresponds to the development of Associations of Supporters based near Manchester, in the UK and also abroad (Malta, Switzerland, Germany, etc.). Competition with City was unparalleled. The map of the branches of supporters clearly revealed the extension of the network of the Reds. No English (or even global) club could boast to have such a vast empire of fans, nationally and internationally. At the beginning of the 1988–1989 season, the club had 63 branches spread across England, Northern Ireland (nine branches), southern Ireland (five branches), Guernsey (one branch) and three foreign countries (Cyprus, Norway, West Germany). At the beginning of the 2002–2003 season, there were 210 branches. The two Irelands, particularly the northern part, was where the greatest number of Manchester United fans could be found (49 groups in total).[8] There, groups of supporters appear to be much larger than those located in Manchester and its suburbs (nine in total). The success of Manchester United in Ireland can be explained by different historical ties between the city and many Irish families.[9] However, the main reason lies in the identification with several glorious players of the club born in the Northern Irish counties of Antrim and Armagh. The successes of Northern players, such as George Best,

Norman Whiteside and Sammy McIlroy, and Southern players, such as Johnny Carey, Johnny Giles, Paul McGrath, Roy Keane and John O'Shea created affinities to the Mancunian club. The incredible expansion of Manchester United fan networks around the world has led casual observers to believe that it was a sign of a club whose membership is more global than local. Thus, some have suggested that Manchester City was the club of local fans and Manchester United is the one of "non-local" fans. This wacky idea was refuted by studies of supporters in the residential areas.[10] Manchester United, before seducing millions of foreign fans, found a special group of supporters in Manchester and throughout the UK.

Since the 2008 arrival of the head of the club, Sheikh Mansour, a wealthy heir from Abu Dhabi, the economic and athletic strength of Manchester City has changed significantly. Now the competition between the two clubs is more competitive. On the field, the Blues distinguish themselves on the transfer market with the signing of Brazilian striker Robinho for a record contract of 32.5 million pounds. In 2012, City won the championship after a 44 year wait. Like the Reds, international policy is actively pursued. The Asian market is covered (with the organizing of tours). Africa is the subject of special attention. The City brand has advertised itself well on the African continent using sport, commercial and charitable projects. This was possible with the support of Patrick Vieira (who was born in Senegal and world champion with France), responsible for the development and the coaching of team U21, and with the help of the Ivorian player Yaya Touré, one of the stars of Man City.

Investing for the common good: The social representation of the club

The desire to remain influential locally is a crucial area that reveals the social visibility of the club. The sports association is in some cases an aid institution and local affiliation to social places like the Working Men's Club and Friendly Societies. The contribution to social works is an aspect in which leaders demonstrate an investment in the community as well as the social position of the club. If there has been a common ground between presidents, it is their commitment to philanthropy. Each of the presidents of Manchester United has found careful ways to involve the club in local areas of concern. The club owes its existence to the generosity of renowned local businessmen, such as the wealthy brewer John Henry Davies and manufacturer James William Gibson. The following presidents had less powerful economic means. Also, their contributions were less personalized. It was through the club that they expressed their interest in relief operations. Whether Harold Hardman, Louis Charles Edwards, Martin Edwards, Peter Kenyon or, more recently, Malcolm Glazer, none of them have moved away from the social dimension of Manchester United. During the presidency of John Henry Davies (1902–1927), his legal provisions and economic affluence allowed the club to be involved in many solidarity activities. Residents of nearby Newton Heath and Old Trafford have benefited from the philanthropic desires of the club which have been initiated by the president. In order to put together funds exclusively devoted to funding charities, friendly matches were organized during the pre-season. The raised funds were then given to various organizations that were sponsored by the club for several years. In the financial statements, there does not appear one year without funding given to charities. The activity represents one of the "normal" expenses for the club. Financial aid constitutes an element of solidarity that is part of the essential and remarkable properties of a club. Schools, specialized homes for adolescents such as youth institutions (Adelphi Lads Clubs), neighboring clubs in financial difficulties (Manchester City), colliers (Wigan Colliery) and local brass band orchestras (St Joseph Industrial Band) have all benefited from the charitable inclinations of the president. Financial contributions have been focused on institutions in which the government policies of the welfare state have not been sufficient enough in improving the conditions of people in economic difficulties. Just as the state, the club has attempted to place itself in situations where it acts as a social representative. Among the costs of annual budgets for various organizations, medical services stand out. They occupy a prominent place. A large part of the sums paid to charity has been for adults' and children's hospitals, along with homes specialized in elderly care. Most institutions have been situated nearby (Newton Heath and Salford). Ancoats Hospital is the place that has received the most funds. An overview of the Minutes Books (records of meeting minutes) is extremely telling. In 1906, when the club was experiencing success on the field, the decision to distribute money to charity raised by charitable games was thus announced:

> It has been decided that the amount of 148 pounds 13 shillings and 6 pence received in friendly matches are to be divided and distributed as follows:
>
> - Ancoats Hospital: 50 pounds
> - Salford Hospital: 25 pounds
> - Rev. J. White: 5 pounds
> - Nurses Home Clayton: 22 pounds 17 shillings and 10 pence
> - Nurses Home Bradford: 22 pounds and 17 shillings
> - Nurses Homes Newton Heath: 22 pounds 17 shillings and 10 pence.[11]

In 1909, the year they won their first Cup, the sum paid to the charities constitutes the fourth-largest source of the club's expenditure totaling 535 pounds 14 shillings and 7 pence. It lags behind the players' salaries, totaling 6,190 pounds and 7 shillings, the signing bonuses, totaling 650 pounds, and travel and other costs, totaling 2,276 pounds 19 shillings and 8 pence. In the 1920s, the cost of charity work continued to play a leading role. Looking at the medical expenses spent on players proving a rather paradoxical situation. The money spent on the medical care of players is far below the money given to charities. During the 1924–1925 and 1925–1926 seasons, the medical expenses were respectively 147 pounds 18 shillings and 3 pence and 214 pounds 16 shillings and pence 10. In comparison, the expenses for subscriptions to charities in the 1924–1925 and the 1925–1926 seasons were respectively 233 pounds 5 shillings and 7 pence and 504 pounds and 8 shillings and 6 pence. In this case, the contributions to charity were apparently more important than the conditions of the players.

In the 1970s, social investment fell under the activities *of Public Relations*. One notices a transformation in the framework of social action. Solidarity operations started to relate to the beginnings of related affinity between the club and local youth or civic projects, including the fight against uncivil behavior in stadiums (hooliganism). To signify interest with the juvenile population, leaders were launching socially prominent actions. They launched an award which honored annually a youth club, developed measures to curb violent behavior at the stadium and finally appointed a public relations expert.

A transition in community action happened in the early 1990s. A diversification of social representation took place. Action for the common good was not restricted to hospital organizations, it occurred in the areas of education, in the economic regeneration of neglected policy areas and in the promotion of football for children and teens (girls and boys). Since 1989, an educational department (installed in the club's museum) has been responsible for informing schools on various social issues. Ruth Hobson, director of the department since its formation, organized its development.

Box 18.4 The education department of Manchester United: a learning values

"When I arrived, I had to do everything. I wrote to the schools, I carried out the program of services that we offer, I was at the cash register. Today (1999) fortunately things have changed. Everything truly changed from 1991 to 1992. We have a team that is built into the structure of a museum. My role is specified because leaders really want the department to be a positive image of the club. The leaders are more aware of the importance of social investment. They want the department involved in several educational projects and especially government initiatives. Today we offer courses to discuss issues of racism, drugs, citizenship, alcoholism, psychological harassment and equal employment opportunities. We are, for example, involved in the campaign against racism, you may have seen the exhibition in the museum devoted to racism. We wanted to link the club with this type of social issue. We also organize workshops where children learn to read, write and count. This is something that is part of the new curriculum requirements [academic program]. Adolescents and adults are not left out here as they can come here and understand how the *business* side of the club functions."

Source: Interview with Ruth Hobson, May 13, 1999, Manchester United Museum, Old Trafford stadium, North Stand.

In the 2000s, the social involvement of the club is maintained, but with noticeably different action modes. The charitable action at the international level was the big news. The people of Manchester were not the only ones to receive assistance from Manchester United. The agreement signed in November 1999 with the global organization dedicated to children, UNICEF, was a decisive step for a charitable activity that goes global. A real changing of the club's image takes place. One sees the intensification of prestigious investments through various significant actions at the local level and representativeness worldwide. In the mid 2000s, the Manchester United Foundation was created. Charitable activities are an essential part of the foundation. During the gala dinner of the 15th anniversary for the partnership between Manchester United and UNICEF, 210,000 books were collected to help needy children. Through associating itself with UNICEF, thereby partnering with a company which has a global reach, Manchester United became an entity which surpassed the norm for sports' clubs.

The invention of myths

One of the attributes of longstanding beliefs about clubs is the ways they endure and also the fact that they are rarely challenged because they are tacitly imposed by management and massively idealized by fans. At Manchester United, the Munich crash in which several young talented players were killed and the style of play epitomized by these flamboyant players have shaped the mythological visions of the club. A range of actions are put in place in order to transform historical elements into true objects of identity for the club identity. The truth is irrelevant: what matters now is how the Munich crash or the players' exploits feed into and perpetuate the United myth.

The tragedy of Munich: building a collective memory

Since February 6, 1958, the club's history has been closely related to the plane crash that occurred in Munich after returning from a European Cup match against Red Star Belgrade. The death of Geoff Bent, Roger Byrne, Eddie Colman, Duncan Edwards, Mark Jones, David Pegg, Tommy Taylor and Billy Whelan can be certainly categorized as the most tragic moment in the history of an English football club after World War II.[12] Various historical reasons may grant the accident a special place in people's memory.

There are conditions in which the leaders and especially coach Matt Busby decided to participate in the competition. It took courage for the coach to break the insular mentality of the leaders of governing bodies, including the Football League. The accident marked the halt of an exceptional generation of young people led by Duncan Edwards and Tommy Taylor. The decline of the England team at international level, especially after the defeat against the modest team from the United States during the 1950 World Cup, and especially the crushing defeat in 1953 against Hungary at Wembley, contributed to the development of the mythologizing of some players by the entire sports community (sports journalists, coaches, managers, players). Duncan Edwards is the player through which the hopes of "all the nation" will remain very high.

The gradual diffusion of television into the homes of thousands of people made the crash more moving because the image was made visible by the debris from the plane and the weather. At any rate, the efforts of the German medical team for the recovery of victims, including Matt Busby, created a sense of sympathy between Germany and England during this Cold War period.

The commemoration procedures for the event constituted a way by which leaders built a space of recognition as well as a space for solidarity between the members of the club. As a result, the Munich accident became a collective mourning, a shared grief, a heritage, a widely respected historical singularity. The tragedy served as a tool for building a collective history, a collective memory. Besides the mythologizing processes of the tragic deaths of some of the Busby Babes exposed in different hagiographic works, the leaders used highly symbolic instruments for marking this historic moment. The terms of creating a collective awareness comes up in public documents (annual reports, match programs, press returns). The private nature unfolds mainly in the *Minute Books*. In these documents that reveal the mental operations of the leaders, we find a series of discussions that focus on ways to honor the deceased and to remember the tragedy for all past and future generations.

Starting from April 1958 the *Munich Memorial* has displayed objects which are related to memories. In a way, this adds to the credibility of leaders as these are concrete actions which are used to convey their sentiments. Several aspects will help to make a visible and poignant tribute. The commemoration should not only memorialize the accident, but also refer to the family and the community, which are important ingredients for the club. To form a highly effective, sensitive remembrance, a set of elements was carefully discussed, among which we note the choice and the material of tribute presentations, the location of memorial sites, disinterest for the sums involved in the work, the concern for maintenance and renewal of tribute presentations, the interest given to certain commemoration dates and people affected directly or indirectly by the accident. In this way, we learn of the initiative taken by the leaders who installed a clock in the stadium, clearly visible to the fans. The defining feature of the clock indicates the time of the accident. Various local personalities (mayors of Manchester and Salford) and foreign personalities (the staff of the Munich hospital) have been invited to the commemorations. To commemorate the 20th anniversary, the leaders unanimously decided to purchase of a new clock that costs 1,350 pounds.

Publicly, the memory of Munich begins with the construction of buildings. The memory is visible surrounding the Old Trafford stadium. February 25, 1960, witnessed the inauguration of the Munich Memorial Plaque and the Munich Clock. The two objects of commemoration are located outside the grandstand. A plaque lists the names of the deceased (secretaries, assistants, coaches and players). The clock displays the month, day and year of the accident. In order to maintain the memory, a museum has been constructed in which the memory of Munich occupies an important place.

Box 18.5 The Manchester Museum: the location of the link

The museum project was initiated in 1984. It is Denzel Haroun, one of the former directors of the club (23 years in the Steering Committee), who thought of the idea of an exhibition space. The design came to him as a result of trips to Real Madrid and Benfica Lisbon museums. He hoped that the place would be dedicated to the attachment that supporters feel towards the club as well as a space to display the grandeur of the Reds. In 1986, the museum space, which occupied 500 m^2 was inaugurated at the entrance of one of the Old Trafford stands. A large part commemorates the memory of Munich. One section is devoted to the Busby Babes, the players who were trained at the club and supervised by coach Matt Busby. Their achievements in youth tournaments and later in the championship are fully narrated and commented on by the fans, who have the privilege to speak. Pictures of the sadness of Matt Busby and Bobby Charlton after the tragedy of February 1958 and the tears of joy after the title of European Champion in May 1968 are explained as a sign of good fortune, of divine justice and club reborn. Many objects recalling the accident are carefully preserved and maintained as significant pieces of the overall memory of the club. The museum is the place of Manchester United's mythological construction, the true location of the link connecting all fans. In 1998, inaugurated by Pelé, the new ultra-modern museum, on three levels, reinforces the memory of Munich with a new set design where the photographic documents are complemented by audiovisuals. The emotional experience is exceptional.

Flamboyant football: the mark of a style of play

During the legendary construction of the club, the coaches and performance of players guarantee discourse shaped by all of the stakeholders (fans, managers, coaches, players). The Scottish coaches, Glasgow native Matt Busby and Alex Ferguson are seen as the architects of this style of play by Manchester United.

From his early years at the club, Busby took the option of building an attack-minded team. He forged a style different than that of his predecessors. His playing philosophy is based on the animation of an offensive game. The success was immediate. The public was enthused by the game played by the Reds. Manchester United attracted thousands of fans who were seduced by the prowess of Charlie Mitten, Tommy Lawton, Denis Law, Bobby Charlton and George Best. The press created the image of a model team capable of ensuring British "superiority" in the international arena. Beaten by Arsenal in 1930, Manchester United became the gold standard for gauging tactical progress of English teams. The success of the Busby method was strengthened by the excellent results at the national and European level. In the 1950s, the backbone of the national team consisted of players from Manchester United. Busby's teams were illustrated by a ferocious appetite for panache football. During the 1950s, the 100-goal bar was reached 4 times. United fascinates all of Europe in the 1960s. The foreign press, as well as the French press, was very impressed by the technical ease and "latin" qualities of George Best and Denis Law. For many observers, the mention of Manchester United is synonymous with beautiful play.

The tradition of offensive play is also accorded to Alex Ferguson. The team he led in the 1990s was seen as an offshoot of Busby style. The prowess of Eric Cantona, Ryan Giggs or Wayne Rooney was matched with the legendary players of yesteryear: Meredith, Law and Best. In the opinion of many United fans, the attacking game, spectacular and eccentric, constitutes the club's DNA. The figures support the facts. During the 5 years with Eric Cantona (1992–1997), the attacking line was very prolific, scoring nearly 65 goals on average. The matches where they won the titles Champion of England and the Cup were broadcast worldwide, with the powerful international channels (BSkyB, Canal +), allowing Manchester United to reach a large audience and above all to delight viewers with their tradition of spectacular play.

Box 18.6 Being a Manchester United player: transmitting a legacy

"Our philosophy here is to maintain the tradition of the club. Tradition is the style of play. You know, attacking is the club's tradition, and our role is to teach it to young people between 9 and 16 years old. It is important to start early so that we can clearly communicate what we expect from them. Football is still a game at 9 years old. For us it is important to have the idea to play, to have fun. Going on the field for pleasure, for fun, is a great way to really enjoy football. It has always been like that here. At any level, you'll see we're playing for fun, the attack, the satisfaction of the audience. . . . The link between the old and young is something we want to preserve. For example, the last time we went to Zurich for the Tournament Blue Star, I said that everything started in Zurich in 1954, what was later called the Busby Babes made themselves known in the tournament where you are. You are the heirs of this generation, this is the history of the club and you are a part of it now. Do justice to the club, because you represent both its image and its history."

Source: Interview with Paul McGuinness, May 18, 1999, at the Cliff, Salford, training center of Manchester United. Inside the club, coaches have become proselytes of the offensive mission. A survey among the assistants of Alex Ferguson looks deep into the story of the mission of transmitting to younger generations the club's identity. The testimony of Paul McGuinness, son of a player from the Busby generation, a former player who was unable to become professional and today is responsible for youth teams, offers us a glimpse into sports policy as well as the mission to perpetuate the offensive tradition.

A club, a business

If there is one area where Manchester United calls attention, it is its sporting and economic stature. For 20 years, the media spotlight has focused on the English club for the way its leaders have so far managed to find a balance between sporting and economic aspirations. Three aspects were important to become a major club: the place given to sporting achievements, the marketing policy and the changes caused by the arrival of Malcolm Glazer to the head of the club.

Improving their record and increasing their capital

The entrepreneurial ambition does not concern itself with the sports ambitions of Manchester United. Just consider the conditions under which the club decided to be listed on the stock exchange in 1991.

Besides personal circumstances, the entrance onto the stock market was a way to establish the club as one of the greatest European teams. The capital was used to renovate the stadium and buy expensive players. That's exactly what took place. Alex Ferguson, under the watchful eye of shareholders, worked to improve the club's record by buying talented players. Manchester United was actively involved on the transfer market by buying more players at record prices. In 1995, the promising English center forward Andy Cole left FC Newcastle for 7 million pounds. In the early 2000s, recruitment abroad became a necessity. In 2001, the Argentine midfielder Veron from Lazio was recruited for 28.1 million pounds. A year later, the defense was strengthened. In 2002, the elegant central defender Rio Ferdinand from Leeds United joined Manchester United for 29.3 million pounds. Two years later, the young hope for English football, Wayne Rooney, was transferred to United for 27 million pounds. To ensure the smooth running of sports and economic performance, a compromise, not without its tensions, was put into place. Manchester United PLC was created and charged with handling economic expansion and economic issues related to the Manchester United Football Club, whose coach Alex Ferguson acted as guarantor and assured the sporting vitality. David Gill,[13] one of the historical managers arrived at the club in 2003, clearly addresses the issue: "the heart of the club's success is on the field, but we must also ensure the sustainability of the club by extreme attention to economic management." Between 1991 and 2005 (the end of the stock exchange listing), Manchester United adopted a phenomenal record with eight league titles in England, four Cup wins and one Champions League trophy, the most prestigious on the European stage. Many players received major trophies which thereby reinforced the aura of the club. Six Manchester United players received the trophy for best player of the championship (PFA award). In 1996, Eric Cantona became the first player of the "market era" to be voted best player by the association of football journalists (the Football Writers' Association).

Commercial policy: loyalty and commitment

The commercial inclination dates back to 1960. It is around the values of loyalty and commitment to the club where the beginnings of commercialization began. The reconstruction of the stadium which was partially damaged by the German air force bombings of 1941 and the will to rebuild a competitive team after the tragic death of players in 1958 forced the directors to think of ways to fill the coffers. In May 1961, the leaders launched MUDA (Manchester United Development Association). The goal of the association was to raise funds to finance sports projects (recruiting players) and projects outside of sports (the layout of the stadium, the acquisition of space to train). The originality of MUDA is reflected by the involvement of fans. The sustainability of the organization was in the hands of the fans, because they are responsible for selling lottery tickets starting with those close to them. Manchester United Development Association became a success. In 1965, the lottery reported 34,823 pounds while the revenue gained from ticket sales was 22,837 pounds. Monies obtained allowed for renovations to begin at the stadium, including dilapidated seating (Stretford End). Wealthy fans were not forgotten. In September 1965, private boxes were inaugurated. The boxes came as of a result of the administrators' prestigious ambition. Inside there is a phone, a TV, a bar, a central heating system and a place to eat with hostesses. Gradually, sporting achievements and the charisma of iconic players (Denis Law, George Best) consolidated the success of mercantile activities. A series of commercial strategies were adopted to grow the attachment to the fan club. A souvenir shop was opened in 1967. There are products that enhance the identification to a player or glorify a specific period. The year 1973 was marked by the creation of Manchester United Commercial Department, a department dedicated to commercial activities. Reception service and restaurant building were important concerns. In 1985, *Manchester United Basketball* is founded. Inside *United Review*, the official journal published at every match, football fans were urged to go encourage basketball. To educate fans, managers brought up the loyalty and grandeur of Manchester United as a supporting argument. The 1990s saw a dramatic change. Men recruited for their expertise in marketing greatly contributed to the economic growth. With them, retention strategies experienced profound change. The entrance onto the stock market in 1991 and the organizational transformation that this caused constituted a decisive moment. The new directions taken by the football federation to improve the image of the game nationally (formation of a new champions' league named the Premier League, renovation of stadiums, the fight against hooliganism, negotiation of TV rights) and international (organization of candidacy high profile competitions) were in favor of Manchester United. The commercial exploitation of the sporting success in which the supporter holds a prominent place became a priority for the administrators of the Red Devils. Perceptions of the supporter changed radically. They are perceived as an actor within the organization's sporting and economic power. The leaders' ambition within the economic sectors was conveyed perfectly by the words of Edward Freedman, the first director of the merchandising department: "Convert the Manchester United fans into real customers."[14] Several methods have been used to animate affiliate membership to the club, regardless of where the support is coming from.

In 1992, the first edition of the *Manchester United Magazine* (renamed *Inside United* in 2001) is released. Its uniqueness is the fact that it is sold in more than 25 countries, as well as translated into Norwegian, Thai and Cantonese for loyal fans installed near Manchester. Today, from an economic point of view, the monthly sports magazine has the biggest draw (more than 300,000 copies) and is also the best-selling inside the UK. Inside, you will discover all of the internal news of the club. The Australian fan can read, for example, an interview with a new player, the story of a memorable match told by a former player, the record of the summer tour that took place in his country or the impressions of Hong Kong fans loyal to Manchester United who gathered during one of the 1-day meetings for official supporters' associations. For leaders, the magazine is an official showcase of the club. For some fans, the monthly issue is an excellent way to get closer to Manchester United, discovering aspects such as of the life of a player, which is showcased very often, the story of his commitment to Manchester United. The year 1998 witnesses an acceleration of affiliate products. Manchester United International Ltd, the department in charge of external relations, including the club's international standing, is founded, and in return for the strong support of the Scandinavian supporters, leaders appoint Angel Kourentis, a Norwegian native, as the head of the organization. Since 1981, this is where all the branches of fans of Scandinavian countries have been centralized. This is the country that has closely followed the news of English football ever since the first matches of the Premier League were broadcast on the cable channel BSkyB. The successes of the old players Ronny Johnsen, Henning Berg and especially the formidable center-forward Ole Gunnar Solskjær strengthened the links between the club and the community of Manchester United fans in Norway. The launch of MUTV (Manchester United Television), in collaboration with the cable channel BSkyB, accentuated global visibility. The club features powerful media exclusives for the strengthening of mythic beliefs about its history or legendary players. The avid Manchester fan will find connections within the different programs that links them back to the club. A range of shows entertains the appetite of every fan.

Box 18.7 Evolution of business activities, 1961–2014

1961: Creation of the Manchester United Development Association whose main activity is the organization of a football lottery
1964: Construction of private boxes
1967: Opening of a souvenir shop in Old Trafford
1968: The club patents its brand, "Manchester United"
1975: Installation of billboards around the stadium. Contract with the English *Admiral*
1982: Sponsorship contract with the Japanese electronics firm, *Sharp*
1985: Manchester United Basketball. Project of a sports club. Agreement with Delta Sport, the company responsible for finding companies willing to sponsor a home game
1986: Inauguration of the museum (the first English club to do so)
1988: Launch of a sales catalog of licensed products
1991: Entrance onto the stock market
1992: Launch of monthly *Manchester United Magazine*
1994: Launch of Manchester United Radio
1995: For the first time in the economic history of the club, the matches of revenue underperformed another business activity: merchandising
1996: Creation of a website
1997: Contract with HSBC Midland, which is strongly established in Asia. Opening a coffee shop in the North Stand, Red Café
1998: Opening of the new museum whose costs reached 4 million pounds. Launch of a TV channel, Manchester United Television (MUTV). Announcement of the Old Trafford stadium carrying a capacity of 67,400 spectators
2000: Opening of three megastores: Old Trafford, 17,500 m^2, Singapore, 17,000 m^2, and Dublin, 15,000 m^2. Thirteen-year contract with Nike US equipment for the sum of 302.9 million pounds
2001: Partnership with the American baseball team New York Yankees. Tour in Southeast Asia (Malaysia, Thailand)
2005: Malcolm Glazer buys the club for €1.04 billion
2014: Record sponsorship contract signed with General Motors: €423 million (for the period of 2014–2021). Record sponsorship contract signed with Adidas: €942 million (for the period of 2015–2025)[a]

[a] Manchester United Annual Report and others.

The Glazer family: a new era

In 2005, the American Malcolm Glazer bought Manchester United for the sum of 1.04 billion euros and became the owner of one of the most lucrative sports institutions. After having bought the Tampa Bay Buccaneers, the famous American football team, Manchester United was bought by Malcolm Glazer who considered the club "as being the most popular in the world". In his first speech to address made to calm the concerns of supporters who feared that the club was turning into a "machine to make money", Glazer announced that the sports sector will remain unchanged, "at the head of the sports sector remains the knighted coach Sir Alex Ferguson. I have too much respect for his work to ever intrude on his work." Until his death in May 2014, the majority owner of Manchester United was never involved in sports business. However, he imposed a profound *turnover* in the policy committee by placing his son on its board composed of 12 renowned finance experts. The continued funding of the Manchester United label maintained itself through its entrance onto the New York Stock Exchange (Wall Street) in August 2012. The arrival of Glazer, while it fundamentally changed the structural direction, had no impact on the operations of coach Sir Alex Ferguson. He continued, until his retirement in 2013, to exercise his influence on the recruitment of expensive players into the sport organization (sustainability of a training policy, extension of overseas recruitment system, staff recruitment).

Manchester United continues to belong to the elite of the richest clubs even if it is second to Real Madrid who occupies the top spot. In 2007, 2008 and 2009, dizzyingly high annual revenues provided a state of good health for the English club: 315.2 million euros, 324.8 million euros and 327 million euros.[15]

In 2014, the directors of Manchester United proudly presented to the press a record breaking annual revenue of 544 million euros (433.2 million pounds), up 19% compared to the previous record. The main source of income came from the business sector, including sponsorship and merchandising, which reported up to 237.8 million euros (189.3 million pounds). The second source of income concerned television rights, which reported 170.6 million euros (135.8 million pounds), up 33.7%: this is partly due to the new contract rights of the Premier League. Finally, the money from game days (tickets, beverages, foods, programs) will make French clubs jealous as they reported 135.8 million euros (108.1 million pounds).[16] The club continues to attract multinationals. The year 2014 was successful. Manchester United signed extremely lucrative long-term contracts. The Chevrolet brand, which is part of General Motors automotive, will spend 559 Million US $ to be the sponsor of the club over the 2014–2021 period and the German supplier Adidas will pay 942 million euros over the period 2015–2025. These are two world records in the sphere of football business.

Since the 1960s, sports results have contributed to the tremendous development of Manchester United. In the 1990s, the club has also taken advantage of the windfall offered by television. The latter has at the same time allowed the club's matches to have international visibility. The leaders have understood the need to look attractive by developing business strategies incorporating the phenomenon of globalization. Manchester United then became an institution whose reputation continues to grow. Since the departure of the legendary coach Sir Alex Ferguson in 2013, the club underwent a relatively inglorious period (lack of participation in the Champions League, no major titles, declining when compared to Manchester City). However, the appeal of Manchester United is still very strong. According to the famous American business magazine *Forbes*, in 2015, the club was one of the top 3 franchises, with an estimated street value of 3.1 billion. Many multinational companies are trying to get closer to Manchester United, who became a real brand. But Manchester United shows that a football club retains some peculiarities, such as a social function, as well as a modern way to do business and the legacy of the past.

Notes

1 Between 1850 and 1900, advances in health are noticed by a reduction in mortality rates from infectious diseases, which guarantees a population potentially able to play football. A. Kidd, *Manchester*, Staffordshire, Keele University Press, 1996, p. 126.

2 Daily Sketch, April 26, 1909; *Manchester Evening News*, April 27, 1909.

3 D. Milliar, "Royal Patronage and Influence", in J.M. Mackenzie (ed.), *The Victorian Vision: Inventing New Britain*, Londres, Victorian and Albert Publications, 2001, p. 43.

4 S. Inglis, *Football Grounds of Britain*, Londres, CollinsWillow, 1996, p. 235.
5 The term "derby" comes from a game played in the city of Derby, between All Saints and St Peter's.
6 B. Murray, *The Old Firm: Sectarianism, Sport and Society in Scotland*, Edinburg, John Donald, 1984.
7 B. Tabner, *Through the Turnstiles*, Harefield, Yore Publication, 1992, pp. 66–67.
8 In 2015, there are 46 Official Manchester United Supporters' Clubs.
9 F. Engels, *La situation de la classe laborieuse en Angleterre*, Paris, Éditions Sociales, 1975, pp. 134–138; Manchester residents' broad country of birth in 2011 compared to the national average, Manchester City Council.
10 The Premier League National Fan Survey. Summary Report 2007–2008 season.
11 *Manchester United Minute Books*, November 6, 1906, p. 25.
12 R. Holt et T. Mason, *Sport in Britain, 1945–2000*, Oxford, Blackwell, 2000, p. 99; P. Howlett, "The 'Golden Age', 1955–1973", in P. Johnson (ed.), *Twentieth Century Britain: Economic, Social and Cultural Change*, Londres, Longman, 1994, pp. 320–339.
13 Interview with David Gill, on November 15, 1999, at the Old Trafford stadium, finance department.
14 Interview with Edward Freedman, on Novembre 20, 1996, Old Trafford stadium, merchandising department.
15 Manchester United Annual Report 2008 and 2010.
16 Manchester United Annual Report 2014, p. 2.

Bibliography

Boli C., *Manchester United, l'invention d'un club. Deux siècles de métamorphoses*, Paris, La Martinière, 2004.

Boli C., "Convertir les supporters en fidèles consommateurs: une politique commerciale à Manchester United", *Communication et Organisation*, n° 27, juin 2005, pp. 73–84.

Boli C., "Manchester United: un empire mondial", *Place publique*, n° 28, juillet-août 2011, pp. 23–26.

Brown A. (ed.), *Fanatics! Power, identity and fandom in football*, Londres, Routledge, 1998.

Cox R., Russel D. et Vamplew W. (eds.), *Encyclopedia of British football*, Londres, Frank Cass, 2002.

Dietschy P., *Histoire du football*, Paris, Perrin, 2010.

Drut B., *Économie du football professionnel*, Paris, La Découverte, 2013.

Gillon P., Grosjean F. et Ravenel L. (eds.), *Atlas mondial du sport mondial*, Paris, Autrement, 2010.

Polley M., *Moving the Goalpost: A history of sport and society since 1945*, Londres, Routledge, 1998.

Questions internationals, n° 44, juillet-août 2010.

Taylor M., *The leaguers: The making of professional football in England, 1900–1939*, Liverpool University Press, Liverpool, UK, 2005.

Taylor M., *The association game: A history of British football*, Harlow, Pearson Education Ltd, 2008.

Thane P., *Twentieth century Britain*, Londres, Cassell, 2001.

Williams J., *Is it all over? Can football survive the Premier League*, Reading, UK, South Press, 1999.

19

PROFESSIONAL FOOTBALL IN CHINA

Retrospect and prospect

Dongfeng Liu

Professionalization of Chinese football: a brief history

Professional sport in China has a relatively short history. Up until the mid-1990s, sport in China remained the prerogative of the government. China was and still is one of the countries that have a ministry-level government department (National Sports Commission or NSC before 1998 and General Administration of Sports or GAS thereafter) that is solely responsible for sport affairs ranging from elite sports to sports for all to sport business regulation and promotion. But the priority has long been on elite sports supported by a state-sponsored high performance sport administration system widely known as "Ju Guo Ti Zhi" in Chinese referring to a centralized system by mobilizing nation-wide resources available in the country. In practice, with a unique system of selecting and training elite athletes supported by a government administration and financial system at its center, this "Ju Guo Ti Zhi" enables China to amass nation-wide resources available to develop its elite sport, with the ultimate goal of winning medals at international competitions, especially at the Olympics, to serve national pride. It was a system modeled after the former Soviet Union, with government playing a dominant role and contributing and controlling most of the resources, and obviously a legacy of the old planned economy. One example of this government domination is the governing system of specific sports. Most of the sports have a national governing body called sports associations as required by their respective international governing bodies, such as Chinese Football Association in the case of football, but in reality, all these associations were only organizations in name without any actual organization with office and full-time staff: they were all governed directly by the NSC.

The situation began to change slowly as the macro-political-economic environment evolved. The year of 1992 marks a decisive year as the Communist Party of China decided to continue with its reform and opening up policy at its 14th National Congress and made it clear that the goal of China's economic reform is to establish a socialist market economy after the late paramount state leader Mr. Deng Xiaoping's inspection tour to South China making remarks of further reform. This means the direction toward a transformation from a planned economy to a market-based economy with the private sector playing an increasingly more important role in national economy. Against this backdrop, the National Sports Commission (NSC), the ministry-level government department responsible for sports in China, started to explore the reform of sport administration and development. Socialization, commercialization and professionalization were some of the major themes put forward by the NSC, meaning the society and private sector vis-à-vis government should play a more important role in terms of supply of sport products and services (Liu, 2008). In June 1992, at the National Football Conference, as a flagship of the sport reform, it was decided by the NSC that the Chinese Football Association (CFA) should become a real governing body of football with office and professional staff, and professional clubs and leagues should be established (Liu, 2008).

Since 1994, as part of the sports governance structure reform, management centers of sports were established one after another for sports governance. Each management center would be an organization responsible for one or more sports governance and share the office with the national associations of the respective sports, called "one office, two organizations" in the media. In the case of football, the Chinese Football Management Center shares the office with Chinese Football Association, but the staff members for the two organizations are essentially the same group of people. While the Chinese Football Management Center operates on behalf of the government as a public body, the Chinese Football Association is supposed to be the non-governmental national governing body as required by FIFA. According to the authorities, this was said to be a stepping stone before these national sports associations become truly non-governmental sports governing bodies running on their own in the end (Liu, 2008).

On April 17, 1994, the first national professional football league was formally launched, with the top flight Series A League consisting of 12 clubs and second tier Series B consisting of 11 clubs. The league was an immediate hit welcomed by the society and football fans, and average attendance rose quickly to 24,300 in 1996, from 16,300 in 1994 (see Figure 19.1).

Despite the initial rapid growth, however, the new financial stakes in football generated far-reaching corruption and problems: match fixing, illegal betting and the bribing of players or referees to influence the results of competitions (so-called Black Whistles scandal) quickly tarnished the image of the championship. According to Xinhua, the crackdown on corruption – which began in 2009 – saw 58 current and former football officials, players and referees indicted for match-fixing and bribery, and Shanghai Shenhua was stripped of its 2003 league title (Guardian, Feb. 20, 2013). Both the level and reputation of professional soccer in China reached a new

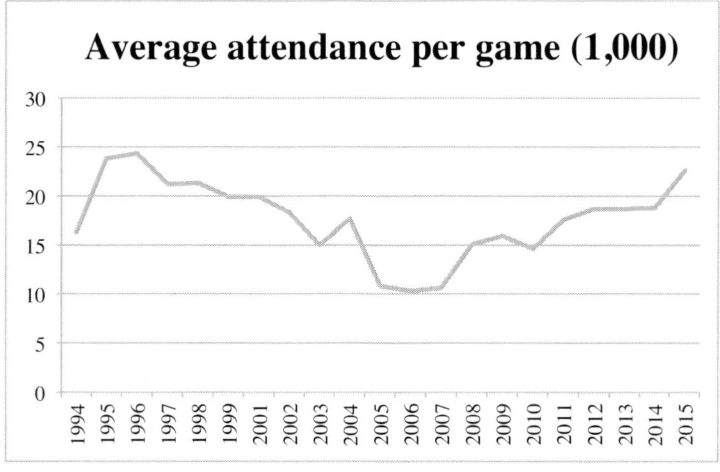

Figure 19.1 Attendance per game for Chinese top flight football (1994–2015)

Source: Edited based on figures released from Chinese Football Association.

low. At its worst, in 2005, only 1 year after the top flight of Chinese football league changed to its current new title "Chinese Super League" from "Chinese Serie A League", the average game attendance reached a record low of 10,000, down by almost 60% from 24,300 in its heyday in 1996 (see Figure 19.1). And what's worse, the league went without a major sponsor after its title sponsor Siemens withdrew its sponsorship due to lack of confidence, which was mocked by the media and fans as "naked running" (South Urban Weekly, Nov. 27, 2005). Corruption with Chinese professional basketball seems less severe than football; but its quality and popularity has also remained limited. Disappointed by the domestic leagues, both Chinese fans and businesses sponsors would then turn to international sports leagues or properties such as European football leagues or FIFA World Cups. China's NYSE-listed Yingli Green Energy Holdings became the first Chinese firm in 2007 sponsoring a Spanish La Liga team, Club Atlético Osasuna, before it became the first Chinese Global Sponsor of the 2010 FIFA World Cup South Africa and the 2014 FIFA World Cup Brazil (Zhang, 2014).

A major challenge regarding sport development in general and professional sport in particular has a lot to do with the centralized governmental sport administration system. Modeled on the former Soviet Union, one of the most fundamental functions of this centralized governing system is to win as many Olympic medals as possible to serve the national prestige, and anything else becomes secondary. Essentially, the Chinese sport governing system for elite sport consists of three sub systems: a highly centralized administrative system (providing governing, funding and supporting), a professional training system, and a sports events organizing system centering around the National Games every 4 years. As a result, all sport governing bodies in China, such as the China Football Association, are all considered quasi-governmental organizations, and actually some 70 national sports associations exist in parallel with 23 sport management centers (governmental departments) controlled and managed by the same group of people. In addition, most athletes trained at the provincial level or national teams are treated as full-time employees with the government. In other words, while a market economy has been largely established in China ever since early 1990s, sport remained in a government-controlled and government-planned system. As a result, the conflict between this planned system and a market based professional and commercial sport is unavoidable. The corruption mentioned above also has a lot to do with this centralized system with little transparency but involving millions of dollars of market potential. It is actually believed that this centralized governing system itself has become one of the major obstacles that should be deregulated and reformed to release the huge market potential of sport industry in China (Liu, 2008).

Despite these problems and challenges mentioned above, based on the figures released by the General Administration of Sport, sport business in China has been growing really fast over the past decade at an annual rate of around 18%, much faster than the growth of the national economy, which is just below 10%. In addition, though sport economy in China is still dominated by sporting goods manufacturing, the structure is improving with the sport service sector now accounting for around 23% of the total sports economy, up from 17% 10 years ago in 2006. Thanks to a growing economy, urbanization and lifestyle change, sports consumption in China is gathering momentum.

Top-down reform in sport and soccer in China and response from the society: the latest development

On October 20, 2014, as part of its agenda for boosting employment, domestic consumption and other areas of the Chinese economy, which is slowing down to 7%–8% percent from the double-digit growth of the previous 2 to 3 decades, China's Cabinet, the State Council, issued a national strategic policy document regarding sport industry targeting the year of 2025 titled "Guidelines on Promotion of Sport Industry and Sport Consumption by State Council" (Guidelines No. 46 of 2014 by State Council, the Guidelines hereafter.) to enhance the country's fast-growing sports industry. The Guidelines marked a milestone in the development of sport business, and their significance was widely applauded by the society and industry in China. This marked the first time that sport industry was singled out by the State Council, China's Cabinet, as a new growth point of the economy with great business potential, and promotion of sport participation was upgraded as a national strategy. Some of the ambitious targets by 2025 set by the Guidelines include, but are not limited to:

- To promote national health and fitness through various sports to see more than 500 million citizens regularly participating in sports and physical activities;
- To generate a gross output of sport industry worth RMB 5 trillion (equivalent to approximately USD 815 billion) per annum; and
- To create an average area of sports grounds in the country that is over 2 square meters per capita.

In addition, the Guidelines also stood out by some of the concrete measures that would be adopted by the government. Actually it has been widely expected that the Guidelines would also mark the beginning of deregulation of the tight control over sport development and resources by the government, and thus the market or private sector would play a leading role in meeting the growing demand for sport products and services.

In less than half a year after the publication of the Guidelines, there came another high profile strategic plan, that is, "The Overall Reform Plan to Boost the Development of Soccer in China" (the Soccer Reform Plan, hereafter), issued on March 16, 2015. The Soccer Reform Plan, involving reform of almost every aspect of the sport, including the professional clubs, leagues, the national teams, youth and grassroots soccer, was approved by China's central reform group, chaired by President Xi Jinping, and issued by the State Council. Some of the highlights of this Soccer Reform Plan include (The State Council, 2015):

- China Football Association should be delinked from its existing affiliation to General Administration of Sport of China and work as a real non-governmental organization; the Association will have no administrative ranks, and thus the management team of the Association will not have any official ranks anymore and cease to be considered governmental officials as they used to be.
- More revenues from sports lottery will be invested in the development of football in the future.
- The total number of elementary and middle schools featuring soccer will increase from the current figure of around 5,000 to 20,000 in 2020 and 50,000 in 2025.
- The long-term goals include bidding for the FIFA World Cup and bringing the national team to the top level of the world.

The significance of this Soccer Reform Plan could not be overstated: it not only shows the determination of the government's will to develop soccer in China, as it comes from the highest level of China's government and endorsed by the most paramount political figure in China, but it is also expected that the reform of soccer will serve as a pilot for other sports in China and thus mark the first concrete steps toward deregulation and further commercialization and professionalization of sports in general.

In spite of widespread suspicion, changes do seem to be happening. On February 24, 2016, within 1 year after the Soccer Reform Plan was issued, as a milestone in the reform of Chinese sport and football, China's Management Center for Football was dissolved, and China's Football Association was announced to be formally detached from the government (i.e. China Generational Administration of Sport). It is expected that the newly restructured football governing body would enjoy much greater autonomy if not independence from government control.

The Soccer Reform Plan has also been supplemented by a series of follow-up policies. In the latest, Mid- to Long-Term Plan for Chinese Soccer Development (2016–2050) (the Soccer Development Plan hereafter), a 35-year soccer development blueprint setting out short, mid and long-term objectives, was unveiled on April 6, 2016, by the National Development and Reform Commission, China's top planning body, through a joint committee of the State General Administration of Sports, the Chinese Football Association and the Ministry of Education. It has set an ambitious goal to become a dominant soccer power in Asia by 2030 and "top class soccer nation" by 2050. The Soccer Development Plan stood out with not only a clear timeline and quantifiable goals, but also many concrete measures addressing some of the bottlenecks of football development. Some of the highlights were as follows (Sun, 2016):

1. **Some of the major short-term (2016–2020) targets and measures include**

- School system: Increasing the number of schools specializing in soccer education from 8,000 to 20,000; encouraging more than 30 million primary and secondary students to practice soccer regularly; and have 5,000 school soccer trainers.
- Social participation: Establishing a three-tier amateur competition system that includes grassroots club teams in 100 cities involving more than 50 million participants.
- Fields: Build 70,000 soccer fields through refurbishment, transformation and new construction to offer at least a half field for every 10,000 participants on average.
- Club: Developing two to three Chinese professional clubs; dominating Asian and well-known leagues in the world. All while expanding the appeal of China's top professional league worldwide.

2. **Major long-term goals (2020–2050) highlighted in the plan**

- Maintaining diverse investments in all aspects of the game to involve more participants while offering at least one full field for every 10,000 participants.
- Boosting soccer-related businesses into a driving force for the sports economy.
- Developing the men's national team into a super power in Asia while driving the women's squad to a world elite group.
- Transforming the country into a world soccer powerhouse, while contributing greatly to the game's international growth and realizing the "soccer dream" for the entire nation.

Response from the society and private sectors

The above-mentioned policies launched from the central government have been well received and applauded in China, with positive reaction from the society and industry, and have significantly raised the profile of sport business and put it into the spotlight in China. The most important and immediate impact of these policy documents can be seen from the unprecedented huge investment into sport industry in general and soccer business, in particular from the private sectors involving some of the richest businessmen in China (see Table 19.1). It is reported that Chinese mergers and acquisitions in domestic and overseas sports markets have seen exponential growth

Table 19.1 High profile soccer deals by Chinese investors

Date	*Sport Property*	*Contract Value (USD)*	*Buyer*	*Owner of the Buying Company*
Jan. 2015	20% of Spanish soccer team Club Atletico de Madrid	52 million	Wanda Group	Wang Jianlin
Mar. 2016	FIFA Partner (up to 2030)	N/A	Wanda Group	Wang Jianlin
June 2014	50% of Guangzhou Evergrande FC	192 million	Alibaba Group	Jack Ma
Dec. 2015	8-year Presenting Partnership of Club World Cup	N/A	Alibaba Group	Jack Ma
Nov. 2015	100% of Jiangsu Football Club	80 million	Suning Group	Zhang Jindong
Oct. 2015	5-year (2016–2020) broadcasting rights of China's Super Football League	1.25 billion	Ti'ao Dongli	Li Ruigang
June 2016	70% club Inter Milan	307 million	Suning Group	Zhang Jindong

Source: based on news releases from major newspaper or Chinese websites such as China Daily, www.sina.com, www.sohu.com

since 2015, when it spent almost 40 billion yuan (around US$5.99 billion) in total investments, with 33 deals valuing over 10 million yuan (around US$1.50 million) (Guo, 2016). In 2015 alone, Wang Jianlin, the real estate tycoon topping China's rich list for years, made at least three major investments in sport business, buying sport properties of close to US$2 billion (see Table 19.1). What is particularly noteworthy is the growing interest in overseas professional soccer clubs from Chinese investors. In June 2016, China's retail giant Suning Holdings Group agreed to pay €270 million (US$307 million) for a 70% stake in Italian soccer club Inter Milan, and Chinese investors also now own Aston Villa, with the purchase price of US$87 million, a 20% portion of Atletico Madrid, and a 13% share of Manchester City (Ogus, 2016). The massive crackdown on corruption in football also helped to clean the sport and restore the image and credibility of the game, and fans are now coming back to the stadium to enjoy the game with stronger competition and better quality, partly thanks to the new investment drawn into the league. In 2015, CSL achieved an average live audience of 23,000 per game, a record high in almost 20 years, which is also the highest among all the Asian football leagues (CCTV, 2015). In October 2015, the Chinese top-flight soccer league sold its 5-year (2016–2020) broadcasting rights for a jaw-dropping record of 8 billion yuan (about US$1.25 billion) with an average of 1.6 billion per season, 26 times higher than the previous 2015 season with an amount of only 60 million yuan. The clubs in the top flight are now also spending huge sums of money buying big-name footballers from the international market. Jiangsu Suning spent a record high of €50 million to sign Shakhtar Donetsk forward Brazilian midfielder Alex Teixeira on February 5, 2016. But the record didn't last long and in less than half a year in July, Shanghai SIPG club signed Brazilian forward Hulk from Zenit St Petersburg for an Asia transfer-record €55.8 million (US$61.92 million), plus possible bonuses if he plays well in China. In total, in the January–February window of 2016, the Chinese football league's overall spending was worth a world-beating €334 million, outstripping the English Premier League's €253 million in January (CCTV, 2016).

Challenges ahead

Despite all the huge investment from private sectors and other positive signs, it would be naive to think that those ambitious goals set by the policy documents will come by easily and the road ahead for sport business is a smooth one. The fact that the reform plan of a sport and its governing system has to come from the country's central government and pushed by the nation's president implies the difficulties and potential resistance from the existing establishment. After all, any reform would involve redistribution of power and interests, and sport is no exception.

The first challenge is still institutional: while the reform of football is in full swing with the China's football management center dissolved, the potential conflict between a centralized governing system with strong government control and a free market based professional football remain unresolved. To what extent the Chinese government is willing to relax control over sports administration is yet to be seen. In fact, the fact that Mr. Cai, the Deputy Minister of GAS, has remained to serve as the President of the newly restructured Chinese Football Association supposed to be detached from the GAS seems to question the autonomy the Association could enjoy as an independent sport governing body.

The second challenge is cultural. While there existed numerous types of physical activities throughout Chinese history, the so-called modern sport, including football, is an imported culture. Over the past hundreds of years in the dynasties in China, excellence in schoolwork and sitting the competitive civil service examination to become a government official was the dream for every average Chinese. As a result, anything else, including leisure activity, was considered as secondary and even a distraction from studying. While today a good degree does not necessarily guarantee a good job in China anymore, schoolwork remains the paramount task for Chinese kids in and after school as required by their parents and teachers. It is reported that increasing numbers of children in large cities across the country are experiencing joyless childhoods due to the lack of playtime (China Daily, 2007). Unlike in the West, where for many sport is a part of life since childhood, it is considered by many parents as a waste of time and distraction from schoolwork. When some more open-minded parents do choose a hobby for their kids, it is often music instruments or painting over sports that would be picked. When a parent decides that his or her kid should play a sport seriously, more often than not, it's out of instrumental concern, and they either think the kid would be an elite athlete or study a sport-related degree in the future. The only time sport is considered important is when people get old and they do exercises for health reasons. This is probably why the participation in sport by senior citizens is far higher in China than in the West (Liu, 2016). Overall, participation in football and sport has to be improved, and a football fan base has to be enlarged to sustain a truly successful and prosperous professional football in China.

Bibliography

CCTV (2015). http://sports.cntv.cn/2015/11/04/ARTI1446598074168490.shtml (accessed May 8, 2016).

CCTV (2016). Chinese Super League on Record Spending. http://english.cntv.cn/2016/02/29/VIDE69rPejl9GV5QYeDc7d9y160229.shtml (accessed May 10, 2016).

China Daily (2007). China's children too busy for playtime, Retrieved July 26, 2016, from China Daily website at http://www.chinadaily.com.cn/china/2007-05/13/content_871182.htm

Coakley, J. (2009). *Sport in society*. (10th ed.). New York: McGraw-Hill.

General Administration of Sport in China (Dec. 29, 2015). Online Resource at http://www.sport.gov.cn/n16/n1077/n1392/n7425138/n7425223/7477924.html (accessed May 3, 2016).

Gratton, C., Liu, D., Ramchandani, G., & Wilson, D. (2012).*The global economics of sport*. London and New York: Routledge.

Guardian (Feb. 20, 2013), http://www.theguardian.com/world/2013/feb/20/match-fixing-bribery-chinese-football (accessed May 5, 2016).

Guo, Y. (Jul. 23, 2016). Chinese buyers' 'shopping' spree for soccer clubs, *China.org.cn*. http://www.china.org.cn/sports/2016-07/23/content_38943040.htm (accessed July 23, 2016).

Kokolakakis, T. (2015). UK Sport Satellite Account, 2011 and 2012, The Sport Industry Research Centre Report Commissioned by Department for Culture, Media and Sport.

Liu, D. (2008). Review of national governing bodies' reform in China, *Academic Journal of Sport*, (9).

Liu, D. (2016). Sport participation and measurement in developed countries with comparison with Shanghai, *Journal of Shanghai University of Sport*, 3.

Madden, Normandy, Wentz, & Laurel. (2005). NBA signs with China's Li-Ning: Advertising Age.

Marshall, S. (2006). *NBA Scores Big In China*. Retrieved October 16, 2014, from Crain's New York Business http://www.crainsnewyork.com/article

Ogus, S. (2016). Chinese Companies Continue Soccer Expansion with Purchase of Italian Team Inter Milan. Retrieved July 26, 2016, from Forbes at http://www.forbes.com/sites/simonogus/2016/06/08/chinese-continue-soccer-expansion-with-purchase-of-italian-team-inter-milan/#3cb629197604

Plunkett Research. Sports Industry Trends & Statistics [EB / OL] (Nov. 11,2014). http://www.plunkettresearch.com/ sports-recreation-leisure-market-research/industry-statistics (accessed June 6, 2015).

South Urban Weekly (Nov. 27, 2005). Summary of Chinese Super League in 2005: Naked Running. http://sports.sina.com.cn/j/2005-11-27/13151903529.shtml

State Council (2015). State Council Sets the Goal of Soccer Reform. Retrieved July 26, 2016, from State Council website at http://english.gov.cn/policies/latest_releases/2015/03/16/content_281475072485440.htm

Sun, X. (2016). The Overall Development Plan of Chinese Soccer. Retrieved July 26, 2016, from China-daily website at http://usa.chinadaily.com.cn/china/2016–04/11/content_24446803.htm

Wang, J. (2003). A study on the factors affecting the number of audience in China's Football League, *Shanghai Sport Science Research*, 24(6).

Xinhuanet (Aug. 3, 2008). http://news.xinhuanet.com/english/2008-08/03/content_8917910.htm (accessed May 3, 2016).

Zhang, Y. (Apr. 10, 2014). MOFCOM body signs deal with La Liga for Chinese firms, *Global Times Business*. http://epaper.globaltimes.cn/2014-04-10/49767.htm (accessed July 23, 2016).

20

MARKETING FOOTBALL

Perspectives from the Japan Football League (J. League)

Yoshifumi Bizen and Shintaro Sato

Introduction

History of J. League

Following the introduction of football to Japan by the British Navy in 1873, the Japanese football society has accumulated a rich history. The national team won the bronze medal in the 1968 Mexico Olympic Games and has qualified for five consecutive FIFA World Cup tournaments since its first appearance in 1998. However, the history of the domestic professional football league is relatively short. The first ever J. League match kicked off on May 15, 1993. Historically in Japan, many sports including football were developed as amateur sports supported by companies for more than a century. Most players became employees of those companies and played for their companies' teams. The discussion towards establishing a Japanese professional football league for future globalization started in the late 1980s. In the new professional football league system, teams were made independent of their corporations and became professional teams known as "clubs." Because teams are representing specific towns, the establishment of the J. League has transformed Japanese sports culture. The J. League put forth a slogan, "The one-hundred-year vision." This means that the J. League aims to contribute to creating a society in which everyone can enjoy any sport through football. In line with the slogan, the league has made great progress not only in raising the level of Japanese football but also in fostering the development of Japan's sporting culture to assist in the healthy mental and physical growth of Japanese people (J. League, 2016b).

Organizational structure of J. League

The J. League started its first season with only 10 clubs in 1993. The number of clubs has been increasing; there are now 53 clubs all over the country in three divisions: J1, J2, and J3. At first, the J. League expected each club to undertake community-based marketing activities under the slogan, "The one-hundred-year vision"; however, many clubs were still run like an old-fashioned business, which depends heavily on large companies such as a parent company. As a result, the J. League faced the dissolution of the Yokohama Flügels owing to the economic recession in 1998. Learning from this critical experience, the J. League is actively trying to reinforce its organizational structure to stabilize the whole management. The regular general meeting consisting of all regular members (i.e., J1, J2, and J3 clubs) is held twice a year, and matters related to business plans, completed and/or ongoing projects, and assets and financial statements are discussed (J. League, 2016a) . The board of directors led by the chairman, who represents the J. League, meets every month to consider matters related to the overall league operation policy. The executive committees, which consist of directors representing J1, J2, and J3 clubs, have been entrusted with deciding issues discussed by the board of directors. In addition, several advisory committees, the rules committee, judicial affairs committee, match commissioner committee, and marketing committee have been established to discuss specific issues and conduct investigations.

Financial condition of J. clubs

To increase the transparency of club management, since 2005, the J. League has disclosed the financial information of all clubs to the public every year. In 2014, business income for all 51 J. League clubs combined was announced to be approximately US$870 million (i.e., 86.85 billion Japanese yen) (J. League, 2015). The total income of 18 clubs in the J. League Division 1 showed a remarkable increase from approximately US$74 million (i.e., 7.45 billion yen) in 2013 to approximately US$590 million (i.e., 59.3 billion yen). It led to the average income of approximately US$33 million (i.e., 3.29 billion yen) for each club. There were 12 clubs that had a revenue of more than US$30 million (i.e., 3 billion yen) in J1. The club with the largest projected revenue increase was the Urawa Red Diamonds, generating approximately US$58 million (i.e., 5.85 billion yen). The breakdown of Urawa's revenue in 2014 showed that their sponsorship fees generated approximately US$24 million (i.e., 2.38 billion yen; 40.66% of total revenue), followed by ticket sales revenue (i.e., US$20 million; 1.98 billion yen; 33.86%), and revenue sharing from the J. League such as TV rights (i.e., US$2.6 million; 0.26 billion yen; 4.49%). However, revenues of J2 teams are only one-third of the average revenue of J1 teams, so J2 teams tend to struggle with their club management. Deloitte Tohmatsu Financial Advisory LLC. assigned a rating to all J league clubs by using the information announced by the J. League in 2014. All clubs were evaluated and quantified in terms of four important business management categories: marketing, managerial efficiency, managerial strategy, and financial condition. As a result of the verification, the Urawa Reds was ranked the best team in business management in J1 (Deloitte Touche Financial Advisory LLC, 2016). The 2014 financial information for J1 clubs is shown in Table 20.1.

How did the Urawa Reds become a successful team from the Japanese football business point of view? In American professional sports settings, team performance is a crucial factor to predict revenue (Fort, 2002). However, there is interesting research about the relationship between revenue and club performance specifically focusing on J. League clubs. Fukuhara and Harada (2013) analyzed the panel data from 2005 to 2010 to examine the relationship between revenue and club performance in the J. League clubs. They found that a club's performance did not significantly influence the revenue. A question then arises: what are the factors influencing the football business in Japan? Understanding Japanese football fans, which we will introduce in the second section, is essential in answering this question.

Club license system

Since the Union of European Football Associations (UEFA) improved the value of its champions' league by successfully introducing a license system, a review system to participate in league competition – first introduced in Germany – has become widespread worldwide. In recent years, many leagues in Asian countries have adopted this system, and the J. League also introduced the

Table 20.1 Financial Information of J1 Clubs in 2014

	Operating Revenue					*Operating Expense*						*Operating Net Profit*
	Sponsorship	*Ticket sales*	*League revenue sharing*	*Others*	*Total*	*Salaries*	*Game related expenses*	*Top team management expenses*	*Service, general administration expense*	*Others*	*Total*	
Urawa	2,380	1,982	263	1,229	**5,854**	2,054	488	404	2,505	191	**5,642**	**212**
Yokohama	2,059	958	226	1,347	**4,590**	1,765	334	508	1,667	310	**4,584**	**6**
Nagoya	2,471	756	204	611	**4,042**	2,053	286	434	1,082	186	**4,041**	**1**
Kashima	1,831	788	222	1,162	**4,003**	1,562	314	295	1,645	159	**3,975**	**28**
G Osaka	1,843	592	238	1,190	**3,863**	1,815	298	242	1,306	117	**3,778**	**85**
Tokyo	1,665	857	205	1,132	**3,859**	1,709	405	376	1,070	263	**3,822**	**37**
C Osaka	1,511	856	232	1,172	**3,771**	1,680	341	679	1,159	0	**3,859**	**–88**
Omiya	2,405	347	205	465	**3,422**	1,720	207	561	868	67	**3,423**	**–1**
Kawasaki	1,794	571	228	766	**3,359**	1,546	185	269	1,214	74	**3,288**	**71**
Shimizu	1,534	539	222	953	**3,248**	1,354	198	220	1,234	195	**3,201**	**47**
Kashiwa	1,943	466	201	555	**3,165**	2,059	138	209	750	39	**3,195**	**–30**
Hiroshima	1,537	505	219	889	**3,149**	1,349	297	299	937	138	**3,019**	**130**
Niigata	1,013	650	210	875	**2,748**	1,085	267	377	932	192	**2,853**	**–105**
Kobe	945	486	211	829	**2,471**	1,348	215	439	828	124	**2,954**	**–483**
Sendai	922	660	203	464	**2,249**	1,141	125	194	811	106	**2,377**	**–128**
Tokushima	1,357	242	202	303	**2,104**	927	82	195	466	33	**1,703**	**401**
Tosu	789	535	222	339	**1,885**	1176	250	120	682	38	**2,266**	**–381**
Kofu	749	422	191	156	**1,518**	759	119	175	437	25	**1,515**	**3**
Average Jl	1,597	678	217	802	**3,294**	1,506	253	333	1,088	116	**3,305**	**–11**
Average J2	534	180	96	306	**1,117**	447	94	135	378	52	**1,105**	**12**
Average J3	155	24	12	80	**271**	97	20	38	123	16	**294**	**–23**

Note: Table was developed based on the official financial report. The unit for the numbers shown is 1 million yen (1 million yen = US$10 thousand).

club license system in 2013 for the purpose of strengthening football competitiveness and the stable management of clubs. The J. League sets benchmarks for evaluating club management of all J. League clubs by focusing on five important areas: (1) facilities, (2) organization structure, (3) legal matters, (4) youth systems, and (5) finances. All clubs that desire to participate in the J. League need to satisfy these specific criteria to receive a club license. In terms of finance, a club can lose its membership if it runs a deficit for 3 consecutive years or is a failed institution with the debts exceeding the assets. All clubs are further encouraged to improve their club management towards fiscal health by the review system. In 2014, there were 15 clubs in J1 and J2 which recorded an annual loss. However, due to the considerable efforts to improve the management system, the number decreased to four (i.e., Kashima, Niigata, Shimizu, and Ehime) in 2015. Sagan Tosu F.C. based in Saga prefecture, which was in the red for the second consecutive year, avoided losing their membership as the club became profitable in 2015. In addition, in terms of facilities, the J. League requires all clubs in J1 to have their home stadium meet the standard for international games and be able to accommodate more than 15,000 spectators. Many clubs renovated their home stadium to meet this criterion.

Market strategies: Asian strategy

The J. League has contributed to improving the total level of competitiveness and business management of the Japanese football society during its first 2 decades (Dolles & Söderman, 2013). However, the J. League could not avoid the loss of its initial vitality over time, which resulted in less powerful organizational leadership in Japan. In addition, there were obvious gaps in the relationship between a club and fans. In other words, the improvement of fan relationship has plateaued. The league as a whole was forced to consider a new direction of marketing strategy that could overcome this difficult situation.

Since it started its Asian strategy in 2012, the J. League has attempted to strengthen its relationship with other leagues around Asia. The goal of its Asian strategy is to (1) increase the value of Asian football in the global market, (2) increase the J. League's presence within Asia, (3) create new business opportunities for the league, its partners, and its clubs, and (4) maximize the potential of Asia's football resources through the sharing of information with other Asian football organizations (J. League, 2016c). The J. League established its Asian Strategy Office and signed partnership agreements with Thailand in 2012. As of June 2016, the J. League has already signed similar agreements with football organizations in 10 different countries. Each club is also trying to develop relationships with several football organizations in the Asian countries under this strategy. For example, Hokkaido Consadole Sapporo has partnerships with professional football teams in Vietnam, and it has acquired the country's national football player, Le Cong Vinh, in July 2013. Le Cong Vinh was the first player to join J. League from Southeast Asia. Owing to his joining the team, Consadole receives increasing attention in Vietnam. A television company in Vietnam started broadcasting some J. League games, and a number of fans actually visited the hometown of Consadole, Sapporo city in Hokkaido, to watch the games, coming all the way from their country (SKY Perfect JSAT Corporation, 2013). This phenomenon is in line with the important policy of the Japanese government that an increase in inbound tourists leads to economic growth. Following Le Cong Vinh from Vietnam, many football players from Asian countries have played in the J. League. However, although a TV station in Thailand also aired J. League games in the country, presently European countries still dominate the football market in Asia. It is reported that the Premier League has proactively sold their TV broadcasting rights to foreign markets. Among all the TV broadcasting rights that they sell to foreign markets annually, approximately 60% of them are obtained by Asian countries. In addition, approximately US$600 million (i.e., 60 billion yen) is paid to the Premier League annually from Asian countries for TV broadcasting rights (Azuma, 2012a). This demonstrates that there is an enormous demand for football spectatorship in Asian countries, but the J. League has not been successful in capitalizing on this potential business opportunity until recently. However, the J. League has been striving to increase its global market share to acquire TV broadcasting contracts with Asian countries.

Specifically, the J. League implements several major strategies to increase its global market share. First, the J. League has increased the number of Asian players with the hope to improve the presence of the J. League within Asia. This can also lead to the expansion of new business opportunities for its partners and clubs. For example, Yanmar Diesel Engine Co., Ltd., a Japanese diesel engine manufacturer and one of the top partners of Cerezo Osaka, started football clinics in Thailand in cooperation with the local agricultural companies. Yanmar Diesel Engine has aimed to increase its presence and strengthen the brand value in Thailand by engaging in philanthropic activities through the J. League club, Cerezo Osaka. The company expects to develop new business in Asian countries after successfully developing a positive brand image in Thailand. Cerezo Osaka also contributes to philanthropic activities by sending coaches from their club to provide football knowledge and techniques to local people in Thailand. The club aims to expand the network within the country and to discover talented local players through these activities (Azuma, 2012a). Thus, if the J. League's Asian strategy is successful in many Asian countries in the long run, the league, its partners, and its clubs will secure tangible and intangible benefits.

Understanding Japanese football fans

As mentioned in the previous section, Japanese football fans can be notably unique. Because of this, applying the general understanding of football fans into marketing strategies may not be as effective in the Japanese football market. The aim of this section is to provide information pertinent for understanding Japanese football fans.

Despite plentiful findings reporting the characteristics of sports fans, efforts that specifically focus on understanding Japanese football fans have been inadequate. Mahony and colleagues (2002) conducted one of the earliest studies that contributed to the understanding of Japanese football fans. They revealed that Japanese football fans' motivations are captured by seven factors: drama, vicarious achievement, aesthetics, team attachment, player attachment, football attachment, and community pride. Among these motivation factors, team attachment is the most important factor to explain how frequently Japanese fans attend the games. Matsuoka and colleagues (2003) study yielded a similar finding, showing that team identification can directly influence Japanese football fans' intention to attend the games. These empirical studies can demonstrate that marketing managers in the Japanese football industry should strive for building fans' psychological attachment/connection to the team.

Nevertheless, the aforementioned findings are somewhat cliché, as numerous studies conducted in a wide variety of professional sports settings provided consistent findings ensuring the positive effect of team identification on fan behavior (e.g., Carlson & Donavan, 2013; Theodorakis, Wann, & Weaver, 2012). What then determines the uniqueness of Japanese football fans? Yoshida and James (2010)* conducted a cross-national study to reveal the differences regarding fan perception of core (i.e., games) and peripheral (i.e., services) sport products. The results showed that Japanese fans' satisfaction toward both games and services uniquely influenced behavioral intentions, whereas American sports fans' behavioral intention was influenced only by

* Although Yoshida and James (2010) study focused on a Japanese professional baseball setting, the unique characteristics of Japanese sports fans are well-documented.

game satisfaction. This demonstrates that Japanese sports fans can be relatively service-demanding consumers who require the qualities of both core and peripheral sport products.

Although these empirical studies provided valuable insights, most are cross-sectional studies and causal inferences cannot be fully justified. As introduced previously, Fukuhara and Harada (2013) employed a time-series analysis and revealed that there was no significant relationship between revenue and club performance in the J. League. Additionally, Yoshida and colleagues' (2015) longitudinal study found that Japanese football fans' actual behavior (i.e., game attendance) is explained by fan community attachment. Specifically, Japanese football fans are more likely to attend the games when they are strongly connected to other fans. These empirical studies can also add to the knowledge regarding the uniqueness of Japanese football fans.

In sum, marketing managers who target the Japanese football industry should understand that (1) Japanese fans are not only game-fanatics, but also service-demanding consumers and (2) connections among fellow fans strongly encourage them to attend the games. Developing the understanding of Japanese football fans will result in a good business spiral that contributes to boosting the revenue from sponsorship, broadcasting rights, and merchandizing.

Sponsorship and media rights

Sponsorship

In the current financial condition, advertising revenue from sponsor companies is the largest revenue source for the J. League. The J. League concluded the newly created title partnership with Meiji Yasuda Life Insurance Company, a Japanese life insurance company, in 2014. Under the title partnership program, the league title of the J. League has been officially named the "Meiji Yasuda J League" for four seasons since 2015. The company is also given the rights to exposure of the company's name with the J. League logo on the official uniform of J. League clubs. The company has been eagerly participating in community contribution activities and holding football clinics for elementary school students throughout Japan with the cooperation of the J. League and the clubs. According to the business report of the Meiji Yasuda (2015), this title partnership contract with the J. League is also one of their community contribution activities. The company aims to not only raise awareness about the company, but also to contribute to the vitalization of local society by cheering J. League and local football clubs. In addition, the J. League has an official partnership contract with many companies in several categories; e.g., top partners, sports promotion partner, and equipment partner. Although the amount of money for each category has not been revealed, it is estimated that total revenue from those sponsorship contracts is approximately US$47 million (i.e., 4.73 billion yen) a year from the statement of income and expense announced by the J. League.

Media (tv broadcasting rights)

The number of clubs running at a loss remains relatively low in the J. League. However, the amount of business income of each J. League club seems to be much lower than that of football clubs in Europe. Real Madrid, the best football club in business in the world in 2015, earned an income of US$75 million (i.e., 75.2 billion yen) a year, which was about 12 times as much as that of Urawa. It is frequently pointed out that the management of TV broadcasting rights is the cause for the low income of J. League clubs. Currently, the League organization itself has centralized control over all television rights in the J. League and distributes revenues from the TV rights to each club. The J. League has concluded a domestic broadcasting rights agreement with SKY

Perfect JSAT Corporation for 2012 through 2016, and also signed a contract for about 3 million dollars (i.e., 300 million yen) with this company in 2015, as regards overseas broadcasting rights for 2015 through 2019. The League was broadcasted in 70 countries during the 2014 season. It is estimated that the J. League has made approximately US$50 million (i.e., 5 billion yen) a year from those TV rights. However, the amount of money that the J. League earns from TV rights is far smaller as compared to those of football leagues in Europe. As of July 2016, it is reported that a domestic broadcasting rights contract from 2017 is still being negotiated with some media companies. If the value of J. League games as media content increases and they can raise the broadcasting contract fee, each club could benefit, thereby strengthening and improving its environment.

Media mix promotions

The explosive growth of the Internet has altered our communication dramatically over the past 20 years. The J. League and the clubs need to consider new promotional strategies not only by using traditional media like TV and radio, but also by using the Internet. The J. League established its official website and also exerts efforts to distribute much information (e.g., game pictures and videos) on the official fan site (J's Goal), Facebook, and Twitter.

The SoftBank Group Corp., a Japanese multinational telecommunications and Internet company, announced that the company has started a sport broadcasting service, Sportsnavi Live, in March 2016. The service is available for a monthly fee of 500 Japanese yen to SoftBank users, and the viewers are able to enjoy several video programs as well as live broadcasting with no limitation on a tablet or smartphone. At present, the service covers seven major sports, that is, Japanese professional baseball, Grand Sumo, women's football league, men's tennis, Major League Baseball, international football, and Japanese men's basketball, and is expected to expand to other sports in the future (SoftBank Group Corp, 2016). It seems that SoftBank expects to create new business opportunities and increase the number of its cell-phone customers through the online distribution service. Since the revenue from TV broadcasting rights has stagnated in recent years, developing new channels such as the online video distribution service should be very important not only as a promotional tool but also as part of another management strategy for the J. League.

Another good example of the use of the Internet for sales promotion is "Ticketbis," an online platform where users can buy and sell tickets to events. Ticketbis was established in Spain in 2009 and is a growing global platform where fans from more than 40 countries have access to a wide range of event tickets in over 20 languages, including sports, concerts, theater, and music festivals. FC Tokyo first introduced the system in the J. League to sell their home game tickets in 2015 (FC Tokyo, 2015). Japanese companies undoubtedly have to overcome the language barrier when trying to break onto the world market. This system has allowed the clubs to expand their brands to the world to reach the fans outside Japan.

However, there is a possibility that information may not reach the target consumers effectively in a multimedia society flooded with information. Selecting the most appropriate method of promotion on a budget has become an important task that the J. League and each club must try to accomplish in these days. In celebration of its 20-year anniversary, the J. League made a movie titled *Detective Conan: The Eleventh Striker* in collaboration with the makers of the famous Japanese animation, *Detective Conan,* in 2012. As a part of the collaboration, players from the J. League actually voiced original characters in the film. The film was officially shown at 351 theaters in Japan, and made approximately US$33 million (i.e., 3.3 billion Japanese yen) in total at the box office. The animation, *Detective Conan* is very popular with families and women in their 20s whom the J. League would like as its new target (Azuma, 2012b). The J. League could conduct an effective marketing promotion through advertising campaigns for the movie. Moreover, it was a good opportunity for the J. League to promote itself overseas because the animation is broadcasted in many countries and well known, especially in Asia.

Stadium

Professional sports teams most often have their own home stadiums/arenas in the franchise cities. Indeed, the stadium has been acknowledged as one of the most important key factors for club management in Japan. The J. League also emphasizes the role of the stadium and has set a high standard regarding facilities in its Club License System. Many Japanese professional teams, however, have not necessarily succeeded in developing fan satisfaction towards football stadiums. Japanese football teams have often utilized multi-sports facilities primarily used for track and field. Athletic tracks play a significant obstruction for the proximity between fans and football fields. There was also another problem regarding stadium capacities. As previously mentioned, in terms of facilities, the J. League requires all clubs in J1 to have a home stadium that meets the standard for the international football games and be able to accommodate more than 15,000 spectators. Although the above issues were acknowledged as major problems, financial as well as political constraints impeded the improvement of stadiums in Japan up until recently.

Nevertheless, the recent football popularity in Japan encouraged many cities and local governments to support their football teams to improve the stadiums, which eventually contribute to building the city brands. The Suita City Football stadium, which is used as a football-oriented home stadium for Gamba Osaka, is a good example, owing to the stadium funding method. The Suita City Football stadium is a 40,000-seat stadium that utilizes solar panels and rainwater recycle systems for effective energy consumption. The stadium was built by numerous supporters that can be divided into two parts: municipal support and donations. First, the land for the stadium was endowed by the city of Suita, which rendered the stadium project realistic as such land acquisition usually involves a large up-front cost and is often recognized as a substantial obstacle for stadium businesses (Aicher, Paule-Koba, & Newland, 2015). Second, a total of approximately US$140 million for the construction cost was covered by donations to the club from a wide variety of stakeholders including local residents, companies, and municipalities. Gamba Osaka currently has designated management rights to fully manage the Suita City Football stadium from 2015 to 2063.

Unlike the stadium business in other countries such as USA, the Japanese sport industry might not be acknowledged as a worthy investment outlet because of the current size and growth potential that prospect investors might be concerned about. However, Gamba Osaka has been trying to sell naming rights for the stadium to further obtain stable financial resources. The efforts in obtaining naming rights for Japanese stadiums in general are not necessarily novel.

Table 20.2 The breakdown of stadium funding

	$US Amount (approximate)	*N*
Corporate Donations	99.5 million	721 companies
Individual Donations	6.2 million	34,627 people
Endowment and Subsidies	35.1 million	
Total	140.8 million	

Note: Table was developed based on the official stadium donation organization report.

Nevertheless, in the case of the Suita City Football Stadium, it can possibly turn into a controversial issue as the city of Suita and local residents greatly contributed to the stadium project. Whether the stadiums include a symbolic name to represent the cities and nurture residents' pride is an issue that deserves careful consideration. Although the Suita City Football stadium is expected to serve as a "city landmark," the relationship between Gamba Osaka and fans cannot be established without carefully considering the above concerns.

Bibliography

Aicher, T., Paule-Koba, A. L., & Newland, B. L. (2015). *Sport facility and event management.* Sudbury: Jones and Bartlett.

Azuma, H. (2012a). Project Design. Vol.3, December 1st. 16–51. The Graduate School of Project Design. Tokyo.

Azuma, H. (2012b). Sendenkaigi. No.836, May 1st. 46–47. Sendenkaigi Co., Ltd. Tokyo.

Carlson, B., & Donavan, D. (2013). Human brands in sport: Athlete brand personality and identification. *Journal of Sport Management, 27,* 193–206.

Deloitte Touche Financial Advisory LLC. (2016). J-League Management Cup 2014. Sport Business Group.

Dolles, H., & Söderman, S. (2013). Twenty years of development of the J-League: Analyzing the business parameters of professional football in Japan. *Soccer & Society, 14,* No. 5, 702–721.

FC Tokyo. (2015). "Ticketbis" to be introduced as online ticket resale platform. *News Release.* June 15.

Fort, R. (2002). *Sports economics.* Upper Saddle River, NJ: Prentice Hall.

Fukuhara, T., & Harada, M. (2013). The relationship between team performance and revenue in the J. League by panel analysis. *Japanese Journal of Sport Management, 6,* 3–15. [in Japanese].

J. League. (2015). Retrieved July 14, 2016, from http://www.jleague.jp/docs/aboutj/club-h26kaiji.pdf. [in Japanese].

J. League. (2016a). About J.League; Organisation. Retrieved July 14, 2016, from http://www.jleague.jp/en/aboutJ/aboutj/soshiki.html

J. League. (2016b). About J.League; Prospectus. Retrieved July 14, 2016, from http://www.jleague.jp/en/aboutJ/aboutj/

J. League. (2016c). From the J. League into Asia, from the Asia to the World. Retrieved July 14, 2016, from http://www.jleague.jp/en/100year/asia/

Mahony, D., Nakazawa, M., Funk, D., James, J., & Gladden, J. (2002). Motivational factors influencing the behaviour of J-League spectators. *Sport Management Review, 5,* 1–24.

Matsuoka, H., Chelladurai, P., & Harada, M. (2003). Direct and interaction effects of team identification and satisfaction on intention to attend games. *Sport Marketing Quarterly, 12,* 244–253.

Meiji Yasuda Life Insurance Company. (2015). Status of Meiji Yasuda NEXT Challenge Program. December 2015.

SKY Perfect JSAT Corporation. (2013). Broadcasting rights agreement signed to relay consadole sapporo soccer matches for broadcast in Vietnam. *News Release.* November 7.

SoftBank Group Corp. (2016). Press Release. March 10th. Retrieved July 14, 2016, from http://www.softbank.jp/corp/group/sbm/news/press/2016/20160310_02/. [in Japanese].

Theodorakis, N. D., Wann, D. L., & Weaver, S. (2012). An antecedent model of team identification in the context of professional soccer. *Sport Marketing Quarterly, 21,* 80–90.

Yoshida, M., Heere, B., & Gordon, B. (2010). Predicting behavioral loyalty through community: Why other fans are more important than our own Intentions, our satisfaction, and the team itself. *Journal of Sport Management, 29,* 318–333.

Yoshida, M., & James, J. D. (2015). Customer satisfaction with game and service experiences: Antecedents and consequences. *Journal of Sport Management, 24,* 338–361.

GENERAL CONCLUSION

This work is fully dedicated to the structural changes of football worldwide. Recent FIFA crises have shown some huge challenges that football can represent. With 209 affiliated countries, FIFA is "more important" than the UN, and its president is welcomed everywhere like a head of state. In certain geographical areas, he is even considered more powerful than some G8 leaders! This geopolitical dimension, and just plain political, is obviously linked to the financial burden that football represents today. When countries win the bid for the World Cup, it is a way to position oneself in the world (South Africa in 2010, Brazil in 2014, Russia in 2018, Qatar in 2022). Countries can be considered as a brand (concept of country branding, often nourished by *soft power*). However, investments in infrastructure are often dizzying, 21 billion for Russia in 2018, and more than 200 billion US dollars for Qatar in 2022![1] In addition, these forecasted budgets for major sporting events are always underestimated a priori and a posteriori!

If national and continental championships do not reach this crazy excess, it must be noted that the accelerated commercialization of football has led authorities to raise questions on the structuring of the system. This system has indeed changed considerably in the last 20 years: in France, although 1998 was a "detonator" with the victory of the national team in the World Cup, the situation today is beyond measure. The intermediaries, the famous "agencies" which previously controlled the system, are no longer as powerful, and the brands (advertisers or clubs) now prefer to manage their marketing rights or television rights themselves. This process, very well analyzed in Chapter 4 by Christophe Bouchet in this work, also applies to major football events. For example, as part of the structure of Euro 2016, UEFA holds 95% of the organizing company.[2] This desire to control its events and its brands is logical, especially when one has only two major events that provide 100% of the revenue like the UEFA (Champions League, Euro), or only one, as is the case with FIFA with the World Cup or the IOC with the Olympic Games.

American professional closed leagues that already existed in "traditional" sports (basketball, football, baseball, ice hockey) formed the basis for the model of the MLS (the league of "soccer" or "football" for Europeans, the most recent league among the major leagues) that we have analyzed in Chapter 3. Therefore, the Americans also consider that sport is a risky activity and that, to reassure potential investors, it is necessary to use a model without relegation or augmentation. Besides, this "model" is gaining ground in the European system. The introduction of groups in the Champions League and the opening of the competition to several clubs in 1992, even though since 1955 the competition only brought together the champions and was held by direct elimination,[3] are directly related to the fact that television, clubs and sponsors want more games "guaranteed", as well as the clubs. Similarly, the decision of the LFP, in France, to limit the number of relegations to 2 (instead of 3) participates in this movement: we have 2 chances in 20 to go down, instead of 3 out of 20![4]

On the European level, the UEFA's attempts to impose financial fair-play are also linked to a desire to make football "more reasonable" on the financial level, to introduce "safeguards", to avoid excesses leading to potential bankruptcy, but also to try to rebalance the system which tends to focus on a few big clubs that are financially stronger and that "monopolize" the titles for years, at the risk of reducing uncertainty and therefore interest in the sporting spectacle. It is in this sense that economics can help the football system, through the ideas of competitive balance highlighted in Chapter 2 by Wladimir Andreff and Nicolas Scelles. This European system, established in the 1950s, seems obsolete today, even on the verge of implosion.[5] However, if regulation and governance can be managed effectively in a unique and closed American sport system, bringing together one country, one language and one currency, it is understandable that it is not the same at the European level.

But this rebalancing by the restructuring of the system is a chimera. There will always be customer areas larger than others, wealthier cities and countries, and therefore television rights or sponsorship deals that are more important. The principle of revenue sharing (the clubs in the situation of earning a profit redistribute their profits to clubs with a deficit) applied in the NHL cannot adapt itself to Europe. The draft (system for distributing the best basketball players from academia by letting the weaker clubs in the last NBA season choose first) is unthinkable since the training clubs are those that participate in national and continental competitions. How can one imagine that they can freely provide a professional football system, when they have committed large sums of money for training? In the United States, the NCAA (organization of university sport) is very rich, as universities do not pay the players, and at the same time the NCAA sells enormous TV rights and marketing rights, which can be compared to those of the professional leagues. This is what allows it to work and to feed the leagues.

Since this adaptation of the American regulatory system is impossible at the level of European football, perhaps outside of an equal sharing of television rights, it is necessary to consider other paths. This is why marketing tools have attained such a high import. Ticket sales, the unique revenue of football when sponsorship and paid TV rights did not exist, are a considerable challenge. The stadiums have to be full, with a good atmosphere, in order to ensure financial revenue, of course (ticketing). But is also crucial for the sporting spectacle in the stands. This show relayed by the media, should be as advanced as possible. But these complex strategies would be of no use if the distribution of the football spectacle did not enjoy today a "special casing", capable of "sublimating" it. These famous "big stadiums", wanted by France for its Euro 2016, or by Brazil or South Africa for the last two World Cups, need to be connected and in tune with social networking strategies (see Chapter 7 by Boris Helleu), even if this has a cost. This connectivity must be at the service of the customer, on his "path" as it is the case at the Allianz Arena in Munich, model for all the presidents of European clubs. Among the many stadiums built in recent years in the world of European football, it is considered the example to follow because this concept of the "connected" stadium is at the service of the consumer hungry to post photos or videos via social networks (the famous "I was there!"), but also allows the provider to increase revenue through online control systems for beverages, catering, parking, etc. In a general way, one can summarize the logic of the supplier in terms of a "customer path" that one seeks to optimize. It is necessary that the viewer arrive as soon as possible in the enclosure, without embarrassment, without waiting, relaxed and in good spirits because all studies show that our consumption levels are proportional to the time we spend at the place of distribution.

This logic of the commodification of players, those from the clubs as well as those from the stadiums (the stadium is considered as "the place of profit" or business unit for the club, and no longer only as the place where one "plays a match") is modeled on American stadiums that are totally dedicated to this market logic but have a huge advantage: infrastructure costs can be depreciated over 41 home games minimum in the NBA or the NHL (because there are 82 season games in a regular season) and 81 in the MLB (because the regular baseball season has 162 games). The only exception is the NFL, where only 16 games are played, and which bases its business model on the scarcity of the product and the record amount of television rights (3 billion US dollars per year over 9 years, according to the contract signed in 2011[6]).

This is why American stadiums, and covered arenas in general, have geared themselves for many decades towards "multi-functionality", a term that evokes the idea that the enclosure can quickly change its configuration to accommodate basketball, ice hockey and concerts. The model of the genre is the Staples Center in Los Angeles, an arena of 18,000 seats which hosts more than 250 events per year,[7] but only half of which are linked to sport, the rest being concerts. This exceptional rate of occupancy holds to the quality of its design, allowing it to switch from basketball to hockey and hockey to basketball in only 2 hours![8]

But it should not be that European football clubs are throwing themselves into this frenzy of construction of "multifunctional" stadiums: indeed, the offer of concerts in Europe, and of spectator sports in general, will never be at the level of the American offer (the Staples Center hosts three professional teams: the Lakers and Clippers in basketball, and the Kings in ice hockey), and the density of European stadiums does not allow either that "everyone has a piece of the cake." A football stadium should therefore be primarily a place dedicated to the sport. Lille has also "bitten off more than it could chew" on this issue: the new stadium, inaugurated in 2012, and whose construction cost was 282 million euros, has not really achieved its goal of welcoming enough non-soccer events (apart from the final of the Davis Cup 2014, Euro 2015 basketball, the semifinals of the Rugby Top 14 in 2014, and some concerts). In this regard, it was necessary that the group be involved in the financing of this enclosure, otherwise its financial equilibrium would be precarious.

This refers to the idea that sport in Europe, and France in particular, can hardly do without the public sector, and that it is not "an industry like any other". Chapter 8, by Christopher Hautbois, shows all this football ambivalence, usually described in the media as a "financial monster", but which, in the end, often involves an SME having a very strong bond with the city that hosts it. Cities like Lyon, Saint-Étienne, Marseille or Bordeaux have also understood the challenge of a big club, able to "sublimate their brand" with a logic of city branding at the international level. Even the "monster" Paris-Saint-Germain, funded by Qatari money, and which does not play in the same league as the other French clubs, has grasped the challenge of good relations with the city of Paris. Yet one would have thought that with its resources it could behave like a 100% private company. The evolution of the PSG logo in 2013 perfectly reflects the direction of the club, "less Saint-Germain" and "more Paris," with a desire to conquer Asia and the world, taking advantage of the glamorous image of the capital, at the risk of frustrating and upsetting "historic" supporters that had seen the birth of the club in 1970 with the help of the city of Saint-Germain-en-Laye. But the globalization of football has gone that route.

Finally, the social roots of football also necessitate the idea that football "does good around it" thanks to the policies of CSR (Corporate Social Responsibility). It's a question of behaving responsibly, environmentally, socially and economically, as in all sustainable development policies. The works of Aurelian François and Emmanuel Bayle (Chapter 9) applied to football clubs show that the logic resembles once again that of the American foundations which have existed since the 1970s, where players, often from disadvantaged backgrounds, prove that they can give back to society what it gave to them.

Figure GC.1 The PSG logo change in 2013

Source: http://leplus.nouvelobs.com/contribution/787619-psg-le-nouveau-logo-gagne-en-simplicite-mais-perd-en-personnalite-et-en-histoire.html – Last accessed on June 14, 2015.

If the social and political roots of football clubs are unquestionable, this book emphasizes how much the weight of marketing and its tools have become essential in a logic of marketization and globalization in a highly competitive environment.

Our case studies applied to big European clubs clearly demonstrate this influence of marketing with regard to strategies, but with variations according to countries, the size of the club, its tradition, its record, its local roots and its capacity for internationalization. As in most management processes, one best way does not exist.

If Paris Saint-Germain, a club with substantial Qatari capital, serves as the "nouveau riche" in the big leagues, and has logically engaged itself in a very rapid internationalization strategy of its brand with important investments, the Olympique Lyonnais is all about the success of its new stadium or "multifunctional park", basing its recapture of Europe for the next 10 years on the model of Bayern Munich with the Allianz Arena or Arsenal with the Emirates Stadium. Saint-Étienne, Liverpool and Dortmund, meanwhile, have fairly similar parallel stories, with a historic working-class tradition and a loyal audience, still representing popular values of football, as opposed to Manchester United or Real Madrid, which are more upper-class clubs. Other clubs, studied in the framework of this book, have more original positions, like Fiorentina in Italy, or Stuttgart in Germany, which is logical when one is in the "soft underbelly" of its championship, with unguaranteed revenue, since these clubs have little sport visibility, and therefore, little financially; indeed, their participation in the Champions League is excluded, and being in the Europa League is not automatic. At the same time, these are the clubs that risk being relegated to the lower level. Once again, that shows that football is not a business like any other, especially in Europe, where athletic risk may have important managerial consequences for SMEs which are not as strong as the media would have liked one to believe.

This level of innovation of some clubs is not unique since in the United States as well, where everything seems to be governed by quasi dictatorial leagues, different development models emerge, contradicting all of the oracles of finance and marketing who think that some mandatory standards apply inescapably.

In the NFL, the Green Bay Packers have managed the unthinkable: winning 4 Super Bowls since 1966 and having a dominant position for a city of only 104,000 inhabitants, while all theories of geomarketing show that only customer areas of several million (New York, Los Angeles, Chicago in the United States; London, Milan, Madrid, Paris, Manchester, Barcelona or Munich in Europe) allow professional teams to develop a continuous and harmonious manner for the long term. The success of the Packers is largely due to its mode of governance: the 364,000 "members" who own the club, a little like the socios in Barcelona.[9]

In baseball, the Chicago Cubs have not won the title since 1908, yet their stadium is full and the franchise is one of the most profitable in the league. In baseball, the Chicago Cubs won the World Series in 2016. But they had not won the title since 1908, yet their stadium was always full and the franchise is one of the most profitable in the league. Obviously, they do not communicate about being the "friendly losers", but the managers promote the club which is a family place, where you can meet friends in a friendly atmosphere, based on conviviality and exchanges. They actually make some "experiential and relational" marketing without realizing it since the 1960s. Certainly, such a success would be impossible in a European context, because the club would come down several times into the lower divisions and would have no existence at the professional level. Nonetheless, this model deserves to be watched closely, and has ultimately inspired several European clubs that are placed in entertainment coupled with sport: "sport + entertainment = sportainment".

In the end, it is marketing and all of its related tools which allow the use of different development models, because not everyone can be Bayern Munich or FC Barcelona. In the coming years, it will be this prominence of marketing in football clubs that will give meaning to the strategy of the clubs while providing them with the means to function financially. However, if all the clubs may have their place, the coexistence of clubs having revenues that are too different seriously pose questions, otherwise marketing remains a makeshift affair that just serves to reduce the gaps which have widened in recent years. If we have seen that the American league's regulatory system is too far off from what the European football could integrate as reforms, the Financial Fair Play (FPF) was introduced (among others) to make this shift. In the coming years, the future and the balance of the European football system will depend on its success (or lack of).

Notes

1 http://www.challenges.fr/economie/20130711.CHA2325/football-le-budget-dementiel-du-qatar-pour-le-mondial-de-2022.html. Last accessed June 14, 2015.
http://www.lequipe.fr/Football/Actualites/La-russie-revoit-a-la-hausse-le-budget/377781. Last accessed June 14, 2015.

2 http://www.challenges.fr/challenges-soir/20150610.CHA6781/pour-l-uefa-l-euro-2016-est-gagne-davance.html. Last accessed June 14, 2015.

3 http://fr.wikipedia.org/wiki/Ligue_des_champions_de_l'UEFA. Last accessed June 14, 2014.

4 http://www.rtl.fr/sport/football/ligue-1-plus-que-deux-descentes-en-ligue-2-au-lieu-de-trois-a-partir-de-la-saison-prochaine-7778436025. Last accessed June 14, 2014.

5 *Cf.* Chapter 5 by Vincent Chaudel.

6 http://www.sports.fr/sports-us/nfl/scans/droits-tv-jackpot-de-27-milliards-de-dollars-pour-la-nfl-152460/. Last accessed June 14, 2015.

7 http://fr.wikipedia.org/wiki/Staples_Center. Last accessed June 14, 2015.

8 http://articles.latimes.com/2012/feb/23/sports/la-sp-sn-staples-center-video-20120223. Last accessed June 14, 2015.

9 http://fr.wikipedia.org/wiki/Packers_de_Green_Bay. Last accessed June 14, 2015.

INDEX

Page numbers in *italics* denote figures, tables or photographs.